C#

For Beginners

The tactical guidebook

Learn by coding

C# For Beginners - The Tactical Guide Book

Source code

The source code accompanying this book is shared under the MIT License and can be downloaded here after registering with the site http://www.csharpschool.com using the code **cfb** or by emailing the author.

About the author

Jonas started a company back in 1994 focusing on education in Microsoft Office and the Microsoft operating systems. While still studying at the university in 1995, he wrote his first book about Widows 95 as well as a number of course materials.

In the year 2000, after working as a Microsoft Office developer consultant for a couple of years, he wrote his second book about Visual Basic 6.0.

Between 2000 and 2004 he worked as a Microsoft instructor with two of the largest educational companies in Sweden. First teaching Visual Basic 6.0, and when Visual Basic.NET and C# were released he started teaching these languages as well as the .NET Framework. Teaching classes on all levels for beginner to advanced developers.

From the year 2005, Jonas shifted his career towards consulting once again, working hands on with the languages and framework he taught.

Jonas wrote his third book *C# programming* aimed at beginners to intermediate developers in 2013 and now in 2015 his fourth book *C# for beginners - The Tactical Guide* was published.

Contents

PART 1 - THE C# LANGUAGE

C# For Beginners

1. Introduction To C#

Who is this book for?

This book is primarily aimed towards developers who are new to C# and have none or very limited prior experience with C# and are up for a challenge. The book does not presuppose that you have any prior C# knowledge since the purpose of the book is to teach you just that. Even if you already have created a couple of small C# projects on your own or have been developing applications for a while you might find the content in this book useful as a refresher.

Disclaimer

If you prefer encyclopaedic books describing everything in minute detail with short examples, then this book is NOT for you. To get the most benefit from the content and learn as much as possible as fast as possible you should read the text and then read through and implement the exercises provided for you.

It's important to mention that this book is not meant to be *encyclopaedic*, it's a practical and tactical book where you will learn as you progress through the examples and build a couple of real applications in the process. Because I personally dislike having to read hundreds upon hundreds of pages of fluff (filler material) that is not relevant to the task at hand, and view it as a disservice to the readers, I will assume that we are of a same mind when it comes to this and will therefore only include important information pertinent to the tasks at hand and thus saving you time and effort in the process. Don't get me wrong, I will describe the important things in great detail, leaving out only the things which are not directly relevant to your first experience with C#. The goal is for you to have created many small and a couple of larger applications with C# using Windows Forms upon finishing this book. You can always look into details at a later time when you have a few projects under your belt.

The examples in this book are presented using Visual Studio 2013 Professional Update 4 but the free express version should do fine if you want to follow along and implement them yourself. Most of the examples and exercises can be implemented with earlier versions of Visual Studio.

The book presupposes that you already have Visual Studio installed on your computer.

Introduction

At the end of this chapter you will have an understanding of what an application is and the parts that make up an application.

What is a program?

An application or a program as it also is called can refer to many different things. It can be a desktop application which runs on Windows or Mac OSX like the calculator, a word processor or a spread sheet, but it can also be a web site or even something smaller like the application built in to a kitchen appliance.

In its simplest form a program is comprised of algorithms that will process data which either is fetched from a data store, such as a database, a file or user input.

Fetched data whether from a data store or user input can then be run through one or more algorithms to reach the goal set up for that algorithm sequence, such as display order data to a customer, calculate the total price for the items in an online shopping cart, or save data back to the data store.

An algorithm is code that describes how data will be entered/fetched from a data store, a keyboard or other types of input devices and subsequently manipulated, calculated, displayed and/or saved back to a data store.

To boil it down: in-data is processed by one or more algorithms that produces a result (out-data).

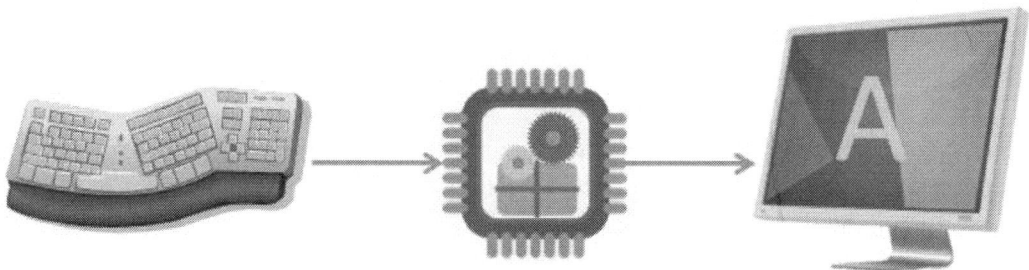

When implementing code using a modern programming language algorithms are often placed in what is known as methods or functions for easier reuse. Though there arguably can be differences between methods and functions in some languages the names will be used interchangeably in this book.

The language of a computer

The core (brain) of a computer is its processor (CPU) which does all the calculations and runs all the algorithms. As of the writing of this book it is very common with multi-core processors meaning that they can execute multiple requests at the same time making the computer work faster. A 4-core processor can run 4 algorithms in parallel and although you in reality can run many more algorithms seemingly at the same time this is achieved by a cleaver use of what is known as threads. Threads are given short time slots in a rotating schedule for one or more of the processor cores.

The processor work with low-level instructions which is specific to certain types of processors. This mean that a program you write for a PC might not work on another personal computer. The low-level instructions are interpreted differently depending on what operating system the application was created for, this means that a program compiled (built) for the Windows operating system cannot be executed on for instance Mac OSX. On more modern Mac computers you can run what is called dual boot where you actually can install Windows on the computer enabling you to run the PC application provided the Mac is booted with Windows.

All instructions sent to the processor is in binary format 0's and 1's. This means that your C# code must be converted into binary machine code somehow. For .NET applications this is a two stage rocket where the C# code first is compiled by Visual Studio into what is known as IL/MSIL (Intermediate language). The IL code can be viewed as C# code which has been turned into intermediate instructions which the .NET framework Just-in-time (JIT) compiler then can turn into low-level machine code (0's and 1's) when the application is run. The JIT compiler is even smart enough to only compile the code that is needed for the task at hand and to cache methods that already have been executed speeding up the execution for subsequent calls.

In short, data and instructions are transferred as binary data, 0's and 1's, which the processor can understand.

High-level languages such as C# and VB.NET has a semantic much like a human readable language which means that it cannot be run directly by a CPU. It first has to be converted into machine code.

Example: C# code → Is compiled to Intermediate Language (IL) in Visual Studio using the Common Type System → The Just-in-time (JIT) Compiler compiles the IL code to machine code → The CPU executes the code.

```
class Program
{
    static void Main(string[] args)
    {
    }
}
```
Build → MyApp.exe (IL Code) → On demand Build → Output

High-level language

```
static void Main(string[] args)
{
    int  x = 10, y = 20, z;

    if (x > y)
    {
        z = 100;
    }
}
```

Intermediate language (MSIL)

```
.method private hidebysig
static void  Main(string[] args)
{
    .entrypoint
    // Code size       24 (0x18)
    .maxstack  2
    .locals init ([0] int32 x,
                  [1] int32 y,
                  [2] int32 z,
                  [3] bool CS$4$0000)|
    IL_0000:  nop
```

You can view the MSIL code for an application by opening a Console window with Visual Studio paths and type in ILDASM followed by a space and the path and name of the application. The full name of the ILDASM tool is *Intermediate Language Disassembler*.

The processor works tightly with the internal memory (RAM) to store instructions between cycles or finished results which will be displayed to the user or saved to a permanent data store.

As an example when the 'A' key is pressed on the keyboard a binary instruction is sent to the processor which will process the request using the RAM memory before displaying the 'A' as output to the user.

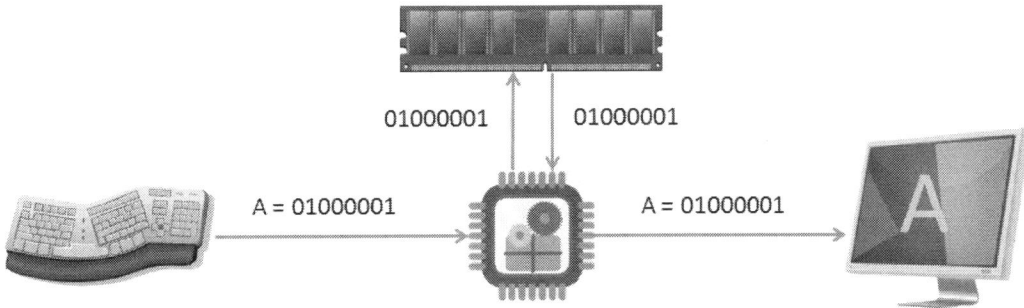

01000001   01000001

A = 01000001   A = 01000001

Bits and bytes

Bit stands for *binary digit* which is the smallest data unit capable of storing a value of 1 or 0 which often represent true or false. Bits are used to store and process data. To be able to work more effectively with data bits are chunked together into bytes where each byte is made up of 8 bits. Each byte can have a value of 0 to 255 which can represent a number, character or a data instruction. Several bytes can be used to store a single value, if more than one byte is used then the subsequent bytes are appended to the left side of the first byte. You always read a binary value from right to left. Because you add a full byte at a time you get the tuples 256, 512, 1024, 2048 and so on.

Byte	8 Bits	1 Byte
KByte	2^{10} Byte	1024 Byte
MByte	2^{20} Byte	1048576 Byte

The following image shows the bit values for one byte, in this case the capital letter A which has a value of 65.

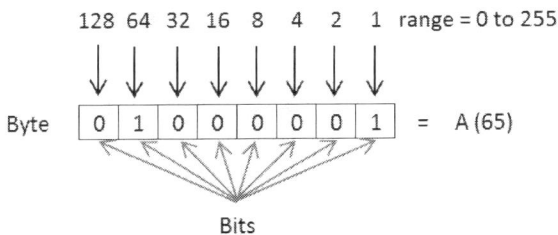

A binary value can be interpreted as an instruction, a memory reference or data depending on the context it is used. If it is a program the CPU will interpret the binary data as instructions and run it, if it is a memory address it will fetch or update data in the memory and if it is in the form of data the data is used with the processor instructions to complete a specific task, such as calculating a value.

Number bases

When creating an application there are three number bases which are frequently used. The number base used daily by most people is the *decimal* base which has a base of 10 hence the name, this is regularly used for measurements, currency and equations. The second number base is the *binary* base with a base of 2. In programming it is regularly used for describing bits which is the smallest storage of data represented by a 0 or a 1 where 1 means that it should be used and 0 that it should be ignored. The third is the hexadecimal base with a base of 16 and is regularly used when working with colors. In order to represent values over 9 the first letters of the alphabet is used to describe 10-15 (A-F).

To distinguish between the different bases when presenting values you use subscript to state the base after the value like 53_{10} for the decimal value 53, and 110101_2 for the binary value 53, and 35_{16} for the hexadecimal value 53.

Let's have a look at how you can convert one base to another. You can use the calculator in *Programmer* mode when converting between bases.

Decimal to binary

Let's convert the decimal number 53 into binary code. Looking at the number 53 you can see that it is smaller than 64 and larger than 32 which tells you that you should start with the binary value for decimal 32.

Can **32 (2^5)** be subtracted from **53**?   Yes   1   53 - 32 = 21
Can **16 (2^4)** be subtracted from **21**?   Yes   1   21 - 16 = 5
Can **8 (2^3)** be subtracted from **5**?   No   0
Can **4 (2^2)** be subtracted from **5**?   Yes   1   5 - 4 = 1
Can **2 (2^1)** be subtracted from **1**?   No   0
Can **1** be subtracted from **1**?   Yes   1   1 - 1 = 0

If you now take the binary 1's and 0's and tip them to the left you get the result 110101_2 which is the decimal value 53 represented in binary code.

Binary to decimal

Let's convert the binary number 110101_2 into a decimal number. When converting a binary number you always start from the left and move to the right where the right most bit represent 1 and the subsequent values to the left are multiples of 2. This means that you end up with a range of decimal values of 1, 2, 4, 8, 16, 32, 64, 128, 256, 1024, 2048 and so on from the left.

If you look at the number and figure out which multiple of 2 is the largest that can be subtracted from the number then working towards the smallest value to the right adding up the decimal values where a 1 is present in the binary value.

$32\ (2^5)$	$16\ (2^4)$	$8\ (2^3)$	$4\ (2^2)$	$2\ (2^1)$	1		
1	1	0	1	0	1		
32	16	0	4	0	1	=	53_{10}

Or if you prefer you can write it as: $110101_2 = 1 \times 2^5 + 1 \times 2^4 + 0 \times 2^3 + 1 \times 2^2 + 0 \times 2^1 + 1 = 53_{10}$

Decimal to hexadecimal

Let's convert the decimal number 1193046_{10} into a hexadecimal number which has a base of 16. The first thing you need to know is what the largest multiple of 16 that can be subtracted from the decimal value is, that will be your starting point. For the example value it is $16^5 = 1048576_{10}$.

How many times can you subtract 16^5 from 1193046_{10}?	1	1193046 - 1048576 = 144470
How many times can you subtract 16^4 from 144470_{10}?	2	144470 - (65536 x 2) = 13398
How many times can you subtract 16^3 from 13398_{10}?	3	13398 - (4096 x 3) = 1110
How many times can you subtract 16^2 from 1110_{10}?	4	1110 - (256 x 4) = 86
How many times can you subtract 16^1 from 86_{10}?	5	86 - (16 x 5) = 6
How many times can you subtract 16^0 from 6_{10}?	6	6 - (16 x 0) = 6

To get the hexadecimal value you simply tip the values in the middle column to the left and read them. $(1193046_{10})_{16} = 123456_{16}$.

Hexadecimal to decimal

Let's convert the hexadecimal number 123456_{16} into a decimal number which has a base of 10. You take one character (0-F) from the left at a time and multiply it by its multiple of 16 and sum up the values. Moving from right to left among the characters of the value you have 0-15, $16^1 = 16$, $16^2 = 256$, $16^3 = 4096$, $16^4 = 65536$, $16^5 = 1048576$.

$16^5 = 1048576$	$16^4 = 65536$	$16^3 = 4096$	$16^2 = 256$	$16^1 = 16$	0-15
1	2	3	4	5	6
1048576 x 1	65536 x 2	4096 x 3	256 x 4	16 x 5	1 x 6
1048576	131072	12288	1024	80	6	= 1193046

Project templates used in this book

When starting a new project, Visual Studio makes it easy by providing templates for the most common scenarios. The templates contain starter code which you can build on when creating your application. Relevant components, controls and references to necessary assemblies (class libraries) for the chosen template are included from the start.

The IDE will be configured according to the template. Below is a brief description of the templates used in this book.

Console Application

The Console Application has no graphical user interface (GUI) instead it is run in a Console window using a command-line interface; as such, it is considered to be very lightweight.

Windows Forms Application

Windows Forms Applications can be used to create desktop forms applications which run directly on top of the Windows operating system, not in a browser.

Class Library

Building a class library will result in a .dll assembly. This is a good way to reuse code and to share it among many applications. All you need to do to reuse the .dll is to reference its assembly.

The Console Application

If you want to create a very light weight application which does not need a graphical user interface (GUI) then the Console Application template in Visual Studio could be the way to go.

The Console application user interface (UI) is completely text based and therefore not very user friendly. One scenario where you might opt for a Console application is when creating server side applications where an administrator need a quick way to enter data or perform some other administrative task.

You will not spend a lot of time learning about every feature of the Console in this book since you most likely won't use it that often, instead you will learn about Windows Forms applications which have a rich user interface for desktop applications.

As the name eludes to the Console application runs in the big black void also known as a Console window. In Visual Studio there are not many windows you need to use when creating a Console application, the Solution Explorer is usually sufficient and sometimes you might want to use debug tools available in other windows (debugging will be covered later in the book).

The Solution Explorer is displayed along the right side of the development environment if you have the default C# language settings in Visual Studio. You can bring up the window again if it is hidden by selecting **View-Solution Explorer** in the main menu or hold down the **Ctrl** key and press **W** followed by **S** on the keyboard (**Ctrl+W, S**).

The Solution Explorer displays the project folders and files in a tree where the folders can be collapsed and expanded as needed. The main file in a Console application is called **Program.cs** and it contains a class called **Program** which is the application container.

The **Program** class contain a method called **Main** which is the application entry point, this is where the execution begin when the user start the application. It is in this method you write the application code you want to execute when the application is started. As you will learn later in the book you are encouraged to split your code into more manageable units called methods and store them in containers called classes for better reuse and to encapsulate the data. But for now you will write the code directly inside the **Main** method when creating your Console applications.

The **Main** method in a Console application has to be declared as **static** so that it can be executed without first having to create an object (instance) of the **Program** class. If you were forced to create an object of the **Program** class it would not be possible to execute the application directly in a Console window. The **Main** method is also not allowed to return a value because a return value cannot be handled after the application ends at the end of the **Main** method.

The images below describe important parts of the development environment and the **Main** method in the **Program.cs** file relating to Console applications.

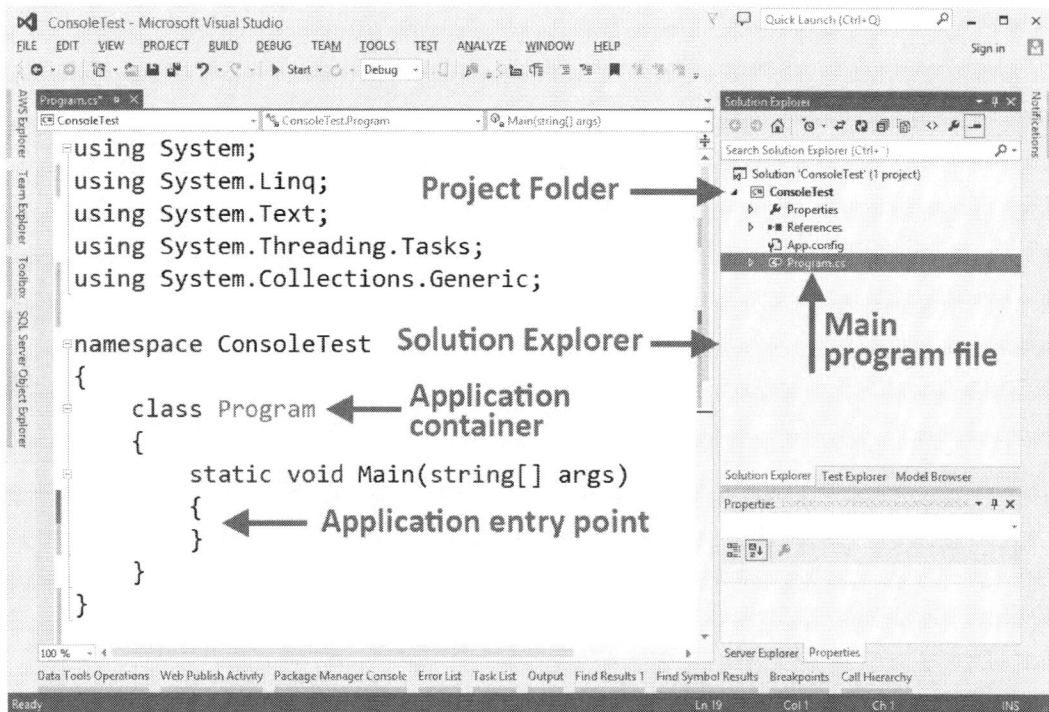

The Application starts here

Execution begin here

```
class Program
{
    static void Main(string[] args)
    {
    }
}
```

Write your code between the method's curly braces

void methods don't return any value

static methods don't require an object to run

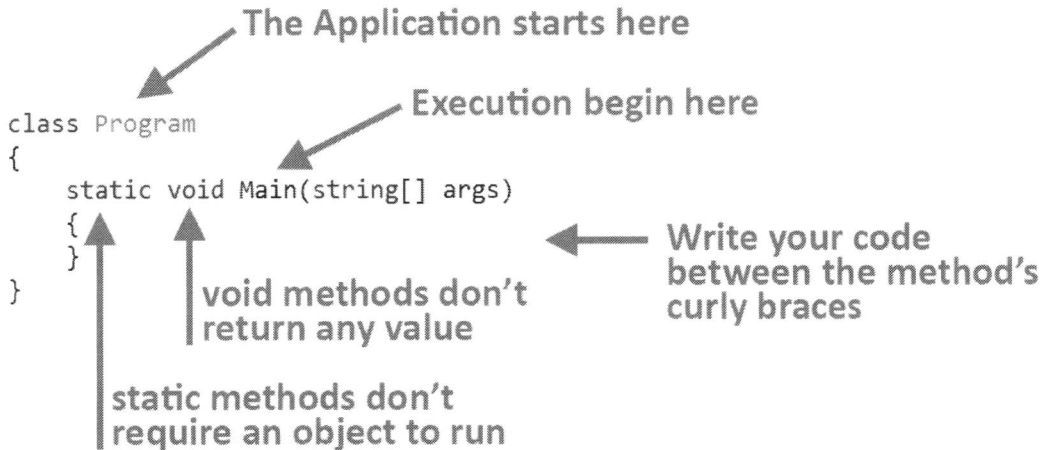

Keyword	Description
Class	In the context of the Program class it is the container for the main application flow.
Static	A static method is a CLASS method which means it belongs to the class and not individual objects which are created from the class. It is imperative that the Main method is declared as static in order for the .NET Framework run-time to execute it when the application is started by the user.
Void	A void declared method do not return any value. The Main method is not allowed to return a value because it cannot be handled by the runtime.

Compiling (building) a Console Application

You will want to continuously build (compile) your application when developing to catch any errors as soon as possible and fix them. You can build the solution by pressing **Ctrl + Shift + B** on the keyboard, the application is also built automatically when you run it by pressing **F5** of **Ctrl + F5** (run without debugging) on the keyboard. If errors are present they will be listed in a window called **Error List** which can be opened by selecting **View-Error List** in the main menu should it be closed. The error list is also reachable through a tab at the bottom of the development environment once it has been opened. You can usually reach the erroneous code by double clicking on the error in the list.

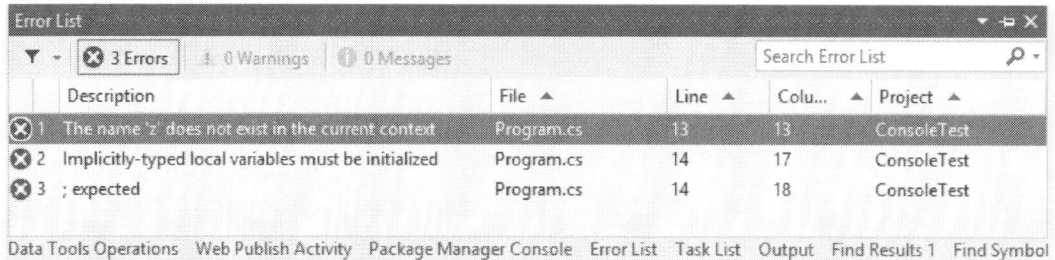

Error List Tab

How to create a Console Application

1. Open Visual Studio.
2. Select **File-New Project** in the menu.
3. Select **Visual C#** in the left tree menu in the dialog.
4. Select **Console Application** in the list of templates.
5. Give the project a name in the **Name** field.
6. Make sure that the **Create directory for solution** checkbox is checked.
7. Click on the **OK** button to have Visual Studio set up the project with the necessary files, folders and references.

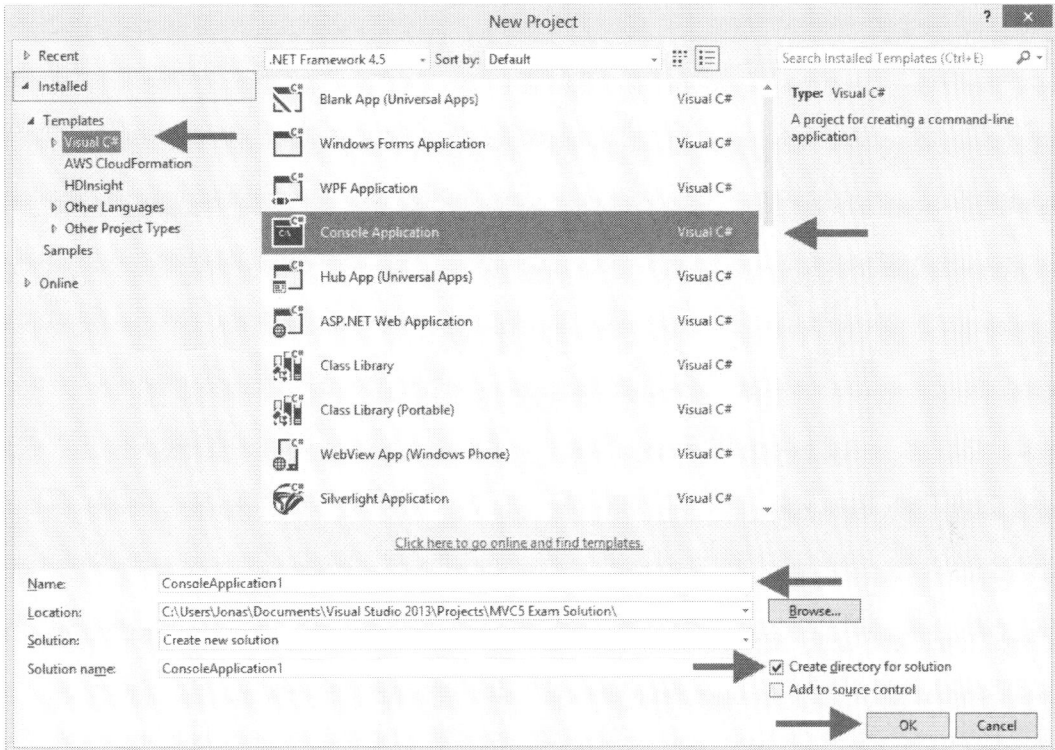

Interacting with the Console Window

The four most commonly used methods when interacting with the Console window are **Write**, **WriteLine**, **ReadLine** and **ReadKey**.

Writing to the Console window

Apart from using the predefined methods of the Console you can also format the output using string commands. You call the **Write** method for outputting text without a line break or the **WriteLine** method which adds a line break at the end of the text. Formatting can be added to the output string using for instance **\n** for an extra line break and **\t** for a tab, this can save you many lines of code not having to add empty **WriteLine** method calls when you desire a line break.

The following examples show how you can write text to the Console window. You can use either the **Write** or the **WriteLine** methods depending on if you want a line break after the text or not.

Note that you can add comments to the code which are ignored when the application is built by starting a code line with two slashes (**//**) or if it is a longer comment you can surround it with slash asterisk-asterisk slash (**/*** this is a comment ***/**).

```
// Add a line break
Console.WriteLine();
// Writes A line of text to the Console without a line break
Console.Write("A line of text");
// Writes the text on a new line using the \n command
Console.WriteLine("\nAnother line of text");
// Writes the text in two columns using \t
Console.WriteLine("\tName\tAge");
/* Formats the string by inserting the name into the string. You can insert
many strings by adding more curly braces and incrementing the index number
and adding the values as a comma separated list. */
Console.WriteLine("Welcome {0}!", "Jonas");
// Create fixed length columns
Console.WriteLine("{0,20}{1,4}yo", "Jonas", 45);
```

Reading user input from the Console window

When reading user input from the Console you might want to store the value for later use. The easiest way to store a value is to use the **var** keyword followed by a variable name through which you can gain access to the stored value (you will learn more about variables in an upcoming chapter).

```
// Prompt the user to enter their name
Console.Write("Enter your name: ");
// Store the name in a variable for later use
var name = Console.ReadLine();
// Writes: Welcome Jonas! to the Console if the name Jonas is entered by
the user
Console.WriteLine("Welcome {0}!", name);
```

Keeping the Console window open when debugging

You can call the **ReadKey** method to keep the Console window open after the last line has been output. The value **true** passed in to the method stop the character from being output to the Console.

```
Console.WriteLine("\nPress any key to exit");
Console.ReadKey(true);
```

Exercise: Create your first Console Application

In this exercise you will create a new Console application which will prompt the user for his or her name with the text "Enter your name: " and store the entered name in a variable called **name**. Then you will use the value stored in the variable to write the text "Welcome *the entered name*!" where *the entered name* represents the actual name stored in the name variable, for instance *Welcome Jonas!* if they entered *Jonas*. The name should be entered on the same line as the text.

Then you will add a line break (**\n**) to the beginning of the text "Enter your age: " and let the user enter their age on the same line as the text, no line break should be added after the text. The age input by the user should be stored in a variable called **age**.

Use a tab (**\t**) to push the text to the right and then output a heading reading "Name Age" with a tab between the words. Then present the name and age on a separate line below the heading.

Next you will use fixed length columns using the **{0, 20}** syntax where the 0 is the index representing the place where the variable value will be inserted and 20 is the fixed number of characters in the column. Use fixed length columns to display the name and the age stored in the variables.

Lastly you will prompt the user to press any key to exit the application and after the text use the **ReadKey** method to wait for the user to press a keyboard key.

Creating the solution

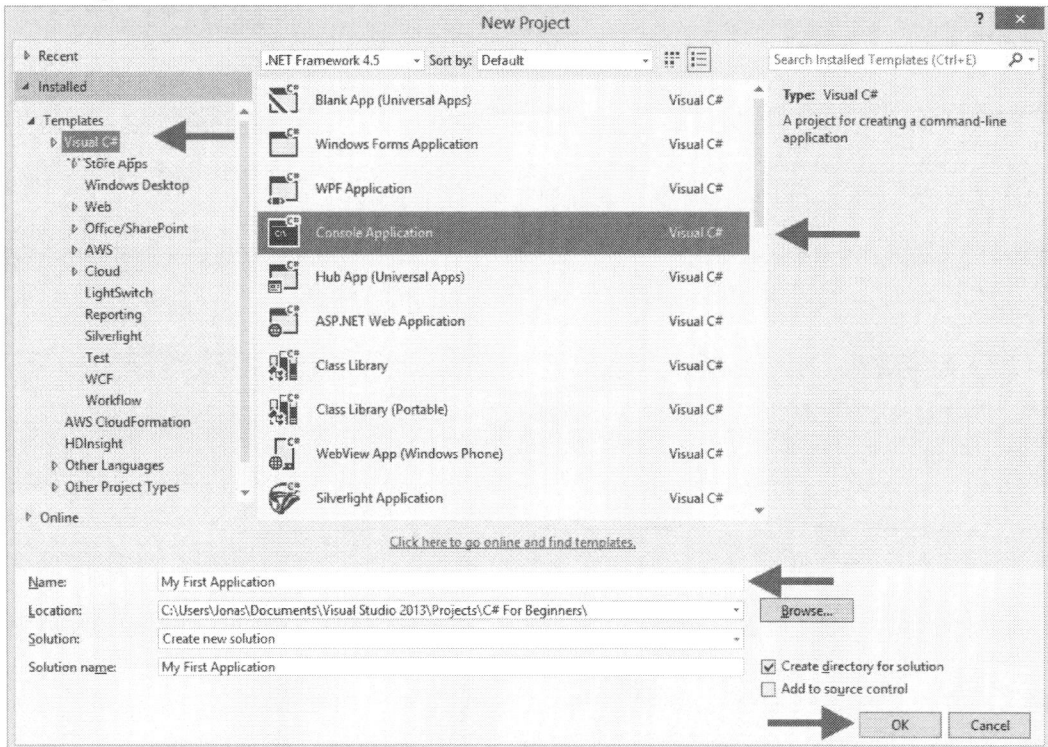

1. Open Visual Studio
2. Click on the **New Project** link or select **File-New Project** in the main menu.

3. Click on **Visual C#** in the tree view on the left side in the *New Project* dialog.
4. Select **Console Application** in the project template list in the middle of the dialog.
5. Name the project *My First Application* in the **Name** text field.
6. Click on the **OK** button.
7. Locate the **Main** method in the **Program.cs** file where you will write your program code.
```
static void Main(string[] args)
{
    // Write your code here
}
```

Keeping the Console window open

The first thing on your to-do list is to make sure that the Console window stays open after the output and user input has finished. If you don't keep the window open it will close as soon as the last line of code has been executed when running it from within Visual Studio.

The output to the Console window should look like this:

1. Create a new line between the curly braces by placing the cursor to the right of the upper curly brace in the **Main** method and press **Enter** on the keyboard.
2. Write the message **"Press any key to exit"** using the **WriteLine** method. Add a line break at the beginning of the string using the **\n** command to move the text down a line so that it isn't flush against the top border of the window.
```
Console.WriteLine("\nPress any key to exit");
```

3. Add a new empty line to your code after the previous code line and add a call to the **ReadKey** method passing in **true** in between the parenthesis to stop the keystroke from being written to the Console window.
```
Console.ReadKey(true);
```

4. Run the application by pressing the **F5** key on the keyboard or click on the **Start** button in the toolbar below the main menu.

The complete code so far looks like this:

```
static void Main(string[] args)
{
    Console.WriteLine("\nPress any key to exit");
    Console.ReadKey(true);
}
```

Ask for the user's name

Now it's time to ask the user for some input and relate the result back to the user by writing text to the console.

The output to the Console window should look similar to this:

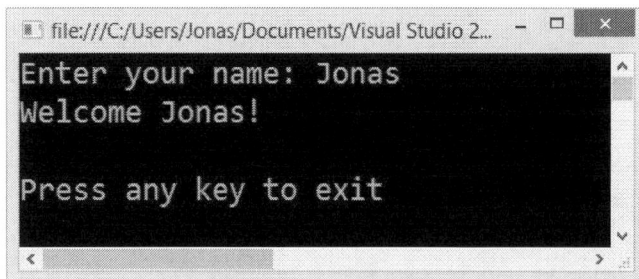

1. Add an empty line above the **Console.WriteLine** method call you added in the previous exercise.
2. Write the text **Enter your name:** to the Console without adding a line break after the text, you can achieve this by calling the **Write** method.
   ```
   Console.Write("Enter your name: ");
   ```
3. Collect the name the user enters in a variable called **name** using the **var** keyword. Call the **ReadLine** method to allow the user to enter their name.
   ```
   var name = Console.ReadLine();
   ```
4. Write the text **Welcome** followed by the name the user enters and end the text with an exclamation mark. The easiest way to achieve this is to use a formatted string. The curly brace with the index inside will be replaced by the text after the comma in the **WriteLine** method's parenthesis. Note that you can use a constant string value if

needed by writing the text between cotes ("the text") or you can use a variable like in the code below.

```
Console.WriteLine("Welcome {0}!", name);
```

5. Run the application, enter your name and press **Enter** on the keyboard. You should end up with an output similar to the one in the image above.

The complete code so far looks like this:

```
static void Main(string[] args)
{
    Console.Write("Enter your name: ");
    var name = Console.ReadLine();
    Console.WriteLine("Welcome {0}!", name);

    Console.WriteLine("\nPress any key to exit");
    Console.ReadKey(true);
}
```

Ask for the user's age

Now let's ask the user for his or her age and display the result using tabular output.

The output to the Console window should look similar to this:

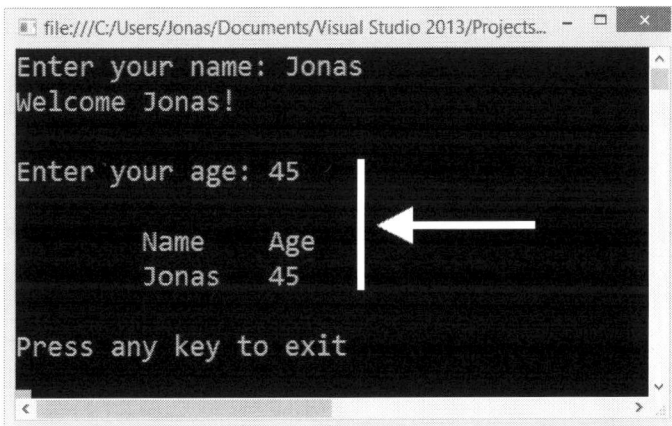

1. Add a new line below the *Welcome* message you added in the previous exercise.

2. Write the message **Enter your age:** without adding a line break after the text using the **Write** method. Add a line break at the beginning of the string using the **\n** command.
```
Console.Write("\nEnter your age: ");
```

3. Store the age entered by the user in a variable called **age** using the **var** keyword. Read the value using the **ReadLine** method.
```
var age = Console.ReadLine();
```

4. Write the **name** and **age** header to the Console and push it in using a tab (**\t**) also use a tab between the words to create the effect of columns. Add a line break (**\n**) at the beginning of the string to push the text down one line creating a space above the text.
```
Console.WriteLine("\n\tName\tAge");
```

5. Write the name and age stored in the variables using a formatted string containing two tabs, to achieve this you have to add two curly braces with indices 0 and 1 and then list the variables in a comma separated list.
```
Console.WriteLine("\t{0}\t{1}", name, age);
```

6. Run the application and make sure that the output is similar to the image above.

The complete code looks like this:

```
static void Main(string[] args)
{
    Console.Write("Enter your name: ");
    var name = Console.ReadLine();
    Console.WriteLine("Welcome {0}!", name);

    Console.Write("\nEnter your age: ");
    var age = Console.ReadLine();
    Console.WriteLine("\n\tName\tAge");
    Console.WriteLine("\t{0}\t{1}", name, age);

    Console.WriteLine("\nPress any key to exit");
    Console.ReadKey(true);
}
```

Namespace and using

Namespaces are a way to physically group classes that belong together and have something in common. To access the classes in a namespace you can either add a using statement at the top of the .cs file you want to access the classes from or you can give the full namespace and class name in the code when using the classes. The latter method of using namespaces is not the recommended way because it adds a lot of extra code which will clutter it up and make it hard to read.

Let's say that you want to calculate the square root of a number, to achieve this you can use a math method called **Sqrt** in a predefined .NET Framework **Math** class. Below are the two ways you can implement it, the namespace paths are usually much longer than the one in the example. You can also note that your **Program** class automatically was placed in a namespace when the project was created.

Implement the calculation using the namespace directly in the code. Note that you have to use the full namespace path every time you make a call to the **Sqrt** method. It might not seem like a lot of extra code to write the namespace path on each line but keep in mind that this is one of the shortest namespace paths in the .NET Framework library, usually they are several levels deep.

```
namespace MyConsoleApplication
{
    class Program
    {
        static void Main(string[] args)
        {
            var result1 = System.Math.Sqrt(5);
            var result2 = System.Math.Sqrt(10);
            var result3 = System.Math.Sqrt(15);
        }
    }
}
```

Implement the code with a **using** statement to declare the namespace and then call the method. Note that you only declare the namespace path once to be able to call the **Sqrt** method directly on the **Math** class as many times as needed.

```
using System;
```

```
namespace MyConsoleApplication
{
    class Program
    {
        static void Main(string[] args)
        {
            var result1 = Math.Sqrt(5);
            var result2 = Math.Sqrt(10);
            var result3 = Math.Sqrt(15);
        }
    }
}
```

Regions

A region is a way to logically group code and not affecting the program flow, it is only used to make the code more readable and easy to follow. A region is a collapsible section of code which hides the code and displays a descriptive text in its place. When the code need to be altered or viewed the region can be expanded again. You collapse and expand a region by clicking on its plus/minus sign in the left margin.

To create a region you add the **#region** keyword followed by the description on the line above the first code line you want to include in the region and add the **#endregion** keyword after the last line of code you want to be part of the region.

If you want to add a region around the mathematical calculations in the previous example the code would look like this:

```
static void Main(string[] args)
{
    #region Math Calculations
    var result1 = System.Math.Sqrt(5);
    var result2 = System.Math.Sqrt(10);
    var result3 = System.Math.Sqrt(15);
    #endregion
}
```

When collapsed the code would only display the heading *Math Calculations*.

```
static void Main(string[] args)
{
    Math Calculations
}
```

When writing a program I usually end up with the following main **regions** in my **classes** or **structs**, you will learn about **structs** and **classes** in upcoming chapters, here I just want to show you the logical sections I often create using **regions**. If there are terms unknown to you in the region descriptions just make a mental note of them and keep them in mind when reading the upcoming chapters. You can always come back to this section if you feel that you need to refresh your knowledge about **regions**. In some applications I don't need all **regions** and in some I need to be more granular and create sub-**regions**.

```
public class MyClass
{
    #region Delegates and Events
    #endregion
    #region Constants
    #endregion
    #region Fields/Variables
    #endregion
    #region Properties
    #endregion
    #region Constructors
    #endregion
    #region Methods
    #endregion
    #region Control Events
    #endregion
}
```

Exercise: Adding regions to the application

Open the application you created in the previous exercise and surround the code fetching and displaying the name with a region which has the description *Fetch user name*. Next place a region around the code that fetches and displays the users age and give it the description *Fetch user's age*. Place a third region around the code that keep the Console window open and give it the description *Exit code*.

23

Once the regions are in place test them by collapsing and expanding them with the plus/minus signs in the left margin of the code window.

Run the application to make sure that the regions does not affect the program flow and that it still works as before.

1. Open the *My First Application* project in Visual Studio.
2. Add a **#region** command above the first **Write** method call and give it the description *Fetch user name*.
   ```
   #region Fetch user name
   Console.Write("Enter your name: ");
   ```
3. Add a **#endregion** command below the **WriteLine** method call writing the *Welcome* message.
   ```
   Console.WriteLine("Welcome {0}!", name);
   #endregion
   ```
4. Add a **#region** command above the **Write** method call asking the user for his or her age and give it the description *Fetch user's age*.
   ```
   #region Fetch user's age
   Console.Write("\nEnter your age: ");
   ```
5. Add a **#endregion** command below the **WriteLine** method call writing the name and age to the Console window.
   ```
   Console.WriteLine("\t{0}\t{1}", name, age);
   #endregion
   ```
6. Add a **#region** command above the **WriteLine** method call asking the user to press any key to exit.
   ```
   #region Exit code
   Console.Write("\nPress any key to exit");
   ```
7. Add a **#endregion** command below the **ReadKey** method call.
   ```
   Console.ReadKey(true);
   #endregion
   ```
8. Now that the regions are in place close them by clicking on the minus sign in the left margin of the code window.
9. Click on the plus signs in the margin to open them again.

10. Now let's collapse all outlines with one command by right clicking in the code window and select **Outlining-Collapse to Definitions (Ctrl+M,O)**. This will collapse all regions and methods in the active code window.

11. Expand the **Main** method by clicking on its plus sign in the margin. This should reveal the method content which should be collapsed and only reveal the region descriptions.

12. Expand all the regions again by right clicking in the code window and selecting **Outlining-Toggle all Outlining (Ctrl+M,L)** or by clicking on their individual plus signs in the margin.

13. Run the application by pressing **F5** on the keyboard or on the **Play** button in the toolbar below the main menu. Make sure that the application is working like it did before the regions were added and that they have not changed the program flow.

14. Close the application.

A first look at Windows Forms

You have just been acquainted with the Console Application which has its limited uses. Now you will have a look at the much more versatile Windows Forms Application project with which you can create fully fledged systems for Windows desktop use. This project type has a Graphical User Interface (GUI) with which the user can interact through the controls you add to it. You can add many types of predefined controls ranging from buttons and text fields to tree view controls and menus.

Creating the solution

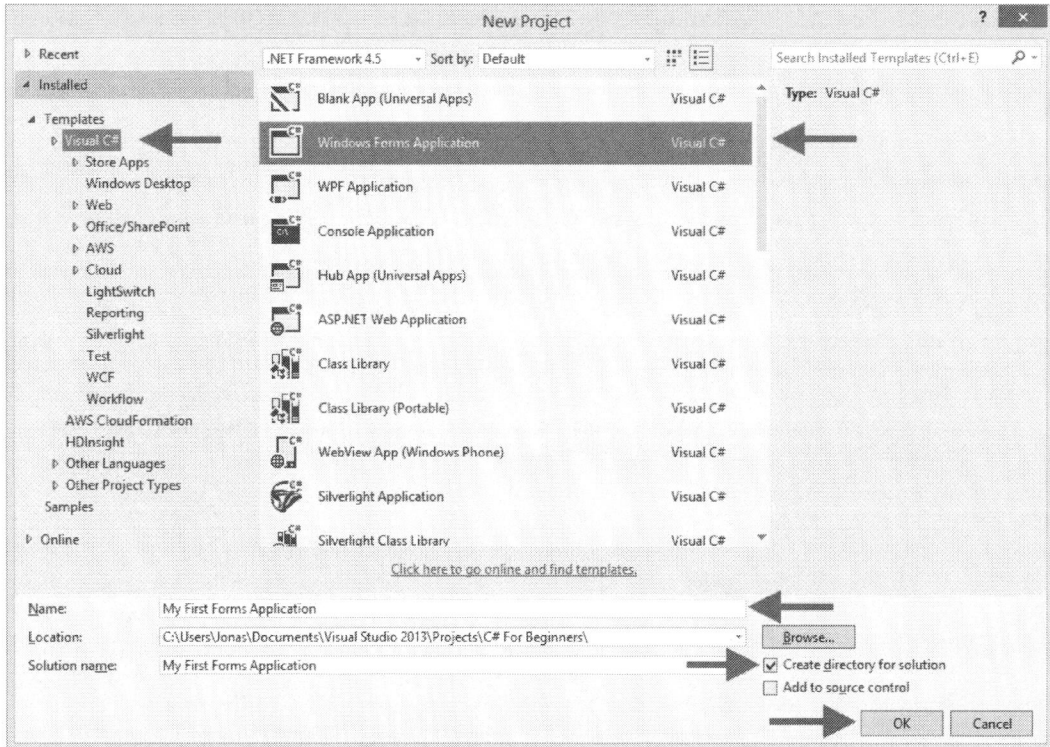

1. Open Visual Studio
2. Click on the **New Project** link or select **File-New Project** in the main menu.
3. Click on **Visual C#** in the tree view on the left side of the *New Project* dialog.
4. Select **Windows Forms Application** in the project template list in the middle of the dialog.
5. Name the project **My First Forms Application** by typing it in the **Name** text field.
6. Click on the **OK** button.

The project content

As you can see the project content is different from what you would find in a Console Application. For starters a gray form is displayed instead of a code window this is deliberate because you have to add controls to the form in order to do anything useful with it, even if it's only a button. The form is the application surface with which the user interacts. To give the user a pleasant experience you want to align the added controls in straight lines and not scatter them around the surface in a chaotic fashion, you also want to use labels to describe the purpose of the controls. If the user is supposed to enter a name in a textbox then you should add a label either above or to the left of the control depending on the layout you have decided to use. You add controls from the **Toolbox** window described in the next section.

All open files are displayed as tabs above the design surface. If you need to open a closed form or other file you can find it in the Solution Explorer. Clicking on the file will open it temporarily and its tab will be replaced by the next file you click on. While double clicking on a file will open it permanently and it will be open the next time you open the solution when it has been closed. You can close a file tab by clicking on its **x**-button.

You might have noticed that there is a **Program.cs** file in this project like in the Console Application project, but in a Windows Forms Application it is only used to start the application and display the main form to the user. You very seldom write any code in this file, the code is instead written in what is known as a code-behind file which is linked to a specific form. The easiest way to open a form's code-behind file is to double click on the its gray background area or expand the form node in the Solution Explorer and click on the sub-node with the same name as the form name. You will learn where to write code in the code-behind throughout the book and new controls will be introduced as needed for the exercises.

The image below show the development environment displaying the **Toolbox** and the form's design surface.

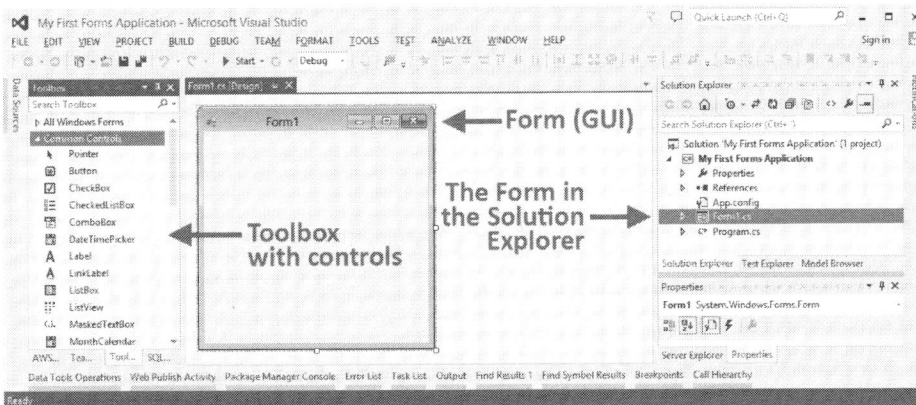

Note that the **Toolbox** is empty when the code-behind is open because it is impossible to add graphical controls to a code file using the **Toolbox**. The code-behind is opened in a second tab and the GUI is in the tab with **[Design]** after the name. You can click on the tabs to toggle between the code-behind and the design view or other open windows.

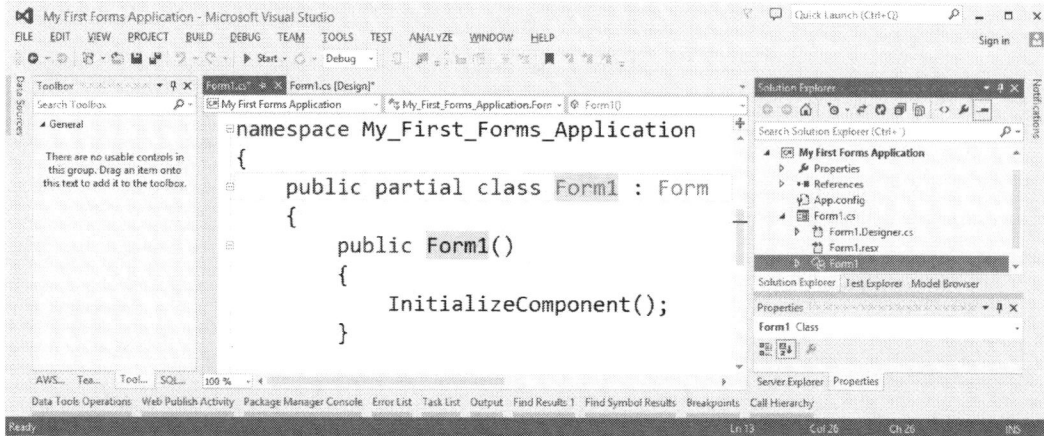

You run the application by pressing **F5** or **Ctrl+F5** on the keyboard or clicking on the **Start** button, the same as for Console Applications. When you run the application the main form is displayed to the user. It will behave as any other standard Windows form you are used to and has the same **minimize**, **maximize** and **close** buttons in the title bar. The form is empty right now, but you will soon add some controls to it.

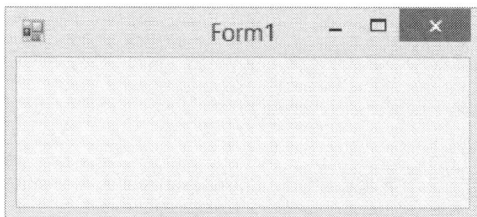

Adding controls to the form

You find the predefined controls you can add to a form in the **Toolbox** window which can be minimized to a tab or a window along the left side of the Visual Studio developer environment. The toolbox can always be opened by selecting **View-Toolbox** in the main menu should you be unable to find it in the development environment.

When working with controls adding them to the form surface it can save time to pin the **Toolbox** window to the developer environment to keep it open, you pin it by clicking on the **pin** icon in the top right corner of the **Toolbox** window. You can unpin it at any time by clicking on the **pin** button again.

You can add controls to the form in many ways the most common are to either double click on the control in the **Toolbox** or to hold down the left mouse button while pointing to the control and drag the control to the form surface.

To design the form well you might need to change the size of the controls you add to its surface, you do this by selecting the control (clicking on it once) and using the control's square sizing handles.

Naming a control

When adding a control to the form you often want to name it (labels can be an exception). To name a control you select it and change the default name in the **Name** property in the **Properties** window which is displayed below the Solution Explorer by default.

You can follow the same instructions when naming a form with the difference that you select the form instead of a control.

1. Open the **Properties** window with **View-Properties Window** in the main menu if it is closed.
2. Select the control in the form you wish to name by clicking on it once.
3. Go to the **Properties** window and scroll to the top where you will find the **(Name)** field.
4. Double click on the **(Name)** label to select all text in it.
5. Write the new name and press **Enter** on the keyboard.

Where to write the code

You add functionality to the form by writing code that will be reachable and executed at different stages depending on where you write the code. The form itself is a class which will be used by the run-time to create a form object on the *Heap* (the slow memory) which then will be displayed to the user.

As you can see in the code below the **Form** class has a section of code called *Form1()* (the name you have given the form) which is a special method known as a *Constructor*. The code written in the *Constructor* will be executed as the form object is created on the *Heap*, you can use this method to initialize variable values before the form, or even its controls, are visible. This is very useful to give the form the correct state before it is accessible by the user.

Below the Constructor is another section called **Form1_Load** (*YourFormName*_Load) which is a special type of method called an event. An event is triggered and executed when the system or a user is interacting with the form or its controls, like clicking on a button, writing in a textbox or when a control or form is loaded or modified. The predefined **Load** event will be executed as the form is loaded into memory after the form object has been created on the *Heap* and before it is displayed to the user. This event can be used to fill form controls with default values or values fetched from a data store such as a database or a file.

```
public partial class Form1 : Form
{
    public Form1()
    {
        InitializeComponent();
        // Code to initialize the Form object
    }

    private void Form1_Load(object sender, EventArgs e)
    {
        // Code to execute before the form is displayed
    }
}
```

Code accessibility

If you declare a variable outside the two previously mentioned methods but inside curly braces of the **Form** class it will be reachable from all methods inside the **Form** class.

Declaring a variable inside a method will narrow its availability to code inside that particular method and it will not be reachable from other methods. In other words, if you declare a variable inside the *Constructor* method that variable can only be used inside the *Constructor* and in no other method.

As you will learn in later chapters there are different types of code blocks which can be declared inside a method. If you declare a variable inside such a block the variable will only be reachable within that block and therefore not in the rest of the method. One example is the **if**-block used to alter the program flow.

The following example code demonstrates the accessibility using three variables. The **total** variable is declared on class level which mean that it can be used throughout the class. The **result** variable is declare inside the **Form1_Load** event method and is therefore only accessible from within that method. The **sum** variable is declared inside the **if**-block and is therefore only accessible inside that block, if you want to use the value in the **sum** value you can assign it to a variable with greater accessibility.

The **total** variable is assigned the value **0** inside the *Constructor* method before the form or its controls have been rendered to the screen. The **result** variable is declared and assigned the value **10** inside the **Load** event and is then used in the **if**-statement (more on **if** in a later chapter) and as part of a calculation inside the **if**-block. The **sum** variable is declared and used to store the result of the calculation inside the **if**-block and its value is then assigned to the class level variable **total** making the value available throughout the class.

```
public partial class Form1 : Form
{
    // Available in all methods of the Form class
    int total;

    public Form1()
    {
        // Assign a value to the total variable
        total = 0;

        InitializeComponent();
    }

    private void Form1_Load(object sender, EventArgs e)
    {
        // result available inside the method and the if block
        var result = 10;

        if (result > 0)
        {
            // sum only available inside the block
```

```
        var sum = result * 100;

        // Assign the sum variable's value to the total variable
        total = sum;
    }
  }
}
```

Exercise: Creating your first Window Forms Application

In this exercise you will implement the same scenario as in the Console Application you crated earlier. You will create a user interface (a form) asking the user for his or her name and age and then display the formatted result in a pop-up dialog box. To achieve this you will need to add two labels with the text *Name* and *Age* respectively and place textboxes which will collect the user input below the labels and lastly you will add a button which will display the dialog box when clicked.

If you haven't already created the Windows Forms Application called *My First Forms Application* described in the section Creating the solution, then do so now.

This is what the form will look like when finished:

Create the form and add controls

1. Open the **Form1 [Design]** tab. If you have closed it you can open it by double clicking on the **Form1** node in the Solution Explorer.
2. Open the **Toolbox** window (**View-Toolbox**) if it's not already open.
3. Double click on the **Label** icon in the **Toolbox** to add a **Label** control to the form and then reposition it on the form surface.
4. Change the text of the label to *Name* in its **Text** property in the **Properties** window.

5. Add a textbox control to the form below the label by double clicking on the textbox icon in the **Toolbox**.

6. Rename the textbox *txtName* in the **Name** field in the **Properties** window.

7. Resize the textbox to make it wider.

8. Add another label below the name textbox and change its text to *Age*.

9. Add another textbox below the *Age* label and change the textbox name to *txtAge*.

10. Add a **Button** control below the age textbox and rename it *btnDisplayData*.

11. Change the text on the **Button** to *Display data*.

12. Resize the form by clicking once on its gray surface and drag the middle bottom square handle upwards and the middle right handle left.

13. Start the application by pressing **F5** on the keyboard.

14. The form is displayed with empty text fields and nothing will happen if you click on the button.

15. Close the application by clicking on the red **x**-button in the upper right corner of the form or click on the **Stop** button (the button with the red square) in the developer environment.

Add code to the button

To make the button perform a task you have to add its **Click** event method in the form code-behind window. The easiest way to add the **Click** event is to double click on the button which will add the event method and take you straight to it in the code window.

The final piece of the puzzle is to make the form display a message in a dialog box when the button is clicked. You can use the **Show** method on the **MessageBox** class to display the dialog box.

1. Double click on the button in the form designer.

2. A **Click** event method with the same name as the button is automatically added to the code-behind window.

   ```
   private void btnDisplayData_Click(object sender, EventArgs e)
   {
       // Your code goes here
   }
   ```

3. Let's start by adding the message box dialog with some static text. Add the following code to the **Click** event.

```
MessageBox.Show("This is my first dialog box");
```

4. Start the application and click on the button to display the dialog box.

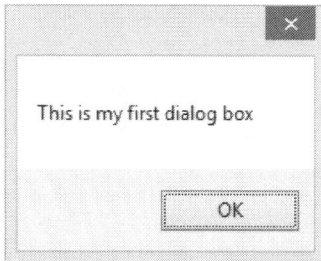

5. Close the dialog box and application.
6. Now let's up the ante to display the text from the **txtName** textbox. Delete the text and quotes (inside the **Show** method parenthesis) and add code that fetch the value form the textbox using its **Text** property. Change the code to this.

```
MessageBox.Show(txtName.Text);
```

7. Start the application and write your name in the **Name** textbox before clicking on the button. The dialog box should display your name.

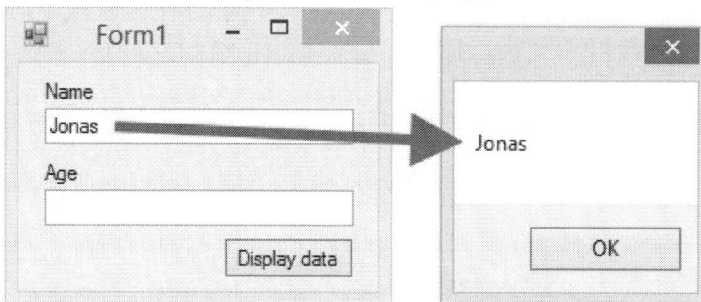

8. Close the application.
9. Now let's up the stakes again by formatting the output string to display name and age from both textboxes and some descriptive text. You can format the string output using the same string formatting technique you used in the Console Application with the difference that you format the string using the **Format** method on **String** class instead of **Console.WriteLine**.

```
MessageBox.Show(String.Format("{0} is {1} years old.", txtName.Text,
txtAge.Text));
```

10. Start the application and enter your name and age in the textboxes and then click the button. The dialog should look similar to this.

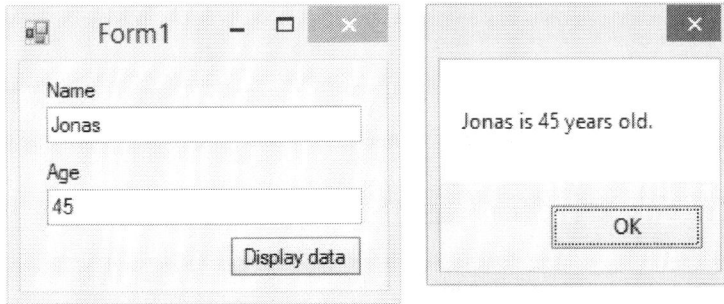

11. Close the application.

2. Conditional Logic

Introduction

Conditional statements are used to determine the flow of the application. For instance, you might pose a question to the user and determine the application flow based on that answer. Although you will use conditional logic to determine the application flow using form controls such as radio buttons and a combo box in this chapter, conditional logic can also be used with constants, variables and even hard coded values. The difference between using controls and the other methods of using conditional logic is that you will use properties of the control instead of declared variables, constants or other values in the **if**- or **switch**-expression.

If

An **if**-statement is used to evaluate if a condition is **true** or **false** and, based on the result, do one of two things or in conjunction with one or more **else**-block or **else if**-blocks to handle multiple scenarios.

If the condition in the **if**-statement evaluates to **true,** the **if**-block is executed; otherwise, the **else** block is executed if one exists.

If **else if**-blocks are defined then the execution will be propagated to the next **else if** statement in line until a statement evaluates to **true** or there are no more **else if**-statements left.

IMPORTANT: *By using two equal signs (==) in an expression you can check if the two values of a condition are equal to one another:* `if (value == otherValue).` *or you can use the* **Equals** *method to achieve the same result:* `if (value.Equals(otherValue)).`

IMPORTANT: *By using a not equals (!=) expression you can check if the two values of a condition differ from one another:* `if (value != otherValue).` *or you can use the* **Equals** *method in conjunction with a negating exclamation mark to achieve the same result:* `if (!value.Equals(otherValue)).`

If statement

```
if (valueToEvaluate == true)
{
    // This code will be executed if the condition
    // evaluates to true
}
```

If...else statement

```
if (valueToEvaluate == true)
{
    // This code will be executed if the condition
    // evaluates to true
}
else
{
    // This code will be executed if the condition
    // evaluates to false
}
```

If...else if statement

```
var someStringValue = "Some text";

if (someStringValue == "Some value")
{
    // This code will be executed if the if
    // condition evaluates to true
}
else if (someStringValue == "Some other value")
{
    // This code will be executed if the else if
    // condition evaluates to true
}
else
{
    // else this code will be executed
}
```

If statement inside another if statement

```
var someStringValue = "Some text";
var someBooleanValue = false;
```

```
if (someStringValue == "Some value")
{
   if (someBooleanValue == true)
   {
       // This code will be executed if the if
       // condition evaluates to true
   }
   else
   {
       // else this code will be executed
   }
}
else
{
}
```

Switch

When writing conditional statements, you should not have too many **if/else** clauses because it makes the code harder to read and understand; instead, you should consider using switch statements. A **switch** block is essentially a more compact and more readable way to write **if/else** clauses.

The **case** choices in a **switch** are defined using constant values.

Each **case** statement ends with a **break** or **return** command which forces the execution to either jump to the end of the **switch** block or exit the current method or event completely without executing any remaining code.

You can have a **default** block in the **switch**, which essentially is the same as an ending **else** clause in an **if/else** statement. This block will be executed if no **case** block is matched.

```
var valueToCheck = "The current value";

switch (valueToCheck)
{
    case "Some value":
        // Do something
```

```
        break;
    case "Some other value":
        // Do something else
        break;
    default:
        // Execute if no case is matched
        break;
}
```

Additional reading: "Selection Statements (C# Reference)"

Exercise: Conditional logic

In the first part of this exercise you will implement **if/else** and **if/else if/else** scenarios. In the **if/else** scenario the user will determine the program flow by checking a checkbox which will enable or disable some other controls. If the checkbox is selected the user can then select a gender with radio buttons taking them into the **if/else if/else** program flow, here the message in the label will be changed when the button is clicked depending on if they have selected any radio button or which radio button has been selected.

In the second part of this exercise you will use a **switch** to control the program flow depending on what country has been selected in the combo box. In the **switch** the primary language of the selected country will be displayed in the label which also will change background color depending on the selected country. You will add the following countries Sweden (Swedish, light green), Norway (Norwegian, LightSkyBlue), Finland (Finnish, LightYellow), Great Britain and USA (English, LightSalmon) and finally Unknown (Unspecified, LightPink). Feel free to add other countries of your choice.

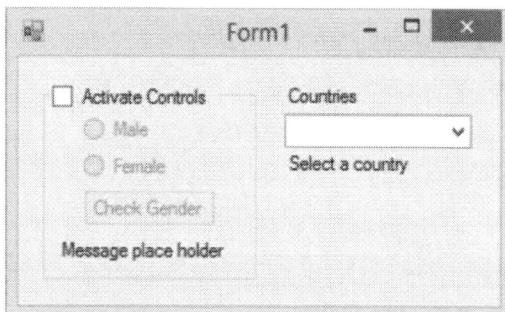

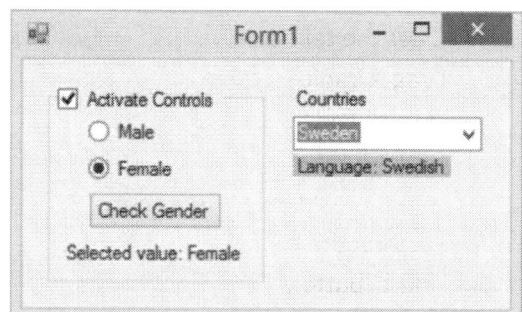

If/else logic

Let's start by adding the controls and then progress to the logic in the code-behind file.

You will need to add a group box control (located in the *All Windows Forms* section of the toolbox) to which you add all the other controls except the checkbox which you will place on top of the group box border (see image above). The reason you need to add a group box is that radio buttons must be placed in a group box to work as a unit, this is especially important if you have several radio button sections which should work independently from one another. If you don't use group boxes for the radio buttons and instead place them on the form directly all radio buttons will be in the same radio button group which will be provided by the form.

Inside the group box you place two radio buttons called *rbnMale* and *rbnFemale* with the text "Male" and "Female" respectively. Below the radio buttons you add a button called *btnCheckGender* with the text "Check Gender" and a label called *lblMessage* with the text "Message place holder".

Lastly you add a checkbox called *chkActivate* with the text "Activate Controls" which will enable or disable the controls in the group box depending on if the checkbox is selected or not. Select the form before adding the checkbox to avoid it being placed inside the group box and then drag it on top of the group box after having removed the group box header text.

Adding the controls

1. Open the form designer.
2. Expand the *All Windows Forms* section of the toolbox.
3. Drag a group box onto the form surface.
4. Clear the text from its **Text** property.
5. Drag a radio button into the group box, change the name to *rbnMale*, its text to "Male" and its **Enabled** property to **false**.
6. Drag a second radio button into the group box, change the name to *rbnFemale*, its text to "Female" and its **Enabled** property to **false**.
7. Position the "Female" radio button below the "Male" radio button.
8. Add a button to the group box, change the name to *btnCheckGender*, its text to "Check Gender" and its **Enabled** property to **false**.

9. Add a label to the group box and change the name to **lblMessage** and its text to "Message place holder".

10. Select the form by clicking on it once.

11. Drag a checkbox to the form surface not inside the group box and change the name to **chkActivate** and its text to "Activate Controls".

12. Move the checkbox on top of the group box where its header used to be displayed making it the checkbox the group box header of sorts.

Enable/disable the controls

1. Select the checkbox control by clicking once on it.

2. Go to the **Properties** window and click on the **Events** button (the one with the flash icon).

3. Locate the **CheckStateChanged** event and double click on its description this will create the event in the form's code-behind file and take you to it. The event will be triggered when the state of the checkbox is changed (checked or unchecked).
```
private void chkActivate_CheckStateChanged(object sender,
EventArgs e)
{
}
```

4. Add an **if**-statement checking if the checkbox is checked using its **Checked** property. When the property or variable used in an **if**-statement is Boolean you don't have to explicitly check if it is equal to **true** or **false** that will be done automatically for you by just stating the property or variable name.
```
if (chkActivate.Checked)
{
}
```

5. Inside the **if**-block curly braces you want to enable the radio buttons and the button because a checked checkbox means that the controls should be enabled. You enable the controls by assigning **true** to their **Enabled** properties.
```
btnCheckGender.Enabled = true;
rbnMale.Enabled = true;
rbnFemale.Enabled = true;
```

6. Add an **else**-block below the **if**-block in which you disable the controls by assigning **false** to their **Enabled** properties.
```
btnCheckGender.Enabled = false;
```

```
rbnMale.Enabled = false;
rbnFemale.Enabled = false;
```

7. Run the application and check and uncheck the checkbox to make sure that the controls are enabled and disabled.

The complete code for the **CheckStateChanged** event looks like this:

```
private void chkActivate_CheckStateChanged(object sender, EventArgs e)
{
    if (chkActivate.Checked)
    {
        btnCheckGender.Enabled = true;
        rbnMale.Enabled = true;
        rbnFemale.Enabled = true;
    }
    else
    {
        btnCheckGender.Enabled = false;
        rbnMale.Enabled = false;
        rbnFemale.Enabled = false;
    }
}
```

Clicking the button

Although you could have one of the radio buttons checked on startup by assigning **true** to its **Checked** property in the **Properties** window they are both unchecked in this exercise because you will implement an **else**-block handling that particular scenario.

The first thing you will add to the button's **Click** event is an **if**-block which will be executed if the *rbnMale* radio button is checked and assign the string "Selected value: Male" to the label *lblMessage* if it is. Then you will add an **else if**-block which will be executed if the *rbnFemale* is checked and assign the string "Selected value: Female" to the label *lblMessage* if it is. The third scenario involves the user clicking on the button when no radio button is checked which will be handled by implementing an **else**-block where you assign the string "No gender selected" to the label *lblMessage*.

1. Double click on the button in the form designer.
2. Add an **if**-statement checking if the **Checked** property of the *rbnMale* radio button is **true** (checked). Remember that you only have to enter the property in the **if**-state-

ment to check a Boolean value, in other words you don't have to compare the property value to true using == or the **Equals** method.

```csharp
if (rbnMale.Checked)
{
    lblMessage.Text = "Selected value: Male";
}
```

3. Next you will check if the value of the *rbnFemale* radio button is **true** using an **else if**-statement.

```csharp
else if (rbnFemale.Checked)
{
    lblMessage.Text = "Selected value: Female";
}
```

4. The last piece of logic you will add is an **else**-block handling all other eventualities such as when no radio buttons are selected.

```csharp
else
{
    lblMessage.Text = "No gender selected";
}
```

5. Run the application and check the checkbox enabling the other controls in the group box.
6. Click the button without selecting any radio button and read the text in the label.
7. Select one of the radio buttons and click the button and read the text in the label.
8. Select the other radio button and click the button and read the text in the label.
9. Uncheck the checkbox to makes sure that the controls in the group box are disabled.
10. Close the application.

The complete code for the **btnCheckGender_Click** event looks like this:

```csharp
private void btnCheckGender_Click(object sender, EventArgs e)
{
    if (rbnMale.Checked)
    {
        lblMessage.Text = "Selected value: Male";
    }
    else if (rbnFemale.Checked)
    {
        lblMessage.Text = "Selected value: Female";
    }
    else
```

```
    {
        lblMessage.Text = "No gender selected";
    }
}
```

Switch logic

In this part of the exercise you will implement a **switch** to handle the selected country in a combo box control and display the language associated with that country. You will also change the background color of the label displaying the information about the country based on what language is spoken in the selected country.

Add a combo box called **cboCountry** to the form and add some countries to it in the form's **Form_Load** event. Add at least the following countries Sweden, Norway, Finland, Great Britain and USA; you can add additional countries if you like.

Add a **switch** which checks the **SelectedIndex** property of the combo box in the combo box's **SelectedIndexChanged** event. Change the label's text and background color in the **switch case**-blocks as per the instructions at the beginning of the exercise.

Adding the controls
1. Drag a label to the form and place it to the right of the group box (see image above).
2. Change the text of the label to "Countries".
3. Add a combo box below the label and name it **cboCountry**.
4. Add a label below the combo box, name it **lblLanguage** and change its text to "Select a country"

Adding the countries to the combo box
1. Double click on the form.
2. use the **Add** method of the combo box to add the countries.
```csharp
private void Form1_Load(object sender, EventArgs e)
{
    cboCountry.Items.Add("Unknown");
    cboCountry.Items.Add("Sweden");
    cboCountry.Items.Add("Norway");
    cboCountry.Items.Add("Finland");
    cboCountry.Items.Add("Great Britain");
    cboCountry.Items.Add("USA");
}
```

3. Go to the form designer and double click on the combo box to add its **Selected-IndexChanged** event to the code-behind.

4. Add a switch block to the event checking the **SelectedIndex** property of the combo box, this index correspond to the item selected in the combo box. The index is zero based meaning that the first item added to the combo box in the **Form_Load** event will have the index **0**.

```
switch (cboCountry.SelectedIndex)
{
}
```

5. Add **case**-blocks for the different country scenarios. Remember that each **case** has to be terminated by a **break** statement to avoid falling through to the next **case**. The **case** implementation for index 4 and 5 are the same so you can let the **case** for index 4 fall through to the index 5 **case** by not adding any code for it except the **case**. Below is a sample implementation of the first case.

```
case 1:
    lblLanguage.Text = "Language: Swedish";
    lblLanguage.BackColor = Color.LightGreen;
    break;
```

6. Use the **default**-block at the end of the **switch** to implement a fallback for all eventualities not handled by any **case**.

```
default:
    lblLanguage.Text = "Language: Unspecified";
    lblLanguage.BackColor = Color.LightPink;
    break;
```

7. Run the application and select different countries in the combo box and see how the background color and the text of the label below the combo box changes.

8. Close the application.

The complete code for the **SelectedIndexChanged** event looks like this:

```
private void cboCountry_SelectedIndexChanged(object sender, EventArgs e)
{
    switch (cboCountry.SelectedIndex)
    {
        case 1:
            lblLanguage.Text = "Language: Swedish";
            lblLanguage.BackColor = Color.LightGreen;
            break;
```

```
    case 2:
        lblLanguage.Text = "Language: Norwegian";
        lblLanguage.BackColor = Color.LightSkyBlue;
        break;
    case 3:
        lblLanguage.Text = "Language: Finnish";
        lblLanguage.BackColor = Color.LightYellow;
        break;
    case 4: // Index 4 will fall through to Index 5
    case 5:
        lblLanguage.Text = "Language: English";
        lblLanguage.BackColor = Color.LightSalmon;
        break;
    default:
        lblLanguage.Text = "Language: Unspecified";
        lblLanguage.BackColor = Color.LightPink;
        break;
    }
}
```

3. Variables

Introduction

A variable is a friendly name (a handle) for a small area in the RAM memory (Random Access Memory) which is used by the computer to store information while executing algorithms; a variable value can be stored for a long time if needed. The RAM used by an application is cleared at the very latest when the application ends but parts of the memory usually is cleared as soon as it's no longer in use.

Data stored in memory can be persisted to a permanent storage such as a hard drive, USB or disc as you will learn in a later chapter.

When declaring a variable you have an option to declare it explicitly using the name of the data type such as **int**, **string** or **bool**, or you can declare it implicitly using the **var** keyword deferring the type evaluation until compile-time.

In many cases, the code will be cleaner and easier to read when using the **var** keyword.

IMPORTANT: *Variable names are case sensitive. The variable name **myValue** is not the same as **myvalue** because the first name has a capital letter V where the second variable does not.*

Both of the declarations below will store the result as integers. The first variable is declared explicitly with the **int** data type and the second implicitly having the .NET Framework assign the data type at compile-time.

```
int myExplicitNumber = 100;
var myImplicitNumber = 200;
```

In C# you must assign a variable before using it. C# is implemented this way to avoid using variables with random values which was a source of problems in C and C++.

Value type vs. reference type

There are two variable types *value type* and *reference type*. Value types also called primitive types are stored in a fast part of the RAM memory called the *Stack* whereas reference types are stored on a larger and slower memory area called the *Heap*. The reason the *Heap* is slower is that it handles large objects which require certain finesse when being removed to ensure that it is done in a safe manner. On the *Stack* however the value can be removed immediately making space for another value.

You can create both user defined value types and reference types using a *struct* when creating a value type and a *class* when creating a reference type. You will learn about this in later chapters.

To put it into a real world context you could view the *Stack* as the shelves in a shop where you store small items and boxes and the *Heap* as the large storage area at the back of the shop where you keep big items and crates that does not fit on the store shelves. You want the customers to have easy and fast access to the small items (the *Stack*) but if they are interested in larger items such as lawnmowers, fancy outdoor grills or patio furniture you will direct them to your large show room or storage area (the *Heap*).

If you for instance declare a value type variable called **myValueType** then its value will be stored on the *Stack*. It's like pulling out a neatly sized box with just enough room to fit the value of the specified data type, placing the value inside the box and attaching a label with the variable name on the outside. When you later need to retrieve the value stored for that particular variable you specify the variable (label) name and get the value back lightning fast.

If you on the other hand use a class to create a reference type which is then used to declare an object associated with a variable name then it will be too large to fit on the *Stack* and will be created on the *Heap* with a reference pointer on the *Stack*. In the previous example you placed the value directly inside the box but now you now place a note with directions to where the actual object is stored, the object is referenced. With that reference you can then go on a treasure hunt among all the objects in the large storage area to find the actual item which off course takes time.

The same goes for destroying or removing a variable. If it is a small item on a shelf (on the *Stack*) you can just toss it in the trash and be done with it but if it is a large object (on the heap) you will first have to dismantle it safely and have the staff (the *Garbage Collector*) toss it in the container out back to be collected by a large garbage truck that eventually will dump it on a land fill, which of course takes more time and resources than throwing a small item it in the trash can.

When an object on the *Heap* is destroyed it cannot be removed directly from memory instead it is given to a *Garbage Collector* called **GC** which then safely removes it from memory, much like in the example above.

The lifespan of a variable differs depending on where it has been declared. If you for instance declare a variable directly in a class its value will be available through its object reference (variable name) for as long as the object is still on the *Heap*. A variable declared in a subroutine (method) will be available throughout that method (until the end curly brace or a return statement is reached). If the variable is declared in a block of code like an **if**-statement then it will only be reachable inside that code block and removed when the end of the code block is reached.

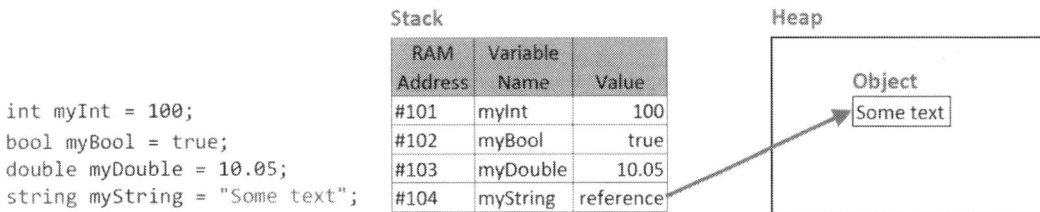

Stack   Heap

RAM Address	Variable Name	Value
#101	myInt	100
#102	myBool	true
#103	myDouble	10.05
#104	myString	reference

Object
Some text

```
int myInt = 100;
bool myBool = true;
double myDouble = 10.05;
string myString = "Some text";
```

Data types

All applications use data from different sources such as user interfaces, databases, network services or other sources. Variables are the way to go when storing values and operators and expressions are used to manipulate those values.

Variables are declared as specific data types and because C# is a type-safe language, the compiler guarantees that the value stored in a variable is the correct type. The table below shows the most commonly used data types and their corresponding system name which is used by the common type system when compiling the solution interpreting the high-level C# code converting it into MSIL code.

Type	Description	Size (bytes)	Range	CLR Alias (System.)	
Int	Whole numbers	4	-2,147,483,648 to 2,147,483,647	Int32	
Long	Whole numbers	8	-9,223,372,036,854,775,808 9,223,372,036,854,775,807	Int64	
Float	Floating point numbers	4	+/-3.4 x 10^38	Single	
Double	Floating point numbers	8	+/-1.7 x 10^308	Double	Value types (Primitive types)
Decimal	Monetary values	16	28 significant figures	Decimal	
Bool	Boolean	1	True or False	Boolean	
Char	Single character	2	N/A	Char	
String	Sequence of characters (text)	2 per char.	N/A	String	String is not a value type but can be used as one from the programmer's perspective
DateTime	Moments in time	8	00:00:00 01/01/0001 to 23:59:59 12/31/9999	DateTime	
Object	Generic type		N/A	Object	

Arithmetic operators

When calculating values it is paramount to know which order the operators are calculated, the list below shows the order of execution.

*	Multiplication
/	Division
%	Remainder (modulo)
+	Addition
-	Subtraction
=	Assignment

Below is a list of assignment and incremental operators you can use to shorten your code. You will use them throughout this book.

++	Increase variable value with 1
--	Decrease variable value with 1

*=	Assignment after multiplication

/=	Assignment after division
%=	Assignment after modulo
+=	Assignment after addition
-=	Assignment after subtraction

Naming rules for variables

When naming variables there are rules to which you must adhere.

Rule 1: An identifier can only contain letters, digits and underscore characters.

Rule 2: An identifier must start with a letter or an underscore character.

Rule 3: The identifier cannot be the same as a reserved C# keyword.

IMPORTANT: *C# is case sensitive which means that you potentially could use the same variable name only changing the casing. The names myVariable and MyVariable would be two different variables. One instance when you might consider using this to your advantage is when naming a property that stores its value in a backing variable.*

There are different naming conventions, *use one convention and stick to it.*

You can declare multiple variables on the same line separating them with commas; all variables declared this way will have the same type.

Declaring a variable

```
int amount;
int vat;
// or
int amount, vat;
```

Assigning a variable

```
int amount;
amount = 100;
```

Declaring and assigning a variable

```
double discount = 0.5;
```

Casting

In an application, it is common to convert a value from one data type to another; one example is when you want to use a value from a text box, or other user interface control, and want to store the value in a variable or use the value in a calculation.

Changing a value form one type to another is called **casting.** There are two types of casting: implicit and explicit.

Implicit casting

Implicit conversion can be made automatically by the CLR as long as no information is lost during the cast; however, this process allows loss of precision.

Widening conversions is allowed; that is going from a smaller data type to a larger data type, for instance casting an **int** to a **long**. The other way around (**long** to **int**) is not permitted because loss of data is possible.

```
int x = 100;
long y;
y = x; // Implicit casting from int to long
```

The following table shows the allowed implicit conversions.

From	To
sbyte	short, int, long, float, double, decimal
byte	short, ushort, int, uint, long, ulong, float, double, decimal
short	int, long, float, double, decimal
ushort	int, uint, long, ulong, float, double, decimal
int	long, float, double, decimal
uint	long, ulong, float, double, decimal
long, ulong	float, double, decimal
float	double
char	ushort, int, uint, long, ulong, float, double, decimal

Explicit casting

An explicit cast require you to write code to perform the cast. This is done when a cast must be made and information potentially could be lost or produce an error. Beware that an explicit cast can produce an unexpected result.

This type of casting can be performed only where it makes sense, such as converting from a **long** to an **int**. You cannot use it to convert from a **string** to an **int** where the format of the data has to physically change.

```
int x;
long y = 1000;
x = (int) y; // Explicit casting from long to int
```

The System.Convert class

You can do explicit conversions using the **System.Convert** class in cases where implicit or explicit casting isn't possible. The class contains conversion functions such as **ToDecimal**, **ToInt32** and **ToString**.

```
string myIntString = "1234";

// Conversion from string to int
int myInt = Convert.ToInt32(myIntString);
```

The TryParse method

You can use the **TryParse** method on the data type to try and see if a conversion is possible. The function takes two parameters; the first is the value to parse and the second is a variable that will contain the parsed value if the conversion succeeds. The second parameter must be passed as an **out** parameter which means that it only can pass a value out from the method.

```
string parseValue = "1234";
int parsedInt = 0;

if (int.TryParse(parseValue, out parsedInt))
{
    // On success
}
else
{
    // On failed parse
}
```

Additional reading: "Casting and Type Conversions (C# Programming Guide)"

Numeric variables

Numeric variables comes in two different flavors whole number and floating point numbers. Whole number variables such as **short**, **int** and **long** can be used as counters and identifiers in data sources such as unique primary and foreign keys in database tables. Floating point variables such as **float**, **double** and **decimal** are often used when doing mathematical calculations where precision is needed. To play around with these type of variables you will now build a simple order form using a Windows Forms Application project.

Exercise: Simple order form

In this exercise you will hone in your skills working with numerical variables by creating a simple order form with a maximum of 5 different products. Values for specific products are entered with controls on horizontal rows and each of the five products use the same type of controls to enter their values. The first control is a textbox for the product name, the second is a textbox for the product price, the third is a numeric up/down control for the number of units ordered of the product and the fourth is a textbox for the line total.

The **Product** name should have a maximum of 30 characters which you can set using the **MaxLength** property in the **Properties** window. Name the textboxes **txtProduct1-txtProduct5** using the **Name** property.

The *Price* textbox should only allow numerical values and a decimal point (comma or period depending on Windows culture settings) which you can achieve using the **KeyPress** event method. The text should also be **right aligned** which you can set using the **TextAlign** property. The default text in the textbox should be zero (**0**). The text should be **bold** which you can set using the **Font** property. Name the textboxes *txtPrice1-txtPrice5*.

The number of **units** ordered will be represented by a NumericUpDown control with a maximum of **10** units per product which you set using the **Maximum** property. The value should be **right aligned** and displayed in **bold**. Name the controls *numUnits1- numUnits5*. When the up or down button in the control is clicked the cost of the ordered product (*price * units*) should be displayed automatically in the *Line Total* textbox, to achieve this you have to add the **ValueChange** event method which you can do by double clicking on the NumericUp-Down control.

The **line total** will be calculated when the NumericUpDown control is used for a specific product; the control can therefore be read only which can be set using its **ReadOnly** property. The background should be yellow to signal that it is a calculated field, it can be set using the **BackColor** property. The text should be displayed in a **bold** font and be **right aligned**. Name the controls *txtLineTotal1- txtLineTotal5*.

The easiest way to implement the subsequent product order rows is to select the controls added for the first order row (product), copy them and change their names. You can select the controls holding down the **Ctrl** key on the keyboard and click on the desired controls, or you can point with the mouse on the form surface to the left of the controls, hold down the left mouse button and drag over the desired controls.

The text in the **discount** textbox should be **right aligned** and displayed with a **bold** font. The value will be deducted from the sum of all the line totals before the VAT is calculated. Name the textbox *txtDiscount*.

VAT has two textboxes one for the VAT percentage and one for the calculated VAT amount. Name the VAT textbox for the percentage *txtVAT* and **right align** its text and make it **bold**. The VAT percentage should be editable. Name the textbox for the calculated VAT amount *txtVATAmt*, its text should be **right aligned** and **bold** as well as have a blue text color which can be set using the **ForeColor** property. The background should be yellow to indicate that it is a calculated field and as such it should be **read only**. The VAT amount is calculated by adding the line totals together, subtracting the discount and finally multiplying the result with the VAT percentage divided by 100. You can do the calculation by first parsing the textbox values using the **Double.TryParse** method and store the resulting values in variables of the **double** data type which you then use in the calculation.

*VatAmt = (lineTotal1 + lineTotal2 + lineTotal3 + lineTotal4 + lineTotal5 - discount) * (vat / 100)*

The example below show how you can parse the value in the discount textbox. Note that the discount variable has to be passed in to the **TryParse** method using the **out** keyword. The **out** keyword can be used to pass out a value from a method as you will learn more about in the chapter on methods. The **TryParse** method will in this case return the string from the textbox converted to a **double** value stored in the **discount** variable. If the conversion fails (the string in the textbox cannot be converted to a **double** value) then **0** will be stored in the **discount** variable. With this example as a template you should be able to parse the values in the other textboxes.

```
double discount;
Double.TryParse(txtDiscount.Text, out discount);
```

The total cost should be displayed in a textbox called ***txtTotal*** when the **Calculate** button (***btnCalculate***) is clicked. The textbox should be **read only**, have a **blue background**, **white right aligned** text displayed with a **bold** font and the default text should be **0**.

Creating the order form
1. Open Visual Studio.
2. Select **New-Project** in the **File** menu.
3. Select the **Windows Forms Application** project template.
4. Name the project ***Order Form*** in the **Name** field and click the **OK** button.
5. The **Form** design surface should now be visible.

Adding the Product textbox
1. Open the **Toolbox** and **pin** it (if not already pinned) by clicking on the small **pin** icon in the top right corner of the **Toolbox**.
2. Double click on the **Label** icon in the **Toolbox** to add a label to the form.

3. Point to the label in the form, hold down the left mouse key and drag the label to reposition it according to the image above. Since the label will not be used to display dynamic data you don't have to name it.

4. Open the **Properties** window if it is closed (**View-Properties Window**). It should be displayed below the **Solution Explorer** along the left border of the development environment.

5. Make sure that the label is selected, if not click on it once to select it.

6. Go to the **Properties** window and locate the **Text** property and change the text to *Product*.

7. Add a textbox to the form using the textbox icon in the **Toolbox**.

8. Reposition it to be displayed below the label you just added (see image above).

9. Select the textbox and rename *txtProduct1* it using the **Name** property in the **Properties** window.

10. While still in the Properties window limit the number of allowed characters by changing the **MaxLength** property to **30**.

11. Make the textbox wider to accommodate all the 30 characters **197px** should do the trick. Change the width using the **Size** (**Width**) property.

Adding the Price textbox

1. Add a textbox to the form from the **Toolbox** window.

2. Rename it *txtPrice1* with the **Name** property.

3. Drag the **Price** textbox to the right of the **Product** textbox.

4. Right align its text by changing the **TextAlign** property to **Right**.

5. Change the text to **bold** by using the **Font** property. Expand the **Font** property and set the **Bold** property to **true** or click on the property text and then the small button with the three dots to open the **Font** dialog (see image below).

6. Set the **Text** property to **0**.

7. Change the width of the textbox to about **65px** to make it smaller.

8. Add a label above the textbox and change its text to *Price*.

The **Font** property settings in the **Properties** window.

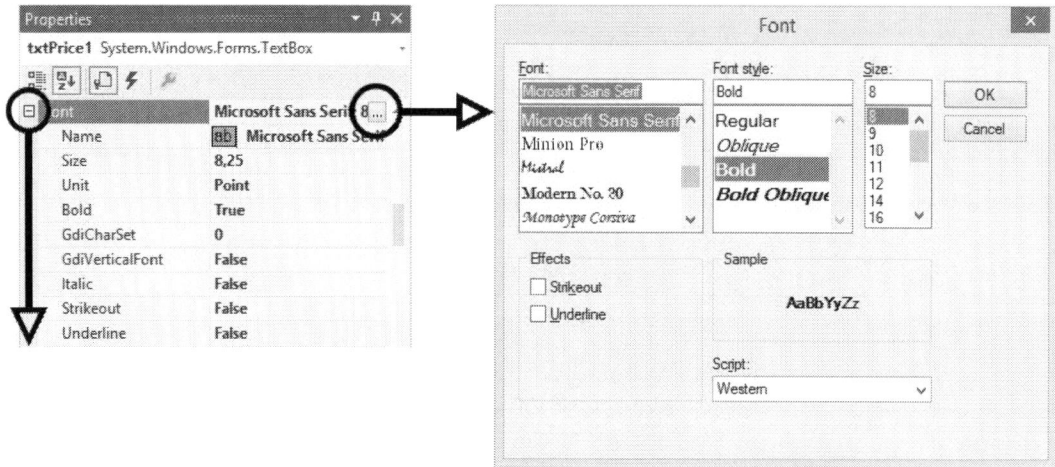

Adding the Units numericUpDown control

1. Add a NumericUpDown control to the form from the **Toolbox** window.
2. Drag it to the right of the **Price** textbox.
3. Rename it *numUnits1* using the **Name** property.
4. Right align the text using the **TextAlign** property.
5. Change the **Maximum** property to **10** to allow values from 0 to 10 being entered.
6. Change the text to be displayed with a **bold** font.
7. Change the width of the textbox to about **39px** to make it smaller.
8. Add a label above the control and change its text to *Units*.

Adding the Line Total textbox

1. Add a textbox to the form from the **Toolbox** window.
2. Drag the textbox to the right of the NumericUpDown control in the form.
3. Change its name to *txtLineTotal1*.
4. Right align the text.
5. Change the text to be displayed with a **bold** font.
6. Change the width of the textbox to about **65px** to make it smaller.
7. Since this is a calculated field you will have to change its **ReadOnly** property to **true**.
8. Change the **BackColor** property to a **yellow** color to signal that it is a calculated field.
9. Add a label above the control and change its text to *Line Total*.

Duplicating the order row

1. Select all the input controls (not the labels) and press **Ctrl+C** on the keyboard to copy them.
2. Paste in the copied controls by pressing **Ctrl+V** on the keyboard.
3. Reposition the controls below the once you created earlier while they are still selected.
4. Rename the controls by increasing the number at the end of the names by one. The copied textbox *txtProduct1* will receive the default name *textBox1* which you will change to *txtProduct2* and so on for the rest of the copied controls.
5. Repeat 1-4 for the remaining 3 order rows.

Adding the Discount textbox

1. Add a textbox to the form from the **Toolbox** window.
2. Drag the textbox below the last order row in the form.
3. Change its name to *txDiscount*.
4. Right align the text.
5. Change the text to be displayed with a **bold** font.
6. Make the textbox as wide as the **Units** and **Line Total** controls combined, **110px** should do the trick.
7. Add a label to the left of the textbox and change its text to *Discount*.

Adding the VAT textboxes

1. Add a textbox called *txtVat* for the VAT percentage value.
2. Align the textbox with the left edge of the **Discount** textbox and place it below the it.
3. Right align the text.
4. Change the text to be displayed with a **bold** font.
5. Change the width of the textbox to about **39px** to make it smaller.
6. Add a second textbox called *txtVatAmt* for the calculated VAT amount.
7. Align the textbox with the left edge of the **Discount** textbox and place it below it.
8. Right align the text.
9. Change the text to be displayed with a **bold** font.
10. Change the width of the textbox to about **64px** to make it smaller.
11. Drag the textbox to the right of the **txtVat** textbox.
12. Since this is a calculated field you will have to change its **ReadOnly** property to **true**.

13. Change the **BackColor** property to a **yellow** color to signal that it is a calculated field.
14. Change the **ForeColor** property to a **blue** color to make it stand out more.
15. Add a label to the left of the **txtVat** textbox and change its text to **VAT %**.

Adding the Total textbox

1. Add a textbox called **txtTotal** for the total amount payable.
2. Align the textbox with the left edge of the **txtVat** textbox and place it below it.
3. Right align the text.
4. Change the text to be displayed with a **bold** font.
5. Change the width of the textbox to about **110px**.
6. Since this is a calculated field you will have to change its **ReadOnly** property to **true**.
7. Change the **BackColor** property to a **blue** color to signal that it is the total amount due.
8. Change the **ForeColor** property to **white** to make it stand out more.
9. Add a label to the left of the textbox and change its text to **Total**.

Adding the Calculate button

1. Add a button called **btnTotal**.
2. Align the button with the left edge of the **txtTotal** textbox and place it below the textbox.
3. Change the button text to **Calculate**.
4. Make the button the same with as the **txtTotal** textbox.
5. Run the application and enter values to the textboxes and the numeric up/down control. As you will notice nothing happens when the Calculate button is clicked nor is the Line Total calculated when the up/down buttons are clicked. The reason for this is that you haven't yet added any code to the code-behind file which will do the calculations, this is your next task.
6. Close the application.

Restricting the input to numerical values

When dealing with numerical input such as a price you might want to limit the input to only numerical characters and a decimal point. It is important to know that the decimal point differs from culture to culture, in Sweden for instance a comma is used to denote a decimal point whereas in the USA a period is used. This can be solved using a more complex imple-mentation using the current culture used in Windows which you will not do in this exercise, instead you will declare a **char** constant called **decimalPoint** holding the decimal symbol. This constant will then be used throughout the calculations which is a way to make the code more maintainable because if you want to change the symbol you only have to change it in one place.

To restrict the allowed characters in the **Price**, **VAT** and **Discount** textboxes you have to add an event called **txtPrice_KeyPress** for those textboxes. Because this is not the default event method for textboxes you cannot just double click on the textboxes to add the event instead you have to use the **Properties** window to add it. You switch from displaying properties to possible events in the **Properties** window by clicking on the button with the **Flash** icon.

Buttons for switching between Properties and Events

You could add a new **KeyPress** event method for each textbox but that would mean a lot of code duplication which is something you should strive to avoid, instead you will create one **KeyPress** event method called **txtPrice_KeyPress** which will be used for all restricted text-boxes. Once you have created that event method you can simply set the **KeyPress** event for the affected textboxes in the **Properties** window by selecting it in the dropdown for that particular event in the list of events.

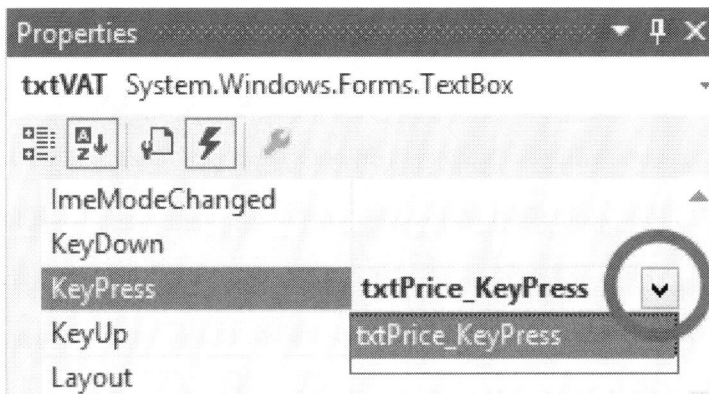

Casting the sender parameter to a textbox

The **KeyPress** event has a **KeyPressEventArgs** parameter called **e** which you find in the event method's parenthesis. This parameter can be used to find out information about the pressed keyboard key such as which character it is using its **KeyChar** property.

To find out if the pressed key is a digit you can use the **char.IsDigit** method and to find out if a control key (**Ctrl, Alt, Shift**) has been pressed you use the **char.IsControl** method. Information of this nature can be extremely valuable when restricting the allowed input in a textbox.

The **KeyPress** event also has an **object** parameter called **sender** which contain the control being used. To get or set property values such as the text of the active textbox you have to cast the **sender** parameter to an actual textbox, you can use the **as** keyword to achieve this. The code below show the **KeyPress** event and how to cast the **sender** object to a textbox. Note that you can use the **var** keyword when declaring the **textbox** variable because the cast will determine which data type will be used when the application is compiled.

```
private void txtPrice_KeyPress(object sender, KeyPressEventArgs e)
{
    var textbox = sender as TextBox;
}
```

Next you need to add a constant called **decimalPoint** of **char** type which holds the decimal point character to be used above the **KeyPress** event. A constant is a variable which only can be assigned once when it is declared. If you live in a region where the decimal symbol is a period you should change this character to a period instead.

```
const char decimalPoint = ',';
```

The **KeyPress**'s **e** parameter has a property called **Handled** which determines whether the character for the pressed key should be added to the textbox or not. If the **Handled** property is set to **true** the character will **not** be added to the textbox. You will create a variable of type **bool** called **isHandled** in the event method which will help determine if the character should be added. Use the following code to determine if the character should be omitted.

```
bool isHandled = !char.IsDigit(e.KeyChar) && !char.IsControl(e.KeyChar) &&
!e.KeyChar.Equals(decimalPoint);
```

IMPORTANT: An exclamation mark (**!**) used in an expression mean **NOT** and will reverse a result making **true** become **false** a vice versa. Two ampersands (**&&**) in an expression mean **AND** forcing both values to be **true** if a result of **true** is to be returned. Two pipes (**||**)in an expression mean **OR** and evaluates to *one or both* values has to be **true** for the result to be **true**.

Check that the pressed key is not a digit (other than a period) and not a control character

Let me explain the code to make it clear what it will do step by step. First you create a variable called **isHandled** which will hold the value **true** if the character should be omitted or **false** if the character should be added to the textbox. The first thing you want to exclude are non-numerical characters using the **char.IsDigit** method passing in the current character using the **e.KeyChar** property, but because the **IsDigit** method return **true** if it is a numerical character you have to reverse the result by placing an exclamation mark before the expression essentially asking if it is not a numerical value. The code looks like this so far, but you will add more code to it later.

```
bool isHandled = !char.IsDigit(e.KeyChar);
```

Next you want to check that no control character has been pressed using the **char.IsControl** method and again you have to use an exclamation mark before the expression to denote that you want the result to reflect if <u>no</u> control key has been pressed.

The double ampersands (**&&**) is used to logically add the two Boolean (**true/false**) method results to find out if the combined result evaluates to **true** or **false**, if one or both are **false** the result will be **false** otherwise it will be **true**. So as an example if you press 7 on the key-board the result would be **false** because the **!char.IsDigit** would return **false** and the **!char .IsControl** would return **true** because no control character was pressed.

```
bool isHandled = !char.IsDigit(e.KeyChar) && !char.IsControl(e.KeyChar);
```

The last thing you need to check is if the character is equal to the **decimalPoint** constant meaning that it is a comma or a period. The reason for checking if it is a decimal point is that you need to do further analysis if it is, so if it isn't a decimal point you can consider the key press handled and to omitted it if the previous checks result in **true**. Use an exclamation mark before the expression to denote that the result should be reversed. The complete result for the **isHandled** variable looks like this. The expression compares the value of the **e.KeyChar** property (the pressed key) to the constant value in the **decimalPoint** constant you added earlier.

```
bool isHandled = !char.IsDigit(e.KeyChar) && !char.IsControl(e.KeyChar) &&
!e.KeyChar.Equals(decimalPoint);
```

Only allow one decimal point

The last thing you need to check to evaluate if the key press is handled is if the pressed key is a decimal point and the textbox already contain a decimal point, you can only have one decimal point after all. You can use the following expression to find out if the pressed key is equal to the decimal point character stored in the **decimalPoint** constant and that no decimal character exist in the textbox. If both these statements return **true** then you can consider the pressed key to be handled and the character should be omitted from the textbox.

```
(e.KeyChar.Equals(decimalPoint) && textbox.Text.Contains(decimalPoint))
```

Adding the KeyPress event

1. Select the first **Price** textbox.
2. Click on the **Flash** button in the **Properties** window to show the events associated with the textbox.
3. Locate the **KeyPress** event in the event list.
4. Write the event name ***txtPrice_KeyPress*** in the text field to the right of the **KeyPress** label.
5. Press enter on the keyboard to create the event method in the code-behind file.
6. Create the textbox constant immediately below the opening curly brace of the form.
   ```
   const char decimalPoint = ',';
   ```

7. In the event method add the following code to cast the sender parameter into a textbox in order to access its **Text** property.
   ```
   var textbox = sender as TextBox;
   ```

8. Add the check to determine if the pressed key is a non-numerical value and also that a control key wasn't pressed. The only non-numerical character allowed is the one stored in the **decimalPoint** constant.

```
bool isHandled = !char.IsDigit(e.KeyChar) &&
!char.IsControl(e.KeyChar) && !e.KeyChar.Equals(decimalPoint);
```

9. Evaluate if the key press is considered handled or if the key character is a decimal point and that the textbox already contain a decimal point if any of these two expressions result in true then the key press should be considered handled and the character be omitted from the textbox.

```
e.Handled = isHandled || (e.KeyChar.Equals(decimalPoint) &&
textbox.Text.Contains(decimalPoint));
```

10. Run the application and make sure that only numerical values and one decimal point can be entered in the first **Price** text box.

11. Close the application.

12. Select all **Price** textboxes except the first one and the **Discount** and **VAT Percentage** textboxes.

13. Locate the **KeyPress** event in the event list in the **Properties** window and select **txtPrice_KeyPress** in the dropdown list in the field to the right of the **KeyPress** label. This will associate the same event method to all the selected textboxes **KeyPress** events.

14. Run the application again and make sure that you have the same restrictions on all the previously selected textboxes.

15. Close the application.

The completed evaluation code looks like this taking both results into account.

```
e.Handled = isHandled || (e.KeyChar.Equals(decimalPoint) &&
textbox.Text.Contains(decimalPoint));
```

The complete code for the **KeyPress** event method looks like this.

```
public partial class Form1 : Form
{
    const char decimalPoint = ',';

    private void txtPrice_KeyPress(object sender, KeyPressEventArgs e)
    {
        // Cast the textbox being edited to a TextBox.
        var textbox = sender as TextBox;

        // The pressed key is not a digit or a
        // period/comma and not a control character.
```

```
        bool isHandled =
            !char.IsDigit(e.KeyChar) &&
            !char.IsControl(e.KeyChar) &&
            !e.KeyChar.Equals(decimalPoint);

        // Allow only one decimal point
        e.Handled =
            isHandled ||
            (e.KeyChar.Equals(decimalPoint) &&
             textbox.Text.Contains(decimalPoint));
    }
}
```

Calculate the line total

The line total for each product row is calculated as *units*price* when the up or down button in the NumericalUpDown control associated with the row is clicked, when the control has focus (the cursor is in the control) and the up or down arrows are used on the keyboard, value changes in the control or when the control loses focus. To implement these scenarios you have to use the **ValueChanged** event of the *numUnits* controls. The result will be presented in the *txtLineItem* textbox associated with the product being entered.

Since the **Value** property of a NumericalUpDown control return a **decimal** value you have to cast it to an **int** before storing the value in a variable called **units**. The casting is necessary in order to use the value as an integer. You can cast it by placing the **int** data type in parenthesis before the control name.

```
var units = (int)numUnits1.Value;
```

Because the value in the **Text** property of the *txtPrice* textbox associated with the product potentially can hold a non-numerical value you have to parse the value to a variable of the **double** data type. The preferred way to convert a value which can contain values other than a **double** is to use the **Double.TryParse** method since it always will return a **double** value even if the parse is unsuccessful in which case **0** is returned. Note that the method return the value as an **out** parameter instead of a return type, this mean that you have to declare a **double** variable (*price*) which you pass in to the method as the second parameter preceded by the **out** keyword, the first parameter being the string value to parse.

```
double price = 0;
Double.TryParse(txtPrice1.Text, out price);
```

Store the result from the actual calculation in a **double** variable called **lineTotal** and assign the variable to the **Text** property of the **txtLineTotal** textbox.

1. Open the Form's design surface.
2. Double click on the first NumericalUpDown control to add its **ValueChanged** event to the code-behind file.
   ```
   private void numUnits1_ValueChanged(object sender, EventArgs e)
   {
   }
   ```
3. Add a variable called units using the **var** keyword and assign the result from the **numUnits1 Value** property cast as an **int** to it.
   ```
   var units = (int)numUnits1.Value;
   ```
4. To be certain a **double** value is used in the calculation you can parse the value in the **txtPrice1 Text** property to a double using the **TryParse** method on the **Double** class. The method requires a variable to be passed in as an **out** parameter through which the method can return the parsed result. A variable declared as **out** can be used in methods to return additional values other than the return type, more on that in the chapter on methods.
   ```
   double price = 0;
   Double.TryParse(txtPrice1.Text, out price);
   ```
5. The line total is calculated with the formula *units*price* and stored in a variable called **lineTotal** declared with the **double** data type.
   ```
   double lineTotal = units * price;
   ```
6. The result in the **lineTotal** variable should be displayed in the **txtLineTotal1** textbox assigning the variable to its **Text** property. Note that you have to use the **ToString** method on the variable when assigning it to the **Text** property in order to convert the value in the variable to a string. The conversion is necessary because the **Text** property requires a string.
   ```
   txtLineTotal1.Text = lineTotal.ToString();
   ```
7. Run the application and test that the line total is displayed when a price has been entered and the number of units changes.
8. Close the application.

9. Repeat 2-8 for all the other NumericalUpDown controls in the form. You can save time by copying the code you just wrote and paste it in to the events you create changing the names of the controls off course.

The complete code for one of the **ValueChanged** events looks like this:

```
private void numUnits1_ValueChanged(object sender, EventArgs e)
{
    var units = (int)numUnits1.Value;
    double price = 0;
    Double.TryParse(txtPrice1.Text, out price);
    double lineTotal = units * price;
    txtLineTotal1.Text = lineTotal.ToString();
}
```

Calculate the order total

The order total for all the line totals, the discount and the VAT is calculated in the **Click** event of the **btnTotal** button. The easiest way to add the **Click** event (since it is the default event for buttons) is to double click on the button in the form.

You will have to parse all the textbox values to be certain that you are performing the calculation with numerical values. Since the **TryParse** method in the **Double** class always return a numerical value even if the value passed in isn't a numerical value itself it will happily handle for instance an empty string returned by an empty textbox yielding a value of **0**.

To handle the values returned as **out** parameters from all the **TryParse** method calls you have to declare all the necessary **double** variables for discount, vat and line totals before calling the first **TryParse** method.

After the values have been parsed and stored in **double** variables it is time to perform the first calculation which is to add all line totals and subtract the discount, store the result in a **double** variable called **lineTotals**.

The second calculation will be to calculate the VAT amount in a **double** variable called **vatTotal** later to be added to the total cost. You calculate the VAT amount by multiplying the value in the **lineTotal** variable with the VAT percentage stored in the **vat** variable divided by **100**. You divide the VAT percentage by 100 because you want the decimal representation of the given percentage value for the calculation.

The third and final calculation is the total stored in a **double** variable called **total**. You calculate the total by adding the value in the **vatTotal** variable to the value in the **lineTotal** variable.

To display the VAT amount and the total in the form you have to assign the variables to their respective textboxes which are ***txtVatAmt*** and ***txtTotal***.

1. Open the Form's design surface.
2. Double click on the Calculate button (***btnTotal***) to add its **Click** event.
   ```
   private void btnTotal_Click(object sender, EventArgs e)
   {
       // The code goes here
   }
   ```
3. Declare all the necessary variables.
   ```
   double discount, vat, ltot1, ltot2, ltot3, ltot4, ltot5;
   double total, lineTotals, vatTotal;
   ```
4. Parse all the values from the textboxes and store the result in the variables you just created.
   ```
   Double.TryParse(txtDiscount.Text, out discount);
   Double.TryParse(txtVAT.Text, out vat);
   Double.TryParse(txtLineTotal1.Text, out ltot1);
   Double.TryParse(txtLineTotal2.Text, out ltot2);
   Double.TryParse(txtLineTotal3.Text, out ltot3);
   Double.TryParse(txtLineTotal4.Text, out ltot4);
   Double.TryParse(txtLineTotal5.Text, out ltot5);
   ```
5. Add the line totals and subtract the discount, store the result in the **lineTotals** variable.
   ```
   lineTotals = ltot1 + ltot2 + ltot3 + ltot4 + ltot5 - discount;
   ```
6. Calculate the VAT amount.
   ```
   vatTotal = lineTotals * (vat / 100);
   ```
7. Calculate the order total by adding the VAT amount to the line totals.
   ```
   total = lineTotals + vatTotal;
   ```
8. Display the result in the ***txtVatAmt*** and ***txtTotal*** textboxes. Remember to use the **ToString** method when assigning the **double** values.
   ```
   txtVatAmt.Text = vatTotal.ToString();
   txtTotal.Text = total.ToString();
   ```

9. The application is now complete. Run the application and enter some values in the fields and click the **Calculate** button to calculate the VAT and total cost.

10. Close the application.

The complete code for the **btnTotal_Click** event look like this:

```
private void btnTotal_Click(object sender, EventArgs e)
{
    double discount, vat, ltot1, ltot2, ltot3, ltot4, ltot5;
    double total, lineTotals, vatTotal;
    Double.TryParse(txtDiscount.Text, out discount);
    Double.TryParse(txtVAT.Text, out vat);
    Double.TryParse(txtLineTotal1.Text, out ltot1);
    Double.TryParse(txtLineTotal2.Text, out ltot2);
    Double.TryParse(txtLineTotal3.Text, out ltot3);
    Double.TryParse(txtLineTotal4.Text, out ltot4);
    Double.TryParse(txtLineTotal5.Text, out ltot5);

    lineTotals = ltot1 + ltot2 + ltot3 + ltot4 + ltot5 - discount;
    vatTotal = lineTotals * (vat / 100);
    total = lineTotals + vatTotal;
    txtVatAmt.Text = vatTotal.ToString();
    txtTotal.Text = total.ToString();
}
```

String variables

Strings are used to store alphanumerical values and can be used, for example, to store values from text boxes in a GUI.

String concatenation

You can use the **+** operator to concatenate strings, but this method of concatenation should be used sparingly because it causes overhead; every time the **+** operator is used, a new string is created in memory and the old string is discarded.

The variable **myString** in the following example would contain the value *First part, second part, third part* after all the strings have been concatenated.

```
string myString = "first part, ";
myString = myString + "second part, ";
```

```
myString = myString + "third part";
```

You should use an instance of the **StringBuilder** class instead of using the **+** operator and append values to the variable because the data is added dynamically and the **StringBuilder** object is only instantiated once on the *Heap*. Use the **Append** method to append data to the **StringBuilder** variable. When you want to use the string built inside the **StringBuilder** instance you have to call the **ToString** method on the variable.

```
StringBuilder myStringBuilder = new StringBuilder("first part");
myStringBuilder.Append("second part");
myStringBuilder.Append("third part");

string concatenatedString = myStringBuilder.ToString();
```

String validation

String validation is very important, especially if the value comes from a GUI, it can help avoid errors in the form of exceptions and it can be used to display validation messages to the user before the data is saved to a data source. One way to implement string validation is to use regular expressions.

The **Regex** class is located in the **System.Text.RegularExpressions** namespace, you can use its **IsMatch** method to validate if the string matches the specified criteria.

The following code validates if the string contains numerical digits.

```
var textToTest = "hell0 w0rld";
var regularExpression = "\\d";
var result = Regex.IsMatch(textToTest, regularExpression,
RegexOptions.None);
{
    // The text matched the expression.
}
```

Additional reading: "Regex Class"

Exercise: StringBuilder and Regex

In this exercise you will use an instance of the **StringBuilder** class called *emailAddresses* to store email addresses entered in a textbox. The email addresses are validated using a regular expression with the **IsMatch** on the **Regex** class before being added to the ***emailAddresses*** variable when the ***btnAdd*** button is clicked. If the email being evaluated is not a true email then the ***txtEmail*** textbox's background should be displayed in a light pink color denoting that the email is incorrect. An email should only be added once to the ***emailAddresses*** variable even if the user tries to enter it multiple times, you can solve this by using the **Contains** method on the string representation of the variable to see if the email already exist in the string.

The actual string representation of a regular expression can mildly put be very difficult to figure out how to create. Unless you really like to dig in to the world of regular expressions I suggest that you use your favorite search engine and scour the internet for already existing viable regular expressions.

One (of many) possible regular expressions derived from the RFC 5322 standard for validating email addresses look like this when added to a read only **string** constant called ***email-Regex***:

```
readonly string emailRegex;
emailRegex =
    @"[a-z0-9!#$%&'*+/=?^_`{|}~-]+(?:\.[a-z0-9!#$%&'*+/=?^_`{|}~-]+)*@" +
    @"(?:[a-z0-9](?:[a-z0-9-]*[a-z0-9])?\.)+[a-z0-9](?:[a-z0-9-]*[a-z0-
9])?";
```

IMPORTANT: *A **readonly** constant can be assigned once at run-time compared to a constant declared with the **const** keyword which has to be assigned a value at compile-time on the same line as the constant is created.*

The following code show how to evaluate is if a string is a match for a specific regular expression. In this case the regular expression stored in the constant is being compared to the string entered into the ***txtEmail*** textbox.

```
var result = Regex.IsMatch(txtEmail.Text, emailRegex);
```

Use the **result** variable in an **if**-statement to figure out which background color (light pink or white) should be displayed in the email textbox and whether the email should be added to the **StringBuilder** variable. Perform the evaluation in the button's **Click** event.

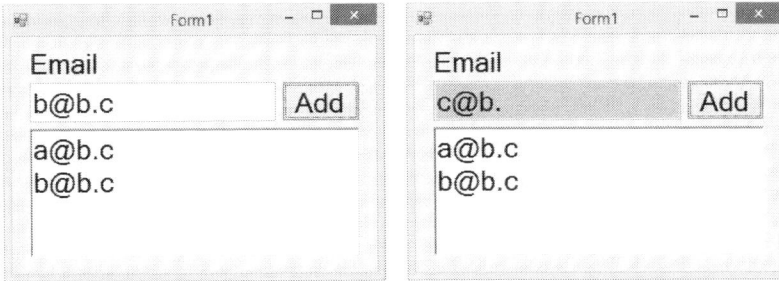

Creating the solution

1. Open Visual Studio and select **New-Project** in the **File** menu.
2. Select **Visual C#** to the left in the dialog.
3. Select **Windows Forms Application** in the middle list.
4. Name the project *Email Regex* in the **Name** textbox.
5. Click the **OK** button.

Adding the form controls

1. Add a label and position it a short distance from the left side and top of the form.
2. Change the text of the label to *Email* with its **Text** property.
3. Add a textbox below the label and name it *txtEmail* with its **Name** property.
4. Add a button to the right of the textbox and name it *btnAdd*.
5. Change the text on the button to *Add* using its **Text** property.
6. Add a rich textbox control below the textbox and make it as wide as the textbox and button combined.
7. Name the rich textbox control *txtEmailList*. This textbox will be used to display the email list as new email addresses are added to the **StringBuilder** variable you will create later.

Adding the regular expression constant and StringBuilder variable

1. Open the form's code-behind file by double clicking on the forms gray surface in the designer.
2. Add a read only string constant called *emailRegex* and an instance of the **String-Builder** called *emailAddresses* to the form class

```
public partial class Form1 : Form
{
    readonly string emailRegex;
    StringBuilder emailAddresses = new StringBuilder();
```

3. Assign the regular expression string to the **emailRegex** variable in the form constructor called **Form1()**. Place an **@**-sign in front of the quote when assigning the string to ensure that all the special characters are treated as characters and keep them from being evaluated by the compiler. Also note that the string is concatenated using the **+** operator.

```
public Form1()
{
    emailRegex =
      @"[a-z0-9!#$%&'*+/=?^_`{|}~-]" +
      @"+(?:\.[a-z0-9!#$%&'*+/=?^_`{|}~-]+)*@" +
      @"(?:[a-z0-9](?:[a-z0-9-]*[a-z0-9])?\.)" +
      @"+[a-z0-9](?:[a-z0-9-]*[a-z0-9])?";

    InitializeComponent();
}
```

4. Add the **btnAdd** button's **Click** event by double clicking on it in the form designer.

```
private void btnAdd_Click(object sender, EventArgs e)
{
}
```

5. Add a variable called **result** inside the **Click** event method which will hold the Boolean result from the **Regex.IsMatch** method call. Pass in the text from the **txtEmail** textbox and the regular expression in the **emailRegex** variable.

```
var result = Regex.IsMatch(txtEmail.Text, emailRegex);
```

6. Add an **if**-statement below the result variable and use it to determine if the email is correct. Use curly braces to create the **if**-block to be executed if the email is correct and change the textbox background color to white inside the block.

```
if (result)
{
    txtEmail.BackColor = Color.White;
}
```

7. Inside the **if**-block, after the change in background color, add a second **if**-statement to check if the email is correct using the **ToString** and **Contains** methods to compare the current content of the **StringBuilder** variable with the text in the **txtEmail** textbox. If the email does not exist (use an exclamation mark to change **true** to **false**) add it to the **emailAddresses StringBuilder**. The **"\n"** string adds a line break after the email.

```
if(!emailAddresses.ToString().Contains(txtEmail.Text))
    emailAddresses.Append(txtEmail.Text + "\n");
```

8. Add an **else**-statement below the closing curly brace of the **if**-block which will be executed if the **if**-statement evaluates to **false** meaning that email is incorrect. Change the background color of the **txtEmail** textbox to light pink to show the user that the email is incorrect.

```
else
    txtEmail.BackColor = Color.LightPink;
```

9. The last thing you need to do is to display the content from the **emailAddresses** variable in the **txtEmailList** rich textbox. Note that you have to call the **ToString** method on the variable to be able to add the content to the control.

```
txtEmailList.Text = emailAddresses.ToString();
```

10. Run the a application and enter an invalid email making the textbox background turn light pink when the button is clicked.

11. Enter a valid email address and click on the button adding it to the large textbox and changing the textbox background color to white.

12. Add another valid email and click the button to add it to the large textbox. Make sure that both email addresses are displayed.

13. Enter an invalid email and click the button making the textbox background turn light pink then change the email to a valid email and click the button to make sure that the background color changes to white and the email is added.

14. Close the application.

The complete code in the form looks like this:

```
public partial class Form1 : Form
{
    readonly string emailRegex;
    StringBuilder emailAddresses = new StringBuilder();

    public Form1()
    {
        emailRegex =
            @"[a-z0-9!#$%&'*+/=?^_`{|}~-]" +
            @"+(?:\.[a-z0-9!#$%&'*+/=?^_`{|}~-]+)*@" +
            @"(?:[a-z0-9](?:[a-z0-9-]*[a-z0-9])?\.)" +
            @"+[a-z0-9](?:[a-z0-9-]*[a-z0-9])?";
```

```
        InitializeComponent();
    }

    private void Form1_Load(object sender, EventArgs e)
    {
    }

    private void btnAdd_Click(object sender, EventArgs e)
    {
        var result = Regex.IsMatch(txtEmail.Text, emailRegex);
        if (result)
        {
            txtEmail.BackColor = Color.White;

            if(!emailAddresses.ToString().Contains(txtEmail.Text))
                emailAddresses.Append(txtEmail.Text + "\n");
        }
        else
            txtEmail.BackColor = Color.LightPink;

        txtEmailList.Text = emailAddresses.ToString();
    }
}
```

Arrays

An array is a sequence of values or objects that are treated as a group and managed as a unit. The most common types of arrays are one-, two- or three-dimensional (list, table and cube, respectively), but you can create arrays with up to 32 dimensions.

Arrays are **zero (0) based**, meaning that the first element of an array is stored at index zero. The size of the array is determined by the number of elements you can store in it. The number of **dimensions** the array holds determines the **rank** of the array. An array always holds values or objects of the same type.

If you need to be able to store different types in the same sequence, consider using collections. Collections are found in the **System.Collections** namespace and are expandable, which means that you can **add** and **remove** objects in the collection as needed.

An array does not allocate physical memory until the **new** operator has been executed; at this time you specify the size of the array implicitly (by assigning values directly) or explicitly (by stating the size).

When reading or writing data to an array, you should check for the **IndexOutOfRangeException** exception; this type of error will occur if you try to use an index that is not available in the array.

One dimensional arrays

The following example shows how you can create a one dimensional array which store values or objects is a sequence starting at index **0**. The value you assign in the declaration of the array (between the two angle brackets after the data type) determine how many items can be stored in the array, not the end index. In the code below the array will contain 5 placeholders to store values of the declared type with the indices 0 through 4.

```
int[] list = new int[5];
```

You can now assign values to the array using the *square bracket* syntax; in the following example the value **10** is stored in the array's first placeholder at index **0**.

```
list[0] = 10;
```

Another way to declare and assign values to an array is to declare it and assign the values at the same time using the *curly brace* syntax. Note that you don't have to specify the number of items the array should hold because it is inferred by the number of items you add within the curly braces.

```
int[] list = new int[] { 1, 5, 45, 75, 2 };
```

You read or use values stored in an array by specifying the name of the array followed by the index of the position you want to fetch the value from. If you are iterating (looping) over the values in an array the hardcoded value in the angle brackets should be replaced by the loop counter.

```
int theValue = list[1];
```

Two dimensional arrays

The following example shows how you can create a two dimensional array which store values or objects in a table like manner where the first index determines the number of dimensions (the rank) of the array and the second the number of items which can be stored in each dimension. The code below would create an array with two dimensions, or two main placeholders if you like, which each can hold three items of the specified data type.

Note that you specify the number of dimensions by adding commas to the first set of square brackets where one comma mean two dimensions.

```
int[,] table = new int[2, 3];
```

You can now store a maximum of six values in the array where the first value is stored in the first dimension at index zero ([0, 0]) and the last in the second dimension at index 2 ([1, 2]). Note that the dimensions also are zero based.

```
table[0, 0] = 1; table[0, 1] = 2; table[0, 2] = 3;
table[1, 0] = 4; table[1, 1] = 5; table[1, 2] = 6;
```

You can also declare and assign values at the same time when declaring a two dimensional array. Use curly braces to indicate the different dimensions.

```
int[,] table = new int[,]
{
    { 1, 2, 3 },
    { 4, 5, 6 }
};
```

To fetch a value from a specific placeholder you have to specify the dimension and the index within that dimension.

```
var tableValue1 = table[0, 1]; // return 2
var tableValue2 = table[1, 2]; // return 6
```

Looping over values in an array

Although you have not yet read about loops it can be worth to mention a way to loop over arrays here just to put loops into an array context. In the example below a for loop is used to iterate over the items in a one dimensional array called list; note that you never should hardcode the end index of a loop (unless absolutely necessary), instead you should use properties and methods such as **Length** and **Count** on the array or collection to determine the number of iterations required for that specific list of values. Here the **Length** property of the **list** array is used to determine the number of iterations needed. To fetch the individual values in the array you use the loop counter (**i** in this case) within the angle brackets of the array variable. It is very common to use counter variables named I, j, k and so on for loop counters if nested loops are used. You start at **i** because a, b, c and so on are usually reserv-ed for placeholders in mathematical calculations. The code below will loop over the values stored in the array and add them together storing the result in a variable called **result**.

```
int result = 0;
for (int i = 0; i < list.Length; i++)
{
    result += list[i];
}
```

Additional reading: "Arrays (C# Programming Guide)"

Exercise: Building a calculator

In this exercise I would urge you to try to implement it without looking at the solution and view it as a test of sorts to see if there are any gaps in your knowledge you need to fill before continuing to the next chapter. The exercise will be presented as a mini use case describing what the fictive customer want you to implement and leave you to figure it out, it is describ-ed this way to model a miniature real world scenario. You will get more exercises of this kind moving forward to make it more fun for you and to keep you on your toes.

IMPORTANT: *If you are using Visual Studio 2015 or later the Windows Forms resolution has changed and you will have to use other control sizes that are appropriate for the UI.*

The use case

The customer is adamant that no hardcoded values should exist in the event methods and that such values should be declared as constants at the beginning of the **Form1** class to make the code more maintainable. Any class level variables should also be declared at the beginning of the class.

The calculator only need to calculate a result using two values. When entering values using the numbered buttons the current value should be displayed with large digits in the value label. When one of the arithmetic buttons (+, -, x, /) is clicked the value should be moved and displayed with a much smaller font in a label displayed over a small portion of the value label (see image below).

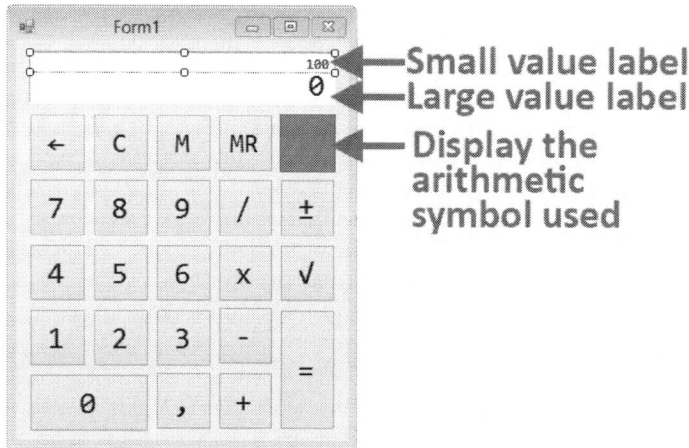

The delete (←), clear (C), memory (M) and memory recall (MR) buttons should be placed below the value label as well as a label (blue background) which should display used the arithmetic character (+, -, x, /) when one of the buttons is clicked.

The delete (←) button should remove the last entered digit (the right most digit). Note that you have to make sure that the minus sign is replaced with a **0** if the last numerical digit of a negative value is deleted. You also have to add a **0** to the large value label if the last numerical digit of a positive value is deleted.

The clear (C) button should clear the value in all the small value label and the label displaying the arithmetic character and assign **0** to the large value label.

The memory (M) button should store the value in the large value label in a **string** variable called **memory** for later use.

The memory recall (MR) button should recall the value in stored in the **memory** variable and display the value in the large value label.

The number buttons should append the digit to the end of the value in the large value label. The same goes for the decimal character which only should be allowed once in the large value label.

When one of the arithmetic buttons is clicked the value in the large value label should be moved to the small value label and the arithmetic symbol should be displayed in the blue label to the right of the memory recall button. This symbol will then be used to determine how the result should be calculated when the button with the equal sign on it is clicked. These buttons should be handled by the same event method called **btnCalculate_Click**.

When the square root (√) button is clicked the square root of the value in the large value label should be calculated using the **Sqrt** method in the **Math** class and the result displayed in the large value label replacing the original value. You should also handle negative values because it is not possible to calculate the square root of a negative value, display a message box with a suitable message.

The negation button (±) should act as a toggle button adding and removing a minus sign (-) to the left of the value in the large value label.

When the calculate button (=) is clicked the result should be calculated using the values from the small and large value labels as well as the symbol store in the blue label.

The number buttons should use the same event method called **btnNumber_Click**. You can cast the sender parameter (from the event parenthesis) to a button using the **Button** class and use the variable you store the clicked button in to access its **Text** property.

```
Button btn = (Button)sender;
```

Rules regarding calculating the result

If one of the labels contain an empty string or if the large value label contain **0** no calculation should take place and the event should be prematurely ended using the **return** keyword.

```
if (...) return;
```

If the last character in either of the two value labels is a decimal sign then that character should be removed prior to the calculation being performed.

The calculation performed should be determined by the arithmetic sign is displayed in the blue label.

After the calculation the blue label and the small value label should be cleared by assigning an empty string to their **Text** properties.

The result should be displayed in the large value label with three (3) decimal digits. You can use the format functionality of the **ToString** method to achieve this. Also if the value is calculated as for instance 10.0 where the value ends with a zero decimal value (,0 or .0) then the zero and the decimal symbol should be removed from the string using the **Replace** method before the value is displayed in the large value label.

```
lblValue.Text = result.ToString("F3").Replace(zeroDecimal, String.Empty);
```

Now structure the information given to you in a document before you start implementing the solution. For instance what constants could be used in place of hard coded text and values. I suggest that you implement the solution in incremental stages to see that one functionality works before proceeding with something new.

The solution

I hope you have tried to implement the solution before deciding to resort to the solution presented here. You will start by creating the GUI and move on from there to implement the button logic culminating in the actual calculation when hitting the button with the equal sign.

The value labels

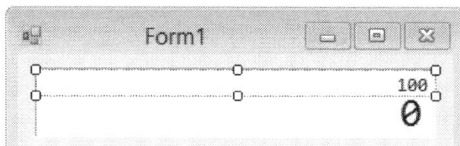

1. Create a new **Windows Forms Application** solution called *Simple Calculator*.
2. Resize the form to **314px** wide and **383px** high.

3. Drag a label to the form which represent the value that the user enters through clicking on the numerical buttons.

4. Rename the label *lblValue*.

5. Set the **AutoSize** property to **false** to be able to resize the label.

6. Change the background color to **white** and the border style to **Fixed3D** to make it look more like a textbox.

7. Change the font to **Consolas 20pt** to make the text larger.

8. Resize the label to **274px** wide and **46px** high.

9. Assign the value **0** to the **Text** property.

10. Align the text to the **bottom right** with the **TextAlign** property.

11. Next drag another label to the form and rename it *lblFirstValue*.

12. Set the **AutoSize** property to **false** to be able to resize the label.

13. Change the background color to **white** and the border style to **None** to remove any border around the label.

14. Change the font to **Consolas 10pt** to make the text smaller.

15. Resize the label to **270px** wide and **14px** high.

16. Clear the **Text** property by deleting any value in it.

17. Align the text to the **middle right** with the **TextAlign** property.

18. Reposition the label on top of the first label so that it appears that it is part of the upper section of the label.

The buttons

All buttons have the same size except the **0** which has double the width of the other buttons and the **equals** button which has double the height of the other buttons. The buttons are **50px** wide and **50px** high. The special characters for the **delete** (←), **square root** (√) and **negation** (±) buttons can be copied from a word processor's *Insert Symbol* functionality and pasted into the **Text** property of the button or you can use the Unicode value for the desired symbol if the value is added programmatically in the form's **Load** event (←, \u2190), (√, \u221A) and (±, \u00B1).

```
btnSign.Text = "\u00B1";
```

The math function label (the blue one)

The purpose of this label is to show the user which mathematical function has been chosen when clicking on one of the (+, -, /, x) buttons. The value stored in this label will then be used to determine how the result will be calculated; you could off course use a variable to store this information but then it would not be visible to the user.

1. Add a label to the form and change its name to *lblMathFunction*.
2. Resize the label to the same height (50px) and width (50px) as the buttons.
3. Reposition the label to the right of the Memory Recall (MR) button.
4. Change the background color to blue.
5. Change the text color to **White** with the **ForeColor** property.
6. Change the text alignment to **MiddleCenter** with the **TextAlign** property.
7. Change the Font to **Consolas 20pt**.
8. Change the border style to **FixedSingle**.

The numerical buttons

Name the numerical buttons *btnOne*, *btnTwo* and so on.

To avoid a lot of duplicated code and to make it more compact and maintainable you should create one **Click** event that is used by all numerical buttons. To access the clicked button's **Text** property (or any other property) you can cast the sender parameter to a **Button**, the sender parameter is sent in through the event's parenthesis.

You have to take into consideration that the value label which contain the current value entered so far could contain the default **0** assigned when the calculator is started or when the value is cleared using either the **delete** or **clear** button. If this is the case then you first have to clear the label by assigning an empty string to it before adding the button's value to the **Text** property of the label.

One way of appending the correct numerical value at the end of the value in the value label is to use the text from the button itself because it holds the necessary number. You can fetch the value from the **Text** property of the variable you cast earlier.

1. Select one of the numerical buttons and enter *btnNumber_Click* in its **Click** event field in the **Properties** window and then press **Enter** on the keyboard. This should create the event method and take you to it.
   ```
   private void btnNumber_Click(object sender, EventArgs e)
   {
   }
   ```

2. Add a variable called **btn** which will hold the cast **sender** parameter and cast the sender parameter to a **Button** to be able to use its properties.
```
Button btn = (Button)sender;
```

3. Because the customer wanted all constant values to be stored as constants you will add a constant named **noValue** to the form's class just inside its opening curly brace and assign the value **0** to the constant.
```
public partial class Form1 : Form
{
    const string noValue = "0";
```

4. Use the constant you just added in an **if**-statement checking if the *lblValue* label is equal to that value, if it is then clear the label by assigning an empty string to it. Note that you don't have to use curly braces to add a block to an **if**-statement that only executes one line of code.
```
if (lblValue.Text == noValue)
    lblValue.Text = String.Empty;
```

5. The last thing you have to do is to append the numerical value of the button to the end of the text in the *lblValue* label, you can do this by using the **+=** operator.
```
lblValue.Text += btn.Text;
```

6. Now that the event method has been implemented you should add it to the **Click** event of all other numerical buttons using the **Events** section of the **Properties** window.

7. Run the application and make sure that the number corresponding to the button you click is appended to the end of the text in the *lblValue* label (the large label).

8. Close the application.

Here's the complete code for the event used with the numerical buttons **Click** events:
```
private void btnNumber_Click(object sender, EventArgs e)
{
    Button btn = (Button)sender;

    if (lblValue.Text == noValue)
        lblValue.Text = String.Empty;

    lblValue.Text += btn.Text;
}
```

The Delete button

The purpose of the **Delete** button is to remove the rightmost character from the *lblValue* label when clicked. There are a couple of edge cases you must take into consideration here:

- You should remove the last digit of the label value only if it contain more than one character otherwise the label value should be reset to **0** using the **noValue** constant you created earlier.
- If the label contain only one digit and it is a minus sign the value of the label should be reset to **0** using the **noValue** constant you created earlier.

1. Name the button *btnDelete*.
2. Double click on the **Delete** (←) button to add its **Click** event method to the code-behind file.
3. Declare a **string** variable called **newValue** and assign the default value store in the **noValue** constant. The variable will hold the new value as it is created throughout the event.
   ```
   string newValue = noValue;
   ```
4. Next fetch the length of the text stored in the *lblValue* label and store it in an **int** variable called **length**. You will need this value to determine if the first edge case should be applied or if the last digit should be removed from the value.
   ```
   int length = Convert.ToInt32(lblValue.Text.Length);
   ```
5. Use the **length** variable to determine if the last digit should be removed and if so remove it using the **Substring** method of the label's **Text** property storing the result in the **newValue** variable you created earlier.
   ```
   if (length > 1)
       newValue = lblValue.Text.Substring(0, length - 1);
   ```
6. Check if the remaining value in the **newValue** is equal to a minus sign denoting that a negative number was used, if it is reset the value of the variable to the value stored in the **noValue** constant. Store the minus character in a **string** constant named **minusSign** at the beginning of the form and use it instead of hard coding the minus sign in the **if**-statement.
   ```
   if (newValue.Equals(minusSign))
       newValue = noValue;
   ```
7. Assign the value in the **newValue** variable to the **Text** property of the *lblValue* label.

8. Run the application and make sure that the **Delete** button works properly.

9. Close the application.

Here's the complete code for the **Delete** button:

```
private void btnDelete_Click(object sender, EventArgs e)
{
    string newValue = noValue;
    int length = Convert.ToInt32(lblValue.Text.Length);

    if (length > 1)
        newValue = lblValue.Text.Substring(0, length - 1);

    if (newValue.Equals(minusSign))
        newValue = noValue;

    lblValue.Text = newValue;
}
```

The Clear button

The purpose of the **Clear** button is to clear the labels and assign default values to them.

1. Name the button *btnClear*.
2. Double click on the **Clear** button in the form to create its **Click** event.
3. Assign the value of the **noValue** constant to the *lblValue* label to reset its value to **0**.
4. Assign an empty string to the *lblFirstValue* and *lblMathFunction* labels to clear them.
5. Run the application and make sure that the **clear** button works properly.
6. Close the application.

Here's the complete code for the **Clear** button:

```
private void btnClear_Click(object sender, EventArgs e)
{
    lblValue.Text = noValue;
    lblFirstValue.Text = String.Empty;
    lblMathFunction.Text = String.Empty;
}
```

The Memory button

The purpose of the **Memory (M)** button is to store the current value from the label *lblValue* in a form level **string** variable called **memory**. The user should then be able to recall that value by clicking on the **Memory Recall (MR)** button.

1. Name the button *btnMemory*.
2. Double click on the **Memory** button in the form to create its **Click** event.
3. Scroll to the beginning of the form and create a new **string** variable called **memory** below the already existing constants and assign an empty string to it.
   ```
   string memory = String.Empty;
   ```
4. Scroll back to the **btnMemory_Click** event.
5. Assign the text in the *lblValue* label to the **memory** variable.
6. Reset the value of the *lblValue* label to the value stored in the **noValue** constant.

Here's the complete code for the **Memory** button:

```
private void btnMemory_Click(object sender, EventArgs e)
{
    memory = lblValue.Text;
    lblValue.Text = noValue;
}
```

The Memory Recall button

The purpose of the **Memory Recall (MR)** button is to recall the value stored in the **memory** variable and assign that value to the *lblValue* label.

1. Name the button *btnMemoryRecall*.
2. Double click on the **Memory Recall** button in the form to create its **Click** event.
3. Assign the value from the **memory** variable you created at form level in the previous section to the *lblValue* label.
4. Run the application to test the **Memory** and **Memory Recall** buttons by entering a value using the numerical buttons and then clicking on the **Memory** button. Clear the label by clicking on the **Clear** button and then click on the **Memory Recall** button to fetch the value in the **memory** variable and display it in the *lblValue* label.
5. Close the application.

Here's the complete code for the **Memory Recall** button:

```
private void btnMemoryRecall_Click(object sender, EventArgs e)
{
    lblValue.Text = memory;
}
```

The Decimal button

The purpose of the **Decimal** (,) button is to append a decimal character to the end of the value in the *lblValue* label. To adhere to the use case specification you have to create another **string** constant for the decimal character (comma or period depending of culture settings in the Windows operating system), name the constant **decimalSign** and assign a comma (,) or a period (.) to it depending of which symbol you use in your country.

1. Name the button *btnDecimal*.
2. Double click on the **Decimal** button in the form to create its **Click** event.
3. Scroll to the beginning of the form and add a **string** constant called **decimalSign** to which you assign the appropriate decimal character.
   ```
   const string decimalSign = ",";
   ```
4. Scroll back down to the **btnDecimal_Click** event.
5. Add a **bool** variable called **hasDecimal** in the event method and assign **true** or **false** to it depending on if the *lblValue* contain the decimal sign stored in the **decimalSign** constant.
   ```
   bool hasDecimal = lblValue.Text.Contains(decimalSign);
   ```
6. Add an **if**-statement to check if the **hasDecimal** variable contain **false** and if it doesn't then append the decimal sign to the label.
   ```
   if (!hasDecimal)
       lblValue.Text += decimalSign;
   ```
7. Run the application and enter a decimal value. Try to add more than one decimal character, it should not be possible.
8. Close the application.

Here's the complete code for the **Decimal** button:

```
private void btnDecimal_Click(object sender, EventArgs e)
{
    bool hasDecimal = lblValue.Text.Contains(decimalSign);
    if (!hasDecimal)
        lblValue.Text += decimalSign;
```

}

The Arithmetic buttons

The purpose of the **Arithmetic (+, -, x, /)** buttons is to determine how the result should be calculated when the calculate (=) button is clicked. When one of the buttons is clicked the arithmetic symbol for the clicked button should be displayed in the *lblMathFunction* label, the value in the *lblValue* label should be moved to the *lblFirstValue* label (the small label on top of the value label) and the value of the **noValue** constant should be assigned to the *lblValue* label. Cast the **sender** parameter to a **Button** to get to the **Text** property of the clicked button which is the value you should display in the *lblMathFunction* label.

1. Select one of the **arithmetic** buttons and add the name *btnCalculate_Click* to its **Click** event field in the **Events** section of the **Properties** window.
2. If you weren't taken to the event method then double click on the button in the form to go to its **Click** event.
3. Cast the **sender** parameter to a **Button** variable called **btn**.
   ```
   Button btn = (Button)sender;
   ```
4. Assign the **Text** property of the **btn** variable (which in reality is the clicked button) to the *lblMathFunction* label. This will display the text of the button in the blue label. You will later use this value when determining how to perform the calculation.
   ```
   lblMathFunction.Text = btn.Text;
   ```
5. Assign the value in the *lblValue* label to the *lblFirstValue* label.
   ```
   lblFirstValue.Text = lblValue.Text;
   ```
6. Set the value of the *lblValue* label to the value of the **noValue** constant.
   ```
   lblValue.Text = noValue;
   ```
7. Run the application and make sure that the arithmetic symbol is displayed in the blue label and that the value is moved from the *lblValue* label to the *lblFirstValue* label.
8. Close the application.

Here's the complete code for the **Calculate** button:

```
private void btnCalculate_Click(object sender, EventArgs e)
{
    Button btn = (Button)sender;
    lblMathFunction.Text = btn.Text;
```

```
    lblFirstValue.Text = lblValue.Text;
    lblValue.Text = noValue;
}
```

The Sign button

The purpose of the **Sign** (±) button is to toggle between displaying a minus sign in the **lblValue** label making the value negative or to remove the minus sign if it is a negative value. Since the use case specifies that no hardcoded values should exist in the code except as constants at the beginning of the form you have to add a **string** constant called **minusSign** which holds a minus sign.

1. Name the button **btnSign**.
2. Double click on the **Sign** button in the form to create its **Click** event.
3. Scroll to the beginning of the form and add a **string** constant called **minusSign** and assign a minus sign to it.
   ```
   const string minusSign = "-";
   ```
4. Scroll back to the **btnSign_Click** event method.
5. Add a **bool** variable called **hasSign** which checks if it is a negative value by using the **Contains** method to check if a minus sign is present in the **Text** property of the **lblValue** label.
   ```
   bool hasSign = lblValue.Text.Contains(minusSign);
   ```
6. Add an **if**-statement checking if the **hasSign** variable is **true** meaning that it is a negative number and the minus sign should be removed. To remove the minus sign you can use the **Replace** method on the **Text** property of the **lblValue** label, replacing the minus sign with an empty string.
   ```
   if (hasSign)
       lblValue.Text = lblValue.Text.Replace(minusSign, String.Empty);
   ```
7. Add an **else if**-statement checking if the value isn't equal to the value stored in the **noValue** constant; that the value is not zero. If that is the case then insert a minus sign at the beginning of the **lblValue** label's **Text** property making the value negative. You can use the Insert method with the **Text** property to add the minus sign at the beginning of the string.
   ```
   else if (lblValue.Text != noValue)
       lblValue.Text = lblValue.Text.Insert(0, minusSign);
   ```
8. Run the application and add toggle between a positive and a negative number.

9. Close the application.

Here's the complete code for the **Sign** button:

```
private void btnSign_Click(object sender, EventArgs e)
{
    bool hasSign = lblValue.Text.Contains(minusSign);

    if (hasSign)
        lblValue.Text = lblValue.Text.Replace(minusSign, String.Empty);
    else if (lblValue.Text != noValue)
        lblValue.Text = lblValue.Text.Insert(0, minusSign);
}
```

The Square Root button

The purpose of the **Square Root (√)** button is to calculate the square root of the value in the **lblValue** label and display the result in the same label. You can use the **Sqrt** method of the **Math** class when calculating the square root. You have to check that the value is positive before calling the **Sqrt** method because it is impossible to calculate the square root of a negative number. Display a message box with an appropriate message if the value is negative.

1. Name the button **btnSqrt**.
2. Double click on the **Square Root** button in the form to create its **Click** event.
3. Add a **bool** variable called **hasSign** that you use to store whether the **lblValue** label contain a minus sign or not. You can use the **Contains** method with the label's **Text** property and the **minusSign** constant you added earlier.
   ```
   bool hasSign = lblValue.Text.Contains(minusSign);
   ```

4. Now use the value of the **hasSign** variable to determine if you should display a message box to the user and then exit out from the event prematurely.
   ```
   if (hasSign)
   {
       MessageBox.Show("Cannot calculate the square root of a negative
           number");
       return;
   }
   ```

5. Next you need to check if the label text ends with a decimal sign using the **EndsWith** method on the **Text** property and the **decimalSign** constant you created earlier. Store the result in a variable called **endsWithDecimalSign**.

94

```
var endsWithDecimalSign = lblValue.Text.EndsWith(decimalSign);
```

6. Next find out the length of the text in the **lblValue** label and store it in an **int** variable called **length**.
   ```
   int length = lblValue.Text.Length;
   ```

7. Check if the **endsWithDecimalSign** variable contain the value **true** in an **if**-statement. If the value is **true** then remove the decimal sign. You can use the **Substring** method with the **Text** property of the **lblValue** label to remove the decimal character; the **Substring** method's first parameter is the start position in the string and the second is how many characters to copy. The user might have clicked the **decimal** button by mistake and forgot to remove it before hitting the **Square Root** button.
   ```
   if (endsWithDecimalSign)
       lblValue.Text = lblValue.Text.Substring(0, length - 1);
   ```

8. Because the **Sqrt** method in the **Math** class requires a **double** value you have the convert the value of the **lblValue** label to a **double** before passing it to the method.
   ```
   var value = Convert.ToDouble(lblValue.Text);
   ```

9. Next calculate the square root by calling the **Math.Sqrt** method passing in the value of the **value** variable from the previous step and store the result in a variable called **result**.
   ```
   var result = Math.Sqrt(value);
   ```

10. You have to call the **ToString** method on the **result** variable when assigning the result to the **lblValue** label.
    ```
    lblValue.Text = result.ToString();
    ```

11. Run the application and try to calculate the square root of a negative number and make sure that the message box is displayed. Calculate the square root of a positive value and make sure that the result is displayed in the **lblValue** label.

12. Close the application.

Here's the complete code for the **Square Root** button:

```
private void btnSqrt_Click(object sender, EventArgs e)
{
    bool hasSign = lblValue.Text.Contains(minusSign);
    if (hasSign)
    {
        MessageBox.Show(
```

```
            "Cannot calculate the square root of a negative number");
        return; // Exit out of the event prematurely
    }

    var endsWithDecimalSign = lblValue.Text.EndsWith(decimalSign);
    int length = lblValue.Text.Length;
    if (endsWithDecimalSign)
        lblValue.Text = lblValue.Text.Substring(0, length - 1);

    var value = Convert.ToDouble(lblValue.Text);
    var result = Math.Sqrt(value);
    lblValue.Text = result.ToString();
}
```

The Equals button

The purpose of the **Equals** (=) button is to calculate the result of the two values using the appropriate arithmetic depending on which arithmetic button was clicked. Since the use case specifies that no hardcoded values should exist in the code except as constants at the beginning of the form you have to add **string** constants for the three remaining arithmetic operators called **plusSign**, **divisionSign** and **multiplicationSign** and assign the values +, / and x to them respectively.

1. Name the button **btnEquals**.
2. Double click on the **Equals** button in the form to create its **Click** event.
3. Scroll to the beginning of the form and add the three **string** constants **plusSign**, **divisionSign** and **multiplicationSign**.
   ```
   const string plusSign = "+";
   const string divisionSign = "/";
   const string multiplicationSign = "x";
   ```
4. Scroll back to the **btnEquals_Click** event.
5. The first thing you need to check is if any of the labels are empty or if the value of the **lblValue** label is **0** and if so exit out of the event prematurely.
   ```
   if (lblFirstValue.Text.Equals(String.Empty) ||
       blMathFunction.Text.Equals(String.Empty) ||
       lblValue.Text.Equals(String.Empty) ||
       lblValue.Text.Equals(noValue))
       return;
   ```
6. Next you need to check if the value of the **lblFirstValue** ends with a decimal character and if so remove it.

```
var endsWithDecimalSign = lblFirstValue.Text.EndsWith(decimalSign);
int length = Convert.ToInt32(lblFirstValue.Text.Length);
if(endsWithDecimalSign)
    lblFirstValue.Text = lblFirstValue.Text.Substring(0, length - 1);
```

7. Next you need to check if the value of the **lblValue** end with a decimal character and if so remove it.
```
length = Convert.ToInt32(lblValue.Text.Length);
endsWithDecimalSign = lblValue.Text.EndsWith(decimalSign);
if (endsWithDecimalSign)
    lblValue.Text = lblValue.Text.Substring(0, length - 1);
```

8. Declare two variables called **value1** and **value2** and store the **double** converted values of the two labels **lblValue** and **lblFirstValue** in them.
```
var value1 = Convert.ToDouble(lblFirstValue.Text);
var value2 = Convert.ToDouble(lblValue.Text);
```

9. Fetch the value stored in the blue **lblMathFunction** label assign it to a **string** variable called **mathFunction**.
```
var mathFunction = lblMathFunction.Text;
```

10. Add a decimal variable called result and assign **0** to it. You can either explicitly declare the variable using the **double** data type or implicitly using the **var** keyword and assign **0d** to it; the **d** after the **0** specifies that the value should be considered a **double** value by the compiler.
```
var result = 0d; //decimal = 0m, double = 0d
```

11. If the sign stored in the **mathFunction** is equal to the **plusSign** constant then calculate the result as **value1** + **value2** and store the result in the **result** variable.
```
if (mathFunction.Equals(plusSign))
    result = value1 + value2;
```

12. Else if the sign is equal to the **minusSign** constant the calculate then result as **value1** - **value2** and store the result in the **result** variable.
```
else if (mathFunction.Equals(minusSign))
    result = value1 - value2;
```

13. Else if the sign is equal to the **divisionSign** constant then calculate the result as **value1** / **value2** and store the result in the **result** variable.
```
else if (mathFunction.Equals(divisionSign))
    result = value1 / value2;
```

14. Else if the sign is equal to the **multiplicationSign** constant then calculate the result as **value1 * value2** and store the result in the **result** variable.

```
else if (mathFunction.Equals(multiplicationSign))
    result = value1 * value2;
```

15. Next empty the two labels *lblMathFunction* and *lblFirstValue*.

```
lblMathFunction.Text = String.Empty;
lblFirstValue.Text = String.Empty;
```

16. Assign the result of the **result** variable with a formatted output of 3 decimal digits using the format option of the **ToString** method.

```
lblValue.Text = result.ToString("F3");
```

17. Run the application and do a few calculations involving +, -, x and /.

18. Close the application.

Here's the complete code for the **Equals** button:

```
private void btnEquals_Click(object sender, EventArgs e)
{
    if (lblFirstValue.Text.Equals(String.Empty) ||
        lblMathFunction.Text.Equals(String.Empty) ||
        lblValue.Text.Equals(String.Empty) ||
        lblValue.Text.Equals(noValue))
        return;

    var endsWithDecimalSign = lblFirstValue.Text.EndsWith(decimalSign);
    int length = Convert.ToInt32(lblFirstValue.Text.Length);
    if(endsWithDecimalSign)
        lblFirstValue.Text = lblFirstValue.Text.Substring(0, length - 1);

    length = Convert.ToInt32(lblValue.Text.Length);
    endsWithDecimalSign = lblValue.Text.EndsWith(decimalSign);
    if (endsWithDecimalSign)
        lblValue.Text = lblValue.Text.Substring(0, length - 1);

    var value1 = Convert.ToDouble(lblFirstValue.Text);
    var value2 = Convert.ToDouble(lblValue.Text);
    var mathFunction = lblMathFunction.Text;
    var result = 0d; //decimal = 0m, double = 0d

    if (mathFunction.Equals(plusSign))
        result = value1 + value2;
    else if (mathFunction.Equals(minusSign))
```

```
        result = value1 - value2;
    else if (mathFunction.Equals(divisionSign))
        result = value1 / value2;
    else if (mathFunction.Equals(multiplicationSign))
        result = value1 * value2;

    lblMathFunction.Text = String.Empty;
    lblFirstValue.Text = String.Empty;

    lblValue.Text = result.ToString("F3");
}
```

4. Loops and Iterations

Introduction

An iteration is a great way to execute a block of code multiple times; it can for instance be an array or a collection of values. The examples in this chapter will use the array below to supply data.

```
string[] animals = { "Cat", "Dog", "Bird", "Fish", "Lizard" };
```

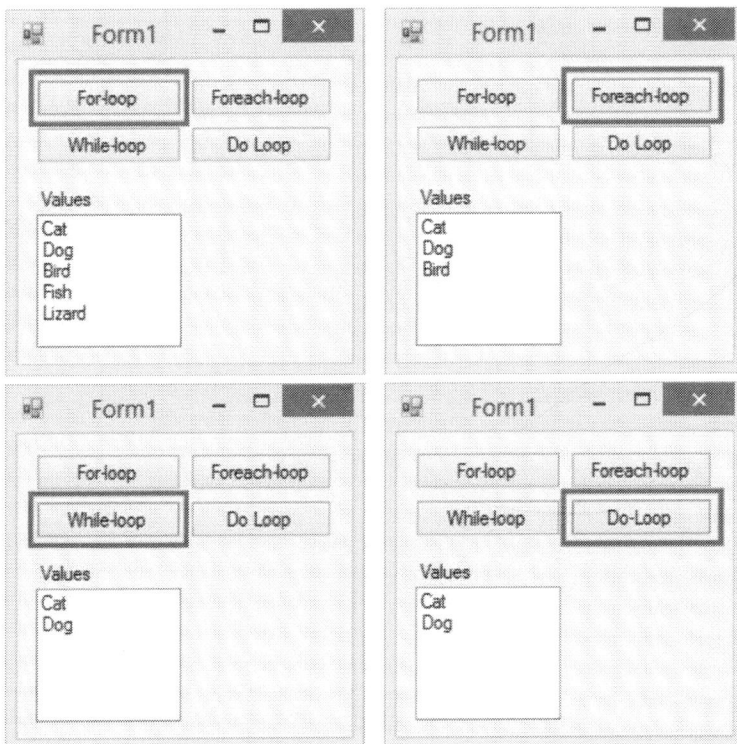

For

A **for** loop is a way to iterate over a set of values until the given expression evaluates to

false. A **for** loop has three parts: a start value for the loop, an expression telling the loop when to stop, and a counter.

In this example `int i = 0` is the start value, `i < 5` is the condition that makes the loop iterate 5 times, `i++` is the iterator.

```
for (int i = 0; i < 5; i++)
{
    lstResult.Items.Add(animals[i]);
}
```

A more dynamic way of determining when the loop should stop iterate is to use the **Length** property or **Count** method on the array or collection variable to find out how many items it contain.

```
for (int i = 0; i < animals.Length; i++)
{
    lstResult.Items.Add(animals[i]);
}
```

Foreach

When using a **foreach** loop, you don't have to know the number of elements that the loop will iterate over because it will iterate over all elements in an array or a collection, unless you explicitly end the loop prematurely with the **break** command. The following code will loop over the animals in the array and stop iterating and end the loop when the current animal of the loop is equal to "Fish", exiting before "Lizard" is even added to the list box.

Note that the **foreach** loop don't have an index and fetch the next item in the array instead. The item is fetched as the type it was created as, in this cases a string, but it could be items created using a **struct** or a **class**.

```
foreach (string animal in animals)
{
    if (animal.Equals("Fish")) break;
    lstResult.Items.Add(animal);
}
```

While

A **while** loop is a way to execute a block of code while a condition is **true**. Important to note is that a while loop will not execute if the condition is **true** from the start. In this example the while loop will end when the animal fetched from the array is equal to "Bird".

```
int counter = 0;

while (!animals[counter].Equals("Bird"))
{
    lstResult.Items.Add(animals[counter]);
    counter++;
}
```

Do

A **do** loop will, contrary to a while loop, always execute at least once.

```
int counter = 0;

do
{
    lstResult.Items.Add(animals[counter]);
    counter++;
} while (!animals[counter].Equals("Bird"));
```

Additional reading: "Iteration Statements (C# Reference)"

Exercise: Loops

In this exercise you will add values in an array to a list box using a **foreach** loop and when the user clicks either the **Move (For)** button or the **Move (While)** button the selected values in the list box will be moved to a second list box.

You can clear the list boxes displaying the selected values after one of the buttons have been clicked by calling its **Items.Clear** method.

```
lstSelected.Items.Clear();
```

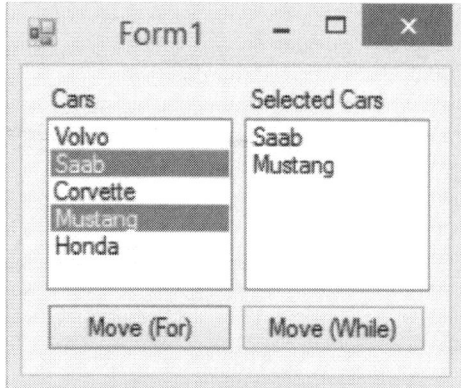

Adding the controls

1. Create a new **Windows Forms Application** in Visual Studio and name it *Loops*.
2. Add a label with the text *Cars* to the form.
3. Add a list box below the label and name it *lstCars*.
4. Add a button below the list box with the text *Move (For)* and name it *btnMoveCarsFor*.
5. Set the **SelectionMode** property of the list to **MultiExtended** to be able to select multiple items while holding down the **Ctrl** or **Shift** key.
6. Add a label with the text *Selected Cars* to the form.
7. Add a list box below the label and name it *lstSelectedCars*.
8. Add a button below the list box with the text *Move (While)* and name it *btnMoveCarsWhile*.

Adding values to the lstCars list box

1. Double click on the form surface (not one of the controls) to add the **Form_Load** event.
2. Locate the beginning of the **From1** class and add a **string** array called **cars** which contain a list of cars.

```
public partial class Form1 : Form
{
    string[] cars = {
        "Volvo", "Saab", "Corvette", "Mustang", "Honda" };
}
```

3. Locate the **Form_Load** event and use a **for** loop to add the items in the **cars** array to the **lstCars** list box. Use the **Length** property of the cars array to determine the number of iterations needed.

```
for (int i = 0; i < cars.Length; i++)
{
    lstCars.Items.Add(cars[i]);
}
```

The complete code of the **Form_Load** event look like this:

```
private void Form1_Load(object sender, EventArgs e)
{
    for (int i = 0; i < cars.Length; i++)
    {
        lstCars.Items.Add(cars[i]);
    }
}
```

Moving the selected values to the lstSelectedCars list box with a foreach loop

1. Double click on **btnMoveCarsFor** button in the form designer, this will create and take you to the button's **Click** event.
2. Clear the **lstSelectedCars** list box.
   ```
   lstSelectedCars.Items.Clear();
   ```
3. Use a **foreach** loop to move the selected items from the **lstCars** list box to the **lstSelectedCars** list box. You find the selected items in the list box's **SelectedItems** property.
   ```
   foreach (string car in lstCars.SelectedItems)
   {
       lstSelectedCars.Items.Add(car);
   }
   ```
4. Run the application and select one or more cars in the list, hold down **Ctrl** or **Shift** to select multiple items when clicking in the list box.
5. Click on the **Move (For)** button to move the selected items to the **lstSelectedCars** list.
6. Close the application.

The complete code of the **btnMoveCarsFor_Click** event look like this:

```
private void btnMoveCarsFor_Click(object sender, EventArgs e)
{
    lstSelectedCars.Items.Clear();
    foreach (string car in lstCars.SelectedItems)
    {
        lstSelectedCars.Items.Add(car);
    }
}
```

Moving the selected values to the lstSelectedCars list box with a while loop

1. Double click on **btnMoveCarsWhile** button in the form designer, this will create and take you to the button's **Click** event.

2. Clear the **lstSelectedCars** list box.
   ```
   lstSelectedCars.Items.Clear();
   ```

3. Use a **while** loop to move the selected items from the **lstCars** list box to the **lstSelectedCars** list box. You find the selected items in the list box's **SelectedItems** property.
   ```
   int index = 0;
   while (index < lstCars.SelectedItems.Count)
   {
       lstSelectedCars.Items.Add(lstCars.SelectedItems[index]);
       index++;
   }
   ```

4. Run the application and select one or more cars in the list, hold down **Ctrl** or **Shift** to select multiple items when clicking in the list box.

5. Click on the **Move (While)** button to move the selected items to the **lstSelectedCars** list.

6. Close the application.

The complete code of the **btnMoveCarsWhile_Click** event look like this:

```csharp
private void btnMoveCarsWhile_Click(object sender, EventArgs e)
{
    lstSelectedCars.Items.Clear();
    int index = 0;
    while (index < lstCars.SelectedItems.Count)
    {
        lstSelectedCars.Items.Add(lstCars.SelectedItems[index]);
        index++;
    }
}
```

5. Debugging

Introduction

Debugging is a skill you have to adopt and learn in order to monitor what's going on in the application at a specific point of the program flow, it is often used to find and fix errors. When debugging you can peek at the current values of variables and control properties by inserting what is known as breakpoints in the code. When a breakpoint is hit the execution halts so that you can switch to the development environment and figure out what is happening at that stage of the application.

There are a number of windows you can utilize when debugging and you will get acquainted with some of them here.

While in debug mode after hitting a breakpoint you are able to step through the code which simplifies the task of finding out where the problem is that you need to fix. To be able to debug an application it must be in **Debug** mode; you can set the mode from the **Standards toolbar** located below the main menu bar.

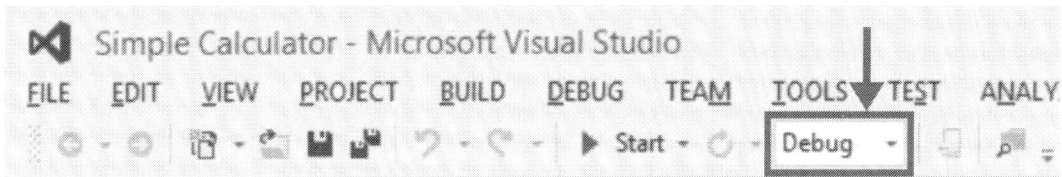

Breakpoints and windows

If you know roughly where the problem you want to debug is located, you can place a breakpoint on the row where you want to halt the execution. This enables you to use the various windows and tools available for debugging.

To set or remove a breakpoint, click on the desired line of code and select **Toggle Breakpoint** from the **Debug menu**, press **F9** on keyboard, or click on the grey area to the left of the desired line of code. A break point is displayed as a filled red circle on the grey area to the left in the code window and the code background is changed to dark red.

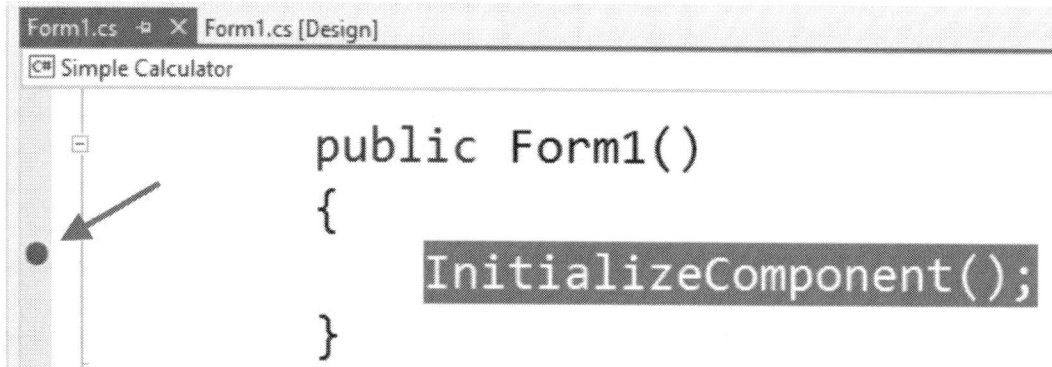

```
public Form1()
{
    InitializeComponent();
}
```

To **start** the application **in debug mode,** press **F5** on the keyboard, select **Debug-Start Debugging** in the main menu or click on the **Play** button in the **Standard** toolbar. If you want to start the application without debugging enabled you can press **Ctrl+F5** on the keyboard or select **Debug-Start Without Debugging** in the main menu.

When the execution encounters a breakpoint the execution halts at that breakpoint making it possible for you to step through the code using the buttons or keyboard keys described in the table below. Note that the line of code where the breakpoint was set gets highlighted in yellow; this highlighting effect will show the next row to be executed when stepping in the code. When stepping in the code you use **F11** to step one line of code at a time jumping into methods if they are called and **F10** to step one line at a time but executing methods in their entirety as they are called without stepping into them.

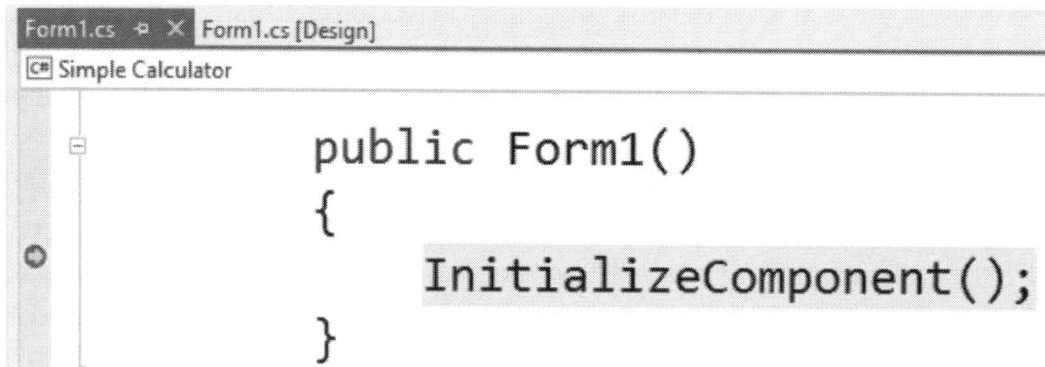

```
public Form1()
{
    InitializeComponent();
}
```

Debug menu	Toolbar button	Keyboard key	Description
Start Debugging	Start/Continue	F5	Start application in Debug mode
Break All	Break all	Ctrl+Alt+Break	Causes a running application to enter break mode.
Stop Debugging	Stop	Shift+F5	Stops debugging and exits the application
Restart	Restart	Ctrl+Shift+F5	Equivalent to stop followed by start
Step Into	Step Into	F11	Steps into method calls
Step Over	Step Over	F10	Executes a method call without stepping into the code
Step Out	Step Out	Shift+F11	Executes the remaining code in the current method and halts execution on the next statement in the method that made the call.

To check values in debug mode you can just hover over a variable name or property. If you want to check or alter values, you can use one of the **Autos**, **Locals** or **Watch** windows.

The **Autos** window displays information about the line of code that was just stepped over while debugging. The information can contain the form controls and variables involved. You can open the window by selecting **Debug-Windows-Autos** in the main menu while in debug mode and a breakpoint has been hit; once opened it will be accessible through a tab located at the bottom of Visual Studio if you are using Visual Studio's default settings.

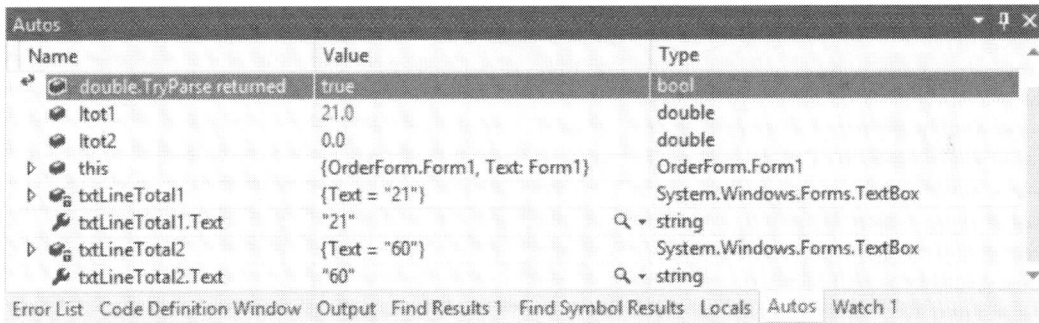

The **Locals** window display information about the currently accessible variables and objects, these variables and objects are often referred to as *being in scope*. You can open the window by selecting **Debug-Windows-Locals** in the main menu while in debug mode and a breakpoint has been hit.

111

Locals			▼ ᄆ ×
Name	Value		Type ▲
▷ ◉ this	{OrderForm.Form1, Text: Form1}		OrderFo
▷ ◉ sender	{Text = "Calculate"}		object {S
▷ ◉ e	{X = 57 Y = 8 Button = Left}		System.E
◉ discount	20.0		double
◉ vat	12.0		double
◉ ltot1	21.0		double
◉ ltot2	0.0		double
◉ ltot3	0.0		double ▼

Error List   Code Definition Window   Output   Find Results 1   Find Symbol Results   Locals   Autos   Watch 1

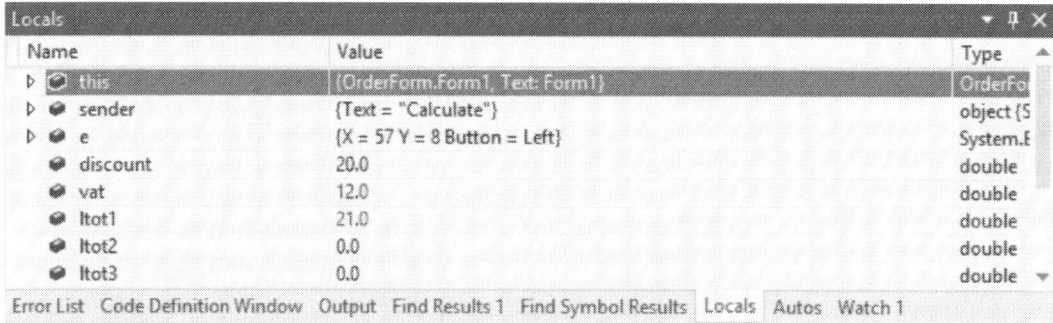

The **Watch** window can be used to keep track of specific variables or control properties. You can open the window by selecting **Debug-Windows-Watch-Watch 1** in the main menu while in debug mode and a breakpoint has been hit. You can add a variable to the watch list by dragging it to the **Watch** window from the code window. To remove a variable from the watch list you simply right click on it in the **Watch** window and select **Delete Watch** in the displayed context menu.

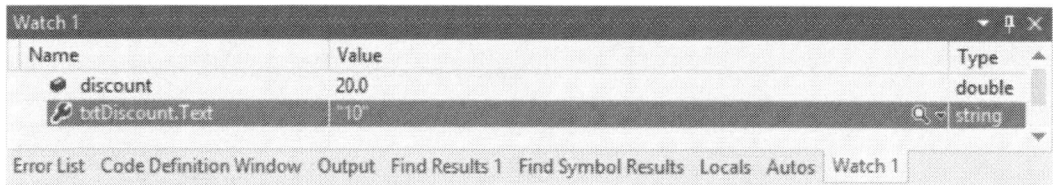

Watch 1			▼ ᄆ ×
Name	Value		Type ▲
◉ discount	20.0		double
🔍 txtDiscount.Text	"10"		string

Error List   Code Definition Window   Output   Find Results 1   Find Symbol Results   Locals   Autos   Watch 1

If you want to print out data while debugging you can use the **Output** window in conjunction with the **Debug.WriteLine** command in your code. You can open the window by selecting **View-Output** in the main menu. You have to add a **using** statement to the **System.Diagnostics** namespace to be able to call the methods on the **Debug** class.

Exercise: Debugging the calculator

1. Open the **Calculator** project you created in the previous chapter.
2. Place breakpoints in the event methods.
3. Start the application in debug mode (**F5**).
4. Step through the code as you click on the buttons.
5. Point to variable names and control properties, for instance the **Text** property of text-boxes, and see what values they contain.

6. Open the **Watch** window and add a variable to it and see what happens in the window as you step through the code.

7. Open the **Locals** window and see what happens in the window as you step through the code.

8. Open the **Autos** window and see what happens in the window as you step through the code.

9. Close the application.

Exercise: Debugging the order form

In this exercise you will open the *Order Form* project you created earlier. You want to print debug information to the **Output** window when the up/down buttons in the **Units** control is clicked for the products. Print the product name, price, units and line total on one line and print the values in separate columns. Add descriptive text to the values (see images below).

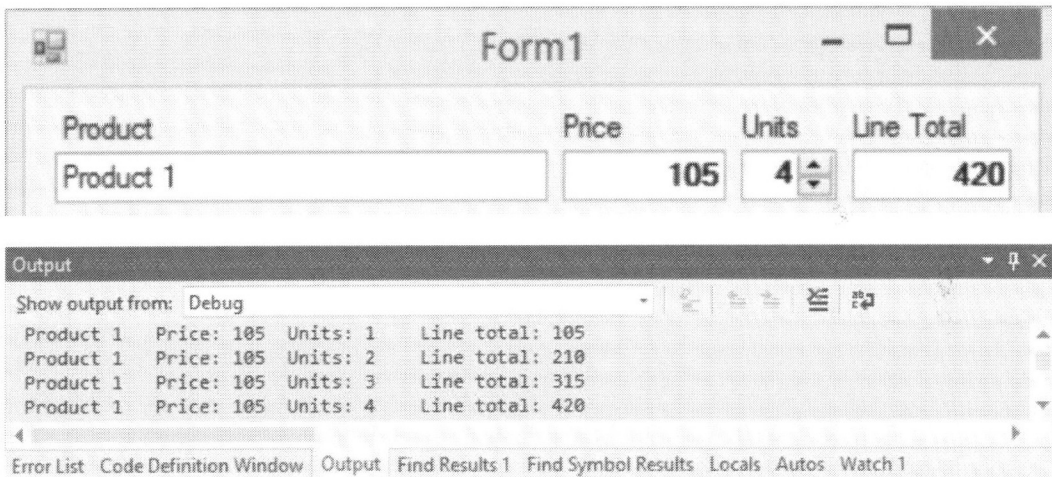

1. Open the *Order Form* solution you created in an earlier exercise.

2. Locate the **numUnits1_ValueChanged** event which will trigger when the up/down buttons in the NumericUpDown controls are clicked.

3. Add the following code below the last line of code in the event.
   ```
   Debug.WriteLine(String.Format("{0}\tPrice: {1}\tUnits: {2}\tLine
   total: {3}", txtProduct1.Text, price, units, lineTotal));
   ```

4. Repeat step 2-3 for the other **ValueChanged** events.

5. Open the **Output** window.
6. Run the application, add data to the form and click the up/down arrows. When the buttons are clicked data should be written to the **Output** window (see image above).
7. Close the application.

6. Simple Types

Introduction

Simple types are user defined types you can create to define your own data types by using the **struct** or **enum** keywords. In some situations a single value is not enough to represent the data you are working with without involving multiple variables; instead of declaring multiple variables you can encapsulate them in a **struct** block which you give an appropriate descriptive name. A variable declared from the **struct** can then be used to gain access to the multiple related values stored in it.

An **enum** is basically a list of constant values which are related to one another.

Enum

If you want to create a variable with a fixed set of values, for instance the names of the weekdays or the months; an **enum** is a good choice. **Enums** are always declared on name-space or class level.

Although you theoretically could use multiple text or numerical variables to achieve a similar result, it is not advisable because the code would be much harder to maintain. There are several benefits to using **enums**:

- Improved manageability
  It is less likely that you will run into invalid arguments and misspelled names using an **enum**. An e**num** restricts what values can be used because it has a fixed set of values.

- Improved developer experience
  Available values in an **enum** will be displayed with IntelliSense.

- Improved code readability
  Using an **enum** makes the code easier to read and understand.

- Improved reusability
  You can easily reuse the same **enum** in different scenarios.

Each **enum** member has a name and a value; the name is the string you list in the braces and the value is a zero-based integer; the first member would get the value 0, the next value 1 and so on. Looking at the next example, *Sunday* would have the value **0** and *Monday* the value **1**.

If you need to, you can assign custom values to the **enum** members by simply giving them integer values. You can access an **enum** either by casting it to an integer **(int)day** or use the value names without casting them **day.Sunday**.

You can use an **enum** as is in **if**-statements or **switch**-expressions. An **enum** can also be used by first declaring a variable using the **enum** as the variable data type or as a parameter in a method definition.

The following example declares an **enum** called **Weekday** which then can be used to create variables or be used in conditional logic.

```
enum Weekday {
    Sunday, Monday, Tuesday, Wednesday, Thursday, Friday, Saturday }
```

The following code can be used to declare a variable using the **enum**.

```
var today = Weekday.Saturday; // implicit declaration
Weekday anotherDay = Weekday.Monday; // explicit declaration
```

The following code will find out if the variable **today** day is a weekend day.

```
var isWeekend = todayday.Equals(Weekday.Saturday) ||
todayday.Equals(Weekday.Sunday);
```

The following code uses the value in the **today** variable in an **if**-statement.

```
if(today.Equals(Weekday.Friday))
{
}
```

The following code use the **today** variable in a **switch**.

```
switch (today)
{
```

```
    case Weekday.Saturday:
    case Weekday.Sunday:
        Debug.WriteLine("Is weekend");
        break;
    default:
        Debug.WriteLine("Is weekday");
        break;
}
```

The following code would cast the day stored in the **today** variable from a **Weekday** data type to an **int** data type.

```
int dayNumber = (int)today;
```

In the following code a **Weekday** parameter is defined for a method. The parameter would be assigned its value when the method is called.

```
void MethodUsingEnum(Weekday day)
{
}
```

If you want to iterate over the names in an **enum** to display the names in a combo box or list box control you will have to use the **enum** type and its methods. Use the **typeof** keyword to fetch the underlying type of the **enum** in order to be able to manipulate it during run-time. Call the **GetEnumNames** method to list the value names. The following code will add the value names of the **Weekday enum** (the name of the days) to a combo box called *cboWeekdays*.

```
cboWeekdays.Items.AddRange(typeof(Weekday).GetEnumNames());
```

Additional reading: "Enumeration Types (C# Programming Guide)"

Exercise: Weekdays (part 1)

In the following exercise you will add an **enum** to a form class in the code-behind file and then use that **enum** to populate a combo box and a list box with the weekdays stored in the **enum**.

When a new day is selected in either control a label should indicate whether the two selected days are the same or not by changing label background color and text. Use **Light-**

Green if they are same otherwise **LightPink**. The text should be "The selected days are equal:" followed by **true** or **false** depending on if they are equal or not.

Both the combo box and the list box should use the same **SelectedIndexChanged** event to determine if the weekdays are the same.

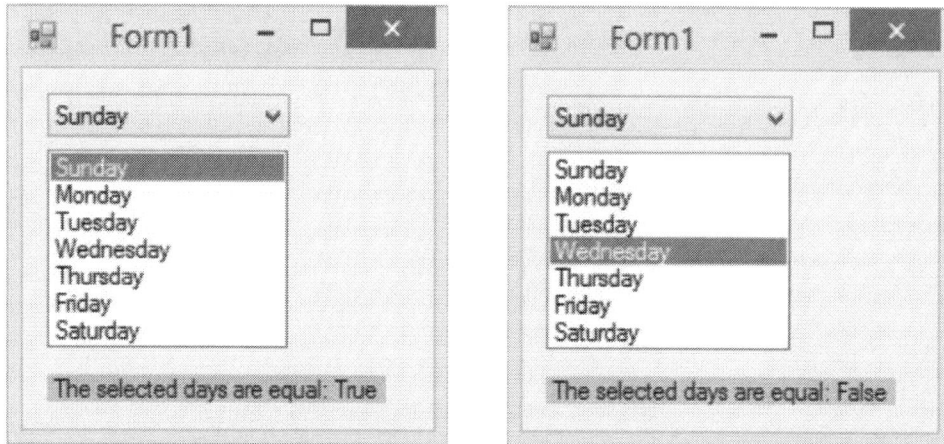

1. Create a new **Windows Forms Application** in Visual Studio and name it *Weekdays*.
2. Drag a combo box control to the form and name it *cboWeekdays*.
3. Change the **DropDownStyle** property of the combo box to **DropDownList** enabling select only mode making it behave like a drop down list instead of a combo box with a text field.
4. Drag a list box control to the form below the combo box and name it *lstWeekdays*.
5. Drag a label to the form below the list box and name it *lblAreEqual*.
6. Double click on the form to get to its **Form_Load** event.
   ```
   private void Form1_Load(object sender, EventArgs e)
   {
   }
   ```
7. Scroll to the beginning of the code-behind file.
8. Add an **enum** called **Weekdays** containing the weekdays just inside the opening curly brace of the form's class.
   ```
   enum Weekday { Sunday, Monday, Tuesday, Wednesday, Thursday, Friday, Saturday }
   ```
9. Scroll back down to the **Form_Load** event.

118

10. Use the **typeof** keyword and its **GetEnumNames** method with the **enum** to fetch the weekday names and add them to the combo box and list box using their **AddRange** method.
```
cboWeekdays.Items.AddRange(typeof(Weekday).GetEnumNames());
lstWeekdays.Items.AddRange(typeof(Weekday).GetEnumNames());
```

11. Next use the **DateTime** data type to get the current day of week (for today's date) and assign it to the **SelectedIndex** property of the combo box and list box to select the current day in the lists.
```
cboWeekdays.SelectedIndex = (int)DateTime.Today.DayOfWeek;
lstWeekdays.SelectedIndex = (int)DateTime.Today.DayOfWeek;
```

12. Switch to the form's design view and select the combo box.

13. Find the **SelectedIndexChanged** event in the event section of the **Properties** window.

14. Add the name **Weekdays_SelectedIndexChanged** to the event field and press enter on the keyboard. You should be taken to the event method automatically.
```
private void Weekdays_SelectedIndexChanged(object sender,
EventArgs e)
{
}
```

15. Fetch the value in the **SelectedItem** property of the combo box and store it in a variable called **cboDay** then do the same for the list box and store the value in a variable called **lstDay**.
```
var cboDay = cboWeekdays.SelectedItem;
var lstDay = lstWeekdays.SelectedItem;
```

16. Change the text on the label to reflect if the selected days are the same or not.
```
lblAreEqual.Text = String.Format("The selected days are equal: {0}",
cboDay.Equals(lstDay));
```

17. Change the background color of the label based on if the selected days are the same or not.
```
lblAreEqual.BackColor = cboDay.Equals(lstDay) ? Color.LightGreen :
Color.LightPink;
```

18. Switch to the form's designer.

19. Select the list box and change its **SelectedIndexChanged** event setting to **Weekdays _SelectedIndexChanged**.

119

20. Run the application and select different days in the two controls and make sure that the label changes according to the rules in the exercise description.
21. Close the application.

Struct

You can use the **struct** keyword to create custom lightweight data structures that contain information related as a single item. An example of data which could be ideal for a **struct** is a point, you could create a **struct** called **Point** which contains variables or properties for x-and y-coordinates. One might argue that you could use a **class** instead, and that is true, but **structs** are faster than **classes** because they are stored on the *Stack* and therefore doesn't have to be passed over to the Garbage Collector (GC) when removed. Most built-in types like **int**, **bool** and **long** are defined by **structs**.

When creating a **struct**, the **struct** keyword is preceded by an access modifier: **public**, **internal** or **private**. **Public** mean that the **struct** can be accessed anywhere. **Internal** (default) mean that the type can be accessed in the same project, but not from other projects; this access modifier is used if the access modifier is omitted. **Private** mean that the **struct** only is accessible to code within the same **struct** or **class**; this requires the **struct** to be located within another type.

You can declare constructors in a **struct** if you want to be able to initialize it when an instance is created. The constructor always has the same name as the **struct** and an empty default constructor is always created by the compiler if you don't provide one. It is possible to add multiple constructors to the same structure as long as they have unique parameter lists.

Important: *When adding constructors with parameters all backing variables or properties in the **struct** have to be initialized with values from within the constructor block.*

To store information in a **struct**, you declare fields (variables) and properties inside it to hold the values. It is not recommended to use **public** fields in a **struct**; instead you should use properties to get and set the **private** field values (see the section on Properties).

This code declares a structure with a constructor.

```
private struct Point
{
    public int x, y;

    public Point(int x, int y)
    {
        this.x = x;
        this.y = y;
    }
}
```

The code below use the **Point struct** when declaring a variable; note that you have to use the **new** keyword when creating a variable based on a **struct**. The variable below could be declared on a **class** level or in an event or method.

```
Point point = new Point(10, 20);
```

You can read or change the value of the variables (or properties) inside your **point** variable at any time by writing a dot (.) after the variable name followed by the name of the variable (or property) you wish to read or change. In the code below the x-variable is changed from its initial value of 10 to 30 before the content of the **point** variable is printed to the **Output** window.

```
private void Form1_Load(object sender, EventArgs e)
{
    point.x = 30;
    Debug.WriteLine(String.Format("x:{0}, y:{1}", point.x, point.y));
}
```

Properties

Properties are used to get and set **private** variable values residing in a **struct** or a **class**. One huge benefit of using properties is that you can perform data checks before assigning or returning a value through a property. Another benefit is that you can change the implemen-tation of the property without impacting the client code (as long as you don't remove the property or change its access modifier or name). A third benefit is that you can bind controls to properties, but not to variables. To the consumer of the **struct** or the **class**, the property looks like a **public** variable.

When implementing a property, you use the **get** and **set** accessors. The **get** accessor is used for returning a value from a **private** field using a **return** statement; the **set** accessor uses a special local variable named **value** to assign the value to the **private** variable. The **value** variable is assigned when the client code assigns a value to the property.

You can decide how a property can be used by the client code by providing both a **get** and a **set** block (read/write), a **get** block (read only), or a **set** block (write only).

There is a predefined property snippet you can use by typing **prop** followed by pressing **Tab** key twice on the keyboard, this template can speed up you coding considerably.

A property can also be used to assimilate data and provide the client code with a result. For instance, you could create a property that return the full name from two private variables or properties containing the first name and last name. Or you could return or assign a value based on business logic. Remember to assign values to all the **private** variables from the constructor.

This example code builds on the previous **Point struct** code where two variables **x** and **y** were added to the **struct** and assigned through a constructor. Now the **public** variables will be changed to properties to make the **struct** conform to best practices.

The variables have been changed from **public** to **private** making them accessible only within the **struct** and two properties have been added to reflect the values out from the **struct** and to make it possible to change the values. Note that property names begin with a upper case letter as opposed to variables and constants which begin with a lower case letter or an underscore character.

```
private struct Point
{
    private int x, y;

    public int X { get { return x; } set { x = value; } }
    public int Y { get { return y; } set { y = value; } }

    public Point(int x, int y)
    {
```

```
        this.x = x;
        this.y = y;
    }
}

Point point = new Point(10, 20);

private void Form1_Load(object sender, EventArgs e)
{
    point.X = 30;
    Debug.WriteLine(String.Format("x:{0}, y:{1}", point.X, point.Y));
}
```

Exercise: Weekdays (part 2)

In this exercise you will alter the *Weekdays* exercise you implemented in the previous section on **enum**. You will encapsulate all information about a weekday in a **struct** called **Day** which you then will use when adding items to the combo box and list box; instead of adding the weekdays to the list controls as strings you will add them as instances of the **Day struct**. Altering the data in the lists will make it possible to cast the selected list items to **Day** instances which you then can extract data from using the **struct** properties.

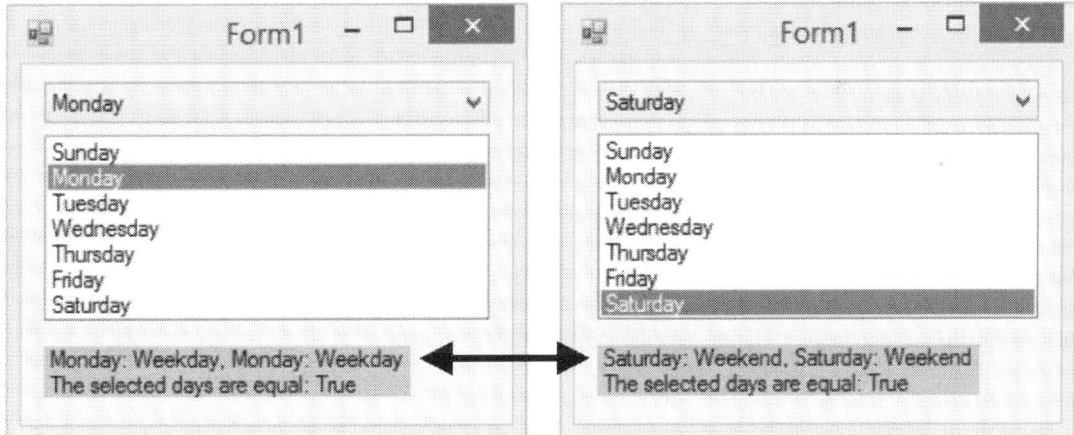

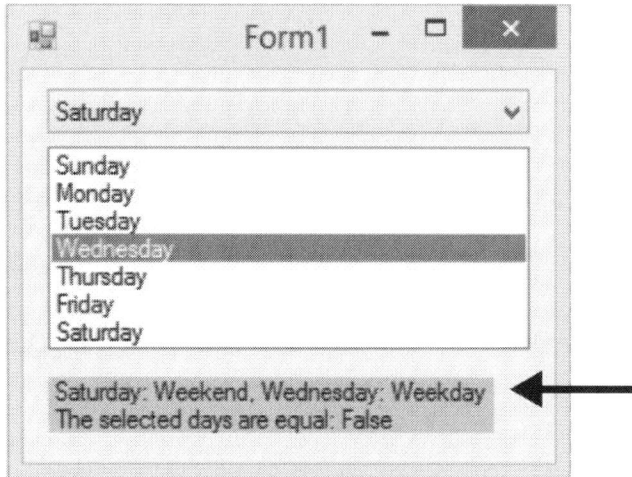

Create a **struct** called **Day** inside the form's **class**, because it is placed inside the **class** it will only be accessible inside the form; if you wanted to give it a wider reach you could declare it as **internal** or **public** outside the form's **class** and inside the namespace.

The **struct** should have a property called **weekday** which can be used to get or set a value of the **Weekday enum** type you created in the previous exercise. It should also have an **int** property called **DayNumber** which keep track of which day of week is being stored in the **struct** variable, a **string** property called **DayName** which keep track of the name of the day and a **bool** property called **IsWeekday** which should return **true** if it is a weekday and **false** otherwise.

The **DayNumber**, **DayName** and **IsWeekday** properties should only return a value, it should not be possible to assign values to them from the code (use only a **get**-block and omit the **set**-block).

The **struct** in this exercise should have two constructors one with a **Weekday** parameter to be able to assign the weekday directly to the **private** local variable **weekday** in the **struct** which is storing the value for the **Weekday** property. The second constructor should have an **int** parameter that is cast to a **Weekday enum** type and thus converted to an actual week-day which then can be stored in the **private** local variable **weekday**.

Delete all code in the form's **Form_Load** event and then create an array which will be used to store the weekdays called **weekdays** using the **Day struct** as its data type. To add days to the array you will have to use a loop in which you create a new **Day** instance for each day in the **Weekday enum** which is then added to the array. Because loops only have been mentioned briefly in an earlier chapter the code will be provided here. Since the weekdays in this exercise start with Sunday you can assume that it will be day 0, knowing this you can have the **for** loop begin with 0 as its initial counter value. Finding out how many iterations the loop should perform is easy in this case because a week always have 7 days, but to show you a more dynamic way of implementing it you will use the **GetEnumValues** of the **Weekday enum** type. Create an instance (variable) of the **Day struct** type inside the loop-block and pass in the day number (the current loop value) to its constructor, this will create the day you store at the array index for the day being processed at the moment. When the loop has finished the **weekdays** array will contain seven instances of the **Day struct** one for each day of the week.

```
Day[] weekdays = new Day[7];

for (int dayNbr = 0; dayNbr < typeof(Weekday).GetEnumValues().Length;
dayNbr++)
{
    var day = new Day(dayNbr);
    weekdays[dayNbr] = day;
}
```

Use the array as the data source for the combo box and a clone of it for the list box. Assign the weekdays array to the **DataSource** property of the combo box and call the **Clone** method on the weekdays array variable to create a copy of the array and assign it to the same property on the list box. Because you are assigning **struct** instances to the list controls you have to specify which property value should be displayed as text in the list controls, you do this by assigning the property's name as a string to the **DisplayMember** property of the list controls, which in this case is **DayName**.

To set the current weekday as the startup value for the list controls you have to create a new variable of the **Day struct** and pass in the **Today.DayOfWeek** property of the **DateTime** class to its constructor and then assign that variable to the **SelectedItem** property of the combo box and list box.

To avoid exception handling (which you haven't learned about yet) you will have to surround the existing code inside the **Weekdays_SelectedItemChanged** event with an **if**-block which checks that the **SelectedItem** property of the combo box and list box controls are <u>not</u> **null**.

Cast the **SelectedItem** property values stored in **cboDay** and **lstDay** variables to the **Day struct** data type. You have to do this because, in the loop, you added seven instances of the **Day struct** (one for each day of the week) to the array which later was used as the data source for the list controls. The cast makes it possible to use the properties values when displaying information about the selected days.

Next you want to add a line of text to the *lblAreEqual* label displaying the name of the two selected weekdays and also if it is a weekday or weekend day, use the **IsWeekday** property of the **Day** variables to figure out if they are a weekdays or part of a weekend. Keep the existing text as the second row in the label, use the **\n** formatting command to create a line break and the **+=** operator to append the old text to the new text.

Keep the logic for the background color as is.

Creating the Day struct
1. Open the **Weekdays** project you created in the **enum** section.
2. Switch to the code-behind window.
3. Locate the **Weekday enum** at the beginning of the class.
4. Add a **struct** called **Day** below the **Weekday enum**.
   ```
   struct Day
   {
   }
   ```
5. Add a **private** variable called **weekday** and its corresponding **public** property called **Weekday** using the **Weekday enum** as the data type inside the **struct**. The variable will be the placeholder for the data stored in the **Day struct** and will be assigned through a constructor or the **Weekday** property.
   ```
   private Weekday weekday;
   public Weekday Weekday { get { return weekday; } set { weekday =
   value; } }
   ```
6. Add a **public int** property called **DayNumber** that return the weekday stored in the **struct** cast to an **int**. The property should be read only.

```
public int DayNumber { get { return (int)weekday; } }
```

7. Add a **public string** property called **DayName** that return the weekday as a **string**, use the **ToString** method on the **weekday** variable. The property should be read only.
```
public string DayName { get { return weekday.ToString(); } }
```

8. Add a **public bool** property called **IsWeekday** which return **true** if the weekday stored in the **struct** is a weekday (mo-fr), you can compare the value stored in the **weekday** variable to the days in the **Weekday enum**. The property should be read only.
```
public bool IsWeekday { get { return !weekday.Equals(Weekday.Sunday)
&& !weekday.Equals(Weekday.Saturday); } }
```

9. Add a constructor method with a parameter called **weekday** of the **Weekday enum** type. Note that a constructor is a method which always has the same name as the **struct**. Assign the **weekday** parameter to the **private weekday** variable in the **struct** to store the value internally for later use.
```
public Day(Weekday weekday)
{
    this.weekday = weekday;
}
```

10. Add a second constructor method which has an **int** parameter called **weekday**. Assign the **weekday** parameter to the **private weekday** variable in the **struct** by casting it using the **Weekday enum**.
```
public Day(int weekday)
{
    this.weekday = (Weekday)weekday;
}
```

The complete code for the **Day struct** looks like this:

```
struct Day
{
    private Weekday weekday;
    public Weekday Weekday
    {
        get { return weekday; }
        set { weekday = value; }
    }
```

```
public int DayNumber { get { return (int)weekday; } }
public string DayName { get { return weekday.ToString(); } }
public bool IsWeekday
{
    get
    {
        return !weekday.Equals(Weekday.Sunday) &&
            !weekday.Equals(Weekday.Saturday);
    }
}

public Day(Weekday weekday)
{
    this.weekday = weekday;
}

public Day(int weekday)
{
    this.weekday = (Weekday)weekday;
}
}
```

The Form_Load event

1. Locate the **Form_Load** event and comment out or delete all the code in it.

2. Create an array called weekdays capable of storing 7 **Day** values one for each day of the week.
   ```
   Day[] weekdays = new Day[7];
   ```

3. Add a **for** loop which iterates over the number of days in the **Weekday enum**. Create a **Day** variable for each iteration and pass in the loop index as a value to the constructor to seed the **Day** variable with a weekday (the second constructor you added will be called). Add the **Day** variable to the position in the array corresponding to the current value of the loop index variable.
   ```
   for (int dayNbr = 0; dayNbr < typeof(Weekday).GetEnumValues().Length;
   dayNbr++)
   {
       var day = new Day(dayNbr);
       weekdays[dayNbr] = day;
   }
   ```

4. Assign the **weekdays** array to the **DataSource** property of the combo box and a copy (clone) of the array to the list box filling them with data. Use the **Clone** method of

the array variable to create the copy. If you don't create a copy of the array both list controls will use the same data linking them together through the shared memory causing undesirable side effects.

```
cboWeekdays.DataSource = weekdays;
lstWeekdays.DataSource = weekdays.Clone();
```

5. Tell the list controls which property value to display in the controls by assigning the name of the property as a string to the **DisplayMember** property of the combo box and list box.

```
cboWeekdays.DisplayMember = "DayName";
lstWeekdays.DisplayMember = "DayName";
```

6. Initialize the two list controls with the current day using the **DateTime** class. Create a variable called **dayOfWeek** which is assigned the day of the week as an **int** using the cast value of the **DateTime.Today.DayOfWeek** property.

```
var dayOfWeek = (int)DateTime.Today.DayOfWeek;
```

7. Create a new variable called **today** using the **Day struct** as its data type passing in the value of the **dayOfWeek** variable you just created to its constructor.

```
var today = new Day(dayOfWeek);
```

8. Assign the **today** variable you just created to the **SelectedItem** property of the combo box and list box to select the corresponding day in the list.

```
cboWeekdays.SelectedItem = today;
lstWeekdays.SelectedItem = today;
```

The complete code of the **Form_Load** event looks like this:

```
private void Form1_Load(object sender, EventArgs e)
{
    Day[] weekdays = new Day[7];
    for (int dayNbr = 0; dayNbr < typeof(Weekday).GetEnumValues().Length;
    dayNbr++)
    {
        var day = new Day(dayNbr);
        weekdays[dayNbr] = day;
    }

    cboWeekdays.DataSource = weekdays;
    lstWeekdays.DataSource = weekdays.Clone();
    cboWeekdays.DisplayMember = "DayName";
    lstWeekdays.DisplayMember = "DayName";
```

```
    var dayOfWeek = (int)DateTime.Today.DayOfWeek;
    var today = new Day(dayOfWeek);
    cboWeekdays.SelectedItem = today;
    lstWeekdays.SelectedItem = today;
}
```

The Weekdays_SelectedIndexChanged Event

1. Locate the **Weekdays_SelectedIndexChanged** event.

2. Add an **if**-statement and block around the code inside the event checking that the **SelectedItem** property of the combo box and list box <u>not</u> is **null**. If you try to cast a **null** value an exception (error) will be thrown but you circumvent this by checking that the values are not **null**. The first time the event is executed the **SelectedItem** of the list box will be **null** since no values have been added to it yet.

    ```
    if (cboWeekdays.SelectedItem != null && lstWeekdays.SelectedItem !=
    null)
    {
    }
    ```

3. Cast the **SelectedItem** property using the **Day struct** as the data type when assigning them to the **cboDay** and **lstDay** variables.

    ```
    var cboDay = (Day)cboWeekdays.SelectedItem;
    var lstDay = (Day)lstWeekdays.SelectedItem;
    ```

4. Add text stating the names of the selected weekdays and if they are weekdays or weekend days. Prepend the already existing text with this new text as well as a line break.

    ```
    lblAreEqual.Text = String.Format("{0}: {1}, {2}: {3}",
        cboDay.DayName, cboDay.IsWeekday ? "Weekday" : "Weekend",
        lstDay.DayName, lstDay.IsWeekday ? "Weekday" : "Weekend");
    lblAreEqual.Text += String.Format(
        "\nThe selected days are equal: {0}",
        cboDay.Equals(lstDay));
    ```

5. Run the application and make sure that the correct text is displayed when selecting days in the combo box and list box.

The complete code of the **Weekdays_SelectedIndexChanged** event looks like this:

```
private void Weekdays_SelectedIndexChanged(object sender, EventArgs e)
{
    if (cboWeekdays.SelectedItem != null &&
        lstWeekdays.SelectedItem != null)
    {
        var cboDay = (Day)cboWeekdays.SelectedItem;
        var lstDay = (Day)lstWeekdays.SelectedItem;

        lblAreEqual.Text = String.Format("{0}: {1}, {2}: {3}",
            cboDay.DayName, cboDay.IsWeekday ? "Weekday" : "Weekend",
            lstDay.DayName, lstDay.IsWeekday ? "Weekday" : "Weekend");

        lblAreEqual.Text += String.Format(
            "\nThe selected days are equal: {0}",
            cboDay.Equals(lstDay));

        lblAreEqual.BackColor = cboDay.Equals(lstDay) ?
            Color.LightGreen : Color.LightPink;
    }
}
```

7. Methods

Introduction

It's important to divide the solution into small, logical components; methods are a way to group code into a separate pieces of work. Writing all code in events without using methods to structure the application would be near impossible to maintain. In this chapter, you will learn how to create and call methods.

A **method** is a way to encapsulate operations designed for a specific purpose and to protect data stored in a type such as a **class** or a **struct**. Many system methods are called when executing an application, one of those methods is called **Main** and defines an entry point to the application which is executed by the CLR when the application is started; you used this method when you created Console applications in the beginning of the book, but it is also used behind the scenes when executing a Windows Forms Application.

There are different types of methods, some are only used internally by the type and are not visible outside of that type, while other methods are **public** and available for other types to request information from that object instance.

.NET Framework itself contain **classes** with methods you can use to interact with the user, computer, or the computer's operating system.

Creating methods

All methods have two parts: a specification and a body. The **specification** defines the method name, its parameters, return type and accessibility (the scope). Each method must have a unique signature which is defined by the name and parameter list. Leaving out the accessibility will give the method **private** scope, making it accessible only inside the type.

Naming methods

When naming a method, you should adhere to similar naming conventions as for variables. Below are some best practices you can follow.

- Use verbs or verb phrases when naming a method; it makes it easier for developers to understand the code structure.
- Use Pascal casing (each word should start with an uppercase letter); do not begin a method name with an underscore or a lowercase letter.

The method body

A **method body** is always enclosed in curly braces and is a block of code that can contain any programming construct. Variables created inside a method will go out of scope (reach) and are destroyed when the method ends and can therefore only be used inside the method.

Method without parameters

The simplest methods have no parameters for in- or out data and return no value. This type of methods are known as **void** methods because the **return** type which must be declared even though no value is returned is called **void**.

If you know that the method only should be accessible inside the **class** or **struct** you are working on then you create it as a **private** method using the keyword with the same name. The **private** keyword can be omitted from the declaration if you want, but I find that it is better to state the intent by specifying the keyword.

In this chapter all methods will be **private**, you will learn about scope in a later chapter.

One scenario when you might want to use a parameter-less method is when initializing controls in a form; extracting that code to one or more methods will keep the **Form_Load** event clean and easy to maintain. You should strive to have as little logic inside the event itself and create separate methods for specific logic and call the methods from the event instead.

The following example shows how you can initialize a label control from a method which is called from the **Form_Load** event. Since no settings will change and the method only is called once no parameters are necessary.

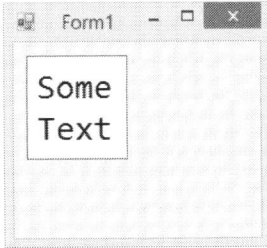

```csharp
public partial class Form1 : Form
{
    private void Form1_Load(object sender, EventArgs e)
    {
        InitializeControls();
    }

    private void InitializeControls()
    {
        lblTest.AutoSize = false;
        lblTest.Size = new Size(80, 80);
        lblTest.Location = new Point(10, 10);
        lblTest.BorderStyle = BorderStyle.FixedSingle;
        lblTest.Font = new Font("Consolas", 20);
        lblTest.TextAlign = ContentAlignment.MiddleCenter;
        lblTest.BackColor = Color.White;
    }
}
```

Method with parameters

All methods have a parameter list which is specified within the method parentheses; if you don't specify any parameters a default empty parameter list will be provided. Each parameter is separated by a comma and is defined by a type and a name. Best practices for parameter names is to use camel case.

In the following example the user can input two numbers into textboxes and when the **Add** button is clicked the two values are added together and displayed in a third textbox. To make the button's **Click** event less cluttered the calculation has been moved into a separate method called **Add** which takes two **double** parameters. In the **Add** method the two numbers are added and displayed in the third textbox and the background of the textbox change based on the calculated result, if the result is negative the background color is changed to **Light Pink** and if it is positive **Light Green**.

135

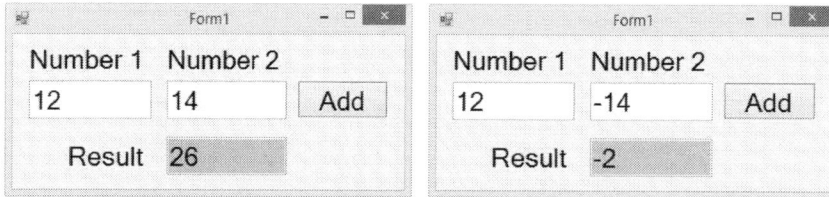

A second method taking a **string** parameter is also created to display error messages in a message box. This logic has been placed in a separate method for easy reuse. Here it is called if the user enters a non-numerical value in one of the two textboxes intended for numerical values.

```csharp
public partial class Form1 : Form
{
    private void Add(double a, double b)
    {
        double result = a + b;
        txtReslut.Text = result.ToString();
        txtReslut.BackColor = result < 0 ? Color.LightPink :
Color.LightGreen;
    }

    private void ErrorMessage(string message)
    {
        MessageBox.Show(message, "Error",
            MessageBoxButtons.OK, MessageBoxIcon.Error);
    }

    private void btnAdd_Click(object sender, EventArgs e)
    {
        double a = 0d, b = 0d;
        var successA = Double.TryParse(txtNo1.Text, out a);
        var successB = Double.TryParse(txtNo2.Text, out b);

        if (successA && successB)
            Add(a, b);
        else
            ErrorMessage("Not a numeric value!");
    }
}
```

Method with reference parameters

When you define a reference parameter using the **ref** keyword you instruct the Common Language Run-time (CLR), to pass a memory reference (pointer) to the passed-in variable instead of passing in the value. This means that you can use the passed-in value as well as assigning a new value to that variable.

In this example the square root is calculated from a value entered in a textbox. When the result has been calculated in the **Sqrt** method it is sent out through the same parameter which received the value to calculate, in the **Click** event the modified value is then displayed in the textbox.

The **double** variable **a** is used as a reference parameter which means that the memory pointer to that variable is set into the **Sqrt** method making it possible to use and alter the variable value in the method as opposed to sending in the value stored in the variable which is the default behavior. As you can see in the **Sqrt** method the **a** parameter is assigned the square root value after calculating it using the same parameter.

Because it is impossible to calculate the square root of a negative number an **if**-statement has been added checking the value passed in through the **a** parameter; if the value is negative the **ErrorMessage** method from the previous example is called.

A value check is also done before calling the **Sqrt** method to make sure that the value is numeric, if not the **ErrorMessage** method is called.

```
public partial class Form2 : Form
{
    private void ErrorMessage(string message)
    {
        MessageBox.Show(message, "Error",
            MessageBoxButtons.OK, MessageBoxIcon.Error);
    }

    private void Sqrt(ref double a)
    {
        if (a >= 0)
            a = Math.Sqrt(a);
        else
            ErrorMessage("Cannot calculate Sqrt from a negative number!");
    }
```

```
private void btnSqrt_Click(object sender, EventArgs e)
{
    double a = 0d;
    var successA = Double.TryParse(txtNo.Text, out a);

    if (successA)
    {
        Sqrt(ref a);
        txtNo.Text = a.ToString();
    }
    else
        ErrorMessage("Not a numeric value!");
}
}
```

Additional reading: "ref (C# Reference)"

Method with out parameters

If you want to pass out more than a return value from a method, you can use output parameters in the parameter list. When you use output parameters, they must be assigned values within the method's body. To specify a parameter as output, you prefix it with the **out** keyword. A parameter defined as **out** cannot pass a value to the method, it can only pass a value out from the method.

This is basically the same example as in the **Method With Parameters** section in this chapter with the difference that the result in the **Add** method is passed out from the method using a **out** parameter; this type of parameter cannot be used in a method other than to return a value, it is not possible to use value passed in through it trying to do so will generate a compile error.

```
public partial class Form1 : Form
{
    private void Add(double a, double b, out double result)
    {
        result = a + b;
    }

    private void ErrorMessage(string message)
    {
        MessageBox.Show(message, "Error",
            MessageBoxButtons.OK, MessageBoxIcon.Error);
    }

    private void btnAdd_Click(object sender, EventArgs e)
    {
        double a = 0d, b = 0d;
        var successA = Double.TryParse(txtNo1.Text, out a);
        var successB = Double.TryParse(txtNo2.Text, out b);

        if (successA && successB)
        {
            double result;
            Add(a, b, out result);
            txtReslut.Text = result.ToString();
            txtReslut.BackColor = result < 0 ?
                Color.LightPink : Color.LightGreen;
        }
        else
            ErrorMessage("Not a numeric value!");
    }
}
```

Additional reading: "out parameter modifier (C# Reference)"

Method with a return type

All methods have return types, even those that don't return a value. You use the **void** return type to specify that a method shouldn't return a value. Methods which return a value must have a **return** statement in the method body and the returned value must have the same data type as in the method declaration. When the method reaches a **return** statement the method is exited; this means that code which occurs after the **return** statement will not be executed.

In this example a return value is used from the **Subtract** method to send back the result to the event where the call originated. The result is collected in a variable which is assigned the result of the method call. Inside the **Subtract** method the **return** keyword is used to send back the result of the arithmetic operation. Note that the **return** data type is specified to the left of the method name, where **void** previously was used for other methods the **double** data type is now used to specify that a value will be returned using the **return** keyword.

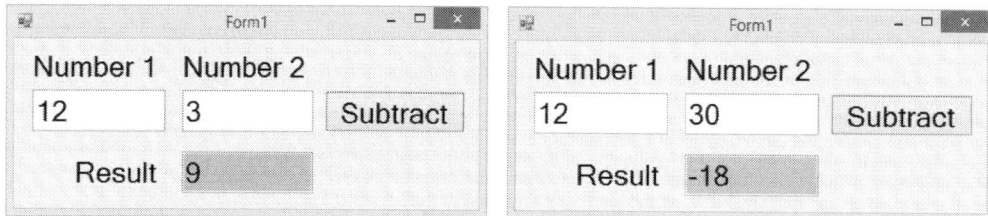

Form1		Form1	
Number 1 Number 2		Number 1 Number 2	
12	3	12	30
	Subtract		Subtract
Result 9		Result -18	

```csharp
public partial class Form1 : Form
{
    private double Subtract(double a, double b) {
        return a - b;
    }

    private void ErrorMessage(string message) {
        MessageBox.Show(message, "Error",
            MessageBoxButtons.OK, MessageBoxIcon.Error);
    }

    private void btnSubtract_Click(object sender, EventArgs e)
    {
        double a = 0d, b = 0d;
        var successA = Double.TryParse(txtNo1.Text, out a);
        var successB = Double.TryParse(txtNo2.Text, out b);

        if (successA && successB)
        {
            var result = Subtract(a, b);
            txtReslut.Text = result.ToString();
            txtReslut.BackColor = result < 0 ?
              Color.LightPink : Color.LightGreen;
        }
        else
            ErrorMessage("Not a numeric value!");
    }
}
```

Calling methods

Because a method encapsulates its logic and "hides" it from the caller you might not have access to the code or know the inner workings of the method; it might be provided by a third-party class library or the .NET Framework.

You call a method by specifying its name followed by its parameters within parentheses. If the method return a value through its return data type you typically assign the value to a variable when calling the method; if you don't need the returned value then you can skip assigning it to a variable.

```
double a = 0d, b = 0d;
var result = Subtract(a, b);
Sqrt(ref a);
Add(a, b);
```

Additional reading: "Methods (C# Programming Guide)"

Overload methods

With overloading, you can create different implementations of methods with the same method name. Sometimes you may want to perform a task with a slight variation depending on the passed-in method parameters; this is when you want to use overloading. You can use the same method name for more than one method, but the signature must be different for each of the methods. The signature consists of the method name and its parameters; the parameters can be declared as output, be optional or named parameters.

Because the return type is not part of the method signature, it is not sufficient to change the return type when creating an overloaded method.

In the example with the **Add** method below an overload is used to be able to call the method with different parameters but with the same end result of adding two numbers.

```
private void Add(double a, double b)
{
    double result = a + b;
    txtReslut.Text = result.ToString();
    txtReslut.BackColor = result < 0 ? Color.LightPink :
Color.LightGreen;
}
```

```
private void Add(double a, double b, out double result)
{
    result = a + b;
}
```

Optional method parameters

One situation where you might want to use optional parameters is when interoperating with Component Object Model (COM) libraries. Since these libraries does not support overloading, you can use optional parameters instead.

Another situation where you might use optional parameters in is when the compiler can't distinguish between method implementations enough to achieve overloading because the parameter list doesn't vary enough.

You declare an optional parameter by assigning it a value in the method's parameter list. All mandatory (non-optional) parameters must be declared before any optional parameters.

When calling a method which has optional parameters you can omit all or some of the optional parameters because they have default values provided by you; if you have more than one optional parameter and omit one, then the rest of the parameters following that parameter must be omitted as well. The method will use the default value when a parameter has been omitted.

In this example you will see how you can implement a more generic method for formatting text controls such as textboxes and labels which have the same properties for formatting and text. To achieve a more generic method optional parameters will be used; in this case the text displayed in the control as well as background and text color will be sent in as optional parameters.

When calling the method for different controls you can choose to omit values to activate the default value for those parameters. As soon as you specify a value for one of the optional parameters you have to specify all parameters to the right of that parameter in the method definition.

Note that you must assign constant compile-time values to the optional parameters like a **string**, the **default** method can be used to get the default value for a type; in this example the **default** method had to be implemented for the **Color** enumeration in the method definition which then is handled in the method body with **if**-statements.

The **Control** class defining the first parameter is inherited (part of) all the controls added to a form and can therefore handle any control passed to the method, you will learn more about inheritance in a later chapter.

The **FormatControls** method is called from the **Form_Load** event and the various labels and textboxes (in the image below) are sent into the method to be formatted.

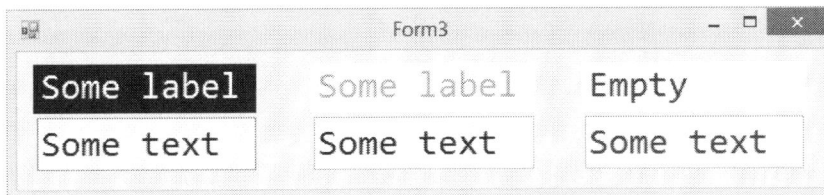

```csharp
public partial class Form3 : Form
{
    private void FormatControls(Control ctrl,
        string text = "Empty", Color color = default(Color),
        Color bkColor = default(Color))
    {
        if (color.Equals(Color.Empty))
            color = Color.DarkRed;
        if (bkColor.Equals(Color.Empty))
            bkColor = Color.White;

        ctrl.BackColor = bkColor;
        ctrl.ForeColor = color;
        ctrl.Text = text;
        ctrl.Font = new Font("Consolas", 20);
    }

    private void Form3_Load(object sender, EventArgs e)
    {
        FormatControls(lblMessage, "Some label text",
            Color.White, Color.DarkBlue);
        FormatControls(txtMessage, "Some text",
            Color.DarkBlue, Color.LightYellow);

        FormatControls(lblMessage2, "Some label text", Color.DarkGray);
```

```
    FormatControls(txtMessage2, "Some text", Color.DarkBlue);

    FormatControls(lblMessage3);
    FormatControls(txtMessage3, "Some text");
  }
}
```

Named method arguments

Using named arguments, you can forego the order in which the parameters have been declared in a method. To use named arguments, specify the parameter name and value separated by a colon.

When used in conjunction with optional parameters, named arguments make it easy to omit parameters. Optional parameters will receive their default values. Omitting mandatory parameters will result in a compilation error.

If you look back at the previous example it has a method called **FormatControls** which implement optional parameters. In that example you learned that you have to specify all subsequent parameters following the first assigned optional parameter, while this is true you can circumvent this by using named arguments. If you wanted to call the **Format-Controls** method sending in text and background color omitting the text color or you only want to send in the text color omitting the other two optional parameters then you need to implement the method call using named parameters.

```
private void Form3_Load(object sender, EventArgs e)
{
    //Using Named Arguments
    FormatControls(txtMessage3, "Some text", bkColor: Color.LightSkyBlue);
    FormatControls(txtMessage3, color: Color.DarkKhaki);
}
```

Additional reading: "Named and Optional Arguments (C# Programming Guide)"

Debugging methods

Debugging is a very powerful tool when testing the application logic. When debugging methods, there are three ways to step through the code; step into, step out and step over.

Step into

Press **F11** on the keyboard to execute the statement at the current position; if that is a call to a function, the debugging will continue in that method. You can click the **Step into** button for the same effect; if you start the application with **Step into,** it will start in break mode.

Step over

Press **F10** on the keyboard to execute the statement at the current position; if that is a call to a function, the debugging will execute the method but not jump into it and continue on the next row of code. The exception is if a breakpoint has been set in that method, then the execution will halt on that line of code.

Step out

Will execute the remaining code in the method and halt on the line of code that called the method.

Exception handling

Exception handling is a good way to enhance the user experience and to avoid unnecessary data loss. Errors can occur in the application logic as well as in external code which has been linked in to the application with references; for instance, you might not know if a file is accessible or if a database is online.

Checking method return values is not sufficient to catch all types of errors, mainly because not all methods return a value. It is important to know why a method failed, not only that it failed. Many errors cannot be handled by checking a return value; one such error could be running out of memory.

You use exceptions to handle all types of errors in your .NET applications. For instance, if a method tries to open a file that does not exist, an exception will be thrown. If the exception is not handled in the method, the exception will propagate to the calling method that has to be ready to handle the exception. The exception will propagate all the way to the application start-up method; if it's not handled by that method, the application will crash and an ugly message will be displayed to the user.

In .NET Framework, all exceptions are derived from the **Exception** class. There are many specialized exceptions that can be thrown by the system, all of which have inherited the

Exception class. You can even create your own exceptions to handle your application logic by deriving them from one of the existing exception classes.

Exception Class	Namespace	Description
Exception	System	Will handle any exception that is raised. Use as failsafe
SystemException	System	Is the base class for all exceptions in the System namespace. Handles all errors raised by the CLR.
ApplicationException	System	Handles all non-fatal exceptions raised by the application.
NullReferenceException	System	Handles exceptions related to null objects.
FileNotFoundException	System.IO	Handles exceptions related to missing files.

Additional reading: "Exception Class"

Try/Catch block

Try/catch blocks are the way you implement Structured Exception Handling (SEH) in an application. To handle exceptions that might arise, you wrap the code in a **try**-block and handle the exceptions in one or more **catch** blocks. It is recommended that you add exception handling using the general **Exception** class as the last **catch**-block in the list of catches; this last **catch** is used to handle any exceptions that you might have overlooked.

Inside the **catch**-blocks you can use properties such as **Message** on the exception variable defined in the **catch**-parenthesis to display or log error information.

```
try
{
    // Code to execute
}
catch (DivideByZeroException ex)
{
    // Specific error handling
}
catch (Exception ex)
{
    // Generic error handling which
    // catches all unhandled exceptions
}
finally
{
    // Will always be executed whether an
```

```
        // exception has been thrown or not
}
```

If **0** is entered in the second textbox in the following example the execution will recognize that you try to divide by zero and the **DivideByZeroException** exception will be thrown and the code in the **catch**-block handling the exception will be executed. If you on the other hand enter a non-numerical value the second **catch**-block will be executed because that will not throw a **DivideByZeroException** exception.

```
private void btnDivide_Click(object sender, EventArgs e)
{
    try
    {
        int value1 = Int32.Parse(txtNo1.Text);
        int value2 = Int32.Parse(txtNo2.Text);

        var result = value1 / value2;
    }
    catch (DivideByZeroException ex)
    {
        MessageBox.Show("Divide by zero exception was thrown!");
    }
    catch (Exception ex)
    {
        MessageBox.Show(ex.Message);
    }
}
```

Finally block

With a **Finally** block at the end of a **Try/Catch** block, you ensure that code that needs to be executed, regardless of if an exception has been handled or not, will be executed. Typically the code in a **Finally**-block make sure that files opened by the application are closed and that open database connections are closed.

The following example is based on the previous example with the addition of a **finally**-block in which the value of the **result** variable is displayed in a message box.

```
private void btnDivide_Click(object sender, EventArgs e)
{
    var result = Int32.MinValue;
```

```
    try
    {
        int value1 = Int32.Parse(txtNo1.Text);
        int value2 = Int32.Parse(txtNo2.Text);

        result = value1 / value2;
    }
    catch (DivideByZeroException ex)
    {
        MessageBox.Show("Divide by zero exception was thrown!");
    }
    catch (Exception ex)
    {
        MessageBox.Show(ex.Message);
    }
    finally
    {
        MessageBox.Show(String.Format("Result: {0}", result.ToString()));
    }
}
```

Additional reading: " try-catch-finally (C# Reference)"

Throwing exceptions

To implement exception handling in your application logic, you will need to know how to throw exceptions as well as handle them. When you throw an exception, the execution of that method ends and the exception will be passed by the CLR to the first exception handler that can handle that particular exception.

Use the **throw** keyword to throw exceptions from your application logic. It's recommended that you create your own exception classes that correspond to your application logic when the system exceptions aren't a good match; consider that you might want to pass application data with the exception; to do that you need to create a new exception class that derives from an existing exception class and implement properties for the data in it.

In the following example, an **ApplicationException** is thrown in the called method when the value of the second parameter (**b**) is **0**. The exception is then handled in the calling event.

```
public partial class Form5 : Form
{
    private double ThrowException(int a, int b)
```

```
    {
        if (b.Equals(0))
            throw new ApplicationException("You cannot divide by Zero!");

        return a / b;
    }

    private void Form5_Load(object sender, EventArgs e)
    {
        try
        {
            ThrowException(1, 0);
        }
        catch (ApplicationException ex)
        {
            MessageBox.Show(ex.Message);
        }
        catch (Exception ex)
        {
            MessageBox.Show(ex.Message);
        }
    }
}
```

You can re-throw an exception if the exception handler can't resolve the problem.

```
public partial class Form5 : Form
{
    private double ReThrowException(int a, int b)
    {
        try
        {
            // Will generate a DivideByZeroException
            return a / b;
        }
        catch (Exception ex)
        {
            // Will propagate the exception
            // to the calling method/event
            throw;
        }
    }
```

```
private void Form5_Load(object sender, EventArgs e)
{
    try
    {
        ReThrowException(1, 0);
    }
    catch (DivideByZeroException ex)
    {
        // The DivideByZeroException
        // will be handled here
        MessageBox.Show(ex.Message);
    }
    catch (Exception ex)
    {
        MessageBox.Show(ex.Message);
    }
}
```

Exercise: Refactoring the calculator application

In this exercise you will do refactoring to the **Calculator** solution you created in an earlier exercise in chapter 3. Refactoring is when you take an existing code base and change it by for instance breaking out code from events to methods making the code cleaner and easier to read and reuse, that is exactly what you will do in this exercise.

The first refactoring you will do is to add regions to logically separate the constructor, events, constants and variables from each other by moving the constants into a **Constants** region, variables into a **Variables** region, the constructor into a **Constructors** region and all the control events into a **Control Events** region. Also add a region called **Methods** for the refactored methods.

Create a method called **AddDigit** which will add a digit to the calculator value; copy the code from the **btnNumber_Click** event and paste it into the **AddDigit** method body. Change the code to use the two **string** parameters you pass into the **AddDigit** method instead of using the label directly. Return the concatenated text from the method using a return statement. Call the **AddDigit** method from the **btnNumber_Click** event passing in the **Text** property values from the *lblValue* label and the currently clicked button as parameters.

```
lblValue.Text = AddDigit(lblValue.Text, btn.Text);
```

Create a **void** method called **DeleteDigit** which takes a reference (**ref**) **string** parameter and a regular **string** parameter. The reference parameter can be used to send in data and to return data from the method. Cut all code except the first and last code lines from the **btnDelete_Click** event and paste it into the **Delete** method then change the pasted code to use the passed in parameters instead of using the label directly. Call the **Delete** method from the **btnDelete_Click** event where the code you cut out was located between the two remaining code lines. Pass in the **newValue** variable as the first parameter by reference using the **ref** keyword and the text in the *lblValue* as the second parameter.

```
DeleteDigit(ref newValue, lblValue.Text);
```

Create a method called **AddDecimal** and modify and use the code form the **btnDecimal _Click** event in it; the method should **return** a **string** and take a **string** as a parameter. Remove all code from the event and assign the result from a call the **AddDecimal** to the *lblValue* label.

```
lblValue.Text = AddDecimal(lblValue.Text);
```

Create a method called **ToggleSign** and modify and use the code form the **btnSign_Click** event in it; the method should **return** a **string** and take a **string** as a parameter. Remove all code from the event and assign the result from a call the **ToggleSign** to the *lblValue* label.

```
lblValue.Text = ToggleSign(lblValue.Text);
```

The **btnEquals_Click** event can be refactored into three methods. Create a method called **CanCalculate** which will check that the labels contain text, call the **CanCalculate** method in the first **if**-statement of the event and exit from the method with a **return** statement if the result of the method call is **true**.

```
if (CanCalculate()) return;
```

Create a method called **EndsWithDecimalSign** which return a **string** and take a **string** as a parameter; the purpose of this method is to make sure that the value in the labels involved in the calculations don't end with a decimal character. Copy the code that checks if a label end with a decimal from the event and modify the code to not use the label directly and instead use the passed in **string** parameter. Replace the two checks in the event with calls to the **EndsWithDecimalSign** method and assign the result to the **Text** property of the *lblFirstValue* and *lblValue* respectively.

```
lblFirstValue.Text = EndsWithDecimalSign(lblFirstValue.Text);
lblValue.Text = EndsWithDecimalSign(lblValue.Text);
```

Create a **void** method called **Calculate** which takes three **double** parameters and a **string** parameter, the first **double** parameter should be declared as an **out** parameter which mean that no value can be passed into the method through that parameter but a value can be passed out through it. Cut out the **if**- and **else if**-statements performing the calculation in the **btnEquals_Click** event and paste it into the **Calculate** method; make sure that the **out** parameter is assigned the result of the calculations and that its default value is **0d**. Call the **Calculate** method from the event where you cut out the code.

```
Calculate(out result, value1, value2, mathFunction);
```

Open the **btnSqrt_Click** event and replace the decimal character check with a call to the **EndsWithDecimalSign** method.

```
lblValue.Text = EndsWithDecimalSign(lblValue.Text);
```

Adding regions

1. Open the Calculator project you created in chapter 3.
2. Create a **region** called **Constants** around the constants in the form's code-behind file.
3. Create a **region** called **Variables** around the **memory** variable.
4. Create an empty **region** called **Methods**; you will add methods in this region as you do refactoring to the code in this exercise.
5. Create a **region** called **Constructors** around the **Form1** constructor.
6. Create a **region** called **Control Events** surrounding all the **Click** events and the **Load** event.

The AddDigit method

1. Add a method called **AddDigit** with a **string** return type and two **string** parameters called **labelText** and **buttonText** to the **Methods** region.
   ```
   #region Methods
   ```

```
private string AddDigit(string labelText, string buttonText)
{
}
#endregion
```

2. Locate the **btnNumber_Click** event and copy all code inside it except the first line where the button is cast.
3. Paste the copied code into the **AddDigit** method body.
4. Replace all the occurrences of *lblValue.Text* with the **labelText** variable name.
5. Replace *btn.Text* with the **buttonText** variable.
6. Add a **return** statement returning the **labelText** variable.

The complete code for the **AddDigit** method look like this:

```
#region Methods
private string AddDigit(string labelText, string buttonText)
{
    if (labelText == noValue)
        labelText = String.Empty;

    labelText += buttonText;

    return labelText;
}
#endregion
```

The btnNumber_Click event

1. Locate the **btnNumber_Click** event and delete all code inside it except the first line where the button is cast.
2. Add a line of code where the result of the **AddDigit** method call is assigned to the **Text** property of the *lblValue* label. Pass in the **Text** properties of the label and button to the method.

The complete **btnNumber_Click** event code look like this:

```
private void btnNumber_Click(object sender, EventArgs e)
{
    Button btn = (Button)sender;
    lblValue.Text = AddDigit(lblValue.Text, btn.Text);
}
```

The DeleteDigit method

1. Add a method called **DeleteDigit** with a **void** return type and two **string** parameters called **newValue** and **value** to the **Methods** region. The **newValue** parameter should be defined with the **ref** keyword making it possible to pass in and return a value through it.

```
private void DeleteDigit(ref string newValue, string value)
{
}
```

2. Locate the **btnDelete_Click** event and cut out all code inside it except the first and last line of code.

3. Paste the copied code into the **DeleteDigit** method body.

4. Replace all occurrences of *lblValue.Text* with the **value** parameter.

The complete code for the **DeleteDigit** method look like this:

```
private void DeleteDigit(ref string newValue, string value)
{
    int length = Convert.ToInt32(value.Length);

    if (length > 1)
        newValue = value.Substring(0, length - 1);

    if (newValue.Equals(minusSign))
        newValue = noValue;
}
```

The btnDelete_Click event

1. Locate the **btnDelete_Click** event.

2. Add a line of code between the two remaining code lines calling the **DeleteDigit** method passing in the **newValue** variable as the first parameter and the *lblValue* label's text as the second parameter. You cannot assign the method call to the label's **Text** property because it is declared as **void** but you can assign the value in the **ref** variable.

The complete **btnDelete_Click** event code look like this:

```
private void btnDelete_Click(object sender, EventArgs e)
{
    string newValue = noValue;
    DeleteDigit(ref newValue, lblValue.Text);
    lblValue.Text = newValue;
}
```

The AddDecimal method

1. Add a method called **AddDecimal** with a **string** return type and one **string** parameter called **value** to the **Methods** region.
   ```
   private string AddDecimal(string value) { }
   ```

2. Locate the **btnDecimal_Click** event and cut out all code inside it.

3. Paste the copied code into the **AddDecimal** method body.

4. Replace all occurrences of *lblValue.Text* with the **value** parameter.

5. Add a **return** statement returning the **value** variable.

The complete code for the **AddDecimal** method look like this:

```
private string AddDecimal(string value)
{
    bool hasDecimal = value.Contains(decimalSign);
    if (!hasDecimal)
        value += decimalSign;

    return value;
}
```

The btnDecimal_Click event

1. Locate the **btnDelete_Click** event.

2. Assign a call to the **AddDecimal** method to the **Text** property of the *lblValue* label passing in the same **Text** property as a parameter to the method.

The complete **btnDecimal_Click** event code look like this:

```
private void btnDecimal_Click(object sender, EventArgs e)
{
    lblValue.Text = AddDecimal(lblValue.Text);
}
```

The ToggleSign method

1. Add a method called **ToggleSign** with a **string** return type and one **string** parameter called **value** to the **Methods** region.

```
private string ToggleSign(string value)
{
}
```

2. Locate the **btnSign_Click** event and cut out all code inside it.
3. Paste the cut code into the **ToggleSign** method body.
4. Replace all occurrences of **lblValue.Text** with the **value** parameter.
5. Add a **return** statement returning the **value** variable.

The complete code for the **ToggleSign** method look like this:

```
private string ToggleSign(string value)
{
    bool hasSign = value.Contains(minusSign);
    if (hasSign)
        value = value.Replace(minusSign, String.Empty);
    else if (value != noValue)
        value = value.Insert(0, minusSign);

    return value;
}
```

The btnSign_Click event

1. Locate the **btnSign_Click** event.
2. Assign a call to the **ToggleSign** method to the **Text** property of the **lblValue** label passing in the same **Text** property as a parameter to the method.

The complete **btnSign_Click** event code look like this:

```
private void btnSign_Click(object sender, EventArgs e)
{
    lblValue.Text = ToggleSign(lblValue.Text);
}
```

The CanCalculate method

1. Add a method called **CanCalculate** with a **bool** return type and no parameters to the **Methods** region.

```
private bool CanCalculate()
```

```
{
}
```

2. Locate the **btnEquals_Click** event and copy all code inside the first **if**-statement.

3. Paste the copied code into the **CanCalculate** method body as a **return** statement.

```
return lblFirstValue.Text.Equals(String.Empty) ||
        lblMathFunction.Text.Equals(String.Empty) ||
        lblValue.Text.Equals(String.Empty) ||
        lblValue.Text.Equals(noValue);
```

The complete code for the **CanCalculate** method look like this:

```
private bool CanCalculate()
{
    return lblFirstValue.Text.Equals(String.Empty) ||
            lblMathFunction.Text.Equals(String.Empty) ||
            lblValue.Text.Equals(String.Empty) ||
            lblValue.Text.Equals(noValue);
}
```

The EndWithDecimalSign method

1. Add a method called **EndWithDecimalSign** with a **string** return type and one **string** parameter called **value** to the **Methods** region.

```
private string EndWithDecimalSign(string value)
{
}
```

2. Locate the **btnEquals_Click** event and copy all code for the first check if the label's text ends with a decimal.

```
var endsWithDecimalSign = lblFirstValue.Text.EndsWith(decimalSign);
int length = Convert.ToInt32(lblFirstValue.Text.Length);
if(endsWithDecimalSign)
    lblFirstValue.Text = lblFirstValue.Text.Substring(0, length - 1);
```

3. Paste the copied code into the **EndWithDecimalSign** method body.

4. Replace all instances of *lblFirstValue.Text* with the **value** variable.

5. Add a **return** statement returning the **value** variable.

The complete code for the **EndWithDecimalSign** method look like this:

```
private string EndsWithDecimalSign(string value)
{
    var endsWithDecimalSign = value.EndsWith(decimalSign);
```

```
    int length = Convert.ToInt32(value.Length);
    if (endsWithDecimalSign)
        value = value.Substring(0, length - 1);

    return value;
}
```

The Calculate method

1. Add a method called **Calculate** to the **Methods** region with a **void** return type and one **double** parameter called **result** declared with the **out** keyword making it possible to pass out but not in values through it. Add two other **double** parameters called **value1** and **value2** and one **string** parameter called **mathFunction**. You must initialize the **result** variable with the value **0d** because an **out** parameter must always be assigned a value.

```
private void Calculate(out double result, double value1, double
value2, string mathFunction)
{
    result = 0d;
}
```

2. Locate the **btnEquals_Click** event and copy all calculation code.
3. Paste the copied code into the **Calculate** method body after the variable assignment.

The complete code for the **Calculate** method look like this:

```
private void Calculate(out double result, double value1, double value2,
string mathFunction)
{
    result = 0d;

    if (mathFunction.Equals(plusSign))
        result = value1 + value2;
    else if (mathFunction.Equals(minusSign))
        result = value1 - value2;
    else if (mathFunction.Equals(divisionSign))
        result = value1 / value2;
    else if (mathFunction.Equals(multiplicationSign))
        result = value1 * value2;
}
```

The btnEquals_Click event

1. Locate the **btnEquals_Click** event.
2. Replace the content of the first **if**-statement with a call to the **CanCalculate** method.
   ```
   if (CanCalculate()) return;
   ```
3. Replace the code checking if the *lblFirstValue* label ends with a decimal with a call to the **EndsWithDecimalSign** method passing in the value *lblFirstValue.Text* property and assign the result to the same property.
   ```
   lblFirstValue.Text = EndsWithDecimalSign(lblFirstValue.Text);
   ```
4. Now do the same for the *lblValue* label.
   ```
   lblValue.Text = EndsWithDecimalSign(lblValue.Text);
   ```
5. Replace the **if**- and **else if**-statements with a call to the **Calculate** method passing in the four variables.
   ```
   Calculate(out result, value1, value2, mathFunction);
   ```
6. Run the application and do some calculations to make sure that the application works as it is supposed to.
7. Close the application.

The complete **btnEquals_Click** event code look like this:

```
private void btnEquals_Click(object sender, EventArgs e)
{
    if (CanCalculate()) return;

    lblFirstValue.Text = EndsWithDecimalSign(lblFirstValue.Text);
    lblValue.Text = EndsWithDecimalSign(lblValue.Text);

    var value1 = Convert.ToDouble(lblFirstValue.Text);
    var value2 = Convert.ToDouble(lblValue.Text);
    var mathFunction = lblMathFunction.Text;
    var result = 0d; // double = 0d

    Calculate(out result, value1, value2, mathFunction);

    lblMathFunction.Text = String.Empty;
    lblFirstValue.Text = String.Empty;

    lblValue.Text = result.ToString("F3");
}
```

The btnSqrt_Click event

1. Locate the **btnSqrt_Click** event.

2. Replace the code checking if the *lblValue* label ends with a decimal with a call to the **EndsWithDecimalSign** method passing in the value *lblValue.Text* property and assign the result to the same property.

   `lblValue.Text = EndsWithDecimalSign(lblValue.Text);`

3. Run the application and calculate some square roots to make sure that the application works as it is supposed to.

4. Close the application.

The complete **btnSqrt_Click** event code look like this:

```
private void btnSqrt_Click(object sender, EventArgs e)
{
    bool hasSign = lblValue.Text.Contains(minusSign);
    if (hasSign)
    {
        MessageBox.Show(
            "Cannot calculate the square root of a negative number");
        return; // Exit out of the event prematurely
    }

    lblValue.Text = EndsWithDecimalSign(lblValue.Text);

    var value = Convert.ToDouble(lblValue.Text);
    var result = Math.Sqrt(value);
    lblValue.Text = result.ToString();
}
```

8. Collections

Introduction

Collections is an essential tool to manage items of the same type as a set where you can add and remove items from and iterate over the items one at a time, as well as count the number of items. You can use any data type such as **int**, **string** and custom types such as **Film** with collections.

Collections are often used in graphical user interfaces where they are data-bound to controls such as list boxes, drop-down lists and menus. Another neat feature is that you can use LINQ to query a collection.

Collection classes are provided by the **System.Collections** namespace and there are several categories of collections you can use depending on the situation below are the most commonly used collection types described.

List

Store items in a linear collection; you can think of a **List** collection as a dynamic one-dimensional array. Can be used to store for example **struct** or **class** instances, **strings** or **int** values.

Let's say that you are working with map information in the form of latitude and longitude, you could then create a **struct** for that purpose and store the coordinates in a **List** collection. When creating a **List** collection you have to specify the data type you want to store objects or values of when declaring it, you do this by stating the data type in angle brackets after the **List** data type.

The code below shows how to create two instances of the **List** collection the first with a **struct** called **MapPoint** and the second with the **int** data type.

```
List<MapPoint> map = new List<MapPoint>();
List<int> values = new List<int>();
```

You add data to a **List** collection by calling the **Add** or **AddRange** methods depending on if you want to add one value or a range of values. Continuing with the previous example you could add data to the collections like this.

```
double latitude = 59.3296842, longitude = 18.0684023;
map.Add(new MapPoint(latitude, longitude));

values.AddRange(new int[] { 1, 2, 3 });
values.Add(10);
```

If you want to fetch a specific item in a **List** collection you can use square brackets after the **List** variable and state the index you wish to fetch from or you can use LINQ which you will look at later in this chapter.

```
var point = map[0];
```

If you need to remove an item from a **List** collection you use the one of the **Remove** or **RemoveAt** methods. Let's say that you want to remove the coordinate you fetched in the previous example, to achieve this you can either call the **RemoveAt** method and pass in the index position of the item you want to remove or you can call the **Remove** method and pass in the actual instance you want to remove which off course mean that you would have had to fetched it earlier. One scenario could be that the user has selected the item in a combo box or list box and then clicked a delete button.

```
var point = map[0];
map.Remove(point);

int index = 0;
map.RemoveAt(index);
```

To iterate over the items in a collection you can use any type of loop you desire, the most commonly used loops for collections are **foreach** and **for**.

```
foreach (var coordinate in map)
{
    lstCoordinates.Items.Add(
        String.Format("Lat: {0}, long: {1}",
        coordinate.Latitude, coordinate.Longitude));
}
```

Exercise: Map coordinates

In this exercise you will store map coordinates in a **List** collection called **map**. Longitude, latitude and the city name will be stored using a **struct** called **MapPoint** which you will create. When the user enters data in the form and clicks the **Add** button the a new **MapPoint** instance will be created and saved in the **map List** collection the data will also be added to a list box called *lstCoordinates* (see image below).

To make sure that the values entered for longitude and latitude are of the **double** data type you have to parse the string values from the textboxes using the **TryParse** method on the **Double** class. Before parsing you might also want to make sure that the decimal sign is a dot (.) and not a comma (,) to be sure that the parse works. Another thing you might want to do is to change the culture used by the application making sure that all users no matter where they live use the same setting when parsing the values, you can achieve this by setting the **CurrentCulture** property on the form's thread. This might be a bit advanced for where you are right now, but let's do it anyway.

Add the following code to the **Form_Load** event to change the culture setting for the form to the US standard.

```
private void Form1_Load(object sender, EventArgs e)
{
    System.Threading.Thread.CurrentThread.CurrentCulture =
        new System.Globalization.CultureInfo("en-US");
}
```

When the user select a city in the list box and click the **Delete** button the selected item should be removed from the list box and the **map List** collection. Use the **SelectedIndex** property of the list box as the index to remove from the **List** collection. The property value correspond with the index at which the coordinate information is stored in the collection because you added them at the same time to the collection and the list box and both are zero based.

Adding the controls

1. Create a new **Windows Forms Application** called *Map Coordinates*.
2. Add a label with the text *Latitude*.
3. Add a textbox called *txtLatitude* below the label.
4. Add a label with the text *Longitude* to the right of the previous label.
5. Add a textbox called *txtLongitude* below the label.
6. Add a label with the text *City* below the latitude textbox.
7. Add a textbox called *txtCity* below the label.
8. Add a button named *btnAddCoordinate* with the text "Add" to the right of the city textbox.
9. Add a list box below the city textbox called *lstCoordinates*.
10. Add a button named *btnDelete* with the text "Delete" below the list box.

Adding the MapPoint struct

1. Double click on the form to get to the code-behind file.
2. Locate the beginning of the **Form1** class.
3. Add a **struct** called **MapPoint** to the class.
   ```
   struct MapPoint
   {
   }
   ```
4. Add two private variables of the **double** data type called **_latitude** and **_longitude**, and one called **_city** of the **string** data type to the **struct**. These variables will store the internal data of the **struct** variable.
   ```
   private double _latitude, _longitude;
   private string _city;
   ```
5. Add the variables' corresponding properties called **Latitude**, **Longitude** and **City**.

164

```
public double Latitude {
    get { return _latitude; }
    set { _latitude = value; }
}
public double Longitude {
    get { return _longitude; }
    set { _longitude = value; }
}
public string City {
    get { return _city; }
    set { _city = value; }
}
```

6. Add a constructor to the **struct** which takes three parameters for the latitude, longitude and city name and assigns them to their respective **private** variable.

```
public MapPoint(double latitude, double longitude, string city)
{
    _latitude = latitude;
    _longitude = longitude;
    _city = city;
}
```

7. Add a **List** capable of storing **MapPoint** values called **map** below the closing curly brace of the **struct**. This collection will store all added coordinates as **MapPoint** instances.

```
List<MapPoint> map = new List<MapPoint>();
```

The code so far look like this:

```
public partial class Form1 : Form
{
    struct MapPoint
    {
        private double _latitude, _longitude;
        private string _city;
        public double Latitude {
            get { return _latitude; }
            set { _latitude = value; }
        }
        public double Longitude {
            get { return _longitude; }
            set { _longitude = value; }
        }
        public string City {
```

```
        get { return _city; }
        set { _city = value; }
    }

    public MapPoint(double latitude, double longitude, string city)
    {
        _latitude = latitude;
        _longitude = longitude;
        _city = city;
    }
}

List<MapPoint> map = new List<MapPoint>();
}
```

The Form_Load event

Here's where it might be a bit tricky to understand what is happening because you will use a thread which is something you haven't done before. What you want to accomplish is to make sure that all users use the same settings when it comes to converting values such as **strings** to **doubles**. In order for you to pull that off you have to change the current culture setting which normally is fetched from the operating system to one of your choice, in this case the US standard (en-US).

The code below is added with the full namespace path but you could add it as a using statement above the namespace surrounding the form. It is added with the full path only to make it easier for you to understand from where the setting originates.

```
private void Form1_Load(object sender, EventArgs e)
{
    System.Threading.Thread.CurrentThread.CurrentCulture = new
    System.Globalization.CultureInfo("en-US");
}
```

The Add button

When the **Add** button is clicked you want to create a new **MapPoint** instance and assign the values from the textbox to its properties. Then you want to add that **MapPoint** to the **map** collection you created earlier and also to the list box.

1. Double click on the **Add** button in the form designer to create its **Click** event.

2. Add two **double** variables called **longitude** and **latitude** which will be used when parsing the textbox values.
```
double latitude, longitude;
```

3. Use the **TryParse** method on the **Double** class to parse the value from the longitude and latitude textboxes. Also save the result from the method calls in two variables called **isLatutude** and **isLongitude**; the result will be **true** if the parse went well and **false** otherwise. Also replace commas (,) for dots (.) in case a user has entered a comma as a decimal sign. Note that the latitude and longitude variables you pass in to the **TryParse** method has the **out** keyword in front of them; this keyword is used when you want to store a value in the variable which is created inside the method you call but you do not want to pass any value into the method, you are only interested in the value sent out from the method.
```
var isLatitude = Double.TryParse(
    txtLatitude.Text.Replace(',', '.'), out latitude);

var isLongitude = Double.TryParse(
    txtLongitude.Text.Replace(',', '.'), out longitude);
```

4. Use the **isLatutude** and **isLongitude** variables in an **if**-statement to determine if you should proceed with adding a **MapPoint** to the **map List** collection and the list box. Only if both are **true** should you add a **MapPoint** to the collection and the list box because then both have been successfully converted to **double** values and can be considered valid coordinates.
```
if (isLatitude && isLongitude)
{
}
```

5. Create a new **MapPoint** called **coordinate** inside the **if**-block using the parsed **double** values for latitude and longitude and the text from the city textbox.
```
var coordinate = new MapPoint(latitude, longitude, txtCity.Text);
```

6. Add the **coordinate** variable to the map collection.
```
map.Add(coordinate);
```

7. Add the data from the **coordinate** variable's properties to the list box.
```
lstCoordinates.Items.Add(String.Format("{0} [{1}, {2}]",
coordinate.City, coordinate.Latitude, coordinate.Longitude));
```

8. Run the application and add some coordinates and cities, below is a list of cities and their coordinates you can use if you like.

```
// Stockholm: Lat:59,3296842, Long: 18,0684023
// New York:  Lat:40,7130838, Long:-74,0057028
// London:    Lat:51,5073509, Long:  0
```

9. Close the application.

This is the complete code for the **Add** button:

```
private void btnAddCoordinate_Click(object sender, EventArgs e)
{
    double latitude, longitude;

    var isLatitude = Double.TryParse(
        txtLatitude.Text.Replace(',', '.'), out latitude);

    var isLongitude = Double.TryParse(
        txtLongitude.Text.Replace(',', '.'), out longitude);

    if (isLatitude && isLongitude)
    {
        var coordinate = new MapPoint(latitude, longitude, txtCity.Text);
        map.Add(coordinate);
        lstCoordinates.Items.Add(
            String.Format("{0} [{1}, {2}]",
            coordinate.City, coordinate.Latitude,
            coordinate.Longitude));
    }
}
```

The Delete button

The purpose of the **Delete** button is to remove the selected list box item from the list box list and also from the **List** collection.

1. Double click on the **Delete** button.
2. Check if the **SelectedIndex** of the list box is greater than -1 which mean that an item is selected.
```
if (lstCoordinates.SelectedIndex > -1)
{
}
```
3. Add a variable called index inside the **if**-block and assign it the **SelectedIndex** value.

```
var index = lstCoordinates.SelectedIndex;
```

4. Use the value of the **index** variable when removing the selected item from the list box and the **map List** collection.
```
map.RemoveAt(index);
lstCoordinates.Items.RemoveAt(index);
```

5. Run the application and add some cities and coordinates. Select a city in the list box and click the **Delete** button to remove it from the collection and the list box.

6. Now I urge you to place breakpoints in the event methods and step through the code when adding and deleting items. This will help you immensely in understanding your code and how everything comes together, it can propel you forward in your understanding of the C# language in ways you cannot imagine. You have to be curious to become a top coder.

7. Close the application when you have finished stepping through the code.

This is the complete code for the **Delete** button:

```
private void btnDelete_Click(object sender, EventArgs e)
{
    if (lstCoordinates.SelectedIndex > -1)
    {
        var index = lstCoordinates.SelectedIndex;
        map.RemoveAt(index);
        lstCoordinates.Items.RemoveAt(index);
    }
}
```

Dictionary

Dictionary collections store items using a key/value pair where each item has one key (object used to index the collection and look up the value with) and one value (the object you want to store). An example could be that you are working on a car registry where the items you want to store are information about cars using their unique registration numbers as key values.

You could solve this by creating a **class** or a **struct** working as a container for the car information and the registration number stored in the **struct** or **class** instances would act as the unique key in the dictionary.

The following **struct** called **Car** will be used in the examples below.

```
struct Car
{
    private string _regNo, _vinNo, _model;
    private int _year;
    public string RegNo { get { return _regNo; } set { _regNo = value; } }
    public string VinNo { get { return _vinNo; } set { _vinNo = value; } }
    public string Model { get { return _model; } set { _model = value; } }
    public int Year { get { return _year; } set { _year = value; } }

    public Car(string regNo, string vinNo, string model, int year)
    {
        _regNo = regNo;
        _vinNo = vinNo;
        _model = model;
        _year = year;
    }
}
```

The code below shows how to create an instance of the **Dictionary** collection using the previously described **Car** a **struct**.

```
Dictionary<string, Car> cars = new Dictionary<string, Car>();
```

You add data to a **Dictionary** collection by calling its **Add** method. Continuing with the example you could add data to the collection like this.

```
var car = new Car("ABC123", "1234567", "Volvo", 1989);
cars.Add(car.RegNo, car);
```

If you want to fetch a specific item in a **Dictionary** collection you can use square brackets after the **Dictionary** variable and state the **key** of the item you wish to fetch or you can use LINQ which you will look at later in this chapter.

```
var fetchedCar = cars["ABC123"];
```

If you need to remove an item from a **Dictionary** collection you use the **Remove** method passing in the **key** to the item you wish to remove. Let's say that you want to remove the car with the **key** (registration number) "ABC123", to achieve this you call the **Remove** method passing in the registration number of the car you want to remove.

```
cars.Remove("ABC123");
```

To iterate over the items in a collection you can use any type of loop you desire, the most commonly used loops for collections are **foreach** and **for**. Because **Dictionary** collections have a **key** and a **value** you can access both in the **loop**-block. The following example would add two cars to the **cars Dictionary** and list them in a list box called *lstCars*.

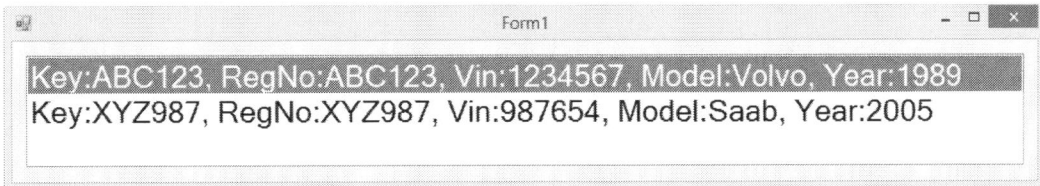

```
private void Form1_Load(object sender, EventArgs e)
{
    var car1 = new Car("ABC123", "1234567", "Volvo", 1989);
    var car2 = new Car("XYZ987", "987654", "Saab", 2005);
    cars.Add(car1.RegNo, car1);
    cars.Add(car2.RegNo, car2);

    foreach (var car in cars)
    {
        lstCars.Items.Add(
            String.Format("Key:{0}, RegNo:{1}, Vin:{2}, Model:{3}, Year:{4}",
            car.Key, car.Value.RegNo, car.Value.VinNo,
            car.Value.Model, car.Value.Year));
    }
}
```

Exercise: Book dictionary

In this exercise you will create a form with which the user can add books to a **Dictionary** collection displayed in a list view control called *lstBooks*. This type of control is designed to display data in different ways where large icons is the default; to display data in a table format you change its **View** property to **Details**. The data in the control is not set to select the entire row by default so that is something you want to change as well by assigning **true** to its **FullRowSelect** property.

You also need to add the desired columns to the list view control by clicking on the small arrow button in the top right corner of the control when it is selected. A menu pops up where you select **Edit Columns** to open the **ColumnsHeader** dialog (see image below). Add three columns for the book information (ISBN, Title and Year) and use the **Name**, **Text** and **Width** columns to modify the columns you add.

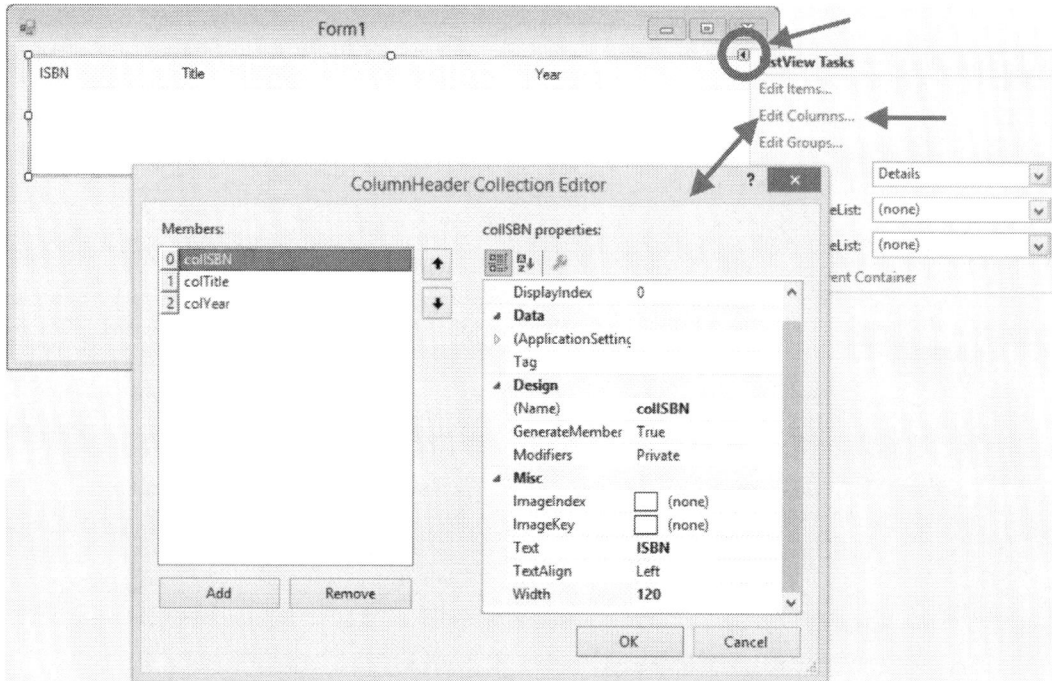

The books should be stored in a **Dictionary** collection called **books** where the **Key** is the ISBN number of the book and **Value** is the complete book information stored using a **Book struct** with properties for **ISBN**, **Title** and **Year**.

Add three books to the **books** collection using the **Book struct** in the form constructor, you can use the following data:

ISBN: 978-0547928227, Title: The Hobbit, Year: 2010
ISBN: 978-0547928210, Title: The Fellowship of the Ring, Year: 2011
ISBN: 978-0547928197, Title: The Return of the King, Year: 2012

Iterate over the books collection in the **Form_Load** event and add the books to the *lstBooks* list view control. You have to assign the **ISBN** number to the **Name** property of the **ListView-Item** instance to make it easier to target specific books in the list when removing books.

The form must have three textboxes for adding new books to the list and an **Add** and a **Delete** button (see image below).

Because the year is entered in a textbox it will be a string when fetched in the **Add** button's **Click** event, you have to parse the value and display an error message to the user and not add the book if the value in the **Year** textbox can't be parsed to an **int** or if the parsed value is negative.

Assuming the **Year** could be parsed and is greater than **0** then you should create a new book using the **Book struct** and add it to the **books** collection. Then you use the book information to add the book to the list view using the **Add** methods of its **Items** collection. Lastly the textboxes should be cleared.

Iterate over the **SelectedItems** collection of the list view control in the **Click** event of the **Delete** button to remove the selected books from the **books** collection and the *lstBooks* list view. Both the list view and the collection has a **Remove** method you can use to remove the current item in the loop. Use the **ToString** method on the current item to get the ISBN number (the **Key**) needed to remove the item from the **books** collection and cast the current item to a **ListViewItem** to remove it from the list view.

173

Adding the Controls

1. Create a new **Windows Forms Application** project called **Books**.
2. Add a list view control to the form.
3. Change its **View** property to **Details** in the **Properties** window.
4. Set the **FullRowSelect** property to **true**.
5. Name the control **lstBooks**.
6. Select the list view control and click on the small arrow button in the top right corner of the control.
7. Click on the **Edit Columns** link in the pop up menu.
8. Add the following columns to the list view control using the **Name**, **Text** and **Width** columns.
    a. colISBN, ISBN, 120
    b. colTitle, Title, 300
    c. colYear, Year, 60
9. Add a label below the list view and change its text to **ISBN**.
10. Add a textbox below the **ISBN** label and name it **txtISBN**.
11. Add a label to the right of the **ISBN** label and change its text to "Title".
12. Add a textbox below the **Title** label and name it **txtTitle**.
13. Add a label to the right of the **Title** label and change its text to "Year".
14. Add a textbox below the **Year** label and name it **txtYear**.
15. Add a button below the **txtYear** textbox called **btnAdd** and change its text to "Add".
16. Add a button to the left of the **Add** button called **btnDelete** and change its text to "Delete".

Adding Book struct

1. Go the form's code-behind and locate the beginning of its class.
2. Add a **struct** called **Book** to the class.
```
struct Book
{
}
```
3. Add two **private string** variables called **_ISBN** and **_Title** and a **private int** variable called **_year** to the **struct**.
```
private string _ISBN, _title;
private int _year;
```

4. Add the properties corresponding to the variables you just added.

```
public string ISBN { get { return _ISBN; } set { _ISBN = value; } }
public string Title { get { return _title; } set { _title = value; }
}
public int Year { get { return _year; } set { _year = value; } }
```

5. Add a constructor with parameters for the three variables.

```
public Book(string isbn, string title, int year)
{
    _ISBN = isbn;
    _title = title;
    _year = year;
}
```

6. Add the **books Dictionary** collection below the **struct**. The **Key** value should be a **string** and the **Value** a **Book**.

```
Dictionary<string, Book> books = new Dictionary<string, Book>();
```

The code looks like this so far:

```
public partial class Form1 : Form
{
    struct Book
    {
        private string _ISBN, _title;
        private int _year;
        public string ISBN { get { return _ISBN; } set { _ISBN = value; } }
        public string Title
        {
            get { return _title; }
            set { _title = value; }
        }
        public int Year { get { return _year; } set { _year = value; } }

        public Book(string isbn, string title, int year)
        {
            _ISBN = isbn;
            _title = title;
            _year = year;
        }
    }

    Dictionary<string, Book> books = new Dictionary<string, Book>();
```

```
   public Form1()
   {
      InitializeComponent();
   }


   private void Form1_Load(object sender, EventArgs e)
   {
   }
}
```

Adding books to the books collection

1. Locate the form's constructor.
2. Create three new book variables using the **Book struct** and the data described in the exercise.
   ```
   var book1 = new Book("978-0547928227", "The Hobbit", 2012);
   ```
3. Add the books to the **books** collection.
   ```
   books.Add(book1.ISBN, book1);
   ```

The complete constructor code looks like this:

```
public Form1()
{
   var book1 = new Book("978-0547928227", "The Hobbit", 2012);
   var book2 = new Book("978-0547928210",
      "The Fellowship of the Ring", 2012);
   var book3 = new Book("978-0547928197",
      "The Return of the King", 2012);
   books.Add(book1.ISBN, book1);
   books.Add(book2.ISBN, book2);
   books.Add(book3.ISBN, book3);

   InitializeComponent();
}
```

Adding Books to the list view

1. Locate the **Form_Load** event.
2. Add a **foreach** loop iterating over the **Values** collection in the **books** collection.
   ```
   foreach(var book in books.Values)
   {
   }
   ```

3. Create a new **ListViewItem** variable called **item** and use the values of the current book in the iteration. Assign the ISBN number to the **Name** property of the **item** variable before adding it to the list view.

```
var item = new ListViewItem(new string[]{book.ISBN, book.Title,
book.Year.ToString() });
item.Name = book.ISBN;
lstBooks.Items.Add(item);
```

4. Run the application and make sure that the books are displayed correctly in the list view.

5. Close the application.

The complete code for the **Form_Load** event look like this:

```
private void Form1_Load(object sender, EventArgs e)
{
    foreach(var book in books.Values)
    {
        var item = new ListViewItem(
            new string[]{ book.ISBN, book.Title, book.Year.ToString() });
        item.Name = book.ISBN;
        lstBooks.Items.Add(item);
    }
}
```

The Add button

1. Add the **Add** button's click event.

2. Add an **int** variable called **year** which will be used when parsing the text from the **txtYear** textbox. Use the variable to store the result from the call to the **Int32.TryParse** method parsing the year, remember that you have to pass in the variable as an **out** parameter. Store the **bool** return value from the method call in a variable called **success**.

```
var year = 0;
var success = Int32.TryParse(txtYear.Text, out year);
```

3. Use the parsed result to determine if the book should be added to the collection and the list view. If the parse is successful the **success** variable should contain **true**. You also want the **year** to be a positive number. If the parse is unsuccessful or the **year** is less than **0** then display a message with an appropriate message.

```
if (success && year > 0)
{
}
else
    MessageBox.Show("Not a valid year");
```

4. Create a new book in the **if**-block and add it to the **books** collection.

```
var newBook = new Book(txtISBN.Text, txtTitle.Text, year);
books.Add(newBook.ISBN, newBook);
```

5. Create a new **ListViewItem** using the book information in the **newBook** variable and add set its **Name** property to the **ISBN** number of the book before adding it to the **lstBooks** list view. The value in the **Name** property will be used when removing books.

```
var item = new ListViewItem(new string[] { newBook.ISBN,
newBook.Title, newBook.Year.ToString() });
item.Name = newBook.ISBN;
lstBooks.Items.Add(item);
```

6. Clear the textboxes.

```
txtISBN.Text = String.Empty;
txtTitle.Text = String.Empty;
txtYear.Text = String.Empty;
```

7. Run the application and add a new book by writing values to the text boxes and clicking the **Add** button.

8. Try to add a book with a year less than **0** or non-numerical text. The message box should be displayed.

9. Close the application.

The complete code for the **Add** button look like this:

```
private void btnAdd_Click(object sender, EventArgs e)
{
    var year = 0;
    var success = Int32.TryParse(txtYear.Text, out year);

    if (success && year > 0)
    {
        var newBook = new Book(txtISBN.Text, txtTitle.Text, year);
        books.Add(newBook.ISBN, newBook);
```

```
        var item = new ListViewItem(new string[] {
            newBook.ISBN, newBook.Title, newBook.Year.ToString() });
        item.Name = newBook.ISBN;
        lstBooks.Items.Add(item);

        txtISBN.Text = String.Empty;
        txtTitle.Text = String.Empty;
        txtYear.Text = String.Empty;
    }
    else
        MessageBox.Show("Not a valid year");
}
```

The Delete button

1. Add the **Delete** button's click event.
2. Add a **foreach** loop iterating over the **SelectedItems** collection of the list view; this collection contain all selected rows in the control.
   ```
   foreach (var item in lstBooks.SelectedItems) { }
   ```
3. Remove the current book in the iteration from the **books** collection calling its **Remove** method passing in the **Dictionary** collection **Key** value (the ISBN number). The **ToString** method of a selected item in the list view will return the value from the first column.
   ```
   books.Remove(item.ToString());
   ```
4. Call the **Remove** method on the list view's **Items** collection passing in the current **item** cast to a **ListViewItem** to remove it from the list view.
   ```
   lstBooks.Items.Remove((ListViewItem)item);
   ```
5. Run the application, select a book in the list and click the **Delete** button to remove it.
6. Close the application.

The complete code for the **Delete** button look like this:

```
private void btnDelete_Click(object sender, EventArgs e)
{
    foreach (var item in lstBooks.SelectedItems)
    {
        books.Remove(item.ToString());
        lstBooks.Items.Remove((ListViewItem)item);
    }
}
```

Queue

Store items on a first in, first out basis; that is, the objects are read in the same order they were added. One example could be an order processing system where the first order in is the first to be processed, another is people standing in line at the checkout counter.

Normally when working with the **Queue** class you only use the **Enqueue** method to add a new item to the queue and **Dequeue** to get the next item in line, but there is a method called **Peek** which can be used to look at items without removing them from the queue.

You can use queues to store any type of data; the code below adds a new item to a **string** queue.

```
Queue<string> myQ = new Queue<string>();
myQ.Enqueue("The string message");
```

The code below retrieves the next item in the queue and stores it in a **string** variable.

```
string value = myQ.Dequeue();
```

Exercise: Order form

In this exercise you will create an order form which adds new orders to a **Queue** called **orders** when the **Add** button is clicked and fetches the next order in the queue when the **Get** button is clicked. The data about the fetched order will be displayed in a message box. There will also be label showing the number of orders in the queue and a list box displaying the queued orders. If there are no orders in the queue when the **Get** button is clicked the event should be exited gracefully using the **return** keyword without causing any errors.

Adding the controls
1. Create a new **Windows Forms Application** called *Order Form*.
2. Add a label and change its text to "OrderNo".

3. Add a textbox below the label and name it *txtOrderNo*.
4. Add a label to the right of the *OrderNo* label and change its text to "Description".
5. Add a textbox below the label and name it *txtDescription*.
6. Add a label below the *OrderNo* textbox, name it *lblInQueue* and change its text to "Orders in Q:".
7. Add a button called *btnAdd* below and right aligned to the *txtDescription* textbox. Change the text on the button to "Add".
8. Add a button called *btnGet* to the left of the **Add** button and change its text to "Get".
9. Add a list box called *lstOrders* to the right of the already added controls.

Adding the Order struct

1. Open the form's code-behind and locate the beginning of its class.
2. Add a **struct** called **Order** to the beginning of the class.
3. Add two properties called **OrderNo** and **Description** and their corresponding **private** variables to the **struct**. The properties should be read only (only have the **get**-block implemented).
4. Add the **Order** constructor with two parameters for the order number and description.
5. Add a **Queue** variable called **orders** which holds instances of the **Order struct**.

The complete code for the **Order struct** and **Queue** look like this:

```
public partial class Form1 : Form
{
    struct Order
    {
        private string _orderNo, _description;
        public string OrderNo { get{ return _orderNo;} }
        public string Description { get{ return _description; } }

        public Order(string orderNo, string description)
        {
            _orderNo = orderNo;
            _description = description;
        }
    }
}
```

```
Queue<Order> orders = new Queue<Order>();
```

The Form_load event

Display the number of orders in the queue in the *lblInQueue* label here in case there already are orders in the queue when the application starts, perhaps read from a database.

```
lblInQueue.Text = String.Format("Orders in Q: {0}", orders.Count);
```

The Add button

1. Add the **Click** event for the **Add** button.
2. Use the **Enqueue** method on the **orders** queue variable to add a new order to the queue.
   ```
   orders.Enqueue(new Order(txtOrderNo.Text, txtDescription.Text));
   ```
3. Use the same code as in the **Form_Load** event to display the number of orders in the queue in the *lblInQueue* label.
4. Clear the list box and use a **foreach** loop to display the orders in the queue in the list box.
   ```
   lstOrders.Items.Add(String.Format("Order [{0}] {1}", order.OrderNo, order.Description));
   ```
5. Run the application and add a couple of orders to make sure that the counter is incremented and that the orders in the queue are displayed in the list box.
6. Close the application.

The complete code for the **btnAdd_Click** event look like this:

```
private void btnAdd_Click(object sender, EventArgs e)
{
    orders.Enqueue(new Order(txtOrderNo.Text, txtDescription.Text));
    lblInQueue.Text = String.Format("Orders in Q: {0}", orders.Count);

    lstOrders.Items.Clear();
    foreach (var order in orders)
    {
        lstOrders.Items.Add(String.Format(
            "Order [{0}] {1}", order.OrderNo, order.Description));
    }
}
```

The Get button

1. Add the **Click** event for the **Get** button.
2. Make sure that no attempt to fetch an order from an empty queue is made. Use the **return** keyword to make sure that the event is exited gracefully.
   ```
   if (orders.Count.Equals(0)) return;
   ```
3. **Dequeue** the next order and store it in a variable called **order**.
   ```
   var order = orders.Dequeue();
   ```
4. Display the number of orders in the queue in the **lblInQueue** label.
5. Display a message box with the order information on the following format:
   ```
   String.Format("Order [{0}] {1}", order.OrderNo, order.Description)
   ```
6. Clear the list box and use it to display the queued orders.
7. Run the application and try to add and remove orders and make sure that the number of orders in the queue is updated in the label and that the orders in queue are displayed in the list box.
8. Close the application.

The complete code for the **btnGet_Click** event look like this:

```
private void btnGet_Click(object sender, EventArgs e)
{
    if (orders.Count.Equals(0)) return;

    var order = orders.Dequeue();
    lblInQueue.Text = String.Format("Orders in Q: {0}", orders.Count);

    MessageBox.Show(String.Format("Order [{0}] {1}",
        order.OrderNo, order.Description));

    lstOrders.Items.Clear();
    foreach (var item in orders)
    {
        lstOrders.Items.Add(String.Format("Order [{0}] {1}",
            item.OrderNo, item.Description));
    }
}
```

Stack

A **Stack** store items on a last in, first out basis; that is, the items are read in the opposite order they were added; the item added last will be read first. One obvious example is a stack of coins; you add coins on top of the coin stack and remove from the top of the stack to avoid coins falling in all directions. Another example is a deck of cards, you shuffle the deck and then draw cards from the top as you deal (at least if you are an honest dealer).

Normally when working with the **Stack** class you use the **Push** method to add a new item to the stack and **Pop** to get the next item from the top of the stack, but there is a method called **Peek** which can be used to look at items without removing them from the stack.

You can store any type of data in a ; the code below adds a new item to a **string** stack.

```
Stack<string> myStack = new Stack<string>();
myStack.Push("Added First");
myStack.Push("Added Second");
myStack.Push("Added Third");
```

When fetching values from the stack the one added last will be the first one received, looking at the previous code snippet the first value to be fetched and stored in the variable by the **Pop** method in the example below would be "Added Third" because it is at the very top of the stack.

```
var nextValue = myStack.Pop();
```

Exercise: Deck of cards

In this exercise you will create a deck of playing cards using two enumerations (**Suit** and **Value**) and a **struct** called **Card** which houses two properties called **Suit** and a **Value**. You will then create the deck of cards as a **Stack** called **deck** and fill it with all the 52 playing cards.

Then you will add a button called **btnDraw** which will draw the next card from the stack and display its data in a list box.

The **Value enum** should hold the card values (*Ace* = 1, *Two*, *Three*, ..., *Jack*, *Queen*, *King*) and the **Suit enum** should hold *Hearts*, *Spades*, *Diamonds* and *Clubs*. Each card is then assigned a value from the **Value enum** and a value from the **Suit enum**.

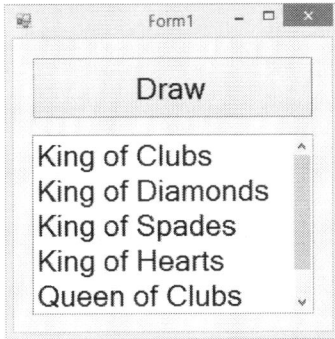

Adding the controls
1. Create a new **Windows Forms Application** called *Deck of Cards*.
2. Add a button called *btnDraw* with the text "Draw".
3. Add a list box called *lstCards* below the button.

Adding the enums
1. Go to the code-behind and locate the beginning of the form's class.
2. Add an **enum** called **Suite** which holds the names of the four card suites. Note that the first **enum** choice is assigned the value **1** to have the enumeration start at that value as opposed to the default **0**.
   ```
   enum Suit { Hearts = 1, Spades, Diamonds, Clubs }
   ```
3. Add an **enum** called **Value** which holds the thirteen card values.
   ```
   enum Value { Ace = 1, Two, Three, Four, Five, Six, Seven, Eight,
   Nine, Ten, Jack, Queen, King }
   ```

Adding the Card struct
1. Add a **struct** called **Card** below the second **enum**.
2. Add a **private** variable called **_suit** using the **Suit enum** as its data type. This will be the placeholder for the specific card's suit.
   ```
   private Suit _suit;
   ```
3. Add a **private** variable called **_value** using the **Value enum** as its data type. This will be the placeholder for the specific card's value.

```
private Suit _value;
```

4. Add the two corresponding properties called **Value** and **Suit**.

5. Add a constructor which takes one **suit** and one **value** as parameters and assigns them to the appropriate variables in the **struct**.
   ```
   public Card(Value value, Suit suit)
   ```

6. Add a **Stack** variable called **deck** below the **Card struct** using the **Card struct** as its data type. This **Stack** will hold all 52 playing cards.
   ```
   Stack<Card> deck = new Stack<Card>();
   ```

The complete code so far look like this:

```
public partial class Form1 : Form
{
    enum Suit { Hearts = 1, Spades, Diamonds, Clubs }
    enum Value { Ace = 1, Two, Three, Four, Five, Six, Seven, Eight, Nine,
        Ten, Jack, Queen, King }

    struct Card
    {
        private Value _value;
        private Suit _suit;
        public Value Value { get { return _value; } }
        public Suit Suit { get { return _suit; } }

        public Card(Value value, Suit suit)
        {
            _value = value;
            _suit = suit;
        }
    }

    Stack<Card> deck = new Stack<Card>();
}
```

Adding the playing cards to the stack

1. Locate the **Form_Load** event.

2. Create one outer for loop which iterates from 1 through 13 (the card values) and add a second inner (nested) loop inside that loop iterating from 1 through 4 (the card suites).

3. **Push** (add) each playing card to the **deck Stack** in the inner loop. You have to cast the loop values to their respective **enum** type (**Suit** or **Value**) when creating the playing cards because the **Card** constructor requires **enum** values as parameters.

The complete code for adding the playing cards look like this:

```
private void Form1_Load(object sender, EventArgs e)
{
    for (int value = 1; value <= 13; value++)
        for (int suit = 1; suit <= 4; suit++ )
            deck.Push(new Card((Value)value, (Suit)suit));
}
```

The Draw button

1. Create the **Draw** button's **Click** event.
2. Check that the **deck Stack** isn't empty before popping (fetching) the next value from it.
   ```
   if(deck.Count > 0)
   ```
3. Fetch the next card using the **Pop** method and store it in a variable called **card**.
   ```
   var card = deck.Pop();
   ```
4. Add the fetched card to the **lstCards** list box displaying the value and suit on the format "Ace of Hearts".
5. Run the application and draw a few cards. Note that the cards are retrieved in the opposite order they were added.
6. Close the application.

The complete code for the **Draw** button look like this:

```
private void btnDraw_Click(object sender, EventArgs e)
{
    if(deck.Count > 0)
    {
        var card = deck.Pop();
        lstCards.Items.Add(String.Format("{0} of {1}", card.Value,
            card.Suit));
    }
}
```

Introduction to LINQ

In this section you will learn how to use LINQ and Lambda expressions to fetch data from a collection and how to **join** (link) collections together to assimilate data from multiple sources before displaying it to the user. Joining collections together can be very useful when dealing with data that are related for instance when displaying customer information in an order header where the customer is connected to the order through a unique customer id.

One of the great features of LINQ is that values are fetched when you ask for them; instances where the data will be fetched include iterating over a query result, using methods such as **First, Last, FirstOrDefault** that fetch one value, or **ToList** that fetch all items produced by the LINQ query.

Because the data isn't retrieved immediately when the data is selected with the query you can actually build on existing queries narrowing down the result even more before fetching the actual data from the source.

Order example

The following code is used by the upcoming examples when creating the **orders** and **customers List** collections used.

```csharp
public partial class Form1 : Form
{
    struct Order
    {
        private int _id, _customerId;
        private double _total;
        private DateTime _date;

        public int Id { get { return _id; } }
        public int CustomerId { get { return _customerId; } }
        public double Total
        {
            get { return _total; }
            set { _total = value; }
        }

        public DateTime Date { get { return _date; } set { _date = value; } }
```

```csharp
    public Order(int id, int customerId, double total, DateTime date)
    {
        _id = id;
        _customerId = customerId;
        _total = total;
        _date = date;
    }
}

struct Customer
{
    private int _id;
    private string _name;

    public int Id { get { return _id; } }
    public string Name { get { return _name; } set { _name = value; } }

    public Customer(int id, string name) {
        _id = id;
        _name = name;
    }
}

List<Order> orders = new List<Order>();
List<Customer> customers = new List<Customer>();

public Form1()
{
    orders.AddRange(new Order[]{
        new Order(1, 2, 100, new DateTime(2015, 01, 10)),
        new Order(2, 1, 200, new DateTime(2015, 01, 20)),
        new Order(3, 2, 300, new DateTime(2015, 01, 15)),
        new Order(4, 3, 400, new DateTime(2015, 5, 1))
    });

    customers.AddRange(new Customer[]{
        new Customer(1, "Carl Smith"),
        new Customer(2, "Jane Doe"),
        new Customer(3, "John Doe"),
    });

    InitializeComponent();
}
}
```

Query syntax

You use the following basic syntax when querying with LINQ:

```
from <variable> in <data source>
join <varible2> in <data source2>
     on <varible.property> equals <varible2.property>
group <grouping criteria>
where <selection criteria>
orderby <result ordering criteria>
select <variable name>
```

A LINQ query always begin with a **from** statement listing the variable names used in the query followed by the **in** keyword and the data source (in this chapter the data sources are collections). The query also always have to have a **select** statement defining what to select from the data source, in simple queries that will be the data source variable returning complete items from the data source.

When working with multiple data sources you might want to link them together to create one result set with data from all data sources, to achieve this you use one or more **join** statements (one per data source you want to join).

it is also possible to group data crating an aggregated result.

The **where** clause is used to filter the data and narrow down the result set; a **where** clause can be very simple only filtering on one property or more complex involving multiple properties.

Use an **orderby** statement if you want to sort the selected data.

Fetch all items

When using LINQ you can fetch all the items in a collection as an **IEnumerable** or as a **List** of items; an **IEnumerable** contain the select query used when fetching the desired data but not the data itself whereas the **ToList** method will use the query to fetch the actual data and store it in a **List** collection.

Create a query and fetch the data later:

```
var allOrders = from o in orders
                select o;

// Execute ToList when you want to fetch the data
allOrders.ToList();
```

Fetch the items directly:

```
var allOrders = (from o in orders
                select o).ToList();

var allCustomers = (from c in customers
                select c).ToList();
```

Fetch a specific item

When using LINQ you can choose two different syntaxes when querying a data source, you can go the all out LINQ query way or you can use predefined query methods which use Lambda expressions. Let's explore both.

In this example you want to fetch a specific order by its order id. With LINQ only the query would involve a **where** clause while using Lambda the **First** or **FirstOrDefault** method would require an expression. The difference between the **First** and **FirstOrDefault** methods is that the latter would return an object with the default settings applied if no matching item was found and the **First** method would return **null**.

Note that both queries uses the **First** method to fetch the first item in a collection of items but since the order id is unique ensuring that only one item is fetched the correct item will be returned. Normally you wouldn't hard code the id off course but it's done here for simplicity.

When it comes to Lambda expressions the **=>** symbol is read as *goes to*. The variable name used in the expression correspond to the current item being evaluated in the collection of items; you can view it as the iteration variable in a **foreach** loop. The **Equals** method is replacing the traditional == operator here but keep in mind that the **Equals** method can yield un-compliable code when comparing the Lambda variable to a **null** value like **o.Id.Equals (null)** in these instances you must resort to the old fashioned syntax **o.Id == null** or **o.Id !=** **null** when checking whether it is **null** or not **null**.

```
//LINQ only
var order = (from o in orders
             where o.Id.Equals(1)
             select o).First();

//LINQ and Lambda
var order = orders.First(o => o.Id.Equals(1));
```

It's a matter of taste which syntax you choose to use except in certain edge cases where you have to use the LINQ method with a Lambda expression; one such occasion is if you want to fetch a certain number of items using the **Take** method or if you want to skip a number of items before fetching your items using the **Skip** method. Both these methods are frequently used when implementing pagination on web pages.

Sorting the fetched items

Sometimes when fetching data you want to sort the result before displaying it to the user, to achieve this you can use an **orderby** clause or call the **OrderBy** method (ascending) or the **OrderByDescending** method (descending) specifying which property to sort by.

```
//LINQ Only
var sortedItems = (from o in orders
                   where o.CustomerId.Equals(2)
                   orderby o.Id
                   select o).ToList();

//LINQ and Lambda
var sortedItems = orders.Where(c =>
c.CustomerId.Equals(2)).OrderByDescending(o => o.Id).ToList();
```

Joining two collections (anonymous object)

Sometimes you need to combine data from two or more data sources using a join expression. When deciding what values to include in the final result set you can use an anonymous object to house the data for each item when the **select** statement is executed, this can be very useful if you don't have access to or don't want to create a new **class** defining the desired properties. Use the **new** keyword and curly braces to define the beginning and end of the anonymous object and inside the curly braces you can specify the desired properties where each property is given a name and a value from one of the **join** variables.

```
var joinedData = (
    from o in orders
    join c in customers on o.CustomerId equals c.Id
    select new
    {
        OrderId = o.Id,
        CustomerId = c.Id,
        OrderDate = o.Date,
        Total = o.Total,
        CustomerName = c.Name
    }).ToList();
```

Joining two collections using an existing class or struct

In the previous section you learned how an anonymous object can be used to collect joined data. In this section you will learn how the joined data can be collected using an existing **struct** or **class**.

To collect the same data as in the previous section you could use a **struct**, but here a **class** is used because it simplifies code and is the recommended way of handling larger objects; just remember that you can substitute the **class** for a **struct** if needs be.

The **class** looks like this:

```
class CustomerOrder
{
    public int OrderId { get; set; }
    public int CustomerId { get; set; }
    public DateTime OrderDate { get; set; }
    public double Total { get; set; }
    public string CustomerName { get; set; }
}
```

The LINQ query would be almost identical to the one in the previous section with the exception of specifying the data type to be used.

```
var joinedData = (
    from o in orders
    join c in customers on o.CustomerId equals c.Id
    select new CustomerOrder
    {
        OrderId = o.Id,
        CustomerId = c.Id,
```

```
      OrderDate = o.Date,
      Total = o.Total,
      CustomerName = c.Name
   }).ToList();
```

Exercise: Order form

In this exercise you will use a **Queue** and two **List** collections to store information about customers and orders which you will display in a list view using LINQ and Lambda expressions. Two **structs** will define the customer and order content and will be used as data types for the queue and lists. The customer should have customer id (**int**) and name (**string**) properties and the order should have order number (**Guid**), total (**double**) and customer id (**int**). The customer id is used to tie a customer to an order.

A Guid is a globally unique identifier meaning that it is virtually impossible to get the same value twice. You can use the **Guid** data type to store this type of values, the **Guid** class can also be used to create new Guids at run-time by calling the **NewGuid** method on the class. An unassigned Guid is filled with zeros and can be checked or assigned using the **Empty** property on the **Guid** class.

The queue should hold new orders and will be a repository for not yet processed orders, by using a queue the orders will be processed on a first in first out basis. The first list should hold customers and the second orders which have been processed.

The GUI is divided into two sections, a tab control at the top with two tabs and a list view control at the bottom (see image below). The **New Order** tab contain the controls for adding a new order; a combo box control for customers, a textbox for the total order amount and a button that will add the order to the queue. The **Manage Orders** tab contain three buttons where the first display the next order in the queue in the list view, the second button processes the next order in the queue and moves it to the processed order list and the third button lists all orders not yet processed in the list view.

When the **New Order** tab is clicked all orders processed and unprocessed should be displayed in the list view; this can be achieved using the **Union** LINQ method to add two query results together and then iterate overt the orders. The same data should be displayed in the list view when the **Add Order** button is clicked, a customer is selected in the combo box or the **Process Next Order** button is clicked. To reuse the code you can place it in a method that is called from the different events.

The next order in the queue should be displayed with a light blue backgound, all unproce-ssed orders with a light pink background and all processed orders with a light green back-grond in the list view.

New orders should only be added to the orders queue if the value in the **Total** textbox can be parsed to a **double**.

The **Close** button should close the window and exit the application. If there are unprocessed orders in the queue a message box should be displayed asking the user if the application should end ("Order Q not empty! Close anyway?"); if the user answers **yes** the application ends otherwise it should remain open. You can change the buttons displayed in a message box and the result can be collected in a **DialogResult** variable. You can optionally display an icon as well.

```
var result = MessageBox.Show("Order Q not empty! Close anyway?", "WARNING",
    MessageBoxButtons.YesNo, MessageBoxIcon.Exclamation);

if (result.Equals(DialogResult.No)) return;
```

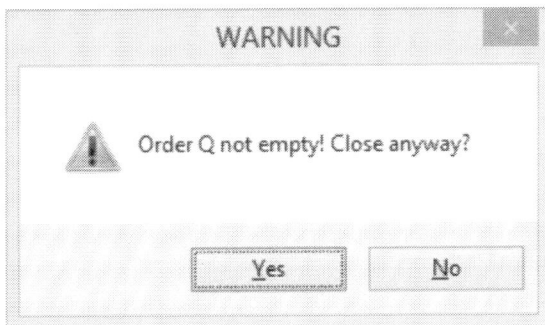

Adding the controls

1. Create a new **Windows Forms Application** called *Orders*.
2. Change its **Text** property to "Orders". This will change the text in the form header.
3. Add a **TabControl** to the form.

4. Click on the first tab and then the white surface below the tab and change the **Text** property to "New Order".
5. Add two labels with the text "Customer" and "Total" to the white tab surface.
6. Add a combo box called *cboCustomers* below the "Customer" label.
7. Add a textbox called *txtTotal* below the "Total" label.
8. Add a button called *btnAddOrder* with the text "Add Order" to the right of the *txtTotal* textbox.
9. Click on the second tab, this should display a white surface again (the second tab's surface), click on the empty white surface and change the text of the tab to "Manage Orders" with its **Text** property
10. Add three buttons called *btnPeekOnNextOrder*, *btnProcessNextOrder* and *btnList-Orders*. Change the text on the buttons to "Peek On Next Order", "Process Next Order" and "List Orders".
11. Add a list view control called *lstOrders* below the tab control.
12. Add a button called *btnClose* with the text "Close" below the list view.

Adding the Order struct

1. Open the code-behind and locate the beginning of the form.
2. Add a new **struct** called **Order** above the form class.
3. Add a **Guid** property called **OrderNo** and its corresponding **private** variable.
4. Add a **int** property called **CustomerId** and its corresponding **private** variable.
5. Add a **double** property called **Total** and its corresponding **private** variable.
6. Add a constructor which takes three parameters corresponding to the **private** variables and assign them to the variables.

This is the complete code for the **Order struct**:

```
struct Order
{
    private int _customerId;
    private double _total;
    private Guid _orderNo;

    public Guid OrderNo {
        get { return _orderNo; }
        set { _orderNo = value; }
    }
```

```
    public int CustomerId {
        get { return _customerId; }
        set { _customerId = value; }
    }
    public double Total {
        get { return _total; }
        set { _total = value; }
    }

    public Order(int customerId, double total, Guid orderNo)
    {
        _total = total;
        _customerId = customerId;
        _orderNo = orderNo;
    }
}
}
```

Adding the Customer struct

1. Add a new **struct** called **Customer** blow the **Order struct**.

2. Add an **int** property called **Id** and its corresponding **private** variable.

3. Add a **string** property called **Name** and its corresponding **private** variable.

4. Add a constructor which takes two parameters corresponding to the **private** variables and assign them to the variables.

This is the complete code for the **Customer struct**:

```
struct Customer
{
    private int _id;
    private string _name;

    public int Id
    {
        get { return _id; }
    }
    public string Name
    {
        get { return _name; }
        set { _name = value; }
    }
```

```
    public Customer(int id, string name)
    {
        _id = id;
        _name = name;
    }
}
```

Adding the collections

1. Locate the beginning of the form class.
2. Add a new **List<Customer>** collection called **customers** to the class.
3. Add a new **List<Order>** collection called **fulfilledOrders**.
4. Add a new **Queue<Order>** collection called **orders**.
5. Add two customers to the **customers** collection in the constructor.
6. Assign the **customers** collection to the *DataSource* property of the *cboCustomers* combo box inside the **Form_Load** event.
7. Specify the **Name** property as the **DisplayMember** inside the **Form_Load** event.
8. Run the application and make sure that the customers are displayed in the combo box.
9. Close the application.

This is the form's code so far:

```
public partial class Orders : Form
{
    List<Customer> customers = new List<Customer>();
    Queue<Order> orders = new Queue<Order>();
    List<Order> fulfilledOrders = new List<Order>();

    public Orders()
    {
        customers.AddRange(new Customer[]{
            new Customer(1, "John Doe"),
            new Customer(2, "Stan Smith")
        });

        InitializeComponent();
    }
}
```

```csharp
    private void Orders_Load(object sender, EventArgs e)
    {
        cboCustomers.DataSource = customers;
        cboCustomers.DisplayMember = "Name";
    }
}
```

Adding ShowCustomerOrder method

To be able to effectively reuse the code for displaying a customer's orders in the list view control you will create a method called **ShowCustomerOrders** which will be called whenever this information should be updated.

1. Add a **region** called **Methods** below the **Form_Load** event.
2. Add a method to the **region** called **ShowCustomerOrders** which takes one **int** parameter called **customerId**.
   ```csharp
   private void ShowCustomerOrders(int customerId)
   {
   }
   ```

3. Use LINQ and Lambda to fetch the customer matching the passed in **customerId** parameter from the **customers** collection.
   ```csharp
   var customer = customers.First(c => c.Id.Equals(customerId));
   ```

4. To avoid the upcoming LINQ expressions to fail if no orders are in the order queue you can only peek at the next order using the **Peek** method if there is at least one order in the queue otherwise an empty **Guid** should be stored for the **nextOrderNo** variable. This order number will be used later to determine which background color should be displayed for the unprocessed orders. If the order number matches one of the orders in the **orders** queue the background color should be **Light Blue** otherwise it should be **Light Pink** when the order is added to the list view control.
   ```csharp
   var nextOrderNo = orders.Count > 0 ? orders.Peek().OrderNo :
   Guid.Empty;
   ```

5. To be able to use one loop when adding the data to the list view control you have to append the orders in the **fulfilledOrders** collection to the **orders** queue for the selected customer using the **Union** LINQ method. Because the backgound color shouldn't be part of the displayed data you will have to add it and the **ListViewItem** containing the customer and order data to an anonymous object which later is accessed in the loop adding the data to the list view control.

```
    var items = (
        from o in orders
        where o.CustomerId.Equals(customer.Id)
        select new
        {
            // The background color used for the
            // order in the list view control
            Color = o.OrderNo.Equals(nextOrderNo) ?
                Color.LightBlue : Color.LightPink,

            // The customer and order data displayed
            // in the list view control
            Item = new ListViewItem(new string[]{
                o.OrderNo.ToString(), o.Total.ToString(),
                customer.Name, customer.Id.ToString()})
        }
    }).Union( /* The fulfilledOrders LINQ query goes here */);
```

6. Add the LINQ query for the **fulfilledOrders** collection inside the **Union** parenthesis.

7. Clear the items in the list view control below the LINQ query.

8. Iterate over the items in the result from the LINQ query and change the background color of the current item and then add it to the list view.

```
lstOrders.Items.Clear();
foreach (var item in items)
{
    item.Item.BackColor = item.Color;
    lstOrders.Items.Add(item.Item);
}
```

This is the complete code for the **ShowCustomerOrders** method:

```
#region Methods
private void ShowCustomerOrders(int customerId)
{
    var customer = customers.First(c => c.Id.Equals(customerId));
    var nextOrderNo = orders.Count > 0 ? orders.Peek().OrderNo : Guid.Empty;

    var items = (
        from o in orders
        where o.CustomerId.Equals(customer.Id)
        select new
        {
            Color = o.OrderNo.Equals(nextOrderNo) ?
                Color.LightBlue : Color.LightPink,
```

```
        Item = new ListViewItem(new string[]{
            o.OrderNo.ToString(), o.Total.ToString(),
            customer.Name, customer.Id.ToString()})
    })
    .Union(
        from o in fulfilledOrders
        where o.CustomerId.Equals(customer.Id)
        select new
        {
            Color = Color.LightGreen,

            Item = new ListViewItem(new string[]{
                o.OrderNo.ToString(), o.Total.ToString(),
                customer.Name, customer.Id.ToString()})
        }
    ); // End of Union

lstOrders.Items.Clear();
foreach (var item in items)
{
    item.Item.BackColor = item.Color;
    lstOrders.Items.Add(item.Item);
}
}
#endregion
```

The cboCustomers_SelectedIndexChanged event

When a customer is selected in the combo box that customer's orders should be displayed in the list view control.

1. Add the **SelectedIndexChanged** event for the *cboCustomers* combo box.
2. Check that the customer combo box contain customers, if it is empty then exit the event gracefully.

   ```
   if (cboCustomers.Items.Count.Equals(0)) return;
   ```

3. Add a variable called **customer** and store the selected customer from the combo box cast as **Customer**.
4. Call the **ShowCustomerorder** passing in the customer id from the **customer** variable.

This is the complete code for the **cboCustomers_SelectedIndexChanged** event:

```
private void cboCustomers_SelectedIndexChanged(object sender, EventArgs e)
{
    if (cboCustomers.Items.Count.Equals(0)) return;
    var customer = (Customer)cboCustomers.SelectedItem;
    ShowCustomerOrders(customer.Id);
}
```

The tab control's SelectedIndexChanged event

When the first tab in the tab control is selected the orders for the selected customer in the combo box should be displayed in the list view control.

1. Add the **SelectedIndexChanged** event for the tab control button. You have to click on one of the tabs in the tab control to add the event.

2. Check that the clicked tab is the first tab in the tab control by accessing its **Selected-Index** property.
   ```
   if (tabControl1.SelectedIndex.Equals(0))
   {
   }
   ```

3. Check that the customer combo box contain customers inside the **if**-block, if it is empty then exit the event gracefully.

4. Fetch the selected customer from the combo box and cast it using the **Customer struct**.

5. Call the **ShowCustomerorder** passing in the customer id from the variable with the cast customer.

This is the complete code for the tab control 's **SelectedIndexChanged** event:

```
private void tabControl1_SelectedIndexChanged(object sender, EventArgs e)
{
    if (tabControl1.SelectedIndex.Equals(0))
    {
        if (cboCustomers.Items.Count.Equals(0)) return;
        var customer = (Customer)cboCustomers.SelectedItem;
        ShowCustomerOrders(customer.Id);
    }
}
```

The Add Order button

1. Add the **Click** event for the **Add Order** button.
2. Because orders only should be added if the value in the **Total** textbox can be parsed to a **double** you have to add a **double** variable called **total** to hold the parsed value.
3. The result returned from the **TryParse** method should be stored in a **bool** variable called **success** and the **total** variable should be passed in to the **TryParse** method as an **out** parameter. **true** will be stored in the **success** variable if the parse succeeds.
4. Add an **if**-statement where the **success** variable must be **true** for the **if**-block to execute.
5. Fetch the customer id from the selected customer in the combo box inside the **if**-block. Use the **SelectedItem** property of the combo box and cast it to a **Customer** then access its **Id** property.
   ```
   var customerId = ((Customer)cboCustomers.SelectedItem).Id;
   ```
6. Create a new variable using the **Order struct** passing in the customer id, the total and a new Guid.
   ```
   var order = new Order(customerId, total, Guid.NewGuid());
   ```
7. Call the **Enqueue** method on the **orders** queue collection to add the order to the queue.
8. Call the **ShowCustomerOrders** method to display the customer and order information in the list view.
   ```
   ShowCustomerOrders(customerId);
   ```
9. Run the application, select a customer in the combo box, enter a value in the **Total** textbox and click the **Add Order** button to add the data as an order to the orders queue. Make sure that the data is displayed in the list view control. The first row should be **Light Blue** and the subsequently added rows should be **Light Pink**. The **Light Blue** color show that it is the next order in the **orders** queue.
10. Close the application.

This is the complete code for the **btnAddOrder_Click** event:

```
private void btnAddOrder_Click(object sender, EventArgs e)
{
    var total = 0d;
    var success = Double.TryParse(txtTotal.Text, out total);
```

```
    if (success)
    {
        var customerId = ((Customer)cboCustomers.SelectedItem).Id;
        var order = new Order(customerId, total, Guid.NewGuid());
        orders.Enqueue(order);

        ShowCustomerOrders(customerId);
    }
}
```

The Peek On Next Order button

The purpose of this button is to peek at the next unprocessed order in the **orders** queue; to achieve this you have to add a LINQ query fetching the customer by customer id and calling the **Peek** method on the queue to fetch the order. Then you have to create a **ListViewItem** with the data from the customer and order and present it in the list view control.

1. Add the **Click** event for the ***btnPeekOnNextOrder*** button.
2. Check that the **orders** queue contain at least one order and that the customers collection contain customers, if either one is empty then exit gracefully from the **Click** event.
    ```
    if (orders.Count.Equals(0) || customers.Count.Equals(0)) return;
    ```
3. Peek at the next order without removing it from the queue by calling the **Peek** method on the queue and store the order in a variable called **order**.
4. Fetch the customer matching the customer id stored in the order and store it in a variable called **customer**. You can either do this with the **First** method and a Lambda expression or a regular LINQ query, both are described here.
    a. With Lambda
    ```
    var customer = customers.First(c =>
    c.Id.Equals(order.CustomerId));
    ```

    b. With LINQ Query
    ```
    var customer = (
        from c in customers
        where c.Id.Equals(order.CustomerId)
        select new Customer(c.Id, c.Name)
    ).First();
    ```
5. Create a new **ListViewItem** with the data from the **order** and **customer** variables.
    ```
    var item = new ListViewItem(new string[]{
    ```

```
order.OrderNo.ToString(), order.Total.ToString(),
customer.Name, customer.Id.ToString()});
```

6. Clear the list view and add the item to it.
7. Run the application and add a couple of orders.
8. Click on the **Manage Orders** tab.
9. Click on the **Peek On Next Order** button; this should display the order and customer data in the list view control.
10. Switch back to the **New Order** tab; this should display all orders for the customer selected in the combo box.

This is the complete code for the **btnPeekOnNextOrder_Click** event:

```
private void btnPeekOnNextOrder_Click(object sender, EventArgs e)
{
    if (orders.Count.Equals(0) || customers.Count.Equals(0)) return;

    var order = orders.Peek();
    var customer = customers.First(c => c.Id.Equals(order.CustomerId));

    var item = new ListViewItem(new string[]{
        order.OrderNo.ToString(), order.Total.ToString(),
        customer.Name, customer.Id.ToString()});

    lstOrders.Items.Clear();
    lstOrders.Items.Add(item);
}
```

The Process Next Order button

The purpose of this button is to simulate that the order is being processed and moved from the **orders** queue to the **fulfilledOrders** collection. You achieve this by fetching the next order in the **orders** queue by calling the **Dequeue** method and adding the fetched order to the collection. Call the **ShowCutomerOrders** method you created earlier to display the various orders in the system after the order has been moved.

1. Add the **Click** event for the **btnProcessNextOrder** button.
2. Check that there are orders in the orders queue, if there are none then exit gracefully from the event.
3. Fetch the next order in the orders queue calling the **Dequeue** method and store the order in a variable called **order**.

```
var order = orders.Dequeue();
```

4. Add the fetched order to the **fulfilledOrders** collection.
5. Call the **ShowCutomerOrders** method to display all orders for the current customer.
   `ShowCustomerOrders(order.CustomerId);`
6. Run the application and add a couple of orders.
7. Switch to the **Manage Orders** tab and note which order is marked with a **Light Blue** background.
8. Click the **Process Next Order** button; this will move the next order in the **orders** queue to the **fulfilledOrder** collection. Note that the order marked with **Light Blue** background has changed because another order is now next in line to be processed. If no order in the list view has a **Light Blue** background the next order belongs to another customer or there are no more orders to process.
9. Close the application.

This is the complete code for the **btnProcessNextOrder_Click** event:

```
private void btnProcessNextOrder_Click(object sender, EventArgs e)
{
    if (orders.Count.Equals(0)) return;
    var order = orders.Dequeue();
    fulfilledOrders.Add(order);
    ShowCustomerOrders(order.CustomerId);
}
```

The List Orders button

The purpose of this button is to display all processed orders in the **fulfilledOrder** collection with their corresponding customer information in the list view. Use a LINQ **join** statement to link the **customers** collection with the **fulfilledOrders** collection and create an anonymous object with the combined data.

1. Add the **Click** event for the *btnListOrders* button.
2. Link the **customers** collection with the **fulfilledOrders** collection using a LINQ **join** and store the result in a variable called **orderList**. Note that you aren't calling the **ToList** method to fetch the items immediately, the items will be fetched automatically when you iterate over the result with a **foreach** loop later.

```
        var orderList =
            from o in fulfilledOrders
            join c in customers on o.CustomerId equals c.Id
            select new
            {
                OrderNo = o.OrderNo,
                Name = c.Name,
                Total = o.Total,
                CustomerId = c.Id
            };
```

3. Clear the list view.

4. Add a **foreach** loop iterating over the result stored in the **orderList** variable. Create a new **ListViewItem** for each iteration inside the **foreach**-block and add it to the list view control.

5. Run the application and add a couple of orders.

6. Click on the **List Orders** button; no orders should be displayed in the list view because all orders are unprocessed.

7. Click the **Process Next Order** button to process at least one order. The processed order should be displayed with a **Light Green** background.

8. Click the **List Orders** button to display only the processed orders without any background color.

9. Close the application.

This is the complete code for the **btnListOrders_Click** event:

```
private void btnListOrders_Click(object sender, EventArgs e)
{
    var orderList =
        from o in fulfilledOrders
        join c in customers on o.CustomerId equals c.Id
        select new
        {
            OrderNo = o.OrderNo,
            Name = c.Name,
            Total = o.Total,
            CustomerId = c.Id
        };

    lstOrders.Items.Clear();
    foreach(var order in orderList)
```

```
    {
        var item = new ListViewItem(new string[]{
            order.OrderNo.ToString(), order.Total.ToString(),
            order.Name, order.CustomerId.ToString()});

        lstOrders.Items.Add(item);
    }
}
```

The Close button

The purpose of this button is to close the application. If the **orders** queue contain unprocessed orders then a message box should be displayed asking the user if the application should be closed anyway.

1. Add the **Click** event for the **Close** button.
2. Check if the **orders** queue contain orders. If it does then display a message box with the header "WARNING", the message "Order Q not Empty, Close anyway?", **Yes/No** buttons and an exclamation icon. Store the button click in a variable called **result**.
   ```
   var result = MessageBox.Show(
       "Order Q not empty! Close anyway?", "WARNING",
       MessageBoxButtons.YesNo, MessageBoxIcon.Exclamation);
   ```
3. If the **No** button is clicked then the event should be exited gracefully and the form remain open.
   ```
   if (result.Equals(DialogResult.No)) return;
   ```
4. Add a call to the form's **Close** method; the form can be reached using the **this** keyword.
   ```
   this.Close();
   ```

This is the complete code for the **btnClose_Click** event:

```
private void btnClose_Click(object sender, EventArgs e)
{
    if (orders.Count > 0)
    {
        var result = MessageBox.Show(
            "Order Q not empty! Close anyway?", "WARNING",
            MessageBoxButtons.YesNo, MessageBoxIcon.Exclamation);

        // Check which button has been clicked
        if (result.Equals(DialogResult.No)) return;
```

```
    }

    this.Close();
}
```

Mini Use Case: Poker application

In this exercise you will create a poker application where the user plays against the computer. You will get a use case describing the different sections of the application and what feature that need to be implemented, try to implement it using only the use case if you can. Some new theory is introduced and described in the use case. The reason for the mini use case layout is to closely mimic a real world scenario. I strongly suggest that you read the whole use case at least once before you start coding.

Description

The application should support playing many hands without restarting the application. It should contain three distinct parts, the **Windows Forms Application** GUI used when playing, a **struct** called **Card** which represent one playing card and a **struct** called **Hand** which represent a dealt hand.

The GUI

The GUI should display the player and dealer hand values in labels as well as the value and suit in one label per card; spades and clubs should be displayed in black while hearts and diamonds are displayed in red (see image below). The card backgrounds should be white. The outcome should be displayed between the two hands with the text "Player wins!" with a light green background if the player wins and "Dealer Wins!" against a light pink background if the dealer wins. A button with the text "DEAL NEW HAND" should deal new hands to the player and dealer when clicked. The dealt cards should be dynamically added to a **Panel** control and should not be present in the GUI when the application is started.

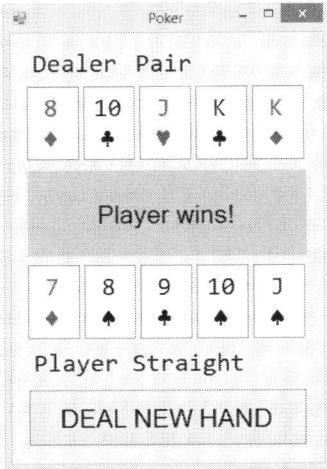

The card

The card consist of two variables storing the value and suit, a property displaying the symbol for the card's suit using the value stored in the **suit** variable and a property displaying the card value in abbreviated form (2, 3, ..., K, A) using the value in the **value** variable; use three **enums** to keep track of the possible values (Two, Three, ..., King, Ace), suit (Heart, Spades, Diamonds, Clubs) and the symbol for each suit (Hearts = '♥', Spades = '♠', Diamonds = '♦', Clubs = '♣').

The **value** and **suit** variables should be declared as types of the respective **enum**.

You will also have to implement an interface called **IComparable** to make it possible to compare two cards on their values (see code and description below).

The hand

The **Hand struct** represent the player or dealer hand. Two **enums** are required outside the **struct**, one called **Hands** which is holding a list of all possible hands (pair, two pairs, ..., Full House, Royal Straight Flush) and one called **Winner** which holds the possible winners (Dealer, Player, Draw). A **Hand** is comprised of data relating to the cards dealt for that hand such as an array able to hold 5 **Card** instances, the hand value in the form of a value from the **Hands enum**, two properties to store the high card during hand evaluation using the **Values enum**, a **List<Value>** collection storing kicker cards using the **Values enum** and an **int** storing the **suit** (hearts, spades, clubs, diamonds).

The Code-behind (form code)

Two variables declared with the **Hand struct** will be needed, one for the dealer called **dealerHand** and one for the player called **playerHand**. A **List<Card>** collection called **deck** is also needed to hold the 52 playing cards in the card deck. An **int** variable called **shuffles** will determine how many times the deck should be shuffled before any cards can be dealt.

Create a method called **Initialize** which is called from the button to instantiate the variables mentioned earlier. This method is used to clear the current hands and deck of cards.

Create a method called **ShuffleDeck** which is called after the **Initialize** method in the button **Click** event. The purpose of this method is to shuffle the card deck as many times as specified by the **shuffles** variable; use the **Random** class to randomize the shuffling.

Create a method called **DealCards** which will assign cards to the dealer and player in an alternating fashion. Don't forget to remove the used cards from the **deck** collection as you deal out the cards. The dealer and player should get 5 cards each stored in the **Cards** array in the **dealerHand** and **playerHand** respectively.

Create a method called **CompareHands** which compare the dealer and player hands using the **Hands enum**, the two **HighCard** and **Kicker** properties of the player and dealer hands. This method need to call another method you will create called **EvaluateHand** taking a **Hand** parameter passed in by reference (**ref**); the method will figure out the hand (pair, two pair, ...) stored in the **Hand** parameter and alter the two **HighCard** and **Kicker** properties in it. To make it easier to evaluate the hand you might want to sort the **Cards** array before evaluating the hand. Call the **EvaluateHand** method twice, once for the player's hand and once for the dealer's hand.

You should also create a method called **CompareCards** which compare the dealer and player cards in the event the hands are equal or both hands don't have a value (only a set of mixed cards).

The last method you need to create is called **RevealCards** which dynamically add the cards to the player and dealer areas in the form and show the winner in the label between the dealer and player cards; the background color of the label should be light pink if the dealer wins and light green if the player wins.

Evaluating the hand

The hand value should be determined by the following hand order: Royal Straight Flush, Straight Flush, Four of a kind, Full House, Flush, Straight, Three of a Kind, Two Pairs, One Pair, High Card.

If the dealer and player have the same hand the winner is determined by the kicker which is the highest of the remaining cards.

How to create a struct in a separate file

1. Right click on the project name in the Solution Explorer and select **Add-Class** in the menu.
2. Give the file a name and click on the **Add** button.
3. Replace the **class** keyword with the **struct** keyword in the file.

How to add controls dynamically

The code below will dynamically add 5 cards to the dealer panel and the player panel.

First the panels are cleared calling the **Clear** method on the **Controls** collection on each panel; the **Controls** collection keep track of what intrinsic controls are placed inside a control or form. You use this collection when adding controls to the panels calling their **Add** methods. Before the labels can be added they have to be created by calling a method called **CreateCard** (which you will create); the purpose of this method is to format the card labels and prepare them to be displayed in a panel.

```
this.panDealer.Controls.Clear();
this.panPlayer.Controls.Clear();
for (int i = 0; i < 5; i++)
{
    //Calculate position
    var x = i * 60;
    var y = 0;
    //Create and format the labels
    var lblDealer = CreateCard(x, y, dealerHand.Cards[i]);
    var lblPlayer = CreateCard(x, y, playerHand.Cards[i]);
    //Add the labels to the Panel's Controls collection
    this.panDealer.Controls.Add(lblDealer);
    this.panPlayer.Controls.Add(lblPlayer);
}
```

```
private Label CreateCard(int x, int y, Card card)
{
    Label lbl = new Label();
    //Format the label text value and symbol on separate rows
    lbl.Text = String.Format("{0}\n{1}",
        card.ValueSymbol, card.SuitSymbol);
    lbl.Size = new Size(55, 76);
    //Position the label in the Panel
    lbl.Location = new Point(x, y);
    //Format border and font
    lbl.BorderStyle = BorderStyle.FixedSingle;
    lbl.Font = new Font("Consolas", 20);
    lbl.TextAlign = ContentAlignment.MiddleCenter;
    lbl.BackColor = Color.White;
    //Set the text color
    lbl.ForeColor =
        card.Suit.Equals(Suit.Hearts) ||
        card.Suit.Equals(Suit.Diamonds) ?
        Color.Red : Color.Black;
    return lbl;
}
```

How to implement the IComparable interface

The **IComparable** interface makes it possible to compare one object with another object based on the criteria you set up. Without implementing this interface objects will be compared on their memory reference instead of a value or criteria.

An interface is a contract describing the method headers for methods that must be implemented, not how they should be implemented. A method called **CompareTo** must be implemented with this particular interface which can then be called on a variable to compare its value with another variable's value. In this case it will be used when sorting the array containing the cards representing a hand.

Value is the property used in the **Card struct** to expose the **private value** variable storing the card's value using the **enum** containing all the possible card values.

```
struct Card : IComparable
{
    public int CompareTo(object obj)
    {
        var obj1 = (int)Value;
```

```
        var obj2 = (int)((Card)obj).Value;
        return obj1.CompareTo(obj2);
    }
}
```

Implementation

You will start by creating the user interface and then add functionality to shuffle a deck and deal two hands, one for the dealer and one for the player, from the shuffled deck. When the two hands have been dealt they should be evaluated and compared to determine the winner; the result should then be displayed in a label between the two hands in the GUI (see image below).

The GUI

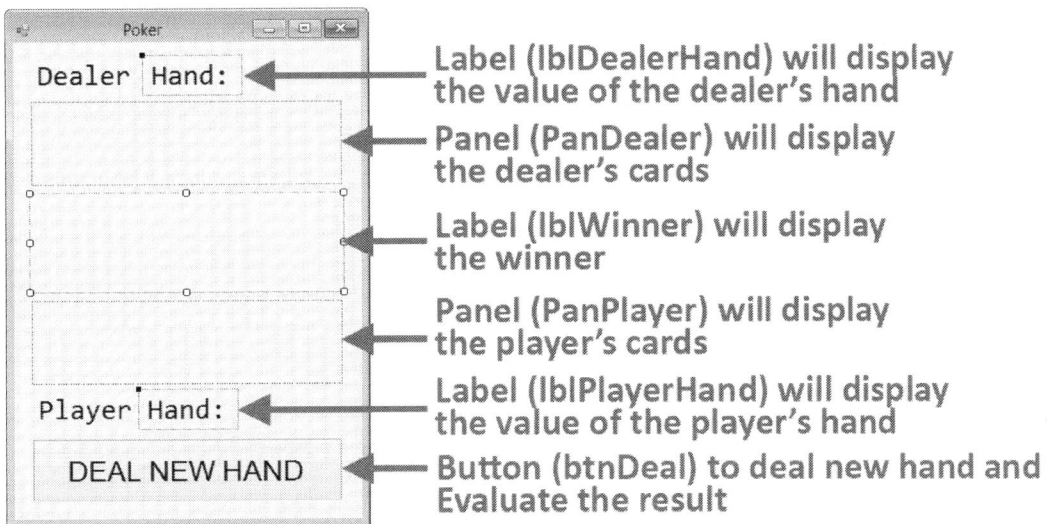

Label (lblDealerHand) will display the value of the dealer's hand

Panel (PanDealer) will display the dealer's cards

Label (lblWinner) will display the winner

Panel (PanPlayer) will display the player's cards

Label (lblPlayerHand) will display the value of the player's hand

Button (btnDeal) to deal new hand and Evaluate the result

1. Create a new **Windows Forms Application** called *Poker*.
2. Change the form's title to **Poker**.
3. Change the form's font to **Consolas, 20pt**.
4. Add a **Label** with the text "Dealer".
5. Add a **Label** called *lblDealerHand* with the text "Hand:" to the right of the previous label.
6. Add a **Panel** called *panDelaer* below the two labels. The **Panel** will hold the dynamically added labels representing the dealer's cards which will be added at run-time.

215

7. Add a an empty **Label** called ***lblWinner*** below the dealer's panel. If you need to change the size of a label then change its **AutoSize** property to **false**. Change the label's **TextAlign** property to **MiddleCenter** to center the text horizontally and vertically.

8. Add a **Panel** called ***panPlayer*** below the winner label. The **Panel** will hold the dynamically added labels representing the player's cards which will be added at run-time.

9. Add a **Label** with the text "Player".

10. Add a **Label** called ***lblPlayerHand*** with the text "Hand:" to the right of the previous label.

11. Add a button called ***btnDeal*** with the text "DEAL NEW HAND" at the bottom of the form.

The Card struct

A **struct** will come in handy to encapsulate all information about a single playing card, add a **struct** called **Card** in a separate .cs file called **Card**. Add three **enums** above the **struct** inside the namespace for the card suits, card values and card symbols.

```
enum Suit { Hearts = 1, Spades, Diamonds, Clubs }
enum Value { Two = 2, Three = 3, ..., King = 13, Ace = 14 }
enum Symbol { Hearts = '♥', Spades = '♠', Diamonds = '♦', Clubs = '♣' }
// Unicode characters "\u2665", "\u2660", "\u2666", "\u2663"
```

The **struct** should have a private variable called **_value** and its corresponding read only property called **Value** storing a value from the **Value enum**. It should also have a variable called **_suit** and its corresponding read only property called **Suit** storing a value of the **Suit enum**.

To display the suit symbol from the **Symbol enum** for the playing card you have to parse the **_suit** value using the **Enum.Parse** method and ultimately cast the result to a **char**.

To display an abbreviated form of the **Value enum** value stored in the **_value** variable you have to add a fourth property called **ValueSymbol** that uses a **switch** to return a **string** representing the card's value (1, 2, 3, ..., J, Q, K, A).

The constructor should have two parameters called **value** and **suit** of the **Value** and **Suit** **enum** data types respectively. The values should be assigned to the appropriate variables in the **struct**.

Implement the **IComparable** interface and its **CompareTo** method comparing the value of the **Value** property cast to an **int** for the two objects being compared. The method is needed later when sorting the cards of a hand. You can read more about how to implement the interface above.

1. Right click on the project name in the Solution Explorer and select **Add-Class** in the menu.
2. Name the file **Card** and click on the **Add** button.
3. Change the type from **class** to **struct**.
   ```
   struct Card
   {
   }
   ```
4. Add three **enums** called **Suit**, **Value** and **Symbol** to the **Poker** namespace , the first for the four card suit, the second for the card values and the third for the card suit symbols. You can find the symbols in a word processor's *insert character* tool or Google it.
   ```
   namespace Poker
   {
       enum Suit { Hearts = 1, Spades, Diamonds, Clubs }
       enum Value { Two = 2, Three = 3, Four = 4, Five = 5,
           Six = 6, Seven = 7, Eight = 8, Nine = 9, Ten = 10,
           Jack = 11, Queen = 12, King = 13, Ace = 14 }
       enum Symbol { Hearts = '♥', Spades = '♠',
           Diamonds = '♦', Clubs = '♣' }
       // Unicode characters "\u2665", "\u2660", "\u2666", "\u2663"
   ```
5. Add a variable called **_value** and its corresponding read only property called **Value** to the **struct** using the **Value enum** as their data types.
6. Add a variable called **_suit** and its corresponding read only property called **Suit** to the **struct** using the **Suit enum** as their data types.
7. Add a read only property called **SuitSymbol** to return the symbol from the **Symbol enum** using the value in the **_suit** variable.

```
public char SuitSymbol
{
    get {
        // return '♥', '♠', '♦' or '♣' based on _suit
        return (char)(Symbol)Enum.Parse(
            typeof(Symbol), _suit.ToString());
    }
}
```

8. Add a property called **ValueSymbol** which uses a **switch** to return a **string** representing the card's abbreviated value (1, 2, 3, ..., J, Q, K, A) based in the value stored in the **_value** variable cast to an **int**.

```
switch ((int)_value)
{
    case 11: return "J";
    ...
    default: return ((int)_value).ToString();
```

9. Add a constructor that has two parameters called **value** and **suit** of the **Value** and **Suit enum** data types respectively and assign their values to the appropriate variables.

```
public Card(Value value, Suit suit)
```

10. Implement the **IComparable** interface by appending : **IComparable** to the **struct** declaration.

```
struct Card : IComparable
```

11. Right click on the interface name and select **Implement Interface** to add the **CompareTo** method from the interface.

```
public int CompareTo(object obj)
{
    throw new NotImplementedException();
}
```

12. Change the code inside the **CompareTo** method to compare on the **Value** property.

```
public int CompareTo(object obj)
{
    var obj1 = (int)Value;
    var obj2 = (int)((Card)obj).Value;
    return obj1.CompareTo(obj2);
}
```

The complete code for the **Card .cs** file look like this:

```
namespace Poker
{
    enum Suit { Hearts = 1, Spades, Diamonds, Clubs }
    enum Value { Two = 2, Three = 3, Four = 4, Five = 5,
        Six = 6, Seven = 7, Eight = 8, Nine = 9, Ten = 10,
        Jack = 11, Queen = 12, King = 13, Ace = 14 }
    enum Symbol { Hearts = '♥', Spades = '♠',
        Diamonds = '♦', Clubs = '♣' }
    // Unicode characters "\u2665", "\u2660", "\u2666", "\u2663"

    struct Card : IComparable
    {
        private Value _value;
        private Suit _suit;

        public Value Value { get { return _value; } }
        public Suit Suit { get { return _suit; } }
        public char SuitSymbol
        {
            get
            {
                return (char)(Symbol)Enum.Parse(
                    typeof(Symbol), _suit.ToString());
            }
        }
        public string ValueSymbol
        {
            get
            {
                switch ((int)_value)
                {
                    case 11: return "J";
                    case 12: return "Q";
                    case 13: return "K";
                    case 14: return "A";
                    default: return ((int)_value).ToString();
                }
            }
        }
    }
```

```
        public Card(Value value, Suit suit)
        {
            _value = value;
            _suit = suit;
        }

        public int CompareTo(object obj)
        {
            var obj1 = (int)Value;
            var obj2 = (int)((Card)obj).Value;
            return obj1.CompareTo(obj2);
        }
    }
}
```

The Hand struct

The **Hand struct** holds information about the dealer's or player's hand such as an array of cards, the hand value, high cards, kicker cards and the suit in case of a flush or straight flush. All variables except the cards array will be assigned and used during the evaluation and comparison process.

You will also have to add two **enums** to the **Poker** namespace, one called **Hands** for all the possible poker hands and one called **Winner** for the possible winners.

```
enum Hands { Nothing, Pair, TwoPair, ..., RoyalStraightFlush }
enum Winner { Dealer, Player, Draw }
```

1. Right click on the project name in the Solution Explorer and select **Add-Class** in the menu.
2. Name the file **Hand** and click on the **Add** button.
3. Change the type from **class** to **struct**.
    ```
    struct Hand
    {
    }
    ```
4. Add an **enum** called **Hands** to the **Poker** namespace for all the possible poker hands.
    ```
    enum Hands { Nothing, Pair, TwoPair, ThreeOfAKind, Straight, Flush,
    FullHouse, FourOfAKind, StraightFlush, RoyalStraightFlush }
    ```
5. Add an array property called **Cards** using the **Card struct** as its data type.
    ```
    public Card[] Cards { get; set; }
    ```

6. Add a property called **HandValue** using the **Hands enum** as its data type.
7. Add two properties called **HighCard1** and **HighCard2** using the **Value enum** as their data types.
8. Add a **List<Value>** collection property called **Kickers**.

```
public List<Value> Kickers { get; set; }
```

9. Add an **int** property called **Suit**.

The complete code for the **Hand .cs** file look like this:

```
namespace Poker
{
    enum Hands { Nothing, Pair, TwoPair, ThreeOfAKind,
        Straight, Flush, FullHouse, FourOfAKind,
        StraightFlush, RoyalStraightFlush }
    enum Winner { Dealer, Player, Draw }

    struct Hand
    {
        public Card[] Cards { get; set; }
        public Hands HandValue { get; set; }
        public Value HighCard1 { get; set; }
        public Value HighCard2 { get; set; }
        public List<Value> Kickers { get; set; }
        public int Suit { get; set; }
    }
}
```

The form variables

You'll need three variables and one constant on form level. The first variable is used to hold the player's hand and the second the dealer's hand, both declared with the **Hand struct**. The third variable is the deck of cards declared as a **List<Card>** collection. An **int** constant called **shuffles** determines how many times the card deck should be shuffled before any cards are dealt.

Place the variables and constant in a region.

1. Open the form's code-behind file and locate the beginning of the form's class.
2. Add a **region** called **Variables**.

3. Add a variable called **playerHand** declared using the **Hand struct**. This variable holds the player's cards.
   ```
   Hand playerHand = new Hand();
   ```

4. Add a variable called **dealerHand** declared using the **Hand struct**. This variable holds the dealer's cards.

5. Add a variable called **deck** declared using a **List<Card>** collection. This variable represent all 52 playing cards in the a deck. It is from this collection the player's and dealer's cards will be dealt.
   ```
   List<Card> deck = new List<Card>();
   ```

6. Add an **int** constant called **shuffles** representing the number of times the deck should be shuffled before any cards are dealt. Assign **1000** to the constant.

The form code so far:

```
public partial class Form1 : Form
{
    #region Variables
    Hand playerHand;
    Hand dealerHand;
    List<Card> deck;
    const int shuffles = 1000;
    #endregion

    public Form1()
    {
        InitializeComponent();
    }
}
```

The Initialize method

The purpose of this method is to create instances for the **playerHand**, **dealerHand** and **deck** variables before each new hand is dealt simulating that the dealer collects the cards and shuffles the deck. Place the method in a **region** called **Methods**.

The **Initialize** method should always be called first in the button **Click** event.

1. Open the form's code-behind file and locate the end of the form class.
2. Add a region called **Methods** at the end of the class.
3. Add a parameter-less **void** method called **Initialize** to the **region**.

```
#region Methods
private void Initialize()
{
}
#endregion
```

4. Create instances for the **playerHand**, **dealerHand** and **deck** variables.

```
playerHand = new Hand();
dealerHand = new Hand();
deck = new List<Card>();
```

5. Add the **btnDeal_Click** event.

6. Call the **Initialize** method from the event.

```
private void btnDeal_Click(object sender, EventArgs e)
{
    Initialize();
}
```

7. Add a breakpoint where the method call is made by placing the cursor on that line of code and press **F9** on the keyboard.

8. Run the application and click the button.

9. When the execution has halted on the breakpoint point to the variables one at a time and see what they contain. The hands should have been created with the default values for the variables in the **Hand struct** and the **List** should be **null**.

10. Press **F11** to step into the method and check the variable values as you step over them with **F11**. The hand variables still contain the default values but the list should have been instantiated and contain **0 Card** instances.

11. Stop the application.

The complete code for the Initialize method look like this:

```
#region Methods
private void Initialize()
{
    playerHand = new Hand();
    dealerHand = new Hand();
    deck = new List<Card>();

}
#endregion
```

```
private void btnDeal_Click(object sender, EventArgs e)
{
    Initialize();
}
```

The ShuffleDeck method

The purpose of this method is to shuffle the deck. To add the playing cards to the deck you can use two nested **foreach** loops iterating over the **Suit enum** in the outer loop and the **Value enum** in the inner loop, this will add cards with the value 2 through 14 for each suit (hearts, spades, diamonds and clubs).

When the 52 cards have been added to the **deck** collection with the loops it is time to shuffle the cards. One way to shuffle the cards is to use the **Random** class to generate random numbers using the number of remaining cards in the collection as the max value for the **Next** method of the **Random** class variable.

Use the random number as the index for the card you fetch and remove from the **deck** collection and add it to a temporary **List<Card>** collection. When the **deck** collection is empty the temporary collection should contain the cards shuffled once. Move the cards to the **deck** collection and empty the temporary collection for each iteration of the randomization process, iterate the number of times stated in the **shuffles** constant. You can use a **for** loop when iterating over the number of shuffles in the **shuffles** constant and a **while** loop to iterate over the cards in the deck, you cannot use a **for** or **foreach** loop when removing items from a collection while iterating because that would mess up the index for the loop.

1. Locate the **Methods region** and add a parameter-less **void** method called **ShuffleDeck**.
   ```
   private void ShuffleDeck()
   {
   }
   ```

2. Add a **foreach** loop iterating over the values in the **Suit enum** to the method. To pull this off you need to use the **GetValues** method **Enum** class passing in the type using the **typeof** method.
   ```
   foreach (Suit suit in Enum.GetValues(typeof(Suit)))
   {
   }
   ```

3. Add a nested **foreach** loop inside the previous **foreach** loop iterating over the values in the **Values enum**.
```
foreach (Value value in Enum.GetValues(typeof(Value)))
{
}
```

4. Create a new **Card** variable inside the nested loop using the **suit** and **value** loop variables to add that card to the **deck** collection.
```
var card = new Card(value, suit);
deck.Add(card);
```

5. Create an instance of the **Random** class called **rnd** below the outer **foreach** loop.
```
Random rnd = new Random();
```

6. Add a **for** loop iterating over the **shuffles** constant and create a new temporary **List<Card>** collection in the loop.
```
for (int i = 0; i < shuffles; i++)
{
    List<Card> tmpDeck = new List<Card>();
}
```

7. Add a **while** loop below the temporary collection iterating for as long as there are cards in the **deck** collection.
```
while (deck.Count > 0)
{
}
```

8. Use the **Next** method on the **rnd** variable to generate a new random number with the number of remaining cards in the **deck** collection as the max value.
```
var index = rnd.Next(deck.Count);
```

9. Use the random number as the index to fetch and remove a card from the **deck** collection. Add the fetched card to the temporary collection.
```
var card = deck[index];
deck.RemoveAt(index);
tmpDeck.Add(card);
```

10. Assign the temporary collection to the deck collection outside the **while** loop when all the cards have been moved to the temporary collection.
```
deck = tmpDeck;
```

11. Add a call to the **ShuffleDeck** method below the **Initialize** method in the button **Click** vent.

12. Add a breakpoint at the end of the button **Click** event.

13. Run the application and click the button.

14. When the breakpoint is hit examine the **deck** collection, it should now contain 52 cards in random order.

15. Stop the application.

The complete code for the **ShuffleDeck** method look like this:

```
private void ShuffleDeck()
{
    foreach (Suit suit in Enum.GetValues(typeof(Suit)))
    {
        foreach (Value value in Enum.GetValues(typeof(Value)))
        {
            var card = new Card(value, suit);
            deck.Add(card);
        }
    }

    Random rnd = new Random();

    for (int i = 0; i < shuffles; i++)
    {
        List<Card> tmpDeck = new List<Card>();
        while (deck.Count > 0)
        {
            var index = rnd.Next(deck.Count);

            var card = deck[index];
            deck.RemoveAt(index);
            tmpDeck.Add(card);
        }
        deck = tmpDeck;
    }
}
```

The DealCards method

The purpose of this method is to deal five cards each to the dealer and player, one card each for each iteration. You will have to initialize the **Cards** array for 5 values in the **playerHand** and **dealerHand** variables. To deal the cards you have to iterate 5 times fetching and removing 2 cards from the **deck** collection with each iteration and placing one card in the **playerHand** and one in the **dealerHand Cards** array.

1. Add a parameter-less **void** method called **DealCards** in the **Methods region**.
2. Initialize the **Cards** array for the player and dealer hands inside the method.

```
private void DealCards()
{
    playerHand.Cards = new Card[5];
    dealerHand.Cards = new Card[5];
}
```

3. Add a **for** loop iterating 5 times fetching two cards that you assign to the player and dealer **Cards** arrays. Then remove the two cards from the **deck** collection simulating that two cards have been dealt from the deck.

```
for (int i = 0; i < 5; i++)
{
    playerHand.Cards[i] = deck.ElementAt(0);
    dealerHand.Cards[i] = deck.ElementAt(1);
    deck.RemoveRange(0, 2);
}
```

4. Add a call to the **DealCards** method in the button's **Click** event.
5. Run the application and explore the **Cards** array in the **dealerHand** and **playerHand** variables. They should contain 5 cards each representing the hands of the player and the dealer.
6. Stop the application.

The complete code for the **DealCards** method look like this:

```
private void DealCards()
{
    playerHand.Cards = new Card[5];
    dealerHand.Cards = new Card[5];
    for (int i = 0; i < 5; i++)
    {
        playerHand.Cards[i] = deck.ElementAt(0);
        dealerHand.Cards[i] = deck.ElementAt(1);
        deck.RemoveRange(0, 2);
    }
}
```

The EvaluateHand method

The purpose of this method is to evaluate a poker hand finding out what hand the dealer or the player has and assign the correct hand to the **HandValue** property of the passed in hand using the **Hands enum**. Most properties in the passed in hand will be used during the evaluation. The **EvaluateHand** method should have one **ref** parameter declared as a **Hand struct**; it needs to be declared as **ref** because you will make permanent changes to it.

This method could be viewed as one of the more complex since it involves a lot of checks that has to be performed in the correct order for the hand to be evaluated correctly.

I suggest that you start by sorting the cards in the **Cards** array using the **Sort** method in the **Array** class to make it easier to evaluate the hand. By sorting the hand cards with the same value will be placed after one another making it easier to find pairs, three of a kind and four of a kind. Finding a straight will also be easier since the cards will be in sequence. Sorting the cards will not only make it easier to determine the hand it will drastically cut down the amount of code you have to write to achieve the end result.

The hand value should be determined using the following hand order: Royal Straight Flush, Straight Flush, Four of a kind, Full House, Flush, Straight, Three of a Kind, Two Pairs, One Pair, High Card, Nothing. You will need to use the **Value** and **Hands enums** when evaluating the hand.

Sorting the cards

After sorting the cards you can create variables called **suit1-suit5** for the cards suits and **value1-value5** for the cards values to make it easier to read the code not having to use the **Cards** array in the **if**-statements.

1. Add a **void** method called **EvaluateHand** taking a **Hand** parameter declared with the **ref** keyword in the **Methods region**.
   ```
   private void EvaluateHand(ref Hand evalHand)
   {
   }
   ```

2. Create a region called **Arranging cards** and sort the cards.
   ```
   #region Arranging cards
   Array.Sort(evalHand.Cards);
   #endregion
   ```

3. Add the **siut1-suit5** and **value1-value5** variables in the region.

```
var suit1 = evalHand.Cards[0].Suit;
...
var value1 = evalHand.Cards[0].Value;
...
```

The complete code for the **Arranging cards** region look like this:

```
private void EvaluateHand(ref Hand evalHand)
{
    #region Arranging cards
    Array.Sort(evalHand.Cards);
    var suit1 = evalHand.Cards[0].Suit;
    var suit2 = evalHand.Cards[1].Suit;
    var suit3 = evalHand.Cards[2].Suit;
    var suit4 = evalHand.Cards[3].Suit;
    var suit5 = evalHand.Cards[4].Suit;
    var value1 = evalHand.Cards[0].Value;
    var value2 = evalHand.Cards[1].Value;
    var value3 = evalHand.Cards[2].Value;
    var value4 = evalHand.Cards[3].Value;
    var value5 = evalHand.Cards[4].Value;
    #endregion
}
```

Has Flush ?

By finding out if the hand is a flush and storing the result in the **Suit** and **HandValue** property of the passed in hand you can use the result to find out the hand is a flush, straight flush or Royal Straight Flush. One way to achieve this is to use LINQ methods and a Lambda expression counting how may cards of the same suit are in the hand, if there are 5 cards with the same suit then you know that it is a flush. You cannot jump out of the method yet however because Straight Flush and Royal Straight Flush are better hands which have to be evaluate first.

1. Add a **region** with the description **Has Flush ?**.
2. Use LINQ and Lambda to count the cards with the same suit and assign **true** if all 5 cards have the same suit otherwise assign **false** to a variable called **hasFlush**.

```
var hasFlush = evalHand.Cards.Count(c =>
c.Suit.Equals(suit1)).Equals(5);
```

3. If **hasFlush** is **true** then save the suit value in the **evalHand** parameter's **Suit** property and **Hands.Flush** in its **HandValue** property.

The complete code for the **Has Flush ?** region look like this:

```
#region Has Flush ?
var hasFlush = evalHand.Cards.Count(c => c.Suit.Equals(suit1)).Equals(5);
if (hasFlush)
{
    evalHand.Suit = (int)suit1;
    evalHand.HandValue = Hands.Flush;
}
#endregion
```

Has Straight ?

By finding out if the hand is a straight and storing the result in three **bool** variables called **hasStraight**, **isHighStraight** (10, J, Q, K, A) and **isLowStraight** (A, 2, 3, 4, 5) you can use the result and the **hasFlush** variable to find out if the hand is a straight, straight flush or Royal Straight Flush.

There are two basic scenarios which have to be addressed; the first is when it is a low straight from A to 5 and all other straights. Use the **value1-value5** variables and the **Value enum** to find out if the hand is a straight.

Don't exit the method with a **return** statement because you still have to find out if the hand is a straight, straight flush or Royal Straight Flush.

1. Add a **region** called **Has Straight ?**.
2. Add a **bool** variable called **hasStraight** that will contain **true** if the hand is a straight. You can achieve this by checking if the current card is equal to the previous card + 1 or if the cards range from A-5.
   ```
   var hasStraight =
       (value2.Equals(value1 + 1) && value3.Equals(value2 + 1) &&
        value4.Equals(value3 + 1) && value5.Equals(value4 + 1)) ||
       (value1.Equals(Value.Two) && value2.Equals(Value.Three) &&
        value3.Equals(Value.Four) && value4.Equals(Value.Five) &&
        value5.Equals(Value.Ace));
   ```
3. Add a **bool** variable called **isHighStraight** that will contain **true** if the hand is a straight from 10 to A.

4. Add a **bool** variable called **isLowStraight** that will contain **true** if the hand is a straight from A to 5.

The complete code for the **Has Straight ?** region look like this:

```
#region Has Straight ?
var hasStraight =
    (value2.Equals(value1 + 1) && value3.Equals(value2 + 1) &&
    value4.Equals(value3 + 1) && value5.Equals(value4 + 1)) ||
    (value1.Equals(Value.Two) && value2.Equals(Value.Three) &&
    value3.Equals(Value.Four) && value4.Equals(Value.Five) &&
    value5.Equals(Value.Ace));

var isHighStraight = hasStraight && value4.Equals(Value.King) &&
    value5.Equals(Value.Ace); // (10, J, Q, K, A)

    var isLowStraight = hasStraight && value2.Equals(Value.Two) &&
    value5.Equals(Value.Ace); // (A, 2, 3, 4, 5)
#endregion
```

Royal Straight Flush

Now that you have figured out if it is a flush or a straight it is time to use that information to figure out if the hand is a Royal Straight Flush. Use the **isHighStraight** and **hasFlush** variables and check if the suit is equal to Hearts, if the expression evaluates to **true** then assign the **value5** variable to the **HighCard1** property and the **RoyalStraightFlush** from the **Hands enum** to the **HandValue** property in the **evalHand** parameter. Exit from the method below the assignments.

1. Add a **region** called **Royal Straight Flush**.
2. Add an **if**-statement checking if it is a Royal Straight Flush.
   ```
   if (isHighStraight && hasFlush && suit1.Equals(Suit.Hearts))
   {
   }
   ```
3. Assign the property values inside the **if**-block and return from the method.

The complete code for the **Royal Straight Flush** region look like this:

```
#region Royal Straight Flush
if (isHighStraight && hasFlush && suit1.Equals(Suit.Hearts))
{
    evalHand.HighCard1 = value5;
    evalHand.HandValue = Hands.RoyalStraightFlush;
    return;
}
#endregion
```

Straight/Straight Flush

Now that you have figured out that it isn't a Royal Straight Flush the next step is to figure out if it is a straight or a Straight Flush.

Use the **hasStraight** variable in an **if**-statement to see if it is a straight. Assign the hand value to the **HighCard1** property of the **evalHand** parameter based on if it is a low straight or any other straight, a low straight should use the **value4** variable and any other straight the **value5** variable.

Use the **hasFlush** variable to figure out if the **HandValue** property should be assigned **StraightFlush** or **Straight** from the **Hands enum**.

1. Add a **region** called **Straight/Straight Flush**.
2. Check if the hand has a straight using the **hasStraight** variable.
   ```
   if (hasStraight)
   {
   }
   ```
3. Assign the **HighCard1** property in the **evalHand** parameter using the **isLowStraight** variable.
   ```
   evalHand.HighCard1 = isLowStraight ? value4 : value5;
   ```
4. Assign the **HandValue** property in the **evalHand** parameter using the **hasFlush** variable.
   ```
   evalHand.HandValue = hasFlush ? Hands.StraightFlush : Hands.Straight;
   ```
5. Exit from the method.

The complete code for the **Straight/Straight Flush** region look like this:

```
#region Straight/Straight Flush
if (hasStraight)
{
    evalHand.HighCard1 = isLowStraight ? value4 : value5;
    evalHand.HandValue = hasFlush ? Hands.StraightFlush : Hands.Straight;
    return;
}
#endregion
```

Flush

Now that you have figured out that it isn't a Royal Straight Flush, Straight Flush or Straight the next step is to exit from the method if the hand is a Flush.

The complete code for the **Flush** region look like this:

```
#region Flush
if (hasFlush) return;
#endregion
```

Four of a Kind

Next you will check if the hand is Four of a Kind, you can do this by checking if there are 4 cards with the same value as the third card because the cards have been sorted. You can use the **Count** LINQ method and Lambda expressions to figure it out.

When assigning the **HighCard1** property in the **evalHand** parameter the **value3** variable will always give you the correct value since it is present in any Four of a Kind hand.

1. Add a **region** called **Four of a Kind**.
2. Evaluate the values for the first and second card to find out if it is a Four of a Kind hand.
   ```
   if (evalHand.Cards.Count(c => c.Value.Equals(value3)).Equals(4))
   {
   }
   ```
3. Assign the **HighCard1** and **HandValue** properties.
4. Exit from the method.

The complete code for the **Four of a Kind** region look like this:

```
#region Four of a Kind
if (evalHand.Cards.Count(c => c.Value.Equals(value3)).Equals(4))
{
    evalHand.HighCard1 = value3;
    evalHand.HandValue = Hands.FourOfAKind;
    return;
}
#endregion
```

Has Three of a Kind ?

Next you will check if the hand contains Three of a Kind, you can do this by checking if there are 3 cards with the same value as the third card because the cads are sorted. You can use the **Count** LINQ method and Lambda expressions to figure it out.

When assigning the **HighCard1** property in the **evalHand** parameter the **value3** variable will always give you the correct value since it is present in any Three of a Kind hand.

Don't exit from the method because you need to check other hands first such as Full House which contain a Three of a Kind.

1. Add a **region** called **Three of a Kind ?**.
2. Evaluate the values for the first, second and third card to find out if the hand contain Three of a Kind hand and store the result in a variable called **hasThreeOfAKind**.
```
var hasThreeOfAKind =
    evalHand.Cards.Count(c => c.Value.Equals(value3)).Equals(3);
```
3. Assign the **HighCard1** and **HandValue** properties if the **hasThreeOfAKind** variable is **true**. Don't add a **return** statement.

The complete code for the **Has Three of a Kind ?** region look like this:

```
#region Has Three of a kind ?
var hasThreeOfAKind =
    evalHand.Cards.Count(c => c.Value.Equals(value3)).Equals(3);

if (hasThreeOfAKind) {
    evalHand.HighCard1 = value3;
    evalHand.HandValue = Hands.ThreeOfAKind;
}
#endregion
```

Full House

To check if the hand is a Full House you use the **hasTreeOfAKind** variable and do a check if there is a pair where the cards have the value of the first or last card in the hand; you only have to check the value of these two cards for pairs since all the other cards have to be part of a Three of a Kind for a hand with a Full House.

Use the **value3** variable when assigning the **HighCard1** property of the **evalHand** parameter that correspond to the card value for the Three of a Kind part of the Full House and the first card value that is <u>not</u> equal to the **value3** variable for the **HighCard2** property corresponding to the pair of the Full House.

Assign **FullHouse** to the **HandValue** property and then **return** from the method.

1. Add a **region** called **Full House**.
2. Add an **if**-statement checking the **hasTreeOfAKind** variable and if there also is a pair present.
   ```
   if (hasThreeOfAKind &&
   (evalHand.Cards.Count(c => c.Value.Equals(value1)).Equals(2) ||
    evalHand.Cards.Count(c => c.Value.Equals(value5)).Equals(2)))
   {
   }
   ```
3. Assign the values to the properties and **return** from the method.

The complete code for the **Full House** region look like this:

```
#region Full House
if (hasThreeOfAKind &&
    (evalHand.Cards.Count(c => c.Value.Equals(value1)).Equals(2) ||
    evalHand.Cards.Count(c => c.Value.Equals(value5)).Equals(2)))
{
    evalHand.HighCard1 = value3; // Three of a kind
    evalHand.HighCard2 = evalHand.Cards.First(c =>
        !c.Value.Equals(value3)).Value; // Pair
    evalHand.HandValue = Hands.FullHouse;
    return;
}
#endregion
```

Return if the hand is Three of a Kind

To check if the hand is Three of a Kind you just check if the **hasTreeOfAKind** variable is **true** and **return** from the method if it is.

The complete code for the **Three of a Kind** region look like this:

```
#region Three of a Kind
if (hasThreeOfAKind) return;
#endregion
```

Has Pairs ?

To check if the hand contain any pairs you only have to check the first, third and fifth card values for matching values to find any pair present in the hand; add the pairs you find to a **List<Value>** collection called **pairs**.

You also need to instantiate the **Kickers** collection in the **evalHand** parameter because when comparing pairs the kicker card or cards may come into play if both hands have the same pairs.

1. Add a **region** called **Has Pairs ?**.
2. Add a **List<Value>** collection variable called **pairs** which will hold the card value for any pairs present in the hand.
   ```
   List<Value> pairs = new List<Value>();
   ```
3. Evaluate the hand to find out if there are pairs present that match the first, third and fifth card values and add the card value to the **pairs** collection if there is a pair present for that value, repeat the code below for the two other scenarios.
   ```
   if (evalHand.Cards.Count(c => c.Value.Equals(value1)).Equals(2))
       pairs.Add(value1);
   ```
4. Instantiate the **Kickers** collection in the **evalHand** parameter.
   ```
   evalHand.Kickers = new List<Value>();
   ```

The complete code for the **Has Pairs ?** region look like this:

```
#region Has Pairs ?
List<Value> pairs = new List<Value>();

if (evalHand.Cards.Count(c => c.Value.Equals(value1)).Equals(2))
    pairs.Add(value1);
if (evalHand.Cards.Count(c => c.Value.Equals(value3)).Equals(2))
    pairs.Add(value3);
if (evalHand.Cards.Count(c => c.Value.Equals(value5)).Equals(2))
    pairs.Add(value5);

evalHand.Kickers = new List<Value>();
#endregion
```

Two Pairs

To check if the hand contain two pairs you can count the number of values in the **pairs** collection since each value correspond to a pair.

Assign the first value in the **pairs** collection to the **HighCard2** property and the second to the **HighCard1** property. Also assign **TwoPair** to the **HandValue** property.

To find the kicker value for the hand you need to add the value of the one remaining card to the **Kickers** collection in the **evalHand** parameter.

1. Add a **region** called **Two Pairs**.
2. Add an **if**-statement checking if the **pairs** collection has two entries.
   ```
   if (pairs.Count.Equals(2))
   {
   }
   ```
3. Assign the first value in the **pairs** collection to the **HighCard2** property.
4. Assign the second value in the **pairs** collection to the **HighCard1** property.
5. Assign **TwoPair** to the **HandValue** property.
6. Find the remaining card and add it to the **Kickers** collection of the **evalHand** parameter.
   ```
   evalHand.Kickers.Add(evalHand.Cards.First(c =>
   !c.Value.Equals(pairs[1]) && !c.Value.Equals(pairs[0])).Value);
   ```
7. Return from the method.

The complete code for the **Two Pairs** region look like this:

```
#region Two Pairs
if (pairs.Count.Equals(2))
{
    evalHand.HighCard1 = pairs[1];
    evalHand.HighCard2 = pairs[0];
    evalHand.HandValue = Hands.TwoPair;
    evalHand.Kickers.Add(evalHand.Cards.First(c =>
        !c.Value.Equals(pairs[1]) &&
        !c.Value.Equals(pairs[0])).Value);
    return;
}
#endregion
```

Pair

To check if the hand contain a pair you can count the number of values in the **pairs** collection since each value correspond to a pair.

Assign the first value in the **pairs** collection to the **HighCard1** property of the **evalHand** parameter. Also assign **Pair** to the **HandValue** property.

To find all the remaining kicker card values for the hand; you need to add the values of all the remaining cards to the **Kickers** collection in the **evalHand** parameter. Reverse the sort order of the **Cards** array to get the kickers from high to low value.

1. Add a **region** called **Pair**.
2. Add an **if**-statement checking if the **pairs** collection has one entry.
   ```
   if (pairs.Count.Equals(1))
   {
   }
   ```
3. Assign the first value in the **pairs** collection to the **HighCard1** property.
4. Assign **Pair** to the **HandValue** property.
5. Find the remaining cards and add them to the **Kickers** collection of the **evalHand** parameter.
   ```
   evalHand.Kickers.AddRange(evalHand.Cards.Reverse().Where(
   c => !c.Value.Equals(pairs[0])).Select(c => c.Value));
   ```
6. Return from the method.

The complete code for the **Pair** region look like this:

```
#region Pair
if (pairs.Count.Equals(1))
{
    evalHand.HighCard1 = pairs[0];
    evalHand.HandValue = Hands.Pair;
    evalHand.Kickers.AddRange(evalHand.Cards.Reverse().Where(c =>
        !c.Value.Equals(pairs[0])).Select(c => c.Value));
}
#endregion
```

Testing the EvaluateHand method

The easiest way to test the **EvaluateHand** method is to create a controlled scenario where no randomizing is involved, to achieve this you can use the **playerHand** variable and assign 5 known cards to its **Cards** array and pass in the **playerHand** variable to the **EvaluateHand** method.

Make sure that you have a breakpoint int he button's **Click** event after the call to the **EvaluateHand** method.

1. Locate the **btnDeal_Click** event.
2. Add the cards to the **Cards** array in the **playerHand** variable after the **DealCards** method call, you can chose to create any poker hand you like.
   ```
   playerHand.Cards = new Card[5]{
       new Card(Value.Ace, Suit.Diamonds),
       new Card(Value.Ace, Suit.Clubs),
       new Card(Value.Eight, Suit.Diamonds),
       new Card(Value.Ace, Suit.Hearts),
       new Card(Value.Five, Suit.Spades)
   };
   ```
3. Add a call to the **EvaluateHand** method and pass in the **playerHand** variable by reference (**ref**) to the method to evaluate the hand.
   ```
   EvaluateHand(ref playerHand);
   ```
4. Start the application in **Debug** mode by pressing **F5** on the keyboard and click the button.
5. Inspect the **playerHand** variable when the breakpoint is reached. The hand you chose to create should be reflected in the **HandValue** property.

6. Test all possible poker hands from Royal Straight Flush to Nothing to make sure that the evaluation works.
7. Close the application.
8. Comment out the test code for the **playerHand** variable.
9. Add a call to the **EvaluateHand** method after the previous **EvaluateHand** method call and pass in the **dealerHand** variable by reference (**ref**) to the method to evaluate the hand.
    ```
    EvaluateHand(ref dealerHand);
    ```

The complete code for the **btnDeal_Click** event look like this:

```
private void btnDeal_Click(object sender, EventArgs e)
{
    Initialize();
    ShuffleDeck();
    DealCards();

    /* Comment out the code for the Cards array
        after testing the EvaluateHand method. */
    playerHand.Cards = new Card[5]{
        new Card(Value.Ace, Suit.Diamonds),
        new Card(Value.Ace, Suit.Clubs),
        new Card(Value.Eight, Suit.Diamonds),
        new Card(Value.Ace, Suit.Hearts),
        new Card(Value.Five, Suit.Spades)
    };

    EvaluateHand(ref playerHand);
    EvaluateHand(ref dealerHand);
}
```

The CompareCards method

Before you can compare the hands you need to create a method that compare the cards of hands with only mixed cards to find out the winner by the highest card value. This method will be called from the **ComapreHands** method you will create next.

The easiest way is probably to create a loop that iterates from 4 to 0 over the cards in the two hands and compare the cards one at a time and when one of the cards is higher than the other you exit the loop by returning one of the values in the **Winner enum**. If both hands are the same the loop will finish and you return the value **Winner.Draw**.

1. Add a method called **CompareCards** using the **Winner enum** as its return data type to the **Methods region**.
   ```
   private Winner CompareCards()
   {
   }
   ```

2. Add a for loop iterating from 4 to 0 inside the method.
   ```
   for (int i = 4; i >= 0; i--)
   ```

3. Add an **if**-statement to the **for** loop checking if the card values at the loop index in the **Cards** arrays differ for the **playerHand** and the **dealerHand**.
   ```
   if (!playerHand.Cards[i].Value.Equals(dealerHand.Cards[i].Value))
   ```

4. If the **if**-expression is **true** then exit the loop with a **return** statement reflecting which hand is the highest using values from the **Winner enum**.
   ```
   return playerHand.Cards[i].Value > dealerHand.Cards[i].Value ?
   Winner.Player : Winner.Dealer;
   ```

5. If the hands are the same then return **Winner.Draw**.

The complete code for the **CompareCards** look like this:

```
private Winner CompareCards()
{
    for (int i = 4; i >= 0; i--)
        if (!playerHand.Cards[i].Value.Equals(dealerHand.Cards[i].Value))
            return playerHand.Cards[i].Value > dealerHand.Cards[i].Value ?
            Winner.Player : Winner.Dealer;

    return Winner.Draw;
}
```

The CompareHands method

This method will compare the **playerHand** and **dealerHand** variables to determine the winner and return the result using the **Winner enum**.

There are three scenarios to investigate where you for the first two only have to compare the **HandValue** property of the two hands and return the winner. The third scenario is a bit more complex since it involves finding the highest cards involved in the hand, or the highest kicker card.

Picture the scenario where both have the same hand value for instance a pair, to find the winner the card values of the pairs have to be compared to see who has the highest pair, or if they have the same pair the kicker cards will help determine the winner. The same goes for the other poker hands except for Royal Straight Flush which is the highest hand and will always win (only one player can have that hand).

1. Add a method called **CompareHands** to the **Methods region** using the **Winner enum** as the method's return data type.

   ```
   private Winner CompareHands()
   {
   }
   ```

2. Add two **if**-statements to check if the dealer or the player is the winner.

   ```
   if (playerHand.HandValue > dealerHand.HandValue) return
   Winner.Player;
   if (playerHand.HandValue < dealerHand.HandValue) return
   Winner.Dealer;
   ```

3. Add a **switch** checking the **playerHand.HandValue** property.

   ```
   switch (playerHand.HandValue)
   {
   }
   ```

4. Return a draw if the switch is not executed.

   ```
   return Winner.Draw;
   ```

The code for the **CompareHands** look like this so far:

```
private Winner CompareHands()
{
    if (playerHand.HandValue > dealerHand.HandValue) return Winner.Player;
    if (playerHand.HandValue < dealerHand.HandValue) return Winner.Dealer;

    // Compare hands if they have the same HandValue
    switch (playerHand.HandValue)
    {
        //Add case statements for the hands here
    }

    return Winner.Draw;
}
```

The StraightFlush case

1. Add a **case** for the **Hands.StraightFlush** hand to the **switch** in the **CompareHands** method.

   ```
   case Hands.StraightFlush:
   ```

2. Compare the **HighCard1** property to see which hand has the highest straight and return the winner using the **Winner enum**.

   ```
   if (playerHand.HighCard1 > dealerHand.HighCard1) return
   Winner.Player;
   if (playerHand.HighCard1 < dealerHand.HighCard1) return
   Winner.Dealer;
   ```

3. If the straights are the same then determine the winner using the **Suit** property of the **playerHand** and **dealerHand** variables.

   ```
   return dealerHand.Suit > playerHand.Suit ? Winner.Player :
   Winner.Dealer;
   ```

The complete code for the **StraightFlush case** look like this:

```
case Hands.StraightFlush:
    if (playerHand.HighCard1 > dealerHand.HighCard1) return Winner.Player;
    if (playerHand.HighCard1 < dealerHand.HighCard1) return Winner.Dealer;
    return playerHand.Suit > dealerHand.Suit ? Winner.Player :
Winner.Dealer;
```

The Straight case

1. Add a **case** for the **Hands.Straight** hand to the **switch** in the **CompareHands** method.
2. Compare the **HighCard1** property to see which hand has the highest straight and return the winner using the **Winner enum**.
3. If the straights are the same then return **Winner.Draw**.

   ```
   return Winner.Draw;
   ```

The complete code for the **Straight case** look like this:

```
case Hands.Straight:
    if (playerHand.HighCard1 > dealerHand.HighCard1) return Winner.Player;
    if (playerHand.HighCard1 < dealerHand.HighCard1) return Winner.Dealer;
    return Winner.Draw;
```

The Four of a Kind, Full House and Three of a Kind cases

1. Add a **case** for the three **HandsFourOfAKind**, **FullHouse** and **ThreeOfAKind** hands to the **switch** in the **CompareHands** method.

```
case Hands.FourOfAKind:
case Hands.FullHouse:
case Hands.ThreeOfAKind:
```

2. Compare the **HighCard1** property to see which player has the best hand and return the winner using the **Winner enum**.

The complete code for the **HandsFourOfAKind**, **FullHouse** and **ThreeOfAKind case** look like this:

```
case Hands.FourOfAKind:
case Hands.FullHouse:
case Hands.ThreeOfAKind:
    return playerHand.HighCard1 > dealerHand.HighCard1 ?
        Winner.Player : Winner.Dealer;
```

The Flush case

1. Add a **case** for the **Hands.Flush** hand to the **switch** in the **CompareHands** method.
2. Add an **if**-statement to check if the hands have the same flush and compare the **HighCard1** property to see which hand has the highest flush and return the winner using the **Winner enum** if they do.
3. If they have flushes of different suits then compare the cards to see which hand has the highest card by returning the result from a call to the **CompareCards** method.
   `return CompareCards();`

The complete code for the **Flush case** look like this:

```
case Hands.Flush:
    if (playerHand.Suit.Equals(dealerHand.Suit))
        return playerHand.HighCard1 > dealerHand.HighCard1 ?
            Winner.Player : Winner.Dealer;

    return CompareCards();
```

The Two Pairs case

Three checks are necessary to figure out the winner of two hands with two pairs. The first is to check the highest pairs and see if they are equal or not, the second is to check the second pairs and see if they are equal or not and the third is to compare the kicker cards. If none of the **if**-statements have been executed then return a draw.

244

1. Add a **case** for the **Hands.TwoPair** hand to the **switch** in the **CompareHands** method.

2. Add an **if**-statement to check if the **HighCard1** property value of the **playerHand** is higher than the value in same property in the **dealerHand**.
   ```
   if (playerHand.HighCard1 > dealerHand.HighCard1) return
   Winner.Player;
   ```

3. Add an **if**-statement to check if the **HighCard1** property value of the **playerHand** is lower than the value in same property in the **dealerHand**.

4. Add an **if**-statement to check if the **HighCard2** property value of the **playerHand** is higher than the same value in property in the **dealerHand**.
   ```
   if (playerHand.HighCard2 > dealerHand.HighCard2) return
   Winner.Player;
   ```

5. Add an **if**-statement to check if the **HighCard2** property value of the **playerHand** is lower than the same value in property in the **dealerHand**.

6. Add an **if**-statement to check if the **Kicker** of the **playerHand** is higher than the **Kicker** in the **dealerHand**.
   ```
   if (playerHand.Kickers[0] > dealerHand.Kickers[0]) return
   Winner.Player;
   ```

7. Add an **if**-statement to check if the **Kicker** of the **playerHand** is lower than the **Kicker** in the **dealerHand**.

8. If the hands are the same then return **Hands.Draw**.

The complete code for the **Flush case** look like this:

```
case Hands.TwoPair:
    if (playerHand.HighCard1 > dealerHand.HighCard1) return Winner.Player;
    if (playerHand.HighCard1 < dealerHand.HighCard1) return Winner.Dealer;
    if (playerHand.HighCard2 > dealerHand.HighCard2) return Winner.Player;
    if (playerHand.HighCard2 < dealerHand.HighCard2) return Winner.Dealer;
    if (playerHand.Kickers[0] > dealerHand.Kickers[0]) return Winner.Player;
    if (playerHand.Kickers[0] < dealerHand.Kickers[0]) return Winner.Dealer;
    return Winner.Draw;
```

The Pair case

There are two checks that has to be made to figure out the winner if both hands have a pair. The first is to check the pairs and see if they are equal or not and the second is to compare the kicker cards. If none of the **if**-statements have been executed then return a draw.

1. Add a **case** for the **Hands.Pair** hand to the **switch** in the **CompareHands** method.
2. Add an **if**-statement to check if the **HighCard1** property value of the **playerHand** is higher than the value of the same property in the **dealerHand**.
3. Add an **if**-statement to check if the **HighCard1** property value of the **playerHand** is lower than the value of the same property in the **dealerHand**.
4. Iterate over the kicker cards in the **Kickers** collection and find out which hand has the highest kicker.
   ```
   for (int i = 2; i >= 0; i--)
       if (!playerHand.Kickers[i].Equals(dealerHand.Kickers[i]))
           return playerHand.Kickers[i] > dealerHand.Kickers[i] ?
               Winner.Player : Winner.Dealer;
   ```
5. Return a draw if none of the **if**-statements have been executed.

The complete code for the **Pair case** look like this:

```
case Hands.Pair:
    if (playerHand.HighCard1 > dealerHand.HighCard1) return Winner.Player;
    if (playerHand.HighCard1 < dealerHand.HighCard1) return Winner.Dealer;

    for (int i = 2; i >= 0; i--)
        if (!playerHand.Kickers[i].Equals(dealerHand.Kickers[i]))
            return playerHand.Kickers[i] > dealerHand.Kickers[i] ?
                Winner.Player : Winner.Dealer;

    return Winner.Draw;
```

The Nothing case

If none of the player's have a hand it comes down to comparing all the cards until the highest card has been found in either hand when compared, you can achieve this by calling the **CompareCards** method you created earlier.

The complete code for the **Pair case** look like this:

```
case Hands.Nothing:
    return CompareCards();
```

Add a call to the CompareHands method

When the hands have been evaluated it is time to compare them and determine a winner which you do by calling the **CompareHands** method from the button's **Click** event and save the result in a variable called **winner**.

1. Locate the button's **Click** event.
2. Add a call to the **CompareHands** method after the calls to the **EvaluateHand** method and save the result in a variable called **winner**.

```
var winner = CompareHands();
```

3. Run the application and look at the value in the **winner** variable to make sure that the correct hand is the winner. Test a few hands to be sure using the commented out test code you added earlier and add the same code for the **dealerHand** variable.
4. Close the application.

The CreateCard method

To add a label dynamically you need to create the labels with similar settings and coordinates this is best done by separating out the label creation code to a method. The **CreateCard** method will return a **Label** and take the **x**- and **y**-coordinates as **int** parameters along with the **Card** being created.

The complete code for the **CreateCard** method look like this:

```
private Label CreateCard(int x, int y, Card card)
{
    Label lbl = new Label();
    lbl.Text = String.Format("{0}\n{1}",
        card.ValueSymbol, card.SuitSymbol);
    lbl.Size = new Size(55, 76);
    lbl.Location = new Point(x, y);
    lbl.BorderStyle = BorderStyle.FixedSingle;
    lbl.Font = new Font("Consolas", 20);
    lbl.TextAlign = ContentAlignment.MiddleCenter;
    lbl.BackColor = Color.White;
    lbl.ForeColor =
        card.Suit.Equals(Suit.Hearts) ||
        card.Suit.Equals(Suit.Diamonds) ?
        Color.Red : Color.Black;
    return lbl;
}
```

The RevealCards method

The purpose of the **RevealCards** method is to display the cards for the player and dealer as labels in the form as well as the winner and the individual hand values. The method has one parameter called **winner** declared using the **Winner enum,** the value will be provided from a call to the **CompareHands** method in the button's **Click** event.

You must clear the two panels where the cards will be added before iterating over the cards and adding them.

To add the cards dynamically to the form you need to call the **CreateCard** method for each card and add the resulting card label to the **Controls** collection of the correct panel.

Then you display the hand values and the winner in the appropriate labels. Change the background color to light green in the winner label if the player wins otherwise change it to light pink.

1. Add a **void** method called **RevealCards** which takes one parameter of the **Winner enum** data type to the **Methods region**.
   ```
   private void RevealCards(Winner winner)
   {
   }
   ```

2. Clear the panels before adding any cards to them.
   ```
   this.panDealer.Controls.Clear();
   this.panPlayer.Controls.Clear();
   ```

3. Add a loop iterating over the cards in the player and dealer hands calling the **CreateCards** method to create the card labels. Duplicate the code for the dealer hand.
   ```
   var lblPlayer = CreateCard(x, y, playerHand.Cards[i]);
   this.panPlayer.Controls.Add(lblPlayer);
   ```

4. Add the dealer hand value to the *lblDealerHand* label and the player hand value to the *lblPlayerHand* label.

5. Add the text "Player wins !", Dealer wins !" or "It's a draw" to the *lblWinner* label depending on the outcome.

6. Change the background color of the *lblWinner* label depending on the outcome.

7. Add a call to the **RevealCards** method to the button's **Click** event below the previous methods passing in the **winner** variable from the call to the **CompareHands** method.

8. Run the application and click the button. Make sure that the information and cards are displayed correctly.

9. Close the application.

10. Comment out the code for the test cards and run the application again. Now randomly generated cards should be displayed when the button is clicked.

11. Close the application.

The complete code for the **RevealCards** method look like this:

```
private void RevealCards(Winner winner)
{
    this.panDealer.Controls.Clear();
    this.panPlayer.Controls.Clear();

    for (int i = 0; i < 5; i++)
    {
        var x = i * 60;
        var y = 0;
        var lblDealer = CreateCard(x, y, dealerHand.Cards[i]);
        var lblPlayer = CreateCard(x, y, playerHand.Cards[i]);
        this.panDealer.Controls.Add(lblDealer);
        this.panPlayer.Controls.Add(lblPlayer);
    }

    lblDealerHand.Text = dealerHand.HandValue.ToString();
    lblPlayerHand.Text = playerHand.HandValue.ToString();
    lblWinner.Text = String.Format("\t{0}",
        winner.Equals(Winner.Player) ? "Player wins!" :
        winner.Equals(Winner.Dealer) ? "Dealer wins!" :
        "It's a draw");
    lblWinner.BackColor = winner.Equals(Winner.Player) ?
        Color.LightGreen : Color.LightPink;
}
```

The button's Click event

Displayed below is the complete code for the **btnDeal_Click** event.

```
private void btnDeal_Click(object sender, EventArgs e)
{
    Initialize();
    ShuffleDeck();
    DealCards();
    EvaluateHand(ref playerHand);
    EvaluateHand(ref dealerHand);
    var winner = CompareHands();
    RevealCards(winner);
}
```

9. Classes

Introduction

Classes are a central part of object-oriented programming; a class is a construct that lets you create custom reference types that are created on the *Heap*. Classes let you encapsulate the behaviors and characteristics of logical entities. A class is like a blueprint for a type; you define the class once and can create as many object instances from it as needed; it's reusable. A class is also extendable, meaning that you can add and change the class without breaking earlier implementations; this is possible using inheritance or changing the class directly.

A **class** is more versatile than a **struct** which is created on the stack as a value type meant to be small and fast. There are things you can do with a class which is impossible with a **struct** one of those things is inheritance. One way to view the difference between the two is that a **struct** is used to create value types that can be used in classes to define a *characteristic* just like a regular value type such as an **int** or a **double** variable or property would do.

The *characteristics* and *behaviors* are defined by variables (fields), properties, methods, and events.

Use the **class** keyword to create a class; best practice is to create one **class** per .cs file even though it is possible to add more than one, the exception to the rule is if you nest the classes. Following this best practice makes it easier to separate concerns and follow the application flow.

Adding a class

To keep the project structured you should consider to create a folder called **Classes** or something pertinent to what the classes you add are used for and create the classes in that folder.

To create a folder you right click on the project or folder you want to crate it in and select **Add-New Folder** and give it a name. To add a class to the folder you right click on the folder, select **Add-Class**, give it a name and click on the **Add** button.

Important: *Best practices is to use Pascal casing when naming classes using an uppercase character for each new word in the name including the first character of the name.*

Access modifiers

You can use access modifiers when declaring a **class** to specify where it should be accessible. The access modifiers come into play when you reference assemblies from the application assembly (project); if you reference a class library from your application then **public** classes will be accessible through the reference in the application while **internal** and **private** will not be accessible.

A **class** declared as **internal** will only be accessible within the assembly (project) it was created; applications referencing the class library will not even know they exist. This is the default setting when omitting the access modifier.

You can only declare a **class** as **private** if you create it inside another class (nesting it) which is common practice in a **class** factory where you need the factory to handle the created instances and not expose them directly to the rest of the application.

```
class MyClass1 // internal (access modifier omitted)
{
}

internal class MyClass2
{
}

public class MyClass3
{
}

class MyClass4 // internal (access modifier omitted)
{
    private class MyNestedClass1
    {
    }

    internal class MyNestedClass2
    {
    }
```

```
}
```

Adding members

To define the *characteristics* of a **class** you add variables (fields) and properties; to define the *behaviors* you add methods and events. The variables and properties declared in a **class** can be value types such as **int** and **double**, they can also be defined by a **struct** or a reference type using a **class**.

A *behavior* could be a method creating a new order or adding a new order row to an order rows collection; another *behavior* could be an event that is raised when a new order row has been added.

You add members to a **class** the same way you do in a **struct**. One difference is that properties don't have to be assigned values when using a constructor and they don't have to have **private** backing variables if you create them using only the **get** and **set** keywords without curly braces.

```
class ClassWithMembers
{
    double _result;
    int _writeOnlyValue;

    public int Value { get; set; }
    public double Result { get { return _result; } set{ _result = value; } }
    public int ReadOnlyValue { get { return Value * 10; } }
    public int WriteOnlyValue { set { _writeOnlyValue = value; } }

    public double SqureRoot(double value)
    {
        if (value < 0)
            throw new ApplicationException("Value must be greater than 0.");
        else
            return Math.Sqrt(value);
    }
}
```

Instantiating classes

To use a **class**, you create *instances* of it; *instances* are also known as *objects*. When you create an instance of a **class**, two things happen; when the variable is declared using the **class** type a reference pointer is created and stored using the variable name and when the **new** keyword is executed an object is created and memory is allocated for it on the *Heap*.

If you like you can skip declaring a variable's data type and let the compiler deduce the type at compile time; you do this by using the **var** keyword when declaring the variable. Using the **var** keyword does not change how the application executes; it is only a shortcut to writing the type name once.

The following code sample shows how you can create an instance of a **class** by using the **class** type or the **var** keyword.

```
private void button1_Click(object sender, EventArgs e)
{
    var cls = new ClassWithMembers();
    // or
    ClassWithMembers cls = new ClassWithMembers();
}
```

When an object has been created, you can use its properties to assign values creating its characteristics. You can also call its methods to achieve certain tasks, and subscribe to its events. When using the dot notation (typing a period after an object name) when writing the code IntelliSense will display a list of all available members for that object.

Constructor

A constructor is a special method that is called when an instance of a **class** is created. You can pass in parameters to the constructor with initial values that you use to set characteristics of the instance using its properties or variables. If no constructor is added to the code, a default constructor will be added by the compiler when the solution is compiled.

It is possible to provide multiple constructors with different parameter lists; this is useful when you want the developer to be able to instantiate instances with different initial values, maybe a sub set of values compared with the constructor taking the most parameters.

In an order **class**, you could make three implementations of the constructor; one empty, one

taking the description and one taking a description and an order id as parameters instantiating the object in different ways.

You can use the **default** method to assign the default value of a given data type to a variable
instead of hard coding the value.

```csharp
public class Order
{
    public int OrderId { get; set; }
    public string Description { get; set; }

    // Instantiate with :
    // OrderRow orderRow = new OrderRow();
    public Order()
    {
        OrderId = 0;
        Description = String.Empty;
    }

    // Instantiate with :
    // OrderRow orderRow = new OrderRow("Row description");
    public Order(string description)
    {
        OrderId = default(int);
        Description = description;
    }

    // Instantiate with :
    // OrderRow orderRow = new OrderRow(1001, "Row description");
    public Order(int orderId, string description)
    {
        OrderId = orderId;
        Description = description;
    }
}
```

Calling an overloaded constructor
To make the previous code more compact and reuse already declared constructors you can
have them call one another using the **this** keyword after the constructor declaration.

In the following example the first constructor calls the second and the second the third constructor when instances are created.

```
public class Order1
{
    public int OrderId { get; set; }
    public string Description { get; set; }

    // Calls the constructor:
    // Order1(string description)
    public Order() : this(String.Empty)  { }

    // Calls the constructor:
    // Order1(int orderId, string description)
    public Order(string description)
        : this(default(int), description) { }

    // Assigns the passed in values to the properties
    public Order(int orderId, string description)
    {
        OrderId = orderId;
        Description = description;
    }
}
```

When an instance is created using the first constructor it calls the second constructor with an empty string and it in turn calls the third constructor with the empty string from the first constructor and pass along the **default** value for the **int** data type.

```
var cls = new Order();
```

When an instance is created using the second constructor the passed in description will be sent to the third constructor along with the **default** value for the **int** data type.

```
var cls = new Order("Some description");
```

When an instance is created using the third constructor both the passed in parameters will be assigned to the properties in the object.

```
var cls = new Order(101, "The description");
```

Exercise: Customer data

In this exercise you will create a **class** called **Customer** and use it to list customers in a combo box and display the selected customer's data in textboxes. It should also be possible to add, update and remove customer information in the **List** collection containing the customers.

The **Customer class** should have four properties and two constructors. The **Id** property should be declared with the **Guid** data type and the **FirstName**, **LastName** and **Name** properties should be declared with the **string** data type. The **Name** property should be read only and return the concatenated value of the **FirstName** and **LastName** properties.

The first constructor should take three parameters for the three assignable properties and assign the passed in values to the appropriate properties in the object. The second constructor should take two parameters for the first name and last name and call the first constructor using the **this** keyword.

Instead of having to iterate over the **customers** collection and write a bunch of add, update and delete code you can use a **BindingList** collection which is specialized at keeping data in form controls in sync when changes are made to the data.

When displaying the collection content in a combo box or list box you simply assign the collection to the **DataSource** property and use the **DataMember** property to specify the property name in the collection's class whose value you want to display in the control.

If you want to bind textboxes to the collection as well to reflect data from the object selected in the combo box you add data binding using the **DataBinding.Add** method on the textbox. The textboxes will then update the data for the selected item in the collection when the text is changed. This might not be the behavior you want and to override that setting you have to pass in two extra parameters where the first can be set to **false** and the second to **DataSourceUpdateMode.Never** which will stop any automatic updates to the collection.

To update data form an item in the collection you have to call the **ResetBindings** method on the collection; you don't have to call this method when adding or removing items.

Don't forget to check that the textboxes contain text when adding or updating data and that there is at least one customer in the collection when trying to update or remove a customer.

The GUI

1. Add three labels with the text "Customers", "First Name" and "Last Name".
2. Add a combo box called **cboCustomers** below the "Customers" label.
3. Add two textboxes called **txtFirstName** and **txtLastName** to display the first name and last name of the customer selected in the combo box.
4. Add three buttons called **btnRemove**, **btnUpdate** and **btnAdd**.

The Customer class

1. Add a new folder to the project by right clicking on the project name and selecting **Add-New Folder**. Name the folder **Classes**.
2. Add a class to the folder by right clicking on the folder and selecting **Add-Class**.
3. Name the class **Customer** and click the **Add** button.
   ```
   class Customer
   {
   }
   ```
4. Add a **Guid** property called **Id**.
   ```
   public Guid Id { get; set; }
   ```
5. Add a **string** property called **FirstName**.
6. Add a **string** property called **LastName**.
7. Add a **string** property called **Name** and remove the **set** keyword.
8. Add a block to the get keyword using curly braces.
   ```
   public string Name { get { } }
   ```
9. Return the concatenated **string** of the **LastName** and **FirstName** properties from the **Name** property.
   ```
   public string Name { get { return String.Format("{0} {1}", LastName, FirstName); } }
   ```

10. Add a constructor which takes three parameters for the three assignable properties in the object and assign their values to the appropriate properties.

```
public Customer(Guid id, string firstName, string lastName)
{
    Id = id;
    FirstName = firstName;
    LastName = lastName;
}
```

11. Add a second constructor taking the first name and last name as parameters and calls the first constructor with the passed in values and a new **Guid** for the id.

```
public Customer(string firstName, string lastName)
: this(Guid.NewGuid(), firstName, lastName)
{
}
```

The complete code for the **Customer** class look like this:

```
class Customer
{
    public Guid Id { get; set; }
    public string FirstName { get; set; }
    public string LastName { get; set; }
    public string Name
    {
        get
        {
            return String.Format("{0} {1}", LastName, FirstName);
        }
    }

    public Customer(string firstName, string lastName)
        : this(Guid.NewGuid(), firstName, lastName)
    {
    }

    public Customer(Guid id, string firstName, string lastName)
    {
        Id = id;
        FirstName = firstName;
        LastName = lastName;
    }
}
```

Binding the data source

1. Add a **BindingList<Customer>** collection called **customers** and instantiate it at the beginning of the form.

   ```
   BindingList<Customer> customers = new BindingList<Customer>();
   ```

2. Locate the form's **Load** event.

3. Assign the **customers** collection to the **DataSource** property of the combo box.

4. Assign the **Name** property to the combo box's **DisplayMember** property.

5. Use the **Add** method of the *txtFirstName*'s **DataBindings** property to bind the **Text** property of the textbox to the **FirstName** property of the objects in the **customers** collection. Disable the automatic updates.

   ```
   txtFirstName.DataBindings.Add("Text", customers, "FirstName",
       false, DataSourceUpdateMode.Never);
   ```

The complete form code so far:

```
public partial class Form1 : Form
{
    BindingList<Customer> customers = new BindingList<Customer>();

    public Form1()
    {
            InitializeComponent();
    }

    private void Form1_Load(object sender, EventArgs e)
    {
        // Binding the combo box to the data source
        cboCustomers.DataSource = customers;
        cboCustomers.DisplayMember = "Name";

        // Binding textboxes to data source
        // Add(Property in the control, data source,
        // Property in the data source, format text, update mode)
        txtFirstName.DataBindings.Add("Text", customers,
            "FirstName", false, DataSourceUpdateMode.Never);
        txtLastName.DataBindings.Add("Text", customers,
            "LastName", false, DataSourceUpdateMode.Never);
    }
}
```

The Add button

1. Add the **btnAdd_Click** event.
2. Exit the event if the textboxes are empty to avoid adding customers without a first- or last name.
   ```
   if (txtFirstName.Text.Equals(String.Empty) ||
   txtLastName.Text.Equals(String.Empty)) return;
   ```
3. Create a new **Customer** instance called **customer** using the values from the textboxes.
   ```
   var customer = new Customer(txtFirstName.Text, txtLastName.Text);
   ```
4. Add the customer to the **customers** collection using the **Add** method of the collection.
   ```
   customers.Add(customer);
   ```
5. Display the added customer in the combo box by assigning its index to the **SelectedIndex** property of the combo box.
   ```
   cboCustomers.SelectedIndex = cboCustomers.Items.Count - 1;
   ```

The complete code for the **btnAdd_Click** event:

```
private void btnAdd_Click(object sender, EventArgs e)
{
    if (txtFirstName.Text.Equals(String.Empty) ||
        txtLastName.Text.Equals(String.Empty)) return;

    var customer = new Customer(txtFirstName.Text, txtLastName.Text);
    customers.Add(customer);
    cboCustomers.SelectedIndex = cboCustomers.Items.Count - 1;
}
```

The Update button

1. Add the **btnUpdate_Click** event.
2. Exit the event if the combo box is empty, you can achieve this by checking if the **SelectedIndex** is **-1**.
   ```
   if (cboCustomers.SelectedIndex.Equals(-1)) return;
   ```
3. Exit the event if the textboxes are empty to avoid saving customers without a first- or last name.
4. Fetch the customer in the **customers** collection corresponding to the **SelectedIndex** value of the combo box.

```
    var customer = customers[cboCustomers.SelectedIndex];
```

5. Change the **FirstName** and **LastName** properties of the fetched customer to the values in the textboxes.
```
customer.FirstName = txtFirstName.Text;
```

6. To reflect the changes made to the collection in the combo box you have to call the **ResetBindings** method on the collection variable to reset the bindings.
```
customers.ResetBindings();
```

The complete code for the **btnUpdate_Click** event:

```
private void btnUpdate_Click(object sender, EventArgs e)
{
    if (cboCustomers.SelectedIndex.Equals(-1)) return;

    if (txtFirstName.Text.Equals(String.Empty) ||
        txtLastName.Text.Equals(String.Empty)) return;

    var customer = customers[cboCustomers.SelectedIndex];
    customer.FirstName = txtFirstName.Text;
    customer.LastName = txtLastName.Text;
    customers.ResetBindings();
}
```

The Remove button
1. Add the **btnRemove_Click** event.
2. Only try to remove the customer if the index is greater than or equal to **0**. Use the **RemoveAt** method of the collection variable to remove the customer at the index corresponding to the **SelectedIndex** property of the combo box.
```
if (cboCustomers.SelectedIndex >= 0)
    customers.RemoveAt(cboCustomers.SelectedIndex);
```
3. Run the application and try to add, update and remove customers.
4. Stop the application.

The complete code for the **btnRemove_Click** event:

```
private void btnRemove_Click(object sender, EventArgs e)
{
    if (cboCustomers.SelectedIndex > 0)
        customers.RemoveAt(cboCustomers.SelectedIndex);
}
```

Class libraries

It is very common to separate out certain functionality and create reusable class libraries especially in large- and enterprise solutions. A class library is essentially a separate project containing classes which are compiled to an assembly (.dll) for a specific purpose; it can be a data access layer, a business layer with business centric logic or a set of helper classes. A class library can be used for any type of scenario that has a specific defined purpose.

The class library can be created as a separate assembly in its own solution or be part of an already existing solution. In both cases you have to add a reference to the assembly or project containing the classes to gain access to them and to create instances from them.

Create a class library

You create a class library in an existing solution by adding a new **Class Library** project to it. In the project you can add as many classes as needed separating them into namespaces and folders.

1. Right click on the solution name in the Solution Explorer and select **Add-New Project**.
2. Select **Class Library** in the dialog.
3. Give the class library a name and click the **OK** button.
4. Add classes to the project in the same way you have done before in an application.

Reference a class library

To gain access to the classes in the class library you have to add a reference to the class library project from the application and add the appropriate **using** statement specifying the namespace path to where the classes reside; you can add the **using** statement by resolving it, right click on the name of the **class** you have added to the code and select **Resolve-using xyz**.

1. Right click on the **References** folder in the application (the main project) and select **Add Reference**.
2. Locate the assembly you want to bring in to the application and use classes form. If the assembly is in the same solution the fastest way to locate it is to select **Solution** in the left dialog menu.
3. Check the checkbox to the left of the assembly name and click the **OK** button.

C# For Beginners

4. Add a **using** statement to where the class is located by hand or write the name of the **class** in your code, right click on it and select **Resolve-using *xyz*** where *xyz* is the namespace path to the **class**.

Mini Use Case: Create a class library

In this exercise you will create a simple order application using a class library to handle the data.

The orders and their corresponding order rows are stored in **private List** collections which will be converted into **BindingList** collections in the application and bound to form controls. The **orders** collection will hold instances of the **Order** class containing an **int** property called **OrderId** and a **string** property called **Description**. The **orderRows** collection will hold instances of the **OrderRow** class containing two **int** properties called **OrderRowId** and **OrderId**, a **string** property called **Product** and a **null-able double** property called **Price**.

The **orders** and **orderRows** collections are created in the simple data layer class you will add called **Data**, this is the class you will use when creating the orders and order rows from the classes. The constructors of the **Order** and **OrderRow** classes will be declared as **internal** to force the creation of objects to take place in the class library project and more specifically in the **Data** class. The **internal** keyword limits the member to be used only within the project it is created in; since the class library is in a separate assembly to the application the instances can only be created in the class library but because the class itself is declared as **public** it can still be used from other assemblies such as the application.

You will have to create methods in the **Data** class for adding, updating and removing **Order** and **OrderRow** instances from the collections; these methods will then be called from the application when an action is taken by the user. You will have to check that the **orders** collection doesn't contain an order with the description the user tries to add when clicking on the **Add Order** button.

Use two **BindingList** collections to bind the data fetched from the class library to the form controls. Use a combo box to display the orders and a data grid view to display the order rows for the selected order. A textbox should be bound to the **orders** collection and display the description of the selected order; the textbox should be used when updating the order description and when adding a new order. To fetch and manipulate the data in the class library you need to create an instance of the **Data** class.

When an order row is added by clicking on the **Add Order Row** button a separate form should be opened where the product information is entered and sent back to the main form when the order row form is closed. If the **OK** button has been clicked in the order row form the order will be added to the orders collection. You can add a new form to the project by right clicking on the project name in the Solution Explorer and select **Add-Windows Form**; name the form *frmAddOrderRow*. When the form has been created you can create a variable using the form's name as the data type when creating an instance of the form. To pass data to and from the form you can alter its constructor sending in an instance of the **OrderRow** class; because it is created from a **class** the object will reside on the *Heap* and have a reference pointer on the stack that is sent to the order row form's constructor effectively changing the same object you sent into it from the main form.

Make sure that the order row form is displayed over the main form when it is opened by assigning **Manual** to its **StartPoisition** property and use its **Location** property to position it.

```
// Create the form instance
var frm = new frmOrderRow(orderRow);

// Position the form
frm.StartPosition = FormStartPosition.Manual;
var location = this.Location;
location.Offset(40, 40);
frm.Location = location;

// Open the form
DialogResult result = frm.ShowDialog();
```

You can check which of the form's buttons was clicked by using the **DialogResult enum** if you assign the appropriate value to the form's **DialogResult** property in the button events of the order row form.

```
// Check the button result
if (result.Equals(DialogResult.Cancel)) return;
```

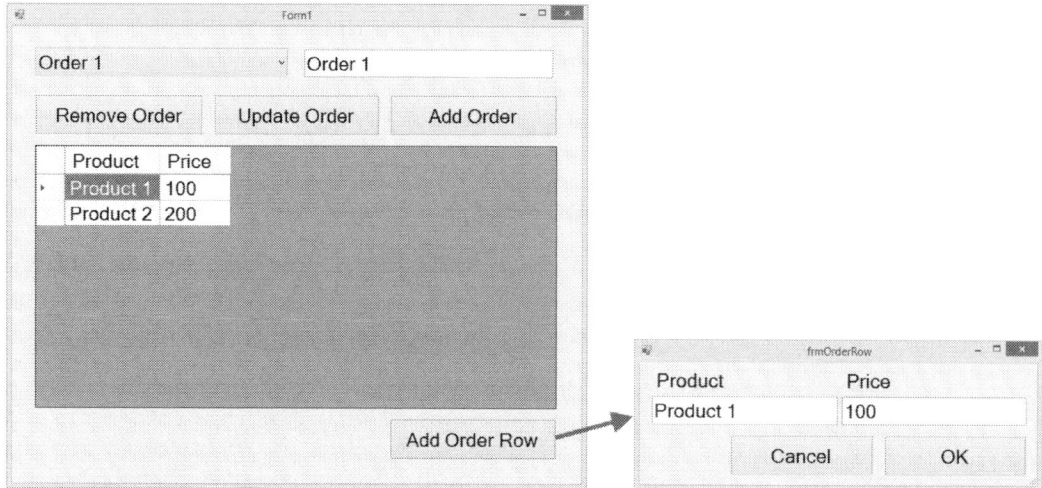

Crating the projects

1. Create a **Windows Forms Application** called **Orders**.

2. Right click on the solution name, not the project name, in the Solution Explorer and select **Add-New Project**.

3. Select **Class Library** in the project list, do <u>not</u> select **Class Library (Portable)**.

4. Name the project **Data Layer** and click on the **OK** button.

5. The new **Data Layer** project contains a class called **Class1.cs** that you can rename and reuse as the **Order** class. Right click on the class name in the Solution Explorer and select **Rename**. Name the class **Order** and press **Enter**; a dialog will ask if you want to rename the **class** as well, click the **Yes** button.

6. You add a reference to the class library in the Windows Forms Application by right clicking on the **References** folder and select **Add Reference**.

7. Click on the **Solution** option in the left menu bar to find the class library.

8. Check the checkbox to the left of the **Data Layer** project name and click the **OK** button.

The Order class

The **Order** class define what information the order objects will hold.

1. Locate the **Order** class in the **Data Layer** class library and double click on it to open it.

2. By default classes are **internal** in a class library so you need to change the class' access modifier to **public**.
   ```
   public class Order
   {
   }
   ```

3. Add an **int** property called **OrderId** which later will contain a unique id.
   ```
   public int OrderId { get; set; }
   ```

4. Add a **string** property called **Description** which later will contain a short order description.

5. Add an **internal** constructor that takes an order id and a description and stores them using the two previously added properties.
   ```
   internal Order(int orderId, string description) { }
   ```

6. Save the solution.

The complete **Order** class code look like this:

```
public class Order
{
    public int OrderId { get; set; }
    public string Description { get; set; }

    internal Order(int orderId, string description)
    {
        OrderId = orderId;
        Description = description;
    }
}
```

The OrderRow class

The **OrderRow** class define what information the order row objects will hold.

1. Right click on the **Data Layer** class library in the Solution Explorer and select **Add-Class**.
2. Name the class **OrderRow** and click the **Add** button.
3. By default classes are **internal** in a class library so you need to change the **class'** access modifier to **public**.
    ```
    public class OrderRow
    {
    }
    ```
4. Add two **int** properties called **OrderRowId** and **OrderId**, the latter id will be foreign key to the order collection keeping track of which order row belong with what order.
5. Add a **string** property called **Product** that will hold the product name.
6. Add a **null**-able **double** property called **Price**. You make a property or variable **null**-able by adding a question mark (?) at the end of the data type name.
    ```
    public double? Price { get; set; }
    ```
7. Add an **internal** constructor to the **class** with parameters for all the properties.

The complete **OrderRow** class code look like this:

```
public class OrderRow
{
    public int OrderRowId { get; set; }
    public int OrderId { get; set; }
    public string Product { get; set; }
    public double? Price { get; set; }

    internal OrderRow(int orderId, int orderRowId, string product,
    double? price)
    {
        OrderId = orderId;
        OrderRowId = orderRowId;
        Product = product;
        Price = price;
    }
}
```

Creating the Data class

The sole purpose of the **Data** class is to work as a layer between the data source (the **orders** and **orderRows** collections) and the application to separate concerns; the forms should not contain any code for manipulating data directly they should use an object of the **Data** class and call its methods. This mean that the Data class need methods that add, update and remove data from the collections; in a real world scenario the collections would most likely be replaced with a database and Entity Framework or ADO.NET.

You will add methods to the **Data** class as you add functionality to the forms, for now you will add the collections and a method called **AddOrder** that will add an order and a method called **GetOrders** that return a **List<Order>**.

Adding the Data class

1. Right click on the **Data Layer** class library in the Solution Explorer and select **Add-Class**.
2. Name the class **Data** and click the **Add** button.
3. Classes are **internal** by default so you need to change the **class**' access modifier to **public**.
   ```
   public class Data
   {
   }
   ```
4. Add a **region** called **Variables**.
5. Add a **List<Order>** collection called **orders** to the **region**.
   ```
   List<Order> orders = new List<Order>();
   ```
6. Add a **List<OrderRow>** collection called **orderRows** to the **region**.

Adding the AddOrder method

1. Add a **region** called **Order Methods**.
2. Add a method called **AddOrder** that return an **Order** object and takes a string parameter called description in the **Order Methods region**.
   ```
   public Order AddOrder(string description)
   {
   }
   ```
3. Add exception handling using **try/catch**-blocks in the method where the **catch**-block throws a new **ApplicationException** for any exception that occurs with the message

"Could not add the order" and the actual exception as its inner exception. By throwing the exception this way it will be propagated as that specific exception to the client for handling.

```
try
{
}
catch(Exception ex)
{
    throw new ApplicationException("Could not add the order", ex);
}
```

4. The first thing you need to do in the **try**-block is to generate a new order id, in this case it will be the highest currently existing order id plus one in a real world scenario it would be automatically generated from the database table or added as a new **Guid**.

```
int newId = orders.Count.Equals(0) ? 1 : orders.Max(o => o.OrderId) + 1;
```

5. Next you have to create a new instance of the **Order class** passing in the **newId** and the **description** as values to its constructor.

```
var order = new Order(newId, description);
```

6. Add the order to the **orders** collection using its **Add** method.
7. Return the order from the method with a **return** statement.

Adding the GetOrders method

1. Add a parameter-less method called **GetOrders** that return a **List<Order>** collection.
2. Return the **orders** collection with a **return** statement.

The **Data** class code look like this so far:

```
public class Data
{
    #region Variables
    List<Order> orders = new List<Order>();
    List<OrderRow> orderRows = new List<OrderRow>();
    #endregion
```

```
#region Order Methods
public Order AddOrder(string description)
{
    try
    {
        int newId = orders.Count.Equals(0) ? 1 :
          orders.Max(o => o.OrderId) + 1;

        var order = new Order(newId, description);
        orders.Add(order);
        return order;
    }
    catch(Exception ex)
    {
        throw new ApplicationException("Could not add the order", ex);
    }
}

public List<Order> GetOrders()
{
    return orders;
}
```

The GUI (the main form)

1. Open the design area of the main form.
2. Add a combo box called **cboOrders** that will list all available orders.
3. Add a textbox called **txtDescription** that will display the selected order's description.
4. Add three buttons called **btnRemoveOrder**, **btnUpdateOrder** and **btnAddOrder**.
5. Add a data grid view control called **dgvOrderRows**.
6. Add a button called **btnAddOrderRow**.

The GUI (the add order row form)

1. Add a new form to the **Orders** project by right clicking on the project name in the Solution Explorer and select **Add-Windows Form**.
2. Name the form **frmAddOrderRow** and click the **Add** button.
3. Add two labels with the text "Product" and "Price".
4. Add two textboxes called **txtProduct** and **txtPrice**.
5. Add two buttons called **btnOK** and **btnCancel**.

Binding the controls in the main form

1. Open the code-behind for the main form.
2. Add a **region** called **Variables** to the beginning of the form.
3. Add a variable called **data** in the **region** that you assign an instance of the **Data** class from the class library. You will have to bring in the correct namespace to gain access to the class.

   ```
   Data data = new Data();
   ```

4. Add two **BindingList** collections called **orders** and **orderRows** which will be used to bind the controls to the current data.

   ```
   BindingList<Order> orders;
   BindingList<OrderRow> orderRows;
   ```

5. Add **try/catch**-blocks to the **Form_Load** event with **catch**-blocks for **Application-Exception** and **Exception**. Add a message box with the text from the exception's **Message** property to the **catch**-block for the **ApplicationException**; this exception will be triggered if an order can't be added in the **AddOrder** method of class library and propagated here.

6. Call the **AddOrder** method on the data instance variable in the **try**-block to add a couple of orders.

   ```
   data.AddOrder("Order 1");
   data.AddOrder("Order 2");
   ```

7. Add the orders from the **orders List** collection in the class library to the **orders BindingList** in the form you link them by calling the **GetOrders** method on the **data** instance variable.

   ```
   orders = new BindingList<Order>(data.GetOrders());
   ```

8. Bind the **BindingList orders** collection in the form to the combo box's **DataSource** property.

9. Assign the name of the property in the **Order** class that you wish to display in the combo box to its **DisplayName** property as a string.

10. Use the **DataBindings.Add** method to bind the **Text** property of the *txtDescription* textbox to the **Description** property of **orders** collection objects.

    ```
    txtDescription.DataBindings.Add("Text", orders, "Description", false,
    DataSourceUpdateMode.Never);
    ```

11. Hide the two first columns in the data grid view to hide the id values of the **Order-Row** objects that will be displayed in the grid.

```
dgvOrderRows.Columns[0].Visible = false;
dgvOrderRows.Columns[1].Visible = false;
```

12. Run the application.

13. The two orders should be displayed in the combo box and the selected order's description should be visible in the textbox.

14. Select the other order and make sure that the text in the textbox changes.

15. Close the application.

The main form code so far:

```
public partial class Form1 : Form
{
    #region Variables
    Data data = new Data();
    BindingList<Order> orders;
    BindingList<OrderRow> orderRows;
    #endregion

    #region Constructor and Form_Load
    public Form1()
    {
        InitializeComponent();
    }

    private void Form1_Load(object sender, EventArgs e)
    {
        try
        {
            data.AddOrder("Order 1");
            data.AddOrder("Order 2");

            orders = new BindingList<Order>(data.GetOrders());

            cboOrders.DataSource = orders;
            cboOrders.DisplayMember = "Description";

            txtDescription.DataBindings.Add(
                "Text", orders, "Description",
                false, DataSourceUpdateMode.Never);
```

```
                dgvOrderRows.Columns[0].Visible = false;
                dgvOrderRows.Columns[1].Visible = false;
            }
        catch (ApplicationException ex)
        {
            MessageBox.Show(ex.Message);
        }
        catch (Exception ex)
        { }
    }
    #endregion
}
```

The ContainsOrder method

The purpose of this method is to make sure that the **orders** collection doesn't already contain an order with the description provided in the textbox. The method will be called when the **Add Order** button is clicked and return **true** or **false** depending on if an order with the provided description already exist; you can use the **Count** method and Lambda expression to check if the **description** exist.

1. Open the **Data** class in the class library.
2. Add a **bool** method called **ContainsOrder** to the **Order Methods region** which take one **string** parameter called **description**.
3. Return the result from checking if the orders collection contain an order with the description passed in to the method. You can use the **Count** method and Lambda expression to check if the **description** exist; if the result is greater than zero then an order with that description already exist.
   ```
   return orders.Count(o => o.Description.Equals(description)) > 0;
   ```

The complete code for the **ContainsOrder** method:

```
public bool ContainsOrder(string description)
{
    return orders.Count(o => o.Description.Equals(description)) > 0;
}
```

The btnAddOrder_Click event

The purpose of this button is to add a new order to the orders collection using the text in the textbox when calling the **AddOrder** method in the **Data** class.

1. Add the **Click** event for the **btnAddOrder** button.

2. Since the **AddOrder** method can throw an **ApplicationException** it must be handled in the **Click** event to keep the application from crashing if an exception occur. Add **try/catch**-blocks to the **Click** event and display a message box with the exception message if the **ApplicationException** is thrown from the **AddOrder** method.

```
try
{
}
catch (ApplicationException ex)
{
    MessageBox.Show(ex.Message);
}
catch (Exception ex)
{ }
```

3. Display the message "Description is empty!" and exit the event if the textbox is empty.

4. Display the message "Description already exist!" and exit the event if an order with the description entered in the textbox already exist. You can perform the check by calling the **ContainsOrder** in the **Data** class.

```
if (data.ContainsOrder(txtDescription.Text))
{
}
```

5. Add a new order after the last **if**-block by calling the **AddOrder** method in the **Data** class and save the returned order in a variable called **order**.

```
var order = data.AddOrder(txtDescription.Text);
```

6. Reset the bindings to the orders collection by calling its **ResetBindings** method.

```
orders.ResetBindings();
```

7. Since a new item automatically will be added to the combo box when a new order has been added and the bindings have been reset you might want to select that order in the combo box. To achieve this you assign the order returned from the **AddOrder** method to the **SelectedItem** property of the combo box.

```
        cboOrders.SelectedItem = order;
```

8. Run the application and enter a description in the textbox.

9. Click the **Add Order** button.

10. The order should be added to the orders collection and be displayed in the combo box.

11. Try to add an order with an already existing description; the message box should pop up.

12. Close the application.

The complete code for the **btnAddOrder_Click** event:

```csharp
private void btnAddOrder_Click(object sender, EventArgs e)
{
    try
    {
        if (txtDescription.TextLength.Equals(0))
        {
            MessageBox.Show("Description is empty!");
            return;
        }

        if (data.ContainsOrder(txtDescription.Text))
        {
            MessageBox.Show("Description already exist!");
            return;
        }

        var order = data.AddOrder(txtDescription.Text);
        orders.ResetBindings();
        cboOrders.SelectedItem = order;
    }
    catch (ApplicationException ex)
    {
        MessageBox.Show(ex.Message);
    }
    catch (Exception ex)
    { }
}
```

The UpdateOrder method

The purpose of this method in the **Data** class is to update an existing order **description** with the text in the textbox.

1. Add a **bool** method called **UpdateOrder** which take two parameters called **orderId** of type **int** and **description** of type **string** to the **Order Methods region** of the **Data** class.

2. Add a **try/catch**-block to the method where the **catch**-block don't have a parameter and return **false** and the **try**-block return **true** as its last statement.

```
try
{
    // Other code goes here
    return true;
}
catch
{
    return false;
}
```

3. Use LINQ and Lambda to fetch the order matching the passed in order id from the **orders** collection and store it in a variable called **order**.

```
var order = orders.FirstOrDefault(o => o.OrderId.Equals(orderId));
```

4. Assign the passed in description to the **order** variable's **Description** property to change it.

The complete code for the **UpdateOrder** method:

```
public bool UpdateOrder(int orderId, string description)
{
    try
    {
        var order = orders.FirstOrDefault(o => o.OrderId.Equals(orderId));
        order.Description = description;
        return true;
    }
    catch
    {
        return false;
    }
}
```

The btnUpdateOrder_Click event

1. Add the **Click** event for the ***btnUpdateOrder*** button.
2. Check that there is at least one order in the orders collection, exit the event if the collection is empty because then there is no order to update.
   ```
   if (orders.Count.Equals(0)) return;
   ```

3. Call the **UpdateOrder** method in the **Data** class and pass in the selected order id from the order selected in the combo box and the description from the textbox. Save the **return** value in a variable called **success**.
   ```
   var success =
   data.UpdateOrder(((Order)cboOrders.SelectedItem).OrderId,
   txtDescription.Text);
   ```

4. If the **success** variable is **true** then the order was updated and you should reset the bindings on the **orders** collection by calling its **ResetBindings** method.
5. Run the application and select an order in the combo box.
6. Change the description in the textbox and click the **Update Order** button.
7. Select another order in the combo box and then select the order you changed to make sure that the description is changed and that the change is reflected in the textbox
8. Close the application.

The complete code for the **btnUpdateOrder_Click** event:

```
private void btnUpdateOrder_Click(object sender, EventArgs e)
{
    if (orders.Count.Equals(0)) return;

    var success = data.UpdateOrder(
        ((Order)cboOrders.SelectedItem).OrderId,
        txtDescription.Text);

    if (success) orders.ResetBindings();
}
```

The RemoveOrder method

The purpose of this method in the **Data** class is to remove an existing order from the **orders** collection and all its associated order rows from the **orderRows** collection.

1. Add a **bool** method called **RemoveOrder** which take one parameter called **orderId** of type **int** to the **Order Methods region** of the **Data** class.
2. Add a **try/catch**-block to the method where the **catch**-block don't have a parameter and return **false** and the **try**-block return **true** as its last statement.
3. Use LINQ and Lambda to remove all the order rows matching the passed in order id from the **ordersRows** collection.
   ```
   orderRows.RemoveAll(or => or.OrderId.Equals(orderId));
   ```
4. Use LINQ and Lambda remove the order matching the passed in order id from the **orders** collection.

The complete code for the **RemoveOrder** method:

```
public bool RemoveOrder(int orderId)
{
    try
    {
        orderRows.RemoveAll(or => or.OrderId.Equals(orderId));
        orders.RemoveAll(o => o.OrderId.Equals(orderId));
        return true;
    }
    catch
    {
        return false;
    }
}
```

The GetOrderRows method

The purpose of this method in the **Data** class is to fetch all order rows from the **orderRows** collection associated with the selected order in the **orders** collection.

1. Add a **region** called **Order Row Methods** to the **Data** class.
2. Add a **List<OrderRow>** method called **GetOrderRows** to the **Order Row Methods region** which take one parameter called **orderId** of type **int**.

3. Use LINQ and Lambda fetch all order rows from the **orderRows** collection matching the passed in order id.

```
return orderRows.Where(or => or.OrderId.Equals(orderId)).ToList();
```

The complete code for the **GetOrderRows** method:

```
public List<OrderRow> GetOrderRows(int orderId)
{
    return orderRows.Where(or => or.OrderId.Equals(orderId)).ToList();
}
```

The UpdateOrderRowBinding method in the main form

The purpose of this method is to update the data bindings between the **orderRows Binding-List** and the data grid view displaying the selected order's order rows.

1. Add a **region** called **Methods** to the main form.
2. Add a parameter-less **void** method called **UpdateOrderRowBindings** to the **region**.
3. The first thing the method has to do is to check that the combo box has a selected item because it is not possible to fetch an order id for an order that does not exist. If the **SelectedItem** property of the combo box is **null** then clear the rows in the data grid view before exiting the method.

```
if (cboOrders.SelectedItem == null)
{
    dgvOrderRows.Rows.Clear();
    return;
}
```

4. Fetch the order id from the order selected in the combo box and store it in an **int** variable called **orderId**.
5. Assign a new instance of the **BindingList<OrderRow>** collection initialized with the **GetOrderRows** method in the **Data** class to the **orderRows** variable.

```
orderRows = new BindingList<OrderRow>(data.GetOrderRows(orderId));
```

6. Assign the **orderRows** collection to the **DataSource** property of the data grid view.

The complete code for the **UpdateOrderRowBindings** method:

```
private void UpdateOrderRowBinding()
{
    if (cboOrders.SelectedItem == null)
    {
```

```
        dgvOrderRows.Rows.Clear();
        return;
    }

    var orderId = ((Order)cboOrders.SelectedItem).OrderId;
    orderRows = new BindingList<OrderRow>(data.GetOrderRows(orderId));
    dgvOrderRows.DataSource = orderRows;
}
```

The btnRemoveOrder_Click event

The purpose of this button is to remove an existing order and its associated order rows.

1. Check that the orders collection contain at least one order, exit the event if it don't.

2. Call the **RemoveOrder** method passing in the order id of the selected order. Save the **return** value from the method in a variable called **success**.

   ```
   var success =
   data.RemoveOrder(((Order)cboOrders.SelectedItem).OrderId);
   ```

3. If the **success** variable is **true** then the order was successfully removed and the bindings on the **orders** and **orderRows** collections have to be reset. You can call the **ResetBindings** method on the **orders** collection and the **UpdateOrderRowBindings** method you created earlier to reset the **orderRows** collection bindings.

4. Run the application and select an order in the combo box.

5. Click the **Remove Order** button.

6. Open the combo box to make sure that the order was successfully removed.

7. Close the application.

The complete code for the **btnRemoveOrder_Click** method:

```
private void btnRemoveOrder_Click(object sender, EventArgs e)
{
    if (orders.Count.Equals(0)) return;

    var success = data.RemoveOrder(((Order)cboOrders.SelectedItem).OrderId);
    if (success)
    {
        orders.ResetBindings();
        UpdateOrderRowBinding();
    }
}
```

The frmAddOrderRow form's constructor

The purpose of this form is to create a new order row that can be added to the **orderRows** collection when the form is closed by clicking on the **OK** button.

1. Open the code-behind of the *frmAddOrderRow* form.
2. Add **region** called **Properties** at the beginning of the form.
3. Add a **private OrderRow** property called **OrderRow** to the **region**.
4. Alter the constructor definition to take an **OrderRow** parameter called **orderRow**.
5. Assign the passed in **orderRow** to the **OrderRow** property.
6. Add a **region** around the constructor with the description **Constructor**.

The form code so far:

```
public partial class frmAddOrderRow : Form
{
    #region Properties
    private OrderRow OrderRow { get; set; }
    #endregion

    #region Constructor
    public frmAddOrderRow(OrderRow orderRow)
    {
        OrderRow = orderRow;

        InitializeComponent();
    }
    #endregion
}
```

The OK button in the frmAddOrderRow form

If the price textbox value can't be parsed to a **double** value when the user clicks this button a message box with the text "Price not valid!" should be displayed and the form should remain open.

If the parse succeeds then the values from the textboxes should be added to the appropriate properties of the **OrderRow** property containing a reference to the passed in **orderRow** object then assign **DialogResult.OK** to the form's **DialogResult** property to signal to the main form that the **OK** button was clicked and then the form should be closed.

1. Add the **Click** event for the **OK** button.

2. Try to parse the value in the *txtPrice* textbox to a **double** value and store the **return** value in a variable called **success** and the parsed value in a variable called **price**.

3. If the **success** variable is **true** then assign the value in the *txtProduct* textbox to the **Product** Property of the **OrderRow** object and the **price** variable to the **Price** property of the **OrderRow** object.

4. Assign **DialogResult.OK** to the form's **DialogResult** property.
   ```
   DialogResult = DialogResult.OK;
   ```

5. Close the form calling its **Close** method; use the **this** keyword to access the form.
   ```
   this.Close();
   ```

6. If the success variable is **false** then display a message box with the text "Price not valid!" and keep the form open.

The complete code for the **btnOK_Click** event:

```
private void btnOK_Click(object sender, EventArgs e)
{
    double price = 0d;
    var success = Double.TryParse(txtPrice.Text, out price);

    if (success) {
        OrderRow.Product = txtProduct.Text;
        OrderRow.Price = price;
        DialogResult = DialogResult.OK;
        this.Close();
    }
    else MessageBox.Show("Price not valid!");
}
```

The Cancel button in the frmAddOrderRow form

1. Add the **Click** event for the **Cancel** button.

2. Assign **DialogResult.Cancel** to the form's **DialogResult** property.

3. Close the form by calling its **Close** method.

The complete code for the **btnCancel_Click** event:

```
private void btnCancel_Click(object sender, EventArgs e)
{
    DialogResult = DialogResult.Cancel;
    this.Close();
}
```

The EmptyOrderRow method

The purpose of this method in the **Data** class is to return an instance of the **OrderRow** class with default values assigned. The instance will be used when a new order row is added to an existing order.

1. Add a parameter-less **OrderRow** method called **EmptyOrderRow**.
2. Return an **OrderRow** instance with the value **0** for both id's, an empty string for the description and **null** for the price.

The complete code for the **EmptyOrderRow** method:

```
public OrderRow EmptyOrderRow()
{
    return new OrderRow(0, 0, String.Empty, null);
}
```

The AddOrderRow method

The purpose of this method in the **Data** class is to add a new order row to an existing order. You will have to create a new order row id based on the highest existing order row id in the **orderRows** collection and assign it to the **OderRowId** property of the passed in **OrderRow** instance. When the order row has been added to the **orderRows** collection the order row instance should be returned with a **return** statement.

1. Add an **OrderRow** method called **AddOrderRow** which as an **OrderRow** parameter called **orderRow** to the **Order Row Methods region** of **Data** class
   ```
   public OrderRow AddOrderRow(OrderRow orderRow)
   {
   }
   ```
2. Add a **try/catch**-block where the catch throws an **ApplicationException** with the message "Could not add the order row" and the actual exception as its inner exception.
3. Calculate the order row id for the new order row and store the result in a variable called **newId** inside the **try**-block.
   ```
   int newId = orderRows.Count.Equals(0) ? 1 : orderRows.Max(o =>
   o.OrderRowId) + 1;
   ```
4. Assign the value of the **newId** variable to the **OrderRowId** property of the passed in **orderRow** parameter.

5. Add the **orderRow** parameter to the **orderRows** collection using its **Add** method.

6. Return the **orderRow** object from the method.

The complete code for the **AddOrderRow** method:

```
public OrderRow AddOrderRow(OrderRow orderRow)
{
    try
    {
        int newId = orderRows.Count.Equals(0) ? 1 :
            orderRows.Max(o => o.OrderRowId) + 1;

        orderRow.OrderRowId = newId;
        orderRows.Add(orderRow);
        return orderRow;
    }
    catch (Exception ex)
    {
        throw new ApplicationException("Could not add the order row", ex);
    }
}
```

The ShowAddOrderRowForm method in the main form

The purpose of this method is to display the **Add Order Row** form and return the result. You can display the form as modal form using the **ShowDialog** method on the form instance variable; a modal form acts like a dialog which has to be closed to be able to use the main form that opened it.

1. Add a **DialogResult** method called **ShowAddOrderRowForm** that takes an **OrderRow** parameter called **orderRow** to the code-behind of the main form.

2. Create an instance of the **frmAddOrderRow** and store it in a variable called **frm**.
   ```
   var frm = new frmAddOrderRow(orderRow);
   ```

3. To be able to position the form 40px from the top and left of the main form you have to assign **Manual** to the **StartPosition** property of the **frm** instance. Use the **Location** property to position the form.
   ```
   frm.StartPosition = FormStartPosition.Manual;
   ```

4. Display the form and save the result of the clicked button in a **DialogResult** variable that you **return** from the method.

```
DialogResult result = frm.ShowDialog();
return result;
```

The complete code for the **ShowAddOrderRowForm** method:

```
private DialogResult ShowAddOrderRowForm(OrderRow orderRow)
{
    // Create the form instance
    var frm = new frmAddOrderRow(orderRow);

    // Position the form
    frm.StartPosition = FormStartPosition.Manual;
    var location = this.Location;
    location.Offset(40, 40);
    frm.Location = location;

    // Open the form and return the result of the clicked button
    DialogResult result = frm.ShowDialog();
    return result;
}
```

The Add Order Row button in the main form

The purpose of this button is to add a new order row to an existing order. To achieve this you have to create an empty order row calling the **EmptyOrderRow** method you created earlier and pass the resulting object to the **ShowAddOrderRowForm** method you created earlier to display the **Add Order Row** form.

If the user fills out the form correctly and click the **OK** button the order id of the order selected in the combo box should be assigned to the order row object's **OrderId** property. Then the order row object should be passed o the **AddOrderRow** method in the **Data** class to add it to the **orderRows** collection.

The last thing you have to do is to add a call to the **UpdateOrderRowBinding** method you created a while back to update the binding between the **orderRows BindingList** collection and the data grid view to reflect the changes.

1. Add the **Click** event for the *btnAddOrderRow* button.
2. Create a new **OrderRow** instance by calling the **EmptyOrderRow** method in the **Data** class and store it in a variable called **orderRow**.
   ```
   var orderRow = data.EmptyOrderRow();
   ```

3. Pass the **orderRow** instance to the **ShowAddOrderRowForm** method to display the form and fill the object with values. Save the **return** value from the form in a variable called **result**.

```
var result = ShowAddOrderRowForm(orderRow);
```

4. Check if the **Cancel** button was clicked in the form and if so exit the event because then the order row shouldn't be added to the **orderRows** collection.

```
if (result.Equals(DialogResult.Cancel)) return;
```

5. Add the order id of the order selected in the combo box to the **OrderId** property of the **orderRow** object.

6. Add the **orderRow** instance to the **orderRows** collection in the **Data** class by calling the **AddOrderRow** method in the **Data** class.

7. Run the application and click the **Add Order Row** button to display the **Add Order Row** form.

8. Enter a product name in the **Product** textbox and an invalid price in the **Price** textbox.

9. When you click the **OK** button a message box should appear. Close the message box.

10. Enter a valid price and click the **OK** button. The form should close and an order row should be displayed in the data grid view.

11. Open the form again and click on the **Cancel** button to make sure that it closes without any message box appearing.

12. Close the application.

The complete code for the **btnAddOrderRow_Click** event:

```
private void btnAddOrderRow_Click(object sender, EventArgs e)
{
    var orderRow = data.EmptyOrderRow();
    var result = ShowAddOrderRowForm(orderRow);

    if (result.Equals(DialogResult.Cancel)) return;

    orderRow.OrderId = orders[cboOrders.SelectedIndex].OrderId;
    orderRow = data.AddOrderRow(orderRow);
    UpdateOrderRowBinding();
}
```

Binding the combo box's SelectedindexChanged event

In order for the order rows in the data grid view to change with the selected order in the combo box you have to update the binding between the **orderRows** collection and the data grid view. You can achieve this by calling the **UpdateOrderRowBinding** method you created a while back from the combo box's **SelectedIndexChanged** event which is called when an item is selected in the combo box.

1. Add the **SelectedIndexChanged** event for the combo box.
2. Add a call to the **UpdateOrderRowBinding** method.
3. Run the application.
4. Add an order row to the selected order.
5. Select another order in the combo box and make sure that the order rows reflect the order rows for the current order.
6. Close the application.

The complete code for the combo box's **SelectedIndexChanged** event:

```
private void cboOrders_SelectedIndexChanged(object sender, EventArgs e)
{
    UpdateOrderRowBinding();
}
```

The RemoveOrderRow method

The purpose of this method in the **Data** class is to remove an order row instance from the **orderRows** collection in the **Data** class.

1. Add a **bool** method called **RemoveOrderRow** which takes an **OrderRow** instance parameter to the **Order Row Methods region** in the **Data** class.
2. Return the result from a call to the **Remove** method on the **orderRows** collection. Pass in the **OrderRow** instance to the method.

The complete code for the **RemoveOrderRow** method:

```
public bool RemoveOrderRow(OrderRow orderRow)
{
    return orderRows.Remove(orderRow);
}
```

Remove an order row

To remove an order row you have to add some code to the **UserDeletingRow** event of the data grid view. You can access the order row being removed from the data grid view through the **DataBoundItem** property of the **e.Row** property; you have to cast it to an **OrderRow**. Then you have to pass that order row instance to the **RemoveOrderRow** method in the **Data** class.

1. Add the **UserDeletingRow** event of the data grid view.
2. Save the order row in the **DataBoundItem** property in a variable called **orderRow**.
   ```
   var orderRow = (OrderRow)e.Row.DataBoundItem;
   ```
3. Call the **RemoveOrderRow** method in the **Data** class passing in the **OrderRow** instance in the **orderRow** variable to the method.
   ```
   data.RemoveOrderRow(orderRow);
   ```
4. Run the application.
5. Add an order row to the current order.
6. Click on the gray area to the left of the order row in the data grid view to select the row. You can select multiple rows by holding down the **Shift** or **Ctrl** key while selecting rows.
7. Press the **Delete** key on the keyboard to remove the order row(s).

The complete code for the **UserDeletingRow** event:

```
private void dgvOrderRows_UserDeletingRow(object sender,
DataGridViewRowCancelEventArgs e)
{
    var orderRow = (OrderRow)e.Row.DataBoundItem;
    data.RemoveOrderRow(orderRow);
}
```

Update the data in an order row

To update the data in an order row you can either double click on the desired cell to enter edit mode or select a cell and start typing. Press **Enter** on the keyboard to save the changes.

Reference types vs. value types

There are two types of variables: value type and reference type. Value types are the built-in **struct**-types such as **int**, **decimal** and **bool** as well as any **structs** you create containing value types. Value types are stored on the *stack* and are therefore much faster than reference types which reside on the *heap*. When working with a value type variable, you interact directly with its value because it contains its data.

Reference types, objects created from classes, work in a different way. A variable created from a **class** will not contain the data directly; instead it contains a reference (a pointer) to an allocated memory area on the *heap*. This means that before you can assign values to the variable, an instance has to be created first. Also, when the variable goes out of scope and no longer is used, the object does not simply vanish; a process called Garbage Collector (GC) will take over the reference and remove the object safely from the memory, which takes time.

Important: *If you copy an object reference to another variable, you are just creating a reference pointer to the same object; you are not creating a new instance of that type. Both variables will point to the same object in memory.*

Additional reading: "Built-In Types Table (C# Reference)"

Boxing and unboxing

Boxing is the mechanism used when converting a value type to a reference type; this is useful in scenarios when a **class** only accepts reference types. Converting values this way is simple because you only have to assign the value type variable to the reference type variable; it is *implicit*.

```
int i = 10;
object obj = i;
```

Unboxing is the mechanism used when converting a reference type variable to a value type variable; this is useful if you have a method returning or a collection storing values of the **object** data type and you need to convert them to another data type. Converting values this way requires casting from one type to another; it is *explicit*.

```
int j;
j = (int)obj;
```

Static classes

There are situations where storing instance data is unnecessary; for instance, you could create a class which contains only methods that don't store any values. It could be conversion methods or methods that return a result of some kind depending on the input parameters, such as mathematical calculations. In cases like these, a **static** class is the choice to go with; a **static** class cannot be instantiated and its members need to be declared with the **static** keyword.

Important: *You access a **static** member through the class directly not a variable.*

Static members

Static members can be useful in circumstances such as if the functionality performed by a **static** method pertains to the type itself like keeping track of how many instances of a type have been created. No matter how many instances that are created, one instance of a **static** member will only ever be created.

Important: *A **static** member is available in all instances of a **class** if the class is not declared as **static** and contains **static** members. If a **static** property value changes, it affects all instances of that **class**.*

Important: *A **static** method cannot access **non-static** members; this is because the **static** member belongs to the type and therefore have no knowledge of any instances.*

Exercise: Calculator with static class and class library

In this exercise you will use refactoring on the latest version of the calculator application you created in an earlier exercise extracting constants and methods to a class library with **static** classes and members.

Open the latest version of the calculator application, the one that you refactored into methods, and add a **Class Library** project called **Calculator Library** to it. Rename the existing class **Calc** in the class library and reference the class library from the application project.

To do refactoring on the constants and methods from the form to the class library you have to cut them out and paste them into the **Calc** class and change them from **private** to **public**. All methods except the **CanCalculate** method can be moved; it cannot be moved since it contain references to form controls.

Prepend all constant and method names in the form code-behind with the **Calc** class (for instance `Calc.noValue`). The easiest way to do that is to do a search and replace for each of them.

Create the class library project

Add a **Class Library** project to the solution and rename the existing class **Calc**. Change the class from an instance class to a **static** class that cannot be instantiated. Reference the class library from the application project.

1. Open the most recent version of the Calculator application you refactored in an earlier exercise.
2. Add a **Class Library** project by right clicking on the Solution in the Solution Explorer and select **Add-New Project**.
3. Name the project **Calculator Library** and click the **OK** button
4. Rename the **Class1.cs** class **Calc.cs** by right clicking on it and select **Rename**. A dialog will pop up, click on the **Yes** button.
5. Change the class from an instance class to a **static** class.
   ```
   public static class Calc
   {
   }
   ```
6. Add a reference to the to the class library in the Calculator application by right clicking on the **References** folder and select **Add Reference**.
7. Select the **Calculator Library** project name in the dialog and click **OK** button.

Move the constants and methods

Cut out all constants and methods except the **CanCalculate** method and paste them into the **Calc** class then change them from **private** to **public**. Prepend all constant and method names with the **Calc** class.

1. Cut out all constants and methods except the **CanCalculate** method and paste them into the **Calc** class.
2. Add the **public** access modifier to the constants.
3. Change the **private** access modifier on the methods to **public static**.
4. Save the **Calc** class.

5. Search and replace **noValue** with **Calc.noValue** in the form code-behind (**Ctrl+Shift+H**). Make sure that the **Look in** drop down is set to **Current Document**.

6. Search and replace **minusSign** with **Calc.minusSign**.

7. Search and replace **AddDigit** with **Calc.AddDigit**.

8. Search and replace **DeleteDigit** with **Calc.DeleteDigit**.

9. Search and replace **AddDecimal** with **Calc.AddDecimal**.

10. Search and replace **ToggleSign** with **Calc.ToggleSign**.

11. Search and replace **EndsWithDecimalSign** with **Calc.EndsWithDecimalSign**.

12. Search and replace **Calculate** with **Calc.Calculate**.

13. Run the application.

14. Do a few calculations to make sure that the calculator works as supposed.

15. Close the application.

10. Interfaces

Introduction

Interfaces are ways to define signatures for methods, properties, events and indexers without specifying how these members are implemented. When implementing an interface in a class, you have to implement all the members that are specified in that interface, guaranteeing the consumer that all members will be implemented. By implementing interfaces, you let the developer use a subset of the class' functionality; it is better to implement several small interfaces than one gigantic interface; remember that you have to implement all members, which can be a daunting task if you only need a small portion of the functionality.

Important: *You can implement many interfaces in one class defining different characteristics and behaviors.*

Important: *Methods defined in an interfaces cannot have any logic (method body) only a definition specifying a return data type and a parameter list if needed. The method body will be added in the class where the interface is implemented.*

Important: *Programming conventions dictate that all interface names should begin with a capital letter "I" to easier distinguish them from classes.*

An interface can only have one of two *access modifiers*, either **public,** which makes it accessible from any assembly; or **internal**, which makes it accessible inside the assembly it was defined in.

Important: *An interface cannot relate to members that are internal to the class such as **fields, constants, operators and constructors**.*

Interface declaration

Suppose that you want to implement a **Movie** class; this could be done by implementing an interface **IMovie** which defines what needs to be implemented in the class; for instance, release date, director, film title, and so on. Note that methods don't have any curly brace bodies in interfaces and are not declared with *access modifiers*.

```
public interface IMovie
{
    // Property declarations
    string Title { get; set; }
    string Director { get; set; }
    DateTime ReleaseDate { get; set; }

    // Method declarations
    int YearsSinceRelease();
}
```

When implementing interfaces in a class you append a colon (:) to the class followed by a comma separated list with the interfaces you want to implement. When adding an interface you will be able to stub out the interface automatically by pointing to the small square at the bottom of the interface name and selecting **Implement interface** from a context menu or you can right click on the interface name and select **Implement Interface**.

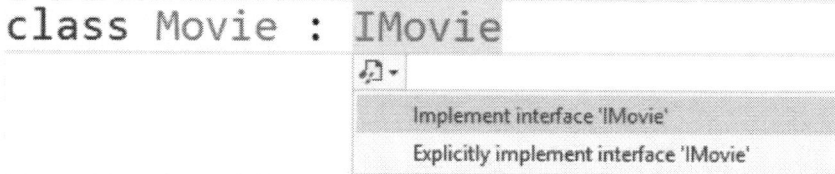

All members will be implemented throwing a **NotImplementedException** that you remove when implementing the actual logic of the member; it's a safety net to indicate that the members have not yet been implemented.

Implicit interface implementation

When implementing an interface implicitly you can reach the interface members directly from the instance variables created from the implementing class without having to cast the object to the interface type first.

```
public class Movie : IMovie
{
    public string Title { get; set; }
    public string Director { get; set; }
    public DateTime ReleaseDate { get; set; }
```

```
    public int YearsSinceRelease()
    {
        throw new NotImplementedException();
    }
}
```

Creating an instance from an implicit interface

```
public partial class Test
{
    public Test()
    {
        var movie = new Movie();
        // Or
        var movie = (IMovie)new Movie();
        // Or
        IMovie movie = new Movie();
    }
}
```

Explicit interface implementation

To implement an interface explicitly means that it is qualified by the interface it belongs to; this can make the code easier to understand, especially if you implement several interfaces. The only time you have to use explicit implementation is if a member with the same name and type is used in more than one of the implemented interfaces.

Important: *When you implement an interface explicitly you can only use the members from that interface by using a variable of that interface type or by casting the class to that interface type.*

```
public class Movie : IMovie
{
    public string IMovie.Title { get; set; }
    public string IMovie.Director { get; set; }
    public DateTime IMovie.ReleaseDate { get; set; }

    public int IMovie.YearsSinceRelease()
    {
        throw new NotImplementedException();
    }
}
```

Creating an instance from an explicit interface

```
public partial class Test
{
    public Test()
    {
        var movie = (IMovie)new Movie();
        // Or
        IMovie movie = new Movie();
    }
}
```

Exercise: Employee class with two interfaces

In this exercise you will create two interfaces **IPerson** and **IEmployee** which will be implemented in the same class called **Employee**. The user interface should contain three radio buttons which will display all accessible data using the full **Employee** instance, the **IPerson** and **IEmployee** interfaces respectively when clicked; you will have to cast the class to the appropriate interface type.

The result from clicking on one of the radio buttons should be displayed in a rich textbox control (see image below).

The **IPerson** interface should define three properties **PersonId (int)**, **Name (string)** and **Born (DateTime)**. It should also define a method called **Age** which when implemented in the class return the age calculated from date in the **Born** property.

The **IEmployee** interface should define three properties **EmployeeId (int)**, **Department (string)** and **Salary (double)**.

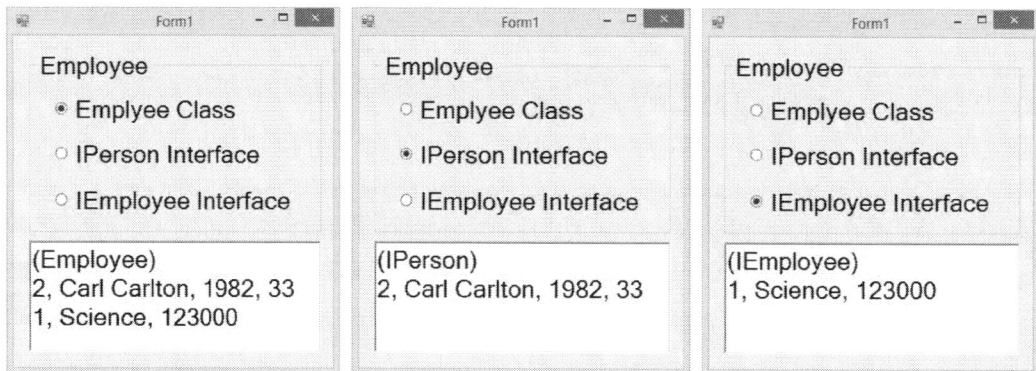

The IPerson interface

1. Create a new Windows Forms Application.
2. Add a folder called **Interfaces** to the project.
3. Right click on the **Interfaces** folder and select **Add-New Item**.
4. Select **Interface** in the dialog, name it **IPerson** and click the **Add** button.
5. Add an **int** property called **PersonId** using only the **get** keyword to make it read only outside the class it is implemented in. *Note that you don't specify any access modi-fier for the members defined by the interface.*
6. Add a **string** property called **Name**.
7. Add a **DateTime** property called **Born**.
8. Add a parameter-less **int** method called **Age**.

The complete code for the **IPerson** interface:

```
interface IPerson
{
    // Property definitions
    int PersonId { get; }
    string Name { get; set; }
    DateTime Born { get; set; }

    // Method definition
    int Age();
}
```

The IEmployee interface

1. Add an **Interface** called **IEmployee** to the **Interfaces** folder.
2. Add an **int** property called **EmployeeId**.
3. Add a **string** property called **Department**.
4. Add a **double** property called **Salary**.

The complete code for the **IEmployee** interface:

```
interface IEmployee
{
    int EmployeeId { get; }
    string Department { get; set; }
    double Salary { get; set; }
}
```

The Employee class

1. Add a folder called **Classes** to the project.
2. Add a class called **Employee** to the **Classes** folder.
3. Add a **public** access modifier to the class so that it can contain **public** properties.
4. Add the Interface names as a comma separated list after the class name, use a colon to separate the class name from the interface list.

    ```
    public class Employee : IPerson, IEmployee
    {
    }
    ```

5. Right click on the both interface names and select **Implement Interface - Implement Interface** to implement their members in the class.
6. Add a **set** keyword with a **private** access modifier to the **PersonId** and **EmployeeId** properties in the class.

    ```
    public int EmployeeId { get; private set; }
    ```

7. Implement the **Age** method body calculating the age from the **Born** property.

    ```
    public int Age()
    {
        return DateTime.Now.AddYears(-Born.Year).Year;
    }
    ```

8. Add a constructor that has parameters for all the properties and assign the passed in values to the appropriate properties.

The complete code for the **Employee** class:

```
public class Employee : IPerson, IEmployee
{
    #region IEmployee Implementation
    public int EmployeeId { get; private set; }
    public string Department { get; set; }
    public double Salary { get; set; }
    #endregion

    #region IPerson Implementation
    public int PersonId { get; private set; }
    public string Name { get; set; }
    public DateTime Born { get; set; }
```

```
public int Age()
{
    return DateTime.Now.AddYears(-Born.Year).Year;
}
#endregion

public Employee(int employeeId, int personId, string department,
double salary, string name, DateTime born)
{
    EmployeeId = employeeId;
    PersonId = personId;
    Department = department;
    Salary = salary;
    Name = name;
    Born = born;
}
}
```

The GUI

1. Open the form's code-behind.

2. Create an instance of the **Employee** class at the beginning of the form class.

   ```
   Employee empl = new Employee(1, 2, "Science", 123000, "Carl Carlton",
   new DateTime(1982, 10, 5));
   ```

3. Add a **Click** event for the radio button displaying the full **Employee** instance data.

4. Assign a formatted string with all the data from the **Employee** instance.

   ```
   private void rbnEmplyeeClass_Click(object sender, EventArgs e)
   {
       // Can use all members from both interfaces
       txtResult.Text = String.Format("(Employee)\n" +
           "{0}, {1}, {2}, {3}\n" + "{4}, {5}, {6}",
           empl.PersonId, empl.Name, empl.Born.Year, empl.Age(),
           empl.EmployeeId, empl.Department, empl.Salary);
   }
   ```

5. Do the same for the radio button displaying the data defined by the **IPerson** interface. Cast the **Employee** instance to an **IPerson** interface pointer. *Note that you only gain access to the members of the interface after casting it.*

   ```
   var person = (IPerson)empl;
   ```

6. Do the same for the radio button displaying the data defined by the **IEmployee** interface. *Note that you can use the **as** keyword when casting if you like.*

```
        var employee = empl as IEmployee;
```

7. Run the application and click the radio buttons to change the text displayed in the rich textbox.
8. Close the application.

The complete code for the **Form** class:

```
public partial class Form1 : Form
{
    Employee empl = new Employee(1, 2, "Science", 123000, "Carl Carlton",
        new DateTime(1982, 10, 5));

    public Form1() {
        InitializeComponent();
    }

    private void rbnEmplyeeClass_Click(object sender, EventArgs e)
    {
        // Can use all members from both interfaces
        txtResult.Text = String.Format("(Employee)\n" +
            "{0}, {1}, {2}, {3}\n" + "{4}, {5}, {6}",
            empl.PersonId, empl.Name, empl.Born.Year, empl.Age(),
            empl.EmployeeId, empl.Department, empl.Salary);
    }

    private void rbnIPersonInterface_Click(object sender, EventArgs e)
    {
        // Cast as IPerson
        // Can only use members from the IPerson interface
        var person = (IPerson)empl;
        txtResult.Text = String.Format("(IPerson)\n{0}, {1}, {2}, {3}",
            person.PersonId, person.Name, person.Born.Year, person.Age());
    }

    private void rbnIEmployeeInterface_Click(object sender, EventArgs e)
    {
        // Cast as IEmployee
        // Can only use members from the IEmployee interface
        var employee = empl as IEmployee;
        txtResult.Text = String.Format("(IEmployee)\n{0}, {1}, {2}",
            employee.EmployeeId, employee.Department, employee.Salary);
    }
}
```

302

Interface polymorphism

Interface polymorphism states that: *A class can be represented as an instance of any interface that it implements*.

Because several classes can implement the same interface, we can use interface pointers to switch between objects at run-time depending on the application flow.

You must use explicit casting to convert from an interface type to a class type implementing the interface; this is because the class may implement other members than those defined by the interface.

Because classes that implement the same interface must implement all the members of that interface, you can use this to your advantage if you need to switch between different instances at run-time. You can use an interface pointer to hold the instance of the currently selected class type.

Suppose you are implementing an application that handles different types of film media such as VHS and Blue Ray; when implementing the classes for VHS and Blue Ray they have some characteristics and behaviors that are similar; for instance, all movies have a title and a release date. You can standardize the members being implemented by using an interface called **IMovie** which contains all the specified members implemented by the classes.

The individual classes implementing the interface can also have unique properties and methods specific to that type of media such as being able to rewind a VHS cassette and clean the surface of a Blue Ray disc.

Note that the **VHS** class has a method called **Rewind** which does not exist in the **BlueRay** class and the **BlueRay** class has a method called **CleanSurface** which does not exist in the **VHS** class. Also note that the implementation of the **YearsSinceRelease** method is implemented differently in the two classes.

```
public class VHS : IMovie
{
    public string Title { get; set; }
    public string Director { get; set; }
    public DateTime ReleaseDate { get; set; }
```

```
    // Method is specific to this class
    public void Rewind()
    {
    }

    public int YearsSinceRelease()
    {
        // Implementation different from Blue Ray
        return DateTime.Now.Year - ReleaseDate.Year;
    }
}

public class BlueRay : IMovie
{
    public string Title { get; set; }
    public string Director { get; set; }
    public DateTime ReleaseDate { get; set; }

    // Method is specific to this class
    public void CleanSurface()
    {
    }

    public int YearsSinceRelease()
    {
        // Implementation different from VHS
        TimeSpan time = DateTime.Now - ReleaseDate;
        return new DateTime().Add(time).Year;
    }
}
```

The **Play** method in the **Player** class has an **IMovie** parameter that can receive an object from any class implementing the **IMovie** interface. In this example the **VHS** and **BlueRay** classes both implement the interface.

Since both classes implement the **IMovie** interface the **IMovie** parameter will be redirected to the correct object based on the interface pointer passed in to it and therefore it can be used to handle all members implementing the interface and no casting is necessary.

You can however cast the interface pointer to the implementing class type to use the specific members implemented in the class that are not part of the interface.

```
public class Player
{
    public void Play(IMovie movie)
    {
        // The same interface properties and methods
        // can be used since both classes implement
        // the interface.
        string info = String.Format(
            "Title: {0} | Released: {1} | Years: {2}",
            movie.Title,
            movie.ReleaseDate.ToShortDateString(),
            movie.YearsSinceRelease());

        // Use the class instance and call a
        // method specific to the defining class
        if (movie is VHS)
        {
            var vhs = (VHS)movie;
            vhs.Rewind();
        }
        else if (movie is BlueRay)
        {
            var blueRay = (BlueRay)movie;
            blueRay.CleanSurface();
        }
    }
}
```

In the code below two movies are created one as a VHS cassette and one as a Blue Ray disc. An instance of the **Player** class is created in the constructor and used to call the **Play** method on the same **Player** instance twice once for the VHS cassette and once for the Blue Ray disc.

The **IMovie** pointer will use the correct movie instance based on what is passed into the **Play** method.

```
public class Test
{
    VHS vhs = new VHS() { Title = "A.I.",
        ReleaseDate = new DateTime(2001, 6, 21) };

    BlueRay blueRay = new BlueRay() { Title = "Alien",
        ReleaseDate = new DateTime(1979, 11, 2)};
```

```
    public Test()
    {
        var player = new Player();

        // Play vhs cassette
        player.Play(vhs);

        // Play Blue Ray disc
        player.Play(blueRay);
    }
}
```

Exercise: Interface polymorphism

In this exercise you will use interface polymorphism to decide which class' implementation will be used when calling a method. You will create an interface called **IAnimal** defining one method called **Walk** that will be implemented in three classes called **Cat**, **Dog** and **Dinosaur** which all will have different implementations of the method. When the user selects one of the radio buttons and click the **Walk** button the object representing the radio button choice will be cast to the **IAnimal** interface, the **Walk** method will be executed and a message box with a message will be displayed.

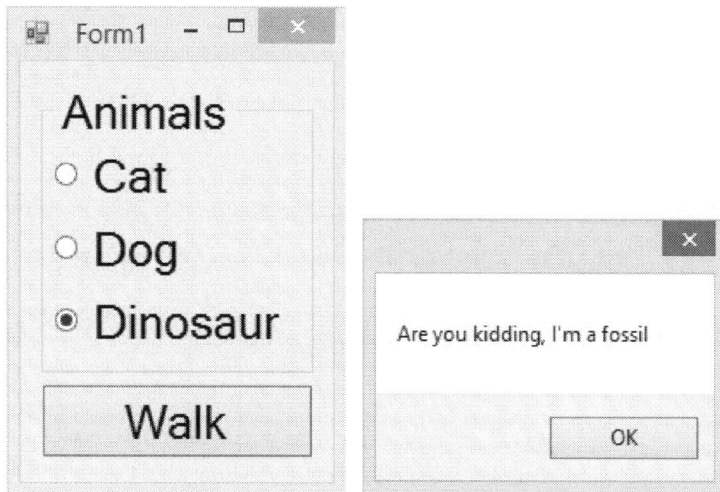

The IAnimal interface

1. Create a new Windows Forms Application.
2. Add a folder called **Interfaces** to the project.
3. Right click on the folder and select **Add-New Item**.
4. Select **Interface** in the list, name it **IAnimal** and click the **Add** button.
5. Add a **string** method definition called **Walk** to the interface and save the interface file.

The complete code for the **IAnimal** interface:

```
interface IAnimal
{
    string Walk();
}
```

The classes

1. Add a folder called **Classes** to the project.
2. Add a class called **Cat** to the folder.
3. Add the **IAnimal** interface name after the class name with a colon in between.
   ```
   class Cat : IAnimal
   {
   }
   ```
4. Implement the interface by right clicking on the interface and select **Implement Interface-Implement Interface**. The **Walk** method will be added to the class, have it return the string "I'm not gonna walk just because you say so".
   ```
   public string Walk()
   {
       return "I'm not gonna walk just because you say so";
   }
   ```

The complete code for the **Cat** class:

```
class Cat : IAnimal
{
    public string Walk()
    {
        return "I'm not gonna walk just because you say so";
    }
}
```

The Dog class

1. Add a class called **Dog** to the **Classes** folder.
2. Add the **IAnimal** interface name after the class name with a colon in between.
3. Implement the interface. The **Walk** method should return the string "Sure, I'll happily go for a walk!".

The complete code for the **Dog** class:

```
class Dog : IAnimal
{
    public string Walk()
    {
        return "Sure, I'll happily go for a walk!";
    }
}
```

The Dinosaur class

1. Add a class called **Dinosaur** to the **Classes** folder.
2. Implement the **IAnimal** interface. The **Walk** method should return the string "Are you kidding, I'm a fossil!".

The complete code for the **Dinosaur** class:

```
class Dinosaur : IAnimal
{
    public string Walk()
    {
        return "Are you kidding, I'm a fossil";
    }
}
```

The GUI

1. Add three radio buttons called **rbnCat**, **rbnDog** and **rbnDinosaur** and a button called **btnWalk**.
2. Add the **Click** event for the **Walk** button.
3. Declare an **IAnimal** interface variable called **animal** in the event. This variable will be the pointer used when deciding which class' object will be used.
   ```
   IAnimal animal;
   ```
4. Assign an instance of the appropriate class to the **animal** variable depending on which radio button has been selected, use an **if**-statement.

```
if (rbnCat.Checked)
    animal = new Cat();
```

5. Display the message "Select an animal" if no radio button have been selected when the button is clicked and exit the event gracefully after the message box has been closed.

6. Call the **Walk** method and display the returned string in a message box after the **if/else if/else**-blocks.

7. Run the application, select a radio button and click the **Walk** button. Try the different radio buttons to make sure that the correct messages are being displayed.

8. If you want to follow the program flow you can place a breakpoint at the beginning of the button's **Click** event and step through the code; you should end up in the method implementations for the different classes depending on the selected radio button.

The complete code for the **Form** class:

```
public partial class Form1 : Form
{
    private void btnWalk_Click(object sender, EventArgs e)
    {
        IAnimal animal;

        //Interface Polymorphism
        if (rbnCat.Checked)
            animal = new Cat();
        else if (rbnDog.Checked)
            animal = new Dog();
        else if (rbnDinosaur.Checked)
            animal = new Dinosaur();
        else
        {
            MessageBox.Show("Select an animal");
            return; // Leave the method gracefully
        }

        MessageBox.Show(animal.Walk());
    }
}
```

The IComparable interface

When .Net Framework collection items are sorted, for instance by calling a **Sort** method on the collection, they use the implementation in the **IComparable** interface. If you want collections to sort the instances of your class in a certain way, you implement the **IComparable** interface and its **CompareTo** method in the class. The **CompareTo** method is used by the .NET Framework whenever a comparison between two instances or values is made. All the built-in data types implement this interface.

The **CompareTo** method takes one argument, the object to compare the current object with, and returns an integer specifying if the current instance should be placed before, in the same position or after the passed-in object instance.

Suppose you have instances of a **Book** class stored in an **List** collection that you want to sort alphabetically by the **Title** property; to do this you implement the **IComparable** interface and its **CompareTo** method comparing the **Title** of the objects when the **Sort** method of the collection is called.

Implementing the IComparable interface

In order to be able to sort the books in the **List<book>** collection on the book titles you need to implement the **CompareTo** method in the **IComparable** interface in the **Book** class, you might also consider overriding the **Equals** method to be able to compare books on their titles using the **Equals** method.

Implement the **IComparable** interface in the **Book** class and compare the **Title** property of the current object with the object passed in to the **CompareTo** method.

The Book Class

```
public class Book : IComparable
{
    public string Title { get; set; }

    public Book(string title)
    {
        Title = title;
    }

    public int CompareTo(object obj)
    {
```

```
      Book book = obj as Book;
      return String.Compare(this.Title, book.Title);
   }

   public override bool Equals(object obj)
   {
      return CompareTo(obj) == 0; // 0 => this == obj
   }
}
```

Sorting a book list

In the **Bookstore** class below a **List\<Book\>** collection will be filled with books and then sorted using the **Sort** method of the collection, you can see the sorted list in the image below.

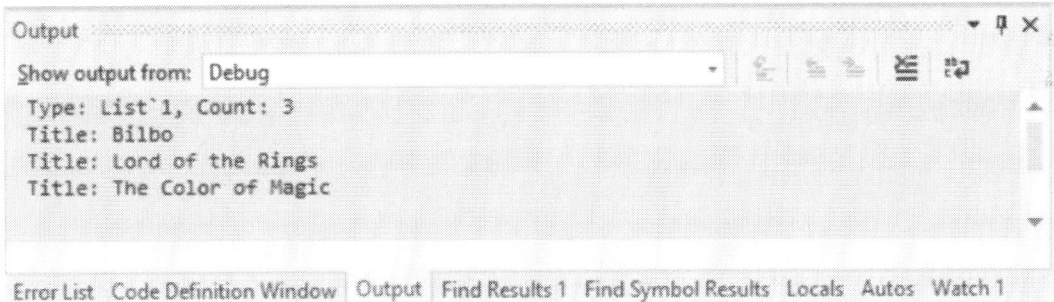

```
class Bookstore
{
   List<Book> books = new List<Book>();

   public Bookstore()
   {
      books.Add(new Book("Lord of the Rings"));
      books.Add(new Book("The Color of Magic"));
      books.Add(new Book("Bilbo"));

      books.Sort();

      PrintCollection();
   }

   private void PrintCollection()
   {
      Debug.WriteLine(String.Format("Type: {0}, Count: {1}",
         books.GetType().Name, books.Count));
```

```
    foreach (var book in books)
    {
        Debug.WriteLine(String.Format("Title: {0}", book.Title));
    }
    }
}
```

The IComparer interface

If you want to compare two objects using a custom comparer class implementation, you implement the **IComparer** interface and its **Compare** method. Using this type of implementation you can create very sophisticated comparisons; you are also very clear what type of comparison is being used because you pass an instance of the comparer class you created to the **Sort** method of the collection. It is also easy to update and reuse the comparison should it be needed.

One major difference between the **IComparer** and the **IComparable** interfaces is that the **IComparer** interface is implemented in a standalone class whereas the **IComparable** interface is implemented in the class that is used to define the collection items.

The Book Class
```
public class Book
{
    public string Title { get; set; }
    public double Rating { get; set; }

    public Book1(string title, double rating) {
        Title = title;
        Rating = rating;
    }
}
```

The BookComparer Class Implementing the IComparer Interface
```
class BookComparer : IComparer<Book>
{
    public int Compare(Book book1, Book book2)
    {
        return book1.Rating.CompareTo(book2.Rating);
    }
}
```

Sorting a book list

In the **Bookstore** class below a **List<Book>** collection will be filled with books and then sorted by rating using the **Sort** method of the collection and the **BookComparer** class, you can see the sorted list in the image below.

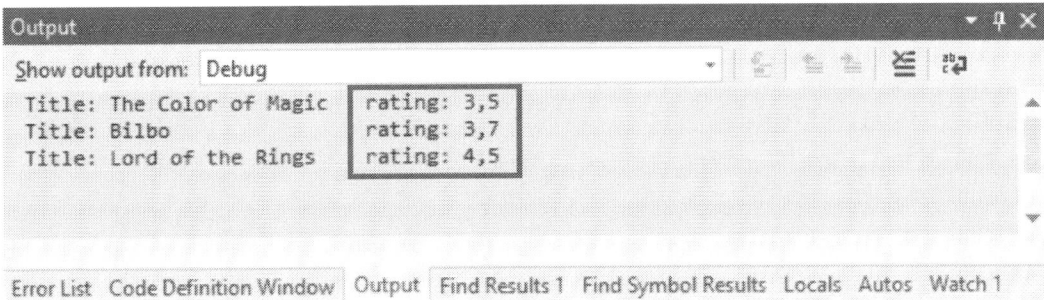

```
Output                                                          ▾ ꝓ ✕
Show output from:  Debug                              ▾   │ 🔍 │ ⤴ ⤵ │ ⪥ │ ⥁
  Title: The Color of Magic   │ rating: 3,5                              ▲
  Title: Bilbo                │ rating: 3,7
  Title: Lord of the Rings    │ rating: 4,5

                                                                        ▼
Error List  Code Definition Window  Output  Find Results 1  Find Symbol Results  Locals  Autos  Watch 1
```

```csharp
class SortedBookstore
{
    List<Book> books = new List<Book>();

    public SortedBookstore()
    {
        books.Add(new Book("Lord of the Rings", 4.5));
        books.Add(new Book("The Color of Magic", 3.5));
        books.Add(new Book("Bilbo", 3.7));

        books.Sort(new BookComparer());
        PrintCollection();
    }

    private void PrintCollection()
    {
        foreach (var book in books)
            Debug.WriteLine(String.Format(
              "Title: {0, -20} rating: {1}",
            book.Title, book.Rating));
    }
}
```

11. Events

Introduction

An event is a way for an object to notify another object that something has happened. One type of events are events that are triggered by a control in a GUI when a user interacts with that control; it could be the **Click** event triggered when the user clicks on a button. You write code that *subscribes* to an event and it can take some action when it is triggered.

Apart from using control events, you can create events for your types defined by **structs** or **classes** that you can *publish* to notify the application or a component as *subscribers* when something happens.

To enable other code to subscribe to an event, you create a delegate; a method signature that defines the return type and parameters for the event function it represents.

An event is associated with a delegate; you subscribe to an event by creating a method, an event handler, that corresponds to the delegate and pass that method name to the *event publisher*, the object that will raise the event.

Defining an event

You use the **delegate** keyword in a struct or class to define a delegate. A system delegate takes two parameters; the first is the object that raised the event and the second is the event argument, an instance of the **EventArgs** class that contains additional information that needs to passed to the subscribers.

You use the **event** keyword to define an event. It takes two parameters: the name of the delegate followed by the name that you want the event to have which is used when subscribing to the event.

The following code sample show how to implement the **OrderRowAdded** event in the **Order** class which will be triggered when a new order row is added to the order.

```
class Order
{
    public delegate void OrderRowAddedHandler(OrderRow row);
    public event OrderRowAddedHandler OrderRowAdded;
}
```

Raising an event

When a **delegate** and an **event** have been defined, you can write code to raise the **event**. When raising an event, all subscribers of that event will be notified and their event handler methods will be executed. It's important to check if that the event is <u>not</u> **null** before raising it because if no one is subscribing to it an exception will be thrown if you try to raise it. The syntax for raising an event is the same as calling a method and passing in the necessary parameters.

The following code sample show how to raise the **OrderRowAdded** event from the method adding the order row.

```
class Order
{
    public delegate void OrderRowAddedHandler(OrderRow row);
    public event OrderRowAddedHandler OrderRowAdded;

    public void AddOrderRow(Product product, int quantity)
    {
        // Add code here to add the order row

        // Raise the event if there are subscribers
        if (OrderRowAdded != null)
            OrderRowAdded(orderRow);
    }
}
```

Subscribing to an event

When subscribing to an event in the client code, there are two things you need to do; first, create a function that matches the event's delegate signature and second, subscribe to the event by using the += operator to attach the client event handler method to the event. In certain cases, you only want to subscribe to an event for a while and then unsubscribe from the event. You do this by using the -= operator.

```
public partial class Form1 : Form
```

```
{
    Order order = new Order();

    private void btnAddOrderRow_Click(object sender, EventArgs e)
    {
        // Subscribe to the event
        order.OrderRowAdded += order_OrderRowAdded;

        // Call the method that add the
        // order row to the order instance
        order.AddOrderRow((Product)cboProducts.SelectedItem,
            (int)numQty.Value);

        // Unsubscribe from the event
        order.OrderRowAdded -= order_OrderRowAdded;
    }

    void order_OrderRowAdded(OrderRow row)
    {
        // Do something when the event is
        // raised in the order instance
    }
}
```

Event example

The following example will simulate a user adding products to order rows in an order. The order will *publish* an event which will be triggered when a new order row is added and the client form will *subscribe* to the event updating the data source in the data grid view control displaying the order rows. The order rows are displayed in ascending order on the order row id and the most recently added order row is displayed with a light green background.

The Product class

This class represent a product that can be added to an order row, it has three properties a unique id, a descriptive title and a price.

```
class Product
{
    public int Id { get; set; }
    public string Title { get; set; }
    public Double Price { get; set; }
}
```

The OrderRow class

This class represent an order row that can be added to an order, all its properties are **public** readable but can only be assigned inside the object or are not assignable at all.

The **private Product** property will hold the product associated with the order row and is not accessible outside the order row to adhere to the encapsulation rules of object oriented programming which states that all data should be **private** and exposed by properties. It can be assigned and read internally and its data is exposed through two read only properties called **Title** and **Price**.

The **Qty** (quantity) and **Id** (order row id) properties are publically readable but can only be assigned within the order row object; their **set**-blocks have been declared as **private**.

The **Total** property is publically accessible and does only contain a **get**-block which return the price multiplied by the quantity.

318

The class' constructor will assign the passed in product and quantity to the appropriate properties and the Id property is assigned a random number with a max value of **1000** (to be able to tell the order rows apart in this example).

```csharp
class OrderRow
{
    private Product Product { get; set; }
    public int Id { get; private set; }
    public string Title { get { return Product.Title; } }
    public double Price { get { return Product.Price; } }
    public int Qty { get; private set; }
    public double Total { get { return Product.Price * Qty; } }

    public OrderRow(Product product, int quantity)
    {
        Product = product;
        Qty = quantity;
        Id = new Random().Next(1000);
    }
}
```

The Order class (event publisher)

This class represent an order that can contain many order rows stored in a **List<OrderRow>** collection. After an order row has been added the **OrderRowAdded** event will be raised signaling to its subscribers (the client) that a new order row is available.

The **AddOrderRow** method will be called by the client when the user clicks the **Add Order Row** button in the GUI. A new order row will be created using the passed in product and quantity and is then added to the **orderRows** collection. After the order row has been added to the collection the **OrderRowAdded** event is raised if there are subscribers to it.

The **GetOrderRows** method will return all order rows in the order sorted in ascending order on the order row id. This method is called by the client when listing all order rows belonging to the order in a data grid view.

```csharp
class Order
{
    public delegate void OrderRowAddedHandler(OrderRow row);
    public event OrderRowAddedHandler OrderRowAdded;

    List<OrderRow> orderRows = new List<OrderRow>();

    public List<OrderRow> GetOrderRows()
    {
        return orderRows.OrderBy(or => or.Id).ToList();
    }

    public void AddOrderRow(Product product, int quantity)
    {
        // Create a new order row with the passed in
        // information and add the order row to the
        // order rows collection
        var orderRow = new OrderRow(product, quantity);
        orderRows.Add(orderRow);

        // Raise the event if there are subscribers
        if (OrderRowAdded != null)
            OrderRowAdded(orderRow);
    }
}
```

The client (event subscriber)

To make the example a bit less complex there is only one order which is declared at the beginning of the form along with a collection that will contain all available products.

The products are added to the **products** collection in the constructor and then the collection is assigned as the combo box's data source listing the product titles .

The button's **Click** event is where the **OrderRowAdded** event is subscribed to and the **AddOrderRow** method of the order instance is called creating a new order row with data from the GUI. The product is fetched from the selected item in the combo box listing the available products and the quantity is fetched from the number up down control.

When the **OrderRowAdded** event is raised in the order object the **order_OrderRowAdded** event method will be called and in it the data source is reassigned by calling the **GetOrderRows** method of the order instance. In this method the data grid view output is formatted assigning column widths and background color to the most recently added order row.

```csharp
public partial class Form1 : Form
{
    Order order = new Order();
    List<Product> products = new List<Product>();

    public Form1()
    {
        products.Add(new Product { Id = 1, Price = 10.5,
            Title = "Product 1" });
        products.Add(new Product { Id = 2, Price = 20,
            Title = "Product 2" });
        products.Add(new Product { Id = 3, Price = 5,
            Title = "Product 3" });

        InitializeComponent();

        cboProducts.DataSource = products;
        cboProducts.DisplayMember = "Title";
    }

    private void btnAddOrderRow_Click(object sender, EventArgs e)
    {
        // Subscribe to the event
        order.OrderRowAdded += order_OrderRowAdded;

        order.AddOrderRow((Product)cboProducts.SelectedItem,
            (int)numQty.Value);

        // Unsubscribe from the event
        order.OrderRowAdded -= order_OrderRowAdded;
    }

    void order_OrderRowAdded(OrderRow row)
    {
        var idx = order.GetOrderRows().IndexOf(row);

        dgvOrderRows.DataSource = null;
        dgvOrderRows.DataSource = order.GetOrderRows();

        foreach (DataGridViewColumn column in dgvOrderRows.Columns)
            column.Width = 90;
```

```
        dgvOrderRows.Columns[1].Width = 180;

        foreach(DataGridViewCell cell in dgvOrderRows.Rows[idx].Cells)
            cell.Style.BackColor = Color.LightGreen;
    }
}
```

Exercise: Video rental with events

In this exercise you will create a simple video rental application using events to signal when all copies of a film is rented out and a copy of a film has been returned and rented.

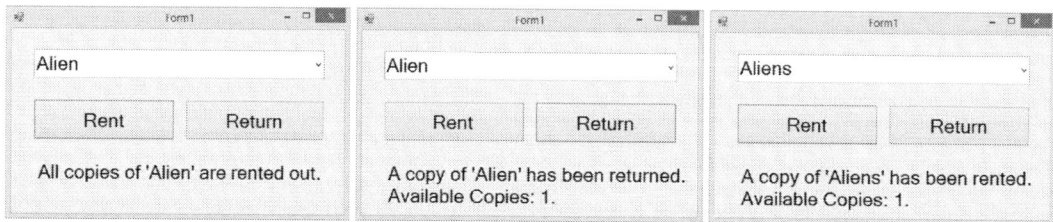

Because there can be more than one copy of a film in the videos collection in the **Video-Rental** class instance you have to select the films using the **Distinct** LINQ method to fetch only one of the films to be displayed in the combo box. To use the **Distinct** method in this way you have to implement a class called **VideoComparer** that implement the **IEquality-Comparer** interface and pass an instance of that class to the **Distinct** method. The interface has two methods defined called **Equals** which compares two instances of a class to determine if they should be considered equal and the **GetHashCode** method which return the unique identifier of the passed in object.

```
class VideoComparer : IEqualityComparer<Video>
{
    public bool Equals(Video video1, Video video2)
    {
        return video1.FilmId.Equals(video2.FilmId);
    }

    public int GetHashCode(Video video) {
        return video.FilmId;
    }
}
```

When calling the **Distinct** LINQ method you pass in an instance of the class defined above to compare the video instances.

```
public List<Video> GetVideos()
{
    return videos.Distinct(new VideoComparer()).ToList();
}
```

When the user clicks the **Rent** button the film id of the film selected in the combo box will be sent to the **RentVideo** method of the **VideoRental** class instance to simulate that the film is being rented. In the **RentVideo** method the **IsRented** property is set to **true** on the first instance of the film matching the passed in film id found in the **videos** collection and the **AllCopiesRentedOut** event is raised if there are no more available copies of the film in the collection otherwise the **VideoInfo** event is raised.

When the **Return** button is clicked the **VideoReturned** event is subscribed to and then the **ReturnVideo** method of the **VideoRental** class instance is called passing in the film id of the film selected in the combo box. After the method call the event is unsubscribed.

When the **AllCopiesRentedOut** event of the **VideoRental** class instance is raised the corresponding event method called **rental_AllCopiesRentedOut** in the client is called where a text message stating that all copies of the film is rented out is displayed in a label (see image above).

When the **VideoInfo** event of the **VideoRental** class instance is raised the corresponding event method called **rental_VideoInfo** in the client is called where a text message showing the number of available copies of the film in a label (see image above).

When the **VideoReturned** event of the **VideoRental** class instance is raised the corresponding event method called **rental_VideoReturned** in the client is called where a text message showing the number of available copies of the film in a label (see image above).

The GUI

The GUI is very simple it consist of a combo box called *cboVideos*, two buttons called *btnRent* and *btnReturn* and a label called *lblResult* (see image above).

The Video class

The **Video** class has three properties called **FilmId**, **Title** and **IsRented**.

1. Add a folder called **Classes** to the project.
2. Add a class called **Video** to the folder.
3. Add an **int** property called **FilmId** to the class.
4. Add a **string** property called **Title** to the class.
5. Add a **bool** property called **IsRented** to the class that will keep track of if the film has been rented or is available.

The complete code of the **Video** class:

```
class Video
{
    public int FilmId { get; set; }
    public string Title { get; set; }
    public bool IsRented { get; set; }
}
```

The VideoComparer class

The **VideoComparer** class implement the **IEqualityComparer** interface specifying the **Video** class as its designated type. The interface define two methods called **Equals** and **GetHash-Code** which have to be implemented in the **VideoComparer** class.

The **VideoComparer** class is used to fetch videos from the **videos** collection using the **Distinct** LINQ method making sure that only one instance of a video is represented in the result even if several instances are present in the collection. This is necessary when listing the films in the combo box in the GUI, fetching films without calling the **Distinct** method will display the same film title multiple times in the combo box.

1. Add a **Class** called **VideoComparer** to the **Classes** folder.
2. Implement the **IEqualityComparer** interface.
   ```
   class VideoComparer : IEqualityComparer<Video>
   {
   }
   ```
3. Implement the **Equals** method and compare the **FilmId** property of the two **Video** instances passed into the method.

4. Implement the **GetHashCode** method and return the **FilmId** property of the passed in **Video** instance.

The complete code of the **VideoComparer** class:

```csharp
class VideoComparer : IEqualityComparer<Video>
{
    public bool Equals(Video video1, Video video2)
    {
        return video1.FilmId.Equals(video2.FilmId);
    }

    public int GetHashCode(Video video)
    {
        return video.FilmId;
    }
}
```

The VideoRental class (event publisher)

The **VideoRental** class is the simulated video store where the videos are rented and returned, it is in this class the events are declared and raised. Apart from the events you also have to add four methods to the class.

The **GetVideos** method return the *distinct* result set of the **videos** collection and is called from the GUI when the combo box is loaded with data. The **AddVideoToList** is used to add a video to the **videos** collection. The **RentVideo** is used to mark a video as rented by assigning **true** to its **IsRented** property in the **videos** collection and then raise either the **AllCopies-RentedOut** or **VideoInfo** events with information about the film. The **ReturnVideo** method is called when a video is returned and the **IsRented** property of the film is set to **false** signaling that it can be rented. After the film has been returned the **VideoReturned** event is raised.

Events and Video collection

1. Add a class called **VideoRental** to the **Classes** folder.
2. Add a delegate called **AllCopiesRentedOutHandler** which is declared as **void** and takes a **Video** instance as a parameter.
   ```csharp
   public delegate void AllCopiesRentedOutHandler(Video video);
   ```

3. Use the delegate to declare an event called **AllCopiesRentedOut**.
   ```csharp
   public event AllCopiesRentedOutHandler AllCopiesRentedOut;
   ```

4. Add a delegate called **VideoHandler** which is declared as **void** and takes a **string** parameter called **title** and an **int** parameter called **count**.
   ```
   public delegate void VideoHandler(string title, int count);
   ```

5. Use the **VideoHandler** delegate to declare two events called **VideoReturned** and **VideoInfo**. You can use the same delegate because the methods are defined exactly the same in the client.

6. Add a **List<Video>** collection called **videos** to the class. This collection will hold all the films both rented and available.

The form's code-behind so far:

```
class VideoRental
{
    public delegate void AllCopiesRentedOutHandler(Video video);
    public event AllCopiesRentedOutHandler AllCopiesRentedOut;

    public delegate void VideoHandler(string title, int count);
    public event VideoHandler VideoReturned;
    public event VideoHandler VideoInfo;

    List<Video> videos = new List<Video>();
}
```

The GetVideos method

Add a method called **GetVideos** which return a **List<Video>** collection with distinct films using an instance of the **VideoComparer** class to compare the **Video** instances when calling the **Distinct** LINQ method.

The complete code for the **GetVideos** method:

```
public List<Video> GetVideos()
{
    return videos.Distinct(new VideoComparer()).ToList();
}
```

The AddVideoToList method

Add a **void** method called **AddVideoToList** which add the passed in **Video** instance to the **videos** collection.

The complete code for the **AddVideoToList** method:

```
public void AddVideoToList(Video video)
{
    videos.Add(video);
}
```

The RentVideo method

1. Add a **void** method called **RentVideo** which takes an **int** parameter called **filmId**.

   ```
   public void RentVideo(int filmId)
   {
   }
   ```

2. Use the passed in film id to fetch the first film in the **videos** collection matching the film id and that is not already rented out. Store the result in a variable called **video**.

   ```
   var video = videos.FirstOrDefault(v => v.FilmId.Equals(filmId) &&
   !v.IsRented);
   ```

3. If the video variable is <u>not</u> **null** then assign **true** to its **IsRented** property marking it as rented and then fetch the first film in the **videos** collection matching the film id that is not already rented out. Store the result in the **video** variable you added earlier.

4. Check if the **video** variable is **null** and the **AllCopiesRentedOut** event has subscribers, if there are subscribers fetch the first video that matches the film id and pass it in to the event when it is raised.

   ```
   if (video == null && AllCopiesRentedOut != null)
   {
       video = videos.FirstOrDefault(v => v.FilmId.Equals(filmId));
       AllCopiesRentedOut(video);
   }
   ```

5. If the previous **if**-statement is evaluated to **false** then count the number of films that are available for rental and store the result in a variable called **count**. Raise the **VideoInfo** event passing in the **Title** property of the video matching the film id and the **count** variable.

   ```
   else
   {
       var count = videos.Count(v => v.FilmId.Equals(filmId) &&
         !v.IsRented);
       VideoInfo(video.Title, count);
   }
   ```

The complete code for the **RentVideo** method:

```
public void RentVideo(int filmId)
{
    var video = videos.FirstOrDefault(
        v => v.FilmId.Equals(filmId) && !v.IsRented);

    // Rent out video if available
    if (video != null)
    {
        video.IsRented = true;

        // Check if there still are videos available
        video = videos.FirstOrDefault(v => v.FilmId.Equals(filmId) &&
            !v.IsRented);
    }

    // Check if event should be triggered
    if (video == null && AllCopiesRentedOut != null)
    {
        video = videos.FirstOrDefault(v => v.FilmId.Equals(filmId));
        AllCopiesRentedOut(video);
    }
    else
    {
        var count = videos.Count(v => v.FilmId.Equals(filmId) &&
            !v.IsRented);
        VideoInfo(video.Title, count);
    }
}
```

The ReturnVideo method

1. Add a **void** method called **ReturnVideo** which take an **int** parameter called **filmId**.
2. Fetch the first video in the **videos** collection that matches the film id and is rented out, store the result in a variable called **video**.
3. If the **video** variable is <u>not</u> **null** then set its **IsRented** property to **false** to indicate that it is available for rental.
4. Count the number of films matching the film id and that are not rented out and store the result in a variable called **count**.
5. Raise the **VideoReturned** event passing in the video **Title** property and the **count** variable to it.

The complete code of the **ReturnVideo** method:

```
public void ReturnVideo(int filmId)
{
    var video = videos.FirstOrDefault(
        v => v.FilmId.Equals(filmId) && v.IsRented);

    // Return video
    if (video != null)
    {
        video.IsRented = false;
        var count = videos.Count(v => v.FilmId.Equals(filmId) &&
            !v.IsRented);
        VideoReturned(video.Title, count);
    }
}
```

The Form class (event subscriber)

The form constructor will add videos to the **videos** collection by calling the **AddVideoToList** method on an instance of the **VideoRental** class called **rental**. It will also add the videos in the **videos** collection as the data source for the combo box by calling the **GetVideos** method.

The form's code-behind code so far:

```
public partial class Form1 : Form
{
    VideoRental rental = new VideoRental();

    public Form1()
    {
        rental.AddVideoToList(new Video { FilmId = 1, Title = "Alien" });
        rental.AddVideoToList(new Video { FilmId = 2, Title = "Aliens" });
        rental.AddVideoToList(new Video { FilmId = 2, Title = "Aliens" });

        InitializeComponent();

        cboVideos.DataSource = rental.GetVideos();
        cboVideos.DisplayMember = "Title";
    }
}
```

The Rent button's click event

Before trying to rent the video selected in the combo box you have to subscribe to the **AllCopiesRentedOut** and **VideoInfo** events. Call the **RentVideo** method on the **rental** instance variable to rent the film then unsubscribe to the events.

1. Add the **Click** event for the **Rent** button.
2. Subscribe to the two events. Press the **Tab** key on the keyboard twice after you have written **+=** to automatically generate the event method.
   ```
   rental.AllCopiesRentedOut += rental_AllCopiesRentedOut;
   rental.VideoInfo += rental_VideoInfo;
   ```
3. Clear the label and fetch the selected video from the combo box.
4. Call the **RentVideo** method on the **rental** instance variable and pass in the video you fetched.
5. Unsubscribe to the events.

The complete code of the **Rent** button's **Click** event:

```
private void btnRent_Click(object sender, EventArgs e)
{
    // Subscribe to event
    rental.AllCopiesRentedOut += rental_AllCopiesRentedOut;
    rental.VideoInfo += rental_VideoInfo;

    // Try to rent a video
    lblResult.Text = String.Empty;
    var video = (Video)cboVideos.SelectedItem;
    rental.RentVideo(video.FilmId);

    // Unsubscribe to event
    rental.AllCopiesRentedOut -= rental_AllCopiesRentedOut;
    rental.VideoInfo -= rental_VideoInfo;
}
```

The AllCopiesRentedOut event method

This method is called when the **AllCopiesRentedOut** event is raised in the **rental** instance's **RentVideo** method. Write a message to the label which states that all copies of the selected film is rented out.

The complete code of the **AllCopiesRentedOut** event:

```
void rental_AllCopiesRentedOut(Video video)
{
    lblResult.Text = String.Format(
    "All copies of '{0}' are rented out.", video.Title);
}
```

The VideoInfo event method

This method is called when the **VideoInfo** event is raised in the **rental** instance's **RentVideo** method. Write a message to the label which states that a copy of the selected film has been rented.

The complete code of the **VideoInfo** event:

```
void rental_VideoInfo(string title, int count)
{
    lblResult.Text = String.Format(
        "A copy of '{0}' has been rented.\nAvailable Copies: {1}.",
        title, count);
}
```

The Return button's Click event

Before the video can be returned you have to subscribe to the **VideoReturned** event which will write a message to the label if the video was successfully returned. You return the video by calling the **ReturnVideo** method on the **rental** instance variable.

1. Add the **Return** button's **Click** event.
2. Subscribe to the **VideoReturned** event.
3. Clear the label text and fetch the selected video from the combo box.
4. Call the **ReturnVideo** method on the **rental** instance variable.
5. Unsubscribe to the **VideoReturned** event.

The complete code of the **VideoReturned** event:

```
private void btnReturn_Click(object sender, EventArgs e)
{
    rental.VideoReturned += rental_VideoReturned;

    // Try to return a video
    lblResult.Text = String.Empty;
    var video = (Video)cboVideos.SelectedItem;
```

```
rental.ReturnVideo(video.FilmId);

    rental.VideoReturned -= rental_VideoReturned;
}
```

The VideoReturned Event Method

This method is called when the **VideoReturned** event is raised in the **rental** instance's **ReturnVideo** method. Write a message to the label which states that the video has been returned.

The complete code of the **VideoReturned** event:

```
void rental_VideoReturned(string title, int count)
{
    lblResult.Text = String.Format(
        "A copy of '{0}' has been returned.\nAvailable Copies: {1}.",
        title, count);
}
```

12. Inheritance

Introduction

Inheritance is the possibility to specialize a class that already exists by reusing it in another class. It is a very powerful tool in your object-oriented developer's toolkit. When inheriting a class, you are reusing the characteristics and behaviors of an already existing class; then you specialize your class by adding new characteristics and behaviors in the form of methods, properties and other programming constructs.

Using inheritance saves money and time by reducing the amount of code you have to write. Object hierarchies that can be used interchangeably depending on requirements are another benefit of using inheritance.

When inheriting, you take an existing class and use it as a base class, as a source of already implemented methods, properties and other constructs, and reuse it in your new class instead of starting from scratch.

Important: *You can only inherit from one class but you can implement several interfaces.*

Suppose you are creating an application that deals with different types of flying machines; you could then build an inheritance chain where you start out with the most general class, **FlyingMachine**, that implements only what is common to all flying machines. Then you inherit the **FlyingMachine** class to more specialized classes, **Plane** and **Saucer**, which are different types of flying machines and therefore have characteristics and behaviors suited to planes and saucers. Then you decide to specialize it further to different sub-categories and the different characteristics and behaviors for each category.

In the flying machine scenario, the **FlyingMachine** class would be the base class for **Plane** and **Saucer** and those two classes respectively would be base classes for the different categories that are created. Another way of putting it is that the category classes are deriving from the **Plane** or the **Saucer** classes; and the **Plane** and **Saucer** classes are deriving from the **FlyingMachine** class.

Important: *You inherit a class by specifying the class name of the class you want to inherit from to the right of the class name of the class you want to inherit to with a colon in between the class names. Example: class InheritingClass : ClassToInherit.*

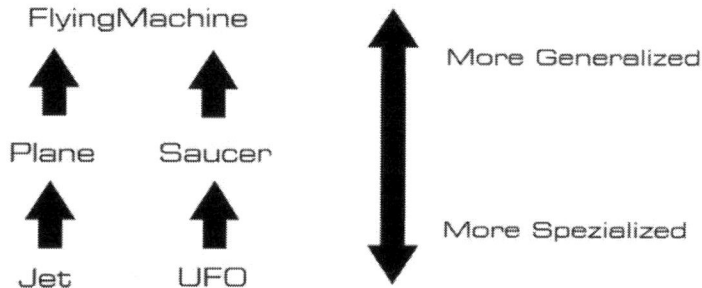

FlyingMachine

Plane   Saucer

Jet   UFO

More Generalized

More Spezialized

Base class: FlyingMachine

The **FlyingMachine** class is the most general class in this inheritance chain and contain members that are used in all types flying machines.

```
class FlyingMachine
{
    public void Drive() { }
    public void Stop() { }
}
```

More specialized classes: Plane and Saucer

The **Plane** and **Saucer** classes are more specialized flying machines than the **FlyingMachine** class and need the same logic as in the **FlyingMachine** class. Instead of rewriting the code from scratch ending up with two code bases that are the same inviting code inconsistencies, you can reuse the code from the **FlyingMachine** class by inheriting it in the **Plane** and **Saucer** class.

By inheriting the **FlyingMachine** class all its **public** members are available in the inheriting classes as if they were implemented in those classes.

```
class Plane : FlyingMachine
{
    public int NumberOfFloors { get; set; }
    public bool HasFirstClass { get; set; }
}
```

```
class Saucer : FlyingMachine
{
    public bool HasAlienTechnology { get; set; }
    public bool IsFromEarth { get; set; }
}
```

Even more specialized classes: Jet and UFO

The **Jet** and **UFO** classes are more specialized planes and flying saucers inheriting the characteristics and behaviors of the **Plane** and **Saucer** classes. By inheriting the **Plane** and **Saucer** classes the **Jet** and **UFO** classes will have access to the members in the **Plane** and **Saucer** classes as well as the members in the **FlyingMachine** class.

```
class Jet : Plane
{
    public bool IsSupersonic { get; set; }
}

class UFO : Saucer
{
    public bool HasWarpSpeed { get; set; }
}
```

Using the classes

The following code sample shows how to use the classes and what is available in each class. Members shown in bold are defined in that class and are not inherited.

```
void UsingTheSpecializedClasses()
{
    FlyingMachine fm = new FlyingMachine();
    fm.Drive();
    fm.Stop();

    Plane plane = new Plane();
    plane.Drive();
    plane.Stop();
    plane.HasFirstClass = true;
    plane.NumberOfFloors = 2;

    Jet jet = new Jet();
    jet.Drive();
    jet.Stop();
```

```
jet.NumberOfFloors = 3;
jet.HasFirstClass = true;
jet.IsSupersonic = false;

Saucer saucer = new Saucer();
saucer.Drive();
saucer.Stop();
saucer.HasAlienTechnology = false;
saucer.IsFromEarth = true;

UFO ufo = new UFO();
ufo.Drive();
ufo.Stop();
ufo.HasAlienTechnology = true;
ufo.IsFromEarth = false;
ufo.HasWarpSpeed = true;
}
```

Base classes

When working in a project, you should ask yourself if and when you or other developers need to use the class you are creating as a base class for inheritance. You have full control over how a class can be inherited if you choose to make it inheritable.

Abstract

It is not uncommon to create **abstract** classes that will be used only as base classes. The members of an abstract class' members do not have to have completely implemented functionality, it can even have missing functionality. It is up to you to decide if a developer can create instances of a class you are creating. If you want the class to be used in inheritance only and don't want the possibility to create instances of the class, then you add the **abstract** keyword to the class declaration.

When adding members to an abstract class, you can choose to create them with the **abstract** keyword, in which case they will be conceptually similar to members defined by interfaces in that they have to be overridden and implemented by the deriving class and no implementation is available in the **abstract** class. It is possible, however, to create fully implemented **non-abstract** members that can be used directly by a deriving class.

Important: *Abstract members cannot have a **private** access modifier.*

Important: *An **abstract** class can only be used in inheritance and cannot be instantiated.*

Creating an Abstract Class

The first two members of the class are implemented and contain logic that can be called directly from the inheriting class. The last two members are declared as **abstract** and need to be overridden in the inheriting class using the **override** keyword.

```
abstract class AbstractBaseClass
{
    // Members with implementations
    internal bool NonAbstractProperty { get; set; }
    internal void NonAbstractMethod()
    {
        // Do something
    }

    // Abstract members that need to be
    // overridden in the inheriting class
    internal abstract bool AbstractProperty { get; set; }
    internal abstract void AbstractMethod();
}
```

Using an Abstract class

Note that the two **abstract** members of the inherited **AbstractBaseClass** class are implemented using the **override** keyword in the **InheritingClass** class before they can be called whereas the two **non-abstract** members can be called directly.

```
class InheritingClass : AbstractBaseClass
{
    // Overridden members of the AbstractBaseClass class
    internal override bool AbstractProperty { get; set; }
    internal override void AbstractMethod()
    {
        // Do something
    }

    void UseMemebers()
    {
        // Using the non-abstract members
        // of the inherited class
        NonAbstractProperty = false;
        NonAbstractMethod();
```

```
        // Overridden members of the inherited class
        // can be called without first being overridden
        AbstractProperty = true;
        AbstractMethod();
    }
}
```

Sealed

In some circumstances, you might want to prevent developers from inheriting a class; you can accomplish this by adding the **sealed** keyword to the class declaration, creating an un-inheritable class.

When creating a class that derives from another class, you might want to prevent further inheritance; you can do that by adding the **sealed** keyword to your class declaration.

Important: *The **sealed** and **abstract** keywords cannot be used on the same class since they are the opposite of one another.*

Important: *Static classes are sealed and <u>cannot</u> be inherited and **static** members in a **non-static** class will not be inherited.*

Creating a Sealed class

This class cannot be inherited and must be instantiated to be used.

```
sealed class SealedClass
{
    public bool PropertyInSealedClass { get; set; }
    public int MethodInSealedClass(int x, int y)
    {
        return x + y;
    }
}
```

Using a Sealed class

The sealed class must be instantiated to be used.

```
class UseSealedClass
{
    public UseSealedClass()
    {
        // Using the sealed class
        var sealedClass = new SealedClass();
        sealedClass.PropertyInSealedClass = true;
        var result   = sealedClass.MethodInSealedClass(10, 20);
    }
}
```

Base class members

Declaring a member of a class with the **virtual** keyword makes it possible for developers to **override** or replace the member in a derived class. When overriding the method in the deriving class, you use the **override** keyword on the method.

The following code define a base class with two methods where the **Subtract** method will throw an exception when called if not overridden. The **Add** method can be called without an exception being throwing because it has valid logic.

```
class BaseClassWithVirtualMember
{
    public virtual int Add(int x, int y)
    {
        return x + y;
    }

    public virtual int Subtract(int x, int y)
    {
        throw new NotImplementedException();
    }
}
```

The following code defines a class inheriting the base class above and overrides the **Subtract** method with valid logic making it possible to call the method on instances of the inheriting class without it throwing an exception.

Note that you can call the **Add** method even though it is not overridden because it is inherited.

```
class OverridingVirtualMember : BaseClassWithVirtualMember
{
    public override int Subtract(int x, int y)
    {
        return x - y;
    }
}
```

The following code creates instances of the base class and the inheriting class and call the methods on the two instances. Note that the base class instance will throw an exception when the **Subtract** method is called but the **Subtract** method of the inheriting class instance will not because it has overridden the method and implemented valid logic.

```
class UseBaseClassMembers
{
    public UseBaseClassMembers()
    {
        var baseClass = new BaseClassWithVirtualMember();
        var baseAdd = baseClass.Add(60, 40);
        // Will throw an exception
        var baseSubtract = baseClass.Subtract(60, 40);

        var overridden = new OverridingVirtualMember();
        var add = overridden.Add(50, 30);
        // Will use the overridden implementation
        var subtract = overridden.Subtract(20, 10);
    }
}
```

New vs. Override

You also can use the **new** keyword to override a member; there is a subtle difference between the **override** and **new** keywords. The result when using the **new** keyword on a base class instance variable that is assigned an instance of a derived class might not be what you expect; the base class instance variable will call the base class implementation of the method overridden with the **new** keyword and not the implementation in the derived class.

The base class

The base class contain two **virtual** declared methods which can be overridden in a deriving class.

```csharp
class BaseClass
{
    public virtual void Method1()
    {
        Console.WriteLine("Base - Method1");
    }

    public virtual void Method2()
    {
        Console.WriteLine("Base - Method2");
    }
}
```

When creating an instance of the base class the methods in the base class will be called no matter how many deriving classes there are because it has no knowledge of those implementations as an instance of the base class.

```csharp
class NewVsOverride
{
    public NewVsOverride()
    {
        BaseClass baseClass = new BaseClass();
        baseClass.Method1();
        baseClass.Method2();

        //Output
        //Base - Method1
        //Base - Method2
    }
}
```

The Deriving class

The deriving class overrides the two virtual declared methods in the base class one with the **override** keyword and one with the **new** keyword.

```csharp
class DerivedClass : BaseClass
{
    public override void Method1()
```

```
    {
        Console.WriteLine("Derived - Method1 (override)");
    }

    public new void Method2()
    {
        Console.WriteLine("Derived - Method2 (new)");
    }
}
```

When creating an instance of the deriving class and calling the methods on that instance variable the overridden methods will be called.

```
class NewVsOverride
{
    public NewVsOverride()
    {
        DerivedClass derivedClass = new DerivedClass();
        derivedClass.Method1();
        derivedClass.Method2();

        //Output
        //Derived - Method1 (override)
        //Derived - Method2 (new)
    }
}
```

Casting the Deriving class as the base class

When casting an instance of the derived class to the base class and calling the methods on that base class instance variable there is one scenario concerning the **new** keyword you should be aware of and that is when the **new** keyword has been used to override a method in the deriving class.

The **new** keyword will override the method implementation in the deriving class and it will be executed when an instance variable of the deriving class is used to call the overridden method. However, if the instance variable of the deriving class is cast to the base class and that instance variable is used to call the overridden methods, the method overridden with the **override** keyword will execute the implementation in the deriving class whereas the one overridden with the **new** keyword will execute the implementation in the base class.

Important: *Note the output for this scenario, the first method will execute the code in the deriving class and the second method will execute the code in the base class.*

```csharp
class NewVsOverride
{
    public NewVsOverride()
    {
        BaseClass baseClassAsDerivedClass = new DerivedClass();
        baseClassAsDerivedClass.Method1();
        baseClassAsDerivedClass.Method2();

        //Output
        //Derived - Method1 (override)
        //Base - Method2
    }
}
```

Additional reading: "Knowing When to Use Override and New Keywords (C# Programming Guide)"

Sealing overridden members

Sealing overridden members is a way for you to force deriving classes to use your implementation. You make a member sealed by using the **sealed** keyword on methods overridden with the **override** keyword.

Important: *Members are **sealed** by default unless you declare them with the **virtual** keyword.*

Important: *You can only use the **sealed** keyword on overridden methods in derived classes.*

```csharp
class BaseClassSealedMembers
{
    // Can be overridden when the
    // class is inherited
    public virtual void DoSomething()
    {
    }
}
```

```csharp
class DerivingClass : BaseClassSealedMembers
{
    // Cannot be overridden if the class
    // is inherited
    public sealed override void DoSomething()
    {
    }
}

class SecondDerivingClass : DerivingClass
{
    // Not possible because the method
    // is sealed in the inherited class.
    // Will cause a compilation error.
    public override void DoSomething()
    {
    }
}
```

Access modifiers

There are five *access modifiers* that control where a class or a member will be accessible. Members are **private** by default and will not be directly accessible from derived classes; to access a **private** member, you have to create a property or method to expose it. A class in **internal** by default.

Access Modifier	Description
Public	Available from any assembly
Protected	Available internally in the class and in classes deriving from the class containing the member.
Internal	Available in the assembly where the class is located.
Protected Internal	Available in the assembly where the class is located and in classes deriving from the class containing the member.
Private	Available in the class containing the member.

Example: Access modifiers (The Godfather)

This example is loosely modeled on the film The Godfather and the Corleone family and the police interrogating them; the purpose is to shed light on the different access modifiers that can be used and their restrictions.

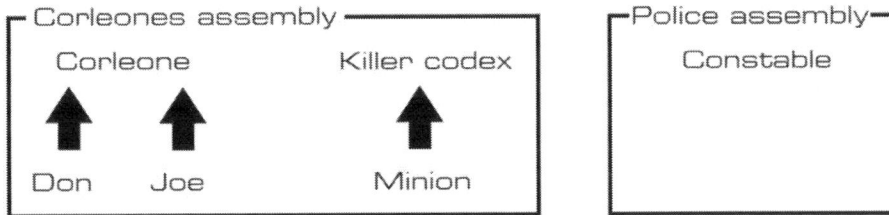

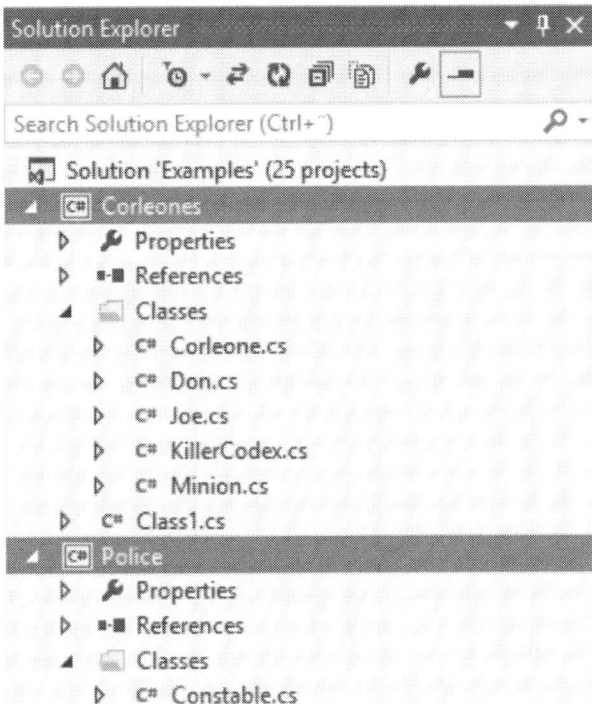

Assemblies, classes and inheritance

In the **Corleones** assembly, we find the classes related to the Corleone family and their minions that do the dirty work for the family. The **Corleone** class is the base class that all Corleone family members inherit from (**Don** and **Joe**). The family has a honor codex that all of their minions who aspire to be hit men have to adhere to. That codex is represented by the **KillerCodex** class; this is the base class for all minions. An instance of the **Minion** class represents a hit man that the family uses.

Outside of the family, we have the constables who chase the family and try to catch them; the **Constable** class is located in the **Police** assembly.

The Corleone class

The **Corleone** class is declared as **public** which means that it can be reached from any assembly. All members are declared as **internal** which means that they can be reached within the **Corleone** assembly, but not from the **Police** assembly.

The **GetMinion** and **AddMinion** methods are declared as **virtual** which means that they can be overridden and implement new logic when the **Corleone** class is inherited. **Don** and **Joe** might have different ways of dealing with the minions and therefore implement the methods with logic specific to their needs.

```csharp
public class Corleone
{
    internal List<Minion> Minions = new List<Minion>();

    internal virtual Minion GetMinion(string name)
    {
        throw new NotImplementedException();
    }

    internal virtual void AddMinion(Minion minion)
    {
        Minions.Add(minion);
    }
}
```

The Don class

This class represents the father of the family and the leader of the organization. This class **inherits** the **Corleone** class and will have access to its members. The **Don** class is declared with the **sealed** keyword which means that it cannot be inherited.

Don Corleone has a family secret that is closely guarded and that only the family knows about; this information and the lie that he tells the police when they are grilling him are declared as **private** because he want the possibility to choose who to share the secret with exposing it through **public** or **internal** properties.

One thing that is public knowledge is that he has a son named Joe. **Joe** is declared as a separate class of which an instance is stored in the **Don** class because he is Don Corelones son and is therefore associated with him; the instance is created in the **Don** class' constructor and the **Don** instance is passed to the **Jon** instance to establish the relationship between father and son using the **this** keyword which represent the current instance of the **Don** class.

```
Son = new Joe(this);
```

What Don tells the family when they ask about the secret is represented by the **TellFamily** property which is declared as **internal** to make sure that only members of the **Corleones** assembly ever can find out the truth. The property **TellPolice** is declared as **public** because anyone, even members of other assemblies, are allowed to hear the lie.

The **GetMinion** method is inherited from the **Corleones** class, but is overridden using the **overrides** keyword to create an alternative implementation that will be used when Don is calling for one of his minions. The method is also declared as **internal** to make sure that only members of the **Corleones** assembly can ask Don to contact his minions.

The **SolveProblem** method is declared without access modifier making it **private.** This means that only members in the **Don** class can call it; whenever Don wants to have a problem solved his son will take care of it hence the call to the **OrderHit** method on the **Son** property containing the **Joe** instance.

```
sealed public class Don : Corleone
{
    private string familySecret = "This is the secret";
    private string lie = "I have no idea";
    public Joe Son { get; set; }

    public Don()
    {
        Son = new Joe(this);
    }

    internal string TellFamily { get { return familySecret; } }
    public string TellPolice { get { return lie; } }

    internal override Minion GetMinion(string name)
    {
        return (from minion in Minions
                where minion.Name == name
                select minion).SingleOrDefault();
    }
}
```

```
void SolveProblem()
{
    Son.OrderHit("Charlie", "Marty");
}
}
```

The Joe class

Joe is the son of Don and helps him run the family business; the **Joe** class is declared as **public** which means that it can be reached from any assembly and has no restrictions on inheritance. Who knows, maybe he will clone himself in the future.

The **AddMinion** method is inherited from the **Corleone** class but is overridden with its own unique implementation, it is also declared as **sealed** which means that if the **Joe** class is inherited, this method cannot be overridden by the deriving class; it is also declared as **internal** which means that it only can be used inside the **Corleones** assembly.

The **GetMinion** method is inherited from the **Corleone** class but is overridden and declared as **internal** which means that it has its own unique implementation and only can be used inside the **Corleones** assembly. Note that it has a different implementation than the same method in the **Don** class.

In the **OrderHit** method which is declared as **internal** and only available in the **Corleones** assembly and the **Kill** method is called on the fetched **Minion** instance using method chaining.

The **AskAboutSecret** method is declared as **public,** making it possible to access it from the **Police** assembly or any other assembly. Note that Joe is thinking about the family secret that he has asked his father about, but speaking the lie.

```
public class Joe : Corleone
{
    private Don father;
    public Joe(Don father)
    {
        this.father = father;
    }

    internal sealed override void AddMinion(Minion minion)
    {
```

348

```
        var exist = GetMinion(minion.Name) != null;
        if(!exist) Minions.Add(minion);
    }

    internal override Minion GetMinion(string name)
    {
        return Minions.SingleOrDefault(m => m.Name.Equals(name));
    }

    internal void OrderHit(string minion, string target)
    {
        GetMinion(minion).Kill(target);
    }

    public string AskAboutSecret()
    {
        Console.WriteLine(
            "[Joe thinking] The Secret is: {0}",
            father.TellFamily);

        return father.TellPolice;
    }
}
```

The KillerCodex class

This class contains two methods that minions who aspire to be hit men must implement or use as is through inheritance. The **KillerCodex** class is declared as **internal** because the police must not be aware of the contract between a minion and the Corleone family. The contract is honored by the minion class **inheriting** the **KillerCodex** class.

The **ChooseWeapon** method is declared as **protected** which means that it has to be inherited to be used outside of the **KillerCodex** class.

The **Kill** method is declared as **protected internal** which means that it can be used either by inheritance or through an instance variable internally in the **Corleones** assembly.

```
internal class KillerCodex
{
    protected void ChooseWeapon()
    {
    }
```

```
    protected internal void Kill(string name)
    {
    }
}
```

The Minion class

This class represents one of the minions working for the family and it **inherits** the **KillerCodex** class and its members. The **Minion** class is declared as **internal** which means that it only is accessible within the **Corleones** assembly and as such not available to the police assembly; this makes the minions a secret group that only the family knows about.

Note that the **Kill** method does not have to be implemented to be used when Joe calls the method from the **OrderHit** method; the **Kill** method can be called by Joe because it is declared as **internal** in the **KillerCodex** class.

```
internal class Minion : KillerCodex
{
    internal string Name { get; set; }

    internal Minion(string name)
    {
        Name = name;
        ChooseWeapon();
    }

    public void Talk()
    {
        Console.WriteLine("I'm not saying anything");
    }
}
```

The Constable class

The **Constable** class resides in a different assembly than all the other classes because it does not belong to the family; the police may be bought but that is not the same, they are still not part of the family. The constables loves to interrogate people and seizes every opportunity to interrogate the Corleones.

The **Constable** class contain one method that asks Don or Joe about the secret; note however that the constable does not have any knowledge of the minions. The **Minion** class is declared as **internal,** making it impossible for other assemblies to access it; you might say that the minions hide as a secret group inside the **Corleones** family assembly.

Note that the person parameter in the **Interrogate** method is declared with the object data type to allow instances of any class to be passed in. The **is** keyword is then used to determine if it is a **Don** or a **Joe** class instance.

Important: *You need to add a reference to the **Corleones** assembly in the **Police** assembly to get access to its classes.*

```
public class Constable
{
    public void Interrogate(object person)
    {
        if (person is Don)
            Console.WriteLine("[Don] {0}", ((Don)person).TellPolice);

        if (person is Joe)
            Console.WriteLine("[Joe] {0}", ((Joe)person).AskAboutSecret());

        // Not possible since the Minion class is declared as internal
        // if (person is Minion)
        // Console.WriteLine("[Minion] {0}", ((Minion)person).TellPolice);
    }
}
```

The base keyword

In some situations, you might want to call a base class' methods or constructor from a derived class even though you have overridden the member in the derived class. You use the **base** keyword to achieve this.

You might have overridden a method in the base class or created a new method and want to call the base class' method as part of your logic; or you want to call the base class' constructor when initializing the derived class. You might also want to call a base class method from a property accessor.

When instantiating a derived class, the base class default constructor will automatically be called before any of the derived class logic is executed. Sometimes you want to call an alternate constructor instead of the default base class constructor; in these situations you use the **base** keyword in the derived class' constructor declaration.

The base class

```
public class Beverage
{
    public string Name { get; set; }
    public bool IsFairTrade { get; set; }

    public Beverage()
    {
        Name = String.Empty;
        IsFairTrade = false;
    }

    public Beverage(string name, bool isFairTrade)
    {
        Name = name;
        IsFairTrade = isFairTrade;
    }

    public virtual bool GetFairTrade()
    {
        return IsFairTrade;
    }
}
```

The deriving class

```
public class Tea : Beverage
{
    public double Weight { get; set; }

    // Call the default base class constructor
    // Is the same as Tea() : base()
    public Tea() { }

    public Tea(string name, bool isFairTrade, double weight)
        : base(name, isFairTrade)
    {
        // Will call the Beverage(string name, bool isFairTrade)
        // constructor before executing any code in this constructor block
        Weight = weight;
    }
```

```
public override bool GetFairTrade()
{
    // Call the GetFairTrade method
    // in the base class
    if (!base.GetFairTrade())
    {
        /* Apply for fair trade status */
    }

    return base.GetFairTrade();
}
}
```

Exercise: Inheritance and access modifiers (Jedi vs. Sith)

This exercise is meant to demonstrate how you can implement inheritance across assemblies and how to use access modifiers to determine where the members of the classes are reachable.

The background story is probably already familiar to you it's a story of good versus evil set in the epic Star Wars science fiction adventures of Jedi versus Sith. As you may well know there can only ever be two Sith, one master and one apprentice. With Jedi it's a bit different since they are the peace keepers of the universe there has to be more than two but a Jedi master can only have one padawan apprentice at any given time.

There are two sides to the force, light and dark, where the Jedi use the light side to uphold peace and the Sith use the dark side to cause mischief and chaos. Once you cross from the light side to the dark it is impossible to turn back. As a Sith you have access to both sides of the force for a while until you have been completely turned to the dark side, like Anakin Skywalker aka Darth Vader.

This application will keep track of who is a Jedi master and who is a padawan apprentice as well as who is the Sith lord and who is the Sith apprentice. To be able to reuse common classes they will be placed in a separate assembly (class library) called **Common Traits** and inherited where needed. The **Jedi** and **Sith** classes will also be placed in separate class libraries called **Jedis** and **Siths** to maintain a barrier between the two. The application will be created as a Console application in a fourth assembly.

In the Console application you want to display information about the characters such as name, race, midichlorian count and what force they use (dark and/or light). You also want to enable the characters to ask one another two questions, the first being whether they are a Sith, a Jedi or neither, the second question is if the character is a Sith; if the character being asked is a Jedi the answer should contain information about if they are a Jedi master or a padawan and if the character has an apprentice. If the character being asked is a Sith and the character asking is a Sith then internal information about being a Sith lord or an apprentice should be revealed otherwise any knowledge about the Sith should be denied.

You will add at least the following four characters Jar Jar Binx (gungan, no force), Senator Palpatine (human, dark side), Anakin Skywalker (human, light side) and Obi Wan Kenobi (human, light side). During the execution Anakin will be turned to the dark side in two steps where the first is becoming Palpatine's apprentice and the second giving in fully to the dark side.

To make it easier to print the information to the Console you will create two methods in the Console Application's **Program** class called **PrintBeing** which outputs the stats about a character and **PrintQuestions** which outputs the answers to the two questions mentioned earlier.

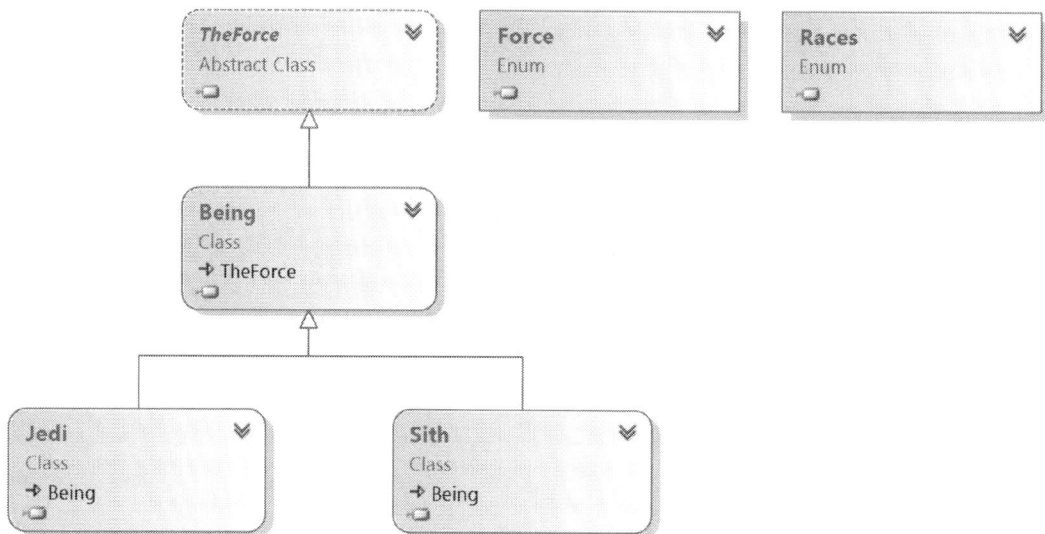

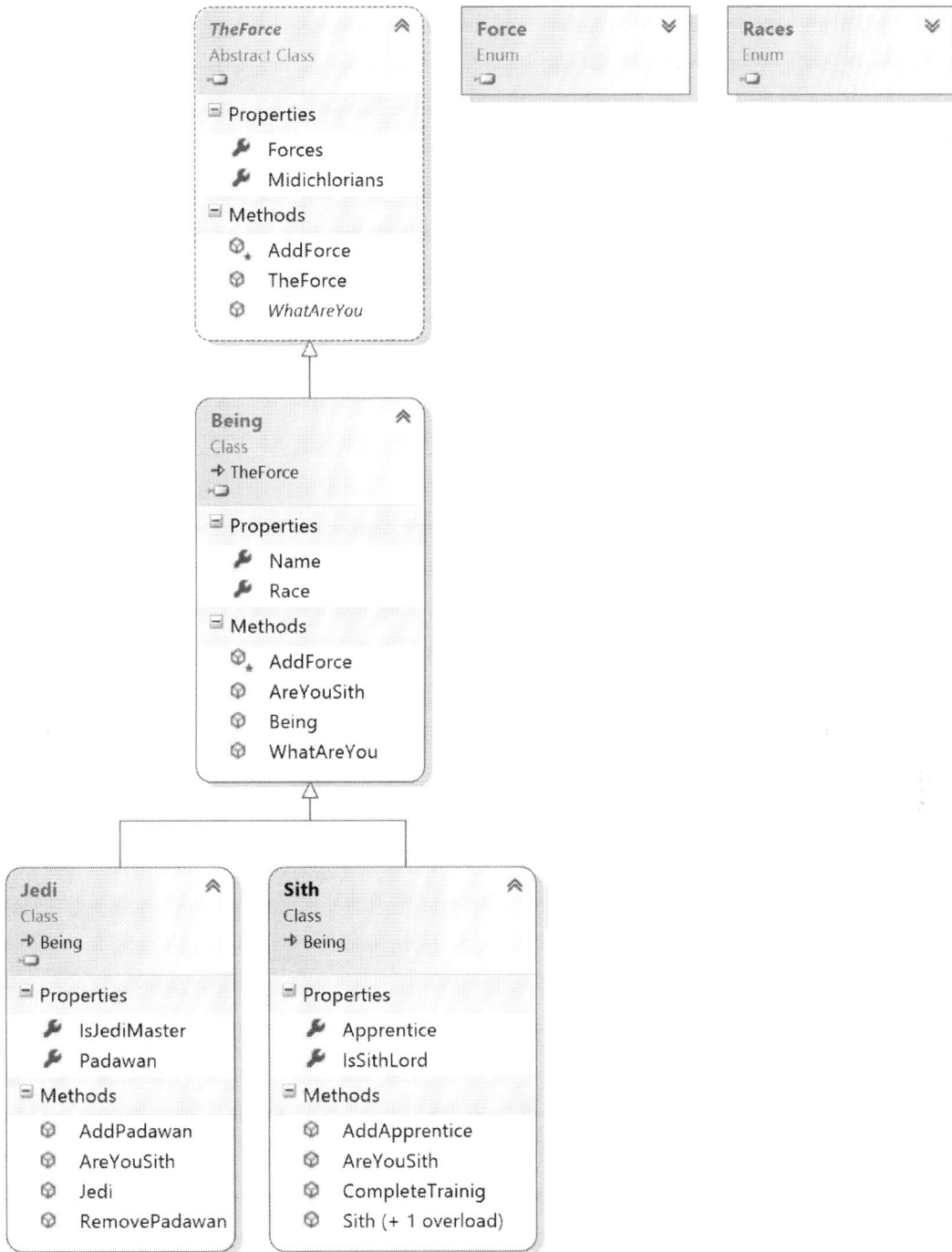

Creating the assemblies

You will need to create four assemblies; start with a Console Application called **JediVsSith** and add the other three Class Library assemblies called **Common Traits**, **Jedis** and **Siths** to the solution.

1. Create a new Console Application called **JediVsSith**.
2. Add a **Class Library** project called **Common Traits** to the solution by right clicking on the solution name in the Solution Explorer and select **Add-New Project**.
3. Add two folders to the **Common Traits** assembly called **Classes** and **Enums**.
4. Add another **Class Library** project called **Jedis**.
5. Add another **Class Library** project called **Siths**.
6. Make sure that the Console Application is the startup project by right clicking on it and select **Set as Startup Project**.

The Common Traits assembly

The **Common Traits** assembly is a **Class Library** which contains classes that are common to all characters whether they are Jedi, Sith or neither.

The Races and Force enumerations

The **Common Traits** assembly also contains one enumeration called **Force** which list the two forces available (**DarkSide** and **LightSide**) and one enumeration called **Races** which list the available races that the characters can be (**Human**, **Gungan**, **Other**). The enumerations have to be **public** to be accessible from any assembly.

1. Add a new class called **Enums** to the **Enums** folder and delete the class' code leaving the namespace block empty.
   ```
   namespace CommonTraits.Enums
   {
   }
   ```
2. Add a **public enum** called **Races** with the following choices: **Human**, **Gungan** and **Other**. You can add more if you like.
3. Add a **public enum** called **Force** with the following choices: **DarkSide** and **LightSide**.

The complete code for the enums:

```
namespace CommonTraits.Enums
{
    public enum Races
    {
        Human,
        Gungan,
        Other
    }

    public enum Force
    {
        DarkSide,
        LightSide
    }
}
```

The TheForce class

This class should only be accessible through inheritance and contains characteristics and behaviors related to the force such a collection of the forces a being possesses and the midichlorian count as well as the **abstract** definition for the method **WhatAreYou** answering that very question when implemented in other classes. A method called **AddForce** which should be available through inheritance and be override-able in the inheriting classes, it should add the specified force to the **Forces** collection.

The class: Should only be accessible through inheritance. The constructor should take an **int** parameter called **midichlorians** which should be assigned to a property with the same name and the **Forces** collection should be initialized here.

The Forces collection: Should be readable from any assembly but only assignable within the class.

The Midichlorians property: Is an **int** property containing the midichlorian count for the character, it should be readable from any assembly but only assignable within the class.

The WhatAreYou method: Should not contain any implementation and should only be implementable by an inheriting class. It should have a **Being** parameter representing the character being questioned, the suspect if you will.

The AddForce method: Should have a **Force** parameter which is added to the **Forces** collection.

1. Add a class called **TheForce** to the **Classes** folder in the **Common Traits** assembly.
2. Change the access modifier of the class to **public abstract**.
   ```
   public abstract class TheForce
   {
   }
   ```
3. Add a **public List<Force>** collection called **Forces** with a **private** setter.
   ```
   public List<Force> Forces { get; private set; }
   ```
4. Add a **public int** property called **Midichlorians** with a **private** setter.
5. Add a constructor with an **int** parameter called **midichlorians** and assign the parameter value to the property with the same name and instantiate the collection.
6. Add an **abstract string** method called **WhatAreYou** which have a **Being** parameter called **suspect**. Being **abstract** the method cannot contain any implementation in the **abstract** class and has to be implemented by an inheriting class.
   ```
   public abstract string WhatAreYou(Being suspect);
   ```
7. Add a **protected virtual void** method called **AddForce** that has a **Force** parameter which is added to the **Forces** collection. Being **protected** the method can only be called from an inheriting class and being declared as **virtual** will make it possible to override the implementation in the inheriting class using either the **override** or **new** keyword.
   ```
   protected virtual void AddForce(Force force) { ... }
   ```

The complete code for the **TheForce** class:

```
public abstract class TheForce
{
    public List<Force> Forces { get; private set; }
    public int Midichlorians { get; private set; }

    public TheForce(int midichlorians)
    {
        Midichlorians = midichlorians;
        Forces = new List<Force>();
    }

    public abstract string WhatAreYou(Being suspect);
```

```
    protected virtual void AddForce(Force force)
    {
        Forces.Add(force);
    }
}
```

The Being class

The **Being** class represent the basic characteristics and behaviors of a character. Use inheritance to shorten the time it takes to develop the class; by inheriting the **TheForce** class you don't have to rewrite everything from scratch. The inheritance will give you direct access to the **AddForce** method implementation making it possible to call it from within the **Being** class, it will also force you to implement the **abstract WhatAreYou** method. You can also read the values from the **Forces** and **Midichlorians** properties.

Apart from the inherited properties you will need to add two properties related to a being called **Name** of type **string** and **Race** of type **Races** (the **enum**). It should be possible to create instances from the **Being** class as well as inherit it and its constructor should have three parameters for name, race and midichlorians; the last parameter should be passed to the base class' constructor.

Three methods called **AddForce** (override), **WhatAreYou** (override) and **AreYouSith** should be implemented (see details below).

The Being class: Should inherit the **TheForce** class and override its **AddForce** and **WhatAreYou** methods. The constructor should take three parameters called **name**, **race** and **midichlorians** with the data types **string**, **Race** (enum) and **int** respectively. The first two parameters should be assigned to properties with the same names in the **Being** class whereas the third should be passed to the base class' (the inherited class') constructor.

The AddForce method: Should override the inherited method with the same name and stop any further overrides if the **Being** class is inherited. The implementation should check if the force being added already exist and if so skip adding it.

The WhatAreYou method: The purpose of this method is to find out if a character is a Jedi, Sith or neither by asking. The **Being** instance passed in as through the **suspect** parameter is the character you are asking. If the instance is **null** then return the **string** "I don't exist" (could be the case when Anakin has been completely turned to the dark side and no longer recognizes himself as Anakin Skywalker), if both the character asking the question and the suspect are capable of using the dark side of the force then return "I'm a Sith", else if the suspect is capable of using the light side of the force then return "I'm a Jedi" or if none of the expressions are valid then return "I'm neither Jedi nor Sith".

The AreYouSith method: Should be **public** and override-able by an inheriting class and have a **Being** parameter called **suspect**. The default implementation in this class should return the **string** "I'm not Sith".

1. Add a class called **Being** to the **Classes** folder in the **Common Traits** assembly.
2. Change the access modifier of the class to **public** and inherit the **TheForce** class.
   ```
   public class Being : TheForce
   {
   }
   ```
3. Add a **string** property called **Name** which can be read from any assembly but only can be assigned within the **Being** class.
4. Add a **Races** property called **Race** which can be read from any assembly but only is assignable within the **Being** class.
5. Add a constructor which has three parameters **name** of type **string**, **race** of type **Races** and **midichlorians** of type **int**. Assign the first two parameters in the constructor and pass the third to the base class' constructor.
   ```
   public Being(string name, Races race, int midichlorians) :
   base(midichlorians){ ... }
   ```
6. Override the inherited **AddForce** method and make it **sealed** to avoid further overrides. Implement it as described above.
   ```
   sealed protected override void AddForce(Force force)
   ```
7. Override the inherited **WhatAreYou** method and make it **sealed** to stop further overrides. Implement it as described above.
8. Add a new **public virtual string** method called **AreYouSith** with a **Being** parameter called suspect and a default return value of "I'm not a Sith". The **virtual** keyword will make it possible to override this implementation in inheriting classes.
   ```
   public virtual string AreYouSith(Being suspect)
   ```

The complete code for the **Being** class:

```csharp
public class Being : TheForce
{
    public string Name { get; private set; }
    public Races Race { get; private set; }

    public Being(string name, Races race, int midichlorians)
    : base(midichlorians)
    {
        Name = name;
        Race = race;
    }

    sealed protected override void AddForce(Force force)
    {
        if(!Forces.Contains(force))
            Forces.Add(force);
    }

    public sealed override string WhatAreYou(Being suspect)
    {
        if (suspect == null)
            return "I don't exist";
        else if (suspect.Forces.Contains(Force.DarkSide) &&
            Forces.Contains(Force.DarkSide))
            return "I'm a Sith";
        else if (suspect.Forces.Contains(Force.LightSide))
            return "I'm a Jedi";

        return "I'm neither Sith nor Jedi";
    }

    public virtual string AreYouSith(Being suspect)
    {
        return "I'm not a Sith";
    }
}
```

The Jedis assembly

This assembly contain one class called **Jedi** which represent a Jedi character. The reason it is created in a separate assembly is to define a clear border between the **Jedi** and **Sith** classes to keep their logic clearly separated.

You will need to add a reference to the **Common Traits** assembly to gain access to all the necessary classes and enumerations.

The Jedi class

The Jedi class: inherit the **Being** class and all its inherent and inherited characteristics and behaviors. The constructor should have three parameters **name** of type **string**, **race** of type **Races** and **midichlorians** of type **int** with a default value of 0. All parameter values should be passed to the base class' constructor. In the constructor the **LightSide** force should be added to the **Forces** collection by calling the inherited **AddForce** method.

The Padawan property: Assigning a **Jedi** instance to this property represent that the **Jedi** has an apprentice. This property should be publicly readable but only privately assignable.

The IsJediMaster property: Will return **true** if the **Jedi** has a padawan apprentice. This property should only have a **get**-block.

The AddPadawan method: This method will add the passed in **Jedi** instance to the **Padawan** property representing that the Jedi has an apprentice.

The RemovePadawan method: Will remove the padawan apprentice from the Jedi by assigning the default value of the **Jedi** class to the **Padawan** property.

The AreYouSith method: This is an overridden version of the inherited method with the same name. The method should return "I'm a Jedi Master, and my apprentice is {name of apprentice}" if the passed in **Being** instance is a **Jedi** master, "I'm a Padawan and my name is {name of padawan}" if the being is a **Jedi** but not a master or "I don't know of any Sith" otherwise.

1. Add a class called **Jedi** to the **Jedis** assembly.
2. Change the access modifier to **public** and inherit the **Being** class.
   ```
   public class Jedi : Being
   {
   }
   ```
3. Add a **public Jedi** property called **Padawan** which only can be assigned from within the **Jedi** class.
   ```
   public Jedi Padawan { get; private set; }
   ```

4. Add a **public bool** property called **IsJediMaster** which only has a **get**-block that return **true** if there is a **Jedi** instance assigned to the **Padawan** property.
```
public bool IsJediMaster { get { return Padawan != null; } }
```

5. Add a constructor with three parameters for name, race and midichlorian count that are passed to the base class' constructor. Call the inherited **AddForce** method from inside the constructor to assign the **LightSide** force to the Jedi.
```
public Jedi(string name, Races race, int midichlorians = 0) :
base(name, race, midichlorians)
{
    AddForce(Force.LightSide);
}
```

6. Add a **public void** method called **AddPadawan** which has a **Jedi** parameter that is assigned to the **Padawan** property.

7. Add a parameter-less **public void** method called **RemovePadawan** which assigns the **default** value of the **Jedi** class to the **Padawan** property.
```
Padawan = default(Jedi);
```

8. Override the inherited method **AreYouSith**. Implement it as described above.

The complete code for the **Jedi** class:

```
public class Jedi : Being
{
    public Jedi Padawan { get; private set; }
    public bool IsJediMaster { get { return Padawan != null; } }

    public Jedi(string name, Races race, int midichlorians = 0)
        : base(name, race, midichlorians)
    {
        AddForce(Force.LightSide);
    }

    public void AddPadawan(Jedi padawan) {
        Padawan = padawan;
    }

    public void RemovePadawan() {
        Padawan = default(Jedi);
    }
```

```
public override string AreYouSith(Being suspect)
{
    if (suspect is Jedi)
    {
        var jedi = suspect as Jedi;

        if (jedi.IsJediMaster)
            return "I'm a Jedi Master, and my apprentice is " +
                jedi.Padawan.Name;
        else
            return "I'm a Padawan and my name is " + jedi.Name;
    }
    else
    {
        return "I don't know of any Sith";
    }
}
}
```

The Siths assembly

This assembly contain one class called **Sith** which represent a Sith character. The reason it is created in a separate assembly is to define a clear border between the **Jedi** and **Sith** classes to keep their logic clearly separated.

You will need to add a reference to the **Common Traits** assembly to gain access to all the necessary classes and enumerations.

The Sith class

The Sith class: inherit the **Being** class and all its inherent and inherited characteristics and behaviors. The constructor should have three parameters **name** of type **string, race** of type **Races** and **midichlorians** of type **int** with a default value of **0**. All parameter values should be passed to the base class' constructor. In the constructor the **DarkSide** force should be added to the **Forces** collection by calling the inherited **AddForce** method. A second constructor with a parameter called **being** of the **Being** data type and a parameter called **name** of the **string** data type should be added calling the first constructor with values from the being parameter and the name parameter.

The Apprentice property: Assigning a **Sith** instance to this property represent that the **Sith** has an apprentice. This property should be publicly readable but only privately assignable.

The IsSithLord property: Will return **true** if the **Sith** has an apprentice. This property should only have a **get**-block.

The AddApprentice method: This method will create a new **Sith** instance from the passed in **Jedi** instance and the name in the **name** parameter. The new **Sith** instance is then assigned to the **Apprentice** property representing that the current **Sith** has an apprentice. Then all the forces in the **Jedi**'s **Forces** collection is added to the **Sith** instance and the **Jedi** instance is assigned the **default** value of the **Jedi** class. Lastly the new apprentice is returned from the method.

The CompleteTraining method: This method will be called when the **Sith** apprentice has taken the final step towards the dark side to remove any traces of the light force.

The AreYouSith method: This is an overridden version of the inherited method with the same name. The method should return "I'm a Sith Lord, and my apprentice is {name of apprentice}" if the passed in **Being** instance is a Sith Lord, "I'm a Sith Apprentice and my name is {name of apprentice}" if the being is a **Sith** but not a Sith Lord or "I don't know of any Sith" otherwise.

1. Add a class called **Sith** to the **Siths** assembly.
2. Change the access modifier to **public** and inherit the **Being** class.
   ```
   public class Sith : Being
   {
   }
   ```
3. Add a **public Sith** property called **Apprentice** which only can be assigned from within the **Sith** class.
   ```
   public Sith Apprentice { get; private set; }
   ```
4. Add a **public bool** property called **IsSithLord** which only has a **get**-block that return **true** if there is a **Sith** instance assigned to the **Apprentice** property.
   ```
   public bool IsSithLord { get { return Apprentice != null; } }
   ```
5. Add a constructor with three parameters for name, race and midichlorian count that are passed to the base class' constructor. Call the inherited **AddForce** method from inside the constructor to assign the **DarkSide** force to the **Sith**.

```
public Sith(string name, Races race, int midichlorians = 0) :
base(name, race, midichlorians)
{
    AddForce(Force.DarkSide);
}
```

6. Add a second constructor which has a **Being** and **name** parameter, use the values in the parameters when calling the first constructor in this class using the **this** keyword.

```
public Sith(Being being, string name)
: this(name, being.Race, being.Midichlorians)
{
}
```

7. Add a **public void** method called **AddApprentice** which has a **Jedi** parameter passed in by reference and a **string** parameter called **name** with the new name the apprentice is given by the Sith lord. The reason the **Jedi** parameter is passed in by reference is that you want to assign the **default** value of the **Jedi** class to it at the end of the method to symbolize that the **Jedi** no longer exist and now is the new born **Sith** Apprentice.

```
public Sith AddApprentice(ref Jedi jedi, string name)
{
    Apprentice = new Sith(jedi, name);
    Apprentice.Forces.AddRange(jedi.Forces);
    jedi = default(Jedi);
    return Apprentice;
}
```

8. Add a **public void** method called **CompleteTraining** with a **Sith** parameter. Remove all **LightSide** values from the Apprentice's **Forces** collection.

```
Apprentice.Forces.Remove(Force.LightSide);
```

9. Override the inherited method **AreYouSith**. Implement it as described above.

The complete code for the **Sith** class:

```
public class Sith : Being
{
    private Sith Apprentice { get; set; }
    internal bool IsSithLord { get { return Apprentice != null; } }
```

```csharp
    public Sith(string name, Races race, int midichlorians = 0)
    : base(name, race, midichlorians)
    {
        AddForce(Force.DarkSide);
    }

    public Sith(Being being, string name)
    : this(name, being.Race, being.Midichlorians)
    {
    }

    public void CompleteTrainig(Sith apprentice)
    {
        Apprentice.Forces.Remove(Force.LightSide);
    }

    public Sith AddApprentice(ref Jedi jedi, string name)
    {
        Apprentice = new Sith(jedi, name);
        Apprentice.Forces.AddRange(jedi.Forces);
        jedi = default(Jedi);
        return Apprentice;
    }

    public override string AreYouSith(Being suspect)
    {
        if (this is Sith && suspect is Sith)
        {
            var sith = suspect as Sith;

            if (sith.IsSithLord)
                return "I'm a Sith Lord, and my apprentice is " +
                    sith.Apprentice.Name;
            else
                return "I'm a Sith Apprentice and my name is " + sith.Name;
        }
        else
        {
            return "I don't know of any Sith";
        }
    }
}
```

The JediVsSith assembly

This is the main application where the information about the characters is displayed. You will need to add a reference to all other assemblies to gain access to the necessary classes and enumerations.

The PrintBeing method: In order to display the information about the characters you will have to add a method called **PrintBeing** which takes one parameter called **being** of the **Being** data type containing the character whose information is to be displayed. Use the **String.Format** method to format an output string containing the name, race, midichlorian count and the forces (dark/light) that the character has and print it to the Console window.

The PrintQuestions method: In order to display the answers to the two questions *What are you?* and *Are you Sith?* you need to add a method called **PrintQuestions** which takes one parameter called **interrogator** of the **Being** data type containing the character asking the questions and one called **suspects** which is a **List<Being>** that contain all the characters being asked the question. The two questions are asked to each of the characters in the suspects collection.

The Main method: Create instances for the four characters Anakin Skywalker (Human, Jedi), Obi Wan Kenobi (Human, Jedi), Senator Palpatine (Human, Sith) and Jar Jar Binx (Gungan, Being) in the **Main** method.

Start by calling the **PrintBeing** for the four characters and then add Anakin as a padawan to Obi Wan Kenobi. Continue by having each of the characters ask the two questions to all the other characters by calling the **PrintQuestions** method. Let Anakin become an apprentice of Senator Palpatine and print the character info by calling the **PrintBeing** method then have Palpatine complete Anakin's training and call the **PrintBeing** method again, note the difference in Anakin's forces. Remove Anakin as a padawan from Obi Wan Kenobi and have Palpatine ask the questions to Darth Vader and Obi Wan, Darth Vader ask Palpatine and Obi Wan and Obi Wan ask Darth Vader.

The PrintBeing method

The **PrintBeing** method should have a parameter called **being** of the **Being** data type. Iterate over the forces stored in the being's **Forces** collection and concatenate a string from the data. Display the name, race, midichlorian count and the forces (dark/light) that the character has in the Console window.

1. Add a method called **PrintBeing** which has a parameter called **being** of the **Being** data type to the **Program** class below the **Main** method.
   ```
   private static void PrintBeing(Being being)
   {
   }
   ```

2. Add a **string** variable called **forces** and assign an empty string to it.

3. Iterate over the forces in the being's **Forces** collection and concatenate a string from the data that you store in the **forces** variable.
   ```
   foreach (var force in being.Forces)
       forces += String.Format("{0}, ", force);
   ```

4. If the **forces** string contain any data after the loop then remove the last two characters from the string to avoid displaying a comma and space at the end of the string.
   ```
   if (!forces.Equals(String.Empty))
       forces = forces.Substring(0, forces.Length - 2);
   ```

5. Write the desired data to the Console window on a single line.

The complete code for the **PrintBeing** method:

```
private static void PrintBeing(Being being)
{
    string forces = String.Empty;
    foreach (var force in being.Forces)
        forces += String.Format("{0}, ", force);

    if (!forces.Equals(String.Empty))
        forces = forces.Substring(0, forces.Length - 2);

    Console.WriteLine(String.Format(
        "Name: {0}, Race: {1}: Midichlorians: {2}, Forces: {3}",
        being.Name, being.Race, being.Midichlorians, forces));
}
```

The PrintQuestions method

The **PrintQuestions** method should have one parameter called **interrogator** of the **Being** data type and one called **suspects** as a **List<Being>** collection. Iterate over the characters in the **suspects** collection and display the interrogator's name, the suspect's name and the result from a call to the **WhatAreYou** method on the **interrogator** instance passing in the current **suspect** as the parameter value, also display the interrogator's name, the suspect's name and the result from a call to the **AreYouSith** method on the **interrogator** instance passing in the current **suspect** as the parameter value. Add an empty line to the Console window after the loop.

1. Add a method called **PrintQuestions** which has one parameter called **interrogator** of the **Being** data type and one called **suspects** as a **List<Being>** collection to the **Program** class below the **Main** method.
   ```
   private static void PrintQuestions(Being interrogator, List<Being>
   suspects)
   {
   }
   ```

2. Add a **foreach** loop iterating over the suspects in the **suspects** collection.

3. For each suspect print the interrogator's name, the suspect's name and the result from a call to the **WhatAreYou** method.
   ```
   Console.WriteLine(String.Format("{0} [WhatAreYou] {1}: {2}",
   interrogator.Name, suspect.Name, interrogator.WhatAreYou(suspect)));
   ```

4. Now do the same as described in bullet 3 calling the **AreYouSith** method instead.

5. Add call to the **Console.WriteLine** method after the loop.

The complete code for the **PrintQuestions** method:

```
private static void PrintQuestions(Being interrogator,
List<Being> suspects)
{
    foreach (var suspect in suspects)
    {
        Console.WriteLine(String.Format("{0} [WhatAreYou] {1}: {2}",
            interrogator.Name, suspect.Name,
            interrogator.WhatAreYou(suspect)));

        Console.WriteLine(String.Format("{0} [AreYouSith] {1}: {2}",
            interrogator.Name, suspect.Name,
            interrogator.AreYouSith(suspect)));
    }

    Console.WriteLine();
}
```

The Main method

Here's where it all comes together and the output is displayed (see above for details about the output and the characters).

1. Add the characters to the **Main** method.

   ```
   var jarJar = new Being("Jar Jar Binx", Races.Gungan, 0);
   var palpatine = new Sith("Senator Palpatine", Races.Human, 10000);
   var anakin = new Jedi("Anakin Skywalker", Races.Human, 50000);
   var obiWan = new Jedi("Obi Wan Kenobi", Races.Human, 10000);
   ```

2. *Output 1*: Call the **PrintBeing** method for the four characters and add a call to the **Console.ReadKey** and **Console.Clear** methods.

   ```
   PrintBeing(obiWan);
   ```

3. Add Anakin as a padawan to Obi Wan Kenobi by calling the **AddPadawan** method on the **obiWan** instance variable passing in the **anakin** instance variable.

   ```
   obiWan.AddPadawan(anakin);
   ```

4. *Output 2*: Call the **PrintQuestion** method for each character passing in the remaining characters as part of the suspects collection. Add a call to the **Console.ReadKey** and **Console.Clear** methods after the **PrintQuestions** method calls.

   ```
   PrintQuestions(palpatine, new List<Being> { anakin, obiWan, jarJar });
   ```

5. Pass in the **anakin** instance by reference to the **AddApprentice** method along with the name "Darth Vader" on the **palpatine** instance variable and store the result in a variable called **darthVader**.

   ```
   var darthVader = palpatine.AddApprentice(ref anakin, "Darth Vader");
   ```

6. Call the **PrintBeing** method passing in the **darthVader** instance.

7. Have Darth Vader complete his training by calling the **CompleteTraining** method on the **palpatine** instance passing in the **darthVader** instance.

   ```
   palpatine.CompleteTrainig(darthVader);
   ```

8. *Output 3*: Call the **PrintBeing** method passing in the **darthVader** instance, note the change in Darth Vader's forces. Add a call to the **Console.ReadKey** and **Console .Clear** methods after the **PrintBeing** method call.

9. Remove Anakin as Obi Wan's padawan by calling the **RemovePadawan** method on the **obiWan** instance variable.

10. *Output 4*: Call the **PrintQuestion** method and have Palpatine ask the questions to Darth Vader and Obi Wan, Darth Vader ask Palpatine and Obi Wan and Obi Wan ask Darth Vader.
11. Add a call to the **Console.ReadKey** method.

The complete code for the **Main** method:

```
static void Main(string[] args)
{
    var jarJar = new Being("Jar Jar Binx", Races.Gungan, 0);
    var palpatine = new Sith("Senator Palpatine", Races.Human, 10000);
    var anakin = new Jedi("Anakin Skywalker", Races.Human, 50000);
    var obiWan = new Jedi("Obi Wan Kenobi", Races.Human, 10000);

    #region Output 1
    PrintBeing(obiWan);
    PrintBeing(anakin);
    PrintBeing(palpatine);
    PrintBeing(jarJar);
    Console.ReadKey();
    Console.Clear();
    #endregion

    obiWan.AddPadawan(anakin);

    #region Output 2
    PrintQuestions(palpatine, new List<Being> { anakin, obiWan, jarJar });
    PrintQuestions(anakin, new List<Being> { palpatine, obiWan, jarJar });
    PrintQuestions(obiWan, new List<Being> { anakin, palpatine, jarJar });
    PrintQuestions(jarJar, new List<Being> { anakin, obiWan, palpatine });
    Console.ReadKey();
    Console.Clear();
    #endregion

    #region Output 3
    var darthVader = palpatine.AddApprentice(ref anakin, "Darth Vader");
    PrintBeing(darthVader);
    palpatine.CompleteTrainig(darthVader);
    PrintBeing(darthVader);
    Console.ReadKey();
    Console.Clear();
    #endregion
```

```
    obiWan.RemovePadawan();

    #region Output 4
    PrintQuestions(palpatine, new List<Being> { darthVader, obiWan });
    PrintQuestions(darthVader, new List<Being> { palpatine, obiWan });
    PrintQuestions(obiWan, new List<Being> { darthVader });
    Console.ReadKey();
    #endregion
}
```

The output from the **Main** method:

```
#region --- Output 1 ---
/*
    Name: Obi Wan Kenobi, Race: Human: Midichlorians: 10000, Forces:
    LightSide
    Name: Anakin Skywalker, Race: Human: Midichlorians: 50000, Forces:
    LightSide
    Name: Senator Palpatine, Race: Human: Midichlorians: 10000, Forces:
    DarkSide
    Name: Jar Jar Binx, Race: Gungan: Midichlorians: 0, Forces:
 */
#endregion
#region --- Output 2 ---
/*
    Senator Palpatine [WhatAreYou] Anakin Skywalker: I'm a Jedi
    Senator Palpatine [AreYouSith] Anakin Skywalker: I don't know of any
    Sith
    Senator Palpatine [WhatAreYou] Obi Wan Kenobi: I'm a Jedi
    Senator Palpatine [AreYouSith] Obi Wan Kenobi: I don't know of any Sith
    Senator Palpatine [WhatAreYou] Jar Jar Binx: I'm neither Sith nor Jedi
    Senator Palpatine [AreYouSith] Jar Jar Binx: I don't know of any Sith

    Anakin Skywalker [WhatAreYou] Senator Palpatine: I'm neither Sith nor
    Jedi
    Anakin Skywalker [AreYouSith] Senator Palpatine: I don't know of any
    Sith
    Anakin Skywalker [WhatAreYou] Obi Wan Kenobi: I'm a Jedi
    Anakin Skywalker [AreYouSith] Obi Wan Kenobi: I'm a Jedi Master, and my
    apprentice is Anakin Skywalker
    Anakin Skywalker [WhatAreYou] Jar Jar Binx: I'm neither Sith nor Jedi
    Anakin Skywalker [AreYouSith] Jar Jar Binx: I don't know of any Sith

    Obi Wan Kenobi [WhatAreYou] Anakin Skywalker: I'm a Jedi
```

```
    Obi Wan Kenobi [AreYouSith] Anakin Skywalker: I'm a Padawan and my
    name is Anakin Skywalker
    Obi Wan Kenobi [WhatAreYou] Senator Palpatine: I'm neither Sith nor Jedi
    Obi Wan Kenobi [AreYouSith] Senator Palpatine: I don't know of any Sith
    Obi Wan Kenobi [WhatAreYou] Jar Jar Binx: I'm neither Sith nor Jedi
    Obi Wan Kenobi [AreYouSith] Jar Jar Binx: I don't know of any Sith

    Jar Jar Binx [WhatAreYou] Anakin Skywalker: I'm a Jedi
    Jar Jar Binx [AreYouSith] Anakin Skywalker: I'm not a Sith
    Jar Jar Binx [WhatAreYou] Obi Wan Kenobi: I'm a Jedi
    Jar Jar Binx [AreYouSith] Obi Wan Kenobi: I'm not a Sith
    Jar Jar Binx [WhatAreYou] Senator Palpatine: I'm neither Sith nor Jedi
    Jar Jar Binx [AreYouSith] Senator Palpatine: I'm not a Sith
*/
#endregion
#region --- Output 3 ---
/*
    Name: Darth Vader, Race: Human: Midichlorians: 50000,
    Forces: DarkSide, LightSide
    Name: Darth Vader, Race: Human: Midichlorians: 50000,
    Forces: DarkSide
*/
#endregion
#region --- Output 4 ---
/*
    Senator Palpatine [WhatAreYou] Darth Vader: I'm a Sith
    Senator Palpatine [AreYouSith] Darth Vader: I'm a Sith Apprentice and
    my name is Darth Vader
    Senator Palpatine [WhatAreYou] Obi Wan Kenobi: I'm a Jedi
    Senator Palpatine [AreYouSith] Obi Wan Kenobi: I don't know of any Sith

    Darth Vader [WhatAreYou] Senator Palpatine: I'm a Sith
    Darth Vader [AreYouSith] Senator Palpatine: I'm a Sith Lord, and
    my apprentice is Darth Vader
    Darth Vader [WhatAreYou] Obi Wan Kenobi: I'm a Jedi
    Darth Vader [AreYouSith] Obi Wan Kenobi: I don't know of any Sith

    Obi Wan Kenobi [WhatAreYou] Darth Vader: I'm neither Sith nor Jedi
    Obi Wan Kenobi [AreYouSith] Darth Vader: I don't know of any Sith
*/
#endregion
```

Mini Use Case: Car rental

In this case study you will be building a portal for renting out cars, like the one they use at gas stations and car rental companies. Obviously you will not build a super detailed and fully fledged system, you will however build a basic system that will serve the purpose of renting out and returning a car.

It is important to know that this solution has been designed this way to illustrate certain aspects of object oriented programming (OOP) and might therefore not be optimal.

Tightly coupled vs. loosely coupled design

Tightly coupled solutions are generally much more difficult to change, making changes to a class generally involves changes to surrounding classes and method calls.

You also paint yourself into a corner in a sense by passing in an instance of a class as a parameter where an interface could be used. The use of interfaces makes it much easier, not only to pass in parts of an instance, but also to pass in other instances all together. Take an instance of a data layer class for instance, by using interfaces you could easily change one implementation for another; for instance switching from a test data layer to a production data layer.

When implementing this use case you will use inheritance to illustrate how abstract classes and members can be used in a solution to re-use code. You will also implement the classes using interfaces to make the solution easier to maintain. By using interfaces you will in the end be able to switch out the business layer and data layer for other implementations by implementing the **IDataLayer** and **IBookingProcessor** interfaces in other classes, this is known as *Interface Polymorphism*. You will also make the solution totally flexible by not defining parameters and types using classes but instead use the interfaces that are implemented in the classes, this is known as interface injection and is part of loosely coupled design patterns. Imagine that you have an interface called **IVehicle** which defines the characteristics and behaviors of any vehicle, by implementing that interface in several classes such as **Car** and **Motorcycle** you can now use the **IVehicle** interface as a parameter in a method definition to pass in either an instance of the **Car** class or the **Motorcycle** class to the method because both implement the same interface. This works because as you might remember from the interface chapter an interface is a contract that has to be implemented in its entirety by the class.

Specification for the Car rental application

Let's begin by looking at the specification and discern what needs to be built, and what technologies to use for this scenario, then you will build the actual loosely coupled application. You will use inheritance where called for and interfaces as data types for variables, parameters and collection types; you will not pass in any parameters using classes.

Important: *An important limitation is that we only allow one vehicle per booking, which means that we get a 1-1 relation where there normally would be a 1-n relationship.*

The system will handle car rentals (rental and return); the system will be used by different companies with varying data storage solutions and user interfaces which lends itself to use a loosely coupled design where the data layer easily can be swapped out.

Your task is to build the application as outlined in the specification below.

Prices

The car category determines how the prices should be calculated, the tariff values may change over time. Common to all calculations are that two types of costs are taken into account: a daily cost and a cost per Km driven.

Sedan: Price = daily cost * number of days

Combi: Price = daily cost * number of days * day tariff + cost per Km * actual Km driven. The day tariff is initially 1.5, but that could be changed over time.

Van: Price = daily cost * number of days * day tariff + cost per Km * actual Km driven * distance tariff. The day tariff is initially 2.0 and distance tariff is initially 2.5, but that could change over time.

Rental

To make it simple the system calculates all rentals during the same day as a full day, half day or hourly rentals are not supported by the system. When a car is rented more than one day the duration should be calculated by subtracting the rental date from the return date.

Specification

The cars are divided into categories where three categories are defined from the start: **Sedan**, **Combi** and **Van**. More categories might be added later.

Every rental must be identifiable by a unique booking number. Every rental is defined as renting one car per booking and every booking can only have one customer.

The classes should be placed in separate assemblies for easy reuse; there are three assemblies with their own folder structures: **Car Rental** which is the Windows Forms Application, **Business Layer** which houses the booking processor that handles all business logic such as user rights (if implemented) and **Data Layer** which houses the entity classes and the data layer classes.

When working with bookings the application will call the appropriate methods on an instance of the **BookingProcessor** class which takes an instance of the **CollectionDataLayer** class to be able to communicate with the data source which in this case is dummy data stored in collections. The **CollectionDataLayer** class is the class that would be switched out if another data source would be implemented and used; it is on an instance of this class that all the method calls from the **BookingProcessor** class instance to the data source is made. The **BookingProcessor** class should have no direct connection to or knowledge of the data source, handling the data is the purpose of the **CollectionDataLayer** class. The dummy data and the collections representing the data source are stored in a class called **TestData**; in a real world scenario this would most likely be implemented using Entity Framework entities to communicate with a database.

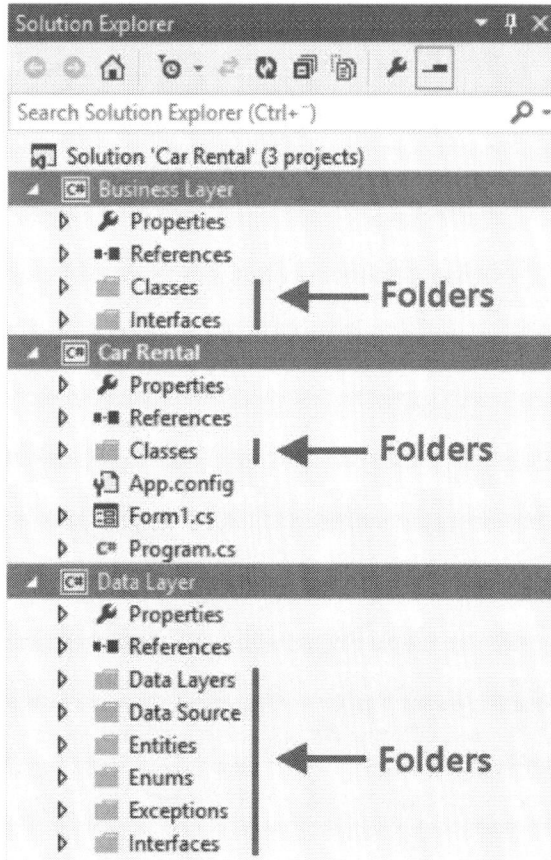

Three assemblies

The solution will contain three assemblies one for the Windows Forms Application called **Car Rental**, one business layer for business rules called **Business Layer** and one that handles communication with the data source called **Data Layer**.

To get access to the classes in the **Business Layer** and **Data Layer** assemblies you have to add references to them in the application assembly.

The Application structure

The application should in this case be created using a Windows Forms Application project called **Car Rental**. Apart from the default project content such as the form, you will add a folder called **Classes** where you will add all classes needed for handling the GUI; you will for instance have to create a class used as model for the data displayed in combo box items and another class used as model for the data displayed in list view.

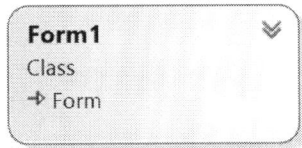

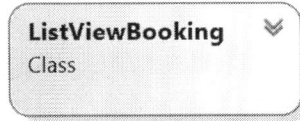

The application GUI

The application GUI consist of one form with a tab control that has four tabs **Rent Vehicle**, **Return Booking**, **Bookings** and **Add Data**.

The **Rent Vehicle** tab has a list view control displaying vehicles available for rental, a combo box with a list of customers and a **Rent** button which uses the information from the other two controls to rent a car to a customer.

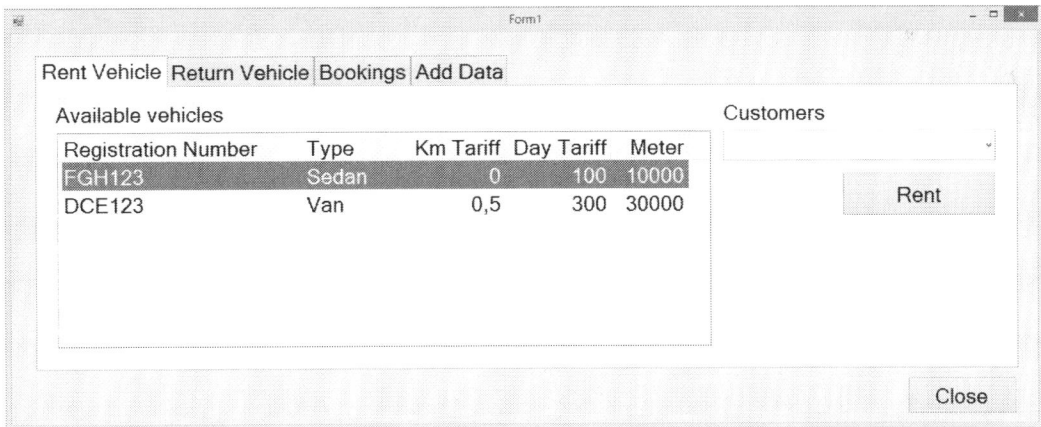

The **Return Vehicle** tab has a list view control displaying rented vehicles that can be returned, a textbox for specifying the vehicle's meter setting when it is returned and a **Return** button which will use the data from the other controls to return the vehicle and calculate the rental cost.

The **Bookings** tab uses a list view control to give an historical overview of all bookings that have been made in the system. Vehicles that are rented don't have a date specified in the **Returned** column.

The **Add Data** tab has the possibility to add new vehicles and customers using textboxes and combo boxes to specify or select data.

The business layer structure

The **Business Layer** assembly should be created using a **Class Library** project, <u>not</u> the **Class Library (Portal)** project as it has limitations you don't want in your project. The assembly only has one class called **BookingProcessor** which implements an interface called **IBooking-Processor** which in turn inherits an interface called **IRentalBase**.

Add two folders called **Classes** and **Interfaces** and place the **BookingProcessor** class in the classes folder and the **IBookingProcessor** interface in the Interfaces folder. The **IRentalBase** interface belong to the **Data Layer** assembly which mean that you need a reference to the **Data Layer** assembly in the **Business Layer** assembly.

The **IRentalBase** interface define most of the methods implemented in the **BookingProcessor** and **CollectionDataLayer** classes; the two classes both implement the same methods because the instance of the **BookingProcessor** class created in the application code-behind will use an instance of the **CollectionDataLayer** calling its methods to reach the data source; having the same name, return data type and parameters for the methods makes it easy to follow the program flow from business layer to data layer, it also enables reuse of the **IRentalBase** interface.

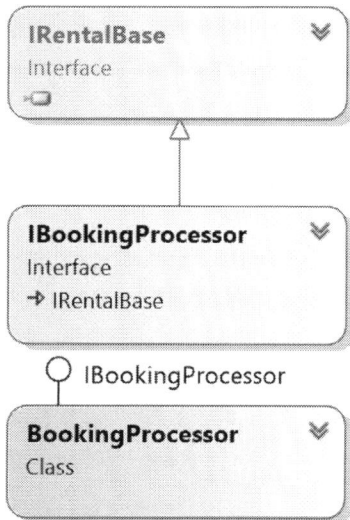

The data layer structure

The **Data Layer** assembly should be created using a **Class Library** project, <u>not</u> the **Class Library (Portal)** project as it has limitations you do not want in your project. This assembly contain most of the classes since it houses all the entity and custom exception classes as well as any implementation of the **IDataLayer** interface such as the **CollectionDataLayer** class.

An instance of the **CollectionDataLayer** class will be injected into (sent in to) an instance of the **BookingProcessor** class; all calls to the data source from the **Car Rental** application will be made through the **BookingProcessor** instance to enforce any business rules before the data layer is called from within the methods of the **BookingProcessor** instance.

There are a number of folders needed to keep the structure clean and easy to navigate. The **Data Layers** folder will house any implementation of the **IDataLayer** interface such as the **CollectionDataLayer** class. The **Data Source** folder will have a class called **TestData** which will act as the data source for the test data used in this implementation of the application. The **Entities** folder will house all data specific classes which could be used to model tables in a database such as **Customer**, **Booking** and **Vehicle**. The **Enums** folder will have a .cs file housing all enumerations needed in the application. The **Exceptions** folder will house all custom defined exceptions used in the application such as **CustomerException** and the **Interfaces** folder will house all interfaces used in the assembly.

The image below show the interfaces involved in implementing a data layer class, in this case the **CollectionDataLayer** class which will be used to fetch and manipulate data in the data source represented by the collections in the **TestData** class. Note that the same **IRentalBase** interface implemented by the **BookingProcessor** class is implemented here as part of an interface inheritance between the **IDataLayer** and the **IRentalBase** interfaces.

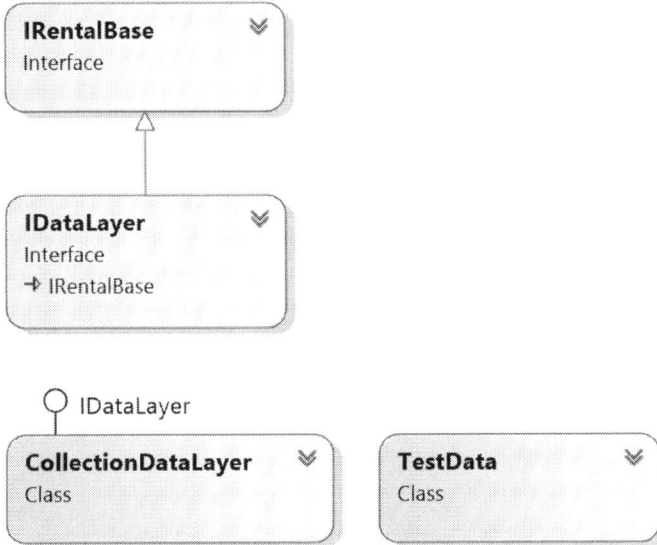

The image below illustrates the custom exceptions needed in the application and their inheritance of the **KeyNotFoundException** class.

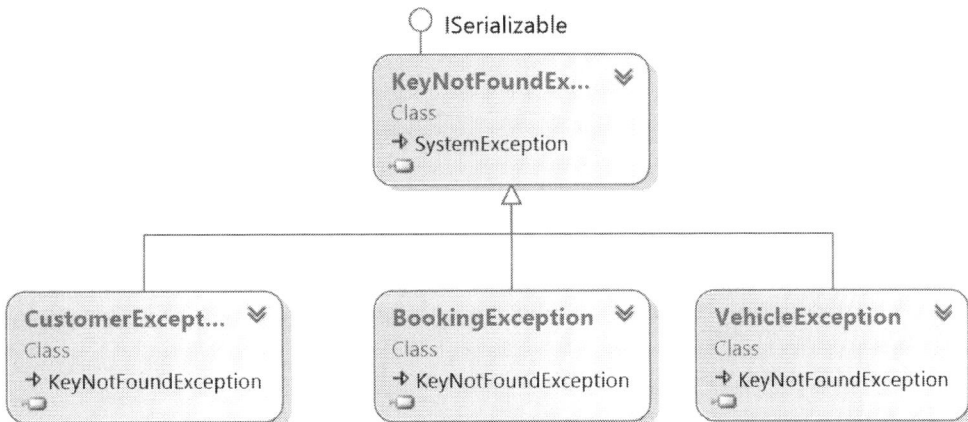

The image below illustrates the implementation of vehicles and the interfaces and inheritance used to implement a specific vehicle like the **Car** class. Note that there is an intermediary class called **Vehicle** being inherited by the **Car** class this is necessary to ensure that default implementations of certain methods are available and it also opens up to using the **IVehicle** interface as a data type for all types of specific vehicle classes that might be added in the future. It also makes the implementation more flexible by using the interface for interface injection in methods instead of using the specific vehicle classes for parameters.

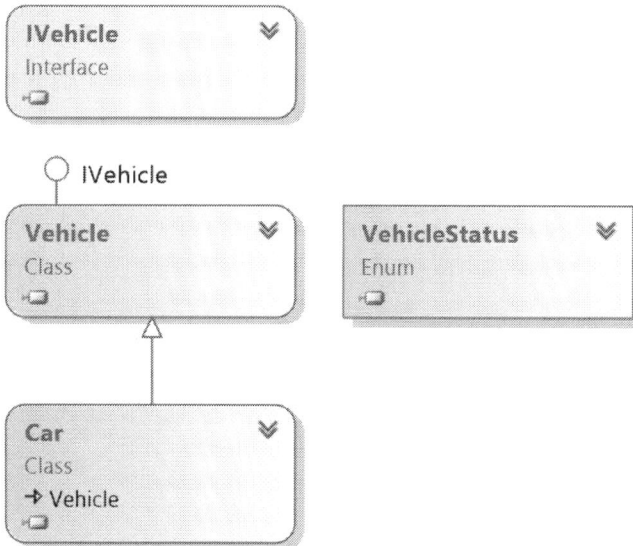

The image below illustrates implementations of the remaining entity classes **Customer**, **Booking** and **VehicleType**. Although it is not strictly necessary to implement these classes using interfaces it is done here for consistency and in the event that sub categories of the entities has to be implemented in the future, you might for instance want to have a more specialized definition of what a customer is and reuse the **ICustomer** interface to implement the default characteristics and behaviors of a customer into the specialized classes making sure that they are customers. Another way of accomplishing a similar result would off course be to use inheritance and override methods.

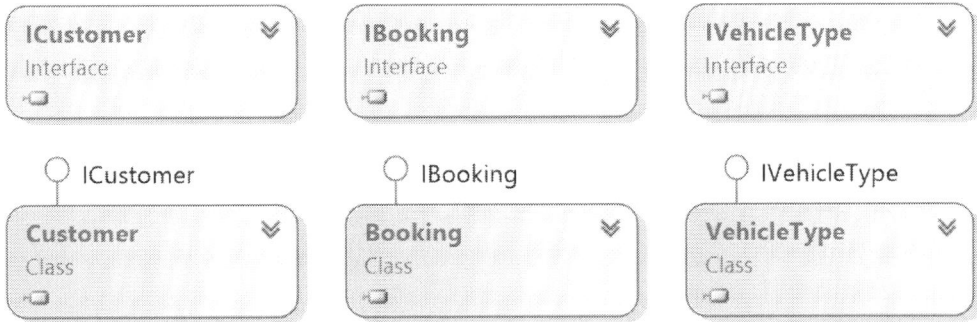

Implementation of the Car rental application

In this section you will implement the different parts of the application starting with the assemblies and folder structures.

The assemblies

You need to create a Windows Forms Application called **Car Rental** as the first assembly in the solution and then add two **Class Library** projects called **Business Layer** and **Data Layer**. When the assemblies are in place you need to add the folder structures as described earlier.

1. Create a **Windows Forms Application** called **Car Rental**.
2. Add a folder called **Classes** to the project.
3. Add a new **Class Library** project (assembly) called **Business Layer** to the solution.
4. Add the following folders to the project: **Classes** and **Interfaces**.
5. Add a new **Class Library** project (assembly) called **Data Layer** to the solution.
6. Add the following folders to the project: **Data Layers**, **Data Source**, **Entities**, **Enums**, **Exceptions** and **Interfaces**.
7. Add a reference to the **Data Layer** assembly in the **Business Layer** assembly.
8. Add a reference to the **Data Layer** and **Business Layer** assemblies in the **Car Rental** assembly.

The Entity interfaces and classes

In this section you will focus on implementing the entity classes and their interfaces according to the specifications given for each scenario. All **Id** properties in the application are declared using the **int** data type.

ICustomer	IBooking	IVehicleType
Interface	Interface	Interface
Properties	**Properties**	**Properties**
FirstName	Cost	BasePricePerDay
Id	CustomerId	BasePricePerKm
LastName	Id	DayTariff
SocialSecurityNumber	Rented	Id
	Returned	KmTariff
	VehicleId	Name

○ ICustomer	○ IBooking	○ IVehicleType
Customer	**Booking**	**VehicleType**
Class	Class	Class

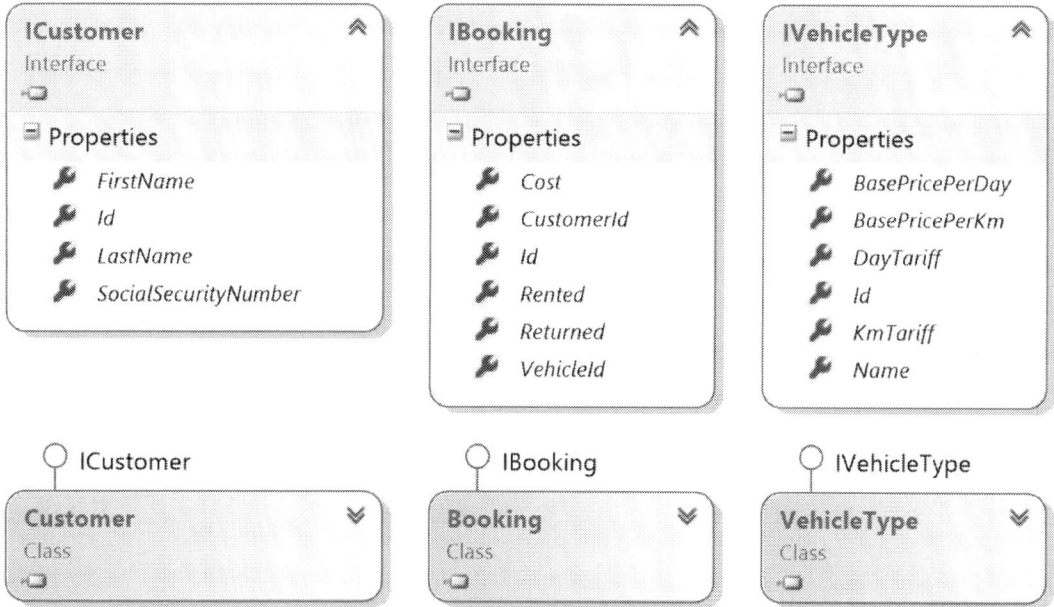

The Customer interface and class

This class will represent the characteristics of a customer meaning that it only contains properties. In this case all properties are **public** to be reachable anywhere, the data types should not be a mystery either, all properties except the **Id** property should be declared using the **string** data type.

1. Add an interface called **ICustomer** to the **Interfaces** folder in the **Data Layer** project and make it **public**.

   ```
   public interface ICustomer
   {
   }
   ```

2. Define all the properties in the interface, remember that you don't specify any access modifiers in an interface.

   ```
   string LastName { get; set; }
   ```

3. Add a **public** class called **Customer** to the **Entities** folder in the **Data Layer** project and implement the interface in the class.

   ```
   public class Customer : ICustomer
   {
   }
   ```

386

4. The fastest way to add the properties is to copy them from the interface and paste them into the class and add the **public** access modifier to them.
```
public string LastName { get; set; }
```

The complete code for the **ICustomer** interface:

```
public interface ICustomer
{
    int Id { get; set; }
    string SocialSecurityNumber { get; set; }
    string FirstName { get; set; }
    string LastName { get; set; }
}
```

The complete code for the **Customer** class:

```
public class Customer : ICustomer
{
    public int Id { get; set; }
    public string SocialSecurityNumber { get; set; }
    public string FirstName { get; set; }
    public string LastName { get; set; }
}
```

The Booking interface and class

This class will represent the characteristics of a booking and as such only contain properties. In this case all properties are **public** to be reachable anywhere, the data types should not be a mystery either, all **Id** properties should be declared using the **int** data type, the **Rented** and **Returned** properties should be declared using the **DateTime** data type and because the cost can contain fractions of a dollar the **Cost** property should be declared using the **double** data type.

1. Add an interface called **IBooking** to the **Interfaces** folder in the **Data Layer** project and make it **public**.
```
public interface IBooking
{
}
```

2. Define all the properties in the interface, remember that you don't specify any access modifiers in an interface.
```
double Cost { get; set; }
```

3. Add a **public** class called **Booking** to the **Entities** folder in the **Data Layer** project and implement the interface in the class.

```
public class Booking : IBooking
{
}
```

4. The fastest way to add the properties is to copy them from the interface and paste them into the class and add the **public** access modifier to them.

```
public double Cost { get; set; }
```

The complete code for the **IBooking** interface:

```
public interface IBooking
{
    int Id { get; set; }
    int VehicleId { get; set; }
    int CustomerId { get; set; }
    DateTime Rented { get; set; }
    DateTime Returned { get; set; }
    double Cost { get; set; }
}
```

The complete code for the **Booking** class:

```
public class Booking : IBooking
{
    public int Id { get; set; }
    public int VehicleId { get; set; }
    public int CustomerId { get; set; }
    public DateTime Rented { get; set; }
    public DateTime Returned { get; set; }
    public double Cost { get; set; }
}
```

The VehicleType interface and class

This class will represent the characteristics of a vehicle type and as such it only contain properties. In this case all properties are **public** to be reachable anywhere, the data types should not be a mystery either, all **Id** properties should be declared using the **int** data type, the base price and tariff properties should be declared using the **double** data type since they can contain fractions of a dollar and the **Name** property should be declared with the **string** data type.

A vehicle type is a not a specific vehicle but a type of vehicle such as Combi, Van and Sedan which all have different base prices and tariffs per Km and day (see the calculations at the beginning of the use case). Whenever a vehicle is returned the system will check these stats to get the values to calculate the cost. Hard coding theses values is not recommended since that would mean rebuilding the entire solution and distributing that version to the users each time the prices change.

1. Add an interface called **IVehicleType** to the **Interfaces** folder in the **Data Layer** project and make it **public**.
2. Define all the properties in the interface, remember that you don't specify any access modifiers in an interface.
3. Add a **public** class called **VehicleType** to the **Entities** folder in the **Data Layer** project and implement the interface in the class.
4. The fastest way to add the properties is to copy them from the interface and paste them into the class and then add **public** access modifiers to them.

The complete code for the **IVehicleType** interface:

```csharp
public interface IVehicleType
{
    int Id { get; set; }
    string Name { get; set; }
    double BasePricePerKm { get; set; }
    double BasePricePerDay { get; set; }
    double DayTariff { get; set; }
    double KmTariff { get; set; }
}
```

The complete code for the **VehicleType** class:

```csharp
public class VehicleType : IVehicleType
{
    public int Id { get; set; }
    public string Name { get; set; }
    public double BasePricePerKm { get; set; }
    public double BasePricePerDay { get; set; }
    public double DayTariff { get; set; }
    public double KmTariff { get; set; }
}
```

The Vehicle interface and class

This class will represent the characteristics and behaviors of a vehicle, besides containing properties it will also have two constructors one without parameters and one that has a parameter declared with the **IVehicle** interface; it might seem strange to send in an object of the same type as the class defines, but it is really not that strange if you envision a scenario where you want to seed a new object with values from an existing object.

In this case the all properties are **public** to be reachable anywhere, the data types should not be a mystery either, all **Id** properties should be dclared with the **int** data type, the meter, base price and tariff properties should be declared with the **double** data type since they can contain fractions and the **RegistrationNumber** property should be declared with the **string** data type.

You might think that it could be a great idea to create the **Vehicle** class as an abstract class and inherit it to the more specialized vehicle classes such as the **Car** class, but in this case it is not recommended since you actually want to pass instances of the **Car** class cast as a **Vehicle** to the **Vehicle** class' constructor to assign values to the **Vehicle** instance's properties when a **Car** instance is crated; this way of implementing the **Car** class saves you the trouble of assigning the property values in the **Car** class' constructor and reuse the code in the **Vehicle** class' constructor keeping the **Car** class much cleaner.

You might wonder why the same set of properties for base prices and tariffs are included in the vehicle interface and class, the reason is that the values might change for the vehicle type between the rental and return and if the rental values are not stored the customer might pay less or more when the vehicle is returned.

IVehicle
Interface

□ Properties
- 🔧 BasePricePerDay
- 🔧 BasePricePerKm
- 🔧 DayTariff
- 🔧 Id
- 🔧 KmTariff
- 🔧 Meter
- 🔧 RegistrationNumber
- 🔧 TypeId

○ IVehicle

Vehicle
Class

VehicleStatus
Enum

- All
- Booked
- Available

Car
Class
→ Vehicle

□ Methods
- ◎ Car (+ 1 overload)

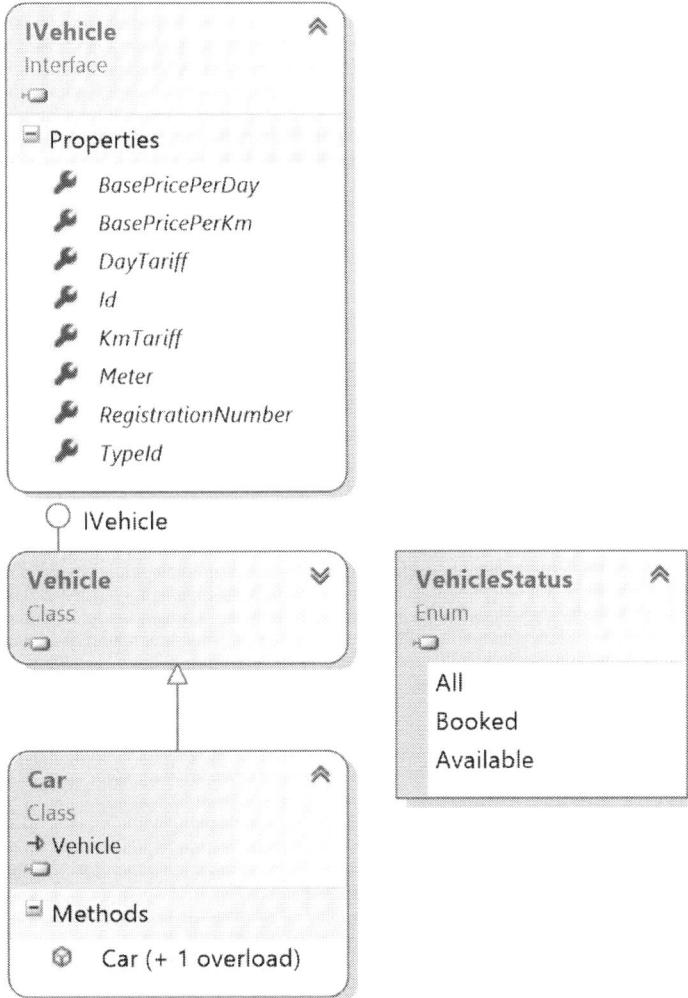

1. Add an interface called **IVehicle** to the **Interfaces** folder in the **Data Layer** project and make it **public**.

2. Define all the properties in the interface, remember that you don't specify any access modifiers in an interface.

3. Add a **public** class called **Vehicle** to the **Entities** folder in the **Data Layer** project and implement the interface in the class.

4. The fastest way to add the properties is to copy them from the interface and paste them into the class and add **public** access modifiers to them.

5. Add two **public** constructors to the class, one without parameters and one with an
IVehicle parameter that assigns the values from the passed in **Vehicle** object to the
properties.

```
public Vehicle() { }
public Vehicle(IVehicle vehicle) { ... }
```

The complete code for the **IVehicle** interface:

```
public interface IVehicle {
    int Id { get; set; }
    int TypeId { get; set; }
    double BasePricePerKm { get; set; }
    double BasePricePerDay { get; set; }
    double DayTariff { get; set; }
    double KmTariff { get; set; }
    string RegistrationNumber { get; set; }
    double Meter { get; set; }
}
```

The complete code for the **Vehicle** class:

```
public class Vehicle : IVehicle {
    public int Id { get; set; }
    public int TypeId { get; set; }
    public string RegistrationNumber { get; set; }
    public double BasePricePerKm { get; set; }
    public double BasePricePerDay { get; set; }
    public double DayTariff { get; set; }
    public double KmTariff { get; set; }
    public double Meter { get; set; }

    public Vehicle() { }
    public Vehicle(IVehicle vehicle)
    {
        BasePricePerDay = vehicle.BasePricePerDay;
        BasePricePerKm = vehicle.BasePricePerKm;
        DayTariff = vehicle.DayTariff;
        KmTariff = vehicle.KmTariff;
        Id = vehicle.Id;
        Meter = vehicle.Meter;
        RegistrationNumber = vehicle.RegistrationNumber;
        TypeId = vehicle.TypeId;
    }
}
```

The Car class

This class will represent the characteristics and behaviors of a car, besides containing properties it also implements two constructors. One constructor without parameters and one with an **IVehicle** parameter that is passed to the base class constructor, now you might see the point with having the **IVehicle** constructor in the **Vehicle** class since that is where the **base** class call ends up.

You might have noticed that there is no mention of an **ICar** interface and the reason is that the **Car** class will inherit the **Vehicle** class which already contain all the properties an **ICar** interface would define.

The complete code for the **Car** class:

```
public class Car : Vehicle
{
    public Car() { }
    public Car(IVehicle vehicle) : base(vehicle) { }
}
```

The data source (the test data)

This class located in the **Data Source** folder in the **Data Layer** assembly will house the collections that will be used to simulate a real data source. Using test data like this can be invaluable since you always know what data will be available when the application start, making it easy to spot logical bugs such as calculation errors or displaying wrong data in the controls.

Because the collections represent tables in a data source you don't want them accessible everywhere, they should only be accessible by and through the data layer; one of the reasons for using different layers is to achieve separation of concerns, one assembly equals one specific area. Another reason for using different layers is to enforce encapsulation; you can encapsulate data in classes and use access modifiers such as **internal** and **private** to ensure that the data only is reachable within the assembly it is created and stored.

Use the **internal** access modifier to limit the scope of the data collections you create to ensure that they only are accessible within the **Data Layer** assembly; the data will then be made accessible outside the assembly using properties and methods in the **CollectionData-Layer** class implementing the **IDataLayer** interface. If you introduce other data sources later on you simply implement the **IDataLayer** interface in a class with the logic needed to access that particular data source and pass an instance of the class to the **BookingProcessor** instance.

To make it easier to access the collections holding the test data you will create them as **static** to avoid having to create an instance of the class which would reset the data. Note that this is not typically how you treat data sources but you will use it for this particular test data scenario.

Four collections are needed. The first is called **VehicleTypes** which is declared using the **IVehicleType** interface and therefore can hold instances of any class implementing the **IVehicleType** interface such as the **VehicleType** class.

The second collection is called **Vehicles** and is declared using the **IVehicle** interface making it possible to store instances of classes implementing that interface such as the **Vehicle** and **Car** class; you might wonder how the **Car** class has access to the interface and the answer is through inheriting the **Vehicle** class that implements the interface.

The third collection is called **Customers** and is declared using the **ICustomer** interface making it possible to store instances of classes implementing that interface such as the **Customer** class.

The fourth collection is called **Bookings** and is declared using the **IBooking** interface making it possible to store instances of classes implementing that interface such as the **Booking** class. Instances of this class is used to represent bookings in the system.

To create a set of test data you need to add a method called **Seed** which adds data to the collections, this keeps the data consistent each time the application is started which is paramount when testing an application.

Add test data for the following vehicle types in the **VehicleTypes** collection : **Sedan**, **Combi** and **Van**.

Add test data for a few vehicles in the **Vehicles** collection using the **Car** class and the vehicle types you just added for the cars' **TypeId** property.

Add test data for a couple of customers in the **Customers** collection.

Add test data for a few bookings in the **Bookings** collection, make sure that at least one booking is marked as returned by adding a date to the **Returned** property.

1. Add a class called **TestData** to the **Data Source** folder in the **Data Layer** project. You don't have to add an access modifier to the class since it is **internal** by default.

2. Add an **internal static List<IVehicleType>** collection called **VehicleTypes** to the class.
   ```
   internal static List<IVehicleType> VehicleTypes = new
   List<IVehicleType>();
   ```

3. Add an **internal static List<IVehicle>** collection called **Vehicles** to the class.

4. Add an **internal static List<ICustomer>** collection called **Customers** to the class.

5. Add an **internal static List<IBooking>** collection called **Bookings** to the class.

6. Add an **internal static** method called **Seed** to the class.
   ```
   internal void Seed()
   {

   }
   ```

7. Add the three vehicle types to the **VehicleTypes** collection in the **Seed** method.
   ```
   VehicleTypes.Add(new VehicleType() { Id = 1, Name = "Sedan",
   BasePricePerDay = 100, BasePricePerKm = 0, DayTariff = 1, KmTariff =
   1 });
   ```

8. Add a few vehicles to the **Vehicles** collection in the **Seed** method.
   ```
   Vehicles.Add(new Car() { Id = 1, TypeId = 1, BasePricePerDay = 100,
   BasePricePerKm = 0, DayTariff = 1, KmTariff = 1, RegistrationNumber =
   "FGH123", Meter = 10000 });
   ```

9. Add a couple of customers to the **Customers** collection in the **Seed** method.
   ```
   Customers.Add(new Customer() { Id = 1, FirstName = "Carl", LastName =
   "Raintree", SocialSecurityNumber = "12324545" });
   ```

10. Add a few bookings to the **Bookings** collection in the **Seed** method.
    ```
    Bookings.Add(new Booking() { Id = 1, VehicleId = 2, Rented =
    DateTime.Now, Returned = DateTime.Now.AddDays(1), Cost = 500,
    CustomerId = 2 });
    ```

The complete code for the **TestData** class:

```
class TestData
{
    #region Collections
    internal static List<IVehicleType> VehicleTypes = new
        List<IVehicleType>();
    internal static List<IVehicle> Vehicles = new List<IVehicle>();
    internal static List<ICustomer> Customers = new List<ICustomer>();
    internal static List<IBooking> Bookings = new List<IBooking>();
    #endregion

    #region Methods
    internal void Seed()
    {
        // Add fake data. This data would normally be fetched
        // from a data source
        VehicleTypes.Add(new VehicleType()
            { Id = 1, Name = "Sedan", BasePricePerDay = 100,
            BasePricePerKm = 0, DayTariff = 1, KmTariff = 1 });
        VehicleTypes.Add(new VehicleType()
            { Id = 2, Name = "Combi", BasePricePerDay = 200,
            BasePricePerKm = 0.5, DayTariff = 1.3, KmTariff = 1 });
        VehicleTypes.Add(new VehicleType()
            { Id = 3, Name = "Van", BasePricePerDay = 300,
            BasePricePerKm = 0.5, DayTariff = 1.5, KmTariff = 1.5 });

        Vehicles.Add(new Car() { Id = 1, TypeId = 1,
            BasePricePerDay = 100, BasePricePerKm = 0,
            DayTariff = 1, KmTariff = 1,
            RegistrationNumber = "FGH123", Meter = 10000 });
        Vehicles.Add(new Car() { Id = 2, TypeId = 2,
            BasePricePerDay = 200, BasePricePerKm = 0.5,
            DayTariff = 1.3, KmTariff = 1,
            RegistrationNumber = "ABC123", Meter = 20000 });
        Vehicles.Add(new Car()
            { Id = 3, TypeId = 3, BasePricePerDay = 300,
            BasePricePerKm = 0.5, DayTariff = 1.5, KmTariff = 1.5,
            RegistrationNumber = "DCE123", Meter = 30000 });

        Customers.Add(new Customer() { Id = 1, FirstName = "Carl",
            LastName = "Raintree", SocialSecurityNumber = "12324545" });
        Customers.Add(new Customer() { Id = 2, FirstName = "Lisa",
            LastName = "Montgomery", SocialSecurityNumber = "95654123" });
```

```
      Bookings.Add(new Booking() { Id = 1, VehicleId = 2,
          Rented = DateTime.Now, Returned = DateTime.Now.AddDays(1),
          Cost = 500, CustomerId = 2 });
      Bookings.Add(new Booking() { Id = 2, VehicleId = 2,
          Rented = DateTime.Now, CustomerId = 1 });
   }
   #endregion
}
```

The IDataLayer interface and DataLayer class

The **IDataLayer** interface inherits the **IRentalBase** interface which also is implemented by the **IBookingProcessor** interface. Most of the methods implemented in the **CollectionData-Layer** and **BookingProcessor** classes are defined in the **IRentalBase** interface.

The **CollectionDataLayer** class located in the **Data Layers** folder implements the **IDataLayer** interface which directly or indirectly define all the members used when communicating with the data source. The class should be declared as **public** since it must be reachable from any assembly.

The data source in this application are the collections you created in the previous exercise but in a real world scenario it would most likely be a data base reached through either ADO.NET or Entity Framework.

The application don't use an instance of the **CollectionDataLayer** class directly instead the instance is passed in to the **BookingProcessor** constructor when its instance is created and then the business layer calls the data layer. This separates concerns and make the solution very flexible since the instance of the **CollectionDataLayer** instance can be swapped out for any class implementing the **IDataLayer** interface when more data sources are added in the future. This fulfills one of the criteria set up by the use case, that the data source can vary.

For right now you will only add an empty **IDataLayer** interface and an empty **CollectionData-Layer** class; you will populate the interface and class as you implement the functionality in the GUI. The only implementation you need to add is a call to the **Seed** method of the **TestData** class from the constructor to populate the collections with data.

1. Add an empty **public** interface called **IRentalBase** to the **Interfaces** folder in the **Data Layer** project.

2. Add an empty **public** interface called **IDataLayer** to the **Interfaces** folder in the **Data Layer** project.

3. Inherit the **IRentalBase** interface in the **IDataLayer** interface.

```
public interface IDataLayer : IRentalBase { ... }
```

4. Add a **public** class called **CollectionDataLayer** to the **Data Layers** folder in the **Data Layer** project.

5. Implement the **IDataLayer** interface in the class.

```
public class CollectionDataLayer : IDataLayer { ... }
```

6. Call to the **Seed** method of the **TestData** class from the constructor.

```
public CollectionDataLayer()
{
    new TestData().Seed();
}
```

The complete code for the **IRentalBase** interface so far:

```
public interface IRentalBase
{
}
```

The complete code for the **IDataLayer** interface so far:

```
public interface IDataLayer : IRentalBase
{
}
```

The complete code for the **CollectionDataLayer** class so far:

```
public class CollectionDataLayer : IDataLayer
{
    public CollectionDataLayer()
    {
        new TestData().Seed();
    }
}
```

The IBookingProcessor interface and BookingProcessor class

The **IBookingProcessor** interface inherit the **IRentalBase** interface and most of the members implemented by the **BookingProcessor** class is defined in the **IRentalBase** interface.

The purpose of this class is to insert a layer of business logic between the application and the data layer to be able to enforce business rules. You can check user rights or create logic that call different methods in the data layer based on set business rules.

In order to gain access to the **IRentalBase** interface and other data layer logic you need to add a reference to the **Data Layer** project in the **Business Layer** project.

Once the reference has been added you will create a **public** interface called **IBooking-Processor** in the **Interfaces** folder in the **Business Layer** project which inherits the **IRental-Base** interface. Add a read only **IDataLayer** property called **DataLayer** to the interface and implement the **IBookingProcessor** interface in a **public** class called **BookingProcessor** in the **Classes** folder.

To force the **BookingProcessor** instances to be created and at the same time receive an instance of a class implementing the **IDataLayer** interface you need to add a constructor that has an **IDataLayer** parameter and stored it in a property called **DataLayer**. It is through this property that the business layer can reach the data layer.

You will later create an instance of the **BookingProcessor** class in the form's code-behind to gain access to the data in the data layer.

1. Add a reference to the **Data Layer** project by right clicking on the **References** folder and select **Add Reference**.

2. Add a **public** interface called **IBookingProcessor** to the **Interfaces** folder.

3. Inherit the **IRentalBase** interface from the **Data Layer** project to the **IBookingProcessor** interface.

4. ```
   public interface IBookingProcessor : IRentalBase { ... }
   ```

5. Add a read only **IDataLayer** property called **DataLayer** to the interface
   ```
   IDataLayer DataLayer { get; }
   ```

6. Implement the interface in the **BookingProcessor** class. Note the **private set** keyword making it possible to add the passed in **IDataLayer** instance to the property internally to the **BookingProcessor** instance.
   ```
   public class BookingProcessor : IBookingProcessor
   {
       public IDataLayer DataLayer { get; private set; }
   }
   ```
   ```

7. Add a constructor with an **IDataLayer** parameter and assign the parameter to the **DataLayer** property.

```
public BookingProcessor(IDataLayer dataLayer)
{
    DataLayer = dataLayer;
}
```

The **IBookingProcessor** interface code so far:

```
public interface IBookingProcessor : IRentalBase
{
    IDataLayer DataLayer { get; }
}
```

The **BookingProcessor** class' code so far:

```
public class BookingProcessor : IBookingProcessor
{
    #region Properties
    public IDataLayer DataLayer { get; private set; }
    #endregion

    #region Constructor
    public BookingProcessor(IDataLayer dataLayer)
    {
        DataLayer = dataLayer;
    }
    #endregion
}
```

The GUI

The GUI is the form the user inputs and selects data from when a car is rented, returned or when additional data is added such as a new customer or vehicle.

There are four action categories a user can choose from: rent out a vehicle, receive a returned vehicle, look at booking history and add new data. One way to display this in an easily understandable manner is to use a tab control with a tab for each action category.

The **Rent Vehicle** tab: Here the user can rent out a vehicle to a customer by choosing a vehicle from a list view called **lvwAvailableVehicles**, select a customer from a combo box called *cboCustomers* and click a button called *btnRent* (see image in the Application GUI section at the beginning of the use case).

The **Return Vehicle** tab: Here the user can process a returned vehicle by choosing a vehicle from a list view called *lvwBookedVehicles*, fill out the current meter setting in a textbox called *txtMeterReturn* and click a button called *btnReturn* (see image in the Application GUI section at the beginning of the use case).

The **Bookings** tab: Here the user can view all bookings in a list view called *lvwBookings* (see image in the Application GUI section at the beginning of the use case).

The **Add Data** tab: Here the user can add a new vehicle filling out two textboxes called *txtRegNo* and *txtMeter*, select a vehicle type from a combo box called *cboTypes* and click the *btnAddVehicle* button. New customers can also be added by filling out three textboxes called *txtSocial*, *txtFirstName* and *txtLastName* and then click the *btnAddCustomer* button (see image in the Application GUI section at the beginning of the use case).

There should also be a button called *btnClose* in the form which will close the form when clicked.

To be able to reach the data in the **TestData** data source you need to create an instance of the **BookingProcessor** class passing in an instance of the data layer class you want to use, in this case the **CollectionDataLayer** class. To gain access to the necessary classes you need to add a reference to the **Business Layer** and **Data Layer** projects in the **Windows Forms Application** project.

1. Add references to the **Business Layer** and **Data Layer** projects.
2. Open the form's code-behind file.
3. Add an **IBookingProcessor** variable called **processor** at the beginning of the form class. It is through this variable you will call the booking processor and get access to the data through the data layer.
   ```
   IBookingProcessor processor;
   ```
4. Create an instance of the **BookingProcessor** class and pass in an instance of the **CollectionDataLayer** class from the **Form_Load** event.
   ```
   processor = new BookingProcessor(new CollectionDataLayer());
   ```

5. Add a region called **Fill Data Methods** below the **Form_Load** event.
6. Add a region called **Action Methods** below the **Fill Data Methods** region.
7. Add a region called **Helper Methods** below the **Action Methods** region.
8. Add a region called **Button Events** below the **Helper Methods** region.

The complete form class code so far:

```
public partial class Form1 : Form
{
    IBookingProcessor processor;

    public Form1()
    {
        InitializeComponent();
    }

    private void Form1_Load(object sender, EventArgs e)
    {
        processor = new BookingProcessor(new CollectionDataLayer());
    }

    #region Fill Data Methods
    #endregion

    #region Action Methods
    #endregion

    #region Helper Methods
    #endregion

    #region Button Events
    #endregion
}
```

Rent Vehicle: List customers

Now it's time to actually use the data in the **TestData** class by implementing the necessary methods in the **BookingProcessor** and **CollectionDataLayer** classes and then calling the methods from the form's code-behind.

The first task is to fill the *cboCustomers* combo box in the **Rent Vehicle** tab with all customers in the data source. In order to be able to fetch all the customers from the **Customers** collection in the **TestData** class (the data source) you need to define a method called **Get-Customers** in the **IRentalBase** interface and implement it in the **CollectionDataLayer** class with logic that fetches data from the **Customers** collection but also in the **BookingProcessor** class with logic that fetches the data by calling the instance of the **CollectionDataLayer** class. When the method has been implemented in both classes the **processor** variable you added to the form's code-behind can be used to call the **GetCustomer** method on the booking processor.

Since you know that the method will return a list of customers it's not a huge leap to come to the conclusion that it should return either a **List<ICustomer>** or **IEnumerable <ICusto-mer>**, the main difference between the two is that the **IEnumerable** defer the actual fetching of the instances until they are used; for instance when looping over the collection. Use the **ICustomer** interface as the collection data type to make the solution as flexible as possible; if you use the **Customer** class then only objects from that class can be stored in the collection, by using the interface instead all classes implementing that interface can be stored in the collection.

The IRentalBase interface

To implement the **GetCustomer** method with the same signature in the **CollectionDataLayer** and **BookingProcessor** class you add it to the **IRentalBase** interface; this will force both classes to implement the method since they implement the interface. Failure to implement the method in either or both classes will result in a compilation exception and the application will not run until the methods has been added.

1. Open the **IRentalBase** interface.
2. Add two regions called **Action Methods** and **Fetch Methods**.
3. Add a definition for an **IEnumerable<ICustomer>** method called **GetCustomer** to the **Fetch Methods** region of interface. Remember that interfaces only define members and never have any logic.
   ```
   IEnumerable<ICustomer> GetCustomers();
   ```

The code for the **IRentalBase** interface so far:

```
public interface IRentalBase
{
    #region Action Methods
    #endregion
```

```
    #region Fetch Methods
    IEnumerable<ICustomer> GetCustomers();
    #endregion
}
```

The CollectionDataLayer class

Add a method called **GetCustomers** to the **CollectionDataLayer** class to implement the method defined in the **IRentalBase** interface; you can copy the definition from the interface, paste it into the class and add the curly braces.

The logic of the method could not be easier, you simply return the **Customers** collection from the **TestData** class.

1. Open the **CollectionDataLayer** class in the **Data Layer** project.
2. Add three regions called **Action Methods**, **Fetch Methods** and **Helper Methods** to the class.
3. Implement the **GetCustomers** method in the **Fetch Methods** region.
4. Return the **Customers** collection in the **TestData** class from the method.
   ```
   public IEnumerable<ICustomer> GetCustomers()
   {
       return TestData.Customers;
   }
   ```

The complete **CollectionDataLayer** class so far:

```
public class CollectionDataLayer : IDataLayer
{
    public CollectionDataLayer() {
        new TestData().Seed();
    }

    #region Action Methods
    #endregion

    #region Fetch Methods
    public IEnumerable<ICustomer> GetCustomers()
    {
        return TestData.Customers;
    }
    #endregion
```

```
    #region Helper Methods
    #endregion
}
```

The BookingProcessor class

Add a method called **GetCustomer** to the **BookingProcessor** class to implement the method defined in the **IRentalBase** interface; you can copy the definition from the interface, paste it into the class and add the curly braces.

Since there is no business logic to implement for this method the logic of the method could not be easier, you simply return the result of a call to the **GetCustomers** method in the **CollectionDataLayer** class that you reach through the **DataLayer** property you added to the **BookingProcessor** class earlier. You should also implement exception handling that re-throws any exception from the data layer.

1. Open the **BookingProcessor** class in the **Business Layer** project.
2. Add three regions called **Action Methods**, **Fetch Methods** and **Helper Methods** to the class.
3. Implement the **GetCustomers** method in the **Fetch Methods** region.
4. Add a **try/catch**-block in the method where the catch re-throws the exception.
5. Return the result from a call to the **GetCustomers** method in the data layer.
   `return DataLayer.GetCustomers();`

The complete **BookingProcessor** class so far:

```
public class BookingProcessor : IBookingProcessor
{
    #region Properties
    public IDataLayer DataLayer { get; private set; }
    #endregion

    #region Constructor
    public BookingProcessor(IDataLayer dataLayer)
    {
        DataLayer = dataLayer;
    }
    #endregion
```

```
    #region Action Methods
    #endregion

    #region Fetch Methods
    public IEnumerable<ICustomer> GetCustomers()
    {
        try
        {
            return DataLayer.GetCustomers();
        }
        catch
        {
            throw;
        }
    }
    #endregion

    #region Helper Methods
    #endregion
}
```

The ComboCustomer class

This class is meant to be the data object stored for each customer in the combo box. The reason you create this class is to be able to display values from many properties in the combo box's text field which normally only accept one property. By creating a property that return the formatted output of the last name, first name and social security number you can assign that property to the **DisplayMember** property of the combo box.

Customers

Raintree Carl (12324545)
Montgomery Lisa (95654123)

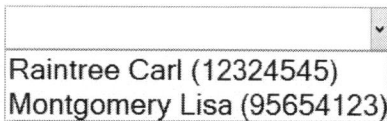

The class should have three properties: **Name** which is the formatted output described above, **SocialSecurityNumber** and **Id** which is the customer id.

1. Add a class called **ComboCustomer** to the **Classes** folder in the Windows Forms Application project.
2. Add two **string** properties called **Name** and **SocialSecurityNumber**.
3. Add an **int** property called **Id**.

The complete **ComboCustomer** class:

```
class ComboCustomer
{
    public string Name { get; set; }
    public string SocialSecurityNumber { get; set; }
    public int Id { get; set; }
}
```

Filling the combo box

Add a method called **FillCustomers** to the form's code-behind and fetch all customers using the **processor** variable to call the **GetCustomers** method in the booking processor. Use a LINQ query to convert the **Customer** objects to **ComboCustomer** objects.

Clear the *cboCustomers* combo box and add the list of **ComboCustomer** objects to it, use the **Name** property as the **DisplayMember**.

1. Open the form's code-behind in the **Car Rental** project.
2. Add a method called **FillCustomers** to the **Fetch Data Methods** region.
3. Add a **try/catch**-block in the method where the **catch**-block is empty ignoring any exception that might occur.
4. Use the result from a call to the **GetCustomers** method in the booking processor in a LINQ query to convert the **Customer** objects to **ComboCustomer** objects.
   ```
   var customer = from c in processor.GetCustomers()
   select new ComboCustomer
   {
       Name = String.Format("{0} {1} ({2})",
           c.LastName, c.FirstName, c.SocialSecurityNumber),
       SocialSecurityNumber = c.SocialSecurityNumber,
       Id = c.Id
   };
   ```
5. Clear the combo box items.
6. Use the **AddRange** method to add the **ComboCustomer** objects to the combo box.
   ```
   cboCustomers.Items.AddRange(customer.ToArray());
   ```
7. Assign "Name" to the **DisplayMember** property of the combo box.
8. Call the **FillCustomers** method below the **processor** variable in the **Form_Load** event
9. Run the application and open the **Customers** combo box to make sure that the customers are in the drop down list.

407

The code for the **GetCustomers** method in the form:

```
public partial class Form1 : Form
{
    IBookingProcessor processor;

    public Form1() ...

    private void Form1_Load(object sender, EventArgs e)
    {
        processor = new BookingProcessor(new CollectionDataLayer());

        FillCustomers();
    }

    #region Fill Data Methods
    private void FillCustomers()
    {
        try
        {
            var customer = from c in processor.GetCustomers()
            select new ComboCustomer
            {
                Name = String.Format("{0} {1} ({2})",
                    c.LastName, c.FirstName, c.SocialSecurityNumber),
                SocialSecurityNumber = c.SocialSecurityNumber,
                Id = c.Id
            };

            cboCustomers.Items.Clear();
            cboCustomers.Items.AddRange(customer.ToArray());
            cboCustomers.DisplayMember = "Name";
        }
        catch
        {
        }
    }
    #endregion
}
```

Rent Vehicle: List available vehicles

Now that the *cboCustomers* combo box has been filled with customers it is time to fill the *lvwAvailableVehicles* in the **Rent Vehicle** tab with all vehicles that are not already rented out. In order to be able to fetch all available vehicles from the **Vehicles** collection in the **Test-Data** class (the data source) you need to define a method called **GetVehicles** in the **IRental-Base** interface and implement it in the **CollectionDataLayer** class with logic that fetches data from the **Vehicles** collection but also to the **BookingProcessor** class with logic that fetches the data by calling the corresponding method in the **CollectionDataLayer** class. When the method has been implemented in both classes the **processor** variable you added to the form's code-behind can be used to call the **GetVehicles** method in the booking processor.

Since you know that the method should return a list of vehicles it should return either a **List <IVehicle>** or **IEnumerable<IVehicle>**. Use the **IVehicle** interface as the collection data type to make the solution as flexible as possible; if you use the **Vehicle** class then only objects from that class can be stored in the collection, by using the interface instead all classes implementing the interface can be stored in the collection.

The **GetVehicles** method should have a **VehicleStatus** parameter called **status** that can be used to filter out the desired vehicles. **VehicleStatus** is an enumeration with the following values: **All**, **Booked** and **Available**.

You need to implement a second method in this scenario called **GetVehicleType** that fetch a vehicle type based on the passed in vehicle type id; this method is used to display the vehicle type name instead of the vehicle type id when displaying vehicles in list view controls.

The VehicleSatus enumeration
To be able to filter on vehicle status you need to implement an enumeration called **Vehicle-Status** that can be used as a parameter data type in the **GetVehicles** method and for filtering in the method. The enumeration should have the following values: **All**, **Booked** and **Available**.

1. Add a **class** called **Enums** to the **Enums** folder in the **Data Layer** project.
2. Delete the **class** code but leave the namespace.
3. Add the **public VehicleStatus enum** to the namespace.

The complete code for the **VehicleStatus** enum:

```
public enum VehicleStatus
{
    All,
    Booked,
    Available
}
```

The IRentalBase interface

To implement the **GetVehicles** and the **GetVehicleType** methods with their signatures in the **CollectionDataLayer** and **BookingProcessor** classes you add them to the **IRentalBase** interface; this will force both classes to implement the methods since they both implement the interface. Failure to implement the methods in either or both classes will result in a compilation exception and the application will not run until the methods has been added.

1. Open the **IRentalBase** interface.
2. Add a definietion for an **IEnumerable<IVehicle>** method called **GetVehicles** which has a **VehicleStatus** parameter called **status**; add it to the **Fetch Methods** region of the interface.
   ```
   IEnumerable<IVehicle> GetVehicles(VehicleStatus status);
   ```
3. Add a definition for an **IVehicleType** method called **GetVehicleType** which has an **int** parameter called **vehicleTypeId**; add it to the **Fetch Methods** region of the interface.
   ```
   IVehicleType GetVehicleType(int vehicleTypeId);
   ```

The complete code for the **IRentalBase** interface so far:

```
public interface IRentalBase
{
    #region Action Methods
    #endregion

    #region Fetch Methods
    IEnumerable<ICustomer> GetCustomers();
    IEnumerable<IVehicle> GetVehicles(VehicleStatus status);
    IVehicleType GetVehicleType(int vehicleTypeId);
    #endregion
}
```

The CollectionDataLayer class

Add a method called **GetVehicles** and another called **GetVehicleType** to the **CollectionData-Layer** class to implement the method defined in the **IRentalBase** interface; you can copy the definition from the interface, paste it into the class and add the curly braces.

The logic in the **GetVehicles** method is a little bit trickier than the **GetCustomers** method because now the returned result set can contain all, available or booked vehicles which mean that you have to implement conditional logic to decide which vehicles to return based on the passed in vehicle status in the **status** parameter. The easiest way to implement this is probably to do a recursive call to the **GetVehicles** method for the **Available** vehicle status with the **Booked** vehicle status as the parameter value; check that the result does not contain any booked vehicles with the current vehicle id in the **where** clause of the **Available** vehicle status LINQ query. If the chained **Count** method on the recursive call is zero then the no booking exist for the vehicle.

```
case VehicleStatus.Available:
    return from c in TestData.Vehicles
    where GetVehicles(VehicleStatus.Booked).Count(b =>
        b.Id.Equals(c.Id)).Equals(0)
    select c;
```

To return the booked vehicles you need to **join** the **Vehicles** collection with the **Bookings** collection on the vehicle id in the LINQ query. You also need to add a **where** clause checking that the vehicle has a booking with the **DateTime.MinValue** in its **Returned** property.

The logic in the **GetVehicleType** is much simpler; you only have to fetch the first or default value for the vehicle type id passed in to the method using a LINQ query on the **Vehicle-Types** collection in the **TestData** class.

1. Open the **CollectionDataLayer** class in the **Data Layer** project.
2. Implement the **GetVehicles** method in the **Fetch Methods** region.
3. Add a switch checking the **status** parameter value.
4. Return all **Vehicles** in the **Vehicles** collection in the **TestData** class if the **status** match **All** in the **VehicleStatus** enum.
   ```
   case VehicleStatus.All:
       return TestData.Vehicles;
   ```

5. Join the **Vehicles** collection with the **Bookings** collection on the vehicle id to return the booked vehicles and check that the vehicle's **Returned** property contain **Date-Time.MinValue**.

```
case VehicleStatus.Booked:
    return from c in TestData.Vehicles
        join b in TestData.Bookings on c.Id equals b.VehicleId
        where b.Returned.Equals(DateTime.MinValue)
        select c;
```

6. Do a recursive call to the **GetVehicles** method for the **Available** vehicle status with the **Booked** vehicle status as the parameter value and check that the result does not contain any booked vehicles n the LINQ query.

```
case VehicleStatus.Available:
    return from c in TestData.Vehicles
        where GetVehicles(VehicleStatus.Booked)
        .Count(b => b.Id.Equals(c.Id)).Equals(0)
        select c;
```

7. Implement the **GetVehicleType** method in the **Fetch Methods** region.

8. Add a LINQ query to the method that uses the **FirstOrDefault** method to fetch the vehicle type using the passed in **vehicleTypeId** parameter.

```
return TestData.VehicleTypes.FirstOrDefault(vt =>
vt.Id.Equals(vehicleTypeId));
```

The code for the **CollectionDataLayer** class so far:

```
public class CollectionDataLayer : IDataLayer
{
    public CollectionDataLayer() ...

    #region Action Methods
    #endregion

    #region Fetch Methods
    public IEnumerable<ICustomer> GetCustomers() ...
    public IEnumerable<IVehicle> GetVehicles(VehicleStatus status)
    {
        switch (status)
        {
            case VehicleStatus.All:
                return TestData.Vehicles;
```

```
        case VehicleStatus.Booked:
            return from c in TestData.Vehicles
                join b in TestData.Bookings on c.Id equals b.VehicleId
                where b.Returned.Equals(DateTime.MinValue)
                select c;
        case VehicleStatus.Available:
            return from c in TestData.Vehicles
                where GetVehicles(VehicleStatus.Booked)
                .Count(b => b.Id.Equals(c.Id)).Equals(0)
                select c;
    }
    return new List<IVehicle>();
}

public IVehicleType GetVehicleType(int vehicleTypeId)
{
    return TestData.VehicleTypes.FirstOrDefault(
        vt => vt.Id.Equals(vehicleTypeId));
}
#endregion

#region Helper Methods
#endregion
}
```

The BookingProcessor class

Add the two methods called **GetVehicles** and **GetVehicleType** to the **BookingProcessor** class as defined in the **IRentalBase** interface; you can copy the definitions from the interface, paste them into the class and add the curly braces.

Since there is no business logic to implement for either of the methods their logic could not be easier, you simply return the result of calls to the **GetVehicles** and **GetVehicleType** methods in the **CollectionDataLayer** class that you reach through the **DataLayer** property you added to the **BookingProcessor** class earlier. You should also implement exception handling that re-throws any exception from the data layer.

1. Open the **BookingProcessor** class in the **Business Layer** project.
2. Implement the **GetVehicles** method in the **Fetch Methods** region.
3. Add a **try/catch**-block in the method where the **catch**-block re-throws the exception.
4. Return the result from a call to the **GetVehicles** method in the data layer.
   ```
   return DataLayer.GetVehicles(status);
   ```

5. Implement the **GetVehicleType** method in the **Fetch Methods** region.
6. Add a **try/catch**-block in the method where the **catch**-block re-throws the exception.
7. Return the result from a call to the **GetVehicleType** method in the data layer.
```
return DataLayer.GetVehicleType(vehicleTypeId);
```

The **BookingProcessor** class so far:

```
public class BookingProcessor : IBookingProcessor
{
    #region Properties
    public IDataLayer DataLayer { get; private set; }
    #endregion

    #region Constructor
    public BookingProcessor(IDataLayer dataLayer) ...
    #endregion

    #region Action Methods
    #endregion

    #region Fetch Methods
    public IEnumerable<ICustomer> GetCustomers() ...
    public IEnumerable<IVehicle> GetVehicles(VehicleStatus status)
    {
        try
        {
            return DataLayer.GetVehicles(status);
        }
        catch
        {
            throw;
        }
    }

    public IVehicleType GetVehicleType(int vehicleTypeId)
    {
        try
        {
            return DataLayer.GetVehicleType(vehicleTypeId);
        }
        catch { throw; }
    }
    #endregion
```

```
#region Helper Methods
#endregion
}
```

The GetVehicles ListViewItem conversion method

Since you want to display vehicles in several list view controls it warrants creating a reusable method called **GetVehicles** that can return a collection of **ListViewItems** needed when adding data to a list view in the **Fill Data Methods** region of the form. What the method do is pretty straight forward, it calls the **GetVehicles** method on the **processor** variable fetching the vehicles matching the vehicle status passed into the method and creates new **ListViewItem** objects using the result from the LINQ query.

When displaying the vehicles you want to show the vehicle type name and not its id value to achieve this you can call the **GetVehicleType** method you created in the previous section of this exercise in the LINQ query.

This method can then be called whenever vehicles are displayed in a list view control.

1. Open the form's code- behind file.

2. Add a **private IEnumerable<ListViewItem>** method called **GetVehicles** that has a **VehicleStatus** parameter called **vehicleStatus** to the **Fetch Data Methods** region.
   ```
   private IEnumerable<ListViewItem> GetVehicles(VehicleStatus
   vehicleStatus)
   {
   }
   ```

3. Return the result from a LINQ query which call the **GetVehicles** method on the **processor** instance variable to fetch the vehicles matching the passed in vehicle status. Create new **ListViewItem** objects for the matching vehicles in the LINQ **select** statement. Call the **GetVehicleType** method in the select statement to fetch the name of the vehicle type.
   ```
   return from v in processor.GetVehicles(vehicleStatus)
       select new ListViewItem(new string[]
       {
           processor.GetVehicleType(v.TypeId).Name,
           ...
       });
   ```

415

The complete code for the **GetVehicles** method:

```
private IEnumerable<ListViewItem> GetVehicles(VehicleStatus vehicleStatus)
{
    return from v in processor.GetVehicles(vehicleStatus)
        select new ListViewItem(new string[]
        {
            v.RegistrationNumber,
            processor.GetVehicleType(v.TypeId).Name,
            v.BasePricePerKm.ToString(),
            v.BasePricePerDay.ToString(),
            v.Meter.ToString(),
            v.Id.ToString(),
            "0" //BookingId
        });
}
```

Filling the list view

Create a method called **FillAvailableVehicles** which fetch all available vehicles by calling the **GetVehicles** method you just created in the form and pass in the **Available** vehicle status.

Use the result from the method call to populate the *lvwAvailableVehicles* list view, don't forget to clear the items in the list view before adding the fetched vehicles to avoid duplicates in the list view.

Available vehicles

Registration Number	Type	Km Tariff	Day Tariff	Meter
FGH123	Sedan	0	100	10000
DCE123	Van	0,5	300	30000

1. Open the form's code-behind file.
2. Add a method called **FillAvailableVehicles** to the **Fill Data Methods** region.
3. Call the **GetVehicles** method passing in **VehicleStatus.Available** and store the result in a variable called **vehicles**.
   ```
   var vehicles = GetVehicles(VehicleStatus.Available);
   ```
4. Clear the **Items** collection of the *lvwAvailableVehicles* list view.
5. Add the fetched vehicles to the **Items** collection by calling the **AddRange** method.
6. Call the **FillAvailableVehicles** method from the **Form_Load** event.

7. Run the application and make sure that the available vehicles are displayed in the list view control on the **Rent Vehicle** tab.

The complete code for the **FillAvailableVehicles** method:

```
private void FillAvialbleVehicles()
{
    var vehicles = GetVehicles(VehicleStatus.Available);
    lvwAvailableVehicles.Items.Clear();
    lvwAvailableVehicles.Items.AddRange(vehicles.ToArray());
}
```

Rent Vehicle: Rent a vehicle

Now that the *cboCustomers* combo box and the *lvwAvailableVehicles* list view in the **Rent Vehicle** tab has been filled with data it is time to implement the functionality to rent a vehicle by clicking the *btnRent* button. In order to rent a vehicle you need the customer id from the selected customer in the combo box and the vehicle id from the selected vehicle in the list view.

Since the **RentVehicle** method you will create isn't fetching data and performing the action of adding a booking to the **Bookings** collection in the **TestData** class (the data source) it should be added to the **Action Methods** regions in the involved classes and the **IRentalBase** interface. Implement the **RentVehicle** method definition from the **IRentalBase** interface in the **CollectionDataLayer** and **BookingProcessor** classes. When the method has been implemented in both classes the **processor** variable you added to the form's code-behind can be used to call the **RentVehicle** method on the booking processor.

Since you want the method to add a booking it can be beneficial to return a **bool** value stating if the booking was successful or not. The method defined in the interface has three parameters, two **int** parameters called **vehicleId** and **customerId** and a **DateTime** parameter called **timeOfRental**.

The IRentalBase interface

To implement the **RentVehicle** method with the same signature in the **CollectionDataLayer** and **BookingProcessor** class you add it to the **IRentalBase** interface; this will force both classes to implement the method since they implement the interface. Failure to implement

417

the method in either or both classes will result in a compilation exception and the application will not run until the methods has been added.

1. Open the **IRentalBase** interface.
2. Add a definition for a **bool** method called **RentVehicle** with three parameters, two **int** parameters called **vehicleId** and **customerId** and a **DateTime** parameter called **timeOfRental** to the **Action Methods** region of the interface. Remember that interfaces only define members and never have any logic.
   ```
   bool RentVehicle(int vehicleId, int customerId, DateTime
   timeOfRental);
   ```

The code for the **IRentalBase** interface so far:

```
public interface IRentalBase
{
    #region Action Methods
    bool RentVehicle(int vehicleId, int customerId, DateTime timeOfRental);
    #endregion

    #region Fetch Methods
    IEnumerable<ICustomer> GetCustomers();
    IEnumerable<IVehicle> GetVehicles(VehicleStatus status);
    IVehicleType GetVehicleType(int vehicleTypeId);
    #endregion
}
```

The CollectionDataLayer class

Add a method called **RentVehicle** to the **CollectionDataLayer** class to implement the method defined in the **IRentalBase** interface; you can copy the definition from the interface, paste it into the class and add the curly braces.

The logic of the method is fairly simple, first you add a **try/catch**-block and then generate a new booking id by adding 1 to the highest existing booking id from the **Bookings** collection in the **TestData** class (note that the booking id would be auto generated from the database in a real world scenario).

Once you have the booking id you use the **Add** method of the **Bookings** collection to add a new booking by creating a new instance of the **Booking** class using the values passed in to the **RentVehicle** method and the new booking id. Return **true** from the method if no exception was thrown by either of the two previous code statements. If an exception is thrown you end up in the **catch**-block where **false** is returned.

1. Open the **CollectionDataLayer** class in the **Data Layer** project.
2. Implement the **RentVehicle** method in the **Action Methods** region.
3. Add a **try/catch**-block to the method.
4. Generate a new booking id by adding 1 to the highest existing booking id from the **Bookings** collection by calling the **Max** method specifying which property you want to fetch the maximum value for.
    var bookingId = TestData.Bookings.Max(b => b.Id) + 1;

5. Add a new booking by calling the **Add** method on the **Bookings** collection passing in a new instance of the **Booking** class.
    TestData.Bookings.Add(new Booking() { Id = bookingId, CustomerId = customerId, Rented = timeOfRental, VehicleId = vehicleId });

6. Return **true** if no exception was thrown otherwise return **false**.

The code in the **CollectionDataLayer** class so far:

```
public class CollectionDataLayer : IDataLayer
{
    public CollectionDataLayer() ...

    #region Action Methods
    public bool RentVehicle(int vehicleId, int customerId,
    DateTime timeOfRental)
    {
        try
        {
            // The booking id would normally be supplied by the database
            var bookingId = TestData.Bookings.Max(b => b.Id) + 1;

            TestData.Bookings.Add(new Booking() {
                Id = bookingId,
                CustomerId = customerId,
                Rented = timeOfRental,
                VehicleId = vehicleId
            });

            return true;
        }
}
```

```
        catch
        {
            throw;
        }
    }
    #endregion

    #region Fetch Methods
    public IEnumerable<ICustomer> GetCustomers() ...
    public IEnumerable<IVehicle> GetVehicles(VehicleStatus status) ...
    public IVehicleType GetVehicleType(int vehicleTypeId) ...
    #endregion

    #region Helper Methods
    #endregion
}
```

The BookingProcessor class

Add a method called **RentVehicle** to the **BookingProcessor** class to implement the method defined in the **IRentalBase** interface; you can copy the definition from the interface, paste it into the class and add the curly braces.

Since there is no business logic to implement for this method the logic of the method could not be easier, you simply return the result of a call to the **RentVehicle** method in the **CollectionDataLayer** class that you reach through the **DataLayer** property you added to the **BookingProcessor** class earlier. You should also implement exception handling that re-throws any exception from the data layer.

1. Open the **BookingProcessor** class in the **Business Layer** project.
2. Implement the **RentVehicle** method in the **Action Methods** region.
3. Add a **try/catch**-block in the method where the catch re-throws the exception.
4. Return the result from a call to the **RentVehicle** method in the data layer.
   ```
   return DataLayer.RentVehicle(vehicleId, customerId, DateTime.Now);
   ```

The complete **BookingProcessor** class so far:

```
public class BookingProcessor : IBookingProcessor
{
    #region Properties
    public IDataLayer DataLayer { get; private set; }
    #endregion
```

```
#region Constructor
public BookingProcessor(IDataLayer dataLayer) ...
#endregion

#region Action Methods
public bool RentVehicle(int vehicleId, int customerId,
DateTime timeOfRental)
{
    try
    {
        return DataLayer.RentVehicle(vehicleId, customerId,
          DateTime.Now);
    }
    catch
    {
        throw;
    }
}
#endregion

#region Fetch Methods
public IEnumerable<ICustomer> GetCustomers() ...
public IEnumerable<IVehicle> GetVehicles(VehicleStatus status) ...
public IVehicleType GetVehicleType(int vehicleTypeId) ...
#endregion

#region Helper Methods
#endregion
}
```

Renting a vehicle

In order to rent a vehicle you need to create a **bool** method called **RentVehicle** that fetch data from the selected items in the *cboCustomers* combo box and the *lvwAvailableVehicles* list view and use that information to call the **RentVehicle** method on the **processor** instance.

The **RentVehicle** method in the **Action Methods** region of the form should return **true** if the booking process was successful otherwise it should return **false**. The returned result will be used in the **Click** event of the *btnRent* button to display a message box if the booking was unsuccessful.

Add a **bool** variable called **success** in the method.

Implement a **try/catch**-block returning **true** in the **try**-block and **false** in the **catch**-block like you have done in previous methods with the difference that you use a variable to store the value and return it after the **catch**-block.

Add an **if**-block checking that a customer is selected in the combo box and display a message to the user and exit gracefully from the method if that is not the case.

Add another **if**-block checking that a vehicle is selected in the list view and display a message to the user and exit gracefully from the method if that is not the case.

Fetch the selected vehicle's id from the list view and store it in a variable called **vehicleId** and the selected customer's id from the combo box and store it in a variable called **customerId**.

Call the **RentVehicle** method on the **processor** instance variable passing in the **vehicleId** and **customerId** variables as well as the current date and store the result in the **returnVehicle** variable.

Call the **FillAvailableVehicles** method you created in the beginning of this exercise to repopulate the list view containing the vehicles available for rental.

1. Open the form's code-behind file.
2. Add a **bool** method called **RentVehicle** to the **Action Methods** region.
3. Add a **bool** variable called **success** to the method and assign **false** to it.
4. Add a **try/catch**-block where the **catch**-block assign **false** to the **success** variable.
5. Return the value of the **success** variable after the **catch**-block.
6. Add an **if**-statement to the **try**-block that check if the **SelectedIndex** of the combo box is less than zero and display a message to the user and return the value of the **success** variable if it is.
7. Add an **if**-statement **try**-block that check if the **SelectedItems.Count** property of the list view is zero and display a message to the user and return the value of the **success** variable if it is.
8. Parse the sixth sub item of the selected item in the list view to get the vehicle id and store the result in a variable called **vehicleId**.
   ```
   var vehicleId = Int32.Parse(lvwAvailableVehicles
       .SelectedItems[0].SubItems[5].Text);
   ```

9. Fetch the customer id from the selected item in the combo box by casting the selected item to a **ComboCustomer** object and read the value in its **Id** property, store the value in a variable called **customerId**.
```
var customerId = ((ComboCustomer)cboCustomers.SelectedItem).Id;
```

10. Call the **RentVehicle** method on the **processor** variable passing in the **vehicleId**, **customerId** and the current date. Store the result form the method call in the **success** variable.
```
success = processor.RentVehicle(vehicleId, customerId, DateTime.Now);
```

11. Call the **FillAvailableVehicles** method to update the *lvwAvailableVehicles* list view. Later you will add calls to two other methods updating the other two list view controls.

12. Add the **Click** event for the *btnRent* button to the **Button Events** region.

13. Call the **RentVehicle** method you just added to the form in the **Click** event and store the result in a variable called **rented**.

14. Add an **if**-statement that display a message box telling the user that the vehicle wasn't rented if the **rented** variable is **false**.

15. Run the application and click the button without selecting a customer and make sure that the correct messages are displayed.

16. Now select a vehicle and customer and click the button. If the booking was successfully added the vehicle should no longer be available for rental in the list view.

The code for the form so far:

```
public partial class Form1 : Form
{
    IBookingProcessor processor;

    public Form1() ...

    private void Form1_Load(object sender, EventArgs e) ...

    #region Fill Data Methods
    private void FillCustomers() ...
    private IEnumerable<ListViewItem> GetVehicles(
        VehicleStatus vehicleStatus) ...
    private void FillAvialbleVehicles() ...
    #endregion
```

```csharp
#region Action Methods
private bool RentVehicle()
{
    bool success = false;

    try
    {
        if (cboCustomers.SelectedIndex < 0)
        {
            MessageBox.Show(
                "A customer must be selected in the drop down list");
            return success;
        }

        if (lvwAvailableVehicles.SelectedItems.Count == 0)
        {
            MessageBox.Show("A vehicle must be selected in the list");
            return success;
        }

        var vehicleId = Int32.Parse(
            lvwAvailableVehicles.SelectedItems[0].SubItems[5].Text);

        var customerId = ((ComboCustomer)cboCustomers.SelectedItem).Id;

        success = processor.RentVehicle(vehicleId, customerId,
            DateTime.Now);

        FillAvialbleVehicles();
    }
    catch { success = false; }

    return success;
}
#endregion

#region Helper Methods
#endregion

#region Button Events
private void btnRent_Click(object sender, EventArgs e)
{
    var rented = RentVehicle();
```

```
        if (!rented) MessageBox.Show("The vehicle was not rented");
    }
    #endregion
}
```

Return Vehicle: Fill the booked vehicles list box

Now that you have enabled the user to rent out a vehicle it's time to add the functionality to return a vehicle on the **Return Vehicle** tab of the form. To return a vehicle the user has to select a vehicle from the *lvwBookedVehicles* list view and enter the current meter setting in the *txtMeterReturn* textbox before clicking on the *btnReturn* button.

In this part of the exercise you will add all booked vehicles to the *lvwBookedVehicles* list view. In order to be able to fetch all the booked vehicles from the **Vehicles** collection in the **TestData** class (the data source) you need to call the **GetVehicles** method you created earlier passing in **VehicleStatus.Booked** in its **vehicleStatus** parameter.

Filling the list view

Add a method called **FillBookedVehicles** to the **Fill Data Methods** region of the form that call the **GetVehicles** method and use the result to fill the list view and then call that method from the **Form_Load** event.

1. Open the form's code-behind file.
2. Add a **void** method called **FillBookedVehicles** to the **Fill Data Methods** region.
3. Call the **GetVehicles** method passing in **VehicleStatus.Booked** to it. Store the result from the method call in a variable called **vehicles**.
   ```
   var vehicles = GetVehicles(VehicleStatus.Booked);
   ```
4. Clear the **Items** collection of the *lvwBookedVehicles* list view.
5. Add the fetched vehicles to the list view using the **AddRange** method.
6. Add a call to the **FillBookedVehicles** method at the end of the **Form_Load** event.
7. Add a call to the **FillBookedVehicles** method after the call to the **FillAvailableVehicles** method in the **RentVehicle** method to update the list view content when a vehicle is rented.
8. Run the application and make sure that there is a booking in the **Booked Vehicles** list view on the **Return Vehicle** tab.

9. Go to the **Rent Vehicle** tab and rent one of the remaining vehicles and make sure that it is removed from the **Available vehicles** list view. Switch to the **Return Vehicle** tab and make sure that the vehicle is displayed in the list view.

The form's code so far:

```
public partial class Form1 : Form
{
    IBookingProcessor processor;

    public Form1() ...

    private void Form1_Load(object sender, EventArgs e) ...

    #region Fill Data Methods
    private void FillCustomers() ...
    private IEnumerable<ListViewItem> GetVehicles(
        VehicleStatus vehicleStatus) ...
    private void FillAvialbleVehicles() ...
    private void FillBookedVehicles()
    {
        var vehicles = GetVehicles(VehicleStatus.Booked);
        lvwBokedVehicles.Items.Clear();
        lvwBokedVehicles.Items.AddRange(vehicles.ToArray());
    }
    #endregion

    #region Action Methods
    private bool RentVehicle() ...
    #endregion

    #region Helper Methods
    #endregion

    #region Button Events
    private void btnRent_Click(object sender, EventArgs e) ...
    #endregion
}
```

Return Vehicle: Return a vehicle

In order to return a rented vehicle the user must select a vehicle in the *lvwBookedVehicles* to get access to the vehicle id, enter the current vehicle meter setting in the *txtMeterReturn* textbox and click the *brnReturn* button.

Since the **ReturnVehicle** method you will create isn't fetching data and performing the action of returning a rented out vehicle it should be added to the **Action Methods** regions in the involved classes and the **IRentalBase** interface. Implement the **ReturnVehicle** method definition from the **IRentalBase** interface in the **CollectionDataLayer** and **BookingProcessor** classes. When the method has been implemented in both classes the **processor** variable you added to the form's code-behind can be used to call the **ReturnVehicle** method in the booking processor.

Since you want the method to return a vehicle by adding the current date to the **Returned** property, calculate the cost and assign that value to the **Cost** property and assign the passed in meter setting to the **Meter** property of an existing booking matching the passed in booking id it can be beneficial to return a **bool** value stating if the actions were successful or not. The method defined in the interface has three parameters, one **int** parameter called **bookingId**, a **double** parameter called **meter** for the current meter setting and a **DateTime** parameter called **returned**.

If something goes wrong with the booking object then a specialized custom exception called **BookingException** should be thrown with a suitable message and the booking id stored in an **Id** property. The **BookingException** should inherit and extend the **KeyNotFoundException** class.

If something goes wrong with the vehicle object then a specialized custom exception called **VehicleException** should be thrown with a suitable message and the vehicle id stored in an **Id** property. The **VehicleException** should inherit and extend the **KeyNotFoundException** class.

To keep the code in the **ReturnVehicle** method clean you have to add two helper methods called **RentalDuration** which calculates how long the vehicle has been rented based on the rental and return date and **CalculatePrice** which calculates the price based on information in the fetched vehicle, the current meter setting and the duration calculated by the **RentalDuration** method.

To do the calculations you have to fetch the booking matching the booking id passed in to the method from the **Bookings** collection in the **TestData** class and the vehicle matching the vehicle id in the fetched booking from the **Vehicles** collection.

The BookingsException, VehicleException and CustomerException classes
To store custom data in an exception you inherit the best existing exception class to a new class, add the necessary properties to the class and add a constructor with the necessary parameters.

In these two exception classes you want to add a property with a **public** getter and a **private** setter called **Id**. The custom message for the exceptions will be stored in the inherited exception class' **Message** property by sending it to inherited class' constructor using the **base** keyword.

The exception classes should be created in the **Exceptions** folder in the **Data Layer** project to be accessible everywhere.

1. Add a class called **BookingException** to the **Exceptions** folder in the **Data Layer** project.
2. Change its accessibility to **public** and inherit the **KeyNotFoundException** class.
   ```
   public class BookingException : KeyNotFoundException
   ```
3. Add a **public int** property called **Id** with a **private** setter.
   ```
   public int Id { get; private set; }
   ```
4. Add a constructor that has an **int** parameter called **id** and a **string** parameter called **message**. Let the constructor call the **base** class' constructor with the **message** parameter and assign the passed in **id** parameter to the **Id** property in the constructor body.
   ```
   public BookingException(int id, string message = "The given booking
   id does not exist") : base(message)
   {
       Id = id;
   }
   ```
5. Repeat the bullets 1-4 for two classes called **VehicleException** and **CustomerException** changing the default text for the message parameter.

The complete code for the **BookingException** class:

```
public class BookingException : KeyNotFoundException
{
    public int Id { get; private set; }
```

```
    public BookingException(int id, string message = "The given booking id
    does not exist") : base(message)
    {
        Id = id;
    }
}
```

The complete code for the **VehicleException** class:

```
public class VehicleException : KeyNotFoundException
{
    public int Id { get; private set; }

    public VehicleException(int id, string message = "The given vehicle id
    does not exist") : base(message)
    {
        Id = id;
    }
}
```

The IDataLayer interface

To implement the **RentalDuration** and **CalculatePrice** methods in the **CollectionDataLayer** class you add it to the **IDataLayer** interface; this will force the class to implement the methods. Failure to implement the methods in the class will result in a compilation exception and the application will not run until the methods have been added.

1. Open the **IDataLayer** interface.
2. Add a definition for an **int** method called **RentalDuration** with two **DateTime** parameters called **rented** and **returned** to the **Helper Methods** region in the interface. Remember that interfaces only define members and never have any logic.
   `int RentalDuration(DateTime rented, DateTime returned);`
3. Add a definition for a **double** method called **CalculatePrice** with three parameters, one **IVehicle** parameter called **vehicle**, a **double** parameter called **returnedMeterSetting** and an **int** parameter called **duration**. Add the method to the **Helper Methods** region in the interface.
   `double CalculatePrice(IVehicle vehicle, double returnedMeterSetting, int duration);`

The complete code for the **IDataLayer** interface:

```
public interface IDataLayer : IRentalBase
{
    #region Helper Methods
    int RentalDuration(DateTime rented, DateTime returned);

    double CalculatePrice(IVehicle vehicle,
        double returnedMeterSetting, int duration);
    #endregion
}
```

The RentalDuration method

This method defined in the **IDataLayer** interface will calculate how long a vehicle has been rented by subtracting the return date from the rental date storing the result in a **TimeSpan** object called **time**. You can use the passed in parameters **TimeOfDay** property to check if the rental duration is within an acceptable range; return 1 if the **time** object's **Days** property is equal to zero and the difference between the **returned** and **rented** parameters' **TimeOfDay** properties is greater than the minimal value for a time span otherwise return the value of the **Days** property of the **time** object.

```
if (time.Days == 0 && returned.TimeOfDay - rented.TimeOfDay >
TimeSpan.MinValue)
```

Add the **RentalDuration** method to the **Helper Methods** region in the **CollectionDataLayer**. The method should have two **DateTime** parameters called **rented** and **returned** and return an **int** value representing the number of days the vehicle has been rented out.

1. Open the **CollectionDataLayer** class.
2. Add a method called **RentalDuration** with two **DateTime** parameters called **rented** and **returned** to the **Helper Methods** region.
   ```
   public int RentalDuration(DateTime rented, DateTime returned)
   ```

3. Add a **TimeSpan** variable called **time** to which you assign the result of the difference between the **returned** and **rented** date parameters.
   ```
   TimeSpan time = returned - rented;
   ```

4. Add an if statement checking if the number of days is equal to zero and return 1 if it is otherwise return the number of days calculated by the **time** variable.

```
    if (time.Days == 0 && returned.TimeOfDay - rented.TimeOfDay >
    TimeSpan.MinValue)
        return 1;
    else
        return time.Days;
```

The complete code for the **RentalDuration** method:

```
public class CollectionDataLayer : IDataLayer
{
    public CollectionDataLayer() ...

    #region Action Methods
    public bool RentVehicle(int vehicleId, int
        customerId, DateTime timeOfRental) ...
    #endregion

    #region Fetch Methods
    public IEnumerable<ICustomer> GetCustomers() ...
    public IEnumerable<IVehicle> GetVehicles(VehicleStatus status) ...
    public IVehicleType GetVehicleType(int vehicleTypeId) ...
    #endregion

    #region Helper Methods
    public int RentalDuration(DateTime rented, DateTime returned)
    {
        TimeSpan time = returned - rented;

        if (time.Days == 0 &&
            returned.TimeOfDay - rented.TimeOfDay > TimeSpan.MinValue)
            return 1;
        else
            return time.Days;
    }
    #endregion
}
```

The CalcualtePrice method

This method defined in the **IDataLayer** interface will calculate how much the customer owe for renting the vehicle using the formulas specified by the use case (see below). The **CalculatePrice** method returning a **double** should be added to the **Helper Methods** region in the **CollectionDataLayer** class and have three parameters, **vehicle** of the **IVehicle** data type, **returnedMeterSetting** of the **int** data type and **duration** of the **int** data type.

Sedan: Price = daily cost * number of days

Combi: Price = daily cost * number of days * day tariff + cost per Km * actual Km driven. The day tariff is initially 1.5, but that could be changed over time.

Van: Price = daily cost * number of days * day tariff + cost per Km * actual Km driven * distance tariff. The day tariff is initially 2.0 and distance tariff is initially 2.5, but that could be changed over time.

1. Open the **CollectionDataLayer** class.
2. Add a method called **CalculatePrice** with three parameters, **vehicle** of the **IVehicle** data type, **returnedMeterSetting** of the **int** data type and **duration** of the **int** data type to the **Helper Methods** region.
   ```
   public double CalculatePrice(IVehicle vehicle, double
   returnedMeterSetting, int duration)
   ```
3. Calculate the price and return it from the method.
   ```
   return vehicle.BasePricePerDay * duration * vehicle.DayTariff +
   vehicle.BasePricePerKm * (returnedMeterSetting - vehicle.Meter) *
   vehicle.KmTariff;
   ```

The complete code for the **CalculatePrice** method:

```
public class CollectionDataLayer : IDataLayer
{
    public CollectionDataLayer() ...

    #region Action Methods
    public bool RentVehicle(int vehicleId, int
        customerId, DateTime timeOfRental) ...
    #endregion

    #region Fetch Methods
    public IEnumerable<ICustomer> GetCustomers() ...
    public IEnumerable<IVehicle> GetVehicles(VehicleStatus status) ...
    public IVehicleType GetVehicleType(int vehicleTypeId) ...
    #endregion

    #region Helper Methods
    public int RentalDuration(DateTime rented, DateTime returned) ...
    public double CalculatePrice(IVehicle vehicle,
```

```
    double returnedMeterSetting, int duration)
{
    return vehicle.BasePricePerDay * duration * vehicle.DayTariff +
        vehicle.BasePricePerKm *
        (returnedMeterSetting - vehicle.Meter) *
        vehicle.KmTariff;
}
#endregion
}
```

The IRentalBase interface

To implement the **ReturnVehicle** and **GetBookings** methods with their signatures in the **CollectionDataLayer** and **BookingProcessor** classes you add them to the **IRentalBase** interface; this will force both classes to implement the methods since they implement the interface. Failure to implement the method in either or both classes will result in a compilation exception and the application will not run until the methods have been added.

The **ReturnVehicle** method is used when returning the vehicle and changing the **Booking** object in the **Bookings** collection in the **TestData** class. The **GetBookings** method return all bookings in the system and is used as a base when fetching a single booking using the **GetBooking** method in the **BookingProcessor** class.

1. Open the **IRentalBase** interface.
2. Add a definition for a **double** method called **ReturnVehicle** with three parameters, one **int** parameter called **bookingId**, a **double** parameter called **meter** and a **DateTime** parameter called **Returned** to the **Action Methods** region of interface. Remember that interfaces only define members and never have any logic.
   ```
   double ReturnVehicle(int bookingId, double meter, DateTime returned);
   ```
3. Add a definition for a parameter-less **IEnumerable<IBooking>** method called **GetBookings** to the **Fetch Methods** region of interface.
   ```
   double ReturnVehicle(int bookingId, double meter, DateTime returned);
   ```

The complete code for the **IRentalBase** interface so far:

```
public interface IRentalBase
{
    #region Action Methods
    bool RentVehicle(int vehicleId, int customerId, DateTime timeOfRental);
    double ReturnVehicle(int bookingId, double meter, DateTime returned);
    #endregion

    #region Fetch Methods
    IEnumerable<ICustomer> GetCustomers();
    IEnumerable<IVehicle> GetVehicles(VehicleStatus status);
    IVehicleType GetVehicleType(int vehicleTypeId);
    IEnumerable<IBooking> GetBookings();
    #endregion
}
```

The ReturnVehicle method in the CollectionDataLayer class

Add a method called **ReturnVehicle** to the **CollectionDataLayer** class to implement the method defined in the **IRentalBase** interface; you can copy the definition from the interface, paste it into the class and add the curly braces.

The logic of the method is more complex than in the previous methods. First you add a **try/catch**-block and then you check a bunch of conditions that can result in booking exceptions and vehicle exceptions before using the booking and vehicle objects to perform the calculations.

The following conditions will result in the method throwing a **BookingException** before calculating the rental duration and cost:

- The fetched booking object is **null**, this mean that no booking object with the passed in booking id exist in the **Bookings** collection.
- The **VehicleId** property in the fetched booking contain **null** or is less than 1.
- The **Date** value of the **Rented** property in the fetched booking is equal to the minimal value for a date.
- The **Date** value of the **Rented** property in the fetched booking is greater than the return date.
- The **returned** parameter passed into the method is equal to the minimal value for a date. This mean that the vehicle is rented and has not been returned.

The following conditions will result in you throwing a **VehicleException** before calculating the rental duration and cost:

- The fetched vehicle object is equal to **null**.
- The **Meter** property of the fetched vehicle object is greater than the meter setting passed in through the method's **meter** parameter.

If no exception has been thrown then the **RentalDuration** and **CalculatePrice** methods can be called to calculate the rental duration and the cost. Use the results to assign values to the **Returned**, **Cost** and **Meter** properties of the fetched booking to return the vehicle.

1. Open the **CollectionDataLayer** class in the **Data Layer** project.
2. Implement the **ReturnVehicle** method in the **Action Methods** region.
3. Add a **try/catch**-block to the method.
4. Fetch the booking matching the passed in bookingId parameter and the **Returned** property contain the minimal value for a date. Store the booking in a variable called **booking**.
   ```
   var booking = TestData.Bookings.FirstOrDefault(b =>
   b.Id.Equals(bookingId) && b.Returned.Equals(DateTime.MinValue));
   ```
5. Add **if**-statements for the conditions that can trigger a booking exception.
6. Fetch the vehicle matching the **VehicleId** property of the fetched booking.
   ```
   var vehicle = TestData.Vehicles.FirstOrDefault(v =>
   v.Id.Equals(booking.VehicleId));
   ```
7. Add **if**-statements for the conditions that can trigger a vehicle exception.
8. Call the **RentalDuration** method passing in the date of the **Rented** property of the **booking** object and the **returned** parameter passed in to the method to calculate how long the vehicle has been rented, store the result in a variable called **duration**.
9. Call the **CalculatePrice** method passing in the **vehicle** object, the **meter** parameter and the calculated **duration**, store the result in a variable called **cost**.
10. Assign the value of the **returned** parameter to the **Returned** property of the **booking** object.
11. Assign the value of the **cost** variable to the **Cost** property of the **booking** object.
12. Assign the value of the **meter** parameter to the **Meter** property of the **booking** object.
13. Return the **cost** variable from the method.
14. Re-throw any exception in the **catch**-block.

The code in the **CollectionDataLayer** class so far:

```
public class CollectionDataLayer : IDataLayer
{
    public CollectionDataLayer() ...

    #region Action Methods
    public bool RentVehicle(int vehicleId, int
        customerId, DateTime timeOfRental) ...
    public double ReturnVehicle(int bookingId, double meter,
    DateTime returned)
    {
        try
        {
            var booking = TestData.Bookings.FirstOrDefault(
                b => b.Id.Equals(bookingId) &&
                b.Returned.Equals(DateTime.MinValue));

            // Throw exception if there is something wrong
            // with the booking object.
            if (booking == null) throw new BookingException(bookingId);
            if (booking.VehicleId == null || booking.VehicleId < 1)
                throw new BookingException(bookingId);
            if (booking.Rented.Date == DateTime.MinValue)
                throw new BookingException(bookingId);
            if (booking.Rented.Date > returned)
                throw new BookingException(bookingId,
                "Rental date is greater than the return date.");
            if (returned == DateTime.MinValue)
                throw new BookingException(bookingId,
                "The car is still rented out.");

            var vehicle = TestData.Vehicles.FirstOrDefault(
                v => v.Id.Equals(booking.VehicleId));

            // Throw exception if there is something wrong
            // with the vehicle object.
            if (vehicle == null) throw new VehicleException(
                vehicle.Id, "The vehicle is not rented out.");
            if (vehicle.Meter > meter)
                throw new VehicleException(vehicle.Id,
                "The meter setting is lower than the current meter
                setting.");
```

```
        // Calculate the cost.
        var duration = RentalDuration(booking.Rented, returned);
        var cost = CalculatePrice(vehicle, meter, duration);
        booking.Returned = returned;
        booking.Cost = cost;
        vehicle.Meter = meter;

        return cost;
    }
    catch
    {
        throw;
    }
}
#endregion

#region Fetch Methods
public IEnumerable<ICustomer> GetCustomers() ...
public IEnumerable<IVehicle> GetVehicles(VehicleStatus status) ...
public IVehicleType GetVehicleType(int vehicleTypeId) ...
#endregion

#region Helper Methods
public int RentalDuration(DateTime rented, DateTime returned) ...
public double CalculatePrice(IVehicle vehicle,
    double returnedMeterSetting, int duration) ...
#endregion
}
```

The ReturnVehicle method in the BookingProcessor class

Add a method called **ReturnVehicle** to the **BookingProcessor** class to implement the method defined in the **IRentalBase** interface; you can copy the definition from the interface, paste it into the class and add the curly braces.

The logic of the method is almost the same as for the **RentVehicle** method. First you add a **try/catch**-block and in the **try**-block you then call the **ReturnVehicle** method on the **Data-Layer** instance property.

1. Open the **BookingProcessor** class in the **Business Layer** project.
2. Implement the **ReturnVehicle** method in the **Action Methods** region.
3. Add a **try/catch**-block to the method.

4. Return the result from a call to the **ReturnVehicle** method in the **try**-block passing in the necessary parameters to the method.
5. Fetch the vehicle matching the **VehicleId** property of the fetched booking.

   `return DataLayer.ReturnVehicle(bookingId, meter, returned);`
6. Re-throwany exceptions in the **catch**-block.

The code for the **ReturnVehicle** method in the **BookingProcessor** class:

```
public double ReturnVehicle(int bookingId, double meter, DateTime returned)
{
    try
    {
        return DataLayer.ReturnVehicle(bookingId, meter, returned);
    }
    catch
    {
        throw;
    }
}
```

The GetBookings method in the CollectionDataLayer class

Add a method called **GetBookings** in the **CollectionDataLayer** class to implement the method defined in the **IRentalBase** interface.

The logic of the method is very simple you only return the **Bookings** collection from the **TestData** class.

1. Open the **CollectionDataLayer** class.
2. Add a parameter-less **IEnumerable<IBooking>** method called **GetBookings** to the **Fetch Methods** region of the class.
3. Return the data in the **Bookings** collection in the **TestData** class.

The code in the **CollectionDataLayer** class so far:

```
public class CollectionDataLayer : IDataLayer
{
    public CollectionDataLayer() ...

    #region Action Methods
    public bool RentVehicle(int vehicleId,
        int customerId, DateTime timeOfRental) ...
```

```
    public double ReturnVehicle(int bookingId, double meter,
        DateTime returned) ...
    #endregion

    #region Fetch Methods
    public IEnumerable<ICustomer> GetCustomers() ...
    public IEnumerable<IVehicle> GetVehicles(VehicleStatus status) ...
    public IVehicleType GetVehicleType(int vehicleTypeId) ...
    public IEnumerable<IBooking> GetBookings()
    {
        return TestData.Bookings;
    }
    #endregion

    #region Helper Methods
    public int RentalDuration(DateTime rented, DateTime returned) ...
    public double CalculatePrice(IVehicle vehicle,
        double returnedMeterSetting, int duration) ...
    #endregion
}
```

The IBookingProcessor interface

You have to add an **IBooking** method called **GetBooking** with an **int** parameter called **vehicleId** to the **IBookingProcessor** interface. The purpose of this method is to return a single **Booking** object from the **Bookings** collection in the **TestClass** based on a vehicle id and that the vehicle has not yet been returned.

1. Open the **IBookingProcessor** interface.
2. Add a definition for an **IBooking** method with an **int** parameter called **vehicleId** called **GetBooking**.

```
IBooking GetBooking(int vehicleId);
```

The code for the **IBookingProcessor** interface so far:

```
public interface IBookingProcessor : IRentalBase
{
    IDataLayer DataLayer { get; }

    IBooking GetBooking(int vehicleId);
}
```

The BookingProcessor class

You have to add two methods called **GetBookings** and **GetBooking** to the **BookingProcessor** class where the first return all bookings in the **Bookings** collection as an **IEnumerable <IBooking>** and the second method call the **GetBookings** method returning one booking.

The logic in the **GetBookings** method is very easy to implement, you simply return the result from a call to the **GetBookings** method in the data layer and re-throw any exceptions that might occur.

The logic in the **GetBooking** method is slightly more difficult because you have to use LINQ to fetch a specific booking from a call to the **GetBookings** method based on a vehicle id and if the booking is marked as returned by having a date other than the min date stored in the **Returned** property; return the default value for an instance of the **Booking** class if no booking is found.

1. Open the **BookingProcessor** class.
2. Add a parameter-less **IEnumerable<Booking>** method called **GetBookings** to the **Fetch Methods** region.
3. Add a **try/catch**-block where the **catch**-block re-throws any exception that might occur.
4. Return the result form a call to the **GetBookings** method on the **DataLayer** property.
   ```
   return DataLayer.GetBookings();
   ```
5. Add a **public IBooking** method called **GetBooking** which has an **int** parameter called **vehicleId** to the **Fetch Methods** region.
   ```
   public IBooking GetBooking(int vehicleId)
   ```
6. Add a **try/catch**-block where the **catch**-block re-throws any exception that might occur.
7. Return the result form a LINQ query using the **GetBookings** method to filter out any booking matching the passed in vehicle id and has the min value for a **DateTime** stored in its **Returned** property.
   ```
   return (from b in DataLayer.GetBookings()
           where b.VehicleId.Equals(vehicleId) &&
               b.Returned.Equals(DateTime.MinValue)
           select b).FirstOrDefault();
   ```

The code for the **BookingProcessor** class so far:

```csharp
public class BookingProcessor : IBookingProcessor
{
    #region Properties
    public IDataLayer DataLayer { get; private set; }
    #endregion

    #region Constructor
    public BookingProcessor(IDataLayer dataLayer) ...
    #endregion

    #region Action Methods
    public bool RentVehicle(int vehicleId, int customerId,
        DateTime timeOfRental) ...
    #endregion

    #region Fetch Methods
    public IEnumerable<ICustomer> GetCustomers() ...
    public IEnumerable<IVehicle> GetVehicles(VehicleStatus status) ...
    public IVehicleType GetVehicleType(int vehicleTypeId) ...
    public IEnumerable<IBooking> GetBookings()
    {
        try
        {
            return DataLayer.GetBookings();
        }
        catch
        {
            throw;
        }
    }
}
```

```
public IBooking GetBooking(int vehicleId)
    {
        try
        {
            return (from b in DataLayer.GetBookings()
                        where b.VehicleId.Equals(vehicleId) &&
                            b.Returned.Equals(DateTime.MinValue)
                        select b).FirstOrDefault();
        }
        catch
        {
            throw;
        }
    }
    #endregion

    #region Helper Methods
    #endregion
}
```

The IsNumeric method

This is a helper method that will check if a string is a numeric value using a regular expression.

```
Regex regex = new Regex(@"^[-+]?[0-9]*\.?[0-9]+$");
```

1. Open the form's code-behind file.
2. Locate the **Helper Methods** region and add a **bool** method called **IsNumeric** with a **string** parameter called **text**.
3. Create a new **RegEx** object and pass in the regular expression to its constructor.
   ```
   Regex regex = new Regex(@"^[-+]?[0-9]*\.?[0-9]+$");
   ```
4. return the result from a call to the **IsMatch** method on the **regex** variable passing in the string in its **text** parameter.
   ```
   return regex.IsMatch(text);
   ```

The complete code for the **IsNumeric** method:

```
#region Helper Methods
bool IsNumeric(string text)
{
    Regex regex = new Regex(@"^[-+]?[0-9]*\.?[0-9]+$");
    return regex.IsMatch(text);
}
#endregion
```

Returning a vehicle

When a user clicks the ***btnReturn*** button, has selected a vehicle in the ***lvwBookedVehicles*** list view and entered a value in the ***txtMeterReturn*** textbox then the vehicle should be marked as returned by assigning the current date to the **Returned** property. The cost should be calculated and assigned to the **Cost** property and the current meter value should be assigned to the **Meter** property of that particular booking. All this is achieved by calling the **ReturnVehicle** method in the booking processor passing in the booking id, meter setting and current date.

To keep the code clean in the button **Click** event you will create a method called **Return-Vehicle** in the **Action Methods** region of the form which is called from the **Click** event.

In the method you have to check that the value entered in the textbox it numeric, if it isn't display a message to the user and return **false**. You also have to check that a vehicle is selected in the list view and display a message and return **false** if no vehicle is selected.

Fetch the vehicle id from the selected item in the list view and store the value in a variable called **vehicleId**. Then fetch the booking id by calling the **GetBooking** method on the **processor** instance and save the result in a variable called **bookingId**.

Call the **ReturnVehicle** method on the **processor** instance passing in the booking id, meter setting and current date to the method to return the selected vehicle.

Call the **FillAvailableVehicles** and **FillBookedVehicles** methods to update the content in the list views.

Assign an empty string to the **Text** property of the textbox and return **true** from the method.

Return **false** if an exception is thrown.

1. Open the form's code-behind file.
2. Locate the **Action Methods** region and add a **private** parameter-less **bool** method called **ReturnVehicle** to it.
3. Add a **bool** variable called **success** and assign **false** to it.
4. Add a **try/catch**-block that assign **false** to the **success** variable in the **catch**-block.
5. Add an **if**-statement checking if the value in the textbox is <u>not</u> numeric by calling the **IsNumeric** method you added earlier and if the statement is **true** then display a message to the user and return the value in the **success** variable.
   ```
   if (!IsNumeric(txtMeterReturn.Text))
   ```
6. Add an **if**-statement checking if <u>no</u> vehicle is selected in the list view and if the statement is **true** then display a message to the user and return the value in the **success** variable.
   ```
   if (lvwBokedVehicles.SelectedItems.Count == 0)
   ```
7. Fetch the vehicle id by parsing the id of the selected vehicle in the list view.
   ```
   var vehicleId = Int32.Parse(lvwBokedVehicles
       .SelectedItems[0].SubItems[5].Text);
   ```
8. Fetch the booking id by calling the **GetBooking** method on the processor instance passing in the vehicle id.
   ```
   var bookingId = processor.GetBooking(vehicleId).Id;
   ```
9. Return the vehicle by calling the **ReturnVehicle** method on the **processor** instance passing in the booking id, meter setting and current date.
   ```
   processor.ReturnVehicle(bookingId, Double.Parse(txtMeterReturn.Text),
   DateTime.Now);
   ```
10. Call the **FillAvailableVehicles** and **FillBookedVehicles** methods to update the list views.
11. Clear the textbox.
12. Assign **true** to the **success** variable.
13. Add a **return** statement at the end of the method returning the value of the **success** variable.
14. Add the **Click** event for the ***btnReturn*** button to the **Button Events** region.

15. Call the **ReturnVehicle** method you added to the form and store the result in a variable called **returned**.

16. if the value of the returned variable is **false** then display a message box with a message stating that the vehicle wasn't returned.

17. Run the application and book a vehicle on the **Rent Vehicle** tab.

18. Open the **Return Vehicle** tab and return the vehicle. Make sure that the vehicle disappears from the list view and appears in the list view in the **Rent Vehicle** tab.

The code in the form code-behind so far:

```
public partial class Form1 : Form
{
    IBookingProcessor processor;

    public Form1() ...

    private void Form1_Load(object sender, EventArgs e) ...

    #region Fill Data Methods
    private void FillCustomers() ...
    private IEnumerable<ListViewItem> GetVehicles(
        VehicleStatus vehicleStatus) ...
    private void FillAvialbleVehicles() ...
    private void FillBookedVehicles() ...
    #endregion

    #region Action Methods
    private bool RentVehicle() ...
    private bool ReturnVehicle()
    {
        bool success = false;

        try
        {
            if (!IsNumeric(txtMeterReturn.Text))
            {
                MessageBox.Show("The meter setting must be a number");
                return success;
            }
```

```
        if (lvwBokedVehicles.SelectedItems.Count == 0)
        {
            MessageBox.Show("A vehicle must be selected in the list");
            return success;
        }

        var vehicleId = Int32.Parse(
            lvwBokedVehicles.SelectedItems[0].SubItems[5].Text);

        var bookingId = processor.GetBooking(vehicleId).Id;
        processor.ReturnVehicle(bookingId,
            Double.Parse(txtMeterReturn.Text), DateTime.Now);

        FillAvialbleVehicles();
        FillBookedVehicles();

        txtMeterReturn.Text = String.Empty;

        success = true;
    }
    catch { success = false; }

    return success;
}
#endregion

#region Helper Methods
bool IsNumeric(string text)
{
    Regex regex = new Regex(@"^[-+]?[0-9]*\.?[0-9]+$");
    return regex.IsMatch(text);
}
#endregion

#region Button Events
private void btnRent_Click(object sender, EventArgs e) ...
private void btnReturn_Click(object sender, EventArgs e)
{
    var returned = ReturnVehicle();

    if (!returned) MessageBox.Show("The vehicle was not returned");
}
#endregion
}
```

Bookings: List bookings

Although this listing look simple enough it actually is the most complex listing in the application since it uses information from all four collections in the **TestData** class. The **Bookings** collection is used to fetch information about a booking and is joined with the **Customers** collection to get the customer name and the **Vehicles** and **VehicleTypes** collections to get the vehicle type. To display the data in the list view a new class called **ListViewBooking** has to be created. Since you already have created all the methods needed to fetch the data the implementation should be fairly quick.

The LINQ query responsible for fetching the data will use the **GetBookings** method and join the customers by calling the **GetCustomers** method and the vehicles by calling the **GetVehicles** method. When collecting the data for each booking using the **ListViewBooking** class you call the **GetVehicleType** method with the value in the current car's **TypeId** property.

The **ListViewBooking** class should contain the following information: booking id, customer id, cost, customer name (Last name and First name in the same property called **Customer**), registration number, vehicle type (fetched with the **GetVehicleType** method), the rented date and the return date. If the vehicle in a booking has not been returned the return date should be empty in the list view and the cost should be zero.

To keep the **Form_Load** event clean and to enable reuse of the code you should place the code in a method called **FillBookings** in the form. You also want to add a method call to this method in the **RentVehicle** and **ReturnVehicle** methods after the call to the **FillBooked-Vehicles** method.

Don't forget to clear the list view's **Items** collection before displaying the bookings to avoid duplicate entries.

Bookings

Booking Id	Reg.No.	Type	Customer	Cost	Rented	Returned
1	ABC123	Combi	Montgomery Lisa	500	2015-07-05 ...	2015-07-06 ...
2	ABC123	Combi	Raintree Carl	0	2015-07-05 ...	

The ListViewBooking class

Add a class called **ListViewBooking** to the **Classes** folder in the **Car Rental** project.

Implement the following properties in it: **BookingId** of type **int**, **CustomerId** of type **int**, **Cost** of type **double**, **Customer** of type **string** (Last name and First name concatenated), **RegistrationNumber** of type **string**, **VehicleType** of type **string** (fetched with the **GetVehicleType** method), **Rented** of type **DateTime**, **Returned** of type **DateTime**.

Implement a method called **ToArray** which return a **string array** with the column data from the properties in the following order: **BookingId**, **RegistrationNumber**, **VehicleType**, **Customer**, **Cost**, **Rented** and **Returned**. The **Returned** property should return an empty string if the date is equal to **DateTime.MinValue** otherwise the date stored in the property. Note that the **CustomerId** property is not included in the array since you don't want to display that piece of data in the list view.

1. Add a **class** called **ListViewBooking** to the **Classes** folder in the **Car Rental** project.
2. Add the two **int** properties **BookingId** and **CustomerId**.
3. Add the **double** property **Cost**.
4. Add the three **string** properties **RegistrationNumber**, **VehicleType** and **Customer**.
5. Add the two **DateTime** properties **Rented** and **Returned**.
6. Add a **string[]** method called **ToArray**.
7. Return a **string array** with the data listed above.

The complete code in the **ListViewBooking** class:

```
class ListViewBooking
{
    public int BookingId { get; set; }
    public int CustomerId { get; set; }
    public string RegistrationNumber { get; set; }
    public string VehicleType { get; set; }
    public double Cost { get; set; }
    public string Customer { get; set; }
    public DateTime Rented { get; set; }
    public DateTime Returned { get; set; }
```

```
public string[] ToArray()
{
    return new string[] {
        BookingId.ToString(),
        RegistrationNumber,
        VehicleType,
        Customer,
        Cost.ToString(),
        Rented.ToString(),
        Returned == DateTime.MinValue ?
          String.Empty : Returned.ToString()
    };
}
}
```

Filling the list view

Add a method called **FillBookings** to the **Fill Data Methods** region of the form and call it from the **Form_Load** event and the two methods **RentVehicle** and **ReturnVehicle** after the call to the **FillBookedVehicles** method.

Add a **try/catch**-block that return **true** at the end of the **try**-block and **false** in the **catch**-block for any exceptions that are thrown.

Use a LINQ query in the **try**-block to fetch a list of all bookings using the **ListViewBooking** class to create the booking objects and store the result in a variable called **bookings**. You will have to join the results from three method calls to **GetBookings**, **GetCustomers** and **GetVehicles** on the **processor** instance variable and call the **GetVehicleType** for each object created to get the vehicle type name.

Once you have the list of **ListViewBooking** objects you clear the **Items** collection of the *lvwBookings* list view and display the bookings stored in the **bookings** variable.

1. Add a parameter-less **bool** method called **FillBookings** to the **Fill Data Methods** region of the form's code-behind.
2. Add a **try/catch**-block that return **false** in the **catch**-block.
3. Add a LINQ query that join the result from a call to the **GetBookings** method with the result from a call to the **GetCustomers** method on the customer id and the **GetVehicles** method on the vehicle id. Store the result of the query in a variable

called **bookings** and use the **ListViewBooking** class to create the objects. Call the **GetVehicleTypes** method to fetch the vehicle type name.

```
var bookings =
    from b in processor.GetBookings()
    join c in processor.GetCustomers()
        on b.CustomerId equals c.Id
    join car in processor.GetVehicles(VehicleStatus.All)
        on b.VehicleId equals car.Id
    select new ListViewItem(new ListViewBooking
    {
        BookingId = b.Id,
        CustomerId = b.CustomerId,
        Cost = b.Cost,
        Customer = String.Format("{0} {1}", c.LastName, c.FirstName),
        RegistrationNumber = car.RegistrationNumber,
        VehicleType = processor.GetVehicleType(car.TypeId).Name,
        Rented = b.Rented,
        Returned = b.Returned
    }.ToArray());
```

4. Clear the **Items** collection on the list view.

5. Add the result stored in the **bookings** variable to the **Items** collection using the **AddRange** method.

6. Return **true**;

7. Add a call to the **FillBookings** method in the **Form_Load** event after the call to the **FillBookedVehicles** method.

8. Add a call to the **FillBookings** method in the **RentVehicle** method after the call to the **FillBookedVehicles** method.

9. Add a call to the **FillBookings** method in the **ReturnVehicle** method after the call to the **FillBookedVehicles** method.

10. Run the application and make sure that there are bookings in the list view on the **Bookings** tab.

11. Add a booking in the **Rent Vehicle** tab and open the **Bookings** tab, the booking should be visible in the list view and the **Returned** column should be empty for the booking.

12. Open the **Return Vehicle** tab and return the vehicle you rented. Open the **Bookings** tab and make sure that the **Returned** column has the current date in it.

The code in the form code-behind so far:

```
public partial class Form1 : Form
{
    IBookingProcessor processor;

    public Form1() ...

    private void Form1_Load(object sender, EventArgs e) ...

    #region Fill Data Methods
    private void FillCustomers() ...
    private IEnumerable<ListViewItem> GetVehicles(
        VehicleStatus vehicleStatus) ...
    private void FillAvialbleVehicles() ...
    private void FillBookedVehicles() ...
    private bool FillBookings()
    {
        try
        {
            var bookings =
                from b in processor.GetBookings()
                join c in processor.GetCustomers()
                    on b.CustomerId equals c.Id
                join car in processor.GetVehicles(VehicleStatus.All)
                    on b.VehicleId equals car.Id
                select new ListViewItem(new ListViewBooking
                {
                    BookingId = b.Id,
                    CustomerId = b.CustomerId,
                    Cost = b.Cost,
                    Customer = String.Format("{0} {1}", c.LastName,
                        c.FirstName),
                    RegistrationNumber = car.RegistrationNumber,
                    VehicleType = processor.GetVehicleType(car.TypeId).Name,
                    Rented = b.Rented,
                    Returned = b.Returned
                }.ToArray());

            lvwBookings.Items.Clear();
            lvwBookings.Items.AddRange(bookings.ToArray());

            return true;
        }
```

```
      catch { return false; }
   }
   #endregion

   #region Action Methods
   private bool RentVehicle() ...
   private bool ReturnVehicle() ...
   #endregion

   #region Helper Methods
   bool IsNumeric(string text) ...
   #endregion

   #region Button Events
   private void btnRent_Click(object sender, EventArgs e) ...
   private void btnReturn_Click(object sender, EventArgs e) ...
   #endregion
}
```

Add Data: List vehicle types

To be able to select the vehicle type from a combo box when adding a new vehicle you need to add a method called **GetVehicleTypes** to the **IRentalBase** interface and implement it in the **CollectionDataLayer** and **BookingProcessor** classes.

The logic for the method in the **CollectionDataLayer** class is very easy to implement you simply return the content in the **VehicleTypes** collection in the **TestData** class.

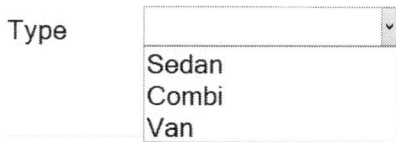

Type

Sedan
Combi
Van

The IRentalBase interface

Add the definition for a parameter-less **IEnumerable<IVehicleType>** method called **Get-VehicleTypes** in the **Fetch Methods** region of **IRentalBase** interface.

1. Open the **IRentalBase** interface.
2. Add a parameter-less **IEnumerable<IVehicleType>** method called **GetVehicleTypes** in the **Fetch Methods** region.

The complete code for the **IRentalBase** interface so far:

```
public interface IRentalBase
{
    #region Action Methods
    bool RentVehicle(int vehicleId, int customerId, DateTime timeOfRental);
    double ReturnVehicle(int bookingId, double meter, DateTime returned);
    #endregion

    #region Fetch Methods
    IEnumerable<ICustomer> GetCustomers();
    IEnumerable<IVehicle> GetVehicles(VehicleStatus status);
    IVehicleType GetVehicleType(int vehicleTypeId);
    IEnumerable<IBooking> GetBookings();
    IEnumerable<IVehicleType> GetVehicleTypes();
    #endregion
}
```

The CollectionDataLayer class

Implement the **GetVehicleTypes** method in the **Fetch Methods** region of the **Collection-DataLayer** class by returning the content in the **VehicleTypes** collection in the **TestData** class.

1. Open the **CollectionDataLayer** class.
2. Add a parameter-less **IEnumerable<IVehicleType>** method called **GetVehicleTypes** to the **Fetch Methods** region.
3. Return the content of the **VehicleTypes** collection in the **TestData** class.

The code in the **CollectionDataLayer** class so far:

```
public class CollectionDataLayer : IDataLayer
{
    public CollectionDataLayer() ...

    #region Action Methods
    public bool RentVehicle(int vehicleId,
        int customerId, DateTime timeOfRental) ...
    public double ReturnVehicle(int bookingId, double meter,
        DateTime returned) ...
    #endregion

    #region Fetch Methods
    public IEnumerable<ICustomer> GetCustomers() ...
```

```
public IEnumerable<IVehicle> GetVehicles(VehicleStatus status) ...
public IVehicleType GetVehicleType(int vehicleTypeId) ...
public IEnumerable<IBooking> GetBookings() ...
public IEnumerable<IVehicleType> GetVehicleTypes()
{
    return TestData.VehicleTypes;
}
#endregion

#region Helper Methods
public int RentalDuration(DateTime rented, DateTime returned) ...
public double CalculatePrice(IVehicle vehicle,
    double returnedMeterSetting, int duration) ...
#endregion
}
```

The BookingProcessor class

Implement the **GetVehicleTypes** method in the **Fetch Methods** region of the **Booking-Processor** class by returning the result from a call to the **GetVehicleTypes** method on the **DataLayer** property. Make sure that the **catch**-block re-throws any exception.

1. Open the **BookingProcessor** class.
2. Add a parameter-less **IEnumerable<IVehicleType>** method called **GetVehicleTypes** to the **Fetch Methods** region.
3. Return the result from a call to the **GetVehicleTypes** method in the data layer in the **try**-block.
   ```
   return DataLayer.GetVehicleTypes();
   ```

The code for the **BookingProcessor** class so far:

```
public class BookingProcessor : IBookingProcessor
{
    #region Properties
    public IDataLayer DataLayer { get; private set; }
    #endregion

    #region Constructor
    public BookingProcessor(IDataLayer dataLayer) ...
    #endregion
```

```
#region Action Methods
public bool RentVehicle(int vehicleId,
    int customerId, DateTime timeOfRental) ...
public double ReturnVehicle(int bookingId, double meter,
    DateTime returned) ...
#endregion

#region Fetch Methods
public IEnumerable<ICustomer> GetCustomers() ...
public IEnumerable<IVehicle> GetVehicles(VehicleStatus status) ...
public IVehicleType GetVehicleType(int vehicleTypeId) ...
public IEnumerable<IBooking> GetBookings() ...
public IBooking GetBooking(int vehicleId) ...
public IEnumerable<IVehicleType> GetVehicleTypes()
{
    try
    {
        return DataLayer.GetVehicleTypes();
    }
    catch
    {
        throw;
    }
}
#endregion

#region Helper Methods
#endregion
}
```

Filling the combo box

Add a parameter-less **void** method called **FillVehicleTypes** to the **Fill Data Methods** region of the form and call it from the **Form_Load** event after the call to the **FillBookings** method.

Add a **try/catch**-block that fills the combo box in the **try**-block and handles any exception by ignoring them with an empty **catch**-block.

Assign the result from a call to the **GetVehicleTypes** method to the **DataSource** property of the *cboTypes* combo box and set its **DisplayMember** property to "Name" to display the names of the vehicle types in the combo box.

1. Open the form's code-behind.

2. Add a parameter-less **void** method called **FillVehicleTypes** to the **Fill Data Methods** region.

3. Add a **try/catch**-block to the method and leave the **catch**-block empty.

4. Assign the result from a call to the **GetVehicleTypes** method to the **DataSource** property of the *cboTypes* combo box.
   ```
   cboTypes.DataSource = processor.GetVehicleTypes();
   ```

5. Assign "Name" to the combo box's **DisplayMember** property.

6. Run the application and click the **Add Data** tab.

7. Make sure that the vehicle types are listed in the *cboTypes* combo box.

The code in the form code-behind so far:

```
public partial class Form1 : Form
{
    IBookingProcessor processor;

    public Form1() ...
    private void Form1_Load(object sender, EventArgs e) ...

    #region Fill Data Methods
    private void FillCustomers() ...
    private IEnumerable<ListViewItem> GetVehicles(
        VehicleStatus vehicleStatus) ...
    private void FillAvialbleVehicles() ...
    private void FillBookedVehicles() ...
    private bool FillBookings() ...
    private void FillVehicleTypes()
    {
        try
        {
            cboTypes.DataSource = processor.GetVehicleTypes();
            cboTypes.DisplayMember = "Name";
        }
        catch { }
    }
    #endregion

    #region Action Methods
    private bool RentVehicle() ...
    private bool ReturnVehicle() ...
    #endregion
```

```
#region Helper Methods
bool IsNumeric(string text) ...
#endregion

#region Button Events
private void btnRent_Click(object sender, EventArgs e) ...
private void btnReturn_Click(object sender, EventArgs e) ...
#endregion
}
```

Add Data: Add a new vehicle

To add a new vehicle the user has to specify a registration number in the ***txtRegNo*** textbox, an initial meter setting in the ***txtMeter*** textbox and select a vehicle type in the ***cboTypes*** combo box before clicking on the ***btnAddVehicle*** button on the **Add Data** tab.

The button calls a method called **AddVehicle** which has an **IVehicle** parameter called **vehicle**. An instance of the desired vehicle class is passed into the method. At the moment there is only one specialized vehicle class and that is the **Car** class. If the vehicle is not added to the **Vehicles** collection a variable called **added** storing the result of the method call will contain **false** and if it does then a message that the vehicle wasn't added should be displayed to the user. The last thing to happen in the **try**-block is that the **Rent Vehicle** tab is displayed.

Since the **AddVehicle** method you will create isn't fetching data and is performing an action by adding a new vehicle it should be added to the **Action Methods** regions in the involved classes and the **IRentalBase** interface. Implement the **AddVehicle** method definition from the **IRentalBase** interface in the **CollectionDataLayer** and **BookingProcessor** classes. When the method has been implemented in both classes the **processor** variable you added to the form's code-behind can be used to call the **AddVehicle** method of the booking processor.

The IRentalBase interface

To implement the **AddVehicle** method with its signature in the **CollectionDataLayer** and **BookingProcessor** classes you add it to the **IRentalBase** interface; this will force both classes to implement the methods since they implement the interface. Failure to implement the method in either or both classes will result in a compilation exception and the application will not run until the methods have been added.

The **AddVehicle** method is used when adding a new vehicle to the **Vehicles** collection in the **TestData** class.

1. Open the **IRentalBase** interface.
2. Add a definition for a **void** method called **AddVehicle** with an **IVehicle** parameter called **vehicle** to the **Action Methods** region of interface. Remember that interfaces only define members and never have any logic.

   ```
   void AddVehicle(IVehicle vehicle);
   ```

The complete code for the **IRentalBase** interface so far:

```csharp
public interface IRentalBase
{
    #region Action Methods
    bool RentVehicle(int vehicleId, int customerId, DateTime timeOfRental);
    double ReturnVehicle(int bookingId, double meter, DateTime returned);
    void AddVehicle(IVehicle vehicle);
    #endregion

    #region Fetch Methods
    IEnumerable<ICustomer> GetCustomers();
    IEnumerable<IVehicle> GetVehicles(VehicleStatus status);
    IVehicleType GetVehicleType(int vehicleTypeId);
    IEnumerable<IBooking> GetBookings();
    IEnumerable<IVehicleType> GetVehicleTypes();
    #endregion
}
```

The CollectionDataLayer class

Implement the **AddVehicle** method in the **Action Methods** region of the **CollectionData-Layer** class by first fetching the highest existing vehicle id in the **Vehicles** collection and store the value incremented by 1 in the **Id** property of the passed in **vehicle** instance. Pass the **vehicle** instance to the **Add** method of the **Vehicles** collection in the **TestData** class.

Note that the vehicle id would be auto generated by the database in a real world scenario.

Surround the code with a **try/catch**-block that re-throws any exception that might occur.

1. Open the **CollectionDataLayer** class.
2. Add a **void** method called **AddVehicle** which has an **IVehicle** parameter called **vehicle** to the **Action Methods** region.

3. Add a **try/catch**-block where the catch re-throws any exception.

4. Calculate the next vehicle id and store it in the **Id** property of the passed in vehicle instance.
   ```
   vehicle.Id = TestData.Vehicles.Max(b => b.Id) + 1;
   ```

5. Add the **vehicle** instance to the **Vehicles** collection in the **TestData** class by calling its **Add** method passing in the **vehicle** instance to it.

The code in the **CollectionDataLayer** class so far:

```csharp
public class CollectionDataLayer : IDataLayer
{
    public CollectionDataLayer() ...

    #region Action Methods
    public bool RentVehicle(int vehicleId,
        int customerId, DateTime timeOfRental) ...
    public double ReturnVehicle(int bookingId, double meter,
        DateTime returned) ...
    public void AddVehicle(IVehicle vehicle)
    {
        try
        {
            // The booking id would normally be supplied by the database
            vehicle.Id = TestData.Vehicles.Max(b => b.Id) + 1;
            TestData.Vehicles.Add(vehicle);
        }
        catch
        {
            throw;
        }
    }
    #endregion

    #region Fetch Methods
    public IEnumerable<ICustomer> GetCustomers() ...
    public IEnumerable<IVehicle> GetVehicles(VehicleStatus status) ...
    public IVehicleType GetVehicleType(int vehicleTypeId) ...
    public IEnumerable<IBooking> GetBookings() ...
    public IEnumerable<IVehicleType> GetVehicleTypes() ...
    #endregion
```

```
    #region Helper Methods
    public int RentalDuration(DateTime rented, DateTime returned) ...
    public double CalculatePrice(IVehicle vehicle,
        double returnedMeterSetting, int duration) ...
    #endregion
}
```

The BookingProcessor class

Implement the **AddVehicle** method in the **Action Methods** region of the **BookingProcessor** class.

Add a **try/catch**-block where the **catch**-block re-throws any exception.

This method implementation differs a bit from previous method implementations in that it has business logic to execute before the call to the **AddVehicle** method can be made.

The business logic consist of an **if**-statement checking property values of the passed in **vehicle** instance; if the **Id** property is greater than zero or the **Meter** property is less than zero or the **RegistrationNumber** property is empty or the **TypeId** property is less than 1 then a new **VehicleException** should be thrown with a message stating that the vehicle has erroneous data.

Call the **AddVehicle** method on the **DataLayer** property to add the **vehicle** instance to the **Vehicles** collection in the **TestData** class.

1. Open the **BookingProcessor** class.
2. Add a **void** method called **AddVehicle** to the **Action Methods** region.
3. Add a **try/catch**-block where the **catch**-block re-throws any exception.
4. Add the business logic described above using an **if**-statement in the **try**-block.
   ```
   if (vehicle.Id > 0 || vehicle.Meter < 0 ||
       vehicle.RegistrationNumber.Equals(String.Empty) ||
       vehicle.TypeId < 1)
       throw new VehicleException(vehicle.Id,
           "The vehicle has erroneous data.");
   ```
5. Call the **AddVehicle** method in the data layer.
   ```
   DataLayer.AddVehicle(vehicle);
   ```

The code for the **BookingProcessor** class so far:

```csharp
public class BookingProcessor : IBookingProcessor
{
    #region Properties
    public IDataLayer DataLayer { get; private set; }
    #endregion

    #region Constructor
    public BookingProcessor(IDataLayer dataLayer) ...
    #endregion

    #region Action Methods
    public bool RentVehicle(int vehicleId, int customerId,
        DateTime timeOfRental)
    public double ReturnVehicle(int bookingId, double meter,
        DateTime returned) ...
    public void AddVehicle(IVehicle vehicle)
    {
        try
        {
            if (vehicle.Id > 0 || vehicle.Meter < 0 ||
                vehicle.RegistrationNumber.Equals(String.Empty) ||
                vehicle.TypeId < 1)
                throw new VehicleException(vehicle.Id,
                    "The vehicle has erroneous data.");

            DataLayer.AddVehicle(vehicle);
        }
        catch
        {
            throw;
        }
    }
    #endregion

    #region Fetch Methods
    public IEnumerable<ICustomer> GetCustomers() ...
    public IEnumerable<IVehicle> GetVehicles(VehicleStatus status) ...
    public IVehicleType GetVehicleType(int vehicleTypeId) ...
    public IEnumerable<IBooking> GetBookings() ...
    public IBooking GetBooking(int vehicleId) ...
    public IEnumerable<IVehicleType> GetVehicleTypes()
    #endregion
```

461

```
    #region Helper Methods
    #endregion
}
```

Adding a vehicle

Add a **void** method called **AddVehicle** with an **IVehicle** parameter called **vehicle** to the **Action Methods** region of the form.

Add a **try/catch**-block with a **catch**-block that re-throws any exceptions.

The **AddVehicle** method should check that all controls involved contain correct information, the **txtRegNo** textbox must not be empty, the **txtMeter** textbox must contain a numerical value that can be parsed into a **double** and the **cboTypes** combo box must have a selected value.

If one or more of the controls contain erroneous data a **string** variable called **errMsg** should be populated with pertinent error messages. The complete message should then be displayed to the user and the method should return **false**.

When the properties of the passed in **vehicle** instance has been assigned using values from the textboxes and the **VehicleType** object stored for the selected vehicle type in the combo box the **AddVehicle** method should be called on the **processor** instance variable.

After the **vehicle** instance has been added to the **Vehicles** collection in the **TestData** class the **FillAvailableVehicles** method should be called to repopulate the list view on the **Rent Vehicle** tab and the textboxes should be cleared.

Return **true** from the method if no exception has been thrown in the **try**-block.

When the **AddVehicle** method has been added it can be called from the **btnAddVehicle** button's **Click** event. Store the result from the method call in a variable called **added** and pass in a new instance of the **Car** class as the method parameter.

If the vehicle could not be added the **added** variable will contain **false** which can be checked with an **if**-statement in order to display a suitable error message to the user.

Open the **Rent Vehicle** tab after the **if**-statement.

1. Open the form's code-behind.

2. Add a **void** method called **AddVehicle** with an **IVehicle** parameter called **vehicle** to the **Action Methods** region of the form.

3. Add a **try/catch**-block where the **catch**-block re-throws any exceptions.

4. Check that the controls has valid data and build an error message in a **string** variable called **errMsg** if any data is invalid.

5. Display the error message and return **false** if the value in the **txtMeter** textbox is not numeric or cannot be parsed to a **double** or the **txtRegNo** textbox is empty or the no item has been selected in the **cboTypes** combo box.
   ```
   if (!IsNumeric(txtMeter.Text) || Double.Parse(txtMeter.Text) < 0 ||
   txtRegNo.TextLength == 0 || cboTypes.SelectedIndex < 0)
   ```

6. Fetch the **VehicleType** object from the selected item in the combo box and store it in a variable called **type**. You have to cast the object using the **VehicleType** class because it is stored using the **object** data type in the combo box.
   ```
   var type = ((VehicleType)cboTypes.SelectedItem);
   ```

7. Assign values to the properties of the passed in **vehicle** object using the form controls and the **type** variable.

8. Call the **AddVehicle** method passing in the **vehicle** object as its parameter to add the vehicle to the **Vehicles** collection in the **TestData** class.
   ```
   processor.AddVehicle(vehicle);
   ```

9. Update the available vehicles in the list view on the **Rent Vehicle** tab by calling the **FillAvailableVehicles** method.

10. Clear the **txtRegNo** and **txtMeter** textboxes.

11. Return **true** from the method.

12. Add the **btnAddVehicle** **Click** event to the **Button Events** region.

13. Add a **try/catch**-block where the **catch**-block displays the exception message in a message box.

14. Call the **AddVehicle** method with a new instance of the **Car** class and store the result from the method call in a variable called **added**.
    ```
    var added = AddVehicle(new Car());
    ```

15. Check if the **added** variable contain **false** and display an error message if that is the case.

16. Switch to the **Rent Vehicle** tab by passing in the tab name to the **SelectTab** method on the tab control.
    `tabBooking.SelectTab(tabRentVehicle);`

17. Run the application and click the **Add Data** tab.

18. Add a new vehicle and make sure that it appears in the vehicle list view on the **Rent Vehicle** tab.

The code in the form code-behind so far:

```
public partial class Form1 : Form
{
    IBookingProcessor processor;

    public Form1() ...

    private void Form1_Load(object sender, EventArgs e) ...

    #region Fill Data Methods
    private void FillCustomers() ...
    private IEnumerable<ListViewItem> GetVehicles(
        VehicleStatus vehicleStatus) ...
    private void FillAvialbleVehicles() ...
    private void FillBookedVehicles() ...
    private bool FillBookings() ...
    private void FillVehicleTypes()
    #endregion

    #region Action Methods
    private bool RentVehicle() ...
    private bool ReturnVehicle() ...
    private bool AddVehicle(IVehicle vehicle)
    {
        try
        {
            // Check the controls for erroneous data
            string errMsg = String.Empty;
            if (txtRegNo.TextLength == 0)
                errMsg = "Incorrect vehicle registration number" +
                Environment.NewLine;
```

```
        if (cboTypes.SelectedIndex < 0)
            errMsg += "No vehicle type selected" +
            Environment.NewLine;

        if (!IsNummeric(txtMeter.Text) ||
            (IsNummeric(txtMeter.Text) &&
            Double.Parse(txtMeter.Text) < 0))
            errMsg += "The meter value is incorrect" +
                Environment.NewLine;

        if (!IsNummeric(txtMeter.Text) ||
            Double.Parse(txtMeter.Text) < 0 ||
            txtRegNo.TextLength == 0 ||
            cboTypes.SelectedIndex < 0)
            {
                MessageBox.Show(errMsg);
                return false;
            }

        // Assign data to the vehicle object
        var type = ((VehicleType)cboTypes.SelectedItem);
        vehicle.Meter = Double.Parse(txtMeter.Text);
        vehicle.RegistrationNumber = txtRegNo.Text;
        vehicle.TypeId = type.Id;
        vehicle.BasePricePerDay = type.BasePricePerDay;
        vehicle.BasePricePerKm = type.BasePricePerKm;
        vehicle.DayTariff = type.DayTariff;
        vehicle.KmTariff = type.KmTariff;

        // Add the vehicle object to the Vehicles collection
        processor.AddVehicle(vehicle);

        // Update the vehicle list on the Rent Vehicles tab
        FillAvialbleVehicles();

        txtRegNo.Text = String.Empty;
        txtMeter.Text = String.Empty;

        return true;
    }
    catch { return false; }
}
#endregion
```

```
#region Helper Methods
bool IsNumeric(string text) ...
#endregion

#region Button Events
private void btnRent_Click(object sender, EventArgs e) ...
private void btnReturn_Click(object sender, EventArgs e) ...
private void btnAddVehicle_Click(object sender, EventArgs e)
{
    try
    {
        var added = AddVehicle(new Car());

        if (!added) MessageBox.Show("The vehicle was not added");

        tabBooking.SelectTab(tabRentVehicle);
    }
    catch (Exception ex)
    {
        MessageBox.Show(ex.Message);
    }
}
#endregion
}
```

Add Data: Add a new customer

To add a new customer the user has to specify a social security number, a first name and a last name in the *txtSocial*, *txtFirstName* and *txtLastName* textboxes before clicking on the *btnAddCustomer* button on the **Add Data** tab.

The button calls a parameter-less **int** method called **AddCustomer** that return the index position of the added customer in the *cboCustomers* combo box so that it can be selected in the **Rent Vehicle** tab. Add a **try/catch**-block to the method where exceptions are ignored by implementing an empty **catch**-block.

The **AddCustomer** method defined by the **IRentalBase** interface as a **void** method with an **ICustomer** parameter called **customer**. Since the **AddCustomer** method performs an action by adding a new customer it should be added to the **Action Methods** regions in the involved classes and the **IRentalBase** interface.

Implement the **AddCustomer** method definition in the **IRentalBase** interface in the **CollectionDataLayer** and **BookingProcessor** classes. When the method has been implemented in both classes use the **processor** variable in the form's code-behind to call the **AddCustomer** method.

Call the **FillCustomers** method after the new customer has been added to update the contents of the *cboCustomers* combo box in the **Rent Vehicle** tab.

The IRentalBase interface

To implement the **AddCustomer** method in the **CollectionDataLayer** and **BookingProcessor** classes you add its definition to the **IRentalBase** interface; this will force both classes to implement the methods since they implement the interface.

The **AddCustomer** method is used when adding a new customer to the **Customers** collection in the **TestData** class.

1. Open the **IRentalBase** interface.
2. Add a definition for a **void** method called **AddCustomer** with an **ICustomer** parameter called **customer** to the **Action Methods** region of the interface.
   ```
   void AddCustomer(ICustomer customer);
   ```

The complete code for the **IRentalBase** interface:

```
public interface IRentalBase
{
    #region Action Methods
    bool RentVehicle(int vehicleId, int customerId, DateTime timeOfRental);
    double ReturnVehicle(int bookingId, double meter, DateTime returned);
    void AddVehicle(IVehicle vehicle);
    void AddCustomer(ICustomer customer);
    #endregion

    #region Fetch Methods
    IEnumerable<ICustomer> GetCustomers();
    IEnumerable<IVehicle> GetVehicles(VehicleStatus status);
    IVehicleType GetVehicleType(int vehicleTypeId);
    IEnumerable<IBooking> GetBookings();
    IEnumerable<IVehicleType> GetVehicleTypes();
    #endregion
}
```

The CollectionDataLayer class

Implement the **AddCustomer** method in the **Action Methods** region of the **CollectionData-Layer** class by first fetching the highest existing customer id in the **Customers** collection and store the value incremented by 1 in the **Id** property of the passed in **customer** instance. Pass the **customer** instance to the **Add** method of the **Customers** collection in the **TestData** class.

Note that the customer id would be auto generated by the database in a real world scenario.

Surround the code with a **try/catch**-block that re-throws any exception that might occur.

1. Open the **CollectionDataLayer** class.
2. Add a **void** method called **AddCustomer** with an **ICustomer** parameter called **customer** to the **Action Methods** region.
3. Add a **try/catch**-block where the **catch**-block re-throws any exception.
4. Calculate the next customer id and store it in the **Id** property of the passed in customer instance.
   ```
   customer.Id = TestData.Customers.Max(c => c.Id) + 1;
   ```
5. Add the **customer** instance to the **Customers** collection in the **TestData** class by calling its **Add** method passing in the **customer** instance to it.

The code in the **CollectionDataLayer** class:

```
public class CollectionDataLayer : IDataLayer
{
    public CollectionDataLayer() ...

    #region Action Methods
    public bool RentVehicle(int vehicleId,
        int customerId, DateTime timeOfRental) ...
    public double ReturnVehicle(int bookingId, double meter,
        DateTime returned) ...
    public void AddVehicle(IVehicle vehicle) ...
    public void AddCustomer(ICustomer customer)
    {
        try
        {
            // The customer id would be auto generated by the database
            customer.Id = TestData.Customers.Max(c => c.Id) + 1;
            TestData.Customers.Add(customer);
        }
```

```
        catch
        {
            throw;
        }
    }
    #endregion

    #region Fetch Methods
    public IEnumerable<ICustomer> GetCustomers() ...
    public IEnumerable<IVehicle> GetVehicles(VehicleStatus status) ...
    public IVehicleType GetVehicleType(int vehicleTypeId) ...
    public IEnumerable<IBooking> GetBookings() ...
    public IEnumerable<IVehicleType> GetVehicleTypes() ...
    #endregion

    #region Helper Methods
    public int RentalDuration(DateTime rented, DateTime returned) ...
    public double CalculatePrice(IVehicle vehicle,
        double returnedMeterSetting, int duration) ...
    #endregion
}
```

The IBookingProcessor interface

You need to add a definition for a **bool** method called **CustomerExist** with a **string** para-meter called **socialSecurityNumber** to the **IBookingProcessor** interface. The purpose of this method is to check if a given social security number already exist in the **Customers** collection in the **TestData** class.

1. Open the **IBookingProcessor** interface.
2. Add a definition for a **bool** method called **CustomerExist** with a **string** parameter called **socialSecurityNumber**.
   ```
   bool CustomerExist(string socialScurityNumber);
   ```

The complete code for the **IBookingProcessor** interface:

```
public interface IBookingProcessor : IRentalBase
{
    IDataLayer DataLayer { get; }

    IBooking GetBooking(int vehicleId);
    bool CustomerExist(string socialScurityNumber);
}
```

The BookingProcessor class

Implement the **AddCustomer** method in the **Action Methods** region and the **CustomerExist** method in the **Helper Methods** region of the **BookingProcessor** class.

The CustomerExist method

Use LINQ to count the number of objects with a social security number equal to the value of the passed in parameter. Return **true** if the result from the LINQ query is greater than zero meaning that the customer already exist.

The AddCustomer method

Add a **try/catch**-block where the **catch**-block re-throws any exception.

This method implementation differs a bit from many of the previous method implementations in that it has business logic to execute before the call to the **AddCustomer** method in the data layer can be made.

The business logic consist of two **if**-statements where the first checks if the **Id** property is greater than zero on the passed in **customer** parameter and to throws a new **Customer-Exception** with a message stating that the customer has erroneous data should the **if**-statement evaluate to **true**.

The second business logic **if**-statement checks if the social security number in the passed in **customer** parameter already exist in the **Customers** collection and throws a new **Customer-Exception** with a message stating that the customer already exist should the **if**-statement evaluate to **true**.

Call the **AddCustomer** method on the **DataLayer** property to add the **customer** instance to the **Customers** collection in the **TestData** class.

1. Open the **BookingProcessor** class.
2. Add a **bool** method called **CustomerExist** with a **string** parameter called **social-SecurityNumber** to the **Helper Methods** region.
3. Count the objects in the **Customers** collection in the **TestClass** whose **SocialSecurity-Number** property is equal to the passed in parameter with the same name. Store the result from the LINQ query in a variable called **social**.
4. Return **true** if there are objects with that social security number.

```
    return social > 0;
```

5. Add a **void** method called **AddCustomer** with an **ICustomer** parameter called **customer** to the **Action Methods** region.

6. Add a **try/catch**-block where the **catch**-block re-throws any exception.

7. Add the business logic for the customer id described above using an **if**-statement in the **try**-block.

```
    if (customer.Id > 0)
        throw new CustomerException(customer.Id,
            "The customer has erroneous data.");
```

8. Add the business logic described above for checking if a customer already exist.

```
    if (CustomerExist(customer.SocialSecurityNumber))
        throw new CustomerException(customer.Id,
            "The customer already exist.");
```

9. Call the **AddCustomer** method in the data layer to add the customer.

```
    DataLayer.AddCustomer(customer);
```

The code for the **BookingProcessor** class:

```
public class BookingProcessor : IBookingProcessor
{
    #region Properties
    public IDataLayer DataLayer { get; private set; }
    #endregion

    #region Constructor
    public BookingProcessor(IDataLayer dataLayer) ...
    #endregion

    #region Action Methods
    public bool RentVehicle(int vehicleId, int customerId,
        DateTime timeOfRental) ...
    public double ReturnVehicle(int bookingId, double meter,
        DateTime returned) ...
    public void AddVehicle(IVehicle vehicle) ...
    public void AddCustomer(ICustomer customer)
    {
        try
        {
            // Business logic to check that the
            // customer does not already exist
```

```
            if (customer.Id > 0)
                throw new CustomerException(customer.Id,
                    "The customer has erroneous data.");

            if (CustomerExist(customer.SocialSecurityNumber))
                throw new CustomerException(customer.Id,
                    "The customer already exist.");

            DataLayer.AddCustomer(customer);
        }
        catch
        {
            throw;
        }
    }
    #endregion

    #region Fetch Methods
    public IEnumerable<ICustomer> GetCustomers() ...
    public IEnumerable<IVehicle> GetVehicles(VehicleStatus status) ...
    public IVehicleType GetVehicleType(int vehicleTypeId) ...
    public IEnumerable<IBooking> GetBookings() ...
    public IBooking GetBooking(int vehicleId) ...
    public IEnumerable<IVehicleType> GetVehicleTypes() ...
    #endregion

    #region Helper Methods
    public bool CustomerExist(string socialScurityNumber)
    {
        var social = (from c in DataLayer.GetCustomers()
            where c.SocialSecurityNumber.Equals(socialScurityNumber)
            select c).Count();

        return social > 0;
    }
    #endregion
}
```

Adding a customer

Add a parameter-less **void** method called **AddCustomer** to the **Action Methods** region of the form.

Add a **try/catch**-block where the first **catch**-block handles any **CustomerException** by displaying the exception message to the user and then return **Int32.MinValue**. The second **catch**-block should be empty to disregard any other exceptions.

The **AddCustomer** method should check that all controls involved contain correct information, if one or more of the textboxes are empty an appropriate message should be displayed and then the method should end gracefully by returning **-1**.

When the properties of the a new instance of the **Customer** class called **customer** has been assigned values from the textboxes the **AddCustomer** method should be called on the **processor** instance variable to add the customer.

After the **customer** instance has been added to the **Customers** collection in the **TestData** class the **FillCustomers** method should be called to repopulate the combo box on the **Rent Vehicle** tab and then the textboxes should be cleared.

Return the index position of the **customer** instance in the combo box if no exception has been thrown.

When the **AddCustomer** method has been added it can be called from the **_btnAddCustomer_** button's **Click** event. Store the result from the method call in a variable called **idx**.

If the vehicle could not be added the **idx** variable will contain **-1** or **Int32.MinValue** which can be checked by **if**-statements in order to display suitable error messages to the user.

Assign the value in the **idx** variable to the **SelectedIndex** property of the **_cboCustomer_** combo box and switch to the **Rent Vehicle** tab.

1. Open the form's code-behind.
2. Add a parameter-less **void** method called **AddCustomer** to the **Action Methods** region of the form.
3. Add a **try/catch**-block with the two **catch**-blocks described above.
4. Check that the controls has valid data and build an error message in a variable called **errMsg** if any data is invalid.
5. Display the error message and return **-1** if any of the textboxes are empty.

6. Create a new instance of the **Customer** class called **customer** assigning the textbox values to its properties.
   ```
   var customer = new Customer() { SocialSecurityNumber =
   txtSocial.Text, FirstName = txtFirstName.Text, LastName =
   txtLastName.Text };
   ```

7. Call the **AddCustomer** method passing in the **customer** object as its parameter to add the customer to the **Customers** collection in the **TestData** class.
   ```
   processor.AddCustomer(customer);
   ```

8. Update the customers in the combo box on the **Rent Vehicle** tab by calling the **FillCustomers** method.

9. Clear the textboxes.

10. Return the index position of the **customer** instance in the combo box.

11. Add the **Click** event for the *btnAddCustomer* button to the **Button Events** region.

12. Call the **AddCustomer** method and store the **return** value in a variable called **idx**.

13. Add an **if**-statement checking if the value of the **idx** variable is equal to **Int32.Min-Value** and if so exit the event with a **return** statement.

14. Add an **if**-statement checking if the value of the **idx** variable is equal to **-1** and if so display a message to the user stating that the customer wasn't added and then exit the event with a **return** statement.

15. Assign the value of the **idx** variable to the **SelectedIndex** property of the *cboCustomers* combo box to select the newly added customer.

16. Open the **Rent Vehicle** tab.
    ```
    tabBooking.SelectTab(tabRentVehicle);
    ```

17. Run the application and add a new vehicle, make sure that it appears in the vehicle list view on the **Rent Vehicle** tab.

The code in the form code-behind:

```
public partial class Form1 : Form
{
    IBookingProcessor processor;

    public Form1() ...

    private void Form1_Load(object sender, EventArgs e) ...
```

```
#region Fill Data Methods
private void FillCustomers() ...
private IEnumerable<ListViewItem> GetVehicles(
    VehicleStatus vehicleStatus) ...
private void FillAvialbleVehicles() ...
private void FillBookedVehicles() ...
private bool FillBookings() ...
private void FillVehicleTypes() ...
#endregion

#region Action Methods
private bool RentVehicle() ...
private bool ReturnVehicle() ...
private bool AddVehicle(IVehicle vehicle) ...
private int AddCustomer()
{
    try
    {
        // Check for erroneous data
        string errMsg = String.Empty;
        if (txtSocial.TextLength == 0)
            errMsg = "Incorrect social security number" +
                Environment.NewLine;

        if (txtFirstName.TextLength == 0)
            errMsg += "Incorrect first name" + Environment.NewLine;

        if (txtLastName.TextLength == 0)
            errMsg += "Incorrect last name" + Environment.NewLine;

        if (txtSocial.TextLength == 0 ||
            txtFirstName.TextLength == 0 || txtLastName.TextLength == 0)
        {
            MessageBox.Show(errMsg);
            return -1;
        }

        // Create the new customer object
        var customer = new Customer() {
            SocialSecurityNumber = txtSocial.Text,
            FirstName = txtFirstName.Text,
            LastName = txtLastName.Text
        };
```

```csharp
        // Add the new customer to the Customers
        // collection and update the combo box
        processor.AddCustomer(customer);
        FillCustomers();

        txtSocial.Text = String.Empty;
        txtFirstName.Text = String.Empty;
        txtLastName.Text = String.Empty;

        return cboCustomers.Items.Count - 1;
    }
    catch(CustomerException ex)
    {
        MessageBox.Show(ex.Message);
        return Int32.MinValue;
    }
    catch { return -1; }
}
#endregion

#region Helper Methods
bool IsNummeric(string text) ...
#endregion

#region Button Events
private void btnRent_Click(object sender, EventArgs e) ...
private void btnReturn_Click(object sender, EventArgs e) ...
private void btnAddVehicle_Click(object sender, EventArgs e) ...
private void btnAddCustomer_Click(object sender, EventArgs e)
{
    var idx = AddCustomer();

    if (idx.Equals(Int32.MinValue)) return;
    if (idx.Equals(-1))
    {
        MessageBox.Show("The customer was not added");
        return;
    }

    cboCustomers.SelectedIndex = idx;
    tabBooking.SelectTab(tabRentVehicle);
}
#endregion
}
```

PART 2 - .NET FRAMEWORK

13. Using Streams

Introduction

When a file, whether in a file system or on a web server fetched over HTTP, reaches a certain size you no longer can use an atomic operation to manipulate the whole file in memory; this is where file streams come into the picture. By streaming a file, you can manipulate it in chunks. A file stream is a sequence of bytes.

Streams are typically used to read data onto a byte array or other types, or fetch data from types and write it to a stream. You can query the stream for the current position when performing reads or writes.

When choosing the stream type, you need to consider what type of data you are manipulating (binary, text ...) and where it is or will be stored; on a web server, in memory or in a file system. The most common file streams are stored in the **System.IO** namespace.

All stream classes derive from the **Stream** class which contains the most commonly used functionality. An instance of the **Stream** class holds a pointer that refers to the current position in the data source; when first created, the pointer points to the byte before the fist byte in the data source. The pointer is then advanced when reading from or writing to the stream.

When using streams, you cannot use the **Stream** class directly, instead you use one of the specialized stream classes such as **FileStream** to connect to a file in a file system, **MemoryStream** storing data in memory, or a **NetworkStream** to connect to a data source on a network source.

The **StreamReader/StreamWriter** reads/writes textual data. The **BinaryReader/BinaryWriter** reads/writes binary data. All these readers and writers use streams like the **FileStream**, **MemoryStream** and the **NetworkStream** to connect to a source.

Streams and binary data

Reading binary data is fast and takes up less space when stored; the drawback is that it is not readable text.

Writing binary data

The **BinaryWriter** class has several properties and functions that you can use when writing to a stream. The **Write** method writes to the stream and advances the pointer. The **Seek** method makes it possible to position the pointer at a specific position; you can then write to that byte. The **Flush** method makes it possible to write the remaining bytes in the buffer to the stream. The **Close** method closes the **BinaryWriter** instance and its underlying stream. The **BaseStream** property makes it possible to access the underlying stream.

Example: Writing a byte array to a file using a BinaryWriter

In this example the values in a **byte array** is saved as binary data to a file using the **Write** method on a **BinaryWriter** instance.

```
private void BinaryWriterTest(string path, byte[] binaryData)
{
    var destinationFile = new FileStream(path, FileMode.Create,
        FileAccess.Write);
    var writer = new BinaryWriter(destinationFile);

    foreach (byte data in binaryData)
        writer.Write(data);

    writer.Close();
    destinationFile.Close();
}
```

Reading binary data

The **BinaryReader** class has several properties and functions that you can use when reading from a stream. The **Read** method reads the remaining bytes in the stream from a specific position. The **ReadByte** and **ReadBytes** methods read the next byte or a number of bytes. The **Close** method closes the **BinaryReader** instance and its underlying stream. The **BaseStream** property makes it possible to access the underlying stream.

Example: Reading a whole file with a BinaryReader

In this example the contents of a binary file is read in its entirety into a **byte array** using the **Read** method on a **BinaryReader** instance and then the data is returned from the method.

```csharp
private byte[] BinaryReaderTest(string path)
{
    FileStream sourceFile = new FileStream(path, FileMode.Open,
        FileAccess.Read);
    BinaryReader reader = new BinaryReader(sourceFile);
    int length = (int)reader.BaseStream.Length;

    // Read all data into an array
    byte[] binaryData = new byte[length];
    reader.Read(binaryData, 0, length);

    reader.Close();
    sourceFile.Close();
    return binaryData;
}
```

Example: Reading from a BinaryReader with a while loop

In this example the contents of a binary file is read byte by byte into a **byte array** using the **ReadByte** method on a **BinaryReader** instance in a **while** loop and then the data is returned from the method.

```csharp
private byte[] BinaryReaderTest(string path)
{
    FileStream sourceFile = new FileStream(path, FileMode.Open,
        FileAccess.Read);
    BinaryReader reader = new BinaryReader(sourceFile);
    int length = (int)reader.BaseStream.Length;

    // Read data with a while loop
    byte[] binaryData = new byte[length];
    while (sourceFile.Position < length)
        binaryData[sourceFile.Position] = reader.ReadByte();

    reader.Close();
    sourceFile.Close();
    return binaryData;
}
```

Example: Reading from a BinaryReader with a for loop

In this example the contents of a binary file is read byte by byte into a **byte array** using the **ReadByte** method on a **BinaryReader** instance with a **for** loop and then the data is returned from the method.

```
private byte[] BinaryReaderTest(string path)
{
    FileStream sourceFile = new FileStream(path, FileMode.Open,
        FileAccess.Read);
    BinaryReader reader = new BinaryReader(sourceFile);
    int length = (int)reader.BaseStream.Length;

    // Read data with a for loop
    byte[] binaryData = new byte[length];
    for (int i = 0; i < length; i++)
        binaryData[i] = reader.ReadByte();

    reader.Close();
    sourceFile.Close();
    return binaryData;
}
```

Streams and text data

When you need to store and read human readable data, you can use the **StreamReader** and **StreamWriter** classes.

Writing text data

The **StreamWriter** class has several properties and functions that you can use when reading from a stream. The **Flush** method writes the remaining data in the buffer to the stream. The **Write** method writes the data to the stream and advances the stream. The **WriteLine** method writes the data to the stream followed by a new line break. The **Close** method closes the **StreamWriter** instance and its underlying stream.

The **AutoFlush** property tells the **StreamWriter** to flush data to the stream after every time it writes data making sure that the write buffer is empty. With the **NewLine** property you can decide which characters that will be used to represent a new line break.

Example: Writing with a StreamWriter

In this example the text in a **string** variable is saved as human readable text to a file using the **WriteLine** method on a **StreamWriter** instance. The path parameter will contain the physical path to the file location and the name of the file.

```
private void StreamWriterTest(string path, string data)
{
    var destinationFile = new FileStream(path, FileMode.Create,
        FileAccess.Write);

    var writer = new StreamWriter(destinationFile);
    writer.WriteLine(data);
    writer.Close();

    destinationFile.Close();
}
```

Reading text data

The **StreamReader** class has several properties and functions that you can use when reading from a stream. The **Peak** method reads the next character, but does not consume it. The **Read** method reads the next character as a binary delivered as an **int**; you might have to explicitly convert the value. The **ReadBlock** method makes it possible to read a block of characters from a specified position. The **ReadLine** method makes it possible to read a line of characters from the stream. The **ReadToEnd** method makes it possible to read the remaining characters from the current position. The **Close** method closes the **StreamReader** instance and its underlying stream. The **EndOfStream** property tells you if you have reached the end of the stream.

Example: Reading characters with a StreamReader

In this example the contents of a text file is read character by character into a **StringBuilder** instance using the **Read** method on a **StreamReader** instance and then the data is returned from the method. The read character is cast to a **char** before it is appended to the **StringBuilder** instance.

```
private string StreamReaderTest(string path)
{
    FileStream sourceFile = new FileStream(path, FileMode.Open,
        FileAccess.Read);
    StreamReader reader = new StreamReader(sourceFile);
```

```
    StringBuilder text = new StringBuilder();

    while (reader.Peek() != -1)
        text.Append((char)reader.Read());

    string data = text.ToString();

    reader.Close();
    sourceFile.Close();
    return data;
}
```

Example: Reading a whole text file with a StreamReader

In this example the entire contents of a text file is read in one go into a **string** variable using the **ReadToEnd** method on a **StreamReader** instance and then the fetched data is returned from the method.

```
private string StreamReaderTest(string path)
{
    FileStream sourceFile = new FileStream(path, FileMode.Open,
        FileAccess.Read);
    StreamReader reader = new StreamReader(sourceFile);
    string data = reader.ReadToEnd();
    reader.Close();
    return data;
}
```

Exercise: Reading/writing data to binary and text files

In this exercise you will create a class called **IO** that will contain two methods for reading and writing data to binary- and text files. By selecting one of the radio buttons in the GUI and clicking on the **Read**- or **Write** button the **ReadFile** or **WriteToFile** methods will be called with a parameter stating if the data should be saved in binary- or text format.

If the **Binary data** radio button is selected and the **Save** button is clicked then the values in a byte array will be saved to a file with a **.bin** extension using the **Write** method on a **BinaryWriter** instance. When the **Read** button is clicked the file with the **.bin** extension will be read using the **Read** method on a **BinaryReader** instance and the data will be displayed in a rich textbox.

If the **Text data** radio button is selected and the **Save** button is clicked then the text in the rich textbox will be saved to a file with a **.txt** extension using the **WriteLine** method on a **StreamWriter** instance. When the **Read** button is clicked the file with the **.txt** extension will be read using the **ReadToEnd** method on a **StreamReader** instance and the data will be displayed in the rich textbox.

The IO class

Add a class called **IO** to a folder named **Classes** and an enum called **DataFormat** above the class with two values **Binary** and **Text**.

Because you will be reading and writing data in different formats (binary and text) the values of the **DataFormat enum** will determine which type of writer to use when saving the data to a file.

The **static WriteToFile** method that you will create have three parameters one called **path** of the **string** data type, a second called **dataFormat** of the **DataFormat** data type and a third called **data** of the **object** data type; the data parameter is declared as **object** because the data can be of different types, a byte array or plain text. The method should return a **bool** value stating if the data was successfully saved to the file in the **try/catch**-block.

The **static ReadFile** method that you will create have three parameters one called **path** of the **string** data type, a second called **dataFormat** of the **DataFormat** data type and a third called **data** of the **object** data type declared as an **out** parameter to return the read data; the data parameter is declared as **object** because the read data can be of different types and as an **out** parameter because the return data type is already used to return a **bool** value stating if the data was successfully read from the file.

1. Create a new Windows Forms Application called **Read and Write**.
2. Add a folder named **Classes** to the project.
3. Add a class called **IO** to the Classes folder.
4. Add an **enum** called **DataFormat** above the class and add the two values **Binary** and **Text**.
5. Add a **static bool** method called **WriteToFile** which has the three parameters described above.

```
public static bool WriteToFile(string path, DataFormat dataFormat,
object data) { ... }
```

6. Add a **try/catch**-block where the **try**-block return **true** as its last statement and the **catch**-block return **false**. This value will indicate whether the write operation succeeded or not.

7. Add a **FileStream** instance called **file** using the **path** parameter for its path, the **FileMode** set to **Create** and the **FileAccess** set to **Write**.
   ```
   var file = new FileStream(path, FileMode.Create, FileAccess.Write);
   ```

8. Since you know that the data will be saved using different formats an **if/else if**-block will be needed to separate the logic using the value from the **dataFormat** parameter.
   ```
   if (dataFormat.Equals(DataFormat.Binary)) { ... }
   else if (dataFormat.Equals(DataFormat.Text)) { ... }
   ```

9. Add a **static bool** method called **ReadFile** which has the three parameters described above.
   ```
   public static bool ReadFile(string path, DataFormat dataFormat, out
   object data) { ... }
   ```

10. Since an out parameter always need to be assigned in the method its first line of code will be assigning a value of **null** to it.
    ```
    data = null;
    ```

11. Add a **try/catch**-block where the **try**-block return **true** as its last statement and the **catch**-block return **false**. This value will indicate whether the write operation succeeded or not.

12. Add a **FileStream** instance called **file** using the **path** parameter for its path, the **FileMode** set to **Open** and the **FileAccess** set to **Read**.
    ```
    var file = new FileStream(path, FileMode.Open, FileAccess.Read);
    ```

13. Since you know that the data will be read using different formats an **if/else if**-block will be needed to separate the logic using the value from the **dataFormat** parameter.
    ```
    if (dataFormat.Equals(DataFormat.Binary)) { ... }
    else if (dataFormat.Equals(DataFormat.Text)) { ... }
    ```

This is the code for the **IO** class so far:

```
class IO
{
    public static bool WriteToFile(string path,
        DataFormat dataFormat, object data)
    {
        try
        {
            var file = new FileStream(path, FileMode.Create,
                FileAccess.Write);

            if (dataFormat.Equals(DataFormat.Binary)) { }
            else if (dataFormat.Equals(DataFormat.Text)) { }

            return true;
        }
        catch
        {
            return false;
        }
    }

    public static bool ReadFile(string path,
        DataFormat dataFormat, out object data)
    {
        data = null;

        try
        {
            FileStream file = new FileStream(
                path, FileMode.Open, FileAccess.Read);

            if (dataFormat.Equals(DataFormat.Binary)) { }
            else if (dataFormat.Equals(DataFormat.Text)) { }

            return true;
        }
        catch { return false; }
    }
}
```

The GUI

The GUI is made up of a label with the text "Message", a rich textbox named *txtMessage*, two radio buttons called *rbnBinary* and *rbnText*, a **Read** button called *btnRead* and a **Save** button called *btnSave*.

The radio buttons don't need any events since their **Checked** property will be used in the buttons **Click** events.

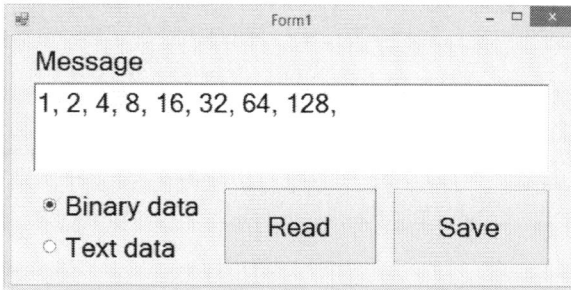

1. Create a new **Windows Forms Application** called **Streams**.
2. Add the controls as described in the image and text above.
3. Add the **Click** event for the **Save** button.
4. Add a **bool** variable called **success** to the **Click** event.
5. Add **if/else if**-blocks checking which of the radio buttons is checked.
   ```
   if (rbnBinary.Checked)
   { }
   else if (rbnText.Checked)
   { }
   ```
6. Add a byte array variable with some data to the **if**-block.
   ```
   byte[] binaryData = { 1, 2, 4, 8, 16, 32, 64, 128 };
   ```
7. Call the **WriteToFile** method in the **IO** class and save the return value in the **success** variable. Pass in the path and file name as its first parameter, **DataFormat.Binary** and the array as the second and third parameters.
   ```
   success = IO.WriteToFile(@"C:\Test\binary.bin", DataFormat.Binary,
   binaryData);
   ```
8. Locate the **else if**-block and call the **WriteToFile** method in the **IO** class and save the return value in the **success** variable. Pass in the path and file name as its first para-

meter, **DataFormat.Text** and the text in the textbox as the second and third parameters.

```
success = IO.WriteToFile(@"C:\Test\text.txt", DataFormat.Text,
txtMessage.Text);
```

9. Display the message "Could not write to file!" if the **success** variable is **false** in the **Write** button's **Click** event.

10. Clear the textbox after the message **if**-statement in the **Write** button.

11. Add the **Click** event for the **Read** button.

12. Add a **bool** variable called **success** to the **Click** event.

13. Clear the textbox after the **success** variable declaration.

14. Add an **if/else if**-block checking which of the radio buttons is checked.

15. locate the **if**-block and add an object variable called **binaryData**.

16. Call the **ReadFile** method in the **IO** class, store the return value in the **success** variable. Pass in the path and file name as its first parameter, **DataFormat.Binary** as its second parameter and the **binaryData** variable as an **out** parameter as its third parameter.

```
success = IO.ReadFile(@"C:\Test\binary.bin", DataFormat.Binary, out
binaryData);
```

17. Since the data is returned with the **object** data type you have to cast it to a **byte[]** when looping over the values to display them in the textbox if the success variable is **true**.

```
foreach (byte data in binaryData as byte[])
```

18. Locate the **else if**-block and add an **object** variable called **text**.

19. Call the **ReadFile** method in the **IO** class, store the return value in the **success** variable. Pass in the path and file name as its first parameter, **DataFormat.Text** as its second parameter and the **text** variable as an **out** parameter as its third parameter.

```
success = IO.ReadFile(@"C:\Test\text.txt", DataFormat.Text, out
text);
```

20. If the success variable is true then assign the **text** variable to the textbox's **Text** property. You will have to call the **ToString** method on the **text** variable.

21. Display the message "Could not read from file!" if the **success** variable is **false** below the **if/else if**-block.

The complete button **Click** events code in the form's code-behind:

```
public partial class Form1 : Form
{
    private void btnSave_Click(object sender, EventArgs e)
    {
        var success = false;

        if (rbnBinary.Checked)
        {
            byte[] binaryData = { 1, 2, 4, 8, 16, 32, 64, 128 };
            success = IO.WriteToFile(@"C:\Test\binary.bin",
                DataFormat.Binary, binaryData);
        }
        else if (rbnText.Checked)
        {
            success = IO.WriteToFile(@"C:\Test\text.txt",
                DataFormat.Text, txtMessage.Text);
        }

        if (!success) MessageBox.Show("Could not write to the file!");
            txtMessage.Clear();
    }

    private void btnRead_Click(object sender, EventArgs e)
    {
        var success = false;
        txtMessage.Clear();

        if (rbnBinary.Checked)
        {
            object binaryData;
            success = IO.ReadFile(@"C:\Test\binary.bin",
                DataFormat.Binary, out binaryData);

            if (success)
                foreach (byte data in binaryData as byte[])
                        txtMessage.Text += data + ", ";
        }
        else if (rbnText.Checked)
        {
            object text;
            success = IO.ReadFile(@"C:\Test\text.txt",
                DataFormat.Text, out text);
```

```
          if (success) txtMessage.Text = text.ToString();
      }

      if (!success)
          MessageBox.Show("Could not read from the file!");
   }
}
```

Saving binary data

In this part of the exercise you will focus on the **if**-block in the **WriteToFile** method where you will add code to save the byte array data to a binary file using a **foreach** loop and the **Write** method on a **BinaryWriter** instance in conjunction with the **FileStream** instance.

1. Open the **IO** class and locate the **if**-block in the **WriteToFile** method.

   ```
   if (dataFormat.Equals(DataFormat.Binary))
   ```

2. Add a region inside the **if**-block with the description **Binary Writer**.

3. Create a **BinaryWriter** instance variable called **writer** inside the region passing in the **file** variable as its only parameter.

   ```
   var writer = new BinaryWriter(file);
   ```

4. Add a **foreach** loop where you loop over the data in the data parameter and write the data to the file using the **Write** method. Note that you have to cast the data to a **byte[]** since it is passed in using the **object** data type.

   ```
   foreach (byte b in data as byte[])
   ```

5. Close the writer and the file stream by calling their **Close** methods.

6. Run the application and make sure that the **Binary data** radio button is selected before clicking the **Save** button.

7. Close the application and open the folder you gave in the **Save** button's **Click** event when calling the **WriteToFile** method.

8. Locate the and open file with the file name you gave when calling the **WriteToFile** method. Note that the data looks like random unreadable characters.

9. Close the file.

The complete code for writing to a file with a **BinaryWriter**:

```
if (dataFormat.Equals(DataFormat.Binary))
{
    #region Binary Writer
    var writer = new BinaryWriter(file);

    foreach (byte b in data as byte[])
        writer.Write(b);

    writer.Close();
    file.Close();
    #endregion
}
```

Reading binary data

In this part of the exercise you will focus on the **if**-block in the **ReadFile** method where you will add code to read the data in the binary file back to a byte array using the **Read** method on a **BinaryReader** instance in conjunction with the **FileStream** instance.

1. Open the **IO** class and locate the **if**-block in the **ReadFile** method.
   ```
   if (dataFormat.Equals(DataFormat.Binary))
   ```

2. Add a region inside the **if**-block with the description **Binary Reader**.

3. Create a **BinaryReader** instance variable called **reader** inside the region passing in the **file** variable as its only parameter.
   ```
   var reader = new BinaryReader(file);
   ```

4. Find out the length of the stream; the number of bytes needed to create the **byte** array that will store the read data.
   ```
   int length = (int)reader.BaseStream.Length;
   ```

5. Create a **byte** array called **binaryData** using the **length** variable.
   ```
   byte[] binaryData = new byte[length];
   ```

6. Read the data into the array by calling the **Read** method on the **reader** variable passing in the array, the start position in the stream and the number of bytes to read.

7. Close the reader and the file stream by calling their **Close** methods.

8. Assign the **binaryData** variable to the **out data** parameter.

9. Run the application and make sure that the **Binary data** radio button is selected before clicking the **Read** button. The data in the file should be displayed in the textbox.

The complete code for reading a file with a **BinaryReader**:

```
if (dataFormat.Equals(DataFormat.Binary))
{
    #region Binary Reader
    var reader = new BinaryReader(file);
    int length = (int)reader.BaseStream.Length;

    // Read all data into an array
    byte[] binaryData = new byte[length];
    reader.Read(binaryData, 0, length);

    reader.Close();
    file.Close();

    data = binaryData;
    #endregion
}
```

Saving text data

In this part of the exercise you will focus on the **else if**-block in the **WriteToFile** method where you will add code to save the text data to a file using the **WriteLine** method on a **StreamWriter** instance in conjunction with the **FileStream** instance.

1. Open the **IO** class and locate the **else if**-block in the **WriteToFile** method.
   ```
   if (dataFormat.Equals(DataFormat.Text))
   ```
2. Add a region inside the **else if**-block with the description **Stream Writer**.
3. Create a **StreamWriter** instance variable called **writer** inside the region passing in the **file** variable as its only parameter.
   ```
   var writer = new StreamWriter(file);
   ```
4. Call the **WriteLine** method on the **writer** instance variable and pass in the content of the data parameter.
5. Close the writer and the file stream by calling their **Close** methods.
6. Run the application and make sure that the **Text data** radio button is selected before clicking the **Save** button.
7. Close the application and open the folder you gave in the **Click** event for the **Save** button when calling the **WriteToFile** method.

8. Locate and open the file with the file name you gave when calling the **WriteToFile** method. Note that the data is in human readable text.
9. Close the file.

The complete code for writing to a file with a **StreamWriter**:

```
else if (dataFormat.Equals(DataFormat.Text))
{
    #region Stream Writer
    var writer = new StreamWriter(file);
    writer.WriteLine(data);
    writer.Close();
    file.Close();
    #endregion
}
```

Reading text data

In this part of the exercise you will focus on the **else if**-block in the **ReadFile** method where you will add code to read the data in the text file back to a string using the **ReadToEnd** method on a **StreamReader** instance in conjunction with the **FileStream** instance.

1. Open the **IO** class and locate the **else if**-block in the **ReadFile** method.
   ```
   if (dataFormat.Equals(DataFormat.Text))
   ```

2. Add a region inside the **else if**-block with the description **Stream Reader**.
3. Create a **StreamReader** instance variable called **reader** inside the region passing in the **file** variable as its only parameter.
   ```
   var reader = new StreamReader(file);
   ```

4. Read the data into the data parameter calling the **ReadToEnd** method on the **reader** variable.
5. Close the reader and the file stream by calling their **Close** methods.
6. Run the application and make sure that the **Text data** radio button is selected before clicking the **Read** button. The data in the file should be displayed in the textbox.

The complete code for reading a file with a **StreamReader**:

```
else if (dataFormat.Equals(DataFormat.Text))
{
    #region Stream Reader
    var reader = new StreamReader(file);
    data = reader.ReadToEnd();
    reader.Close();
    file.Close();
    #endregion
}
```

Exercise: Car Rental - Saving customers to a file

In this exercise you will add an **IO** class to the **Car Rental** application. The purpose of the **WriteToFile** method will be to list all customers in a text file as tabular data. Because you know what information will be saved to the file it is easy to determine what data type to use to pass the data to the method, an **IEnumerable<ICustomer>** parameter named **customers** will do the trick. The method should return a **bool** value indicating if the data was successfully saved.

Because you want to save the data as human readable text the **StreamWriter** is a good choice to pass the data to the file. In the **foreach** loop used to iterate over the customers the **WriteLine** method of the writer instance can be used to write each customer on a separate line. The **String.Format** method can be used to format the data into columns using **\t** to create the columns.

The data should be saved when the user clicks a button called **btnSave** on the **Rent Vehicle** tab.

Adding the WriteToFile method

1. Open the most recent version of the **Car Rental** solution.
2. Add a class called **IO** to the **Classes** folder.
3. Add a **public static bool** method called **WriteToFile** which has two parameters a **string** called **path** and an **IEnumerable<ICustomer>** called **customers**.

4. Add a **try/catch**-block where the **try**-block return **true** as its last statement and the **catch**-block return **false**. This value will show if the data was successfully saved to the file.

5. Add a **FileStream** instance called **file** using the **path** parameter as its first parameter and **FileMode.Create** and **FileAccess.Write** as its second and third parameters.

6. Add a **StreamWriter** instance called **writer** and pass in the **file** variable to its constructor.

7. Iterate over the customers in the passed in **customers** collection and use the **WriteLine** method to write the customer data on separate lines in the file.

```
foreach (var customer in customers)
    writer.WriteLine(String.Format("{0}\t{1}\t{2}\t{3}",
        customer.Id, customer.SocialSecurityNumber,
        customer.LastName, customer.FirstName));
```

8. Call the **Close** method on the **writer** and **file** objects.

The complete code for the **IO** class:

```
class IO
{
    public static bool WriteToFile(string path,
    IEnumerable<ICustomer> customers)
    {
        try
        {
            var file = new FileStream(path, FileMode.Create,
                FileAccess.Write);
            var writer = new StreamWriter(file);

            foreach (var customer in customers)
                writer.WriteLine(String.Format("{0}\t{1}\t{2}\t{3}",
                    customer.Id, customer.SocialSecurityNumber,
                    customer.LastName, customer.FirstName));

            writer.Close();
            file.Close();
            return true;
        }
```

```
    catch
    {
        return false;
    }
    }
}
```

Saving the customers

1. Add a **Save** button called ***btnSave*** to the **Rent Vehicle** tab.
2. Add the **Save** button's **Click** event to the **Button Events** region in the code-behind.
3. Add a call to the **WriteToFile** method in the **IO** class and pass in a suitable path and file name as the first parameter and a call to the **GetCustomers** method on the **processor** instance to fetch the customers from the data source through the booking processor. Save the **return** value from the method call in a variable called **success**.

```
var success = IO.WriteToFile(@"C:\Test\Customers.txt",
    processor.GetCustomers());
```

4. If the **success** variable is **true** then display a message telling the user that the customers were saved to the file and display a message teling the user that the customers couldn't be saved to the file if it is **false**.
5. Run the application and click the **Save** button. The resulting file's content should look something like this:

1	12324545	Raintree	Carl
2	95654123	Montgomery	Lisa

The code for the **Save** button:

```
private void btnSave_Click(object sender, EventArgs e)
{
    var success = IO.WriteToFile(@"C:\Test\Customers.txt",
        processor.GetCustomers());

    if (success) MessageBox.Show("The customers were saved to the file.");
    else MessageBox.Show("Could not save the customers to the file!");
}
```

14. Serialization

Introduction

Serialization can be used to persist or transport object data that later can be de-serialized back to object instances. We will look at how we can use Binary, XML and JSON serialization/de-serialization. The format needs to be lightweight for transportation over HTTP and SOAP.

One scenario could be that you want to save user settings. You could have an object containing the settings as properties be serialized when the settings are changed and de-serialized when starting the application. Another scenario could be that you are taking orders from your front-end GUI and the orders are serialized and placed in a queue for later processing. The back-end order processing process will then de-serialize the order data into objects that it can use to store the data.

Binary serialization is often used when transporting objects between applications on the same platform; it is lightweight, has little overhead and preserves fidelity and state between instances.

XML serialization is often used when transporting objects over the SOAP protocol to and from web services; it has overhead because it is verbose being formatted using XML which makes it more processor intensive. The upside is that it can be used cross-platform and between different applications. Another drawback is that it does not preserve type fidelity and only serializes **public** members. The **System.Runtime. Serialization.Formatters.Soap** assembly has to be referenced.

Alternatively you can use easier to use **XmlSerializer** class in the **System.Xml.Serialization** namespace when serializing to XML (see example below).

The following code shows an example XML output:

```
<?xml version="1.0"?>
<ArrayOfCustomer xmlns:xsi="http://www.w3.org/2001/XMLSchema-instance"
xmlns:xsd="http://www.w3.org/2001/XMLSchema">
  <Customer>
    <Id>1</Id>
    <SocialSecurityNumber>12324545</SocialSecurityNumber>
    <FirstName>Carl</FirstName>
    <LastName>Raintree</LastName>
  </Customer>
  <Customer>
    <Id>2</Id>
    <SocialSecurityNumber>95654123</SocialSecurityNumber>
    <FirstName>Lisa</FirstName>
    <LastName>Montgomery</LastName>
  </Customer>
</ArrayOfCustomer>
```

JSON serialization is based on a subset of JavaScript and is often used when asynchronous calls from JavaScript using AJAX are involved. You are not limited to the same domain and JSON is lightweight, human readable, easy to parse and platform independent. The **System .Runtime.Serialization** assembly has to be referenced and a using statement added to **System .Runtime.Serialization.Json**.

Alternatively you can use **JavaScriptSerializer** class in the **System.Web.Extensions** assembly when serializing to JSON (see example below).

The following code shows an example JSON output:

```
[{"Id":1,"SocialSecurityNumber":"12324545",
  "FirstName":"Carl","LastName":"Raintree"},
 {"Id":2,"SocialSecurityNumber":"95654123",
  "FirstName":"Lisa","LastName":"Montgomery"}]
```

Serializing and deserializing

To make a class serializable when using a **BinaryFormatter**, you have to add some serialization code; add the **[Serializable]** attribute above the class definition and implement the

ISerializable interface; this interface contain the method definition for **GetObjectData** that is used when serializing the data. You also need to add a constructor that takes two para- meters **SerializationInfo** and **StreamingContext.** This constructor is used when de-serializing data into an object. If you want to omit fields from the serialization process then add the **[NonSerialized]** attribute to the fields.

```
[Serializable]
public class Customer
{
    public int Id { get; set; }
    public string SocialSecurityNumber { get; set; }
    public string FirstName { get; set; }
    public string LastName { get; set; }

    [NonSerialized]
    public string TempValue { get; set; }
}
```

Binary serialization

Binary serialization requires the class to be marked with the **[Serializable]** attribute. To seria- lize an object using binary serialization, you need to create an instance of the **Binary- Formatter** class. Next you create the file you want to persist the object to using the **File** or **FileStream** class. To serialize the object, you call the **Serialize** method on the **Binary- Formatter** instance passing in the file stream and the object you want to serialize. Don't forget to close the file stream using the **Close** method on the file stream instance.

The **GetCustomers** method in the example return a **List<Customer>** collection.

```
var formatter = new BinaryFormatter();
using (var stream = File.Create(@"C:\Test\binary.txt"))
{
    formatter.Serialize(stream, GetCustomers());
}
```

Binary deserialization

To deserialize a persisted object to an object instance stored in binary format you need to create an instance of the **BinaryFormatter** class. To open the file containing the object data you use the **OpenRead** method on the **File** or **FileStream** class. To recreate the object you call the **Deserialize** method on the **BinaryFormatter** instance passing in the file stream and store the result in an instance variable of the serialized type. Don't forget to close the file stream using the **Close** method on the file stream instance.

```
var formatter = new BinaryFormatter();
using (var stream = File.OpenRead(@"C:\Test\binary.txt")) {
    var customers = (List<Customer>)formatter.Deserialize(stream);
}
```

XML serialization

To serialize an object using binary serialization you need to create an instance of the **XmlSerializer** class located in the **System.Xml.Serialization** namespace. Create the file you want to persist the object to using the **File** or **FileStream** class. To serialize the object you call the **Serialize** method on the **XmlSerializer** instance passing in the file stream and the object you want to serialize. Don't forget to close the file stream using the **Close** method on the file stream.

The **GetCustomers** method in the example return a **List<Customer>** collection.

```
var serializer = new XmlSerializer(typeof(List<Customer>));
using (var stream = File.Create(@"C:\Test\xml.txt"))
{
    serializer.Serialize(stream, GetCustomers());
}
```

XML deserialization

To de-serialize a persisted object stored in binary format to an object instance you need to create an instance of the **XmlSerializer** class. Open the file containing the object data and use the **OpenRead** method on the **File** or **FileStream** class. To recreate the object you call the **Deserialize** method on the **XmlSerializer** instance passing in the file stream and store the result in an instance variable of the serialized type. Don't forget to close the file stream using the **Close** method on the file stream instance. You have to cast the de-serialized data to the correct data type, in this case **List<Customer>**.

```
var xml = File.ReadAllText(@"C:\Test\xml.txt");
var deserializer = new XmlSerializer(typeof(List<Customer>));
using (var reader = new StringReader(xml))
{
    var customers = (List<Customer>)deserializer.Deserialize(reader);
}
```

JSON serialization

You need to create an instance of the **JavaScriptSerializer** class and pass in the object type of the class you are serializing to serialize an object using JSON serialization. Create the file you want to persist the object to using the **File** or **FileStream** class and use the **WriteAllText** method to persist the data.

Important: *You need to reference the **System.Web.Extensions** assembly to get access to the **JavaScriptSerializer** class.*

Note: *There are other .NET and third party (Json.NET) assemblies that can be used when serializing to JSON.*

The **GetCustomers** method in the example return a **List<Customer>** collection.

```
string json = new JavaScriptSerializer().Serialize(GetCustomers());
File.WriteAllText(@"C:\Test\json.txt", json);
```

JSON deserialization

To de-serialize a persisted object to an object instance stored in JSON format you need to open the file containing the object data using the **ReadAllText** method on the **File** or **File-Stream** class. To recreate the object, you call the **Deserialize** method on the **JavaScriptSerializer** instance passing in the data you read from the file and store the result in an instance variable of the serialized type.

```
string json = File.ReadAllText(@"C:\Test\json.txt");
var customers = new
JavaScriptSerializer().Deserialize<List<Customer>>(json);
```

Exercise: Car Rental - Persisting data

In this exercise you will add data persisting functionality to the **Car Rental** application using JSON serialization and de-serialization.

The first thing you need to do is to add a reference to the **System.Web.Extensions** assembly in the **Data Layer** project.

Add a new region with the description **Serialize/Deserialize** to the **CollectionDataLayer** class and place all methods you create in this exercise that region.

Add a new **public** interface called **ISerialize** which contain one **void** method called **Serialize** that has a **string** parameter called **path**. The **IDataLayer** interface should inherit the **ISerialize** interface. Implement the **Serialize** method in the **CollectionDataLayer** class; use a **Serialize** method on a **JavaScriptSerializer** object to serialize the four collections in the **TestData** class and the **File** class to persist the data to files calling its **WriteAllText** method.

```
File.WriteAllText(path + @"Bookings.txt", new JavaScriptSerializer()
.Serialize(TestData.Bookings));
```

Add four methods called **DeserializeBookings**, **DeserializeCustomers**, **DeserializeVehicles** and **DeserializeVehicleTypes** to the **CollectionDataLayer** class which deserialises the data in their respective files and return an appropriate collection with the fetched data. In each method the file containing the data for that particular collection should be read using the **ReadAllText** method on the **File** class. Pass the fetched data to the **Deserialize** method on an instance of the **JavaScriptSerializer** class and **return** the result from the method.

```
string json = File.ReadAllText(path);
return new JavaScriptSerializer().Deserialize<List<Booking>>(json);
```

Add a **void** method called **Seed** which has a **string** parameter called **path** that will load the data into the respective collections by calling the four **Deserialize** methods you just added. Once the files have been created with a call to the **TestClass.Seed** method you replace it with a call to this method in the **CollectionDataLayer** class' constructor.

You can use the **FormClosing** event of the form to persist the data to the files each time the form closes. Call the **Serialize** method on the **DataLayer** instance within the **processor** instance.

```
processor.DataLayer.Serialize(@"C:\Test\");
```

Adding the ISerialize interface

1. Add an interface called **ISerialize** to the to the **Interfaces** folder in the **Data Layer** project.
2. Change the interface accessibility to **public**.

3. Add a method definition for a **void** method called **Serialize** which has a **string** parameter called **path**.

4. Open the **IDataLayer** interface and inherit the **ISerialize** interface.
   ```
   public interface IDataLayer : IRentalBase, ISerialize
   ```

The complete code for the **ISerialize** interface:

```
public interface ISerialize
{
    void Serialize(string path);
}
```

Implementing the ISerialize interface

1. Open the **CollectionDataLayer** class.
2. Add a region with the description **Serialize/Deserialize**.
3. Add a **void** method called **Serialize** which has a **string** parameter called **path** to the region.
4. Call the **WriteAllText** method on the **File** class to persist the serialized data. Pass a path to where you want the file to be created and the name of the file as its first parameter and the serialized data as the second parameter. As you can see in the code below the call has been condensed into one row of code.
   ```
   File.WriteAllText(path + @"Bookings.txt", new
   JavaScriptSerializer().Serialize(TestData.Bookings));
   ```

The complete code for the **Serialize** method:

```
public void Serialize(string path)
{
    /* Requires a reference to the System.Web.Extensions assembly */
    File.WriteAllText(path + @"Bookings.txt",
        new JavaScriptSerializer().Serialize(TestData.Bookings));
    File.WriteAllText(path + @"Customers.txt",
        new JavaScriptSerializer().Serialize(TestData.Customers));
    File.WriteAllText(path + @"Vehicles.txt",
        new JavaScriptSerializer().Serialize(TestData.Vehicles));
    File.WriteAllText(path + @"VehicleTypes.txt",
        new JavaScriptSerializer().Serialize(TestData.VehicleTypes));
}
```

Implementing the four deserialize methods

1. Open the **CollectionDataLayer** class.
2. Locate the **Serialize/Deserialize** region.
3. Add a **private List<Booking>** method called **DeserializeBookings** which has a **string** parameter called **path**.
4. Fetch the JSON data stored in the file specified by the **path** parameter using the **ReadAllText** method on the **File** class. Store the result in a **string** variable called **json**.
   ```
   string json = File.ReadAllText(path);
   ```
5. Return the result from a call to the **Deserialize** method on an instance of the **JavaScriptSerializer** class to which you pass the JSON data you just fetched.
   ```
   return new JavaScriptSerializer().Deserialize<List<Booking>>(json);
   ```
6. Repeat the previous steps for the three other methods called **DeserializeCustomers**, **DeserializeVehicles** and **DeserializeVehicleTypes** and their corresponding collections in the **TestData** class called **Customers**, **Vehicles** and **VehicleTypes**.

The complete code for the four **Deserialize** methods:

```
/* Requires a reference to the System.Web.Extensions assembly */
private List<Booking> DeserializeBookings(string path)
{
    string json = File.ReadAllText(path);
    return new JavaScriptSerializer().Deserialize<List<Booking>>(json);
}

private List<Customer> DeserializeCustomers(string path)
{
    string json = File.ReadAllText(path);
    return new JavaScriptSerializer().Deserialize<List<Customer>>(json);
}

private List<Vehicle> DeserializeVehicles(string path)
{
    string json = File.ReadAllText(path);
    return new JavaScriptSerializer().Deserialize<List<Vehicle>>(json);
}
```

```
private List<VehicleType> DeserializeVehicleTypes(string path)
{
    string json = File.ReadAllText(path);
    return new JavaScriptSerializer().Deserialize<List<VehicleType>>(json);
}
```

Implementing the Seed method

1. Open the **CollectionDataLayer** class.

2. Locate the **Serialize/Deserialize** region.

3. Add a **private void** method called **Seed** which has a **string** parameter called **path**.

4. Assign the result from a call to the **DeserializeBookings** method to the **Bookings** collection in the **TestData** class. Note that you have to call the **Cast** method to cast the data from a list of **Booking** objects to a list of **IBooking** objects. You also have to call the **ToList** method to force the objects to be fetched as a list.
   TestData.Bookings = DeserializeBookings(path + @"Bookings.txt").Cast<IBooking>().ToList();

5. Repeat the previous step for the three remaining collections in the **TestData** class changing the method calls to **DeserializeCustomers**, **DeserializeVehicles** and **DeserializeVehicleTypes**.

The complete code for the **Seed** method:

```
private void Seed(string path)
{
    TestData.Bookings = DeserializeBookings(path +
        @"Bookings.txt").Cast<IBooking>().ToList();
    TestData.Customers = DeserializeCustomers(path +
        @"Customers.txt").Cast<ICustomer>().ToList();
    TestData.Vehicles = DeserializeVehicles(path +
        @"Vehicles.txt").Cast<IVehicle>().ToList();
    TestData.VehicleTypes = DeserializeVehicleTypes(path +
        @"VehicleTypes.txt").Cast<IVehicleType>().ToList();
}
```

Implementing the FormClosing event

1. Open the form designer and select the form.

2. Double click on the **FormClosing** event in the event list in the **Properties** window.

3. Call the **Serialize** method on the **DataLayer** property of the **processor** instance from the **FormClosing** event passing in the path to the location where you want the files to end up.
   ```
   processor.DataLayer.Serialize(@"C:\Test\");
   ```
4. Run the application and close it immediately.
5. Open a Windows Explorer window and go to the location where the files have been created. Open them and make sure that they contain the expected data.
6. Go back to Visual Studio.
7. Locate the **CollectionDataLayer** class's constructor and comment out or remove the call to the **TestData** class' **Seed** method and add a call to the local **Seed** method you created earlier.
   ```
   public CollectionDataLayer()
   {
       //new TestData().Seed();
       Seed(@"C:\Test\");
   }
   ```
8. Run the application and make sure that the data from the files have been loaded correctly.
9. Add and change some data and close the application.
10. Start the application again and make sure that the data was persisted to the files and read back correctly.

The complete code for the **FormClosing** event:

```
private void Form1_FormClosing(object sender, FormClosingEventArgs e)
{
    processor.DataLayer.Serialize(@"C:\Test\");
}
```

The complete code for the **CollectionDataLayer** class' constructor:

```
public CollectionDataLayer()
{
    //new TestData().Seed();
    Seed(@"C:\Test\");
}
```

15. Reflection

Introduction

Reuse of code and components is something you always want to keep in mind when building an application. Reflection is a way to use existing assemblies in your application and to inspect their metadata at run time; just keep in mind that it is marginally slower than static C# code. Use the classes in the **System.Reflection** namespace to implement reflection in your applications.

An example of where reflection is used is the **System.Runtime.Serialization** namespace that uses reflection to determine which type members to serialize.

You can examine a third-party assembly with unknown types and members to see if your application satisfies the dependencies of the assembly. In some cases, such as if you are implementing a generic storage repository, you might want to use reflection to inspect each type and its attributes before storing it. In other cases, you might want to have pluggable assemblies that load at run-time; one way to implement this is to look for specific interfaces with reflection. If you are building a virtualized platform that uses types and methods created in a language such as JavaScript you might want to define and execute methods at run-time.

Apart from the reflection classes listed below you might also find the **System.Type** class useful when implementing reflection; one method of particular interest is the **GetFields** method that fetches the fields defined within the type into a list of **FieldInfo** objects.

This is a list of some of the classes in the **System.Reflection** namespace.

Class	Description
Assembly	Inspect an assembly's metadata and types. Can also be used to load an assembly into memory.
TypeInfo	Inspect a type's characteristics.
ParameterInfo	Inspect what parameters a member has.
ConstructorInfo	Inspect a type's constructor.
FieldInfo	Inspect the fields' of a type.
MemberInfo	Inspect the members exposed by a type.
PropertyInfo	Inspect the properties of a type.
MethodInfo	Inspect the methods of a type.

Additional reading: "MSDN Type Class" and "Reflection in the .NET Framework"

Loading assemblies

The **Assembly** class of the **System.Reflection** namespace has two contexts; one that is for reflection-only operations that you can use to examine the assembly metadata using **static** methods but not execute any code. The other is the execution context that you use to execute code in an assembly that has been loaded.

Trying to execute code in an assembly using the reflection-only context will result in an **InvalidOperationException** exception being thrown. This context is faster than the execution context.

The **Assembly** class contains the following **static** methods for loading an assembly at run time.

Static Method	Description
LoadFrom	Use an absolute file path to load an assembly in execution context.
ReflectionOnlyLoad	Will load an assembly into a binary BLOB object using a reflection-only context.
ReflectionOnlyLoadFrom	Use an absolute file path to load an assembly in reflection-only context.

The following code shows the three ways of loading an assembly; you only have to use one of them when implementing your solution.

```
string assemblyPath = @"C:\Sample Files\TestAssembly.dll";

// Execute context
Assembly assembly = Assembly.LoadFrom(assemblyPath);

// Reflection-only context
Assembly assembly = Assembly.ReflectionOnlyLoadFrom(assemblyPath);

// Reflection-only context - BLOB
var rawBytes = File.ReadAllBytes(assemblyPath);
Assembly assembly = Assembly.ReflectionOnlyLoad(rawBytes);
```

When the assembly is loaded, you can use the following methods and properties to inspect and execute it.

Method	Description
FullName	Retrieves the full name of the assembly that contains the assembly version and public key token.
GetReferencedAssemblies	Fetches a list of all the names of the assemblies that the loaded assembly references.
GlobalAssemblyCache	States if the assembly was loaded from the GAC.
Location	The absolute path to the assembly file.
ReflectionOnly	States if the assembly was loaded using a reflection-only context.
GetType	Fetches an instance of a Type in the assembly with the type name.
GetTypes	Fetches an array of all the types in the assembly; the array elements are represented by the Type type.

Additional reading: "Assembly Class"

Examining types

With reflection you can examine an assembly fetching information about individual members or all members of a type. The following code examples build on the code in the previous example.

GetType/GetTypes

Use the **GetType** method to fetch a type in an assembly by its fully qualified name, **null** will be returned if the type does not exist. Use the **GetTypes** method to fetch all types in an array of **Type** objects.

The following code shows how you can get a specific type (class, struct, ...) from a loaded assembly.

```
public static Type GetType(Assembly assembly, string typeName)
{
    return assembly.GetType(typeName);
}
```

The following code shows how you can get a list of all type names from a loaded assembly.

```
public static List<string> GetTypeNames(Assembly assembly)
{
    return assembly.GetTypes().Select(t => t.FullName).ToList();
}
```

GetConstructors

Use the **GetConstructors** method to fetch all constructors of a type; it returns an array of **ConstructorInfo** objects. Use the **GetParameters** method to get each constructor's parameters.

The following example show how you can iterate over the constructors in a type and fetch each constructor's parameters.

```
public static List<string> GetConstructors(Type type)
{
    // Iterate over the constructors
    foreach (var constructor in type.GetConstructors())
    {
        var parameters = new StringBuilder();

        // Iterate over the constructor's parameters
        foreach (var parameter in constructor.GetParameters())
            parameters.Append(String.Format("{0} {1}, ",
                parameter.ParameterType.Name, parameter.Name));
    }
}
```

GetFields

Use the **GetFields** method to fetch all fields (variables) of a type; it returns an array of **Field-Info** objects. Use the **BindingFlags** collection to select which fields are to be fetched. The fields will be listed on the form *[private/public] Fieldname*.

Add a where clause removing all variable names that contain a "<" character to remove backing properties created by the system to store property values in variables,

```
public static List<string> GetFields(Type type)
{
    var flags = BindingFlags.Instance | BindingFlags.NonPublic |
                BindingFlags.Public | BindingFlags.DeclaredOnly;

    return (
        from t in type.GetFields(flags)
        where !t.Name.Contains("<")
        select String.Format("{0} {1}",
            t.IsPrivate ? "private" : "public", t.Name)
        ).ToList();
}
```

GetProperties

Use the **GetProperties** method to fetch all fields of a type; it returns an array of **PropertyInfo** objects. Use the **BindingFlags** collection to select which properties are to be fetched. The properties will be listed on the form *[private/public] Propertyname {[public/private] get; [public/private] set;}*. The **GetMethod.IsPrivate** property states if the property is **public** or **private** and the **GetGetMethod.IsPrivate** and **GetSetMethod.IsPrivate** property states if the property's getter and setter blocks are **public** or **private**.

```
public static List<string> GetProperties(Type type)
{
    var flags = BindingFlags.Instance | BindingFlags.NonPublic |
                BindingFlags.Public | BindingFlags.DeclaredOnly;

    return (
        from t in type.GetProperties(flags)
        select String.Format(
            "{0} {1} {{ {2} get; {3} set; }}",
            t.GetMethod.IsPrivate ? "private" : "public",
            t.ToString(),
```

```
            t.GetGetMethod(true).IsPrivate ?
            "private" : "public",
            t.GetSetMethod(true).IsPrivate ?
            "private" : "public")
    ).ToList();
}
```

GetMethods

Use the **GetMethods** method to fetch all methods of a type; it returns an array of **Method-Info** objects. Use the **BindingFlags** collection to select which methods are to be fetched. The methods will be listed on the form *[private/public] Methodname*.

```
private List<string> GetMethods(Type type)
{
    var flags = BindingFlags.Instance | BindingFlags.NonPublic |
                BindingFlags.Public | BindingFlags.DeclaredOnly;

    return (
        from t in type.GetMethods(flags)
        select String.Format("{0} {1}", t.IsPrivate ?
            "private" : "public", t.Name)
    ).ToList();
}
```

Invoking members

In .NET you can invoke objects using reflection which is done in the same basic way as with regular instantiations using C#; you first create an instance of the type then you call methods and use properties.

If you are using **static** members, there is no need to create an instance explicitly when using reflection.

A class named **Student** will be used from the assembly named *TestAssembly.dll*. The following code will be the set-up for coming examples.

```csharp
public class Student
{
    private int _id;

    public int Id { get { return _id; } set { _id = value; } }
    public string FirstName { get; set; }
    public string LastName { get; set; }
    public DateTime DateOfBirth { get; private set; }
    public static string School { get; set; }

    public Student()
    {
        DateOfBirth = DateTime.MinValue;
    }

    public Student(DateTime dateOfBirth)
    {
        DateOfBirth = dateOfBirth;
    }

    public int GetAge()
    {
        TimeSpan difference =
            DateTime.Now.Subtract(DateOfBirth);

        int ageInYears = (int)(difference.Days / 365.25);
        return ageInYears;
    }

    public int GetAge(DateTime dateOfBirth)
    {
        if (DateOfBirth == DateTime.MinValue ||
            dateOfBirth != DateOfBirth)
            DateOfBirth = dateOfBirth;

        return GetAge();
    }
}
```

Creating an instance of a type

To create an instance of **Type,** you use the **GetType** method on the assembly that you have loaded with the **LoadFrom** method of the **Assembly** class. When you have the **Type** loaded, you can use the **GetConstructor** method to fetch the desired constructor; matching the parameter signature with the array of **Types** that you pass in to the **GetConstructor** method, to get the default constructor, you pass in an empty array with a length of zero (0).

This sample code shows how you create an instance of a **Type** in an assembly loaded with reflection. Note that the return data type is **object** since the instance type is unknown at design time.

```
public static object CreateWithDefaultConstructor(Type type)
{
    try
    {
        var constructor = type.GetConstructor(new Type[0]);

        return constructor.Invoke(new object[0]);
    }
    catch { throw; }
}

public static object CreateWithSpecificConstructor(Type type)
{
    try
    {
        var constructor = type.GetConstructor(
            new Type[1] { typeof(DateTime) });

        return constructor.Invoke(
            new object[1] { new DateTime(1970, 5, 4) });
    }
    catch { throw; }
}
```

Calling methods

To call a method on a type in an assembly using reflection you call the **GetMethod** method on the instance's **Type** (use the **GetType** method), then call the **Invoke** method on the **MethodInfo** object returned from the **GetMethod** method; pass in the **Type** instance and the list of arguments (as an **object** array). Pass in an empty **object** array if it is a parameter-less method.

In the following example the method must return an **int** since that is the return data type of the **ExecuteMethod** method. You could make the method more generic with a little after-thought.

```
public static int ExecuteMethod(object instance, string methodName)
{
    try
    {
        var method = instance.GetType().GetMethod(methodName, new Type[0]);
        var value = method.Invoke(instance, new object[0]);
        return Convert.ToInt32(value);
    }
    catch
    {
        return Int32.MinValue;
    }
}
```

Setting property values

To assign a value to an instance property using reflection you first have to fetch the property from the instance **Type** calling the **GetProperty** method and then call the **SetValue** method on the **PropertyInfo** object returned from the **GetProperty** method to set the value of the property.

This example shows how you assign a value to an instance property using reflection.

```
public static void SetPropertyValue(object instance, string propertyName,
object value)
{
    var property = instance.GetType().GetProperty(propertyName);
    property.SetValue(instance, value);
}
```

To assign a value to a **static** property using reflection you first have to fetch the property from the **Type** calling the **GetProperty** method, no instance is needed. You can then call the **SetValue** method on the **PropertyInfo** object returned from the **GetProperty** method to set the value of the property.

This example shows how you assign a value to a **static** property using reflection.

```
private void SetStaticPropertyValue(Type type, string propertyName,
object value)
{
    var property = type.GetProperty(propertyName);
    property.SetValue(null, value);
}
```

Getting Property Values

To fetch a value from an instance property using reflection you first have to fetch the property from the instance **Type** calling the **GetProperty** method; you can then call the **GetValue** method on the **PropertyInfo** object returned from the **GetProperty** method to get the value of the property.

This example shows how you fetch a value from an instance property using reflection.

```
public static string GetPropertyValue(object instance, string propertyName)
{
    var property = instance.GetType().GetProperty(propertyName);
    var value = property.GetValue(instance);
    return value.ToString();
}
```

To fetch a value from a **static** property using reflection you first have to fetch the property from the Type calling the **GetProperty** method, no instance is needed; you can then call the **GetValue** method on the **PropertyInfo** object returned from the **GetProperty** method to set the value of the property.

This example shows how you fetch a value from a **static** property using reflection.

```
private string GetStaticPropertyValue(Type type, string propertyName)
{
    var property = type.GetProperty(propertyName);
    var value = property.GetValue(null);
    return value.ToString();
}
```

Exercise: Reflection

In this exercise you will use your knowledge about reflection to create a Windows Forms Application that uses a class library you will build with reflection methods to read information from the **Student** class type described earlier in this chapter, you will also read and update information in an instance of the **Student** class using reflection. The **Student** class will be created in a third assembly called **Test Assembly** and you will *reflect* over the .dll assembly crated when the project is built.

The first thing you want to display in the GUI is a list of all the types (classes) in the **TestAssembly** using a combo box called *cboTypes*. When a type is selected in the list the application will use reflection to list all the variables, properties, methods and constructors in the type using a list box called *lstInfo*.

Then you will add a button called *btnCallMethod* which will call the **GetAge** method on an instance of the **Student** class and display the result in a label called *lblResult*.

The last part of the exercise will be to change a value of the **FirstName** property when the button *btnSetProperty* is clicked using the value from a textbox called *txtValue* and then read that value back and display it in the *lblResult* label when the *btnGetProperty* is clicked.

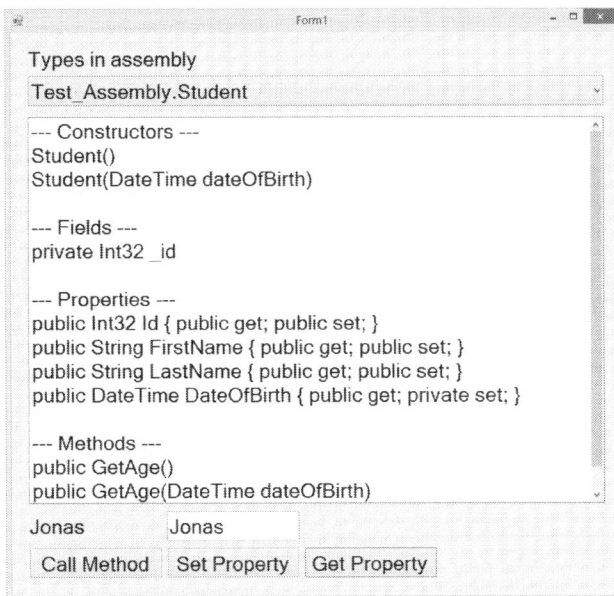

519

The solution setup

The solution consist of three projects one Windows Forms Application called **Reflection Application**, a class library for the reflection methods you will create called **Reflection Library** and a class library containing the **Student** class called **Test Assembly**.

You will create two classes in the **Reflection Library** assembly one called **LoadAssembly** which will contain the methods needed to load an assembly and another called **Members** which will contain the methods for reading and altering data in the assembly types.

1. Create a new Windows Forms Application called **Reflection Application**.
2. Add a new **Class Library** project called **Reflection Library** to the solution.
3. Add two classes called **LoadAssembly** and **Members**.
4. Change their accessibility to **public**.
5. Add a new **Class Library** project called **Test Assembly** to the solution.
6. Add a **public** class called **Student** and implement it according to the specification provided in the <u>Invoking Members</u> section of this chapter.

The GUI

1. Open the form's designer in the **Reflection Application** project (see image above).
2. Add a label with the text "Types in assembly".
3. Add a combo box called **cboTypes**; will later be filled with the names of all the types (classes) in the **Test Assembly.dll** assembly.
4. Add a list box called **lstInfo**; will list all the members of the type selected in the combo box.
5. Add a label called **lblResult** below the list box.
6. Add a textbox called **txtValue** beside the label to the right.
7. Add a button called **btnCallMethod** which will be used to call a method on the loaded type.
8. Add a button called **btnSetProperty** which will be used to assign a value to a property on the loaded type.
9. Add a button called **btnGetProperty** which will be used to read a value from a property on the loaded type.

Loading the assembly type

To be able to load the names of all the types in an assembly you need to load the assembly into memory calling the **Assembly.ReflectionOnlyLoadFrom** method and then the **GetTypes** method on the assembly instance. You then assign the result to the **DataSource** property of the *cboTypes* combo box.

To make the assembly code reusable you will create a **public static Assembly** method called **LoadReflectionOnly** with a **string** parameter called **assemblyPath** in the **LoadAssembly** class. The method loads the assembly using the **Assembly.ReflectionOnlyLoadFrom** method and returns the resulting readable assembly instance.

Important: *Creating the methods as **static** mean that you can call them without having to first create an instance of the class.*

The LoadAssembly class

1. Open the **LoadAssembly** class in the **Reflection Library** project.
2. Add a region called **Load Assembly**.
3. Add a **public static Assembly** method called **LoadReflectionOnly** with a **string** parameter called **assemblyPath**. This method will return a reflection only instance of the loaded assembly.
   ```
   public static Assembly LoadReflectionOnly(string assemblyPath)
   ```
4. Return the .dll assembly loaded from the path in the parameter. Use the **ReflectionOnlyLoadFrom** method on the **Assembly** class to load the assembly into memory.
   ```
   return Assembly.ReflectionOnlyLoadFrom(assemblyPath);
   ```

The code in the **LoadAssembly** class so far:

```
public class LoadAssembly
{
    #region Load Assembly
    public static Assembly LoadReflectionOnly(string assemblyPath)
    {
        // Reflection-only context
        return Assembly.ReflectionOnlyLoadFrom(assemblyPath);
    }
    #endregion
}
```

The Members class

1. Open the **Members** class in the **Reflection Library** project.
2. Add a region called **Type Methods**.
3. Add a **public static List<string>** method called **GetTypeNames** with an **Assembly** parameter called **assembly**. This method will return a list of the names of all types (classes, structs, ...) in the passed in assembly.

    ```
    public static List<string> GetTypeNames(Assembly assembly)
    ```

4. Return the **FullName** property of the types. The **GetTypes** method on the passed in assembly will fetch all types in the assembly. Use the **Select** LINQ method to fetch only the **FullName** property value of each type and chain on the **ToList** method at the end to create a list of the result.

    ```
    return assembly.GetTypes().Select(t => t.FullName).ToList();
    ```

The code in the **Members** class so far:

```
public class Members
{
    #region Type Methods
    public static List<string> GetTypeNames(Assembly assembly)
    {
        return assembly.GetTypes().Select(t => t.FullName).ToList();
    }
    #endregion
}
```

The form's Load event

To load a reflection only instance of the **Test Assembly** you need to provide the full path and file name to the **LoadReflectionOnly** method that you call from the form's **Load** event. Because the same path will be used multiple times you can create a **string** constant on form level to hold the value. You will also need to create an **Assembly** variable on form level to hold the instance you create. The last thing you will do in the **Load** event is to assign the result from a call to the **LoadReflectionOnly** method to the *cboTypes* combo box's **Data-Source** property; you don't need to specify a **DisplayMember** value since the collection you are assigning only contain a list of strings.

1. Open the form and add the its **Load** event to the code-behind.

2. Add a **string** constant called **assemblyPath** to the form's class and assign the path and file name to the **Test Assembly** .dll file. If you think that the path is overly long to where the .dll file is located you can always copy the .dll file to another directory closer to the root directory; don't place the file in the root directory because it often has safety restrictions.

3. Add an **Assembly** variable called **assembly** to the form class.
   ```
   Assembly assembly;
   ```

4. Add a call to the **LoadReflectionOnly** method from the **Load** event and store the **return** value in the **assembly** variable. Pass in the **assemblyPath** constant as the method's parameter.
   ```
   assembly = LoadAssembly.LoadReflectionOnly(assemblyPath);
   ```

5. Call the **GetTypeNames** method in the **Members** class and assign the result to the **DataSource** property of the *cboTypes* combo box.

6. Run the application and make sure that the **Students** class is listed in the combo box.

The form class so far:

```
public partial class Form1 : Form
{
    const string assemblyPath = @"C:\Sample Files\Test Assembly.dll";
    Assembly assembly;

    public Form1()
    {
        InitializeComponent();
    }

    private void Form1_Load(object sender, EventArgs e)
    {
        assembly = LoadAssembly.LoadReflectionOnly(assemblyPath);

        cboTypes.DataSource = Members.GetTypeNames(assembly);
    }
}
```

Fetching the constructors in the type

In this part of the exercise you will use the loaded assembly to fetch the information about its constructors and display that information in the *lstInfo* list box with one row per constructor.

To be able to fetch the type itself you will need to add a method called **GetType** which takes an **Assembly** parameter called **assembly** and a **string** parameter called **typeName**. The passed in assembly will be used when extracting the type specified by the **typeName** parameter using the **GetType** method on the assembly instance.

Once the type has been extracted in the **SelectedIndexChanged** event of the *cboTypes* combo box the **GetConstructor** method you will add to the **Members** class will fetch the information about the constructors and return it as a list of strings which are displayed in the *lstInfo* list box.

A nested loop is required to iterate over the constructors by calling the **GetConstructors** method on the passed in type and the **GetParameters** method on each constructor. Use the information to build a formatted **string** containing the constructor name and any parameters within parenthesis.

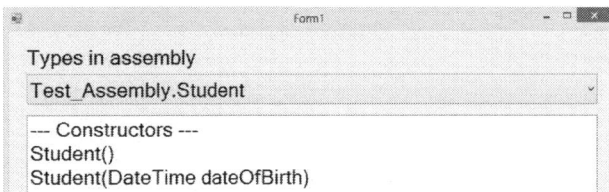

The GetType method

1. Locate the **Type Methods** region in the **Members** class.
2. Add a **public static Type** method called **GetType** which has an **Assembly** parameter called **assembly** and a **string** parameter called **typeName**.
   ```
   public static Type GetType(Assembly assembly, string typeName)
   ```
3. Return the result from a call to the **GetType** method on the **assembly** parameter passing in the **typeName** parameter to the method.

524

The **Members** class so far:

```
public class Members
{
    #region Type Methods
    public static List<string> GetTypeNames(Assembly assembly) ...
    public static Type GetType(Assembly assembly, string typeName)
    {
        return assembly.GetType(typeName);
    }
    #endregion
}
```

The GetConstructors method

1. Add a region called **Fetch Type Members** below the previously added region in the **Members** class.

2. Add a **public static List<string>** method called **GetConstructors** which has a **Type** parameter called **type**.
   ```
   public static List<string> GetConstructors(Type type)
   ```

3. Add a **List<string>** variable called **constructors** to the method and instantiate it.

4. Add a foreach loop iterating over the constructors returned from a call to the **Get-Constructors** method on the passed in type.

5. Add a new instance of the **StringBuilder** class called **ctor** which will be used to create the **string** representing the constructor and its parameters. Send in the **type** name and an open parenthesis to the **StringBuilder** constructor; you use the type name because a constructor always has the same name as the type it resides in and an open parenthesis because all methods has a at least an opening and a closing parenthesis after the method name.
   ```
   var ctor = new StringBuilder(String.Format("{0}(", type.Name));
   ```

6. Add another **StringBuilder** instance called **parameters** which will be used when building the list of parameters belonging to the constructor. Instantiate it with an empty constructor.

7. Add a foreach loop iterating over the result from a call to the **GetParameters** on the current constructor instance in the **constructor** variable in the outer loop.

8. Use the **Append** method on the **parameters StringBuilder** variable to add the constructor parameters to it using the **String.Format** method to add the parameter type and the parameter name with a space in between and a comma at the end.
```
parameters.Append(String.Format("{0} {1}, ",
parameter.ParameterType.Name, parameter.Name));
```

9. Add an **if**-statement checking if the length of the **parameters StringBuilder** variable is equal to **0**; if it is then there are no parameters and a closing parenthesis can be added to the **ctor** variable. If there are parameters then they have to be added to the **ctor** variable along with a closing parenthesis. Be sure to remove the ending comma and space from the **parameters** variable before adding the parameters to the **ctor** variable.
```
if(parameters.Length.Equals(0))
    ctor.Append(")");
else
    ctor.Append(String.Format("{0})",
parameters.ToString().Substring(0, parameters.Length - 2)));
```

10. Add the **ctor** variable to the **constructors** collection.

11. Return the **constructors** collection at the end of the method outside the loops.

The **Members** class so far:

```
public class Members
{
    #region Type Methods
    public static List<string> GetTypeNames(Assembly assembly) ...
    public static Type GetType(Assembly assembly, string typeName) ...
    #endregion

    #region Fetch Type Members
    public static List<string> GetConstructors(Type type)
    {
        // Iterate over the constructors
        var constructors = new List<string>();

        foreach (var constructor in type.GetConstructors())
        {
            var ctor = new StringBuilder(String.Format("{0}(", type.Name));
            var parameters = new StringBuilder();
```

```
        foreach (var parameter in constructor.GetParameters())
            parameters.Append(String.Format("{0} {1}, ",
                parameter.ParameterType.Name, parameter.Name));

        if(parameters.Length.Equals(0))
            ctor.Append(")");
        else
            ctor.Append(String.Format("{0})",
                parameters.ToString().Substring(0,
                parameters.Length - 2)));

        constructors.Add(ctor.ToString());
    }

    return constructors;
    }
}
#endregion
```

The SelectedIndexChanged event

1. Add the **SelectedIndexChanged** event for the *cboTypes* combo box.
2. Add a call to the **GetType** method and store the returned type in a variable called **type**. Pass in the assembly variable you added to the form class earlier and the text from the combo box to the method.
    ```
    var type = Members.GetType(assembly, cboTypes.Text);
    ```
3. Clear the content in the *lstInfo* list box.
4. Add an item with the text "--- Constructors ---" to the list box.
5. Add the list of constructors to the list box by passing in the result from a call to the **GetConstructors** method on the **Members** class to the **AddRange** method on the list box's **Items** collection.
    ```
    lstInfo.Items.AddRange(Members.GetConstructors(type).ToArray());
    ```
6. Add an empty item to the list box as a separator for the upcoming information.
7. Run the application and make sure that the constructors of the **Student** class are listed in the list box.

The form class so far:

```
public partial class Form1 : Form
{
    const string assemblyPath = @"C:\Sample Files\Test Assembly.dll";
    Assembly assembly;

    public Form1() ...

    private void Form1_Load(object sender, EventArgs e) ...
    private void cboTypes_SelectedIndexChanged(object sender, EventArgs e)
    {
        var type = Members.GetType(assembly, cboTypes.Text);

        lstInfo.Items.Clear();
        lstInfo.Items.Add("--- Constructors ---");
        lstInfo.Items.AddRange(Members.GetConstructors(type).ToArray());
        lstInfo.Items.Add("");
    }
}
```

Fetching the fields in the type

In this part of the exercise you will use the loaded assembly to fetch information about its fields (variables) and display that information in the *lstInfo* list box with one row per field.

Add a **public static List<string>** method called **GetFields** which has a **Type** parameter called **type** to the **Members** class; it will fetch the information about the fields and return it as a list of strings. The returned data will be displayed in the *lstInfo* list box using the **SelectedIndex-Changed** event of the *cboTypes* combo box.

You can use a LINQ query in the **GetFields** method on the passed in type and the **String .Format** method to format the output. You want to exclude any field with a "<" in its name because that is a field added by the system to back a property. The output should reflect whether the field is **public** or **private**, its data type and its name separated by spaces.

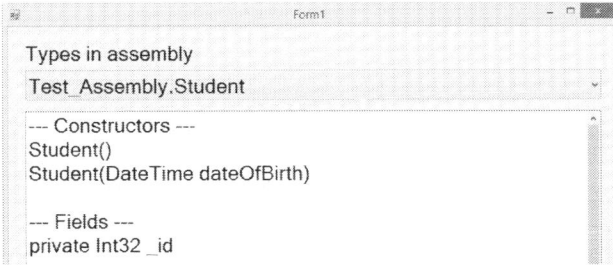

The GetFields method

1. Open the **Members** class and add a new region at the top of the class called **Constants**.

2. Add **BindingFlags** constant called **flags** to the region and assign the following values to it: **Instance**, **NonPublic**, **Public** and **DeclaredOnly**. These flags determine which members to include from the type.

   ```
   static BindingFlags flags =
         BindingFlags.Instance | BindingFlags.NonPublic |
         BindingFlags.Public | BindingFlags.DeclaredOnly;
   ```

3. Locate the **Fetch Type Members** region in the **Members** class.

4. Add a **public static List<string>** method called **GetFields** which has a **Type** parameter called **type**.

   ```
   public static List<string> GetFields(Type type)
   ```

5. Return the result from a LINQ query fetching the fields by calling the **GetFields** method on the **type** parameter passing in the list of **BindingFlags** from the **flags** constant to the method.

   ```
   from t in type.GetFields(flags)
   where !t.Name.Contains("<")
   select String.Format("{0} {1} {2}", t.IsPrivate ?
         "private" : "public", t.FieldType.Name, t.Name)
   ```

The **Members** class so far:

```
public class Members
{
    #region Constants
    static BindingFlags flags =
        BindingFlags.Instance | BindingFlags.NonPublic |
        BindingFlags.Public | BindingFlags.DeclaredOnly;
    #endregion
```

```
#region Type Methods
public static List<string> GetTypeNames(Assembly assembly) ...
public static Type GetType(Assembly assembly, string typeName) ...
#endregion

#region Fetch Type Members
public static List<string> GetConstructors(Type type) ...
public static List<string> GetFields(Type type)
{
    return (
        from t in type.GetFields(flags)
        where !t.Name.Contains("<")
        select String.Format("{0} {1} {2}", t.IsPrivate ?
            "private" : "public", t.FieldType.Name, t.Name)
    ).ToList();
}
#endregion
```

The SelectedIndexChanged event

1. Locate the **SelectedIndexChanged** event for the *cboTypes* combo box in the form's code-behind file.
2. Add an item with the text "--- Fields ---" to the list box.
3. Add the list of fields to the list box by passing in the result from a call to the **Get-Fields** method on the **Members** class to the **AddRange** method on the list box's **Items** collection.
    ```
    lstInfo.Items.AddRange(Members.GetFields(type).ToArray());
    ```
4. Add an empty item to the list box as a separator for the upcoming information.
5. Run the application and make sure that the fields of the **Student** class have been added to the list box.

The combo box's **SelectedIndexChanged** event so far:

```
private void cboTypes_SelectedIndexChanged(object sender, EventArgs e)
{
    var type = Members.GetType(assembly, cboTypes.Text);

    lstInfo.Items.Clear();
    lstInfo.Items.Add("--- Constructors ---");
    lstInfo.Items.AddRange(Members.GetConstructors(type).ToArray());
    lstInfo.Items.Add("");
```

```
lstInfo.Items.Add("--- Fields ---");
lstInfo.Items.AddRange(Members.GetFields(type).ToArray());
lstInfo.Items.Add("");
}
```

Fetching the properties in the type

In this part of the exercise you will use the loaded assembly to fetch information about its properties and display that information in the *lstInfo* list box with one row per property.

Add a **public static List<string>** method called **GetProperties** to the **Members** class which has a **Type** parameter called **type**; it will fetch the information about the properties and return it as a list of strings. The returned data will be displayed in the *lstInfo* list box using the **SelectedIndexChanged** event of the *cboTypes* combo box.

You can use a LINQ query in the **GetProperties** method on the passed in type and use the **String.Format** method to format the output. The output should reflect whether the property is **public** or **private**, its data type, its name, whether the getter and setters are **public** or **private**; use the following format: "{0} {1} {2} {{ {3} get; {4} set; }}".

Use the **GetGetMethod** and **GetSetMethod** methods on the current type to fetch information about the getter and setter.

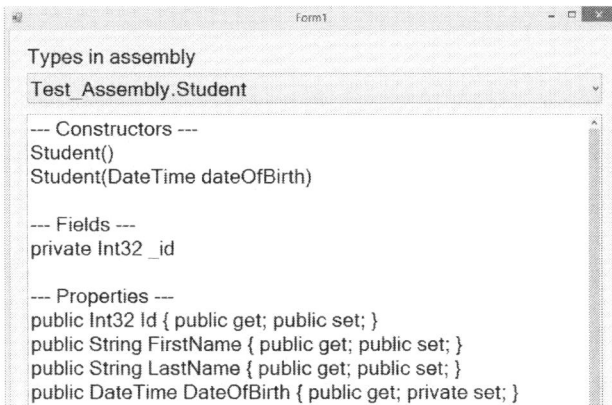

The GetProperties method

1. Open the **Members** class and locate the **Fetch Type Members** region.
2. Add a **public static List<string>** method called **GetProperties** which has a **Type** parameter called **type**.

```
public static List<string> GetProperties(Type type)
```

3. Return the result from a LINQ query fetching the properties by calling the **GetProp-erties** method on the **type** parameter passing in the list of **BindingFlags** from the **flags** constant to the method.

The **Members** class so far:

```
public class Members
{
    #region Constants
    static BindingFlags flags = ...
    #endregion

    #region Type Methods
    public static List<string> GetTypeNames(Assembly assembly) ...
    public static Type GetType(Assembly assembly, string typeName) ...
    #endregion

    #region Fetch Type Members
    public static List<string> GetConstructors(Type type) ...
    public static List<string> GetFields(Type type) ...
    public static List<string> GetProperties(Type type)
    {
        return (
            from t in type.GetProperties(flags)
            select String.Format(
                "{0} {1} {2} {{ {3} get; {4} set; }}",
                t.GetMethod.IsPrivate ? "private" : "public",
                t.PropertyType.Name,
                t.Name,
                t.GetGetMethod(true).IsPrivate ?
                    "private" : "public",
                t.GetSetMethod(true).IsPrivate ?
                    "private" : "public")
        ).ToList();
    }
    #endregion
```

The SelectedIndexChanged event

1. Locate the **SelectedIndexChanged** event for the *cboTypes* combo box in the form's code-behind file.

2. Add an item with the text "--- Properties ---" to the list box.

3. Add the list of fields to the list box by passing in the result from a call to the **Get-Properties** method on the **Members** class to the **AddRange** method on the list box's **Items** collection.
   `lstInfo.Items.AddRange(Members.GetProperties(type).ToArray());`

4. Add an empty item to the list box as a separator for the upcoming information.

5. Run the application and make sure that the properties of the **Student** class have been added to the list box.

The combo box's **SelectedIndexChanged** event so far:

```
private void cboTypes_SelectedIndexChanged(object sender, EventArgs e)
{
    var type = Members.GetType(assembly, cboTypes.Text);

    lstInfo.Items.Clear();
    lstInfo.Items.Add("--- Constructors ---");
    lstInfo.Items.AddRange(Members.GetConstructors(type).ToArray());
    lstInfo.Items.Add("");
    lstInfo.Items.Add("--- Fields ---");
    lstInfo.Items.AddRange(Members.GetFields(type).ToArray());
    lstInfo.Items.Add("");
    lstInfo.Items.Add("--- Properties ---");
    lstInfo.Items.AddRange(Members.GetProperties(type).ToArray());
    lstInfo.Items.Add("");
}
```

Fetching the methods in the type

In this part of the exercise you will use the loaded assembly to fetch information about its methods and display that information in the *lstInfo* list box with one row per method.

Add a **public static List<string>** method called **GetMethods** which has a **Type** parameter called **type** to the **Members** class which will fetch the information about the methods and return it as a list of strings. The returned data will be displayed in the *lstInfo* list box using the **SelectedIndexChanged** event of the *cboTypes* combo box.

You can use the result from a LINQ query in conjunction with a loop in the **GetMethods** method on the passed in type and use the **String.Format** method to format the output. The output should reflect whether the method is **public** or **private**, its data type, its name, and a list of its parameters; use the following format: "{0} {1} {2}({3})".

You want to exclude any method with a name that contain **get_** or **set_** because that is a property.

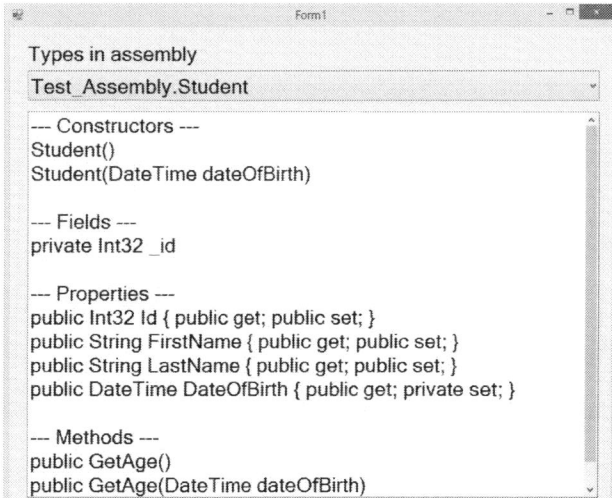

```
                          Form1                    - □ ×
Types in assembly
Test_Assembly.Student                                      ▼

--- Constructors ---                                        ▲
Student()
Student(DateTime dateOfBirth)

--- Fields ---
private Int32 _id

--- Properties ---
public Int32 Id { public get; public set; }
public String FirstName { public get; public set; }
public String LastName { public get; public set; }
public DateTime DateOfBirth { public get; private set; }

--- Methods ---
public GetAge()
public GetAge(DateTime dateOfBirth)                         ▼
```

The GetMethods method

1. Open the **Members** class and locate the **Fetch Type Members** region.
2. Add a **public static List<string>** method called **GetMethods** with a **Type** parameter called **type**.
   ```
   public static List<string> GetMethods(Type type)
   ```
3. Add a **List<string>** variable called **result** and instantiate it.
4. Save the result from a LINQ query fetching the methods by calling the **GetMethods** method on the **type** parameter in a variable called **methods**, pass in the list of **BindingFlags** from the **flags** constant to the method. You also want to exclude any methods with a name that contain **get_** or **set_** because that is a property.
   ```
   var methods =
       from method in type.GetMethods(flags)
       where !method.Name.Contains("get_") &&
           !method.Name.Contains("set_")
       select method;
   ```
5. Add a **foreach** loop which iterates over the methods in the **methods** variable.
6. Add a **StringBuilder** variable called **parameters** to the loop.
7. Add a nested loop iterating over the parameters in each method by calling the **GetParameters** method on the current method in the outer loop.

```
        foreach (var parameter in method.GetParameters())
```

8. Append the parameter info to the **parameters StringBuilder** variable; display the data type and parameter name for each parameter.

9. Remove any trailing comma and space in the **parameters** variable.

10. Add the method information to the **result** collection where each string represent one method's data. The string should show if the method is **public** or **private**, its return data type, its name, and its list of parameters inside parenthesis. Use the following format: "{0} {1} {2}({3})".

11. Return the **result** collection at the end of the method outside the loops.

The **Members** class so far:

```
public class Members
{
    #region Constants
    static BindingFlags flags = ...
    #endregion

    #region Type Methods
    public static List<string> GetTypeNames(Assembly assembly) ...
    public static Type GetType(Assembly assembly, string typeName) ...
    #endregion

    #region Fetch Type Members
    public static List<string> GetConstructors(Type type) ...
    public static List<string> GetFields(Type type) ...
    public static List<string> GetProperties(Type type) ...
    public static List<string> GetMethods(Type type)
    {
        var result = new List<string>();
        var methods =
            from method in type.GetMethods(flags)
            where !method.Name.Contains("get_") &&
                !method.Name.Contains("set_")
            select method;

        foreach (var method in methods)
        {
            var parameters = new StringBuilder();
```

```
        foreach (var parameter in method.GetParameters())
            parameters.Append(String.Format("{0} {1}, ",
                parameter.ParameterType.Name, parameter.Name));

        if (parameters.Length > 0)
            parameters.Remove(parameters.Length - 2, 2);

        result.Add(String.Format("{0} {1} {2}({3})",
            method.IsPrivate ? "private" : "public",
            method.ReturnType.Name,
            method.Name,
            parameters.ToString()));
    }
    return result;
}
#endregion
```

The SelectedIndexChanged event

1. Locate the **SelectedIndexChanged** event for the *cboTypes* combo box in the form's code-behind file.

2. Add an item with the text "--- Methods ---" to the list box.

3. Add the list of methods to the list box by passing in the result from a call to the **Get-Methods** method on the **Members** class to the **AddRange** method on the list box's **Items** collection.
   ```
   lstInfo.Items.AddRange(Members.GetMethods(type).ToArray());
   ```

4. Add an empty item to the list box as a separator for the upcoming information.

5. Run the application and make sure that the methods of the **Student** class have been added to the list box.

The complete code for the combo box's **SelectedIndexChanged** event:

```
private void cboTypes_SelectedIndexChanged(object sender, EventArgs e)
{
    var type = Members.GetType(assembly, cboTypes.Text);

    lstInfo.Items.Clear();
    lstInfo.Items.Add("--- Constructors ---");
    lstInfo.Items.AddRange(Members.GetConstructors(type).ToArray());
    lstInfo.Items.Add("");
    lstInfo.Items.Add("--- Fields ---");
    lstInfo.Items.AddRange(Members.GetFields(type).ToArray());
```

```
lstInfo.Items.Add("");
lstInfo.Items.Add("--- Properties ---");
lstInfo.Items.AddRange(Members.GetProperties(type).ToArray());
lstInfo.Items.Add("");
lstInfo.Items.Add("--- Methods ---");
lstInfo.Items.AddRange(Members.GetMethods(type).ToArray());
}
```

Calling a method in the type

In this part of the exercise you will use the assembly instance to call an **object** method called **ExecuteMethod** which has an **object** parameter called **instance** that holds the instance of the desired type and a **string** parameter called **methodName** which holds the name of the method to call on the instance. Call the **GetMethod** method on the **GetType** method on the passed in instance to specify which method you want to call, store the definition in a variable called **method**; pass in the **methodName** parameter and an empty **Type** array (because you are not passing in any parameters to the method). To call the method you have to call the **Invoke** method on the **method** variable, store the return value from the method call in a variable called **result**. return the **result** variable from the method if no exception was thrown and **null** from the **catch**-block if an exception was thrown.

Display the returned value from the **ExecuteMethod** method call in a label called *lblResult*.

To be able to call a method on an instance of a type created with reflection you have to call the **LoadFrom** method on the **Assembly** class, you will add a method to the **LoadAssembly** class called **LoadExecutable** which returns the created assembly. You cannot use the **Load-ReflectionOnly** method since it only return reflection data and not a fully created assembly instance.

Add an **object** method called **CreateWithSpecificConstructor** to the **Members** class which has a **Type** parameter called **type** and a **DateTime** parameter called **date**. Add a **try/catch**-block where the **catch**-block re-throws any exception. In the **try**-block you first have to add a variable called **constructor** that will hold the definition of the constructor and then invoke that constructor by calling the **Invoke** method on the **constructor** variable. Pass in the list of necessary parameters as a comma separated list in a **Type** array to the **GetConstructor** method and the values for those parameters in a comma separated list in an **object** array to the **Invoke** method.

```
var constructor = type.GetConstructor(new Type[1] { typeof(DateTime) });
return constructor.Invoke(new object[1] { date });
```

Add a **try/catch**-block to the **_btnCallMethod_** button and display the exception message in a message box if an exception is thrown.

Load the assembly into memory by calling the **LoadExecutable** method in the **LoadAssembly** class and store the result in the **assembly** variable on form level.

Fetch the selected type name from the combo box and pass it and the assembly as parameter values to the **GetType** method in the **Members** class to get the type definition of the class with the selected type name in the assembly, store the type in a variable called **type**.

Call the **CreateWithSpecificConstructor** method in the **Members** class to create an instance of the type and store it in a variable called **instance**.

Call the **ExecuteMethod** method with the **instance** variable and the name of the method (**GetAge**) you want to call and display the **return** value in the **_lblResult_** label.

The LoadExecutable method
1. Open the **LoadAssembly** class and locate the **Load Assembly** region.
2. Add a **public static Assembly** method called **LoadExecutable** which has a **string** parameter called **assemblyPath**.
   ```
   public static Assembly LoadExecutable(string assemblyPath)
   ```
3. Return the result from a call to the **Assembly.LoadFrom** method passing in the **assemblyPath** parameter to it.

The **LoadAssembly** class so far:

```
public class LoadAssembly
{
    #region Load Assembly
    public static Assembly LoadReflectionOnly(string assemblyPath) ...
    public static Assembly LoadExecutable(string assemblyPath)
    {
        // Executable context
        return Assembly.LoadFrom(assemblyPath);
    }
    #endregion
}
```

The CreateWithSpecificConstructor method

1. Open the **Members** class and add a region called **Instance Members**.
2. Add a **public static object** method called **CreateWithSpecificConstructor** which has a **Type** parameter called **type** and a **DateTime** parameter called **date**.
   ```
   public static object CreateWithSpecificConstructor(Type type,
   DateTime date)
   ```
3. Add a **try/catch**-block where the **catch**-block re-throws any exception.
4. Add a **List<string>** variable called **result** and instantiate it.
5. Call the **GetConstructor** method on the passed in type specifying that the construct-or definition should have a **DateTime** parameter.
   ```
   var constructor = type.GetConstructor(new Type[1] { typeof(DateTime)
   });
   ```
6. Return the result from a call to the **Invoke** method on the constructor variable pass-ing in the date from the **date** parameter.
   ```
   return constructor.Invoke(new object[1] { date });
   ```

The **Members** class so far:

```
public class Members
{
    #region Constants
    static BindingFlags flags = ...
    #endregion

    #region Type Methods
    public static List<string> GetTypeNames(Assembly assembly) ...
```

```
public static Type GetType(Assembly assembly, string typeName) ...
#endregion

#region Fetch Type Members
public static List<string> GetConstructors(Type type) ...
public static List<string> GetFields(Type type) ...
public static List<string> GetProperties(Type type) ...
public static List<string> GetMethods(Type type) ...
#endregion

#region Instance Members
public static object CreateWithSpecificConstructor(Type type,
DateTime date)
{
    try
    {
        var constructor = type.GetConstructor(
          new Type[1] { typeof(DateTime) });

        return constructor.Invoke(new object[1] { date });
    }
    catch { throw; }
}
#endregion

}
```

The ExecuteMethod method

1. Open the **Members** class and locate the **Instance Members** region.

2. Add a **public static object** method called **ExecuteMethod** that has an **object** parameter called **instance** which is the instance crated from the class and a **string**
parameter called **methodName** which is the name of the method to call.
```
public static object ExecuteMethod(object instance, string
methodName)
```

3. Add a **try/catch**-block where the **catch**-block return **null**.

4. Call the **GetMethod** method on the **GetType** method on the **instance** parameter,
store the result in a variable called **method**. Pass in the **methodName** parameter
and an empty **Type** array to the **GetMethod** method.
```
var method = instance.GetType().GetMethod(methodName, new Type[0]);
```

5. Return the result from a call to the **Invoke** method on the **method** variable passing in the **instance** parameter and an empty **object** array.

```
return method.Invoke(instance, new object[0]);
```

The **Members** class so far:

```
public class Members
{
    #region Constants
    static BindingFlags flags = ...
    #endregion

    #region Type Methods
    public static List<string> GetTypeNames(Assembly assembly) ...
    public static Type GetType(Assembly assembly, string typeName) ...
    #endregion

    #region Fetch Type Members
    public static List<string> GetConstructors(Type type) ...
    public static List<string> GetFields(Type type) ...
    public static List<string> GetProperties(Type type) ...
    public static List<string> GetMethods(Type type) ...
    #endregion

    #region Instance Members
    public static object CreateWithSpecificConstructor(Type type,
        DateTime date) ...
    public static object ExecuteMethod(object instance, string methodName)
    {
        try
        {
            var method = instance.GetType().GetMethod(methodName,
              new Type[0]);
            return method.Invoke(instance, new object[0]);
        }
        catch
        {
            return null;
        }
    }
    #endregion
}
```

The Call Method button Click event

1. Add the ***btnCallMethod*** button's **Click** event to the code-behind.
2. Add a **try/catch**-block where the **catch**-block displays the exception message in a message box.
3. Call the **LoadExecutable** method on the **LoadAssembly** class and pass in the **assemblyPath** constant to it, store the resulting assembly in the **assembly** variable that you added to the form class in the beginning of the exercise.

   ```
   assembly = LoadAssembly.LoadExecutable(assemblyPath);
   ```

4. Call the **GetType** method on the **Members** class passing in the **assembly** variable and the text from the selected item in the combo box. Store the resulting type in a variable called **type**.

   ```
   var type = Members.GetType(assembly, cboTypes.Text);
   ```

5. Create an instance of the type definition in the **type** variable by calling the **Create-WithSpecificConstructor** method on the **Members** class passing in the **type** variable and a date. Store the result in a variable called **instance**.

   ```
   var instance = Members.CreateWithSpecificConstructor(type,
       new DateTime(1970, 5, 4));
   ```

6. Call the **ExecuteMethod** method on the **Members** class passing in the **instance** variable and the name of the method to call (**GetAge**); display the result in the ***lblResult*** label.

   ```
   lblResult.Text = Members.ExecuteMethod(instance,
       "GetAge").ToString();
   ```

7. Run the application and click the **Call Method** button and the age should appear in the label.

The form class so far:

```
public partial class Form1 : Form
{
    const string assemblyPath = @"C:\Sample Files\Test Assembly.dll";
    Assembly assembly;

    public Form1() ...

    private void Form1_Load(object sender, EventArgs e) ...
```

```
private void cboTypes_SelectedIndexChanged(object sender,
    EventArgs e) ...
private void btnCallMethod_Click(object sender, EventArgs e)
{
    try
    {
        assembly = LoadAssembly.LoadExecutable(assemblyPath);
        var type = Members.GetType(assembly, cboTypes.Text);
        var instance = Members.CreateWithSpecificConstructor(
            type, new DateTime(1970, 5, 4));
        lblResult.Text = Members.ExecuteMethod(instance,
            "GetAge").ToString();
    }
    catch (Exception ex)
    {
        MessageBox.Show(ex.Message);
    }
}
}
```

Saving and reading a value from a property

In this part of the exercise you will use the assembly instance to assign and read a value stored in a property.

Since you already have called a constructor with a parameter you will now call the default constructor when creating the instance of the type. To achieve this you will add a new method to the **Members** class called **CreateWithDefaultConstructor** which has a **Type** parameter called **type**. In the method you will fetch the constructor definition and create the instance from the type like before only this time you will pass in an empty **Type array** to the **GetConstructor** method and an empty **object** array to the **Invoke** method.

Add an **object** method called **SetPropertyValue** which have an **object** parameter called **instance**, a **string** parameter called **propertyName** and an **object** property called **value** to the **Members** class. In the method you call the **GetProperty** method with the **propertyName** parameter on the **GetType** method on the **instance** parameter to fetch the property definition into a variable called **property**. Call the **SetValue** method on the **property** variable passing in the **instance** and the **value** parameters to assign the value to the property.

Add an **object** method called **GetPropertyValue** which has an **object** parameter called **instance** and a **string** parameter called **propertyName** to the **Members** class. In the method you call the **GetProperty** method with the **propertyName** parameter on the **GetType** method on the **instance** parameter to fetch the property definition into a variable called **property**. Return the result from a call to the **SetValue** method on the **property** variable passing in the **instance** parameter to read the value from the property.

Since both buttons involved in reading and writing to the property must use the same instance of the type you have to add an **object** variable called **instance** to the form class that will hold the instance created when the value is assigned to the property in the ***btnSetProperty*** button's **Click** event.

Both the ***btnSetProperty*** and ***btnGetProperty*** buttons will have **try/catch**-blocks where the exception message is displayed to the user with a message box in the **catch**-block.

The **LoadExecutable** method will be called in the ***btnSetProperty*** button's **try**-block to load the assembly into memory. Then the **GetType** method will be called to load the type (class) into memory and that type will be used to create the instance by calling the **CreateWith-DefaultConstructor** method. When the instance has been created it can be passed into the **SetPropertyValue** method along with the name of the property you want to assign the value to and the actual value fetched from the ***txtValue*** textbox.

The SetProperty and GetProperty methods

1. Open the **Members** class and locate the **Instance Members** region.
2. Add a **public static void** method called **SetProperty** which has an **object** parameter called **instance** (the instance crated from the class), a **string** parameter called **propertyName** which is the name of the property to assign the value to and an **object** parameter called **value** which is the value to assign to the property.
   ```
   public static void SetPropertyValue(object instance, string
   propertyName, object value)
   ```
3. Add a **try/catch**-block where the **catch**-block re-throws any exception.
4. Call the **GetProperty** method on the **GetType** method on the **instance** parameter, store the result in a variable called **property**. Pass in the **propertyName** parameter to the **GetProperty** method.
   ```
   var method = instance.GetType().GetProperty(propertyName);
   ```

544

5. Call the **SetValue** method on the **property** variable passing in the **instance** and **value** parameters to assign the value to the property.
   ```
   property.SetValue(instance, value);
   ```

6. Add a **public static object** method called **GetProperty** which has an **object** parameter called **instance** (the instance crated from the class) and a **string** parameter called **propertyName** which is the name of the property to retrieve the value from.
   ```
   public static object GetPropertyValue(object instance, string
   propertyName)
   ```

7. Add a **try/catch**-block where the **catch**-block re-throws any exception.

8. Call the **GetProperty** method on the **GetType** method on the **instance** parameter, store the result in a variable called **property**. Pass in the **propertyName** parameter to the **GetProperty** method.
   ```
   var method = instance.GetType().GetProperty(propertyName);
   ```

9. Return the result from a call to the **GetValue** method on the **property** variable passing in the **instance** parameter to fetch the value stored in the property.
   ```
   return property.GetValue(instance);
   ```

The **Members** class so far:

```
public class Members
{
    #region Constants
    static BindingFlags flags = ...
    #endregion

    #region Type Methods
    public static List<string> GetTypeNames(Assembly assembly) ...
    public static Type GetType(Assembly assembly, string typeName) ...
    #endregion

    #region Fetch Type Members
    public static List<string> GetConstructors(Type type) ...
    public static List<string> GetFields(Type type) ...
    public static List<string> GetProperties(Type type) ...
    public static List<string> GetMethods(Type type) ...
    #endregion
```

```
#region Instance Members
public static object CreateWithSpecificConstructor(Type type,
    DateTime date) ...
public static object ExecuteMethod(object instance,
    string methodName) ...
public static void SetPropertyValue(object instance,
string propertyName, object value)
{
    try
    {
        var property = instance.GetType().GetProperty(propertyName);
        property.SetValue(instance, value);
    }
    catch { throw; }
}

public static object GetPropertyValue(object instance,
string propertyName)
{
    try
    {
        var property = instance.GetType().GetProperty(propertyName);
        return property.GetValue(instance);
    }
    catch { throw; }
}
#endregion
}
```

The CreateWithDefaultConstructor method

1. Open the **Members** class and locate the **Instance Members** region.

2. Add a **public static object** method called **CreateWithDefaultConstructor** which has a
   Type parameter called **type**.
   ```
   public static object CreateWithDefaultConstructor(Type type)
   ```

3. Add a **try/catch**-block where the **catch**-block re-throws any exception.

4. Call the **GetConstructor** method on the **type** parameter passing in an empty **Type**
   array. Store the result in a variable called **constructor**.
   ```
   var constructor = type.GetConstructor(new Type[0]);
   ```

5. Return the result from a call to the **Invoke** method on the **constructor** variable passing in an empty **object array**.

```
        return constructor.Invoke(new object[0]);
```

The complete code for the **Members** class:

```
public class Members
{
    #region Constants
    static BindingFlags flags = ...
    #endregion

    #region Type Methods
    public static List<string> GetTypeNames(Assembly assembly) ...
    public static Type GetType(Assembly assembly, string typeName) ...
    #endregion

    #region Fetch Type Members
    public static List<string> GetConstructors(Type type) ...
    public static List<string> GetFields(Type type) ...
    public static List<string> GetProperties(Type type) ...
    public static List<string> GetMethods(Type type) ...
    #endregion

    #region Instance Members
    public static object CreateWithSpecificConstructor(Type type,
        DateTime date) ...
    public static object ExecuteMethod(object instance,
        string methodName) ...
    public static void SetPropertyValue(object instance,
        string propertyName, object value) ...
    public static object GetPropertyValue(object instance,
        string propertyName) ...
    public static object CreateWithDefaultConstructor(Type type)
    {
        try
        {
            var constructor = type.GetConstructor(new Type[0]);
            return constructor.Invoke(new object[0]);
        }
        catch { throw; }
    }
    #endregion
}
```

The Set Property button's Click event

1. Add the ***btnSetProperty*** button's **Click** event to the code-behind.
2. Add an **object** variable called **instance** to the form's class.
3. Add a **try/catch**-block to the **Click** event where the **catch**-block displays the exception message in a message box.
4. Call the **LoadExecutable** method on the **LoadAssembly** class passing in the **assemblyPath** constant. Store the result in the **assembly** varaible on form level.
5. Call the **GetType** method on the **Members** class passing in the **assembly** variable and the text from the item selected in the combo box. Store the result in a variable called **type**.
6. Call the **CreateWithDefaultConstructor** method on the **Members** class passing in the **type** variable. Store the result in the **instance** variable you just added to the form's class.
   ```
   instance = Members.CreateWithDefaultConstructor(type);
   ```
7. Call the **SetPropertyValue** method on the **Members** class passing in the **instance** variable, the name of the property to store the value in (**FirstName**) and the value to store from the ***txtValue*** textbox.
   ```
   Members.SetPropertyValue(instance, "FirstName", txtValue.Text);
   ```

The complete code for the ***btnSetProperty*** button's **Click** event:

```
private void btnSetProperty_Click(object sender, EventArgs e)
{
    try
    {
        assembly = LoadAssembly.LoadExecutable(assemblyPath);
        var type = Members.GetType(assembly, cboTypes.Text);
        instance = Members.CreateWithDefaultConstructor(type);
        Members.SetPropertyValue(instance, "FirstName", txtValue.Text);
    }
    catch (Exception ex)
    {
        MessageBox.Show(ex.Message);
    }
}
```

The Get Property button's Click event

You don't have to create the instance of the type since that was done in the ***btnSetProperty-Value*** button's **Click** event and stored in a form level variable called **instance**.

1. Add the ***btnGetProperty*** button's **Click** event to the code-behind.
2. Add a **try/catch**-block to the **Click** event where the **catch**-block displays the exception message in a message box.
3. Assign the result from a call to the **GetPropertyValue** method on the **Members** class passing in the **instance** variable and the name of the property to fetch the value from to the ***lblResult*** label.
   ```
   lblResult.Text = Members.GetPropertyValue(instance,
       FirstName").ToString();
   ```
4. Run the application and enter a value in the textbox.
5. Click the **Set Property** button to save the value in the **FirstName** property of the **Student** class instance.
6. Click the **Get Property** button to fetch the value stored in the **FirstName** property. The value should be displayed in the label.

The complete code for the ***btnGetProperty*** button's **Click** event:

```
private void btnSetProperty_Click(object sender, EventArgs e)
{
    try
    {
        assembly = LoadAssembly.LoadExecutable(assemblyPath);
        var type = Members.GetType(assembly, cboTypes.Text);
        instance = Members.CreateWithDefaultConstructor(type);
        Members.SetPropertyValue(instance, "FirstName", txtValue.Text);
    }
    catch (Exception ex)
    {
        MessageBox.Show(ex.Message);
    }
}
```

16. Generics

Why use generics?

In this section you will learn about why you might want to use generics and why they are a powerful tool in your C# coding tool belt.

Generics is a powerful way of reusing code in a type safe manner. Imagine what would happen if you executed the following code:

```
public void UseArrayList()
{
    ArrayList books = new ArrayList();
    books.Add(new Book("Lord of the Rings"));
    books.Add(new Book("The Color of Magic"));

    // We can add an object which is not of the Books class
    books.Add(new Car());

    // The run-time will throw an exception because
    // you cannot cast a Car to a Book
    Book book = (Book)books[2];
}
```

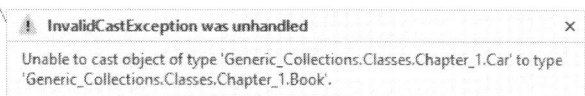

The application would throw an exception because it is not possible to cast an object created with the **Car** class to an object of the **Book** class. You could of course circumvent the problem by adding additional checks to the code like if-blocks, but that would be cumbersome and unmanageable. You would essentially have to add checks for every existing and future type to be "safe".

```
Book book = (Book)books[2];
```

⚠ **InvalidCastException was unhandled**   ✕

Unable to cast object of type 'Generic_Collections.Classes.Chapter_1.Car' to type 'Generic_Collections.Classes.Chapter_1.Book'.

Collections

Wouldn't it be nice if there was a way to state what type of object should be stored in a collection without the hassle of adding a lot of extra logic to your code such as casting objects and avoiding boxing and un-boxing of value types being stored?

Constraining a collection

As you probably already have guessed, there is. The name of the valiant knight on the white steed saving the day is *Generics*. Generics is a way to postpone stating the type to be used until the instance of the class is created.

Note that as you write the open angle bracket after the **List** class a gray pop-up message is telling you that it is a generic list which takes types of **T** where **T** is substituted with the actual type you want to use with the list. Once you state the type the generic list becomes a *closed* generic list which only can work with the provided type.

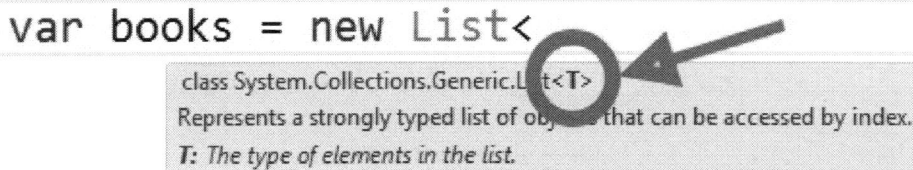

```
var books = new List<
```
class System.Collections.Generic.List<T>
Represents a strongly typed list of objects that can be accessed by index.
T: The type of elements in the list.

Note that a closed generic list is used as a return type for the method returning the book list that is created in the method.

```csharp
public List<Book> UseGenericCollection()
{
    var books = new List<Book>
    {
        new Book{ ISBN = "1234567890", Title = "Lord of the Rings"},
        new Book { ISBN = "0987654321", Title = "The Color of Magic" }
    };

    // It is no longer possible to add objects other than Books to the list
    //books.Add(new Car { ChassiId = "1223ABDS23", Make = "Volvo" });

    return books;
}
```

```
books.Add(new  Car  { ChassiId = "1223ABDS23", Make = "Volvo" });|
```
(local variable) List<Book> books

Error:
   The best overloaded method match for 'System.Collections.Generic.List<Generic_Collections.Classes.Chapter_1.Book>.Add(Generic_Collections.Classes.

If you try to add a **Car** to the **Book** list a pre-compile error will be displayed.

Creating a specialized collection using generics

Let's say that you have realized that your application framework could use a specialized collection which easily can reverse the content of a collection. To achieve this you could create a class which takes a generic type and implements the **IEnumerable** interface making it possible to iterate over the stored items.

This example is a bit contrived, I know, but it serves the purpose to show you how you can use generics with classes, methods, method parameters, fields and as a return type. You will also learn how to use the **yield** keyword to create a list result when looping.

To begin you have to add a class called **ReversableCollection** which implements the generic **IEnumerable<T>** version of the **IEnumerable** interface.

Important: *The **yield** keyword builds a state machine which will implement an IEnumerator <T> and return the modified or sorted items when the iteration has finished.*

```csharp
class ReverasbleCollection<T> : IEnumerable<T>
{
    #region Implementation of IEnumerable<T>

    public IEnumerator<T> GetEnumerator()
    {
        foreach (var item in collection)
        {
            yield return item;
        }
    }

    IEnumerator IEnumerable.GetEnumerator()
    {
        // Calls the other GetEnumerator
        // method and return its result
```

```
        return GetEnumerator();
    }

    #endregion
}
```

Next you need to enable to save items of type **T** in an **private** collection which cannot be reached outside the class. The list will store the items added through the **Add** and **AddRange** methods which you will add next.

Because you have implemented the class with the generic type of **T** which means that **T** now can be used throughout the whole class. You will take advantage of this when adding a **List<T>** named **collection** which will store the items added to the collection. You will also use the generic type **T** when creating the **Add(T item)** and **AddRange(T[] item)** methods to the class.

In the **Add** method you simply add the passed in item to the **List<T>** collection by calling its **Add** method. You do the same in the **AddRange** method but call the **AddRange** method on the **List<T>** collection.

Because the items are passed in as items of type **T** any type can be stored in the **Reversable-Collection**, but it can only handle one type once assigned as it then becomes a closed generic.

```
List<T> collection = new List<T>();

public void Add(T item)
{
    collection.Add(item);
}

public void AddRange(T[] items)
{
    collection.AddRange(items);
}
```

Next you will implement the **Reverse** method which will reverse the order of the items in the collection. This method takes no parameters and return an **IEnumerable<T>**, the reversed list. Note that you can use the **yield** keyword when looping to build the reversed list.

```
public IEnumerator<T> Reverse()
{
    foreach (var item in collection.Reverse<T>())
    {
        yield return item;
    }
}
```

Lastly you want to use the **ReversableCollection** from a button in the form.

```
private void btnOpenGenericList_Click(object sender, EventArgs e)
{
    var books = new ReversableCollection<Book>
    {
        new Book{ ISBN = "1234567890", Title = "Lord of the Rings"},
        new Book { ISBN = "0987654321", Title = "The Color of Magic" },
        new Book { ISBN = "6789054321", Title = "Bilbo" }
    };

    lstResult.DataSource = books.Reverse<Book>().ToList();
    lstResult.DisplayMember = "Title";
}
```

Exercise: Generic collections

In this exercise you will use a generic collection and constrain it to store data of one type. This will make the collection type safe storing only values of one type per instantiation.

Using a collection

Let's start by looking at what happens if you use a regular collection to store values of multiple types.

1. Create a new Windows Forms Application solution.
2. Add a folder called **Classes** to the project.
3. Add a class called **Car** to the **Classes** folder. The **Car** class should have two properties: **RegNo** of type **string** and **Model** of type **string**.
4. Add a class called **Motorcycle** to the **Classes** folder. The **Motorcycle** class should have two properties: **RegNo** of type **string** and **Model** of type **string**.
5. Add a combo box control named **dboCars** to the form.
6. Add a button named **btnCollections** to the form and open its **Click** event.

7. Create an **ArrayList** collection named **vehicles** to the form's class (not in the button **Click** event).

8. Add two cars and one motorcycle to the **vehicles** collection in the form's constructor or in the form's **Load** event.

```
vehicles.Add(new Car { RegNo = "ABC123", Model = "Volvo" });
vehicles.Add(new Car { RegNo = "XYZ123", Model = "Saab" });
vehicles.Add(new Motorcycle { RegNo = "QWE987", Model = "Honda" });
```

9. In the button **Click** event add a **foreach** loop iterating over the vehicles in the **vehicles** collection.

10. Because you only want to display cars in the **cboCars** combo box you cast the objects using the **Car** class before adding them to the combo box.

```
foreach (var vehicle in vehicles)
    cboCars.Items.Add((Car)vehicle);
```

11. When you run the application and push the button an **InvalidCastException** exception is displayed because the **Motorcycle** object cannot be cast to a **Car** object.

```
foreach (var vehicle in vehicles)
        cboCars.Items.Add(((Car)vehicle).RegNo);
```

⚠ **InvalidCastException was unhandled** ⬅ ✕

Unable to cast object of type 'Generic_Collections.Classes.Motorcycle' to type 'Generic_Collections.Classes.Car'.

The complete code for the **Car** class:

```
class Car
{
    public string RegNo { get; set; }
    public string Model { get; set; }
}
```

The complete code for the **Motorcycle** class:

```
class Motorcycle
{
    public string RegNo { get; set; }
    public string Model { get; set; }
}
```

The code for the form's class so far:

```csharp
public partial class Form1 : Form
{
    ArrayList vehicles = new ArrayList();

    public Form1()
    {
        InitializeComponent();

        #region ArrayList collection
        vehicles.Add(new Car { RegNo = "ABC123", Model = "Volvo" });
        vehicles.Add(new Car { RegNo = "XYZ123", Model = "Saab" });
        vehicles.Add(new Motorcycle { RegNo = "QWE987", Model = "Honda" });
        #endregion
    }

    private void btnCollections_Click(object sender, EventArgs e)
    {
        foreach (var vehicle in vehicles)
            cboCars.Items.Add(((Car)vehicle).RegNo);
    }
}
```

The interface solution

You could solve this by using an intermediary interface called **IVehicle** implemented by both the **Car** and the **Motorcycle** classes and use that interface to avoid the exception. This will however present another challenge which you will explore in this exercise.

1. Add a new folder to the project named **Interfaces.**
2. Add an Interface named **IVehicle** to the **Interfaces** folder.
3. Add the two properties **RegNo** and **Model** to the **IVehicle** interface.
4. Implement the **IVehicle** interface in the **Car** and **Motorcycle** classes.
   ```csharp
   class Car : IVehicle
   class Motorcycle : IVehicle
   ```
5. Add another button to the form named *btnCollectionWithInterface*.
6. Go to the button's **Click** event and add a **foreach** loop iterating over the **vehicles** collection.
7. This time you will cast the objects to **IVehicle** instead of **Car** when adding them to the combo box.

8. Run the application. This time no exception is thrown. However if you look in the combo box list you can see that now the motorcycle object is displayed alongside the car objects in the combo box's drop down list.

Clearly this wasn't the outcome you wished for when the goal was to display only cars in the combo box.

The code for the form's class so far:

```
public partial class Form1 : Form
{
    ArrayList vehicles = new ArrayList();

    public Form1() ...

    private void btnCollections_Click(object sender, EventArgs e) ...
    private void btnCollectionsWithInterface_Click(object sender,
    EventArgs e)
    {
        foreach (var vehicle in vehicles)
            cboCars.Items.Add(((IVehicle)vehicle).RegNo);
    }
}
```

The generic solution

A better way to solve displaying only cars would be to use a collection dedicated only to car objects when working with cars and a collection dedicated to motorcycles when working with motorcycles. To achieve this you will use generics.

1. Add a **List<T>** collection called **cars** which is used to store cars to the form's class (not the button's **Click** event).
   ```
   List<Car> cars;
   ```
2. Add two cars to the **cars** collection.
   ```
   cars = new List<Car>
   {
       new Car { RegNo = "ABC123", Model = "Volvo" },
       new Car { RegNo = "XYZ123", Model = "Saab" }
   ```

```
};
```

3. Try to add a **Motorcycle** instance to the **cars** collection, this should raise a pre-com-pile error underlining the code with a red squiggly line. As you can see it is impossi-ble to store anything but cars in the a generic list once it has been instantiated with a type and has become a closed generic collection.

4. Comment out or remove the line of code trying to add the motorcycle.

5. Create a new button called **btnGenericCollection** and add its **Click** event.

6. In the button's event use the **DataSource** property of the combo box to display the registration numbers using the **DisplayMember** property.

7. Run the application and click the button. As you can see the list is only displaying cars.

```
ABC123           ▾
ABC123
XYZ123
```

The code for the form's class:

```csharp
public partial class Form1 : Form
{
    ArrayList vehicles = new ArrayList();
    List<Car> cars;

    public Form1()
    {
        InitializeComponent();

        #region ArrayList collection ...

        #region Generic collection
        cars = new List<Car>
        {
            new Car { RegNo = "ABC123", Model = "Volvo" },
            new Car { RegNo = "XYZ123", Model = "Saab" }
        };
        #endregion

    }

    private void btnCollections_Click(object sender, EventArgs e) ...
```

```
private void btnCollectionsWithInterface_Click(object sender,
    EventArgs e) ...
private void btnGenericCollection_Click(object sender, EventArgs e)
{
    cboCars.DataSource = cars;
    cboCars.DisplayMember = "RegNo";
}
}
```

Constraining generics

When working with generics it is sometimes necessary to constrain the usage of the generic type to be of a specific class, implement a certain interface or make sure that it has a default parameter-less constructor. By doing this you can use the generic in a more flexible way. You can for instance defer execution of a method or property defined by the constraining interface because the compiler will know that that method or property exist because it belong to the interface (remember that an interface has to be implemented in its entirety to ensure that the members exist in the implementing class).

Constraints

The table below describe constraints you can use with generics.

Constraint	Description
where T : <name of interface>	The type argument must be, or implement, the specified interface.
where T : <name of base class>	The type argument must be, or derive from, the specified class.
where T : U	The type argument must be, or derive from, the supplied type argument U; for instance where T : Vehicle.
where T : new()	The type argument must have public default constructor.
where T : struct	The type argument must be a value type.
where T : class	The type argument must be a reference type.

Must be a class

This type of constraint is very useful if you know that the generic type must be a class. It could be that it handles different entities in a data base for instance which have to be classes. By limiting the generic type to only work with classes (reference types) it won't work with value types.

```
class Repository<T> where T : class
{
    public T Get(int id)
    {
        return (T)new object();
    }

    public void Add(T entity)
    {
    }
}
```

There is a limitation to what we can do with the passed in generic type inside the methods because the compiler does not know what the type contains. The only methods available are the default methods available in all reference types (see image above).

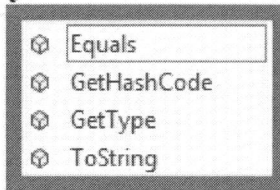

If you need access to other methods you can specify a specific class the generic type must be or inherit from but then it will no longer be a true generic.

Must derive from a specific base class

Using the pervious example as a starting point you can change the constraint to a specific base class from which all instances of the generic type must inherit. Let's say you have a base class called **Entity** which all generic types used in the **Repository** class must inherit from, then you could change the class definition of the **Repository** class to:

```
class Repository<T> where T : Entity
```

If the **Entity** base class implements a property called **IsValid** then you would have access to that property using the generic type within the **Repository** class.

```
class Entity
{
    public bool IsValid { get; set; }
}
```

```
public void Add(T entity)
{
    entity.
}
```

Must have a default constructor

You can also specify that the generic type must have a default constructor implemented. A default constructor takes no parameters. The **new()** constraint must be the last constraint in the list of constraints.

```
class Repository<T> where T : Entity, new()
```

Must implement a specific interface

Using the same basic example as a starting point you can change the constraint to a specific interface which all instances of the generic type must implement. This is more flexible because you are not narrowing down the constraint to a specific base class, instead you are allowing any class implementing the interface to be passed in as the generic type.

Let's say you have an interface called **IEntity** which all generic types used in the **Repository** class must implement, then you could change the class definition of the **Repository** class to:

```
class Repository<T> where T : IEntity
```

If the **IEntity** interface defines a property called **IsValid** which all classes passed in as the generic type must implement then you would have access to that property using the generic type within the **Repository** class. This works because the compiler can defer the type assignment and thus point at the right method at run-time when the type is known.

```
interface IEntity
{
    bool IsValid { get; set; }
}

class Repository<T> where T : IEntity
{
    public void Add(T entity)
    {
        if (entity.IsValid) { }
    }
}
```

Exercise: Creating a specialized collection

In this exercise you will create a generic repository class which will have two methods **Add** and **Get** and only allows types implementing the **IRegisterable** interface that you will create.

Create and implement the IRegisterable interface

In this part of the exercise you will create a new interface called **IRegisterable** which contain one property called **IsRegistered** of type **bool**.

1. Create a new Windows Forms Application.
2. Add a new interface named **IRegisterable**.
3. Add a **bool** property called **IsRegistered** to the interface.
4. Add a class called **Car**.
5. Implement the **IRegisterable** interface in the **Car** class.
6. Also add a read only **string** property called **DisplayValue** that return the registration number, model and if the car is registered (use **String.Format**). *The **DisplayValue** property belongs to the **Car** class and is not part of the interface.*
7. Add a class called **Motorcycle** with two **string** properties called **RegNo** and **Model**. Do not implement the **IRegisterable** interface in this class.

The code for the **IRegisterable** interface:

```
public interface IRegisterable
{
    bool IsRegistered { get; set; }
}
```

The complete code for the **Car** class:

```
class Car : IRegisterable
{
    public string RegNo { get; set; }
    public string Model { get; set; }

    public bool IsRegistered { get; set; }
    public string DisplayValue
    {
        get
        {
            return String.Format("{0} : {1} : {2}",
                RegNo, Model, IsRegistered.ToString());
        }
    }
}
```

The code for the **Motorcycle** class so far:

```
class Motorcycle
{
    public string RegNo { get; set; }
    public string Model { get; set; }
}
```

Create the Repository class

In this part of the exercise you will add a generic class called **Repository<T>**, **T** will determine the type of object that can be stored in the list collection the class contain. The generic type **T** defining the class should be constrained by the interface you crated in the previous exercise. The **Repository<T>** class should contain a **List<T>** collection called **items** which will store the items being added through its **Add** method that which you will create in a later exercise.

1. Add a new generic **Repository<T>** class.
2. Constrain the type **T** to only allow objects that implement the **IRegisterable** interface.
3. Add a private **List<T>** collection called **items** in the class.

```
class Repository<T> where T : IRegisterable
{
    List<T> items = new List<T>();
}
```

Create the Add and Get methods in the Repository class

In this part of the exercise you will add two methods **Add** and **Get** to the **Repository<T>** class. The **Add** method will take an item of type **T** and add it to the collection. The **Get** method will return an **IEnumerable<T>** with all items if its **null**-able **bool** parameter **registered** is **null** otherwise it will return the items where the **IsRegistered** property is equal to the value of the parameter.

1. Add a method named **Add** to the **Repository<T>** class, it should have a parameter of type **T**.
2. The passed in item should be added to the **items** collection in the method.
3. Add a method called **Get** that has a **null**-able **bool** parameter (**bool?**) called **registered**. The method should return an **IEnumerable<T>**. The **bool?** parameter should have a default value of **null**.
4. Add an **if**-statement checking if the passed in parameter is **null**. If it is then return the whole list of items (cars). If the parameter is **true** then return registered cars otherwise return the unregistered cars. You can us a LINQ statement with a Lambda expression to fetch the registered or unregistered cars with only one *else*-block.

The complete code for the **Repository<T>** class:

```
public class Repository<T> where T : class, IRegisterable, new()
{
    List<T> items = new List<T>();

    public void Add(T item)
    {
        items.Add(item);
    }
```

```
public IEnumerable<T> Get(bool? registered = null)
{
    // If registered is null then return all items
    // otherwise return registered items if true
    // and not registered items if false
    if (registered == null)
        return items;
    else
        return items.Where(item => item.IsRegistered.Equals(registered));
}
}
```

The GUI

In this part of the exercise you will create the GUI.

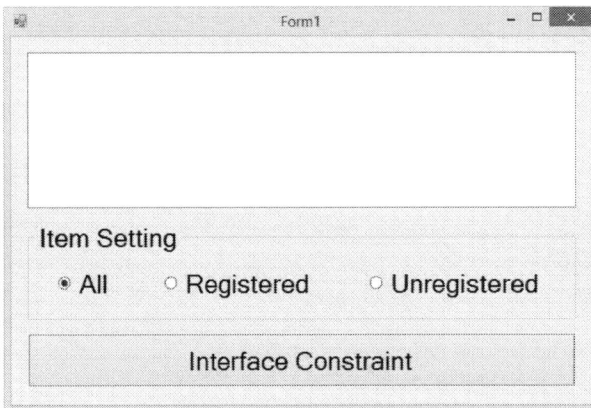

1. Add a list box called *lstItems* to the form.
2. Add a group box control in which you place three radio buttons.
3. Name the radio buttons *rbnAll* (if selected all items will be returned from the **Get** method in the **Repository<T>** class), *rbnRegistered* (will return registered items) and *rbnUnregistered* (will return unregistered items).
4. Make sure that the *rbnAll* is preselected when the application is started.
5. Go to the form's code-behind file and add an instance of the **Repository<T>** class called **repository** to the form's class.
   ```
   Repository<Car> carRepository= new Repository<Car>();
   ```
6. Add four **Car** instances to the to the **repository<T>** instance by calling its **Add** method. Two instance should be registered and two unregistered.

```
carRepository.Add(new Car { RegNo = "ABC123", Model = "Volvo",
    IsRegistered = false });
carRepository.Add(new Car { RegNo = "GFD123", Model = "Corvette",
    IsRegistered = false });
carRepository.Add(new Car { RegNo = "XYZ123", Model = "Saab",
    IsRegistered = true });
carRepository.Add(new Car { RegNo = "LKJ123", Model = "Koenigsegg",
    IsRegistered = true });
```

7. Add a button called **btnInterfaceConstraint** to the form and create its **Click** event.

8. Add an **if**-statement checking if the **rbnAll** is selected and call the **Get** method of the **repository<T>** instance without any value if it is.

9. Add an **else**-statement that call the **Get** method with either **true** if **rbnRegistered** is checked or **false** if the **rbnUnregistered** is checked. You can use the short notation for an **if**-statement (*expression to check ? true : false*) to avoid having to implement two else statements. Assign the returned **IEnumerable<T>** from the method call to the **DataSource** property of the list box control and set its **DisplayMember** property to "DisplayValue" (the property you added to the **Car** class earlier).

10. Run the application and click the button. All the cars should be displayed in the list box.

11. Select the **rbnRegistered** radio button and click the button. Only the registered cars should be displayed in the list box.

12. Select the **rbnUnregistered** radio button and click the button. Only the unregistered cars should be displayed in the list box.

The code for the form's class so far:

```
public partial class Form1 : Form
{
    Repository<Car> carRepository = new Repository<Car>();

    public Form1()
    {
        InitializeComponent();

        carRepository.Add(new Car {
            RegNo = "ABC123", Model = "Volvo", IsRegistered = false });

        carRepository.Add(new Car {
            RegNo = "GFD123", Model = "Corvette", IsRegistered = false });
```

```
        carRepository.Add(new Car {
            RegNo = "XYZ123", Model = "Saab", IsRegistered = true });

        carRepository.Add(new Car {
            RegNo = "LKJ123", Model = "Koenigsegg", IsRegistered = true });
    }

    private void btnInterfaceConstraint_Click(object sender, EventArgs e)
    {
        if (rbnAll.Checked)
            lstItems.DataSource = carRepository.Get();
        else
            lstItems.DataSource = carRepository.Get(
                rbnRegistered.Checked ? true : false).ToList();

        lstItems.DisplayMember = "DisplayValue";
    }
}
```

Testing the Repository with the Motorcycle class

In this part of the exercise you will create an instance of the **Repository<T>** class called **mcRepository** which takes instances of the **Motorcycle** class.

1. Go to the form's code-behind.
2. Add an instance of the **Repository<T>** class below the **carRepository** instance called **mcRepository** which is defined by the **Motorcycle** class.
3. You should get an exception saying that the interface **IRegisterable** isn't implemented by the **Motorcycle** class.
4. Implement the **IRegisterable** interface in the **Motorcycle** class.
5. Add the **DisplayValue** property to the **Motorcycle** class (see the **Car** class). It is needed to print the result to the list box in the form.
6. The exception should disappear when you build the solution.

The code for the form's class so far:

```
public partial class Form1 : Form
{
    Repository<Car> carRepository = new Repository<Car>();
    Repository<Motorcycle> mcRepository = new Repository<Motorcycle>();
```

```
    public Form1() ...

    private void btnInterfaceConstraint_Click(object sender,
        EventArgs e) ...
}
```

The code for the **Motorcycle** class so far:

```
class Motorcycle : IRegisterable
{
    public string RegNo { get; set; }
    public string Model { get; set; }

    public bool IsRegistered { get; set; }
    public string DisplayValue
    {
        get
        {
            return String.Format("{0} : {1} : {2}",
                RegNo, Model, IsRegistered.ToString());
        }
    }
}
```

Constrain with class and default constructor

In this part of the exercise you will constrain the generic type **T** used with the **Repository<T>** class further by adding the constraints **class** and **new()** to it. The **class** constraint forces the **Repository<T>** class to only handle reference types (classes) and the **new()** constraint checks that the instances represented by the generic type implements a default constructor.

1. Go to the **Repository<T>** class and change its constraint to:
   ```
   class Repository<T> where T : class, IRegisterable, new()
   ```
2. Go to the **Motorcycle** class and implement a constructor which takes three parameters for the assignable properties in the class (**RegNo**, **Model** and **IsRegistered**)
3. This should generate a compile error making it impossible to build the solution
   ```
   Repository<Motorcycle> mcRepository = new Repository<Motorcycle>();
   ```
   '_02_Constraints.Motorcycle' must be a non-abstract type with a public parameterless constructor in order to
   use it as parameter 'T' in the generic type or method '_02_Constraints.Classes.Chapter_2.Repository<T>'

The reason for this exception is that when you implement a constructor the default constructor is automatically disregarded by the compiler.

4. To solve this you have to implement a default constructor in the **Motorcycle** class. You do this by adding a constructor without parameters.

5. The error should go away.

6. Run the application and click the button. All the cars should be displayed in the list box.

   The reason they are displayed even though you changed the constraint on the **Repository<T>** class is that the **Car** class is a class which has a default constructor and implement the **IRegisterable** interface.

The code for the **Motorcycle** class so far:

```
class Motorcycle : IRegisterable
{
    public string RegNo { get; set; }
    public string Model { get; set; }

    public bool IsRegistered { get; set; }
    public string DisplayValue
    {
        get
        {
            return String.Format("{0} : {1} : {2}",
                RegNo, Model, IsRegistered.ToString());
        }
    }

    public Motorcycle(string regNo, string model, bool isRegistered)
    {
        RegNo = regNo;
        Model = model;
        IsRegistered = isRegistered;
    }

    // Default constructor
    public Motorcycle()
    {
    }
}
```

Extension methods

Inheritance is often used when extending classes but in some cases, such as when dealing with a sealed class where inheritance is not an option, *extension methods* could be the answer. One scenario might be that you want to lift out some functionality and create a more generic version which can be used with many different types.

An extension method does not change the underlying type. They must be declared as **public static** and the first parameter must specify the type to extend; you do this by prefixing the first parameter with the **this** keyword. Note that you don't pass in a value for the **this** parameter to the method when calling the it because it represents the type on which the extension method is used. The class containing the extension methods must be declared with the **static** keyword.

Extension methods are frequently used in MVC applications to output HTML.

Important: *You must place a **using statement** to the class containing the extension method in the .cs file where you intend to use the them.*

Example: Extension method

This sample code shows how to create an extension method for the sealed **Sytem.String** type that checks if the string contains numbers.

```
public static class StringExtensions
{
    public static bool ContainsNumbers(this string value) {
        return Regex.IsMatch(value, @"\d");
    }
}
```

This sample code shows how to call an extension method.

```
public class UseExtensions
{
    void UseExtensionMethod(string str) {
        // The extension method is called on the type variable
        bool hasNumbers = str.ContainsNumbers();
    }
}
```

Chaining extension methods

If the extension method returns a value of the same type it was initiated with then other extension methods working with that type can be chained to the original extension method with the dot (.) notation. Let's say the extension method will receive a collection and reverse the order of its items and then return the modified collection. If you then wanted to retrieve the top 10 items from the collection you could chain on the LINQ **Take** extension method.

Example: Chaining extension methods

In this example **Person** objects are stored in a collection added with an **Add** extension method with a **string** parameter called **name** and returns a modified version of the passed in **List<Person>** collection. The extension method should also return the number of times a name exist in the collection by calling another extension method called **Count** which has a **string** parameter called **name**.

When implemented the **static** class containing the extension methods should have two methods called **Add** and **Count**.

```
public class Person
{
    public string Name { get; set; }
}

public static class ChainingExtensions
{
    public static List<Person> Add(this List<Person> persons, string name)
    {
        persons.Add(new Person { Name = name });
        return persons;
    }

    public static int Count(this List<Person> persons, string name)
    {
        var count = persons.Count(p => p.Name.Equals(name));
        return count;
    }
}
```

In the previous example the **Add** method can be chained several times if more than one person will be added because it return the same collection that was passed in to the method. As soon as the **Count** method has been called chaining is no longer possible on the **List<Person>** collection because the **Count** method returns an **int**.

```
List<Person> persons = new List<Person>();

public int ChainingExtensionMethods(string searchName)
{
    var count = persons.Add("Jonas")
                      .Add("Lisa")
                      .Add("Jonas")
                      .Count(searchName);
    return count;
}
```

Generic methods

Generics are very useful when an undetermined type has to be used with the method. A generic method can work with any type and will be a closed generic method when the type is determined at run-time. Reflection can be used with the generic type to glean information and to call its methods and properties.

Example: Generic extension methods

In this example items in a **List<T>** collection will be manipulated using extension methods. Two generic extension methods will be created, **AddItem** which adds an item to the collection and **CountItems** which counts the number of times a value exist in the collection. Note the similarities with the pervious example, the difference is that the methods are generic.

Also note that the **AddItem** and **CountItems** methods are constrained to implement the **ICounter** interface which defines a **CompareValue** property that is used when comparing the generic item's value with a passed in value. Using the interface ensures that reflection don't have to be used access the value stored in the **CompareValue** property of the generic item. Because the compiler can be certain that the **CompareValue** property exist it can defer the execution until run-time.

In this example the **CompareValue** implemented in the **Animal** class will return the value stored in the **Race** property, but it any value could be returned that should be used when comparing the values.

```
public interface ICounter
{
    string CompareValue { get; }
}

public class Animal : ICounter
{
    public string Race { get; set; }
    public string CompareValue { get { return Race; } }
}
```

Continuing with the example. The generic extension method **AddItem** takes two parameters a generic **List<T>** collection and an item of type **T** that will be added to the collection. Note that the method name is decorated with the generic type **T**, this is necessary for passing in generic types in the method parameters.

The generic extension method **CountItems<T>** has two parameters a generic **List<T>** collection and a **string** containing the value to filter on when counting the items. Note that the method name is decorated with the generic type **T**, this is necessary for passing in a generic **List<T>** collection as a method parameter.

Note that both methods are constrained to implement the **ICounter** interface to ensure that the type **T** contains the **CompareValue** property used in the **CounterItem** method.

```
public static class GenericExtensionMethods
{
    public static List<T> AddItem<T>(this List<T> list, T item)
    where T : ICounter
    {
        list.Add(item);
        return list;
    }

    public static int CountItems<T>(this List<T> items, string value)
    where T : ICounter
    {
        var count = items.Count(item => item.CompareValue.Equals(value));
        return count;
    }
}
```

The **Animal** class used when creating the objects stored in the collection implement the **ICounter** interface enabling the use of the **CountItem** extension method.

```
public class UseExtensions
{
    List<Animal> items = new List<Animal>();

    public int GenericExtensionMethods(string filter)
    {
        var count =
            items.AddItem(new Animal { Race = "Cat", Type="Egyptian Mau" })
                .AddItem(new Animal { Race = "Dog", Type = "Boxer" })
                .AddItem(new Animal { Race = "Cat", Type = "Siberian" })
                .CountItems(filter);
        return count;
    }
}
```

Create an instance of the **UseExtensions** class from the ***btnGenericExtensionMethods*** button's **Click** event and call the **GenericExtensionMethods** method to use the extension methods.

```
private void btnGenericExtensionMethods_Click(object sender, EventArgs e)
{
    var extensions = new UseExtensions();

    var count = extensions.GenericExtensionMethods("Cat");
    lblResult.Text = count.ToString();
}
```

Exercise: Generic extension methods

In this exercise you will create an extension method called **Search** which will filter out vehicles on any of their **string** properties and display the result in a list box.

Creating the Search extension method

Create an extension method called **Search** that will search through all the available readable **string** properties of the items in the **items** collection located in the **Repository** class. The **Search** method will return an **IEnumerable<T>** containing all items where at least one **string** property contains the search string provided by the method parameter.

You will have to pretend that you don't have access to the code in the **Repository** class, as if it was part of a third party class library. You will use reflection in a loop to find the properties of the items one at a time and in a second (inner) loop you will iterate over the available readable properties of the generic type **T** to find out if the property name exist in the generic type. Use the property names to find out if the corresponding properties in the current item contains the value from the passed in **string search** parameter.

1. Create a new class called **Extensions** and change it to **static**.
2. Create a **public static** method called **Search** which is declared with the generic type **T**.
3. Add two parameters to the method:
    a. The first is the object the method should act upon, this parameter should be decorated with the **this** keyword. Name the parameter **rep** and declare it as a **Repository<T>**. Because you don't have direct access to the collection in the **Repository<T>** class you can gain access to its items through the **rep** object's **Get** method.
    b. The second is a **string** parameter called **search** which contains the string to search for.
4. Because the **Repository<T>** class has constraints this method must have the same constraints.

```
public static class Extensions
{
    public static IEnumerable<T> Search<T>(this Repository<T> rep,
      string search) where T : class, IRegisterable, new()
    { ... }
}
```

5. Find all the **string** properties defined in the passed in type **T**. To do this you have to:
    a. Call the **GetProperties** method on the type **T** using **typeof** to get the actual type of **T**.
    b. Use the LINQ **Where** method to find the properties that are declared as **string** and are readable:
        i. To find out if a property is of a certain type you can use the **PropertyType** property of the current item in the **Where** method's Lambda variable and compare it to the desired type you are after.

      ii.   To find out if a property is readable you can check the **CanRead** property of the current item in the Where method's Lambda variable.

  c.   Save the resulting properties in a variable called **readProps**.

```
var readProps = typeof(T).GetProperties()
    .Where(p => p.PropertyType.Equals(typeof(string)) &&
                p.CanRead);
```

6.   Create a **List<T>** called **result** which will hold the items matching the passed in **string** search value.

7.   Add a **foreach** loop that iterates over all the items in the **Repository<T>** class collection; you can get access to the items by calling the **Get** method on the **rep** parameter passed in to the **Search** method.

8.   Add an **if**-statement inside the loop which checks if the current item already is in the **result** collection (see step 6). If it exist then immediately jump to the next item by using the **continue** keyword.

```
var result = new List<T>();
foreach (var item in rep.Get())
{
    if (result.Contains(item)) continue;
}
```

9.   Iterate over all the properties of **string** types you fetched in step 5 after the **if**-statement. You want to use the names of these properties when checking their corresponding values in the current loop item.

  a.   To check the property value of the current loop item you need to:

      i.   Call the **GetType** method on the item.

      ii.   Call the **GetProperty** method on the **GetType** method passing in the **name** of the current property from the collection of properties you are iterating over in the inner loop.

      iii.   To get the value of the property you have to call the **GetValue** method on the **GetProperty** method passing in the current item as a parameter.

      iv.   Convert that value to an upper case string and check if the upper case version of the **search** string is somewhere within that property string.

```
    foreach (var prop in readProps)
        if (item.GetType().GetProperty(prop.Name).GetValue(item)
            .ToString().ToUpper().Contains(search.ToUpper()))
        {
            ...
        }
```

10. Add another **if**-block inside the **if**-block of the inner loop that checks if the **result** collection does **not** contain the current item. If that is the case then add the current item to the **result** collection and use the **continue** keyword to continue to the next item.

```
if (!result.Contains(item))
{
    result.Add(item);
    continue;
}
```

11. Return the **result** collection from the **Search** method.

The **Extensions** class so far:

```
public static class Extensions
{
    public static IEnumerable<T> Search<T>(this Repository<T> rep,
    string search) where T : class, IRegisterable, new()
    {
        var readProps = typeof(T).GetProperties()
            .Where(p => p.PropertyType.Equals(typeof(string)) &&
                p.CanRead);

        var result = new List<T>();
        foreach (var item in rep.Get())
        {
            if (result.Contains(item)) continue;

            foreach (var prop in readProps)
                if (item.GetType().GetProperty(prop.Name).GetValue(item)
                    .ToString().ToUpper().Contains(search.ToUpper()))
                {
                    if (!result.Contains(item))
                    {
                        result.Add(item);
```

```
                    continue;
                }
            }
        }
        return result;
    }
}
```

The GUI

The GUI contains a list box called *lstResult* which will display the search results, a label with the text "Search", a textbox called *txtSearch* where the search text will be entered and a button called *btnSearch* that will initiate the search and display the result in the list box.

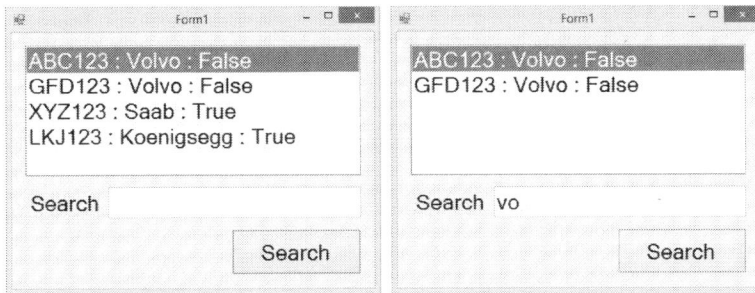

1. Create a new Windows Forms Application.
2. Add a list box called *lstResult* to the form.
3. Add a label with the text "Search" to the form.
4. Add a textbox called *txtSearch* to the right of the label in form.
5. Add a button called *btnSearch* below the textbox in the form.

Calling the Search extension method

In this part of the exercise you will call the **Search** extension method that you created earlier. When the **Search** button is clicked a value from the textbox is passed to the **Search** method and the result from the method call is displayed in the list box.

1. Add a an instance of the **Repository<T>** called **carRepository** to the form's class.
2. Add the same cars to the repository in the form's constructor as in previous exercises.

3. In the button's **Click** event assign the collection of cars returned from a call to the **Search** method of the **carRepository** instance to the **DataSource** property of the list box. Don't forget to pass in the text value from the textbox to the **Search** method.

4. Set the **DisplayMember** property of the list box to "DisplayValue" which is the property value you want to display from **Car** objects.

```csharp
private void btnSearch_Click(object sender, EventArgs e)
{
    lstResult.DataSource = carRepository.Search(txtSearch.Text);
    lstResult.DisplayMember = "DisplayValue";
}
```

5. Run the application and enter a value in the textbox then click the button. For a **Car** object to be displayed in the list box one or more of its **string** property values must contain the text entered in the textbox.

The form class so far:

```csharp
public partial class Form1 : Form
{
    Repository<Car> carRepository = new Repository<Car>();

    public Form1()
    {
        InitializeComponent();

        carRepository.Add(new Car {
            RegNo = "ABC123", Model = "Volvo", IsRegistered = false });
        carRepository.Add(new Car {
            RegNo = "GFD123", Model = "Volvo", IsRegistered = false });
        carRepository.Add(new Car {
            RegNo = "XYZ123", Model = "Saab", IsRegistered = true });
        carRepository.Add(new Car {
            RegNo = "LKJ123", Model = "Koenigsegg", IsRegistered = true });
    }


    private void btnSearch_Click(object sender, EventArgs e)
    {
        lstResult.DataSource = carRepository.Search(txtSearch.Text);
        lstResult.DisplayMember = "DisplayValue";
    }
}
```

Delegates and generics

A delegate is essentially a variable that can point to a method and later be used when you want to call that method. It defines a method header and its return type making it possible to call the method associated with that delegate in a type safe way.

Example: Outputting data without a delegate using a generic approach

To be able to output the **CompareValue** of the items stored in the **List<T>** collection you can implement an **Output** method in the **GenericExtensionMethods** class; there is a drawback and that is that it is not very flexible and only allow printing the values to one type of output control or window, in the example code it's the *Output* window in the Visual Studio IDE.

```
public static void Output<T>(this List<T> items) where T : ICounter
{
    foreach(var item in items)
    {
        Debug.WriteLine(item.CompareValue);
    }
}
```

Example: Using a delegate

To make the **Output** method more flexible it can be implemented using delegate to pass in a function pointer. The function pointer can then be directed to a print method which will handle the actual printing. This approach will enable reuse of the **Output** method by pointing the delegate to different print methods. The print method will be determined by the method sent in to the **Printer** delegate.

You need to add a **public delegate** which takes a parameter of the **object** data type outside the class; by using the **object** data type the delegate can handle any type of data.

```
public delegate void Printer(object data);
```

To be able to use the delegate the **Output** extension method in the **GenericExtension-Methods** class has to be altered to take the delegate as its second parameter. This will enable the **Output** method to call the passed in method associated with the delegate when printing.

Swap out the **Debug.WriteLine** call for an invocation call to the delegate.

```
public static void Output<T>(this List<T> items, Printer print)
where T : ICounter
{
    foreach (var item in items)
    {
        print(item.CompareValue);
    }
}
```

By making this change to the **Output** method it is possible to print to any output control you desire.

Let's add a method that writes to the form's list box instead of the *Output* window. To achieve this the print method added to the form's class has to match the delegate definition. As you can see in the example code below it's a **void** method that has a parameter of the **object** data type just like the delegate definition dictates. You can give the individual print methods appropriate names according to their intended purposes.

```
void PrintToListBox(object data)
{
    lstResult.Items.Add(data);
}
```

Add a button called ***btnPrintingUsingDelegate*** and add its **Click** event to the form's class. Create a delegate using the **PrintToListBox** method you just added. Call the **Output** method passing in the delegate as its parameter.

```
private void btnPrintingUsingDelegate_Click(object sender, EventArgs e)
{
    Printer print = new Printer(PrintToListBox);
    var extensions = new DelegatesAndGenerics();
    extensions.items.Output(print);
}
```

You can create as many delegate methods as you need displaying data in other controls or windows.

Example: Using a generic delegate

The code can be made more generic by passing in a type of **T** to the print methods. Start by changing the delegate to take a generic type of **T**.

```
public delegate void Printer<T>(T data);
```

The **Output** method has to be modified to take a **Printer<T>** delegate and pass the items in the loop as the parameter to the **print** delegate pointer. Remember to add the correct constraint to the method.

```
public static void Output<T>(this List<T> items, Printer<T> print)
where T : ICounter
{
    foreach (var item in items)
    {
        print(item);
    }
}
```

Change the **PrintToListBox** delegate method parameter to the generic type **T**. To get access to the **CompareValue** in the class you need to restrict the generic type **T** to types implementing the **ICounter** interface like you have done on other methods.

```
void PrintToListBox<T>(T data) where T : ICounter
{
    lstResult.Items.Add(data.CompareValue);
}
```

Add a button called ***btnPrintingUsingGenericDelegate*** and add its **Click** event to the form's class. Create a delegate with a specific type for and pass in the **PrintToListBox** method you just altered as its parameter. Call the **Output** method passing in the delegate as its parameter.

Connect the **PrintToListBox** method to the delegate and call **Output** method on the list from a button click event.

```
private void btnPrintingUsingGenericDelegate_Click(object sender,
EventArgs e)
{
    var extensions = new DelegatesAndGenerics();
    var print = new Printer<Animal>(PrintToListBox);
    extensions.items.Output(print);
}
```

Action/Func/Predicate delegates

Another way of handling delegate calls is to use one of the three predefined delegates **Action**, **Func** and **Predicate**. **Action** and **Func** can take up to 16 generic type arguments and **Predicate** only 1.

Action	Defines a delegate method that always return **void**.
Func	Defines a delegate method that always return a type.
Predicate	Defines a delegate method that always return **bool**.

Action Delegate

Instead of writing all that cumbersome code in the previous example an **Action** delegate can be used to achieve the same result. There are several different ways to implement the code, let's look at them one at a time.

Example: Replacing a delegate

The first step is to replace the delegate and still use the **PrintToListBox** method. To do this you need to change the **Output** method (or overload the existing one) to take an **Action<T>** as its **print** parameter.

```
public static void Output<T>(this List<T> items, Action<T> print)
where T : ICounter
{
    foreach (var item in items)
    {
        print(item);
    }
}
```

Then you have to change the definition of the delegate call to use an **Action** instead of the delegate you removed.

```
private void btnPrintingUsingAction_Click(object sender, EventArgs e)
{
    var extensions = new DelegatesAndGenerics();
    Action<Animal> print = PrintToListBox;
    extensions.items.Output(print);
}
```

Example: Inline delegate

The second step is to get rid of the **PrintToListBox** method replacing it with an inline delegate, placing the code directly inside the button's **Click** event. This type of **Action** can be very useful when using LINQ and Lambda expressions.

By changing the code in this way you can delete the **PrintToListBox** method.

```
private void btnPrintingUsingAction_Click(object sender, EventArgs e)
{
    Action<Animal> print = delegate(Animal data) {
        lstResult.Items.Add(data.Race);
    };

    extensions.items.Output(print);
}
```

Example: Using Lambda

The third step is to get rid of the delegate definition and the code block all together; to achieve this you can use a Lambda expression. You read the Lambda expression (a =>) as *'a'* *goes to*.

```
private void btnPrintingUsingAction_Click(object sender, EventArgs e)
{
    Action<Animal> print = a => lstResult.Items.Add(a.Race);
    extensions.items.Output(print);
}
```

Pretty significant change wouldn't you say! You can take it one step further though by using a Lambda expression directly in the function call.

```
private void btnPrintingUsingAction_Click(object sender, EventArgs e)
{
    extensions.items.Output(a => lstResult.Items.Add(a.Race));
}
```

Func delegate

A **Func** differs from an **Action** in that it always has to return a value and thus always has to take at least one generic type, the return value. The last generic type in a **Func** is always the return type.

Example: Calling a Func

Let's say you want to create a function that returns the first **Animal** instance from a **List<Animal>** collection by the specified race. To achieve this you could use a **Func** to which you pass in two parameters, a **string** for the race and **Animal** for the return type. When the **Func** has been declared it can be called like any other function. The 'a' in the Lambda expression below is the **string** (*"Cat"*) passed in to the **animal Func**.

```
var extensions = new DelegatesAndGenerics();

// Defining the function that can be called
Func<string, Animal> animal = a =>
    extensions.items.FirstOrDefault(f => f.Race.Equals(a));

// Calling the function
var result = animal("Cat");
```

Predicate delegate

A **Predicate** differs from an **Action** in that it always has to return a Boolean value and take one generic type, the in-parameter value.

Example: Calling a predicate

In the following example a **Predicate** function called **HasRace** is used to find out if the specified animal race exist in the animals collection. The **race** in the Lambda expression below is the **string** (*"Cat"*) passed in to the **HasRace** function.

```
private void btnPredicate_Click(object sender, EventArgs e)
{
    var extensions = new DelegatesAndGenerics();
```

```
Predicate<string> HasRace = race =>
    extensions.items.Count(f => f.Race.Equals(race)) > 0;

var result = HasRace("Cat");
lblResult.Text = result.ToString();
}
```

Exercise: Action/Func/Predicate delegates

In the exercises in this section you will create an **Action** to output information to different controls, a **Func** to return an object and a **Predicate** to find out if one or more items match the search string in a textbox.

The GUI

The GUI needs a few more controls for this exercise. Add a label with the text "Result:" and to the right of that label add a label called *lblResult* with the text "No result". Add a combo box called *cboResult* and four buttons called **btnPrintToListBox**, **btnPrintToComboBox**, **btnCallFunc** and **btnCallPredicate** (see image below).

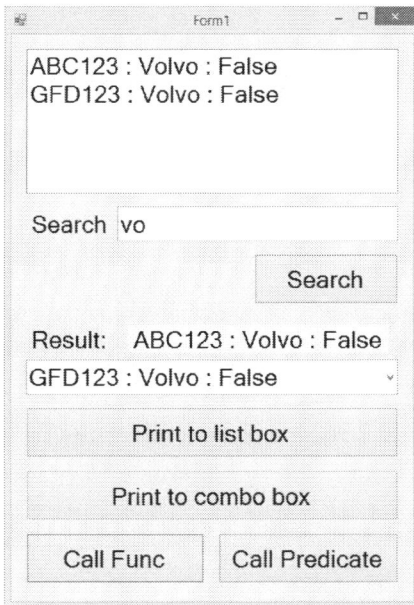

1. Add a label with the text "Result:" below the **Search** button.
2. Add a label called *lblResult* with the text "No result" to the right of the previous label.

3. Add a combo box called **cboResult** below the two labels.
4. Add a button called **btnPrintToListBox** below the combo box.
5. Add a button called **btnPrintToComboBox** below the previous button.
6. Add a button called **btnCallFunc** below the previous button.
7. Add a button called **btnCallPredicate** to the right of the **btnCallFunc** button.

Adding an Action

In this section you will call the **Search** extension method you created in a previous exercise and output the result to a list box and a combo box by calling an extension method called **Output** which you will create. This demonstrates how an **Action** can be used to divert the output to the chosen type of control without having to change the implementation of the extension method.

1. Open the **Extensions** class an add an extension method called **Output** which takes an **IEnumerable<T>** called **items** as its first parameter and an **Action<T>** called **print** as its second parameter. The method should return **void**
2. Add a **foreach** loop to the method that iterates over the items in the passed in collection.

The complete code of the **Extensions** class:

```
public static class Extensions
{
    public static IEnumerable<T> Search<T>(this Repository<T> rep,
    string search) where T : class, IRegisterable, new() ...

    public static void Output<T>(this IEnumerable<T> items, Action<T> print)
    where T : class, IRegisterable, new()
    {
        foreach (var item in items)
        {
            print(item);
        }
    }
}
```

Using the Action

Now you will call the **Search** extension method you created in a previous exercise. Output the result to a list box and a combo box by calling the **Output** extension method you just created. This demonstrates how an **Action** can be used to divert the output to the chosen type of control without having to change the implementation of the extension method.

1. Add the **Click** event for the ***btnPrintToListBox*** button.
2. Clear the list box's items.
3. Call the **Output** method on the result from a call to the **Search** method. You can attach the call to the **Output** method directly to the **Search** method chaining them together. Use a Lambda expression in the call to the **Output** method pointing to the **Add** method of the list box.

```
carRepository.Search(txtSearch.Text).Output(
    a => lstResult.Items.Add(a.DisplayValue));
```

4. Start the application, enter a value in the text box and click the ***btnPrintToListBox*** button. The list box should display information about the matching cars.
5. Add the **Click** event for the ***btnPrintToComboBox*** button.
6. Repeat step 5 but clear the combo box and point to its **Add** method in the Lambda expression.
7. Start the application, enter a value in the text box and click the ***btnPrintToCombo-Box*** button. The combo box should display information about the matching cars.

The form's class so far:

```
public partial class Form1 : Form
{
    Repository<Car> carRepository = new Repository<Car>();

    public Form1() ...

    private void btnSearch_Click(object sender, EventArgs e) ...

    private void btnPrintToListBox_Click(object sender, EventArgs e)
    {
        lstResult.Items.Clear();
        carRepository.Search(txtSearch.Text)
            .Output(a => lstResult.Items.Add(a.DisplayValue));
    }
```

```
private void btnPrintToComboBox_Click(object sender, EventArgs e)
{
    cboResult.Items.Clear();
    carRepository.Search(txtSearch.Text)
        .Output(a => cboResult.Items.Add(a.DisplayValue));
}
}
```

Using a Func

In this exercise you will create a **Func** called **FirstMatch** which return the first item matching the search text entered into the textbox.

1. Add the **Click** event for the ***btnCallFunc*** button.

2. Create a **Func** delegate called **FirstMatch** that takes a **string** input parameter and calls the **Search** method on the **carRepository** returning the first car matching the search string. Use a Lambda expression to call the **Search** method
   ```
   Func<string, Car> FirstMatch = search => // Defines the Func delegate
       carRepository.Search(search).FirstOrDefault();// The method to
   call
   ```

3. Call the **FirstMatch Func** and pass in the text from the textbox; store the result in a variable called **result**.
   ```
   var result = FirstMatch(txtSearch.Text);
   ```

4. Display the **DisplayValue** property value in the label ***lblResult*** if the result variable is not **null** otherwise display the text "No car found".
   ```
   lblResult.Text = result != null ? result.DisplayValue : "No car
   found";
   ```

5. Run the application, enter a value in the textbox and click the button. If the value matches a text value in one or more of the car objects then the information of the first car is displayed in the label otherwise the text "No car found" is displayed.

The form's class so far:

```
public partial class Form1 : Form
{
    Repository<Car> carRepository = new Repository<Car>();

    public Form1() ...
```

```
private void btnSearch_Click(object sender, EventArgs e) ...
private void btnPrintToListBox_Click(object sender, EventArgs e) ...
private void btnPrintToComboBox_Click(object sender, EventArgs e) ...

private void btnCallFunc_Click(object sender, EventArgs e)
{
    // Create a Func which takes a string (search)
    // and return a Car object by calling the
    // Search method with the search text and
    // returning the first item found.
    Func<string, Car> FirstMatch = search =>
        carRepository.Search(search).FirstOrDefault();

    // Call the Func
    var result = FirstMatch(txtSearch.Text);

    // Display the result
    lblResult.Text = result != null ?
        result.DisplayValue : "No car found";
}
}
```

Using a Predicate

In this exercise you will create a **Predicate** called **Contains** which return **true** if there is a matching item and **false** if no matching item was found.

1. Add the **Click** event for the ***btnCallPredicate*** button.
2. Create a **Predicate** delegate which takes a **string** input parameter and calls the **Search** method on the **carRepository**. Use a Lambda expression to call the **Search** method

   ```
   Predicate<string> Contains = search => // Defines the Predicate
   delegate
       carRepository.Search(search).Count() > 0; // The method to call
   ```

3. Call the **Contains Predicate** method passing in the text from the textbox and store the result in a variable called **result**.

   ```
   var result = Contains(txtSearch.Text);
   ```

4. Display the result in the ***lblResult*** label

5. Run the application, enter a value in the textbox and click the button. If the value matches a text value in one or more of the car objects then display **True** in the label otherwise display **False**.

The form's class so far:

```
public partial class Form1 : Form
{
    Repository<Car> carRepository = new Repository<Car>();

    public Form1() ...

    private void btnSearch_Click(object sender, EventArgs e) ...
    private void btnPrintToListBox_Click(object sender, EventArgs e) ...
    private void btnPrintToComboBox_Click(object sender, EventArgs e) ...
    private void btnCallFunc_Click(object sender, EventArgs e) ...

    private void btnCallPredicate_Click(object sender, EventArgs e)
    {
        // Create a Predicate which takes a string (search) and
        // return true if a match is found otherwise false.
        Predicate<string> Contains = search =>
            carRepository.Search(search).Count() > 0;

        // Call the Predicate and display the result
        var result = Contains(txtSearch.Text);
        lblResult.Text = result.ToString();
    }
}
```

Events and generics

It can be very useful to be able to send information from an object to the caller using generic events. Using regular events you have to specify the data type in advance forcing the event to work with that type an no other type. With generic events however you can specify the type to use when registering for that event making it possible to use the event with any type.

To declare a generic event you use the **EventHandler<T>** class which coincidentally saves you one line of code since you don't have to explicitly specify a delegate for it; one is provided behind the scenes.

Every event takes two parameters **sender** of type **object**, which is the object or control from where the event originated and **EventArgs** which can contain data about the object or control that needs to be sent to the subscriber (the recipient). To pass your own data with the event you have to create your own **EventArgs** class containing the properties.

To create the **EventArgs** class you add a new class deriving from the **EventArgs** class and add properties to it. Since the generic type of **T** will be available throughout the class raising the event you can safely use it in your **EventArgs** class.

Example: Generic event

In this example you will see how a generic event can be used to pass data to the event subscriber.

In the specification handed to you for this task it's stated that you should be able to remove an item from a list in a class called **Buffer** end raise an event when the item is removed. The first thing on the agenda is to create a class called **RemovedItemEventArgs** which inherits the **EventArgs** class.

Note that the generic type **T** is passed in to the class and used to store the removed item.

```
public class RemovedItemEventArgs<T> : EventArgs
{
    public T RemovedItem { get; set; }

    public RemovedItemEventArgs(T removedItem)
    {
        RemovedItem = removedItem;
    }

}
```

The Buffer class takes a generic type **T** and contains a collection to store the items in.

```
public class Buffer<T>
{
    public List<T> items = new List<T>();
}
```

Add the event to the **Buffer** class. The event will be triggered when an item is removed from the collection.

```
public event EventHandler<RemovedItemEventArgs<T>> ItemRemoved;
```

Add the **RemoveItem** method to the **Buffer** class, it will remove an item from the collection at the given index and raise the event to the subscriber.

```
public void RemoveItem(int index)
{
    var item = items.ElementAtOrDefault(index);

    // Create the EventArgs and raise the event
    var eventArgs = new RemovedItemEventArgs<T>(item);
    ItemRemoved(this, eventArgs);

    items.RemoveAt(index);
}
```

With the **Buffer** class complete we move on to the form where the event will be subscribed to in a button event. An instance of the **Buffer** class is added to the form and filled with the following data.

```
Buffer<string> buffer = new Buffer<string>();
buffer.items.Add("First string");
buffer.items.Add("Second string");
buffer.items.Add("Third string");
```

Subscribe to the event in the button's **Click** event and remove the second item from the collection and display the remaining strings in a list box.

```
private void btnEvent_Click(object sender, EventArgs e)
{
    // Subscribe to the event
    buffer.ItemRemoved += buffer_ItemRemoved;

    // Remove the second item "Second string"
    buffer.RemoveItem(1);

    //Display the remaining items in a list box
    lstResult.Items.Clear();
```

```
    foreach (var item in buffer.items)
        lstResult.Items.Add(item);
}
```

In the **buffer_ItemRemoved** event method created when subscribing to the event you want to display the removed string in a Label. Note that Visual Studio automatically detected the type that was used with the **Buffer** class and used that type with the **RemovedItemEvent-Args** class.

```
void buffer_ItemRemoved(object sender, RemovedItemEventArgs<string> e)
{
    // Display the removed item in a Label
    lblResult.Text = e.RemovedItem;
}
```

Mini Use Case: Car rental - Generic business rules engine

In this exercise you will refactor and redefine how business rules are added and evaluated. The rules are defined in the form and evaluated in the business layer. This is possible by creating objects of a class called **BusinessRule** which defines what property to compare with a given value and what operator to use specified by an enum.

Important: *I strongly suggest that you create a copy of the Car Rental solution before continuing with the use case so that you can go back to the starting point if anything goes wrong. I also suggest that you continually make copies of the solution as you refactor it.*

The rule will be evaluated by an instance of the **RuleComparer** class which implements the **IComparer** interface in order to define how two **object** values will be compared. It will also implement a generic method called **EvaluateRules<T>** which will take an item of **T** and a list of **BusinessRule<T>** objects. The methods uses reflection to fetch the property value from the item of **T** and a property called **Property** in each rule object, the property is compared to the value in the **Value** property of each of the rule objects. So in essence you take the value from a property in an object (of type **T**) use reflection to fetch the property value for a given property specified by the rule object and compare it to another property value supplied by the rule object.

Each rule object in the **List<BusinessRule<T>>** collection sent into the method will be evaluated separately and the weighted result from all rules will determine if the **EvaluateRules<T>** method will return success (**true**) or fail (**false**).

To make this work you need to add two classes and one enum.

The enum: The enum called **RuleOperator** will define the different types of comparisons that can be made by the **EvaluateRules<T>** method when it evaluates the rules. Each rule object will have a property specifying how the property value and the specified value should be compared. The operators you will add are: **GreaterThan**, **LessThan**, **Equal**, **NotEqual**, **Contains** and **NotContains**; the two last values will be used when checking whether a list contains a value or not.

The BusinessRule<T> class: The first class is the generic **public BusinessRule<T>** class which will define a single business rule for an item of the given type **T**. The class has five **public** properties:

- A **string** property called **Property** which will hold the name of the property in the item that you wish to compare to the value in the second **object** property called **Value**.
- The third property is an **IEnumerable<T>** called **Items** which is a list of items of the same type as the rule will evaluate; the method scans all the items in the collection to determine if the rule is successful or not.
- The fourth is a **RuleOperator** property called **Comparer** will hold one of the values from the **RuleOperator** enum, it will determine how the two values are compared.
- The last property is a **null**-able **bool** (**bool?**) called **Success**; it will be **null** until the rule has been evaluated, **true** if the **EvaluateRules<T>** method returned *success* for the rule and **false** if the evaluation was *unsuccessful* or *failed*.

The RuleComparer class: The **RuleComparer** instance will evaluate a list of **BusinessRule<T>** rules against one item of type **T**. In order to compare **object** values using the standard comparison operators such as **<** and **>** the class has to implement the **IComparer** interface because otherwise **object** values cannot be compared using those operators.

.NET Framework has a couple of comparer classes that you can use if you don't want to implement you own; the one you will use here is called **CaseInsensitiveComparer** and works on **string** values. The **Compare** method implemented by the **IComparer** interface return an **int** where a negative value mean that the first object's value is less than the second object's value, zero mean that they are equal and a positive value mean that the first object's value is greater than the second object's value. Since this particular comparer will compare numerical values as **double** values and strings as **string** values you have to create two scenarios where the first compare the values parsed to **double** values and the second where the values are compared as strings. You can implement the same **IsNumeric** method that you created a while back to check whether the values are numerical or not.

The class will have three methods where the first is called **IsNumeric** and will check if an **object** value is numerical or not and return **true** or **false** depending in the outcome. The second **int** method is called **Compare** which has two **object** parameters called **value1** and **value2** and is part of the **IComparer** interface, its task is to evaluate whether two **objects** values are equal or not. The third method is called **EvaluateRules<T>** with a **T** parameter called **item** and a **List<BusinessRule<T>>** parameter called **rules**. The purpose of this method is to iterate through the rules in the collection and evaluate each rule against a given property in the passed in **T** instance stored in the **item** object. You can read how the method works at the beginning of this use case.

Defining a rule: You define the rules in the form's methods by creating a **List<BusinessRule <T>>** collection which you then pass to the booking processor for evaluation through one of its methods, for instance the generic **Add** method you will create in another use case. All rules have to be successful for the evaluation to be considered a success.

```
// Create rules to be evaluated by the booking processor
var rules = new List<BusinessRule<ICustomer>>() {
    new BusinessRule<ICustomer> {
        Property = "Id", Value = 1, Comparer = RuleOperator.LessThan
    },
    new BusinessRule<ICustomer> { Property = "SocialSecurityNumber",
        Items = processor.Get<ICustomer>(),
        Comparer = RuleOperator.NotContains
    }
};

// Passing the rules collection to the Add method
var success = processor.Add(customer, rules);
```

The BusinessRule<T> class

Here you will implement the **RuleOperator** enum and the **BusinessRule<T>** class; they will be placed in the same .cs file for simplicity but you can place them in separate files if you want.

1. Create a copy of the **Car Rental** solution so that you can go back to the starting point if something goes wrong.
2. Open the **Car Rental** solution.
3. Add a class called **BusinessRule** in the **Classes** folder in the **Business Layer** project.
4. Change the accessibility of the class to **public**.
5. Make the class generic of type **T**.
   ```
   public class BusinessRule<T>
   ```
6. Add a **public** enum called **RuleOperator** above the class and inside the namespace.
7. Add the following values to the enum: **GreaterThan**, **LessThan**, **Equal**, **NotEqual**, **Contains** and **NotContains**.
8. Add the following **public** properties to the class: **Property** of type **string**, **Value** of type **object**, **Items** of type **IEnumerable<T>**, **Comparer** of type **RuleOperator**, **Success** of type **bool?** (**null**-able **bool**).

The complete code for the **BusinessRule** class and the **RuleOperator** enum:

```
public enum RuleOperator
{
    GreaterThan,
    LessThan,
    Equal,
    NotEqual,
    Contains,
    NotContains
}

public class BusinessRule<T>
{
    public string Property { get; set; }
    public object Value { get; set; }
    public IEnumerable<T> Items { get; set; }
    public RuleOperator Comparer { get; set; }
    public bool? Success { get; set; }
}
```

The RuleComparer class

The purpose of the methods in this class is to evaluate the business rules of type **Business-Rule<T>** that you pass in to it.

The Compare method

1. Add a class called **RuleComparer** to the **Classes** folder in the **Business Layer** project.

2. Implement the **IComparer** interface in the class. This will add a method called **Compare** which takes two parameters of the **object** data type that will be compared with one another.

3. To be able to evaluate the values in the **Compare** method you need to add a method called **IsNumeric** which checks if an **object** value is numeric. You have already created this method in the form so you can simply copy it and paste it into the **RuleComparer** class.

4. Use the **IsNumeric** method in the **Compare** class to determine if the values in the **value1** and **value2** parameters defined by the method are numerical.

   ```
   if (IsNumeric(value1) && IsNumeric(value2))
   ```

5. If both values are numerical then parse them to the **double** data type before sending them in to the **CaseSensitiveComparer's Compare** method to compare them.

   ```
   return ((new CaseInsensitiveComparer()).Compare(
       Double.Parse(value1.ToString()),
       Double.Parse(value2.ToString()))
   );
   ```

6. If the values are not numerical you can call the **CaseSensitiveComparer's Compare** method without first parsing the values.

   ```
   return ((new CaseInsensitiveComparer()).Compare(value1, value2));
   ```

The complete code for the **Compare** and **IsNumeric** methods:

```
class RuleComparer : IComparer
{
    bool IsNumeric(object value)
    {
        Regex regex = new Regex(@"^[-+]?[0-9]*\.?[0-9]+$");
        return regex.IsMatch(value.ToString());
    }
```

```
public int Compare(object value1, object value2)
{
    if (IsNumeric(value1) && IsNumeric(value2))
    {
        return ((new CaseInsensitiveComparer()).Compare(
            Double.Parse(value1.ToString()),
            Double.Parse(value2.ToString()))
        );
    }

    return ((new CaseInsensitiveComparer()).Compare(value1, value2));
}
}
```

The EvaluateRules<T> method

The purpose of this method is to evaluate the rules against properties in an object of type **T**. To achieve this you will need to use reflection to look at the properties of the object and to fetch the value from a property named by the **Property** property of the rule.

1. Add a generic **bool** method called **EvaluateRules<T>** which has a **T** parameter called item and a **List<BusinessRule<T>>** collection parameter called rules. The **T** parameter is the instance you want to evaluate the rules against and the collection is the list of rules to evaluate.
   ```
   public bool EvaluateRules<T>(T item, List<BusinessRule<T>> rules)
   {
   }
   ```

2. Add a **bool** variable called **success** and assign **true** to it. The variable will be used to determine the weighted success of all the rules in the collection passed into the method. If all rules are successful then the variable will contain **true** otherwise it will contain **false**.

3. Add a **foreach** loop which iterates over the rules in the collection.

4. Fetch the property value from the **item** of type **T** using reflection inside the **foreach**-block. You need to use reflection in order to get to the property values. Call the **GetType** method on the **item** variable to get its type definition (the class and its content), then call the **GetProperty** method on the type to fetch a specific property definition based on the name stored in the **Property** property in the current rule in the iteration. Use that property to call the **GetValue** method passing in the **item** of **T** object to it.

```
var value = item.GetType().GetProperty(rule.Property).GetValue(item);
```

5. Add an **int** variable called **result** and assign **0** to it. This variable will be used to store the result from a call to the **Compare** method when evaluating if the two values being compared are equal, less than or greater than one another.

6. To find out what operator to use and how to evaluate the comparison between the two object values you need to add a **switch** checking the **Comparer** property of the current rule in the iteration.

```
switch (rule.Comparer)
{
}
```

7. Add the **case** for **RuleOperator.LessThan** by making a call to the **Compare** method passing in the value from the property of the item of **T** that you fetched earlier with reflection and the value from the **Value** property of the **rule**. Store the result in the **result** variable you created earlier. To determine if the result is successful you assign **result < 0** to the **Success** property of the rule and use a Boolean and (**&**) to determine the result of the **success** variable (**success & result < 0**) that way the result in the **success** variable can only be **true** if both values are **true**; you can expand the result to encompass all the rules in the collection.

```
case RuleOperator.LessThan:
    result = Compare(value, rule.Value);
    rule.Success = result < 0;
    success = success & result < 0;
    break;
```

8. The **case** for **RuleOperator.Equal** is very similar to the previous **case**, the difference is that instead of evaluating **result < 0** you evaluate **result.Equals(0)**.

9. The **case** for **RuleOperator.GreaterThan** is very similar to the previous **case**, the difference is that instead of evaluating **result.Equals(0)** you evaluate **result > 0**.

10. The **case** for **RuleOperator.NotEqual** is very similar to the previous **case**, the difference is that instead of evaluating **result > 0** you evaluate **!result.Equals(0)**.

11. The **case** for **RuleOperator.Contains** is different than the other cases in that it has to iterate over all the items in the collection in order to evaluate the rule fully. Begin by assigning **false** to the **Success** property of the **rule**.

12. Add a **foreach** loop iterating over all the items in the **rule**'s **Items** collection.

601

13. Fetch the current item's value In the loop for the same property you fetched the value for the **item** of **T** earlier, use the name in the **Property** property of the **rule** (**itm** is the current item in the iteration).
```
var propValue =
itm.GetType().GetProperty(rule.Property).GetValue(itm);
```

14. Since you want to figure out if there is an item in the collection that is equal to the **item** of **T** based on the given property you can assume that if there is one or more matches the **rule** is successful and the **Success** property of the **rule** should be assigned **true**. You can do this evaluation by calling the **Compare** method and evaluate if the result is equal to **0** (**value** is the variable holding the value stored in the property in the **item** of **T**)
```
if(Compare(propValue, value).Equals(0))
{
    rule.Success = true;
}
```

15. Use a Boolean and (**&**) when determining if the result is successful and assign the result to the **success** variable. You have to cast the **rule.Success** variable since it is declared as a **null**-able **bool** (**bool?**)
```
success = success & (bool)rule.Success;
```

16. The **case** for **RuleOperator.NotContains** is very similar to the previous **case** but you begin by assigning **true** to the **Success** property of the **rule**, **false** to the **Success** property of the **rule** and then **break** out of the loop if the comparison is successful (if there is a comparable item in the collection).
```
if (Compare(propValue, value).Equals(0))
{
    rule.Success = false;
    break;
}
```

17. The final evaluation if the **rule** is successful or not is the same as for the previous **case**.

18. The last thing you need to do in the method is to **return** the **success** variable from the method outside the loop (before the closing curly brace of the method).

The complete code for the **EvaluateRules<T>** method:

```csharp
public bool EvaluateRules<T>(T item, List<BusinessRule<T>> rules)
{
    var success = true;

    foreach (var rule in rules)
    {
        var value = item.GetType().GetProperty(rule.Property).GetValue(item);
        int result = 0;

        switch (rule.Comparer)
        {
            case RuleOperator.LessThan:
                result = Compare(value, rule.Value);
                rule.Success = result < 0;
                success = success & result < 0;
                break;
            case RuleOperator.Equal:
                result = Compare(value, rule.Value);
                rule.Success = result.Equals(0);
                success = success & result.Equals(0);
                break;
            case RuleOperator.GreaterThan:
                result = Compare(value, rule.Value);
                rule.Success = result > 0;
                success = success & result > 0;
                break;
            case RuleOperator.NotEqual:
                result = Compare(value, rule.Value);
                rule.Success = !result.Equals(0);
                success = success & !result.Equals(0);
                break;
            case RuleOperator.Contains:
                rule.Success = false;
                foreach (var itm in rule.Items)
                {
                    var propValue = itm.GetType()
                        .GetProperty(rule.Property).GetValue(itm);

                    if(Compare(propValue, value).Equals(0))
                    {
                        rule.Success = true;
                    }
```

```
            }

            success = success & (bool)rule.Success;
            break;
        case RuleOperator.NotContains:
            rule.Success = true;
            foreach (var itm in rule.Items)
            {
                var propValue = itm.GetType()
                    .GetProperty(rule.Property).GetValue(itm);

                if (Compare(propValue, value).Equals(0))
                {
                    rule.Success = false;
                    break;
                }
            }

            success = success & (bool)rule.Success;
            break;
    }
}

return success;
}
```

Adding and testing rules

Let's add the rules that will be used later and test them to see that they actually work. The rules will be used when adding a new vehicle or customer on the **Add Data** tab and the rules are the same as the rules in the **AddVehicle** and **AddCustomer** methods of the **Booking-Processor** class.

The following rules are evaluated when a vehicle is added:

- The vehicle **Id** must be less than **1**.
- The vehicle's **Meter** setting must be greater than or equal to **0**.
- The vehicle's **RegistrationNumber** must not be an empty string.
- The vehicle's **TypeId** must be greater than **0**.

The following rules are evaluated when a customer is added:

- The customer **Id** must be less than **1**.

- The customer's **SocialSecurityNumber** must not exist in the **Customer** collection in the **TestData** class (the data source).

Adding the rules:

1. Locate the **AddVehicle** method in the form's code-behind.
2. Add the rules above the call to the **processor.AddVehicle** method.
3. Create a variable called **rules** and assign an instance of **List<BusinessRule< IVehicle>>** to it. Create rules in the collection by adding new instances of the **BusinessRule<IVehicle>** class and assign values to their properties (see the rules above).

```
var rules = new List<BusinessRule<IVehicle>>() {
    new BusinessRule<IVehicle> {
        Property = "Id", Value = 1,
        Comparer = RuleOperator.LessThan },
    new BusinessRule<IVehicle> {
        Property = "Meter", Value = -1,
        Comparer = RuleOperator.GreaterThan },
    new BusinessRule<IVehicle> {
        Property = "RegistrationNumber", Value = String.Empty,
        Comparer = RuleOperator.NotEqual },
    new BusinessRule<IVehicle> {
        Property = "TypeId", Value = 0,
        Comparer = RuleOperator.GreaterThan }
};
```

4. To evaluate the rules you will have to temporarily change the access modifier on the **RuleComparer** class to **public**.
5. Add a call to the **EvaluateRules<T>** method on an instance of the **RuleComparer** class and assign the **return** value to a variable called **success**. Pass in the **vehicle** instance being created in the **AddVehicle** method to the **EvaluateRules** method along with the **rules** collection.

```
var success = new RuleComparer().EvaluateRules(vehicle, rules);
```

6. Place a breakpoint on the call to the **processor.AddVehicle** method.
7. Run the application and add a new vehicle on the **Add Data** tab.
8. The value of the **success** variable should be **true**.
9. Stop the application.
10. Change the **Id** rule's **Value** property to **0**.

11. Run the application and add a new vehicle on the **Add Data** tab.

12. The value of the **success** variable should be **false**. because one of the rules has been evaluated to **false**. Remember that all rules have to return **true** for the final result of all rules to be **true**.

13. Stop the application.

14. Change the **Id** rule's value back to **1**.

15. Remove the call to the **EvaluateRules** method that you added in step 5.

16. Locate the **AddCustomer** method in the form's code-behind.

17. Add the rules above the call to the **processor.AddCustomer** method.

18. Create a variable called rules which you assign a **List<BusinessRule<ICustomer>>** instance, create rules in the collection by adding new instances of the **BusinessRule< ICustomer>** class and assign values to their properties (see the rules above). Note that the **Items** property is assigned the **Customers** collection by calling the **Get-Customers** method and the **Comparer** property is assigned **NotContains**.

```
var rules = new List<BusinessRule<ICustomer>>() {
    new BusinessRule<ICustomer> {
        Property = "Id", Value = 1,
        Comparer = RuleOperator.LessThan },
    new BusinessRule<ICustomer> {
        Property = "SocialSecurityNumber",
        Items = processor.GetCustomers(),
        Comparer = RuleOperator.NotContains }
};
```

19. Add a call to the **EvaluateRules<T>** method on an instance of the **RuleComparer** class and assign the **return** value to a variable called **success**. Pass in the **customer** instance being created in the **AddCustomer** method to the **EvaluateRules** method along with the **rules** collection.

```
var success = new RuleComparer().EvaluateRules(customer, rules);
```

20. Place a breakpoint on the call to the **processor.AddCustomer** method.

21. Run the application and add a new customer on the **Add Data** tab.

22. The value of the **success** variable should be **true**.

23. Stop the application.

24. Change the **Id** rule's **Value** property to **0**.

25. Run the application and add a new customer on the **Add Data** tab.

26. The value of the **success** variable should be **false**. because one of the rules has been evaluated to **false**.

27. Stop the application.

28. Change the **Id** rule's **Value** property back to **1**.

29. Run the application and try to add a customer with an existing social security number and make sure that the result in the **success** variable is **false**. You can find existing social security numbers in the **Seed** method in the **TestData** class.

30. Remove the call to the **EvaluateRules** method that you added in step 19.

31. Remove the **public** access modifier you added to the **RuleComparer** class making it **internal** again.

Mini Use Case: Car rental - Generic reflection data layer

In this exercise you will refactor the data- and business layer's methods to make them more flexible using reflection and by doing so cutting down the number of methods needed to accomplish tasks such as fetching and adding entities. For instance, up until now there has been one method for each fetch scenario with methods like **GetCustomer** and **GetVehicle**; that will be a thing of the past as you move forward. You will be able to remove all those methods from the data layer and most of them in the business layer when refactoring to one **Get** method and one **Add** method in the data layer. You might be wondering how that is possible, well, it is possible because with reflection, as you know, you can look into a class' definition and call methods on a "reflection" instance of that class.

This task of switching to generic methods would involve pretty significant changes to the **IBookingProcessor** and **IDataLayer** interfaces rendering them useless to other applications, so what you will do instead is to create two new interfaces (version 2.0) that you will implement in new data layer and business layer classes. This way the only affected application will be the one you are working on and older systems can still use the previous version of the interfaces and class implementations. You can then communicate to all your customers that the old interfaces are scheduled for removal in a future release giving them time to adapt their systems to the new implementations.

To make it really visible for you what changes are being made they will be made in copies of the existing classes and interfaces. Let's take it step by step and incrementally change everything that has to be altered.

Creating the interfaces and classes

Copy the **IBookingProcessor** interface and **BookingProcessor** class and rename them **IGenericProcessor** and **GenericProcessor**. Do the same for the **IDataLayer**, **IRentalBase** and **CollectionDataLayer** and rename them **IGenericDataLayer**, **IGenericBase** and **GenericDataLayer**.

Don't forget to change the names of the implemented and inherited interfaces as well as the constructors of the involved classes. So far no code has been removed, changed or added apart from the changes stated above.

You can copy a .cs file by:

1. Right clicking on the file in the Solution Explorer and select **Copy**.
2. Right click on the folder where you want the copy and select **Paste**.
3. Select the file you pasted in and press **F2** on the keyboard to rename the file, this does not change the name in the file however.
4. Open the file and change the name of the class or interface and the constructor name if it is a class.

The changes to the copied and renamed interfaces and classes in the **Data Layer** project:

```
public interface IGenericBase
{
    // Other available methods are not displayed here
}

public interface IGenericDataLayer : IGenericBase, ISerialize
{
    // Other available methods are not displayed here
}

public class GenericDataLayer : IGenericDataLayer
{
    public GenericDataLayer()
    {
        // The code is not displayed here
    }

    // Other available methods are not displayed here
}
```

The changes to the copied and renamed interfaces and classes in the **Business Layer** project:

```
public interface IGenericProcessor : IGenericBase
{
    IGenericDataLayer DataLayer { get; }

    // Other available methods are not displayed here
}

public class GenericProcessor : IGenericProcessor
{
    #region Properties
    public IGenericDataLayer DataLayer { get; private set; }
    #endregion

    #region Constructor
    public GenericProcessor(IGenericDataLayer dataLayer)
    {
        DataLayer = dataLayer;
    }
    #endregion

    // Other available methods have been left out
}
```

The generic Get method

To be able to implement the generic **Get** method it will first have to be implemented in the **IGenericBase** interface, that way it has to be implemented in both the **GenericProcessor** and **GenericDataLayer** class. But what should that method return and what, if any, parameters should it have?

If you look at the old **Get** methods in the interface you can see that they return an **IEnumerable** of the type they fetch data for; this mean that it is a great opportunity for using generics since it is the type that determine what will be returned; those types can easily be replaced with the generic type **T**. The tricky part is that a generic type **T** doesn't give you access to the type members which mean that you will have to use reflection to access them in the generic **Get** method.

To make it less complicated you will deal with the parameter-less **Get** methods as one case and the other **Get** methods as separate cases, you will still be able to use the generic **Get** method for those methods as well in a secondary capacity. So the **GetCustomers, Get-Bookings** and **GetVehicleTypes** methods will all be replaced by the new parameter-less generic **Get** method.

The new generic interface method definition will thus be **IEnumerable<T> Get<T>()**. Add that method definition to the **IGenericBase** interface but don't remove the old **Get** method definitions yet.

Implement the new **Get** method in the **GenericProcessor** and **GenericDataLayer** classes.

Call the **Get** method in the **GenericDataLayer** class from the **Get** method in the **Generic-Processor** class.

Adding the Get method to the IGenericBase interface

1. Open the **IGenericBase** interface.
2. Add a **region** with the description **Generic Methods**.
3. Add the method definition to the region.

The alterations to the **IGenericBase** interface:

```
public interface IGenericBase
{
    #region Generic Methods
    IEnumerable<T> Get<T>();
    #endregion

    #region Action Methods ...
    #region Fetch Methods ...
}
```

Implementing the Get method in the GenericProcessor class

1. Open the **GenericProcessor** class.
2. Add a **region** with the description **Generic Methods**.
3. Add a **public Get** method with the same definition as in the **IGenericBase** interface.
4. Call the new **Get** method in the **GenericDataLayer** class through the **DataLayer** property and return the result.
   ```
   public IEnumerable<T> Get<T>() {
       return DataLayer.Get<T>();
   }
   ```

Implementing the Get method in the GenericDataLayer class

This method is a bit tricky since it involves a lot of reflection. The first thing you need to do is to fetch the type definition for the generic type **T** in order to get access to its member definitions. You then create an instance of the **TestData** class and fetch its type definition in order to get access to its member definitions and later its collections.

Use the type definition of the **TestData** class to fetch the first field that has a generic argument with a type name matching the type name of the generic type **T**. This will locate the collection that has the same type in its angle brackets as the type stored in the generic type **T**. In other words, if **T** is **ICustomer** that type will be used to locate the **IEnumerable <ICustomer>** collection in the **TestData** class matching them on the type name and return it as a **FieldInfo** object.

```
var colFieldInfo = testDataType.GetFields().FirstOrDefault(f =>
f.FieldType.GetGenericArguments().First().Name.Equals(type.Name));
```

```
var colFieldInfo =
    testDataType.GetFields() // Get the variables in the TestData class
        .FirstOrDefault(f => // Find the first matching field
        f.FieldType // Get the variable's data type (IEnumerable)
        .GetGenericArguments() // Get the angle bracket's data types
        .First() // Get the first generic type (you only use one)
        .Name // Get the name of that generic type
        .Equals(type.Name)); // Is it equal to the type name of T
```

Use the **FieldInfo** object, the collection, to fetch its values by calling the **GetValue** method on it passing In the instance of the **TestData** class.

1. Open the **GenericDataLayer** class.
2. Add a **region** with the description **Generic Methods**.
3. Add a **public Get** method with the same definition as in the **IGenericBase** interface.
4. Fetch the type definition of the type **T** and store it in a variable called **type**.
   ```
   var type = typeof(T);
   ```
5. Create an instance of the **TestData** class and store it in a variable called **testDataObj**.
6. Fetch the type definition of the type **TestData** class and store it in a variable called **testDataType**.
   ```
   var testDataType = testDataObj.GetType();
   ```

7. Fetch the FieldInfo object describing the collection you are seeking and store it in a variable called **collectionField** (see detailed description above).
```
var collectionField = testDataType.GetFields().FirstOrDefault(f =>
f.FieldType.GetGenericArguments().First().Name.Equals(type.Name));
```

8. Fetch the collection and cast it to a **IEnumerable<T>**. Store the collection in a variable called **collection**. You need to pass in the **TestData** instance to the **GetValue** method to gain access to the data.
```
var collection =
    (IEnumerable<T>)collectionField.GetValue(testDataObj);
```

9. Return the collection from the method.

The complete code for the **Get** method in the **GenericDataLayer** class:

```
#region Generic Methods
public IEnumerable<T> Get<T>()
{
    var type = typeof(T);
    var testDataObj = new TestData();
    var testDataType = testDataObj.GetType();

    var collectionField = testDataType.GetFields()
        .FirstOrDefault(f => f.FieldType.GetGenericArguments()
        .First().Name.Equals(type.Name));

    var collection = (IEnumerable<T>)collectionField
        .GetValue(testDataObj);

    return collection;
}
#endregion
```

Replacing the Get method calls in the form

This is basically a search and replace scenario where you replace all the calls to the **GetCustomers**, **GetBookings** and **GetVehicleTypes** methods with a call to the generic Get method specifying the type you want to fetch collection data for; an example would be that the **GetCustomers()** call would be replaced with a call to **Get<ICustomer>()**.

Changing the access modifiers to **public** on the collections in the **TestData** will make it easier for you to work with the data in the class through reflection.

1. Open the **TestData** class and change the access modifier from **internal** to **public** for all the collections.
2. Open the form's code-behind.
3. Locate the **IBookingProcessor processor** variable at the beginning of the form and change it to **IGenericProcessor processor**.
4. Change the instance creation of the **BookingProcessor** in the **Form_Load** event to create an instance of the **GenericProcessor** class.
   ```
   processor = new GenericProcessor(new GenericDataLayer());
   ```
5. Locate the **FillCustomers** method.
6. Replace the call to the **GetCustomers** method in the LINQ query with a call to the generic **Get** method.
   ```
   var customer = from c in processor.Get<ICustomer>()
   ```
7. Locate the **FillBookings** method.
8. Replace the call to the **GetBookings** and **GetCustomers** methods in the LINQ query with calls to the generic **Get** method.
   ```
   var bookings = from b in processor.Get<IBooking>()
   join c in processor.Get<ICustomer>() on b.CustomerId equals c.Id
   ```
9. Locate the **FillVehicleTypes** method.
10. Replace the call to the **GetVehicleTypes** method in the LINQ query with a call to the generic **Get** method.
    ```
    cboTypes.DataSource = processor.Get<IVehicleType>();
    ```
11. Locate the **GetBooking** method.
12. Replace the call to the **GetBookings** method in the LINQ query with calls to the generic **Get** method.
    ```
    return (from b in DataLayer.Get<IBooking>()
    ```
13. Locate the **AddCustomer** method.
14. Replace the call to the **GetCustomers** method in the **SocialSecurityNumber** rule with a call to the generic **Get** method.
    ```
    new BusinessRule<ICustomer> { Property = "SocialSecurityNumber",
        Items = processor.Get<ICustomer>(),
        Comparer = RuleOperator.NotContains }
    ```
15. Locate the **CustomerExist** method.

16. Replace the call to the **GetCustomers** method in the LINQ query with calls to the generic **Get** method.
```
var social = (from c in DataLayer.Get<ICustomer>()
```

17. Locate the **btnSave_Click** event.

18. Replace the call to the **GetCustomers** method in the call to the **WriteToFile** method with a call to the generic **Get** method.
```
var success = IO.WriteToFile(@"C:\Test\Customers.txt",
    processor.Get<ICustomer>());
```

19. Run the application and make sure that all the list views and combo boxes have data.

20. Close the application.

21. Now that you know that the application works it's time to do some clean up and remove code that is no longer in use.

22. Open the **IGenericBase** interface and remove (or comment out) the **GetCustomers**, **GetBookings** and **GetVehicleTypes** methods.
```
//IEnumerable<ICustomer> GetCustomers();
//IEnumerable<IBooking> GetBookings();
//IEnumerable<IVehicleType> GetVehicleTypes();
```

23. Open the **GenericProcessor** class and remove (or comment out) the **GetCustomers**, **GetBookings** and **GetVehicleTypes** methods.

24. Open the **GenericDataLayer** class and remove (or comment out) the **GetCustomers**, **GetBookings** and **GetVehicleTypes** methods.

25. Run the application and make sure that all the list views and combo boxes have data.

26. Close the application.

Refactoring the GetVehicles method

This method will no longer be needed in the **GenericDataLayer** class since it will be calling the generic **Get** method from the **GetVehicles** method in the **GenericProcessor** class. You will therefore move the method's interface definition from the **IGenericBase** to the **IGenericProcessor** interface.

The **GetVehicles** method contain logic about which vehicles to fetch that you need to preserve by moving it to the **GenericProcessor** version of the method.

1. Open the **IGenericBase** interface and cut out the **GetVehicles** definition.
2. Open the **IGenericProcessor** interface and paste the **GetVehicles** definition into the interface.
   ```
   IEnumerable<IVehicle> GetVehicles(VehicleStatus status);
   ```
3. Open The **GetVehicles** method in the **GenericDataLayer** class and cut out the **switch**-block and delete what's remaining of the method.
4. Open the **GenericProcessor** version of the **GetVehicles** method and replace the call to the **DataLayer.GetVehicles** method with the **switch** you cut out.
   ```
   // Replace this code with the switch
   return DataLayer.GetVehicles(status);
   ```
5. The code will light up like a Christmas tree, but not to worry. Just replace the direct collection uses with calls to the generic **Get** method for the specified collection types; as an example the **TestData.Vehicles** would become **DataLayer.Get<IVehicle>()**.
   ```
   case VehicleStatus.All:
       // return TestData.Vehicles;
       // Would become
       return DataLayer.Get<IVehicle>();
   ```
6. Run the application and make sure that all list views contain information.
7. Close the application.

The complete code for the **GetVehicles** method in the **GenericProcessor** class:

```
public IEnumerable<IVehicle> GetVehicles(VehicleStatus status)
{
    try
    {
        switch (status)
        {
            case VehicleStatus.All:
                return DataLayer.Get<IVehicle>();
            case VehicleStatus.Booked:
                return from c in DataLayer.Get<IVehicle>()
                join b in DataLayer.Get<IBooking>() on c.Id equals b.VehicleId
                where b.Returned.Equals(DateTime.MinValue)
                select c;
```

```
        case VehicleStatus.Available:
            return from c in DataLayer.Get<IVehicle>()
            where GetVehicles(VehicleStatus.Booked)
                .Count(b => b.Id.Equals(c.Id)).Equals(0)
            select c;
        default:
            return null;
        }
    }
}
catch
{
    throw;
}
}
```

Refactoring the GetVehicleTypes method

This method will no longer be needed in the **GenericDataLayer** class since it will be calling the generic **Get** method from the **GetVehicleTypes** method in the **GenericProcessor** class. You will therefore move the method's interface definition from the **IGenericBase** to the **IGenericProcessor** interface.

The **GetVehicleTypes** method contain logic about which vehicles to fetch that you need to preserve by moving it to the **GenericProcessor** version of the method.

1. Open the **IGenericBase** interface and cut out the **GetVehicleTypes** definition.
2. Open the **IGenericProcessor** interface and paste the **GetVehicleTypes** definition into the interface.
    ```
    IVehicleType GetVehicleType(int vehicleTypeId);
    ```
3. Open The **GetVehicleTypes** method in the **GenericDataLayer** class and cut out the code fetching the first vehicle type matching the **vehicleTypeId** parameter.
    ```
    return TestData.VehicleTypes.FirstOrDefault(vt =>
    vt.Id.Equals(vehicleTypeId));
    ```
4. Open the **GenericProcessor** version of the **GetVehicleTypes** method and replace the call to the **DataLayer.GetVehicleTypes** method with the code you cut out.
    ```
    // Replace this code with the cut out code
    return DataLayer.GetVehicleType(vehicleTypeId);
    ```
5. Replace the direct usage of the **VehicleTypes** collection with a call to the generic **Get** method for the **IVehicleType** type **DataLayer.Get<IVehicleType>()**.

```
//return DataLayer.GetVehicleType(vehicleTypeId);
// Would become
return DataLayer.Get<IVehicleType>()
    .FirstOrDefault(vt => vt.Id.Equals(vehicleTypeId));
```

6. Run the application and make sure that the list views display the vehicle type in the **Type** column and that the combo box on the **Add Data** tab contain the vehicle types.

7. Close the application.

The complete code for the **GetVehicleTypes** method in the **GenericProcessor** class:

```
public IVehicleType GetVehicleType(int vehicleTypeId)
{
    try
    {
        return DataLayer.Get<IVehicleType>()
            .FirstOrDefault(vt => vt.Id.Equals(vehicleTypeId));
    }
    catch
    {
        throw;
    }
}
```

The Refactored IGenericBase interface

```
public interface IGenericBase
{
    #region Generic Methods
    IEnumerable<T> Get<T>();
    #endregion

    #region Action Methods
    bool RentVehicle(int vehicleId, int customerId, DateTime timeOfRental);
    double ReturnVehicle(int bookingId, double meter, DateTime returned);
    void AddVehicle(IVehicle vehicle);
    void AddCustomer(ICustomer customer);
    #endregion
}
```

The Refactored IGenericProcessor interface

```
public interface IGenericProcessor : IGenericBase
{
    IGenericDataLayer DataLayer { get; }

    bool CustomerExist(string socialScurityNumber);
    IBooking GetBooking(int vehicleId);
    IEnumerable<IVehicle> GetVehicles(VehicleStatus status);
    IVehicleType GetVehicleType(int vehicleTypeId);
}
```

The generic Add method

One version of the generic **Add** method will be implemented in the **GenericDataLayer** class and another in the **GenericProcessor** class where the **Add** method in the **GenericProcessor** class will call the **Add** method in the **GenericDataLayer** class.

The **Add** method in the **GenericDataLayer** class will use reflection to find the correct collection based on the data type of the item of **T** passed in to it. It will also use reflection to generate a new id for the added item.

The **Add** method in the **GenericProcessor** class will evaluate the passed in business rules and if they report back a successful outcome call the **Add** method in the **GenericDataLayer** class.

The **AddVehicle** method in the form's code-behind will call the new **Add** method in the **GenericProcessor** class passing in the vehicle object and a list of rules to evaluate (the rules you added and tested in an earlier exercise).

The IGenericDataLayer interface

You will add a **void Add** method which has a parameter called **item** of type **T**.

1. Open the **IGenericDataLayer** interface.
2. Add a **region** with the description **Generic Methods**.
3. Add a **void Add** method which has a parameter called **item** of type **T** to the region.
   ```
   void Add<T>(T item);
   ```

The complete **IGenericDataLayer** interface:

```
public interface IGenericDataLayer : IGenericBase, ISerialize
{
    #region Generic Methods
    void Add<T>(T item);
    #endregion

    #region Helper Methods
    int RentalDuration(DateTime rented, DateTime returned);
    double CalculatePrice(IVehicle vehicle,
        double returnedMeterSetting, int duration);
    #endregion
}
```

Implementing the Add method in the GenericDataLayer class

This method is a bit tricky since it involves a lot of reflection. The first thing you need to do is to fetch the type definition for the generic type **T** in order to get access to its member definitions. You then have to create an instance of the **TestData** class to fetch its type definition and use it to access its member definitions and later be able to get access to the data in the collections.

Use the type definition of the **TestData** class to fetch the first field that has a generic argument with a type name matching the type name of the generic type **T**. This will locate the collection that has the same type in its angle brackets as the type stored in the generic type **T**. In other words, if **T** is **ICustomer** that type will be used to locate the **IEnumerable <ICustomer>** collection in the **TestData** class matching them on the type name and return it as a **FieldInfo** object.

```
var collectionVariable = testDataType.GetFields().FirstOrDefault(f =>
f.FieldType.GetGenericArguments().First().Name.Equals(type.Name));


var collectionVariable =
    testDataType.GetFields() // Get the variables in the TestData class
        .FirstOrDefault(f => // Find the first matching field
        f.FieldType // Get the variable's data type (IEnumerable)
        .GetGenericArguments() // Get the angle bracket's data types
        .First() // Get the first generic type (you only use one)
        .Name // Get the name of that generic type
        .Equals(type.Name)); // Is it equal to the type name of T
```

Use the **collectionVariable** to fetch the values in the collection by calling the **GetValue** method on it passing in the instance of the **TestData** class, store the result in a variable called **collection**.

Use the **collection** variable to fetch the highest id value and assign that value incremented by 1 to the **Id** property of the **item** of **T** object passed in to the method.

Add the updated **item** object to the collection using its **Add** method.

1. Open the **GenericDataLayer** class.
2. Add a **region** with the description **Generic Methods**.
3. Add a **public Add** method with the same definition as in the **IGenericDataLayer** interface.
4. Fetch the type definition of the type **T** and store it in a variable called **type**.
   ```
   var type = typeof(T);
   ```
5. Create an instance of the **TestData** class and store it in a variable called **testDataObj**.
6. Fetch the type definition of the type **TestData** class and store it in a variable called **testDataType**.
   ```
   var testDataType = testDataObj.GetType();
   ```
7. Fetch the FieldInfo object describing the collection you are seeking and store it in a variable called **collectionVariable** (see detailed description above).
   ```
   var collectionVariable = testDataType.GetFields().FirstOrDefault(f =>
   f.FieldType.GetGenericArguments().First().Name.Equals(type.Name));
   ```
8. Fetch the collection and cast it to an **IEnumerable<T>**. Store the collection in a variable called **collection**. You need to pass in the **TestData** instance to the **GetValue** method to gain access to the data.
   ```
   var collection =
   (IEnumerable<T>)collectionVariable.GetValue(testDataObj);
   ```
9. Assign a value to the **item** object's **Id** property.
   ```
   item.GetType().GetProperty("Id").SetValue(item, collection.Max(b =>
   (int)b.GetType().GetProperty("Id").GetValue(b) + 1));
   ```
10. Add the updated **item** object to the collection.

The complete code for the **Add** method in the **GenericDataLayer** class:

```
public void Add<T>(T item)
{
    // Get the type that defines the collection
    var type = typeof(T);
    // Create an instance of the TestData Class,
    // the instance is needed when adding the
    // item to the collection
    var testDataObj = new TestData();
    // The type definition of the TestData class
    // which is needed to find the collection
    var testDataType = testDataObj.GetType();
    // Find the collection based on its generic type
    // for instance <ICustomer> and the type name of
    // T (ICustomer, IVehicle, ...)
    var collectionVariable = testDataType.GetFields()
        .FirstOrDefault(f => f.FieldType.GetGenericArguments()
        .First().Name.Equals(type.Name));

    // Get the actual collection as a List<T>
    // using the collection variable
    var collection = (List<T>)collectionVariable.GetValue(testDataObj);

    // Highest Id + 1
    item.GetType().GetProperty("Id").SetValue(item,
    collection.Max(b => (int)b.GetType().GetProperty("Id").GetValue(b) +
        1));

    // Add the instance of T to the collection
    collection.Add(item);
}
```

The IGenericProcessor interface

You will add a **void Add** method which has one parameter called **item** of type **T** and another called **rules** of type **List<BusinessRule<T>>**.

1. Open the **IGenericProcessor** interface.
2. Add a **region** with the description **Generic Methods**.
3. Add a **void Add** method which with the two parameters described above to the region.
   ```
   bool Add<T>(T item, List<BusinessRule<T>> rules);
   ```

The complete **IGenericProcessor** interface:

```
public interface IGenericProcessor : IGenericBase
{
    IGenericDataLayer DataLayer { get; }

    #region Generic Methods
    bool Add<T>(T item, List<BusinessRule<T>> rules);
    #endregion

    bool CustomerExist(string socialScurityNumber);
    IBooking GetBooking(int vehicleId);
    IEnumerable<IVehicle> GetVehicles(VehicleStatus status);
    IVehicleType GetVehicleType(int vehicleTypeId);
}
```

Implementing the Add method in the GenericProcessor class

This Add method takes an **item** parameter of type **T** and a **List<BusinessRule<T>>** parameter called **rules**. It implements a **try/catch**-block where the **catch**-block re-throws any exception.

The first thing to happen in the **try**-block is that the rules are evaluated by the **EvaluateRules** method on an instance of the **RuleComparer** class. If the method return a successful outcome the **Add** method is called on the **DataLayer** instance. The **Add** method result is then returned from the **EvaluateRules** method call.

1. Open the **GenericProcessor** class.
2. Add the **Add** method as described above to the **Generic Methods** region.
   ```
   public bool Add<T>(T item, List<BusinessRule<T>> rules)
   ```
3. Add a **try/catch**-block where the **catch**-block re-throws any exception.
4. Evaluate the rules by calling the **EvaluateRules** method on an instance of the **Rule-Comparer** class and store the result in a variable called **success**.
   ```
   var success = new RuleComparer().EvaluateRules(item, rules);
   ```
5. Call the **Add** method on the **DataLayer** instance if the **success** variable is **true**.
6. Return the value in the **success** variable from the method.

The complete code for the **Add** method in the **GenericProcessor** class:

```
public bool Add<T>(T item, List<BusinessRule<T>> rules)
{
    try
    {
        var success = new RuleComparer().EvaluateRules(item, rules);
        if (success) DataLayer.Add(item);
        return success;
    }
    catch
    {
        throw;
    }
}
```

Altering the AddVehicle method in the form's code-behind

Replace the call to the **processor.AddVehicle** method call with a call to the new generic **Add** method passing in the **vehicle** object and the collection of **rules** you added in an earlier exercise.

1. Open the form's code-behind and locate the call to the **AddVehicle** method.
2. Replace the call to the **AddVehicle** method with a call to the generic **Add** method.
   ```
   // processor.AddVehicle(vehicle);
   // Replace with
   var success = processor.Add<IVehicle>(vehicle, rules);
   ```
3. Open the **IGenericBase** interface and remove the **AddVehicle** method.
4. Open the **IGenericDataLayer** interface and remove the **AddVehicle** method.
5. Open the **IGenericProcessor** interface and remove the **AddVehicle** method.
6. Run the application and make sure that you can add a vehicle on the **Add Data** tab.
7. Try to add a vehicle with a negative meter setting and make sure that it has not been added to the **Available Vehicles** list on the **Rent Vehicle** tab.
8. Close the application.

The code in the form's **AddVehicle** method:

```
private bool AddVehicle(IVehicle vehicle)
{
    try
    {
        // Code for checking the form input
        // fields has been omitted to save space

        // Code for adding values to the vehicle
        // has been omitted to save space

        // Business rules that are evaluated
        // in the Add method of the GenericProcessor
        var rules = new List<BusinessRule<IVehicle>>() {
            new BusinessRule<IVehicle> { Property = "Id",
                Value = 1, Comparer = RuleOperator.LessThan },
            new BusinessRule<IVehicle> { Property = "Meter",
                Value = -1, Comparer = RuleOperator.GreaterThan },
            new BusinessRule<IVehicle> {
                Property = "RegistrationNumber", Value = String.Empty,
                Comparer = RuleOperator.NotEqual },
            new BusinessRule<IVehicle> { Property = "TypeId",
                Value = 0, Comparer = RuleOperator.GreaterThan }
        };

        var success = processor.Add<IVehicle>(vehicle, rules);

        FillAvialbleVehicles();

        txtRegNo.Text = String.Empty;
        txtMeter.Text = String.Empty;

        return true;
    }
    catch { return false; }
}
```

Altering the AddCustomer method in the form's code-behind
Replace the call to the **processor.AddCustomer** method call with a call to the new generic
Add method passing in the **customer** object and the collection of **rules** you added in an
earlier exercise.

1. Open the form's code-behind and locate the call to the **AddCustomer** method.
2. Replace the call to the **AddCustomer** method with a call to the generic **Add** method. Note that you don't have to specify the interface type when calling the **Add** method on the processor instance, it will be inferred by the compiler.

```
// processor.AddCustomer(vehicle);
// Replace with
var success = processor.Add(customer, rules);
```

3. Open the **IGenericBase** interface and remove the **AddCustomer** method.
4. Open the **IGenericDataLayer** interface and remove the **AddCustomer** method.
5. Open the **IGenericProcessor** interface and remove the **AddCustomer** method.
6. Open the **IGenericProcessor** interface and remove the **CustomerExist** method.
7. Open the **GenericProcessor** interface and remove the **CustomerExist** method.
8. Run the application and add a customer, make sure that the customer is added in the combo box on the **Rent Vehicle** tab.
9. Try to add a customer with a social security number that already exist and make sure that the customer isn't added to the combo box on the **Rent Vehicle** tab.
10. Close the application.

The code in the form's **AddCustomer** method:

```
private int AddCustomer()
{
    try
    {
        // Code for checking the form input
        // fields has been omitted to save space

        var customer = new Customer() {
            SocialSecurityNumber = txtSocial.Text,
            FirstName = txtFirstName.Text,
            LastName = txtLastName.Text
        };

        // Business rules that are evaluated
        // in the Add method of the GenericProcessor
        var rules = new List<BusinessRule<ICustomer>>() {
            new BusinessRule<ICustomer> { Property = "Id",
                Value = 1, Comparer = RuleOperator.LessThan },
```

```
        new BusinessRule<ICustomer> {
            Property = "SocialSecurityNumber",
            Items = processor.Get<ICustomer>(),
            Comparer = RuleOperator.NotContains }
    };

    processor.Add(customer, rules);

    FillCustomers();

    txtSocial.Text = String.Empty;
    txtFirstName.Text = String.Empty;
    txtLastName.Text = String.Empty;

    return cboCustomers.Items.Count - 1;
}
catch(CustomerException ex)
{
    MessageBox.Show(ex.Message);
    return Int32.MinValue;
}
catch { return -1; }
}
```

17. Multithreading

Introduction

To enhance the user experience, you should take advantage of the possibility to distribute the work load to multiple threads simultaneously. We will see how the *Task Parallel Library* will solve this and how we can perform long-running tasks without blocking threads as well as how to access resources concurrently from multiple threads.

You should avoid executing long-running tasks on the UI thread because that will render the UI unresponsive. Most of the processors today have multiple cores; be sure to utilize that by using multiple threads in the application to improve performance.

Tasks

The **Task** class will enable you to perform multiple tasks in parallel on different threads. The *Task Parallel Library* handles the thread pool in the background to assign tasks to threads; with this library you can chain and pause tasks, wait for tasks to complete and perform other operations.

You create a task by using an instance of the **Task** class passing in an **Action** delegate that points to the method to be executed; this *static* method must be implemented and cannot return a value. If you need to return a value, you can use the **Func** class or a **Task<TResult>** instead.

Example: Use an Action delegate to perform a Task:

```
public partial class Form1 : Form
{
    Task taskWithMethod = new Task(new Action(ActionMethod));

    private void TaskWithMethod_Click(object sender, EventArgs e)
    {
        taskWithMethod.Start();
    }
}
```

```
    private static void ActionMethod()
    {
        // Do some long running operation
        Thread.Sleep(3000);
        MessageBox.Show("Finished: " +
            DateTime.Now.ToLongTimeString());
    }
}
```

Example: Using an anonymous delegate to perform a Task

If you want to execute a method that has a single purpose you can implement it using an anonymous delegate.

```
public partial class Form1 : Form
{
    Task taskWithDelegate = new Task(delegate
    {
        Thread.Sleep(3000);
        MessageBox.Show("Finished: " +
            DateTime.Now.ToLongTimeString());
    });

    private void TaskWithDelegate_Click(object sender, EventArgs e)
    {
        taskWithDelegate.Start();
    }
}
```

Creating tasks using Lambda expressions

Lambda is a shorthand way to define anonymous delegates that can take parameters and return a value; Lambda expressions follow the form *(input parameters) => expression*; the Lambda operator (=>) reads as "Goes to". You can pass in variables to the expression in the parenthesis on the left side of the operator; for instance the expression **(x, y) => x > y** would return **true** if **x** is greater than **y**, otherwise it would return **false**.

A Lambda expression can be used with a simple expression, target an implemented method or an anonymous method defined by a code block within curly braces on the form *(input parameters) => { C# code }*.

Using Lambda expressions is the recommended way to implement **Tasks** because it is a concise way of declaring delegates that have a tendency to become complex.

Example: Task and Lambda expression with an implemented function

```
public partial class Form1 : Form
{
    // Equivalent to:
    // Task taskName = new Task(delegate(TaskMethod));
    Task taskWithLambda = new Task(() => TaskMethod());

    private void TaskWithLambda_Click(object sender, EventArgs e)
    {
        taskWithLambda.Start();
    }

    private static void TaskMethod()
    {
        Thread.Sleep(3000);
        MessageBox.Show("Finished: " +
            DateTime.Now.ToLongTimeString());
    }
}
```

Example: Task and Lambda expression with an Anonymous delegate

```
public partial class Form1 : Form
{
    Task taskWithLambdaAnonymous = new Task(() =>
    {
        Thread.Sleep(3000);
        MessageBox.Show("Finished: " +
            DateTime.Now.ToLongTimeString());
    });

    private void TaskWithLambdaAnonymous_Click(object sender, EventArgs e)
    {
        taskWithLambdaAnonymous.Start();
    }
}
```

Additional reading: "Lambda Expressions (C# Programming Guide)"

Controlling Task execution

You can use three different methods to start queuing a **Task** for execution; the **Task.Factory .StartNew** method is highly configurable using its parameters.

Example: Three ways to start a Task

```
public partial class Form1 : Form
{
    private void ThreeWaysToStartATask_Click(object sender, EventArgs e)
    {
        Task task1 = new Task(() =>
            Console.WriteLine("Task 1 has completed.")
        );
        task1.Start();

        var task2 = Task.Factory.StartNew(() =>
            Console.WriteLine("Task 2 has completed.")
        );

        // A shorter way of calling the
        // Task.Factory.StartNew method
        var task3 = Task.Run(() =>
            Console.WriteLine("Task 3 has completed. ")
        );
    }
}
```

Waiting on Tasks

Sometimes you need to wait on the execution of a **Task**; for instance if you need to use the result of the **Task** or if you need to handle exceptions that might be thrown by the **Task**.

There are three methods that you can use to wait on a **Task**; the **Task.Wait** method waits on a specific **Task**; the **Task.WaitAll** will wait on multiple **Tasks** to finish, and the **Task.WaitAny** will wait until any one **Task** in a collection of tasks has finished.

The following methods and variable will be used in the upcoming code samples.

```
public partial class Form1 : Form
{
    private static string result = String.Empty;

    private static void LongRunningTaskA()
    {
        Thread.Sleep(3000);
        result = "LongRunningTaskA";
    }

    private static void LongRunningTaskB()
    {
        Thread.Sleep(1000);
        result = "LongRunningTaskB";
    }

    private static void LongRunningTaskC()
    {
        Thread.Sleep(3000);
        result = "LongRunningTaskC";
    }
}
```

Example: "Wait On One" Task

The execution will wait until the **Task** has completed; the label will display *LongRunning-TaskA* when the task has completed.

```
public partial class Form1 : Form
{
    private static string result = String.Empty;

    private static void LongRunningTaskA() ...
    private static void LongRunningTaskB() ...
    private static void LongRunningTaskC() ...

    private void WaitOnOneTask_Click(object sender, EventArgs e)
    {
        var taskA = Task.Run(() => LongRunningTaskA());
        taskA.Wait();

        lblTest.Text = result;
    }
}
```

Example: "Wait On Any" Task

The execution will wait until one of the tasks in the **Task** collection has completed; the Label will display *LongRunningTaskB* when the task has completed because that **Task** finishes first.

```
public partial class Form1 : Form
{
    private static string result = String.Empty;

    private static void LongRunningTaskA() ...
    private static void LongRunningTaskB() ...
    private static void LongRunningTaskC() ...

    private void WaitOnOneTask_Click(object sender, EventArgs e) ...
    private void WaitOnAnyTask_Click(object sender, EventArgs e)
    {
        Task[] tasks = new Task[3]
        {
            Task.Run( () => LongRunningTaskA()),
            Task.Run( () => LongRunningTaskB()),
            Task.Run( () => LongRunningTaskC())
        };

        // Wait for any of the tasks to complete
        // Only one Task has to complete
        Task.WaitAny(tasks);
        lblTest.Text = result;
    }
}
```

Example: "Wait On All" Tasks

The execution will wait until all of the tasks in the **Task** collection have completed; the label will display *LongRunningTaskC* when tasks have completed because that **Task** finishes last.

```
public partial class Form1 : Form
{
    private static string result = String.Empty;

    private static void LongRunningTaskA() ...
    private static void LongRunningTaskB() ...
    private static void LongRunningTaskC() ...

    private void WaitOnOneTask_Click(object sender, EventArgs e) ...
    private void WaitOnAnyTask_Click(object sender, EventArgs e) ...
```

```
private void WaitAllTask_Click(object sender, EventArgs e)
{
    Task[] tasks = new Task[3]
    {
        Task.Run( () => LongRunningTaskA()),
        Task.Run( () => LongRunningTaskB()),
        Task.Run( () => LongRunningTaskC())
    };

    // Wait for all of the tasks to complete
    Task.WaitAll(tasks);
    lblTest.Text = result;
}
}
```

Return a value from a Task

To return a value from **Task,** you need to use the generic **Task<TResult>** class; when the **Task<TResult>** has finished its execution, the return value will reside in a property named **Result** in the **Task<TResult>** instance variable.

Example: Return a value from a Task

When the **Task** finishes its execution, a **Student** instance is returned in the **Return** property.

```
class Student
{
    public string FirstName { get; set; }
    public string LastName { get; set; }
    public DateTime DOB { get; set; }
}

public partial class Form1 : Form
{
    private void ReturnAValueFromATask_Click(object sender, EventArgs e)
    {
        Task<Student> studentTask = Task.Run<Student>(() => new Student()
                { FirstName = "Jonas", LastName = "Fagerberg" });

        lblTest.Text = String.Format("{0} {1}",
            studentTask.Result.FirstName,
            studentTask.Result.LastName);
    }
}
```

Cancel a Task

In certain circumstances, you might want to give the user the possibility to cancel a long-running **Task**; it would however be dangerous to just end the **Task,** so the *Task Parallel Library* uses cancellation tokens to support cooperative cancellations.

To be able to cancel a **Task** a cancellation token has to be created when creating the **Task**. The token is then passed to the delegate method. You cancel the **Task** by calling the **Cancel** method on the **CancellationTokenSource** instance that created the token instance. You can check the status of cancellation token in the method where the **Task** was created.

Example: Cancel a Task without throwing an exception

First, you create a variable to hold the **Task**, a **CancellationTokenSource** instance to create the cancellation token and a **CancellationToken** variable to hold the token. Assign a newly created token to the **CancellationToken** variable in the **Click** event where the **Task** is created and start the **Task**. Cancel the **Task** in the cancellation **Click** event method.

The **DoWork** method is executed by the **Task**; note that a check if cancellation has been requested is made to see if the **Task** should be cancelled.

```csharp
public partial class Form1 : Form
{
    Task task;
    CancellationTokenSource cts = new CancellationTokenSource();
    CancellationToken ct;

    private void CancelATask_Click(object sender, EventArgs e)
    {
        result = String.Empty;
        ct = cts.Token;
        task = Task.Run(() => doWork(ct));
    }

    private void CancelTheTask_Click(object sender, EventArgs e)
    {
        cts.Cancel();
        lblTest.Text = result;
    }
```

```
    private void doWork(CancellationToken token)
    {
        for (int i = 0; i < 3; i++)
        {
            // Check for cancellation.
            if (token.IsCancellationRequested)
            {
                result = "Cancelled";
                return;
            }

            Thread.Sleep(1000);

            // Continue if the task has not been cancelled
            result = "Finished";
        }
    }
}
```

Example: Cancel a Task throwing an exception

If you want the **Task** to throw an exception if canceled, then you need to call the **ThrowIf-CancellationRequested** method on the token instance; an **OperationCanceledException** exception will be thrown if the **Task** is canceled.

```
public partial class Form1 : Form
{
    Task task;
    CancellationTokenSource cts = new CancellationTokenSource();
    CancellationToken ct;

    private void CancelATaskThrow_Click(object sender, EventArgs e)
    {
        result = String.Empty;
        ct = cts.Token;
        task = Task.Run(() => doWorkThrow(ct));
    }
```

```
    private void CancelTheTaskThrow_Click(object sender, EventArgs e)
    {
        try
        {
            cts.Cancel();
            if (ct.IsCancellationRequested)
                throw new OperationCanceledException(ct);
        }
        catch (OperationCanceledException ex)
        {
            lblTest.Text = "Cancelled";
        }
    }

    private void doWorkThrow(CancellationToken token)
    {
        token.ThrowIfCancellationRequested();
        Thread.Sleep(5000);
    }
}
```

Additional reading: "How to: Cancel a Task and Its Children" and "Task Cancellation C#"

Parallel Tasks

The **Parallel** class in the *Task Parallel Library* contains a number of methods that can be used if you want to execute several tasks simultaneously.

Example: A fixed set of Tasks

If you have a fixed set of **Tasks** that you want to execute simultaneously, you can use the **Parallel.Invoke** method.

The result after executing this **Task** list would be *MethodC MethodB MethodA* because that's the order the methods finish.

```
public partial class Form1 : Form
{
    private static void MethodA(){
        Thread.Sleep(3000);
        result += "MethodA ";
    }
```

```
    private static void MethodB()
    {
        Thread.Sleep(2000);
        result += "MethodB ";
    }

    private static void MethodC()
    {
        Thread.Sleep(1000);
        result += "MethodC ";
    }

    private void ExecuteFixedSetOfTasks_Click(object sender, EventArgs e)
    {
        result = String.Empty;

        Parallel.Invoke(
            () => MethodA(),
            () => MethodB(),
            () => MethodC()
        );

        lblTest.Text = result;
    }
}
```

Parallel iterations

If you have a need to run loops in parallel, you can do so using the **Parallel.For** or **Parallel.Foreach** methods; both have many overloads for different scenarios.

Example: Parallel For

The *from* and *to* parameters of the loop are of type **Int32** and the *index* parameter is executed as an **Action<Int32>** once per iteration.

```
public partial class Form1 : Form
{
    private void ParallelLoops_Click(object sender, EventArgs e)
    {
        double[] array = ParallelFor();
    }
```

```
    private double[] ParallelFor()
    {
        int from = 0;
        int to = 500000;
        double[] array = new double[to];
        Parallel.For(from, to, index =>
        {
            array[index] = Math.Sqrt(index);
        });

        return array;
    }
}
```

Example: Parallel Foreach

The simplest version of this overloaded method takes two parameters one collection of type **IEnumerable<TSource>** that you want to iterate over and one **Action<TSource>** which is the delegate function that will be executed once per iteration.

```
public partial class Form1 : Form
{
    private void ParallelForeach_Click(object sender, EventArgs e)
    {
        var students = new List<Student>();
        students.Add(new Student() { FirstName = "Jonas",
            LastName = "Fagerberg"});
        students.Add(new Student() { FirstName = "Lisa",
            LastName = "Ericsson" });

        Parallel.ForEach(students, student =>
            ParallelForeach(student));
    }

    private void ParallelForeach(Student student)
    {
        if(student.FirstName.Equals("Jonas"))
            student.FirstName = "Demo Name";

        Debug.WriteLine(student.FirstName);
    }
}
```

Additional reading: "MSDN Data Parallelism (Task Parallel Library)"

Parallel LINQ

Language-Integrated Query (LINQ) supports parallel execution through an implementation called *Parallel LINQ (PLINQ)*. You can use *PLINQ* when iterating over **IEnumerable** collections by calling the **AsParallel** method

Additional reading: "MSDN Parallel LINQ (PLINQ)"

```
public partial class Form1 : Form
{
    private void ParallelLinq_Click(object sender, EventArgs e)
    {
        var students = new List<Student>();
        students.Add(new Student()
            { FirstName = "Jonas", LastName = "Fagerberg" });

        students.Add(new Student()
            { FirstName = "Lisa", LastName = "Ericsson" });

        // Parallel LINQ (PLINQ)
        var selectedStudents =
            from student in students.AsParallel()
            where student.LastName.Equals("Fagerberg")
            select student;
    }
}
```

Handling Task exceptions

When exceptions are thrown from tasks, the *Task Parallel Library* will bundle any exceptions from joined tasks into an **AggregateException** object where all thrown exceptions are stored in the **InnerExceptions** collection property.

You can handle exceptions by waiting until the **Task** has finished; this is done by calling the **Task.Wait** method in a **try** block and implementing a **catch**-block for the **AggregateException** exception.

Additional reading: "MSDN Exception Handling (Task Parallel Library)"

```csharp
public partial class Form1 : Form
{
    private void HandleException_Click(object sender, EventArgs e)
    {
        CancellationTokenSource cts = new CancellationTokenSource();
        CancellationToken ct;
        ct = cts.Token;
        var task = Task.Run(() => doThrow(ct), ct);
        // Will trigger the exception
        cts.Cancel();

        try
        {
            task.Wait();
        }
        catch (AggregateException ae)
        {
            foreach (var inner in ae.InnerExceptions)
            {
                if (inner is TaskCanceledException)
                {
                    lblTest.Text = "Task Cancelled";
                }
                else
                {
                    // re-throw any other exception
                    throw;
                }
            }
        }
    }

    private void doThrow(CancellationToken token)
    {
        token.ThrowIfCancellationRequested();
        Thread.Sleep(5000);
    }
}
```

Concurrent collections

When using **Tasks** or other multi-threading techniques, you must ensure that the collections you use are thread-safe, which standard collections are not. There are several thread-safe collections that you can utilize when building a multi-threaded application. The reason you need thread safe collections is to keep the integrity of the data intact; no two resources should be able to use the same data simultaneously and cause corrupt data. You find the thread-safe collections in the **System.Collections.Concurrent** namespace.

Thread-safe collections

These collections are designed to work in a thread-safe manner in a multi-threaded application.

Collection	Description
ConcurrentBag<T>	Stores an unordered collection of items.
ConcurrentDictionary<TKey, TValue>	Stores a collection of dictionary items using key-value pairs.
ConcurrentQueue<T>	Works the same way as the Queue<T> class.
ConcurrentStack<T>	Works the same way as the Stack<T> class.
BlockingCollection<T>	Is a wrapper for the IProducerConsumerCollection<T> interface. It can block read requests until a read lock is available. It can block items being added to the underlying collection until space is available.
IProducerConsumerCollection<T>	This interface defines methods that are implemented by classes that distinguish between producers that add items and consu-mers that read items. The interface is implemented by the ConcurrentBag<T>, ConcurrentQueue<T> and ConcurrentStack<T> collections.

Example: Thread-safe ConcurrentQueue and ConcurrentBag

This sample code shows how you can implement a thread-safe **ConcurrentQueue** and **ConcurrentBag**. When we click the button orders will begin pouring in to the queue and the processing will begin by one of three people. When all processing is done, the result is presented in a list box.

The Order class

```
class Order
{
    public Order(string name, string description)
    {
        Name = name;
        Description = description;
    }

    public string Name { get; set; }
    public string Description { get; set; }
    public int Id
    {
        get { return Convert.ToInt32(Description.Substring(5)); }
    }
}
```

The Form

Because the application uses multiple threads to service the customers, one per waiter or waitress, you have to use thread safe collections. The collections chosen for this particular task are the **ConcurrentQueue** and **ConcurrentBag**; the queue is perfect for handling orders as they are placed because the items are handled on a first-in-first-out basis and the bag is useful to store orders as they are serviced to the customer.

The **PlaceOrders** method will add orders with a slight delay between each order on a separate thread.

The **ProcessOrders** method is called by each waiter or waitress to enable them to deliver the finished orders to the customers. The **while** loop ensures that they continue to serve the customers indefinitely and tries to de-queue orders and add them to the orders collection to show that they have been delivered.

In the button's **Click** event the **PlaceOrders** method is executed on a separate thread using a **Task** and is awaited further down the code to ensure that all orders have been processed before displaying the orders in a list box.

All waiters and waitresses are also started on separate threads using **Tasks** to ensure that they can operate simultaneously.

This means that there are at least five thread running at the same time, the UI thread running the form, the thread placing orders and the three waiter and waitress threads.

```csharp
public partial class Form1 : Form
{
    ConcurrentQueue<string> queue = new ConcurrentQueue<string>();
    ConcurrentBag<Order> orders = new ConcurrentBag<Order>();

    private void PlaceOrders()
    {
        for (int i = 1; i <= 25; i++)
        {
            Thread.Sleep(5);
            var order = String.Format("Order {0}", i);
            queue.Enqueue(order);
        }
    }

    private void ProcessOrders(string name)
    {
        string order;
        while (true) //continue indefinitely
            if (queue.TryDequeue(out order))
                orders.Add(new Order(name, order));
    }

    private void ConcurrentQueue_Click(object sender, EventArgs e)
    {
        var taskPlaceOrders = Task.Run(() => PlaceOrders());

        Task.Run(() => ProcessOrders("Carl"));
        Task.Run(() => ProcessOrders("Lisa"));
        Task.Run(() => ProcessOrders("Mary"));

        taskPlaceOrders.Wait();

        lstOrders.DataSource =
            from o in orders
            orderby o.Id ascending
            select String.Format("{0} processed by {1}",
                o.Description, o.Name);
    }
}
```

Additional reading: "System.Collections.Concurrent Namespace"

Exercise: Restaurant

In this exercise you will create a restaurant application where orders are placed until the is restaurant closed (the tasks are cancelled). When the start button is clicked the restaurant opens and the cashier begin taking orders that are added to a thread safe **Queue** called **orders**. The restaurant menu is stored in a thread safe collection called **menu**; a randomly chosen dish is added to the order to simulate that a customer has ordered something from the menu.

The orders are added to the **orders** queue in a method called **PlaceOrders** in a **while** loop that will run until the cancel button is clicked and the **Tasks** are cancelled through a **CancellationTokanSource**. In the **while** loop the **Thread.Sleep** method is used to simulate that it took a while for the cashier to register the order and then a random number between 1 and the number of dishes in the **menu** collection is generated that is used to fetch the ordered dish; the dish is then used to create a new order that is added to the **orders** queue. If the order was successfully added to the queue an **orderId** variable is incremented by 1.

To simulate that the waiters and waitresses are serving food to the customers a method called **ProcessOrders** is called. Here is where it gets a bit tricky because the order information that will be presented in a list box originates from a different thread than the form that contain the control. If you try to add the order information directly to the list box you will commit a *cross-thread operation violation* that throws an **InvalidOperationException**. The solution is to create an **Action<string>** delegate called **AddToListBox** that is used in a call to the **this.BeginInvoke** method that sends the information to the form's thread. A **while** loop will be added to the **ProcessOrders** method which will iterate until the current **Task** has been cancelled. The purpose with the loop is to fetch the next order in the **orders** queue, add the waiters name to it and send the information to be displayed to the list box; you do this by calling the **BeginInvoke** method on the form passing it the **AddToListBox Action** and the string to display.

To open the restaurant the **OpenRestaurant** method is called where a **CancellationToken** is created that is passed to all the **Tasks** that are used to run the restaurant; this is the token that will determine when no more orders will be added to the orders queue and when the waiters and waitresses quit for the day. The first **Task** in the **OpenRestaurant** method will call the **PlaceOrders** method with the **CancellationToken** to begin adding orders to the **orders** queue; it has to be executed on a separate thread because it must be able to add new orders while the waiters and waitresses service the customer with already placed orders.

Next the waiters and waitresses will sign in for their shift by you creating one **Task** per staff member which call the **ProcessOrders** method to begin serving the customers. The method is passed the name of the employee and the **CancellationToken**.

The form should have a list box called *lstOrders* and two buttons called *btnStart* and *btnCancel*. When the **Start** button is clicked the **OpenRestaurant** method is called on a separate thread using a **Task** to free up the UI thread; if it ran on the UI thread the user would not be able to click **Cancel** button to close the restaurant.

The **Cancel** button will call the **Cancel** method on the **CancellationTokanSource** instance to cancel all the **Tasks**.

Both buttons should be disabled when clicked.

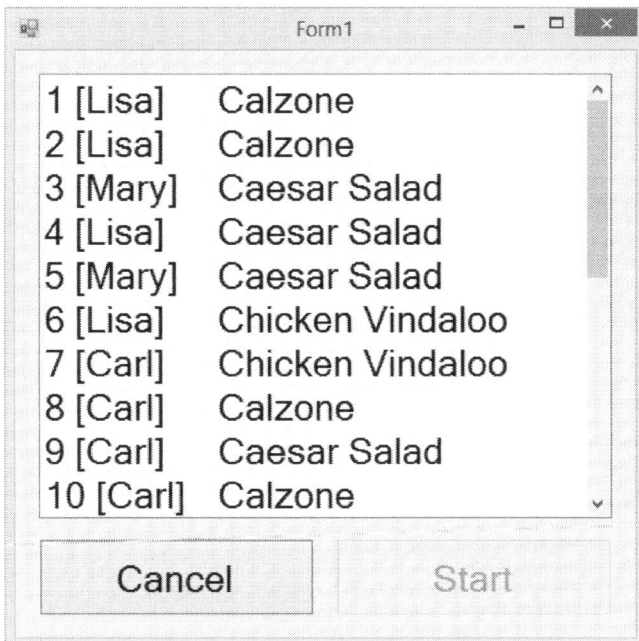

The Dish class

Objects of this class represent the different dishes on the menu and are added to a **Concur-rentBag<Dish>** called **menu** in the form's code-behind. Each placed order has a **Dish** object stored in it. The **Dish** class has a **public int** property called **Id** and a **public string** property called **Name**.

The complete code for the **Dish** class:

```
class Dish
{
    public int Id { get; set; }
    public string Name { get; set; }
}
```

The Order class

Objects of this class represent orders that the customers place. The **Order** objects are placed in a **ConcurrentQueue<Order>** collection called **orders**. The **Order** class has a constructor that takes three parameters called **id** of type **int**, **dish** of type **Dish** and **waiter** of type **string**. Assigned the **default** value for the **string** data type to the **waiter** parameter.

Four properties are needed in the class. **Id** of type **int**, **Waiter** of type **string**, **Dish** of type **Dish** and a read only property called **OrderInfo** that return information about the order and the dish. The **OrderInfo** property is displayed in the list box.

The complete code for the **Order** class:

```
class Order
{
    public Order(int id, Dish dish, string waiter = default(string))
    {
        Id = id;
        Waiter = waiter;
        Dish = dish;
    }
    public string Waiter { get; set; }
    public Dish Dish { get; set; }
    public int Id { get; set; }
    public string OrderInfo
    {
        get
        {
```

```
                return String.Format("{0} [{2}]\t{1}",Id, Dish.Name, Waiter);
        }
    }
}
```

The GUI

The GUI contains a list box called **lstOrders** and two buttons called **btnStart** and **btnCancel**. The form's code-behind has a **ConcurrentQueue<Order>** called **orders** that keep track of the un-serviced orders, a **ConcurrentBag<Dish>** called **menu** to keep track of the dishes on the menu, a **CancellationTokenSource** called **cts** and a **CancellationToken** called **ct** that will be used to end the executing **Tasks**.

Add the **Click** events for the buttons to the code-behind.

The form's code-behind so far:

```
public partial class Form1 : Form
{
    ConcurrentQueue<Order> orders = new ConcurrentQueue<Order>();
    ConcurrentBag<Dish> menu = new ConcurrentBag<Dish> {
        new Dish{ Id = 1, Name = "Chicken Vindaloo"},
        new Dish{ Id = 2, Name = "Calzone"},
        new Dish{ Id = 3, Name = "Caesar Salad"},
        new Dish{ Id = 4, Name = "Pasta Carbonara"}
    };

    CancellationTokenSource cts = new CancellationTokenSource();
    CancellationToken ct;

    public Form1()
    {
        InitializeComponent();
    }

    private void btnStart_Click(object sender, EventArgs e)
    {
    }

    private void btnCancel_Click(object sender, EventArgs e)
    {
    }
}
```

The PlaceOrders method

Add the **PlaceOrders** method to the form's code-behind; it will add orders to the **orders** queue and assign a unique order id and a randomly chosen dish from the menu to each order.

To be able to cancel the **while** loop adding orders a **CancellationToken** instance is passed to the method, the **IsCancellationRequested** property of the token can be used to check if a cancellation request has been made by clicking on the **Cancel** button.

Use a **try/catch**-block that ignores any exceptions and only adds the order to the queue in the **try**-block if no exception has been thrown.

Add a **Thread.Sleep(300)** method call to simulate that it takes a while to register the order. Use the **Random** class to generate a random number from 1 to the number of items in the **menu** collection; this id will then be used to fetch a dish from the **menu** collection.

Create a new **Order** instance and pass in the order id and the dish to its constructor; add the order to the **orders** queue.

Increment the order id by 1.

1. Add a **private void** method called **PlaceOrders** with a **CancellationToken** parameter called **token** to the form's code-behind.
2. Add a variable called **orderId** and assign **1** to it.
3. Add a **while** loop that iterates for as long as no cancellation request has been made with the **token** parameter.
   ```
   while(!token.IsCancellationRequested)
   ```
4. Add a **try/catch**-block with an empty **catch**-block to the **while** loop.
5. Add a **Thred.Sleep(300)** to the **try**-block.
6. Create a random number between 1 and the number if dishes in the menu collection. Use the random number to fetch the dish with the matching id.
   ```
   var idx = random.Next(1, menu.Count);
   var dish = menu.First(m => m.Id.Equals(idx));
   ```
7. Create a new instance of the **Order** class and pass in the order id and the dish to its constructor.

8. Add the order to the **orders** queue.

9. Increment the **orderId** variable by **1**.

The complete code for the **PlaceOrders** method:

```
private void PlaceOrders(CancellationToken token)
{
    var orderId = 1;
    while(!token.IsCancellationRequested)
    {
        try
        {
            Thread.Sleep(300);
            var random = new Random();
            var idx = random.Next(1, menu.Count);
            var dish = menu.First(m => m.Id.Equals(idx));

            var order = new Order(orderId, dish);
            orders.Enqueue(order);
            orderId++;
        }
        catch { }
    }
}
```

The ProcessOrders method

Add the **ProcessOrders** method to the form's code-behind; it will try to de-queue an order from the **orders** queue and display order information and the waiter's name in the list box. This is achieved by calling the **BeginInvoke** method on the form passing in an **Action <string>** delegate to it along with the data to display.

A **while** loop that iterates for as long as no cancellation request has been made will be used when the waiter or waitress processes orders from the **orders** queue. The cancellation request will be triggered by a **CancellationToken** called **token** passed in to the method as a parameter.

For each iteration the waiter or waitress associated with the method will try to de-queue an order from the **orders** queue; if successful the name of the person will be added to the order and the **Action<string>** delegate method will be called to add the value of the **OrderInfo** property to the list box. To make a cross-thread call you have to use the form's **BeginInvoke** method.

The method should have a **string** parameter called **name** and a **CancellationToken** called **token**.

1. Add a method called **ProcessOrders** with a **string** parameter called **name** and a **CancellationToken** parameter called **token** to the form's code-behind.
2. Add an **Action<string>** delegate called **AddToListBox**.
   ```
   Action<string> AddToListBox = orderInfo =>
   lstOrders.Items.Add(orderInfo);
   ```
3. Add an **Order** variable called **order** that will be used when de-queuing the next order in the orders queue.
4. Add a **while** loop that iterates for as long as no cancellation request has been made with the **token** parameter.
   ```
   while(!token.IsCancellationRequested)
   ```
5. Add an **if**-statement to the **while** loop that will be executed if an order is successfully de-queued from the **orders** queue.
   ```
   if (orders.TryDequeue(out order))
   ```
6. Add the name of the waiter or waitress to the de-queued **order** in the **if**-block.
7. Call the **BeginInvoke** method on the form to activate the **Action<string>** delegate that calls the **Add** method on the list box from within the **if**-block. pass in the **Action** method name and the value of the **OrderInfo** property of the de-queued **order** object.
   ```
   this.BeginInvoke(AddToListBox, new object[] { order.OrderInfo });
   ```

The complete code for the **ProcessOrders** method:

```
private void ProcessOrders(string name, CancellationToken token)
{
    Action<string> AddToListBox = orderInfo =>
        lstOrders.Items.Add(orderInfo);
    Order order;

    while (!token.IsCancellationRequested)
        if (orders.TryDequeue(out order))
        {
            order.Waiter = name;
```

```
            this.BeginInvoke(AddToListBox, new object[] { order.OrderInfo });
        }
}
```

The OpenRestaurant method

This method will start the **Task** which add orders to the **orders** queue and the **Tasks** that are used by the waiters and waitresses when they are servicing the customers de-queuing orders from the **orders** queue.

A token has to be created for the **CancellationToken** variable that will be passed as a parameter to the **Task** methods making it possible to cancel the ongoing **Tasks** and close the restaurant.

1. Add a parameter-less **private void** method called **OpenRestaurant** to the form's code-behind.

2. Create a Token for the **CancellationToken** variable using the **CancellationToken-Source** variable.
   ```
   ct = cts.Token;
   ```

3. Add a **Task** that executes the **PlaceOrders** method passing in the **CancellationToken** variable.
   ```
   Task.Run(() => PlaceOrders(ct));
   ```

4. Add three **Tasks** that executes the **ProcessOrders** method passing in the name of the waiter or waitress (Carl, Mary and Lisa) and the **CancellationToken** variable.
   ```
   Task.Run(() => ProcessOrders("Carl", ct));
   ```

The complete code for the **OpenRestaurant** method:

```
private void OpenRestaurant()
{
    ct = cts.Token;

    Task.Run(() => PlaceOrders(ct));

    Task.Run(() => ProcessOrders("Carl", ct));
    Task.Run(() => ProcessOrders("Lisa", ct));
    Task.Run(() => ProcessOrders("Mary", ct));
}
```

The btnStart_Click event

The restaurant opens and the **OpenRestaurant** method is called using a **Task** when the user clicks the button. The button should be disabled when it has been clicked.

1. Locate the **btnStart_Click** event in the form's code-behind.
2. Add a **try/catch**-block where the **catch**-block ignores all exceptions.
3. Add a **Task** that executes the **OpenRestaurant** method.
4. Disable the button.

The complete code for the **btnStart_Click** event:

```
private void btnStart_Click(object sender, EventArgs e)
{
    try
    {
        Task.Run(() => OpenRestaurant());
        btnStart.Enabled = false;
    }
    catch { }
}
```

The btnCancel_Click event

Clicking this button will close the restaurant by calling the **Cancel** method on the **CancellationTokenSource** instance. The button should be disabled when it has been clicked.

1. Locate the **btnCancel_Click** event in the form's code-behind.
2. Add a **try/catch**-block where the **catch**-block ignores all exceptions.
3. Call the **Cancel** method on the **CancellationTokenSource** instance.
4. Disable the button.

The complete code for the **btnCancel_Click** event:

```
private void btnCancel_Click(object sender, EventArgs e){
    try
    {
        cts.Cancel();
        btnCancel.Enabled = false;
    }
    catch { }
}
```

18. Async

Introduction

When you want to execute an operation on a separate thread from the one that initiated the operation and you don't want to wait for the initial thread to complete, then an asynchronous operation is the answer.

.NET Framework 4.5 makes it easier than before to create asynchronous operations; operations that create tasks in the background and coordinate their actions. The **async** keyword lets you create asynchronous operations without blocking the thread and the **await** keyword waits for the result, all within a single method.

async and await

In .NET Framework 4.5, the **async** and **await** keywords were introduced; they make it much easier to write asynchronous operations. You use the **await** keyword to suspend execution of the **async** decorated method while a long-running task completes; the main thread can continue with its work while the **async** method is suspended.

The unique thing about running an asynchronous operation using **async** and **await** is that they enable you to run asynchronous operations on a *single* thread; this makes them especially useful when updating the GUI from asynchronous operations.

Blocked GUI thread

When executing this code, the GUI thread will be blocked until the **Task** has completed.

```
public partial class Form1 : Form
{
    private void btnBlockingUIThread_Click(object sender, EventArgs e)
    {
        Task<string> task = Task.Run<string>(() =>
        {
            Thread.Sleep(5000);
            return "Finished";
        });
```

```
      // Blocks the UI thread until the task has completed.
      lblResult.Text = task.Result;
   }
}
```

Suspend execution

To suspend the execution and let the GUI thread continues its work, you use the **async** and **await** keywords. Note that the **async** keyword is decorating the method header.

```
public partial class Form1 : Form
{
   private async void btnAsyncAndAwait_Click(object sender, EventArgs e)
   {
      Task<string> task = Task.Run<string>(() =>
      {
         Thread.Sleep(5000);
         return "Finished";
      });

      // Will be called when the Task has a result
      lblResult.Text = await task;
   }
}
```

Additional reading: "Asynchronous Programming with Async and Await (C# and Visual Basic)"

Awaitable methods

The **await** operator waits on a **Task** to complete in a non-locking manner. An await-able method should return a **Task** for **void** methods or a **Task<TResult>** for methods that return a value; one exception is event methods that are allowed to return **void**.

This code shows an implementation of a synchronous method that will be altered to an asynchronous method in the next example.

```
public partial class Form1 : Form
{
    private Student GetDataSynchronous()
    {
        var task = Task.Run<Student>(() =>
        {
            Thread.Sleep(3000);
            return new Student()
            {
                FirstName = "Jonas"
            };
        });

        return task.Result;
    }
}
```

The code below shows an implementation of an asynchronous method returning a value.
Note that both the asynchronous method and the event method have to be decorated with
the **async** keyword and that the **await** operator is used in the event method when calling the
asynchronous method. The **Text** property of the label will be assigned when the asynchronous method has completed.

```
public partial class Form1 : Form
{
    private async Task<Student> GetDataAsynchronously()
    {
        var task = await Task.Run<Student>(() =>
        {
            Thread.Sleep(3000);
            return new Student() { FirstName = "Jonas" };
        });

        return task;
    }

    private async void btnAwaitableMethod_Click(object sender, EventArgs e)
    {
        var student = await GetDataAsynchronously();
        lblResult.Text = student.FirstName;
    }
}
```

Additional reading: "Async Return Types (C# and Visual Basic)"

Callback methods

You can configure an asynchronous operation to invoke a callback method when it completes its task; the asynchronous method can pass data back to the callback method that processes the information or updates the GUI.

A delegate must be created to handle the callback method and it must be passed as a parameter to the asynchronous method. A callback method typically has parameters and returns **void**; this makes the **Action<T>** delegate suitable when declaring a callback method because it can take up to 16 **Type** parameters, **T** is the type you want to return.

In the following example a new student is enrolled into school using an asynchronous method and in the callback method a message box will confirm to the user that the student was added.

When the button is clicked the **EnrollStudent** method is called asynchronously using the **await** keyword with the callback method and the name of the student as its parameters.

The **EnrollStudent** method is declared using the **async** keyword and returning a **Task** making it an asynchronous method. The callback parameter handling the incoming callback method pointer is declared as an **Action<Student>** since it will be receiving a **Student** instance as its parameter.

In the **EnrollStudent** method an awaited **Task** adds a new student to the **Students** collection (or database table in a real world scenario) and return the **Student** object. Then another **Task** is awaited executing the callback method with the **Student** object as its parameter.

When both these tasks have been completed the **EnrollStudent** method will have finished its work.

In the **DisplayStudentCallback** method a message box displays the newly enrolled student.

```
public partial class Form1 : Form
{
    List<Student> Students = new List<Student>();

    private async void btnCallbackMethod_Click(object sender, EventArgs e)
    {
        await EnrollStudent(DisplayStudentCallback, "Lisa", "Smith");
    }

    private async Task EnrollStudent(Action<Student> callback,
    string firstName, string lastName)
    {
        var student = await Task.Run(() =>
        {
            Students.Add(new Student {
                FirstName = firstName, LastName = lastName });

            return Students.Last();
        });

        // Invoke the callback method asynchronously.
        await Task.Run(() => callback(student));
    }

    private void DisplayStudentCallback(Student student)
    {
        MessageBox.Show(String.Format(
            "Student {0} {1} was enrolled",
            student.FirstName, student.LastName));
    }
}
```

Additional reading: "Action<T> Delegate"

Synchronizing concurrent data access

Responsiveness and performance are two benefits of multitasking, but there are challenges as well. One of them is concurrent data access; if two resources update the same data problem can arise leaving the data in an unpredictable state.

To solve these challenges, you can use locking mechanisms and concurrent collections.

Lock block

If multiple threads access the same data simultaneously, there is a risk of corrupt data being used and stored. Let's say you have a warehouse application that has different methods that updates and checks the stock level of an item. If the stock level is being updated by one thread when a request for the current stock level, then there is a chance that the request is being made before the update to the stock level has completed.

The solution is to use a **lock**-block to implement mutual-exclusion locks where critical updates are made; a lock of this type will lockout any other threads than the one currently holding the lock. Use the following syntax to implement a lock: **lock** *(object) {statement block}*. The **object** in the lock should be declared as **private** in the class and serve only one purpose, to hold the lock with something that is unique. Write the critical code within the *statement block*.

Example: Class with a method using lock

When an instance of the **Warehouse** class is created an initial stock balance has to be provided with the constructor and is stored in the **int stock** variable.

The **GetStockLevel** method returns the number of items in stock.

When the **FetchItemsFromStorage** method is called the passed in number of sold items represented by the **soldItems** parameter is subtracted from the current **stock** count and saved back to the **stock** variable if a **lock** has been achieved on the **stockLock** instance.

```
class Warehouse
{
    private object stockLock = new object();
    int stock;

    public Warehouse(int initialStock)
    {
        stock = initialStock;
    }

    public int GetStockLevel()
    {
        return stock;
    }
```

```
public bool FetchItemsFromStorage(int soldItems)
{
    lock (stockLock)
    {
        if (stock >= soldItems)
        {
            Thread.Sleep(3000);
            // Calculate new stock level
            stock = stock - soldItems;
            return true;
        }
        else
        {
            // Insufficient stock available
            return false;
        }
    }
}
```

Example: Calling method using a lock

The following code shows the class that calls to the method with the lock implemented. If both buttons are clicked in sequence then the second call will have to wait for the first call to end. To be able to click both buttons we have to run the calls on separate threads hence the **async** and **await** keywords.

If you executed this code with the lock, you would get the following result: firstUpdateTask = true, firstStockLevelCountTask = 1, secondUpdateTask = false, secondStockLevelCountTask = 1.

If you removed the **lock** and executed the code, you would get the following result: firstUpdateTask = true, firstStockLevelCountTask = 1, secondUpdateTask = true, second-StockLevelCountTask = -2. The second call yields corrupt data because the stock level updates was not locked and could be executed simultaneously with the first call.

```
public partial class Form1 : Form
{
    Warehouse w = new Warehouse(4);
    bool firstUpdateTask, secondUpdateTask;
    int firstStockLevelCountTask, secondStockLevelCountTask;

    private async void FirstUser_Click(object sender, EventArgs e)
    {
        firstUpdateTask = await Task.Run<bool>(() =>
            w.FetchItemsFromStorage(3));

        firstStockLevelCountTask = await Task.Run<int>(() =>
            w.GetStockLevel());
    }

    private async void SecondUser_Click(object sender, EventArgs e)
    {
        secondUpdateTask = await Task.Run<bool>(() =>
            w.FetchItemsFromStorage(3));

        secondStockLevelCountTask = await Task.Run<int>(() =>
            w.GetStockLevel());
    }
}
```

Additional reading: "lock Statement (C# Reference)" and "Thread Synchronization (C# and Visual Basic)"

Exercise: Stock history

In this exercise you will use multithreading through **Tasks** and asynchronous calls using **async** and **await** to fetch stock information from Yahoo and Nasdaq. The web requests will be made on separate threads and the information from the fastest service will be used; this accomplished by setting it up as **Tasks** that are executed using the **Task.WaitAny** method. Each **Task** will call the **Task.Factory.FromAsync** method to fetch the data asynchronously from the web sites.

When stock history have been fetched for all desired stock symbols the data is presented nicely formatted in a rich textbox. Apart from creating a **StockFactory** class that do all the heavy lifting you will also create a **Stock** class that holds the data for each stock symbol being processed.

The Stock class

The Stock class will hold the data for one stock symbol. The **decimal Max**, **Min** and **Avg** properties of the class will be calculated and assigned by a method called **ProcessStock**. The rest of the properties will be assigned through the constructor. The **string** properties **Symbol**, **Site** and **DataSource** will hold the name of the stock symbol, the site address and information about how the data was obtained. The **bool** property **HasPrices** will return **true** if any prices were obtained for the stock and the **decimal** property **DataPoints** will return the number of data points (prices) that were used to obtain the calculated values for the **Max**, **Min** and **Avg** properties.

The constructor should have the following parameters: **string symbol**, **string site**, **string dataSource** and **List<decimal> prices**.

The **ProcessStock** method is called from the constructor after the properties have been assigned their values from the constructor parameters. It has one **List<decimal>** collection parameter called **prices** that will contain all the historical prices for the stock symbol.

To avoid exceptions when trying to calculate data for empty values the first thing to do in the method will be to check if the collection is empty or **null** and return from the method if that is the case. This can happen if the **HttpWebRequest** object used when calling the web sites returns an error code.

Next three **Tasks** will be defined using the **Task.Run** method to call the **Min**, **Max** and **Average** methods on the **prices** collection to calculate the values for the **Max**, **Min** and **Avg** properties.

The **Task.WaitAll** method will be called within a **try**-block to execute all the defined **Tasks** and wait until they all have finished before assigning their return values to the properties. The **catch**-block should ignore any exceptions.

1. Create a new Windows Forms project called **Stock History**.
2. Add a folder called **Classes**.
3. Add a class called **Stock** to the folder.

4. Add three **string** properties called **Symbol**, **Site** and **DataSource** with **private setters** to the class.

5. Add a **bool** property called **HasPrices** that has a **private setter**.

6. Add four **decimal** properties called **DataPoints**, **Max**, **Min** and **Avg** with **private setters**.

7. Add a constructor that has **string** parameters called **symbol**, **site** and **dataSource**. Also add a parameter called **prices** of type **List<decimal>** for all the price points. The last parameter should not be stored in a property or variable, it should only be sent to the **ProcessStock** method.

8. Assign values to the **Symbol**, **Site**, **DataSource**, **HasPrices** and **DataPoints** properties in the constructor.

9. Add a **private void** method called **ProcessStock** that has a **List<decimal>** parameter called **prices**.

10. Add an **if**-statement that checks if the **prices** collection is empty or **null** and return from the method with a **return** statement if that is the case.

11. Add three **Tasks** called **T_min**, **T_max** and **T_avg** that will hold the **Task** definition for the calls to the **Min**, **Max** and **Average** methods of the **prices** collection. The purpose of the **Tasks** is to find the minimum and maximum values in the collection and to calculate the average of all the values using separate threads to speed up the execution.
    ```
    var T_min = Task.Run<decimal>(() => prices.Min());
    ```

12. Add a **try/catch**-block where the **catch**-block ignores any exceptions.

13. Execute all the **Tasks** inside the **try**-block by calling the **Task.WaitAll** method. This will halt the execution temporarily in the method until all the **Tasks** have returned a result.
    ```
    Task.WaitAll(new Task[] { T_min, T_max, T_avg });
    ```

14. Assign the results from the **Tasks** to the appropriate properties.
    ```
    Min = T_min.Result;
    ```

15. Add a call to the **ProcessStock** method after all the property assignments in the constructor.

The complete code for the **Stock** class:

```csharp
class Stock
{
    #region Properties
    public string Symbol { get; private set; }
    public string Site { get; private set; }
    public string DataSource { get; private set; }
    public bool HasPrices { get; private set; }
    public decimal DataPoints { get; private set; }
    public decimal Min { get; private set; }
    public decimal Max { get; private set; }
    public decimal Avg { get; private set; }
    #endregion

    #region Constructor
    public Stock(string symbol, string site, string dataSource,
    List<decimal> prices)
    {
        Symbol = symbol;
        Site = site;
        DataSource = dataSource;
        HasPrices = prices.Count > 0;
        DataPoints = prices.Count;
        ProcessStock(prices);
    }
    #endregion

    #region Methods
    private void ProcessStock(List<decimal> prices)
    {
        if (prices == null || prices.Count.Equals(0)) return;

        var T_min = Task.Run<decimal>(() => prices.Min());
        var T_max = Task.Run<decimal>(() => prices.Max());
        var T_avg = Task.Run<decimal>(() => prices.Average());

        try
        {
            Task.WaitAll(new Task[] { T_min, T_max, T_avg });
            Min = T_min.Result;
            Max = T_max.Result;
            Avg = T_avg.Result;
        }
```

```
        catch { }
    }
    #endregion
}
```

The GUI - Part 1

The GUI will have two controls, a rich textbox called *txtResult* and a button called *btnGet-StockData*. The button's **Click** event should be asynchronous to prevent locking the GUI when the stock history is fetched and when the text is formatted and presented.

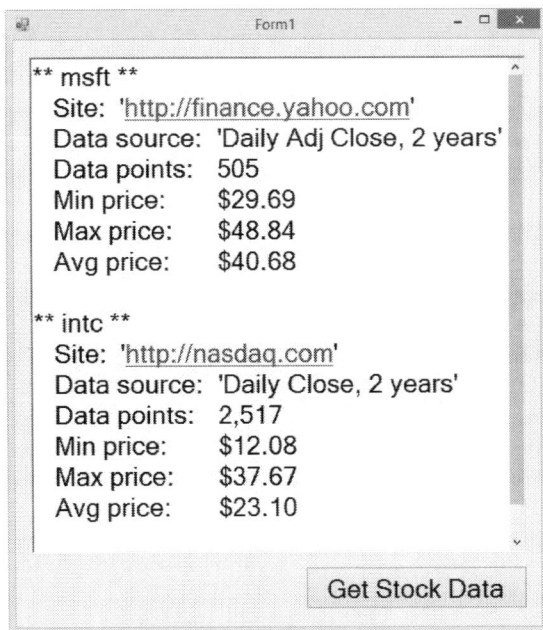

When the user clicks the button a **List<string>** called **symbols** will be created holding the Microsoft (msft) and Intel (intc) stock symbols, you can add more stock symbols if you like.

Because the **Click** event is asynchronous the **Tasks** executing the **GetData** method that fetches the data and the **FormatOutput** method that formats the data can both be **awaited** to free up the GUI thread.

Once both **Tasks** have finished the output generated by the **FormatOutput** method is assigned to the **Text** property of the rich textbox.

The button should be disabled when clicked and enabled when the data has been displayed.

In this section you will create the two methods **GetData** and **FormatOutput** and implement a delay in them using the **Task.Delay** method to verify that the form remains responsive when work is performed by the methods. You will add the real implementation in an upcoming section of this exercise.

1. Add a rich textbox control to the form called ***txtResult***.
2. Add a button called ***btnGetSTockData*** with the text **Get Stock Data**.
3. Add a **private List<Stock>** method called **GetData** with a **List<string>** parameter called **symbols** and an **int** parameter called **yearsOfHistory** to the form's code-behind. Assign a default value of 1 to the **yearsOfHistory** parameter.
   ```
   private List<Stock> GetData(List<string> symbols, int yearsOfHistory
   = 1)
   ```
4. Add a delay of 2 seconds to the method using the **Thread.Sleep** method.
5. Return **null** from the method.
6. Add a **string** method called **FormatOutput** with a **List<Stock>** parameter called **stocks**.
7. Add a delay of 2 seconds to the method using the **Thread.Sleep** method.
8. Return **null** from the method.
9. Add the **Click** event for the ***btnGetSTockData*** button and make it asynchronous by adding the **async** keyword to it..
10. Add a **try/catch**-block to the **Click** event where the **catch**-block displays the exception message in a **MessageBox**.
11. Disable the button and clear the rich textbox in the **try**-block.
12. Add a **List<string>** collection variable called **symbols** and add the symbols for Microsoft (msft) and Intel (intc) to it.
    ```
    var symbols = new List<string> { "msft", "intc" };
    ```
13. Add a **Task** variable called **stocks** that **awaits** the result from a **Task** calling the **GetData** method with the **symbols** collection and the number of years you want to fetch data for.
    ```
    var stocks = await Task.Run(() => GetData(symbols, 2));
    ```
14. Add a **Task** variable called **output** that **awaits** the result from a **Task** calling the **FormatOutput** method with the **stocks** collection returned from the previous **Task**.

```
var output = await Task.Run(() => FormatOutput(stocks));
```

15. Assign the value in the **output** variable to the **Text** property of the *txtResult* rich textbox.

16. Enable the button.

17. Run the application and click the button.

18. You should be able to move the form while the button is disabled.

19. Close the application.

The StockFactory class

This class does the heavy lifting when it comes to fetching stock history data from the Nasdaq and Yahoo websites.

Constants, properties and constructor

To fetch data you need correctly formatted Url's which unfortunately are long with a lot of numbers; create two string constants in the class called **urlTemplateYahoo** and **urlTemplateNasdaq** to hold the Url's.

```
#region Constants
private const string urlTemplateYahoo =
    "http://ichart.finance.yahoo.com/table.csv?s=" +
    "{0}&d={1}&e={2}&f={3}&g=d&a={1}&b={2}&c={4}&ignore=.csv";

private const string urlTemplateNasdaq =
    "http://charting.nasdaq.com/ext/charts.dll?2-1-14-0-0,0,0,0,0|
    0,0,0,0,0|0,0,0,0,0|0,0,0,0,0|0,0,0,0,0|0,0,0,0,0|0,0,0,0,0|0,0,0,0,0|0,
    0,0,0,0|0,0,0,0,0|0,0,0,0,0|0,0,0,0,0|0,0,0,0,0|0,0,0,0,0|0,0,0,0,0|0,0,
    0,0,0|0,0,0,0,0|0,0,0,0,0|0,0,0,0,0|0,0,0,0,0|0,0,0,0,0|0,0,0,0,0|0,0,0,
    0,0|0,0,0,0,0|0,0,0,0,0|0,0,0,0,0|0,0,0,0,0|0,0,0,0,0|0,0,0,0,0|0,0,0,0,
    0|0,0,0,0,0|0,0,0,0,0|0,0,0,0,0|0,0,0,0,0|0,0,0,0,0|0,0,0,0,0|0,0,0,0,0|
    0,0,0,0,0|0,0,0,0,0|0,0,0,0,0-5120-03NA000000{0}-&SF:4|5-WD=539-HT=395--
    XXCL-";
#endregion
```

You will also need to add a **bool** property called **IsInternetAvailable** that will return the result from a call to the **GetIsNetworkAvailable** method of the **NetWorkInterface** class in the **System.Net.NetworkInformation** namespace. This property will be used to ensure that an internet connection is available on the computer.

Because you will be using asynchronous web requests you need to implement the **Unob-servedTaskException** event in the **TaskScheduler** class to handle **Tasks** that are cancelled. Because only the first web request to return a result will be used and the rest will be cancelled the .NET Framework demands that the cancelled **Tasks** will be observed to avoid that the Garbage Collection throws exceptions for those **Tasks**. Cancelled **Tasks** can be ignored by calling the **e.SetObserved** method in the **UnobservedTaskException** event.

1. Add a class called **StockFactory** to the **Classes** folder.
2. Add a **private string** constant called **urlTemplateYahoo** (see description above for the Url template to use).
3. Add a **private string** constant called **urlTemplateNasdaq** (see description above for the Url template to use).
4. Add a **bool** property called **IsInternetAvailable** that return **true** if an internet connection is available on the computer.
   ```
   public static bool IsInternetAvailable {
       get { return NetworkInterface.GetIsNetworkAvailable(); } }
   ```
5. Add a **public** constructor and wire up the **UnobservedTaskException** event.
   ```
   TaskScheduler.UnobservedTaskException += new EventHandler
   <UnobservedTaskExceptionEventArgs>(TaskUnobservedException_Handler);
   ```
6. Make the event method **static** so that the it can be used for all instances.
7. Call the **e.SetObserved** method in the event to tell the Garbage Collection that you have observed the cancelled **Task** object and that it can be removed.

The code for the **StockFactory** class so far:

```
class StockFactory
{
    #region Constants
    private const string urlTemplateYahoo =
        "http://ichart.finance.yahoo.com/table.csv?s=" +
        "{0}&d={1}&e={2}&f={3}&g=d&a={1}&b={2}&c={4}&ignore=.csv";

    private const string urlTemplateNasdaq =
        "http://charting.nasdaq.com/ext/charts.dll?2-1-14-0-0,0,0,0,0|
        0,0,0,0,0|0,0,0,0,0|0,0,0,0,0|0,0,0,0,0|0,0,0,0,0|0,0,0,0,0|
        0,0,0,0,0|0,0,0,0,0|0,0,0,0,0|0,0,0,0,0|0,0,0,0,0|0,0,0,0,0|
        0,0,0,0,0|0,0,0,0,0|0,0,0,0,0|0,0,0,0,0|0,0,0,0,0|0,0,0,0,0|
        0,0,0,0,0|0,0,0,0,0|0,0,0,0,0|0,0,0,0,0|0,0,0,0,0|0,0,0,0,0|
```

```
0,0,0,0,0|0,0,0,0,0|0,0,0,0,0|0,0,0,0,0|0,0,0,0,0|0,0,0,0,0|
0,0,0,0,0|0,0,0,0,0|0,0,0,0,0|0,0,0,0,0|0,0,0,0,0|0,0,0,0,0|
0,0,0,0,0|0,0,0,0,0|0,0,0,0,0-5120-03NA000000{0}-&SF:4|
5-WD=539-HT=395--XXCL-";
#endregion

#region Properties
public static bool IsInternetAvailable
{
    get { return NetworkInterface.GetIsNetworkAvailable(); }
}
#endregion

#region Constructor
public StockFactory()
{
    /* When an async requests is canceled exceptions are thrown.
       These exceptions must be observed to avoid exceptions
       being thrown by the Garbage Collection during clean-up
       of the Task objects. */
    TaskScheduler.UnobservedTaskException += new
        EventHandler<UnobservedTaskExceptionEventArgs>(
        TaskUnobservedException_Handler);
}
#endregion

#region Event Handlers
/* In this application several Tasks are started to get the stock
   data but only the first one to return is processed, the other
   Tasks are cancelled. Cancelled Tasks need to be observed
   otherwise the Garbage Collection will throw exceptions during
   clean-up of the Task objects. The following event handler is a
   work-around this problem.
   NOTE: that this event handler is registered with the class'
   static constructor to only be registered once. */
private static void TaskUnobservedException_Handler(object sender,
UnobservedTaskExceptionEventArgs e)
{
    /* Ignore all subsequent Tasks since the result from the first
       Task to return a result already has been processed */
      e.SetObserved();
  }
  #endregion
}
```

The ParsePrices method

This **static List<decimal>** method will be called from the **GetStockAsync** method and will use the **WebResponse** object passed in to it to read its response stream and separate out the historical price information returned from the called web site.

Add a **try/finally**-block where the **finally**-block closes the response stream passed in through the **response** parameter to the method.

Use the **GetResponseStream** method on the **response** object to get the response stream containing the data in the **try**-block..

Use a **StreamReader** to read the data; continue to read the stream until the **EndOfStream** stream property is **true**.

Read one line at a time from the stream reader and split it up using the **Split** method and the **separators** parameter. Store the result in a **string[]** variable called **tokens**.

Check that the first token in the **tokens** array is a valid date and that the price stored at the position determined by the passed in **dataIndex** parameter is parse-able to a **decimal** value. Use the **en-US** culture to make sure that the data is parsed correctly. Add the price to a **List<decimal>** collection called **prices**.

Return the **prices** collection below the **using**-blocks reading the response stream.

1. Add a **private static List<decimal>** method called **ParsePrices** to the **StockFactory** class. The method should have three parameters **response** of type **WebResponse**, **separators** of type **char[]** and **dataIndex** of type **int**.
2. Add a **try/finally**-block to the method where the **finally**-block closes the response stream.
3. Add a **List<decimal>** collection called **prices** to the **try**-block.
4. Add a **using**-block for the **GetResponseStream** method call on the **response** object.
   ```
   using (Stream WebStream = Response.GetResponseStream())
   ```
5. Add a **using**-block for the **StreamReader** that will read the content of the response stream.
   ```
   using (StreamReader Reader = new StreamReader(WebStream))
   ```
6. Add a **while** loop that iterates for as long as there is content in the stream.

```
while (!Reader.EndOfStream)
```

7. Read one line at a time inside the while loop and store the data in a **string** variable called **record**.

8. Split the **record** string using the **separators** parameter and the **Split** method. Store the result in a **string[]** variable called **tokens**.

9. Add a **DateTime** variable called **date** and a **decimal** variable called **data** that will hold the values returned from the **TryParse** method calls.

10. Try to parse the first value in the tokens array to a date and the value at the position corresponding to the value in the **dataIndex** parameter. Add the price to the **prices** collection if the parsing is successful.

```
if (DateTime.TryParse(tokens[0], out date))
    if (Decimal.TryParse(tokens[dataIndex],
        NumberStyles.AllowDecimalPoint,
        new CultureInfo("en-US"), out data))
            prices.Add(data);
```

11. Return the **prices** collection from the method below the outer **using**-block.

The complete code for the **ParsePrices** method:

```
/// <summary>
/// Parses prices from the Response stream containing the stock data
/// </summary>
private static List<decimal> ParsePrices(WebResponse Response, char[]
separators, int dataIndex)
{
    // Open data stream and parse the data
    try
    {
        List<decimal> prices = new List<decimal>();

        using (Stream WebStream = Response.GetResponseStream())
        {
            using (StreamReader Reader = new StreamReader(WebStream))
            {
                // Read data stream
                while (!Reader.EndOfStream)
                {
                    string record = Reader.ReadLine();
                    string[] tokens = record.Split(separators);

                    DateTime date;
```

```
                    decimal data;

                    // Add prices that have valid dates.
                    // Use the specific culture of en-US to ensure that the
                    // decimal parse works in cultures where a comma is used
                    // as separator
                    if (DateTime.TryParse(tokens[0], out date))
                        if (Decimal.TryParse(tokens[dataIndex],
                            NumberStyles.AllowDecimalPoint,
                            new CultureInfo("en-US"), out data))
                                prices.Add(data);
                }
            }
        }

        return prices;
    }
    finally
    {
        try
        {
            // Close the response stream before the data is returned
                Response.Close();
        }
        catch { }
    }
}
```

The GetStockAsync method

This **static** method will be called from the **GetStockData** method and will fetch the stock information for the passed in stock symbol by making an asynchronous call to the web site named in the method's **url** parameter. The method has the following parameters: **url** of type **string**, **site** of type **string**, **dataSource** of type **string**, **symbol** of type **string**, **separators** of type **char[]**, **dataIndex** of type **int**, **yearsOfHistory** of type **int** and **request** of type **HttpWebRequest** declared as **out**.

To make the asynchronous web request you first have to create the web request using the **url** parameter and store it in the **request** parameter defined with the **out** keyword. You create the request by calling the **Create** method on the **HttpWebRequest** class.

To make the asynchronous call you have to create a **Task** called **webTask** with the **From-Async** method on the **Task's Factory** property passing in the **BeginGetResponse** and **EndGet-Response** methods of the **request** variable you created earlier.

Because you want to use the result from the **webTask** in another **Task** called **resultTask** you will have to continue where the first **Task** ends its execution using the **ContinueWith** method.

The parameter called **antecedent** passed in through the Lambda expression to the **result-Task Task** contains the response from the first **Task**. If its **Status** property isn't equal to **TaskStatus.Faulted** then call the **ParsePrices** method to read the response stream and read the price information for the stock; store the result in a **List<decimal>** collection called **prices**. Return a new instance of the **Stock** class and pass in the values from the **symbol**, **site** and **dataSource** parameters along with the **prices** collection.

If the **antecedent** parameter is equal to **TaskStatus.Faulted** then return a new instance of the **Stock** class and pass in the values from the **symbol**, **site** and **dataSource** parameters along with the an empty **List<decimal>** collection.

Return the value of the **resultTask** variable from the method.

1. Add a **Task<Stock>** method called **GetStockData** to the **StockFactory** class with the parameters described above.
   ```
   private static Task<Stock> GetStockAsync(string url, string site,
   string dataSource, string symbol, char[] separators, int dataIndex,
   int yearsOfHistory, out HttpWebRequest request)
   ```

2. Create an **HttpWebRequest** instance using the Url in the **url** parameter and store it in the **request** parameter that was passed into the method with the **out** keyword.
   ```
   request = (HttpWebRequest)HttpWebRequest.Create(url);
   ```

3. Create the asynchronous **Task** that will use the request object in the **request** para-meter to fetch data from the web site specified by the **url** parameter.
   ```
   var webTask = Task.Factory.FromAsync<WebResponse>(
       request.BeginGetResponse,
       request.EndGetResponse,
       null);
   ```

4. Add the callback **Task** called **resultTask** that will use the result from the asynchronous call.

```
var resultTask = webTask.ContinueWith<Stock>(antecedent =>
{
}
```

5. Add an **if**-statement to the callback **Task** checking if the **webTask Task** returned with a faulty state.

```
if (!antecedent.Status.Equals(TaskStatus.Faulted))
```

6. Store the response result from the **webTask Task** in a variable called **response**.

7. Call the **ParsePrices** method passing in the **response** variable and the **separators** and **dataIndex** parameters to it. Store the result in a **List<decimal>** collection variable called **prices**.

8. Return a new **Stock** instance from the **resultTask** passing in the **symbol**, **site** and **dataSource** parameters along with the **prices** collection.

9. Return a new **Stock** instance from the **resultTask** passing in the **symbol**, **site** and **dataSource** parameters along with an empty **List<decimal>** collection (outside the **if**-block).

10. Return the **resultTask** variable from the method below the **Tasks**.

The complete code for the **GetStockAsync** method:

```
/// <summary>
/// Tries to download stock data asynchronously from Yahoo or Nasdaq.
/// </summary>
private static Task<Stock> GetStockAsync(string url, string site, string
dataSource, string symbol, char[] separators, int dataIndex, int
yearsOfHistory, out HttpWebRequest request)
{
    // Request data from site
    request = (HttpWebRequest)HttpWebRequest.Create(url);

    var webTask = Task.Factory.FromAsync<WebResponse>(
        request.BeginGetResponse,
        request.EndGetResponse,
        null);

    var resultTask = webTask.ContinueWith<Stock>(antecedent =>
    {
        if (!antecedent.Status.Equals(TaskStatus.Faulted))
```

```
    {
        var response = (HttpWebResponse)antecedent.Result;

        List<decimal> prices = ParsePrices(response, separators,
            dataIndex);

        return new Stock(symbol, site, dataSource, prices);
    }

    return new Stock(symbol, site, dataSource, new List<decimal>());
});

    return resultTask;
}
```

The GetStockData method

This **static** method will be called from the **GetData** method in the form to fetch the stock history data. It should return a **Stock** instance containing the returned historical prices for the stock symbol and take to parameters. The first parameter is called **symbol** of type **string** that will contain the symbol for the stock to investigate and the second parameter is called **yearsOfHistory** of type **int** that determines how many years of data to fetch for the stocks.

The method should throw an **ApplicationException** exception with the message "No internet available" if there is no internet available. Use the **IsInternetAvailable** property to determine if internet is available.

Declare two **HttpWebRequest** variables called **req_yahoo** and **req_Nasdaq** that will hold the returned request object for the calls to the web sites. The reason you need to store the request objects is so that the remaining request can be cancelled when one of the sites has returned with a result. It is unnecessary to continue with ongoing requests once one has finished, because the historical stock data already has been obtained.

Use the **urlTemplateYahoo** and **urlTemplateNasdaq** constants and **String.Format** to create two variables called **urlYahoo** and **urlNasdaq** that will hold the complete Urls to the sites. The Yahoo variable will need the symbol, the current month - 1, day - 1, year and year - **yearsOfHistory**; use a **DateTime** instance to get the information. The Nasdaq variable will need the symbol.

Create two **Task<Stock>** variables called **yahoo** and **nasdaq** that are assigned the result from a call to the **GetStockAsync** method. The **GetStockAsync** method need the following information: the value in the **urlYahoo** or **urlNasdaq** variables, the site (to be displayed in the output), the data source specifying how the data was obtained, for instance *Daily Close 2 years* (to be displayed in the output), the character that separates the data returned from the web site, the index position in the data that contain the prices, the number of years to fetch data for and the **HttpWebRequest** variable to receive the request object from the method declared with the **out** keyword.

Add a **List<Task<Stock>>** collection called **tasks** that will hold the tasks and a **List<HttpWebRequest>** collection called **requests** that will hold the web request objects returned from the GetStockAsync method calls. Add the **yahoo** and **nasdaq Tasks** to the **tasks** collection and the **req_yahoo** and **req_nasdaq** object to the **requests** collection.

Add a **Stock** variable called **result** and assign **null** to it; this variable will hold the stock from the winning web request **Task**.

Add a **while** loop that iterates over the **Tasks** in the **tasks** collection. Add a variable called **taskIndex** to the loop; this variable will hold the collection index of the winning **Task** or a negative value indicating that a timeout occurred. Assign the result of a call to the **Task .WaitAny** method that takes the **tasks** collection converted to an array and a 15 second timeout as parameters.

Jump out of the loop with a **break** statement if a timeout occurred.

Assign the **Task** result to the **result** variable if no exceptions were reported by the **Task** and the **Task** result contains prices. You can check **Exceptions** property of the current **Task** for exceptions and the **Result** property for prices.

Remove the **Task** from the **tasks** collection and the **request** object from the **requests** collection using the current index in the **taskIndex** variable.

Add a **foreach** loop below the **while** loop that iterates over the remaining requests in the **requests** collection and aborts them by calling their **Abort** method.

Add an **if**-statement below the **foreach** loop that return the value of the **result** variable if it isn't **null**. Add an **else**-block that throws an **ApplicationException** exception with the text "Could not fetch data from any of the web sites."

1. Add a **static Stock** method called **GetStockData** that has a **string** parameter called **symbol** and an **int** parameter called **yearsOfHistory**.
   ```
   public static Stock GetStockData(string symbol, int yearsOfHistory)
   ```

2. Check if internet is available and throw an exception if it's not.

3. Add the two **HttpWebRequest** variables.
   ```
   HttpWebRequest req_yahoo, req_nasdaq;
   ```

4. Assemble the Yahoo Url.
   ```
   DateTime today = DateTime.Now;
   string urlYahoo = string.Format(urlTemplateYahoo, symbol, today.Month
   - 1, today.Day - 1, today.Year, today.Year - yearsOfHistory);
   ```

5. Assemble the Nasdaq Url.
   ```
   string urlNasdaq = string.Format(urlTemplateNasdaq, symbol);
   ```

6. Create the **Task** that calls the Yahoo site for stock history data.
   ```
   Task<Stock> yahoo = GetStockAsync(
       urlYahoo, http://finance.yahoo.com",
       string.Format("Daily Adj Close, {0} years",
       yearsOfHistory), symbol, new char[] { ',' },
       6, yearsOfHistory, out req_yahoo);
   ```

7. Create the **Task** that calls the Nasdaq site for stock history data.
   ```
   Task<Stock> nasdaq = GetStockAsync(
       urlNasdaq, "http://nasdaq.com",
       string.Format("Daily Close, {0} years",
       yearsOfHistory), symbol, new char[] { '\t' },
       4, yearsOfHistory, out req_nasdaq);
   ```

8. Create a **List<Task<Stock>>** collection called **tasks** that will hold the tasks.

9. Create a **List<HttpWebRequest>** collection called **requests** that will hold the web request objects returned from the **GetStockAsync** method calls.

10. Add the **Tasks** to the **tasks** collection.

11. Add the request objects (the **req_yahoo** and **req_nasdaq**) to the **requests** collection.

12. Add a **Stock** variable called **result**.

13. Add a **while** loop that iterates over the **Tasks** in the **tasks** collection.

14. Call the **Task.WaitAny** method and save the result in an **int** variable called **taskIn-dex**. The **WaitAny** method will wait until one of the **Tasks** in the **tasks** collection return a result and then terminate the remaining **Tasks**.

```
int taskIndex = Task.WaitAny(tasks.ToArray(), 15000);
```

15. Jump out of the loop with a **break** statement if a timeout has occurred.

16. Assign the **Task** result to the **result** variable if no exceptions were reported by the **Task** and the **Task** result contains prices.

```
if (tasks[taskIndex].Exception == null &&
tasks[taskIndex].Result.HasPrices)
    result = tasks[taskIndex].Result;
```

17. Remove the **Task** from the **tasks** collection and the request object from the requests collection using the current index in the **taskIndex** variable.

18. Use a **foreach** loop to abort any remaining requests in the **requests** collection by calling the **Abort** method.

```
foreach (HttpWebRequest r in requests)
    r.Abort();
```

19. Add an **if**-statement below the **foreach** loop that return the value of the **result** variable if it isn't **null** or throws an **ApplicationException** exception if it is.

The complete code for the **GetStockData** method:

```
/// <summary>
/// Tries to fetch historical Stock data from Yahoo or Nasdaq
/// </summary>
public static Stock GetStockData(string symbol, int yearsOfHistory)
{
    if (!IsInternetAvailable)
        throw new ApplicationException("No internet available.");

    HttpWebRequest req_yahoo, req_nasdaq;
    DateTime today = DateTime.Now;

    string urlYahoo = string.Format(urlTemplateYahoo, symbol,
        today.Month - 1, today.Day - 1, today.Year, today.
        Year - yearsOfHistory);

    string urlNasdaq = string.Format(urlTemplateNasdaq, symbol);

    Task<Stock> yahoo = GetStockAsync(urlYahoo, "http://finance.yahoo.com",
```

```
        string.Format("Daily Adj Close, {0} years", yearsOfHistory),
        symbol, new char[] { ',' }, 6, yearsOfHistory, out req_yahoo);

    Task<Stock> nasdaq = GetStockAsync(urlNasdaq, "http://nasdaq.com",
        string.Format("Daily Close, {0} years", yearsOfHistory),
        symbol, new char[] { '\t' }, 4, yearsOfHistory, out req_nasdaq);

    var tasks = new List<Task<Stock>>();
    var requests = new List<HttpWebRequest>();

    tasks.Add(yahoo);
    tasks.Add(nasdaq);

    requests.Add(req_yahoo);
    requests.Add(req_nasdaq);

    Stock result = null;

    // Use the result from the first Task that returns without exception
    while (tasks.Count > 0)
    {
        // The index of the completed task in the tasks array,
        // or if taskIndex < 0 then a timeout occurred
        int taskIndex = Task.WaitAny(tasks.ToArray(), 15000);

        if (taskIndex < 0) break; // timeout occurred

        // Get the result from the task if it was successful
        if (tasks[taskIndex].Exception == null &&
        tasks[taskIndex].Result.HasPrices)
            result = tasks[taskIndex].Result;

        // Remove the Task from the tasks collection
        // and the request from the requests collection
        tasks.RemoveAt(taskIndex);
        requests.RemoveAt(taskIndex);
    }

    // Cancel any remaining requests
    foreach (HttpWebRequest r in requests)
        r.Abort();
```

```
// Return the result if it contains data
if (result != null)
    return result;
else
    // Throw exception if none of the websites could produce data
    throw new ApplicationException(
        "Could not fetch data from any of the web sites.");
}
```

The GUI - Part 2

The last thing you have to do before you can run the application and fetch stock data is to implement the two methods **GetData** and **FormatOutput** in the form's code-behind. If you haven't already removed the two code lines you added to them before then do so while implementing them.

The GetData method

The **GetData** method has two parameters **symbol** of type **List <string>** and **yearsOfHistory** of type **int**. Assign **1** to the latter parameter. You want to create a new **Task** for each stock symbol. The **Tasks** should call the **GetStockData** on the **StockFactory** class and add the returned **Stock** object in a **List<Stock>** collection called **stocks**. Each **Task** should be added to a **List<Task>** collection called **tasks** that is passed as a parameter to the **Task.WaitAll** method executing the **Tasks**. The method should return the resulting **List<Stock>** collection.

1. Add a **List<Stock>** method called **GetData** with two parameters **symbols** of type **List <string>** and **yearsOfHistory** of type **int**. Assign **1** to the latter parameter.
2. Add a **List<Stock>** collection called **stocks**.
3. Add a **List<Task>** collection called **tasks**.
4. Add a **foreach** loop that iterates over the **symbols** collection.
5. Create a new **Task** for each symbol using the **Task.Factory.StartNew** method that you pass an anonymous **Action** delegate block and the current symbol of the loop. Call the **GetStockData** method on the **StockHistory** class inside the **Action**-block and pass it the symbol from the **Action** parameter and the **yearsOfHistory** parameter.

```
foreach (var symbol in symbols)
{
    Task task = Task.Factory.StartNew((t_symbol) =>
    {
        var stock = StockFactory.GetStockData(t_symbol.ToString(),
            yearsOfHistory);
```

```
        stocks.Add(stock);
    }, symbol);

    tasks.Add(task);
}
```

6. Call the **Tasks.WaitAll** method below the **foreach** loop and pass it the **tasks** collection converted to an array.
7. Return the **stocks** collection from the method.

The complete code for the **GetData** method:

```
private List<Stock> GetData(List<string> symbols, int yearsOfHistory = 1)
{
    var tasks = new List<Task>();
    var stocks = new List<Stock>();

    foreach (var symbol in symbols)
    {
        Task task = Task.Factory.StartNew((t_symbol) =>
        {
            var stock = StockFactory.GetStockData(t_symbol.ToString(),
                yearsOfHistory);

            stocks.Add(stock);
        }, symbol);

        tasks.Add(task);
    }

    // Wait for all tasks to complete
    Task.WaitAll(tasks.ToArray());

    return stocks;
}
```

The GetData method
The **FormatOutput** method has a **List<stock>** parameter called **stocks** and returns a **string** containing the formatted output from the historical stock data. Use the **en-US** formatting when displaying currency information.

Use a **StringBuilder** object and append the formatted stock information for each stock in the **stocks** collection.

1. Add a **string** method called **FormatOutput** with a **List<Stock>** collection parameter called **stocks** to the form's code-behind.
2. Add a **StringBuilder** variable called **output**.
3. Add a **CultureInfo** variable targeting the **en-US** culture called **culture**. This object will be used with the **String.Format** method when adding currency information.
   ```
   var culture = new CultureInfo("en-US");
   ```
4. Add a **foreach** loop that iterates over the **stocks** collection.
5. Use **String.Format** when appending data about the stock to the **StringBuilder** object. Pass in the **culture** object to **String.Format** when adding the price information for the stock to get the correct currency symbol.
   ```
   output.Append(string.Format(culture, "\n   Data points:\t{0:#,##0}",
   stock.DataPoints));
   output.Append(string.Format(culture,  "\n      Min  price:\t\t{0:C}",
   stock.Min));
   ```
6. Return the value of the **output** variable as a **string** from the method.
7. Run the application and click the button to fetch some historical stock data.

The complete code for the **FormatOutput** method:

```
private string FormatOutput(List<Stock> stocks)
{
    var output = new StringBuilder();
    var culture = new CultureInfo("en-US");

    foreach (var stock in stocks)
    {
        output.Append(string.Format("** {0} **", stock.Symbol));
        output.Append(string.Format("\n   Site:  '{0}'", stock.Site));
        output.Append(string.Format("\n   Data source:\t'{0}'",
            stock.DataSource));
        output.Append(string.Format(culture, "\n   Data points:\t{0:#,##0}",
            stock.DataPoints));
        output.Append(string.Format(culture, "\n   Min price:\t\t{0:C}",
            stock.Min));
        output.Append(string.Format(culture, "\n   Max price:\t{0:C}",
            stock.Max));
```

```
        output.Append(string.Format(culture, "\n   Avg price:\t\t{0:C}\n\n",
            stock.Avg));
    }

    return output.ToString();
}
```

Made in the USA
San Bernardino, CA
18 February 2019